The Java Simulation Handbook –
Simulating Discrete Event Systems with UML and Java

Bernd Page, Wolfgang Kreutzer
(main authors)

Coauthored by Björn Gehlsen, Johannes Göbel,
Gunnar Kiesel, Nicolas Knaak, Julia Kuck, Tim Lechler
Ruth Meyer, Gaby Neumann, Volker Wohlgemuth

Berichte aus der Informatik

**Bernd Page,
Wolfgang Kreutzer**

The Java Simulation Handbook

Simulating Discrete Event Systems
with UML and Java

Shaker Verlag
Aachen 2005

Bibliographic information published by Die Deutsche Bibliothek
Die Deutsche Bibliothek lists this publication in the Deutsche
Nationalbibliografie; detailed bibliographic data is available in
the internet at http://dnb.ddb.de.

Copyright Shaker Verlag 2005
All rights reserved. No part of this publication may be reproduced, stored in a
retrieval system, or transmitted, in any form or by any means, electronic,
mechanical, photocopying, recording or otherwise, without the prior
permission of the publishers.

Printed in Germany.

ISBN 3-8322-3771-2
ISSN 0945-0807

Shaker Verlag GmbH • P.O. BOX 101818 • D-52018 Aachen
Phone: 0049/2407/9596-0 • Telefax: 0049/2407/9596-9
Internet: www.shaker.de • eMail: info@shaker.de

Introduction

Computer simulation is an important tool for modelling and analysing a complex system. Its applications range widely; from the natural to the engineering sciences, from the social sciences to economics, from medicine to studying environmental concerns. Within computer science, simulation has been used in such diverse areas as chip design, system and communication network performance analysis, database design, and for the study of operating systems and other software. When applied to commercial problems, computer simulation offers a flexible and highly successful method to explore and optimize information and material flows in an enterprise.

Designing and implementing suitable algorithms and programs for such a wide range of applications, however, remains a challenging task; particularly since it seems highly desirable to base models on unified and transferable architectures, and since usable and powerful modelling software can be a key ingredient to the success of a simulation study.

Simulation is one of the earliest applications of computing technology. In addition to mastery of the respective domains (e.g. production, computer, telecommunication, or logistics systems), its application demands competence in a large number of areas, such as system analysis, system design, statistical methods, experimental design, software design and programming. Because of its wide ranging applications, its high degree of practical relevance, and its demand for a unique blend of skills in both system design and implementation, simulation plays also an important and easily motivated part in teaching academic computer science programmes. Good software is needed to support exploration of the whole spectrum of simulation development, from system analysis to model implementation and experimentation. Programming a simulation model, in particular, places high cognitive demands on the model designer. By offering prepackaged functionality to support specific modelling contexts, object-oriented frameworks help to master this complexity. Good modelling frameworks ensure that many *programming aspects* of a simulation study are already taken care of, so that a model designer's mind becomes free to concentrate on *problem-specific aspects* of a system under investigation.

For many years the Faculty of Informatics at the University of Hamburg has been involved in developing software for discrete event simulation frameworks, hosted in different programming languages. These frameworks package core functionality for implementing discrete event simulations and therefore leave students more time to analyse, design, experiment with, and evaluate relevant system models. Studying their architecture also aids understanding of important structural aspects and control patterns in simulation software.

Prompted by Java's increasing popularity as a programming tool for both teaching at universities and use in industrial practice, we have, for a number of years, designed and

I

implemented a Java-based discrete event simulation framework called DESMO-J (Discrete Event Simulation and MOdelling in Java). We plan to continue maintaining and improving DESMO-J as public domain software under the GNU Lesser General Public License. From 2000 to 2004 a close cooperation with the University of Canterbury has been supported by the Federal Ministry of Education and Research (BMBF)[1].

In drawing on the results of this cooperation, the Java Simulation Handbook presents a broad palette of important and timely topics within the context of discrete event simulation. All contributions were written by competent specialists in the respective areas from different universities, coordinated by the two main authors, who have provided the content framework for the book. The book's 16 chapters build on each other and present information in a common style. Although chapters often refer to each other's examples and discussions, each still remains reasonably self-contained. The fact that each chapter can stand on its own means that they may be read both sequentially, in the specified order, or more selectively, whenever particular information is needed. This makes the Java Simulation Handbook suitable to serve as either a textbook (e.g. for a university course) or as a reference.

The book presents its contents in four parts. The first, *Foundations*, discusses fundamental concepts of discrete event simulation. The next part, *Software*, concerns the implementation of discrete event simulation in general as well as in DESMO-J, while *Advanced Methodology* addresses current research, such as agent-based and distributed simulation. The *Applications* part then summarizes simulation's contributions to e-learning, logistics, and industrial practice. For the practitioner, it finally offers some guidelines for the successful completion of real-world simulation projects.

Systematic design and development of discrete event models is the dominant focus of the book. To support our presentation, we use the well established UML 2 (Unified Modelling Language, Version 2.0) notation for model design and the above mentioned DESMO-J Java-based simulation framework for model implementation. To give better support to the simulation domain, we also enrich UML 2 with some simulation-specific extensions.

Although this focus on model design and implementation distinguishes this handbook from many others, which favour a statistical perspective on simulation technology, the handbook also includes chapters dealing with relevant statistical aspects and other foundational issues.

It is one of this book's aspirations to teach by example. To further this purpose, it contains many examples of models, programs, and exercises, the completion of which will hopefully inspire the reader to explore further. This aspect and its associated web-based resources make the book particularly well-suited for teaching a course which emphasises the programming aspects of discrete event simulation.

---

[1] BMBF Programme for Scientific-Technological Collaboration with New Zealand, project number NZL 00/02

The Java Simulation Handbook is supported by a number of web-based resources. Readers can access a web server at http://www.desmoj.de with the DESMO-J software, a web-based DESMO-J tutorial, and a link to the cooperation platform CommSy (with a CommSy project room *JavaSimulationHandbook*). It contains a simulation laboratory with many example programs and some applet-based animations. These materials were developed as part of an e-learning project, which was financed by the E-Learning Consortium Hamburg from 2003 until 2005. The handbook itself is one of the results of this project and would not exist without this support. The web-based resources are a useful add-on to the book. In addition to its role as a repository for teaching materials, the project's online cooperation platform also offers a means for discussing the book's contents. User access to the CommSy-platform is open to readers of this book using the guest account *JavaBeans* and the password *snoopy*. The same account and password allow for access to the DESMO-J laboratory on the Internet.

The intended readership of this handbook and the DESMO-J framework are students and teachers of computer science, at both academic and other, possibly more applied, tertiary educational institutions. Readers should feel confident in using object-oriented programming styles and Java. Moreover, they should be interested in acquiring core competence in system analysis, model design, and the implementation of discrete event simulation programs. Some elementary knowledge of probability theory and statistics is assumed. Since the book only uses a small range of techniques, this can be obtained rather quickly. Suitable recommendations for further reading are given under *Further Reading* at the end of those chapters where additional background information seemed to be helpful for certain readers. Some knowledge of UML may prove helpful. To provide some background, the handbook presents those parts of UML that are particularly relevant to simulation.

The authors would like to thank all contributors, without whose participation a handbook of this depth and size would not have been possible. The DESMO-J software has been developed and extended by many colleagues and students, among who the main developers of the DESMO-J core Java foundation, Tim Lechler and Sönke Claasen, deserve particular thanks. Editorial work on the manuscript and its markup in LaTeXwas done by Johannes Göbel, with assistance by Ruth Meyer. Ruth Meyer also wrote the current version of the DESMO-J tutorial. Other e-learning materials for this book were created by Alexander Bentz and Gunnar Kiesel. At the end we must thank Kirsten-Verena Bull, Frank Heitmann, and Alexander Bentz for their final corrections, which have prevented many errors and inconsistencies to slip through.

We are very grateful to the BMBF and its New Zealand counterpart, for their financial support over many years. Among other things this has enabled us to travel in order to cooperate and communicate effectively over the large physical distance between Germany and New Zealand. Ultimately, this has provided a sound scientific basis on which the Java Simulation Handbook could be built. Further thanks go to the E-Learning Consortium Hamburg, for its financial support in writing the handbook and, in particular, for assistance in developing the accompanying electronic materials.

Finally, we thank the Shaker Verlag for the professional and timely publication of this handbook in its Informatik series. We are particularly pleased with the book's electronic version, which reflects our vision of a *blended* learning environment for the teaching of simulation rather well.

Bernd Page, \
University of Hamburg

Wolfgang Kreutzer, \
University of Canterbury

Hamburg and Christchurch, September 2005

Contents

I Foundations — 1

1 Introduction and Basic Terms — 3
- 1.1 Motivation and Overview — 3
- 1.2 Systems — 4
- 1.3 Models — 5
- 1.4 Simulation — 9
- 1.5 The Modelling Cycle — 12
- 1.6 Application — 17
- 1.7 Potential and Limitations of Simulation — 18
    - 1.7.1 Advantages of Modelling and Simulation — 18
    - 1.7.2 Limitations of Modelling and Simulation — 20
- Bibliography — 21

2 Basic Concepts in Discrete Event Simulation — 23
- 2.1 Motivation and Overview — 23
- 2.2 Discrete Event Simulation Model Components — 24
- 2.3 Relations between Model State and Time Advance — 24
- 2.4 Discrete Event Model Components — 28
- 2.5 Executing a Discrete Event Simulation — 29
- 2.6 Simulating Random Events — 31
- 2.7 From Event to Event: A Paper and Pencil Exercise — 32
- Bibliography — 35

3 Object-Oriented System Development and Simulation — 39
- 3.1 Motivation and Overview — 39
- 3.2 History & Core Concepts of Object-Orientation — 42
    - 3.2.1 Some History — 42
    - 3.2.2 Core Concepts — 43
- 3.3 Object-Oriented Analysis and Design — 49
- 3.4 Object-Oriented Programming Tools — 53
- 3.5 Summary and Perspectives — 54
- Further Reading — 56
- Bibliography — 57

Contents

4 Simulation Model Descriptions with UML 2 — 59
- 4.1 Motivation and Overview — 59
- 4.2 Introduction to the Unified Modelling Language — 60
  - 4.2.1 The Road to UML 2 — 61
  - 4.2.2 Diagram Types and Design Principles of the UML — 62
- 4.3 Modelling Static System Structures — 65
- 4.4 Modelling Dynamic Behaviour — 69
  - 4.4.1 Statecharts — 70
  - 4.4.2 Activity Diagrams — 77
- 4.5 Modelling Interactions — 87
  - 4.5.1 Sequence Diagrams of Interaction Scenarios — 88
  - 4.5.2 High Level Sequence Diagrams — 90
  - 4.5.3 Timing Diagrams — 92
- Further Reading — 93
- Bibliography — 93

5 Discrete Event Model Design — 97
- 5.1 Motivation and Overview — 97
- 5.2 Dominant Discrete Event Modelling Styles — 98
  - 5.2.1 Process-Oriented Simulation Modelling — 98
  - 5.2.2 Event-Oriented Simulation Modelling — 108
  - 5.2.3 Comparison and Evaluation — 117
- 5.3 Other Modelling Styles — 129
  - 5.3.1 Transaction-Oriented Modelling — 129
  - 5.3.2 Activity-Oriented Modelling — 131
- 5.4 Object-Oriented Model Construction — 133
- 5.5 Combined Modelling Styles — 134
  - 5.5.1 Embedding Events in a Process-Oriented Model — 134
  - 5.5.2 Example: A Combined Process/Event Model — 135
- Bibliography — 140

6 First Steps in Simulation Programming — 143
- 6.1 Motivation and Overview — 143
- 6.2 Java as a "Simulation Language" — 144
  - 6.2.1 General Requirements — 144
  - 6.2.2 Simulation-Specific Requirements — 146
  - 6.2.3 Advantages of Java as a Simulation Language — 149
- 6.3 A Simple Java Class Library for Event-Oriented Simulation — 149
  - 6.3.1 Event List — 150
  - 6.3.2 Entities, Events, and Event Scheduling — 152

Contents

		6.3.3	Distribution Sampling, Data Collection, and Queueing	153
		6.3.4	Example	156
	Further Reading			157
	Bibliography			157

7 Simulation Statistics   159
- 7.1 Motivation and Overview 159
- 7.2 Creating Random Numbers 161
  - 7.2.1 General Approach 161
  - 7.2.2 The Java Random Number Generator 168
- 7.3 Estimating an Input Distribution 170
- 7.4 Analysing a Simulation Experiment 173
  - 7.4.1 Repeating a Simulation Run 173
  - 7.4.2 Stationary Model States 174
  - 7.4.3 Warm-up Phases and Steady States 174
  - 7.4.4 Analysing Simulation Results 179
- 7.5 Observing a Simulation Experiment 185
  - 7.5.1 Independent Replications 185
  - 7.5.2 Batch Means 186
  - 7.5.3 Terminating and Non-Stationary Systems 188
- 7.6 Sample Size and Simulation Experiments 188
- 7.7 Choosing Good Model Parameters 189
- 7.8 Conclusion 191
- Further Reading 192
- Bibliography 192

8 Validation, Verification, and Testing of Simulation Models   195
- 8.1 Motivation and Overview 195
- 8.2 Foundations of Model Validation 197
  - 8.2.1 Basic Terms 197
  - 8.2.2 The Validation Process 199
  - 8.2.3 A Philosophical View of Model Validation 203
  - 8.2.4 Principles and Guidelines for Model Validation 205
  - 8.2.5 Classification of Validation Techniques 210
- 8.3 Selected Validation Techniques 211
  - 8.3.1 Conceptual Model Validation 212
  - 8.3.2 Model Verification and Testing 215
  - 8.3.3 Operational Validation of Model Behaviour 221
- 8.4 Summary 230
- Further Reading 231
- Bibliography 231

Contents

II Software 237

9 Simulation Software **239**
9.1 Motivation and Overview 239
9.2 Requirements 240
   9.2.1 General Requirements 240
   9.2.2 Simulation-Specific Requirements 241
9.3 Some History 243
9.4 Classification 247
9.5 Examples 251
   9.5.1 Extend 252
   9.5.2 eM-Plant 254
9.6 The Role of Animation 257
9.7 Criteria for Choosing Simulation Software in Practice 259
9.8 Commercial Discrete Event Modelling Tools 260
Bibliography 261

10 DESMO-J – A Framework for Discrete Event Modelling & Simulation **263**
10.1 Motivation and Overview 263
10.2 Simulation with DESMO-J 266
   10.2.1 The Event-Oriented World View 268
   10.2.2 The Process-Oriented World View 273
   10.2.3 Combining Events and Processes in a Single Model 274
   10.2.4 Some Core Model Components 276
10.3 Experimentation with DESMO-J 280
10.4 Advanced Concepts 284
   10.4.1 Higher-Level Modelling Constructs 284
   10.4.2 Hierarchical Modelling Constructs 291
   10.4.3 Graphical Interfaces 293
10.5 Example: Modelling Container Traffic in the Baltic Sea 293
   10.5.1 Model Description 293
   10.5.2 An Event-Oriented Implementation 294
   10.5.3 A Process-Oriented Implementation 307
   10.5.4 Using Higher-Level Modelling Constructs 314
10.6 Development and Evaluation 334
Bibliography 335

III Advanced Methodology 337

11 Multi-Agent-Based Simulation (MABS) 339
11.1 Motivation and Overview 339
11.2 Multi-Agent Systems 340
    11.2.1 The Agent Metaphor 340
    11.2.2 Characteristics of MAS 341
    11.2.3 Architectures for Agent Design 342
11.3 Different Views of Agent-Oriented Simulation 347
11.4 Foundations of Multi-Agent-Based Simulation 348
    11.4.1 Applications of MABS 349
    11.4.2 Comparison of Agent-Based and Classical World Views 351
    11.4.3 Components of Multi-Agent-Based Simulation Models 353
    11.4.4 Conceptual Modelling Methods 357
    11.4.5 Tools for Agent-Based Simulation 360
11.5 Conclusion: Potentials, Limitations, and Prospects for MABS 365
Further Reading 367
Bibliography 368

12 Parallel and Distributed Simulation 373
12.1 Motivation and Overview 373
12.2 Synchronization 374
12.3 Modes of Distribution 376
    12.3.1 Parallel Simulation 377
    12.3.2 Component-Based Simulation 378
    12.3.3 Web-Based Simulation 380
Further Reading 382
Bibliography 383

13 Simulation-Based Optimization 387
13.1 Motivation and Overview 387
13.2 Integration of Simulation and Optimization 388
13.3 A Formal Model for Simulation-Based Optimization Problems 391
13.4 Characteristics of Simulation-Based Objective Functions 392
13.5 Genetic Algorithms 394
    13.5.1 Terminology 395
    13.5.2 General Strategy 395
    13.5.3 Parallelization 397
Further Reading 397
Bibliography 398

IV Applications 399

14 Simulation and E-Learning 401
14.1 Motivation and Overview 401
14.2 E-Learning Foundations 403
    14.2.1 Definition 403
    14.2.2 Technological Development 404
    14.2.3 Three Theories of Learning 407
    14.2.4 Requirements for the Design and Implementation of E-Learning . 410
14.3 Computer Simulation to Improve E-Learning 412
    14.3.1 Simulation and Learning 412
    14.3.2 Simulation and E-Learning 413
    14.3.3 Simulation-Based Learning in LogEduGate 415
14.4 E-Learning to Support Simulation Learning 419
    14.4.1 Using DESMO-J to Teach Simulation Courses .. 420
    14.4.2 The DESMO-J Web Tutorial 421
    14.4.3 The DESMO-J Internet Laboratory 422
    14.4.4 Using Java Applets to Demonstrate Key Simulation Concepts . . 424
14.5 A Web Platform for Cooperative Teaching and Learning 427
14.6 Conclusions 429
Further Reading 430
Bibliography 431

15 Simulation and Logistics 435
15.1 Motivation and Overview 436
15.2 Introduction to Logistics 436
15.3 Modelling and Simulation in Logistics 440
    15.3.1 Application of Simulation in Logistics 440
    15.3.2 Logistics Simulation Tools 442
    15.3.3 Simulation Experiments in Logistics Problem Solving 443
15.4 Knowledge Acquisition and Knowledge Sharing in Logistics Simulation . 446
    15.4.1 Logistics Simulation Knowledge 446
    15.4.2 Cooperative Knowledge Sharing in Logistics Simulation Projects 448
    15.4.3 Simulation Model as Knowledge Repository 450
    15.4.4 Experiment-Based Knowledge Creation 451
    15.4.5 Knowledge Management and Logistics Simulation 452
15.5 Cases in Logistics Simulation 453
    15.5.1 Simulation to Support Logistics Planning:
        The Case of a Paper Store 453
    15.5.2 Simulation to Support Modification:
        The Case of a Pallet Flow System 458
    15.5.3 Simulation to Support Logistics Operation:
        The Case of an Order Picking System 461

15.6	Conclusions	465
	Further Reading	467
	Bibliography	468

16 Simulation in Practice — 469

16.1	Motivation and Overview	469
16.2	Introduction	470
16.3	General Requirements for a Successful Simulation Study	472
16.4	Simulation Project Organization	477
	16.4.1 Roles and Responsibilities in a Simulation Project Team	477
	16.4.2 Simulation as a Consulting Service	478
	16.4.3 Costs and Time Requirements for a Simulation Study	480
16.5	Methods of Data Collection	481
16.6	Typical Errors and Pitfalls in a Simulation Study	483
16.7	Conclusion	484
	Further Reading	485
	Bibliography	486

Authors — 487

Index — 493

Part I

Foundations

Chapter 1

Introduction and Basic Terms

Bernd Page, Wolfgang Kreutzer

Contents

1.1	Motivation and Overview	3
1.2	Systems	4
1.3	Models	5
1.4	Simulation	9
1.5	The Modelling Cycle	12
1.6	Application	17
1.7	Potential and Limitations of Simulation	18
	1.7.1 Advantages of Modelling and Simulation	18
	1.7.2 Limitations of Modelling and Simulation	20
	Bibliography	21

1.1 Motivation and Overview

Simulation is an experimental technique for modelling real or imaginary systems whose behaviour we wish to explore. Studying a system from multiple points of view and predicting how, as well as understanding why it will react to different inputs are main motivations for users of modelling tools. Since simulation can explore models with any degree of complexity, it can further these goals where other techniques may fail. Whenever a problem's solution requires a model too complex for mathematical optimization, simulation should be the tool of choice.

This chapter will explain some basic concepts, discuss how simulation differs from other modelling techniques (e.g. mathematical optimization), and summarize how simulations can be designed and constructed. After reading the chapter a student will

❑ understand important *terms* used in systems analysis and simulation;

❑ understand how simulation can be *used* in a modelling project; and

Chapter 1 Introduction and Basic Terms

❑ understand the importance of thinking in terms of *systems* as networks of complex connections.

As computing technology evolved from simple data processing to decision support systems and knowledge management systems based on complex networks of information, managing complexity has become an ever increasing concern of computer science. Competence in model design, construction, and analysis is an important skill for addressing this concern, and simulation techniques, while interdisciplinary and applicable to a wide range of problems, have proved particularly useful for analysing computer and communication systems at many levels in both the hardware and software domains.

Outside a computing technology context, model-based analyses have also grown in importance in many other areas, such as general systems analysis and design, logistics planning, and management of production facilities. To make relevant contributions to these areas, computer professionals need competence and skills to quickly acquire domain knowledge and communicate with a wide variety of computer users. The ability to model and simulate an application system at a suitable level of detail and validity furthers these goals by helping to understand basic terminology, structures, and processes of a task domain and by providing insights into an application's structure and context.

Simulation modelling is often associated with a set of techniques referred to as *operations research* (OR), which aims at providing support for both tactical and strategic decision making and planning. OR uses models, based on quantifiable information, to derive optimal solutions (with *analytical* models) or to explore state spaces (with *simulation* models) for a given system. While computer science views simulation as a subfield of its application, operations research considers it a subfield of OR. While OR perhaps focuses more strongly on methodology, for which computer science provides suitable software support, both disciplines have made many contributions to the state of the art of simulation modelling.

1.2 Systems

A *system* is a subset of reality which we study to answer a question; i.e. its *boundary* to the environment in which it is embedded will be determined by the questions we wish to ask. A system must have a number of distinct and clearly identifiable *components*, which may themselves be considered as systems at a "lower" level. Systems must be closed under a common purpose. Interactions between components generate behaviour, which is often counter-intuitive and hard to predict. Systems can encompass material as well as immaterial aspects; i.e. they may consist of ideas as well as real world objects.

To increase our understanding of many important systems, *science* has made good use of a range of techniques for abstraction and aggregation – particularly in the natural and engineering sciences. *Systems Analysis* is part of this programme to provide methods and tools to investigate the behaviour of a system over time; e.g. for *predict-*

ing the consequences of human activities. Often such studies are conducted on *models* rather than real systems, where great care must be taken to ensure that all *relevant* aspects of the real system are preserved. This requires knowledge of all relevant objects, properties, and actions, as well as their interactions. *Linear* analyses allow complex systems to be split into parts, which can then be studied in isolation. More recently interest has shifted to systems with interdependent and dynamically changing components, which are less amenable to linear analysis. Computer-based modelling offers a means for studying such *non-linear* phenomena.

System theory investigates patterns formed by relationships between systems and their components. It tries to discover how general principles of composition determine a system's structure and functions and how they are reflected within different scientific disciplines. Within this context, the following terms are commonly used:

- *Elements* or *objects* of a system are components of a system which are not decomposed any further (relative to a system's purpose).
- *Properties* or *attributes* of a system are variables storing an element's state.
- *System state* is defined by the set of values of all state variables (properties) of a system at any given point in time.
- *System behaviour* is a vector of system states over time.
- *System complexity* depends on the number of state variables and the density of their connections.
- *System boundary* is a border separating a system from its environment; i.e. from everything not included as part of the system.
- *Open* systems have at least one interaction with their environment; for example a factory with materials, orders, and energy as its inputs and products and waste as its outputs.
- *Closed* systems have no interactions with their environment; for example an aquarium or the dome of the American Biosphere II project.
- *Static* systems contain no time reference.
- *Dynamic* systems show time-dependent behaviour.
- *Cybernetic* systems contain feedback connections between their components.

Figure 1.1 summarizes and illustrates some of these terms.

1.3 Models

A *model* is a system's representation within a chosen experimental frame; i.e. a model must have a *purpose* or set of questions it can answer.

> "Models are material or immaterial systems which represent other systems in such a way that experimental manipulation of the modelled structures and states becomes possible" (Niemeyer 1977, p. 57).

Chapter 1 Introduction and Basic Terms

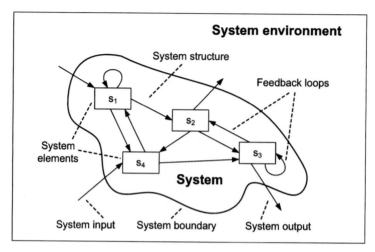

Figure 1.1: Some terms for describing a system

While *mental* models are involved in most of our thinking, we often employ an *external* model (e.g. maybe with the help of pencil and paper, twigs and stones, or computer-supported scenarios) to communicate our ideas or clarify thoughts whenever a system becomes too complicated to keep in mind. *Formal* models are needed for mathematical reasoning and whenever models need to be cast into code.

Models can help us improve understanding of system behaviour and the effects of interactions among components. We use *abstraction* and *idealization* to map real world systems to models. A model is therefore always a simplification of its original. This makes it possible for the human mind to analyse complex systems in a manageable fashion. Which system properties are considered essential and which can be safely ignored will always depend on a model's purpose. If needed, we can define many different models for a given part of reality, and each may reflect a different purpose and/or subjective point of view of a model designer. Models can be categorized in many different ways, e.g. according to their medium of representation or form of analysis:

- *physical* model: a scale model of a ship
- *verbal* model: verbal instructions for how to get to a place in a city
- *graphical* descriptive model: a UML activity diagram
- graphical *mathematical* model: a Petri net
- abstract *equation-based* model: a set of differential equations
- abstract *algorithmic* model: a discrete event simulation model

1.3 Models

Figure 1.2 shows a classification based on properties of a model's *state variables' values*, while Figure 1.3 differentiates four types of models by *purpose*.

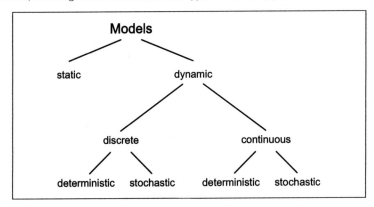

Figure 1.2: Model classification by state variable values

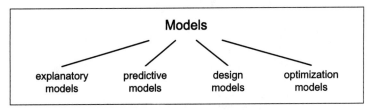

Figure 1.3: Model classification by purpose

Explanatory models serve understanding, *predictive* models derive a system's future states, *design* models explore alternative configurations (e.g. in warehouse planning) or sequencing (e.g. in logistics), and *optimization* models seek to maximize objectives.

Models reflect empirical observations and theoretical hypotheses so that logical conclusions about a system's behaviour can be drawn. This leads to improved understanding and better conceptual frameworks for predicting effects caused by actions. Within this context we can experiment with scenarios which are impossible or infeasible to observe in reality; for example:

- evolution of galaxies (beyond our control)
- continental drift (life's too short)
- emergency procedures in nuclear power stations (too dangerous)

Chapter 1 Introduction and Basic Terms

- admission schedules for a hospital ward (too disruptive)
- different manufacturing strategies used in semiconductor production (too expensive)

It is very important to remember that models are *always* abstractions of reality and must be built with a clear purpose in mind. Deriving models from systems is a subjective and *creative* activity, the results of which strongly depend on a modeller's knowledge, goals, experiences, cognitive style etc. What is considered "obvious" or important depends on what is already known. System boundaries are often fuzzy and the influence of the model environment may initially be quite unclear. This becomes even more important if a "real" system is not available or does not (yet) exist. According to Shannon (1975) modelling is "more art than science". There is therefore no "correct" model, only an appropriate or adequate one; i.e. a model that serves its purpose. The goal of a modelling project is always to understand, predict, or control, not to build the model itself.

Since a model should only be used for a purpose for which it has been *validated*, i.e. for which a "close enough" correspondence between system and model behaviour has been established (see Section 1.5 below), models cannot be reused uncritically. This means that *Occam's razor*[1] for reducing complexity should be applied to shave a model down to the simplest form serving its purpose; although this may require a depth of understanding which can only be gained through a lengthy sequence of modifications.

There are many ways in which models can be simplified; e.g.:

- removing elements and actions of no importance to model goals
- ignoring interactions of no importance to model goals
- aggregating elements and actions of little importance to model goals
- mapping specific elements into more general ones; e.g. by identifying a smaller number of object, action, or relationship types
- restricting the number of values state variables may take
- replacing detailed causal scenarios by mathematical functions (e.g. model seasonal variations in sunshine hours by a sine function) or probabilistic descriptions (e.g. model a trace of delay times by a distribution)

Goal-directed model design requires identification of relevant elements and their interactions. *Graphical visualizations* can aid this activity, particularly where dynamic interactions between processes are involved. Beyond this goal graphical representations also aid communication between model developers and application experts; both during model design and validation. Cause-effect diagrams, block diagrams, and *UML diagrams* are often used for this purpose.

---

[1] See http://www.webster-dictionary.org/definition/Occam%27s%20Razor

1.4 Simulation

Simulation (from Latin: *simulare*) is a term for which a range of definitions can be found in literature; for example:

- Simulation is "the imitation of a dynamic process in order to derive insights which can be applied to reality" (VDI 1993).
- Simulation is "the process of describing a real system and using this model for experimentation, with the goal of understanding the system's behaviour or to explore alternative strategies for its operation" (Shannon 1975).
- Simulation "involves playing out a model of a system by starting with the system status at an initial point in time and evaluating the variables in the model over time to ascertain the dynamic performance of the model" (Banks 1998).

In this book we favour a more precise definition of simulation in which the model building process is explicitly mentioned. Furthermore, we consider simulation a special modelling methodology in contrast to analytical models. Thus, we define *simulation* as the modelling of dynamic processes in real systems, based on real data, and seeking predictions for a real system's behaviour by tracing a system's changes of state over time (starting from some initial state). In computer-based simulations *models* are represented by (simulation) programs, and simulation experiments ("runs") are performed by a model's execution for a specified data set. Figure 1.4 shows the relations between system, model, and model user (observer).

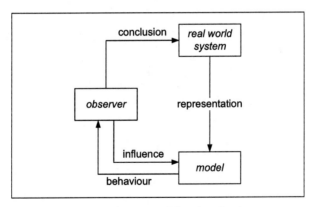

Figure 1.4: System, model, and application

Chapter 1 Introduction and Basic Terms

Analytical models differ from simulations in that they provide a set of equations for which closed-form solutions can be obtained. Examples are:

- analytical queueing models; e.g. an $M/M/1$ waiting system with expected value $ET = \frac{1}{\mu(1-\rho)}$ of residence time T for service rate μ and utilization ρ
- optimization models for maximizing or minimizing an objective function under constraints; e.g. (derived from Domschke and Drexl 1998, Ch. 1)

$$g_i(\mathbf{x}) \begin{cases} \geq \\ = \\ \leq \end{cases} 0 \quad \text{for } i = 1 \ldots m,$$

where $\mathbf{x}$ is a vector of variables with n components, and

$\mathbf{x} \in \mathbb{R}_n^+$ (ensures non-negativity),
$\mathbf{x} \in \mathbb{Z}_n^+$ (ensures that x_j ($j \in \{1, \ldots, n\}$) is a whole number), or
$\mathbf{x} \in \mathbb{B}_n$ (ensures that x_j ($j \in \{1, \ldots, n\}$) is a binary number)

In contrast to analytical models, simulation can only compute step-by-step traces of a state variable's values while the modeller must decide which variables should be traced at what level of detail. This strategy provides only a means of exploring a model's state spaces and does not guarantee to find solutions. Skilful experimentation with simulations is needed to make them as effective as problem solving tools. Simulation techniques should therefore only be used when analytical models fail to capture relevant aspects of a complex system; e.g. because of invalid linearity assumptions, inappropriate simplifications of complex connections and behaviour, or non-well-behaved forms of statistical distributions.

On the positive side, simulations need not be constrained by assumptions about linearity, distribution types, uniformity, and independence. This means that they can be made more realistic and can capture patterns of interactions whose complexity extends well beyond any analytical model's reach. Although simulation models cannot be "solved" for an optimum, they can help us explore models at different levels of detail and let us perform sensitivity analyses, based on e.g. different distributions and alternative system structures. Since they are typically mathematically simpler than analytical models, they are easier to understand and communicate to domain experts. The capability to trace simulations in a step-by-step fashion also makes them more credible to mathematically less sophisticated users.

The price paid for this flexibility is that valid and useful simulations need skill and much effort to be constructed and that optimal solutions cannot be guaranteed. However, in many cases a better solution than a current state of affairs will suffice and optimization, while desirable, may be impossible or too costly to obtain. Simulation models may also require considerable computational resources, and at higher levels of detail they will need large amounts of reliable data about the systems they represent.

1.4 Simulation

While there are many different types of simulation models, this book focuses on discrete event simulation, where all system state changes are mapped onto discrete events and assuming that nothing relevant happens between; i.e. that states remain constant and no computations are needed during such intervals. Such models' *time trajectory* can therefore be represented as a finite sequence of states. This class of models is particularly suitable for systems whose states do not fluctuate in a steady pattern and in which relevant changes of state happen suddenly and in irregular intervals. Within the general framework of discrete event simulation, *event-driven* (next event) models often lead to more precise and efficient model representations than the alternative *time-driven* ("fixed Δt") approach.

In so-called *continuous simulations* states change steadily over time, and models are framed in terms of differential equations with time as the free variable. Here simulation consists of solving the model equations, using numerical integration. Implementing this framework on a digital rather than analogue computer in a *quasi-continuous* fashion means that the model equations must be solved in a sequence of steps separated by a discrete time interval. Such simulations are often used to analyse engineering designs which involve feedback loops, as well as complex physical or biological processes; e.g. in fluid mechanics, weather prediction, or ecosystem analysis. The model classification based on the representation of time is summarized in Figure 1.5.

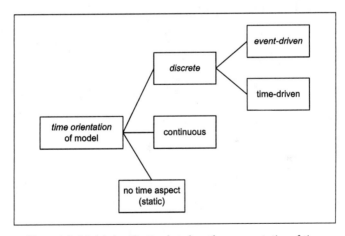

Figure 1.5: Model classification based on the representation of time (from Page et al. 2000, p. 6)

Chapter 1 Introduction and Basic Terms

A mathematical formulation of a continuous simulation model often consists of
- a set of time-dependent *state variables*: $x_1(t)\ldots x_n(t)$;
- a set of *input variables*: $u_1(t)\ldots u_m(t)$;
- a set of state *rates* at which state variables change: $x'_1(t)\ldots x'_n(t)$;
- a set of output variables (*results*): $y_1(t)\ldots y_r(t)$; and
- a system of *differential equations* describing the model dynamics:

$$x'_1(t) = f_1(x_1(t)\ldots x_n(t), u_1(t)\ldots u_m(t))$$
$$\vdots$$
$$x'_n(t) = f_n(x_1(t)\ldots x_n(t), u_1(t)\ldots u_m(t))$$
$$y_1(t) = h_1(x_1(t)\ldots x_n(t))$$
$$\vdots$$
$$y_r(t) = h_r(x_1(t)\ldots x_n(t)).$$

The so-called *predator-prey* model is a classic representative of this model type. For example, a population of hares can be modelled as a passive resource, actively preyed on by a population of foxes for which they are the only source of food. In a scenario for which simplifying assumptions abound, a suitable quasi-continuous model may consist of equations relating the two populations, which a continuous simulation would need to solve in a sequence of equidistant instants of model time, in order to trace both populations' (hares and foxes) temporal evolution. A rise in the fox population would be followed by a lagged decrease in hares (through kills) and a fall of the hare population would show a lagged decrease in foxes (through starvation). Each computation of system state at a model time instant plots one point on a corresponding chronological graph, which would show a sine curve if the system is in equilibrium. Otherwise all hares would be killed and all foxes would starve. A relevant purpose for such a model would be to determine how an equilibrium between the two populations can be achieved and maintained.

1.5 The Modelling Cycle

Clustered around model design and construction, a simulation project goes through a number of phases; as depicted in Figure 1.6. Here, the *conceptual model* is the result of the relevant abstractions and deliberations in the mind of the modeller while the *computer model* facilitates simulations by casting the model to code.

A closer look at this so-called *modelling cycle* reveals activities such as:
- problem definition and system identification
- model design
- data collection

1.5 The Modelling Cycle

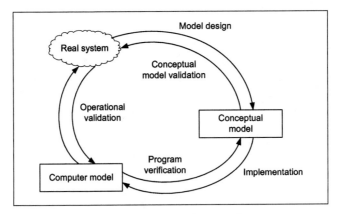

Figure 1.6: A process model of simulation

- model implementation
- model validation
- experimentation
- analysis of results
- presentation and documentation
- putting recommendations into practice

While listing activities in this way can be very useful, one should not expect a project to rigidly follow these steps in a linear sequence. As software engineering has learned over time, model development is a complex task, which needs to observe many cross connections between phases and may require many iterations until an acceptable outcome emerges. Figure 1.7 shows a possible sequence of steps.

Problem definition and system identification (1) Problem definition and system identification is based on a clarification of questions and goals, which determines appropriate levels of details and decides where system boundaries should be drawn. This phase also settles all basic assumptions and should result in a plan which includes estimates for costs, benefits, needed resources, and time. It should also sketch any expectations of interactions between model developers and model users.

Model design (2a) A first iteration of the conceptual model is built in this phase. Based on the modelled system's goals, boundaries and level of detail, relevant objects, properties, relationships, actions, events, and processes are identified and a suitable

Chapter 1 Introduction and Basic Terms

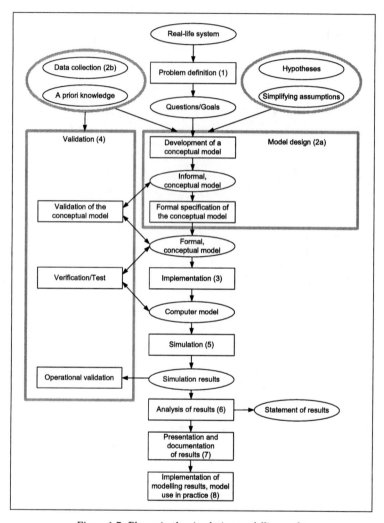

Figure 1.7: Phases in the simulation modelling cycle

1.5 The Modelling Cycle

modelling framework (e.g. analytical or simulation model, discrete or continuous, deterministic or stochastic) is chosen. This phase also includes suitable decomposition into modular units and identification of relevant patterns of interaction between them.

Graphical representations in the form of structure diagrams, flow charts, or UML diagrams can help model design, whose result will be a precise and formal, i.e. mathematical or algorithmic, representation of the informal conceptual model in the modeller's mind.

Data collection (2b) Planning for data collection to initialise model constants and variables, generate workloads, and estimate distributions should commence in parallel with model design. Relevant information can be derived from observation and measurement of the modelled system or obtained from domain experts. If all else fails, missing data can be roughly approximated (e.g. via estimated minimum, mean and maximum values). Chapter 16.5 presents further details on data collection.

Model implementation (3) Suitable implementation tools are determined during this phase. For computer-based models this includes choice of a programming language. While Chapter 9 discusses simulation software in detail, some alternatives of a programming language are:

- a general purpose high-level programming language
- a general purpose high-level programming language augmented by a package of suitable simulation related library procedures
- a general purpose simulation language
- a special purpose simulation language (e.g. for modelling computer networks)
- a ready-made simulation system that can be parametrized

The result of model implementation should be a syntactically and semantically correct (i.e. well tested) computer model.

Model validation (4) Validation is needed to ensure that a model's results will be credible. Since models are always abstractions of the systems they model, it is impossible to *prove* a model's correctness in general. It is, however, very important for a model's acceptance to do all that is possible to ensure that it is plausible, transparent, and that its behaviour can be easily reproduced. Validation can be performed at different levels:

- **Validation of a conceptual model** focuses on the correspondence between a system and a more abstract representation. This representation may be in an informal textual or graphical form. The goal here is to reach a common understanding between all participants in the modelling process and an agreement on model design.
- **Program verification** focuses on the correctness of mapping a conceptual model into a program. The term is somewhat misleading since *correctness* is an un-

Chapter 1 Introduction and Basic Terms

decidable property of programs, which cannot be verified but only be tested for. Here the term means that we must convince ourselves (and others) that a computer implementation is an accurate reflection of the model design.

❏ **Operational model validation** considers a large range of factors, such as model robustness, model calibration, and output comparison. Validation is most convincing when it can be confirmed empirically; e.g. by comparing a model's predictions to the modelled system's response. This assumes that sufficient empirical data about the modelled system is available. Major differences in the model's and modelled system's responses can point to modelling errors while small differences may possibly be corrected by modifying model parameters. If insufficient empirical information can be obtained (e.g. if the modelled system is not accessible or does not exist), we can still perform plausibility tests; e.g. the trend of a model's predictions could be compared to the results of a simpler analytical one.

Due to its importance and complexity, validation will be covered in detail in Chapter 8.

Experimentation (5) Simulation is an experimental technique which requires data to be collected during a model run (experiment). Since simulation uses models in place of a real system, many standard techniques for experimental design must be modified to take account of this difference. This holds particularly for *stochastic* models (i.e. models in which statistical distributions are used). In Chapter 7 we will therefore return to this topic and survey the application of relevant statistical methods to simulation experiments.

Analysis of results (6) Drawing conclusions from model experiments requires detection of patterns from which relevant and useful conclusions (e.g. "the network controller is a bottleneck") can then be drawn. This task requires both statistical compression of information (e.g. means, deviations, frequency distributions) and graphical representation (e.g. charts and plots). Since simulation runs generate a huge amount of data, it is particularly important to make it as easy as possible to detect interesting patterns. Although final, problem-relevant interpretation of data remains a task for the model user, "the goal is to generate insight, not numbers" (Hamming 1962).

Presentation and documentation (7) Presenting both model and data to domain experts in pleasing and easily understandable form is an important factor for model acceptance. Graphical representation is of particular value in this context and should be used to document both model (e.g. via UML diagrams) and simulation results (via bar charts, pie charts, chronological plots). All material should be commented and interpreted and inputs and outcomes for all phases of a simulation project should be explained.

1.6 Application

Putting recommendations into practice (8) The final step in the simulation modelling cycle concerns the practical application of model results to solve or improve the problem the model was meant to study. For example, additional trucks could be deployed in a logistics system as a result of a simulation study. Chapter 16 will discuss the problem of implementing simulation results in detail. Sometimes a model is intended to be used as a tool for recurring decisions (e.g. for controlling a power station). In this case user acceptance and ease of use becomes even more important. Ease of understanding, a high degree of transparency, highly visual interfaces, and adaptability to system changes and user requirements are additional criteria for success in such cases.

1.6 Application

Simulation is an interdisciplinary technique, which is used for many different problem types across a wide range of disciplines; e.g.:

- in the natural and engineering sciences
- in economics and social sciences
- in computer science
- in psychology and medicine
- in environmental science
- in the humanities

Some representative examples of applications are:

- *management science:* Planning of factory schedules, personnel planning, inventory management, business processes
- *production systems:* Planning and control of automated manufacturing systems
- *computer and information technology:* Computer configuration, simulation of operating systems, computer network analysis, database design, computer security issues, modelling of system failures, emergency management, chip design, client-server architectures
- *transportation and logistics systems:* Airport and seaport design, planning container terminals, transportation system design, product delivery scheduling, road network routing and capacity planning, scheduling traffic signals

While information technology uses simulation as an important tool for systems design and analysis, it also provides much of the infrastructure which makes simulation possible; e.g.:

- programming languages and software tools
- design methods
- Petri nets and graphical documentation and visualization tools
- databases and parallel computers
- standards for interfaces between system components

1.7 Potential and Limitations of Simulation

While modelling and simulation has long established itself as a proven tool for systems analysis, it remains important to be aware that well planned and correctly executed simulation studies are crucial for its success. Prudent application of simulation results also calls for awareness of the importance of informed and critical analyses, based on clear goals and realistic expectations according to the model's specifications regarding e.g. accuracy and level of detail. Responsibility for decisions on how to choose such requirements rests with a modeller and remains outside the scope of simulation as a technique.

This chapter has already mentioned some of the capabilities and advantages of simulation, and subsequent chapters will add to this. Like all things in life these are balanced by a number of problems and limitations. Figure 1.8 summarizes these aspects, which are then commented on in more detail below.

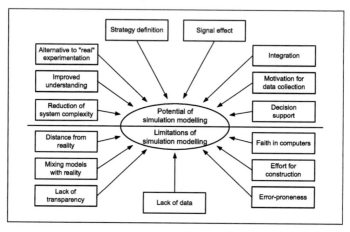

Figure 1.8: Potential and pitfalls of simulation

1.7.1 Advantages of Modelling and Simulation

Simulation can offer a number of advantages as a tool for systems design and analysis:

- **Capability for modelling high levels of complexity:** Our limited short-term memory puts constraints on the complexity of phenomena we can "keep in mind". We find it particularly difficult to reason about change over time or to trace consequences across long chains of events. As a result, we have developed

1.7 Potential and Limitations of Simulation

strategies to "divide and conquer"; by studying a complex system's components in isolation. Complex dynamic systems are composed of many interacting processes, for which such decompositions of wholes into independent and simpler parts is often impossible. Computer simulations provide the only available tool for analysing such complex scenarios, and their interdisciplinary aspect can further improve our capability for tackling many difficult problems.

- **Potential for improved understanding of system behaviour:** Building a model requires detailed system analysis and reflection. These activities often improve understanding even without making use of the model. The need to explicitly consider all aspects in preparation for coding highlights many formerly "tacit" premises (e.g. a-priori knowledge, hypotheses, background assumptions) and clarifies a model's logical structure. Inconsistencies and incomplete specifications become easy to spot.
- **Capability to offer alternatives to experimentation with real systems:** Studying models in place of reality can be very useful whenever manipulating a real system is either impossible, too expensive, or not advisable. In many such cases simulation offers the only way to experiment without disrupting the modelled system in unacceptable ways.
- **Capability to derive consequences associated with complex strategies:** Simulation can help making decisions which of a number of strategies controlling a complex system should be used; e.g. different scheduling strategies in a computer operating system.
- **Potential for "signal effects":** Exploring a simulation can warn of undesirable consequences of planned changes in complex systems; e.g. the danger of resource depletion.
- **Capability to use models as model components:** Provided they fulfil all constraints on their context of use, models or sub-models can be integrated as components in other models. In spite of the many difficulties which plague their design, reusable libraries of components have long been a Holy Grail of software engineering, and reusable simulation models can *in principle* assemble such collections. This may, however, prove difficult to accomplish in practice.
- **Potential for stimulating data collection:** Simulation models need reliable data; e.g. to instantiate model components and generate workloads. Such data can be of use independent of a simulation's requirements, and data collection motivated by the needs of a simulation study may well serve as a catalyst for regular gathering of such data in future.
- **Improvements to the quality of decisions and the competence of decision makers:** Because it can deal with high level complexity, modelling and simulation allows decision makers to widen their viewpoints. Since no "mechanical" automatism can take responsibility, these techniques cannot and should not *make* a decision. They can, however, *support* complex decision making and

Chapter 1 Introduction and Basic Terms

planning; e.g. by predicting the outcomes of hypothetical courses of action. Making it possible to evaluate large numbers of alternatives from different angles can also improve the quality of normative (i.e. value-driven) decisions.

1.7.2 Limitations of Modelling and Simulation

To use modelling and simulation in an informed and responsible way, knowing its limitations and risks is just as important as knowing its merits. The following issues must therefore be borne in mind by all model developers.

- **Conceptual gap between model and reality:** Modelling suggests simplification and can lead to scenarios where the gap between a model and the system it represents can be large. Experience shows that it is easy to interpret relationships wrongly, overlook relevant aspects, or assume inadequate goals. Such modelling errors become more likely at higher degrees of abstraction. Socio-economic or ecological systems in particular are full of qualitative factors which are difficult to quantify. This leads to challenges to a model's credibility and doubts of the validity of its conclusions. Careful validation becomes more important than ever.
- **Confusing a model with its reality:** The attraction and power of models can easily lead to an overestimation of their significance and accuracy. Simulation results are not "facts" and should not be treated as such. A model represents only one of a number of possible ways from which a real system can be viewed. Depending on purpose, different models emphasise different aspects and describe systems at different levels. All these perspectives are equally valid and must be kept clearly apart. Often our modelling goals seek only a snapshot of a system's steady state behaviour, from which a specific state may substantially differ.
- **Lack of transparency:** Transparency of all steps in a model's development is an important condition for a simulation's reproducibility. All important factors must be visible for and controllable by any interested outsider. Unfortunately obscure structural details, overly simplifying assumptions, heroic hypotheses, and tacit premises often make models and simulations very difficult to understand and trace with acceptable effort. Cleaner model structures, well commented implementation, and better documentation of models and experiments can help to avoid this pitfall.
- **Inadequate data:** In many applications models are built without suitable data. This can lead to the use of empirically inadequately supported estimates and has the potential to significantly devalue a model's result. All important data should be available at the start of a simulation study or should at least be obtainable with reasonable effort. If this is not the case, the advisability of using simulation should be carefully reassessed. Gathering data specifically for the needs of a simulation study requires adequate financial resources. These may be more readily available where such data can also be used for other purposes.

1.7 Potential and Limitations of Simulation

- **Propensity for errors:** The internal complexity of simulation models increases the risk of modelling errors during all phases of the modelling cycle (see Section 1.5). Model implementation, for example, can easily introduce unintended deviations from a model's design. Such errors can be difficult to find and will sometimes never be detected. Proper validations should guard against the effects of such errors, but many modelling projects skip or treat this important step much too lightly. In some models the effects of *numerical* errors should also not be underestimated. In lengthy simulations these can accumulate and produce biased (and therefore invalid) results. These effects can be exacerbated in stochastic models, where proper generation of random numbers and sampling from specified distributions can create additional biases, which may be extremely hard to detect. In many cases unfortunate choices for initial values can also have a significant influence on the accuracy of a model's results.

- **High degrees of construction effort:** Like most computer software, simulation models are complex artefacts, which take considerable time to construct. It is easy to underestimate this, which can subsequently lead to a project's failure. Another danger associated with the long duration of modelling projects lies in the fact that some relevant characteristics of the modelled system may change; and thus make a partially completed model invalid.

- **Misplaced confidence in computer generated data:** Since our society treats computers as embodiments of rationality, there is always a danger that computer generated predictions will be falsely endowed with an aura of objectivity. Simulation models are *not* objective; rather they may embody highly personal theories on how a complex system may function. Any objectivity must be granted through validation; for a particular problem and for a particular range of questions which can be asked. Uncritical interpretation of simulation results may conveniently ignore these facts and use the computer's rational aura to invalidly justify a preferred point of view. While this danger is common to all models or lines of argument, it is particularly grave in the case of a complex simulation; largely because hidden assumptions in the underlying model may be very hard to discover, and its computer-based nature may give it a false sense of objectivity. Avoiding this danger requires transparent models and comprehensive documentation as much as a willingness for critical consideration on the part of a user.

All the above mentioned issues are not equally problematic in all areas of application. For example, they are more acute for highly aggregated models formulated at *macro* levels. Models of this type are common in the social sciences, economics, and the ecological sciences. More specific and less aggregated *micro* models, which include the class of time dynamic models discussed in this book, are less threatened by some of these problems. However, the prudent modeller as well as a competent user would do well to keep modelling and simulation's limitations and risks firmly in mind.

Bibliography

J. Banks, editor. *Handbook of Simulation – Principles, Methodology, Advances, Applications, and Practice*. Wiley, New York, 1998. Chapter 1.

W. Domschke and A. Drexl. *Einführung in Operations Research* ("Introduction to Operations Research", in German). Springer, Berlin, 4th edition, 1998. Chapter 1.

R. W. Hamming. *Numerical Methods for Scientists and Engineers*. McGraw-Hill, New York, 1962.

A. M. Law and W. D. Kelton. *Simulation Modeling and Analysis*. McGraw-Hill, New York, 3rd edition, 2000. Chapter 1.

G. Niemeyer. *Kybernetische System- und Modelltheorie, System Dynamics* ("Cybernetic System and Model Theory, System Dynamics", in German). Vahlen, Munich, 1977.

L. Oakshott. *Business Modelling and Simulation*. Pitman, London, 1997. Chapters 1, 2, and 6.

B. Page. *Diskrete Simulation – Eine Einführung mit Modula-2* ("Discrete Simulation – An Introduction with Modula-2", in German). Springer, Berlin, 1991. Chapter 1.

B. Page, T. Lechler, and S. Claassen. *Objektorientierte Simulation in Java mit dem Framework DESMO-J* ("Object-Oriented Simulation in Java with the Framework DESMO-J", in German). Libri Book on Demand, Hamburg, 2000.

R. E. Shannon. *Systems Simulation – The Art and Science*. Prentice Hall, Englewood Cliffs, 1975.

Verein Deutscher Ingenieure (VDI). *Simulation von Logistik-, Materialfluss- und Produktionssystemen – VDI-Richtlinie 3633* ("Simulation of Systems in Materials Handling, Logistics, and Production – VDI-Guideline 3633", in German). Beuth, Berlin, 1993.

Chapter 2

Basic Concepts in Discrete Event Simulation

Bernd Page, Wolfgang Kreutzer

Contents

2.1	Motivation and Overview	23
2.2	Discrete Event Simulation Model Components	24
2.3	Relations between Model State and Time Advance	24
2.4	Discrete Event Model Components	28
2.5	Executing a Discrete Event Simulation	29
2.6	Simulating Random Events	31
2.7	From Event to Event: A Paper and Pencil Exercise	32
	Bibliography	35

2.1 Motivation and Overview

This chapter aims to give the reader some motivation and basic understanding of how simulations can be realized as computer programs, we will first explain some core concepts and then demonstrate how discrete event simulation programs work.

Although discrete event simulation can take many forms and can be used to solve many different problems, a small number of basic ideas underlie all modelling and simulation techniques and the most important are summarized in Section 2.2. The most characteristic aspect of computer-based discrete event simulation models is the representation of system states and their change over time; a requirement for which Section 2.3 highlights some commonly used modelling strategies. Section 2.4 surveys common properties and components of discrete event simulation models. This includes the initialisation module, the notion of a simulation clock, the event list, statistical instrumentation, and the display of reports. Section 2.5 will then offer a glimpse "behind the scenes" of a running simulation, which will include a preliminary discussion of *stopping rules*; i.e. when and how simulations should terminate. Most discrete event simulations are stochastic; i.e. they describe mathematical experiments which may have non-deterministic results. So-called *pseudo-random numbers* are therefore a central component of discrete event simulations. How to use them to model random events is touched on in Section 2.6. A "hand-simulated" step-by-step paper and pencil example in Section 2.7 concludes the chapter and is intended to help readers understand how a discrete event simulation can function.

2.2 Discrete Event Simulation Model Components

A simulation model consists of objects called *entities*. Entities model a real system's components and may interact with each other. The terms *entity* and *object*, as used in object-oriented programming, are closely related. An entity can be viewed as an object whose behaviour is defined throughout a simulation's duration.

> "An entity is an object which can (actively) move through simulated time."
> (Spaniol and Hoff 1995, p. 9)

Entities are characterized by their *state* (defined by their attributes' values) and a set of *methods* or *rules* for their state's change over time. To trigger such state transformations at specified (model) times, we must attach a *time* property to a method, which can then be asked to execute when required.

The example in Figure 2.1 shows entities modelling vehicles, a road, and two traffic lights as part of a traffic simulation.

2.3 Relations between Model State and Time Advance

Models are representations of a real system's (static) structure and (dynamic) behaviour. In addition to showing all relevant states, a dynamic model must also describe how these may change over time. A number of elementary concepts serve this purpose in time-discrete simulations.

The time whose passing is modelled internally during a simulation is referred to as *model time*. In contrast to *real time*, which passes during a simulation's execution, model time is fictitious and independent of the length of a computation. For example, the simulation of a 45 second phone call in a mobile network may well need more than an hour to execute (since many other calls will also be simulated during this period), while an inventory system simulation of a year's transactions may only require a few minutes of computation.

Queueing networks, in which customers request the attention of capacity-constrained servers, are typical examples of time discrete models. If a server is busy, customers must wait their turn. The resulting queue, e.g. in front of a group of machines in a manufacturing facility, changes only with the arrival or departure of items which are to be processed by this facility. Such arrivals and departures can be viewed as *discrete*

2.3 Relations between Model State and Time Advance

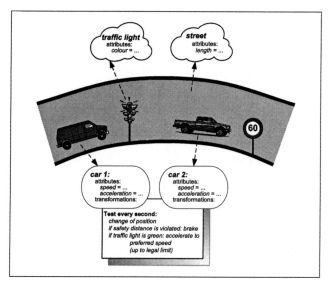

Figure 2.1: Entities of a traffic simulation (derived from Spaniol and Hoff 1995, p. 6)

events, which occur at discrete points along a simulated model's time axis. Often such models trace the behaviour of particular classes of entities (e.g. tasks, products, or machines) and, to answer some relevant questions, it is often advantageous or even necessary to model such entities as objects with a history or "lifecycle" of their own. In addition to aiding performance analysis of production facilities, such models can also be used to study breakdowns and interruptions. This allows us to predict system availability or compare alternative scheduling strategies for servers. Inventory systems, in which distributions and deliveries occur as discrete events, also map well into a discrete event model. Other important applications of simulation technology include computer system and network simulations, models of telecommunication systems, and efficiency studies of a variety of different supply and logistics systems.

Discrete event simulation techniques can be contrasted with modelling frameworks where the effects of steady fluctuations of system states are modelled for a specified time period. In Section 1.4 we have already taken a glimpse at such *quasi-continuous* simulation models.

In this book we will concentrate on the foundations of *discrete event simulation*. Here, simulation time jumps from event to event, triggered by relevant changes in an entity's state. In between such events no changes are made to the model. To support

Chapter 2 Basic Concepts in Discrete Event Simulation

such a strategy, each event must record its type, which entities it involves, and the event time; i.e. the time at which the event will occur. Whenever an event occurs, a model time clock will be updated to the event's event time and any required state transformation will be performed (see Figure 2.2). Most state transformations will in turn lead to further events, whose occurrence will be recorded for future consideration. Once the current event has been processed, the next event – i.e. the one with the now lowest event time – will be chosen and attended to. To facilitate this, a simulation controller (or "monitor") keeps all candidate events (planned to occur in the future) in a data structure called an *event list*. A simulation run then iterates this strategy (select next event, update model time, change model state, record new events) across all items in the event list; until this list becomes empty or other criteria (e.g. number of samples or end of a time interval) terminate the cycle.

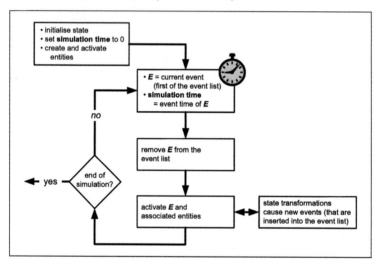

Figure 2.2: Simplified flow of a discrete event simulation
(derived from Spaniol and Hoff 1995, p. 8)

Events with the same event time are referred to as parallel events and can be processed in any order (e.g. *FCFS*, "first come, first served"), unless specific priorities are attached to individual events or event classes. Typical operations on an event list include reordering, insertion, access, or deletion of events.

All dynamic system behaviour can ultimately be mapped into event sequences; as shown in Figure 2.3. The model time management of next event simulations is reflected in the model clock's discrete and variable length jumps from the current event's time of

2.3 Relations between Model State and Time Advance

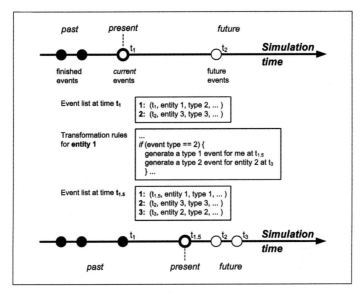

Figure 2.3: Example of event list processing when using a next event strategy (derived from Spaniol and Hoff 1995, p. 9)

occurrence to the next event's time of occurrence. In contrast to a simpler strategy based on a fixed time increment ("time slicing"), discrete event simulation allows more precise and realistic schedules of state transformations and avoids any potential inaccuracies of executing events in the "wrong" order, or inefficiencies caused by long "idle" periods associated with an unfortunate choice of a fixed update interval.

Discrete event simulation offers three different frameworks for synchronizing a model's state changes with the passage of simulation time (see Figure 2.4):

1. Using *events* which describe changes of an entity's state at specified points in model time. Such events can be generated
   - externally; i.e. their occurrence is determined solely by the environment. Modelling electricity blackouts or customer arrivals are good examples;
   - internally; i.e. their occurrence is caused by state transformations of model entities.

   Event times can be deterministic or stochastic (e.g. beginning and end of a customer service).

27

Chapter 2 Basic Concepts in Discrete Event Simulation

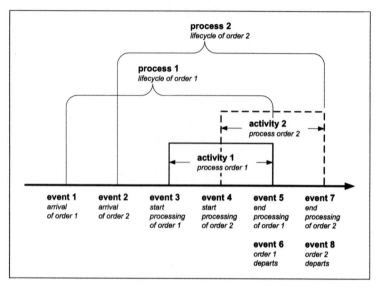

Figure 2.4: Relationships between events, activities, and processes in an order-processing system (from Page 1991, p. 27)

2. Using *activities* composed of a set of operations performed during a model time interval. State changes are then performed at an activity's beginning and end; e.g. the acquisition (at a service's beginning) and release (at a service's end) of a server in a queueing scenario.

3. Using *processes* composed of sequences of activities related to a class of entities' lifecycle. We could, for example, use a process to describe a machine's operation in a manufacturing simulation; i.e. as it attends to a sequence of orders with different processing requirements.

2.4 Discrete Event Model Components

A variety of components are required to implement discrete event simulation models. These include:

- ❑ A representation of *system state*; i.e. a set of state variables describing the modelled system at model time t.
- ❑ A *simulation clock*; i.e. a variable which stores current model time.

- A *process or event list* whose elements store time and type of processes or events whose occurrence is planned in the future; this list is ordered by time.
- *Statistical counters* which collect relevant results of simulation runs, each of which defines a simulation experiment.

A number of methods are also needed to simulate typical discrete event simulation models; e.g.:

- A main process to control initialisation and termination of simulation experiments.
- Methods for *initialisation* at the start of a simulation experiment.
- Some *process descriptions* or *event routines* which define changes in model state. One process description is needed for each class of model process, and one event routine must be defined for each type of event.
- Methods for statistical instrumentation and the display of performance measures during and at the end of a simulation run.
- An internal control loop, runtime control system, or monitor routine, whose execution drives it through the simulated model time dimension. It loops through a set of common repeating activities (see Figure 2.2):
  - select the next imminent event from the event list
  - update the system clock to the time aspect of this event, i.e. jump to the time of the "next event"
  - activate the relevant process phase or event routine

2.5 Executing a Discrete Event Simulation

Figure 2.5 summarizes the internal processing strategy used in a typical discrete event simulation.

To serve as a tool for performance prediction, we must take great care that the data we collect during a simulation is valid; i.e. that it adequately characterizes the behaviour of the real system the model is meant to represent. Among other things this means that we need to pay careful attention when to terminate a simulation once it has run "long enough". For this a number of strategies can be used, e.g.:

1. Specify a fixed length model time for the simulation to run. Termination can be achieved through either a special termination event or by continually polling the model time and comparing it to the stop time.
2. Prescribe a fixed sample size; e.g. in terms of a number of transactions, messages, customer lifecycles to be simulated.
3. Require specific confidence intervals to be reached for a model's key output variables.

Chapter 2 Basic Concepts in Discrete Event Simulation

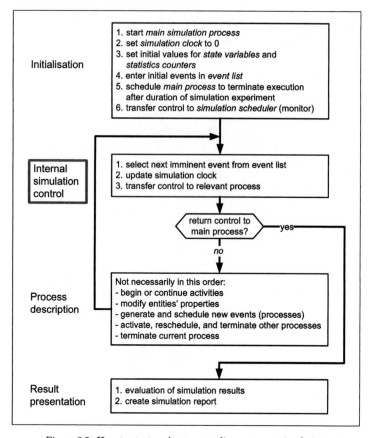

Figure 2.5: How to start and process a discrete event simulation

4. Define termination in terms of the model's state; e.g it may stop when all capacity has been depleted or when key performance indicators seem to be in steady state (don't seem to change much any more).
5. Run a simulation until it terminates; e.g. until its event list is empty.

2.6 Simulating Random Events

Most discrete event simulations are stochastic; i.e. they describe mathematical experiments which may have non-deterministic results. So-called *pseudo-random numbers* are therefore a central component of discrete event simulation software.

In a model an invocation of a generator of pseudo-random numbers is used to simulate a "random" event or behaviour. A typical example is the arrival of customers in a queueing scenario. An *arrival event* models this system aspect. To determine the model time when such events should be scheduled, we could draw on empirical data collected in the real system our model is a model of, and use these to create model arrivals. However, such data is typically just a short sample whose size would limit the length of model time our simulation could be run for.

A better alternative may be to use statistical analysis of the empirical samples to derive a suitably representative *distribution function*. If such a function is known or can be estimated and calibrated from the available data (see Page 1991, Ch. 4.3), it can be used to create a stream of synthetic samples. To do this, we create uniformly distributed random numbers over the interval [0,1] (called *normalized* random numbers) and then use an inverse transformation to map these into the sample we need. There are other ways to generate suitable samples if an inverse transformation does not exist (e.g. for normal distributions). Samples created in this fashion can, for example, model the intervals between successive customer arrivals. Such intervals are often adequately characterized by a negative exponential distribution. Modelling service time delays in a queueing network is another example for where samples drawn from a specified distribution are typically needed.

While the potential for unlimited creation and their potential reproducibility for the purpose of model debugging is clearly attractive, an algorithmic creation of random numbers has also a number of drawbacks. Sequences of numbers created by the commonly used "congruential" methods will repeat themselves after some finite period (i.e. once a cycle hits the same number again, see Section 7.2.1). After this happens, such number streams cease to be statistically independent and should not be used any further. The great advantage of synthetically generated pseudo-random numbers, however, is their reproducibility; i.e. when grown from the same initial value (called seed) the same sequence will start again. Since we can use this property to rule out effects caused by different random numbers, we can have more confidence in comparisons of models using different strategies. It is advisable to use stochastically independent streams of random numbers for each stochastic variable in a model, which requires separate generators for each stream.

In this book we cannot do justice to the wealth of complex issues governing the proper use of statistical methods in discrete event simulation because our main focus is on model design and implementation. We discuss statistical methods in some detail in Chapter 7. Interested readers should consult other textbooks which cover this topic more comprehensively; e.g. Law and Kelton (2000, Ch. 4 and Ch. 6–12) or Banks (1998).

2.7 From Event to Event: A Paper and Pencil Exercise

In this section we will now step through a simple example that takes a closer look at how a discrete event simulation is executed. The example models transportation aspects of a gravel pit as a queueing system and will be manually traced over 25 cycles of the simulation monitor, where changes in model clock, system states, event list, and statistical instrumentation are shown at each step. We suggest that you use paper and pencil to record progress.

System Description

A gravel pit uses six trucks for transporting gravel to a closely located train station. Each of these trucks has the following lifecycle:

- Unloaded trucks access one of two loading docks and become loaded. The distribution of relevant loading times is shown below in Table 2.1. If both loading stations are busy, trucks join a FIFO (first in, first out; i.e. the first truck entering the queue will be the first leaving) queue which feeds both stations.
- Loaded trucks drive directly to an adjacent weighing station. If necessary, the trucks have to join a FIFO queue here, too. Because the distance is short, we abstract from driving times and model this without time delays. The distribution of weighing times is listed below.
- Weighed trucks transport their loads to a train station and return to the gravel pit's loading dock after unloading. We will not model this in detail, but will rather just sample a time delay distribution (see Table 2.1) to represent this task.

Figure 2.6 shows a graphical summary of the model.

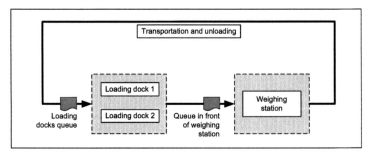

Figure 2.6: A summary of the gravel pit model

2.7 From Event to Event: A Paper and Pencil Exercise

Model Structure

System state at a given time t can be viewed as a tuple

$$\langle l, q_l, w, q_w \rangle_t$$

where l is the number of trucks in the two loading docks (0, 1, or 2), q_l is the number of trucks in the loading docks queue, w is the number of trucks in the weighing station (0 or 1), and q_w the number of trucks in the weighing station queue.

Model Entities

Relevant entities for this model are trucks (6 objects), loading docks (2 objects), and weighing station (1 object).

Event Types

At a minimum we need only three types of events to prescribe changes of state in this model (see Section 5.2.2):
- arrival of $truck_i$ at the loading docks (or their queue) at time t (AT, t, $truck_i$)
- end of loading $truck_i$ at time t (EL, t, $truck_i$)
- end of weighing $truck_i$ at time t (EW, t, $truck_i$)

Queues

Since processing of trucks at the gravel pit proceeds in two stages, the model contains two queues:
- a joint FIFO queue in front of the two loading docks
- a FIFO queue in front of the weighing station

Activities Which Consume Model Time

To represent any activity with fluctuating duration, we need a statistical basis (see Table 2.1). This stochastic aspect of model time intervals is typical for discrete event simulations and is often based on empirical data from which relevant frequency or probability distributions can be derived. While a simulation is running, these are then sampled to obtain time delays in a model.

Note that the column "numeric encoding" is used to assist "random" selections based on a Table of random numbers (see table 2.4 at the end of this section) during the manual execution of simulations.

Chapter 2 Basic Concepts in Discrete Event Simulation

Table 2.1: Durations of model activities

Loading a truck in a loading dock:	*loading time*	*probability*	*cumulative probability*	*numeric encoding*
	5	0,3	0,3	1–3
	10	0,5	0,8	4–8
	15	0,2	1,0	9–0
Weighing a truck in a weighing station:	*weighing time*	*probability*	*cumulative probability*	*numeric encoding*
	12	0,7	0,7	1–7
	16	0,3	1,0	8–0
Transportation (inclusive unloading) delays:	*transport time*	*probability*	*cumulative probability*	*numeric encoding*
	40	0,4	0,4	1–4
	60	0,3	0,7	5–7
	80	0,2	0,9	8–9
	100	0,1	1,0	0

Model Initialisation

Before a simulation can start, models must be in some well-defined initial state (possibly empty) at model time 0. In our model we assume that there is one truck in the weighing station (for which a weighing activity will start immediately) and that the other five trucks are all queued in front of the loading docks; i.e. two trucks can be loaded immediately.

Model Execution

To better our understanding of a discrete event simulation's execution, we trace 25 of the monitor's processing cycles (i.e. simulation steps) and record system states after each cycle. To determine each loading, weighing, and transport time, we use the random numbers in Table 2.4 at the end of this chapter; specifically those in rows 1, 2, and 3. Based on the numeric encoding of Table 2.1, we obtain the sequence of times shown in Table 2.2. As long as they can be established as suitably *random*, other numbers would serve just as well. However, while the model's long term behaviours would hopefully be very similar, specific event sequences would differ from our results. All delays associated weighing and transportation can be modelled in the same way.

Table 2.2: Samples for loading, weighing, and transportation delays

Loading times	(from Table 2.4, row 1)	5	5	10	5	10	5	10	5	10	10	15	5	10	...
Weighing times	(from Table 2.4, row 2)	12	12	12	16	16	12	16	12	16	12	12	16	12	...
Transportation times	(from Table 2.4, row 3)	60	60	60	60	40	40	60	100	40	40	40	40	80	...

2.7 From Event to Event: A Paper and Pencil Exercise

Table 2.3 shows an extract from the record of system states for 25 steps of simulating our sample model. The interested reader should complete all missing steps (i.e. step 6 to 24) on his or her own. To aid computation of estimates for mean utilizations of loading docks and weighing station, the table offers two additional columns in which their cumulative use is recorded. These values will be increased by each time interval during which a loading dock or the weighing station has been in use. It should be obvious that 25 steps can hardly even approximate any accurate performance predictions and that any credible simulation experiment must be run for much longer.

Table 2.3: A step-by-step view of the gravel pit simulation

Step	Clock	System state l	q_l	w	q_w	Stations loading	Stations weighing	Queues loading	Queues weighing	List of events	Cumulative usage times Dock	Cumulative usage times Weighing Station
1.	0	2	3	1	0	$truck_2$ $truck_5$	$truck_1$	$truck_4$ $truck_3$ $truck_6$	–	(EL, 0 + 5, $truck_2$) (EL, 0 + 5, $truck_5$) (EW, 0 + 12, $truck_1$)	0	0
2.	5	2	2	1	1	$truck_3$ $truck_4$	$truck_1$	$truck_5$ $truck_6$	$truck_2$	(EL, 5, $truck_3$) (EW, 12, $truck_1$) (EL, 5 + 10, $truck_4$)	10	5
3.	5	2	1	1	2	$truck_4$ $truck_5$	$truck_1$	$truck_6$	$truck_2$ $truck_3$	(EW, 12, $truck_1$) (EL, 5 + 5, $truck_5$) (EL, 15, $truck_4$)	10	5
4.	10	2	0	1	3	$truck_4$ $truck_6$	$truck_1$	–	$truck_2$ $truck_3$ $truck_5$	(EW, 12, $truck_1$) (EL, 15, $truck_4$) (EL, 10 + 10, $truck_6$)	20	10
5.	12	2	0	1	2	$truck_4$ $truck_6$	$truck_2$	–	$truck_3$ $truck_5$	(EL, 15, $truck_4$) (EL, 20, $truck_6$) (EW, 12 + 12, $truck_2$) (AT, 12 + 60, $truck_1$)	24	12
...	...	...	...	...	...	...	...	...	...	...	...	...
25.	122	1	0	1	2	$truck_6$	$truck_3$	–	$truck_4$ $truck_5$	(EW, 124, $truck_3$) (EL, 135, $truck_6$) (AT, 156, $truck_1$) (AT, 208, $truck_2$)	77	122

When we look at the results of this simulation, we should again bear in mind that such a short duration will most probably lead to highly skewed and unrealistic results and that the model's initial state will have an undesirably strong influence.

Utilizations for loading docks and the weighing station can be derived from their cumulative usage – as recorded in the rightmost two columns of Table 2.3. Their computation divides this usage by the maximally available capacity. Since the example run simulated 122 model time units and the two loading docks were in use for 77 time units, their utilization is $77/122 \approx 0.631$ or 63.1%. The utilization statistic for the weighing station is $122/122 = 1.0$; i.e. 100%. This result suggests the conclusion that the weighing station is more highly utilized than the loading docks, and that the weighing station is the gravel pit model's bottleneck. Is this a valid conclusion? To answer this question, we must again look at the distributions for loading and weighing times in Table 2.1. While the mean time delay of a truck at a loading dock ranges from 5 to 15 minutes, the weighing station needs an average time of 12 to 16 minutes to weigh a truck. Since there are two loading docks but only one weighing station, it is not surprising that the weighing station is more highly utilized and it seems very unlikely that lengthier simulations will suggest any different conclusion.

Chapter 2 Basic Concepts in Discrete Event Simulation

Table 2.4: A table of random numbers

Row	1	2	3	4	5	6	7	8	9	10
1	33628	17364	01409	87803	65641	33433	48944	64299	79066	31777
2	51199	49794	49407	10774	98140	83891	37195	24066	61140	65144
3	55672	16014	24892	13089	00410	81458	76156	28189	40595	21500
4	87331	82442	28104	26432	83640	17323	68764	84728	37995	96106
5	78702	98067	61313	91661	59861	54437	77739	19892	54817	88645
6	54680	13427	72496	16967	16195	96593	55040	53729	62035	66717
7	18880	58497	03862	32368	59320	24807	63392	79793	63043	09425
8	10242	62548	62330	05703	33535	49128	66298	16193	55301	01306
9	54993	17182	94618	23228	83895	73251	68199	64639	83178	70521
10	22686	50885	16006	04041	08077	33065	35237	02502	94755	72062
11	42349	03145	15770	70665	53291	32288	41568	66079	98705	31029
12	18093	09553	39428	75464	71329	86344	80729	40916	18860	51780
13	11535	03924	84252	74795	40193	84597	42497	21918	91384	84721
14	35066	73848	65351	53270	67341	70177	92373	17604	42204	60476
15	57477	22809	73558	96182	96779	01604	25748	59553	64876	94611
16	48647	33850	52956	45410	88212	05120	99391	32276	55961	41775
17	86857	81154	22223	74950	53296	67767	55866	49061	66937	81818
18	20182	36907	94644	99122	09774	29189	27212	79000	50217	71077
19	83687	31231	01133	41432	54542	60204	81618	09586	34481	87683
20	81315	12390	46074	47810	90171	36313	95440	77583	28506	38808
21	87026	52826	58341	76549	04105	66191	12914	55348	07907	06978
22	34301	76733	07251	90524	21931	83695	41340	53581	64582	60210
23	70734	24337	32674	49508	49751	90489	63202	24380	77943	09942
24	94710	31527	73445	32839	68176	53580	85250	53243	03550	00128
25	76462	16987	07775	43162	11777	16810	75158	13894	88945	15539
26	14348	28403	79245	69023	34196	46398	05964	64715	11330	17515
27	74618	89317	30146	25606	94507	98104	04239	44973	37636	88866
28	99442	19200	85406	45358	86253	60638	38858	44964	54103	57287
29	26869	44399	89452	06652	31271	00647	46551	83050	92058	83814
30	80988	08149	50499	98584	28385	63680	44638	91864	96002	87802
31	07511	79047	89289	17774	67194	37362	85684	55505	97809	67056
32	49779	12138	05048	03535	27502	63308	10218	53296	48687	61340
33	47938	55945	24003	19635	17471	65997	85906	98694	56420	78357
34	15604	06626	14360	79542	13512	87595	08542	03800	35443	52823
35	12307	27726	21864	00045	16075	03770	86978	52718	02693	09096
36	02450	28053	66134	99445	91316	25727	89399	85272	67148	78358
37	57623	54382	35236	89244	27245	90500	75430	96762	71968	65838
38	91762	78849	93105	40481	99431	03304	21079	86459	21287	76566
39	87373	31137	31128	67050	34309	44914	80711	61738	61498	24288
40	67094	41485	54149	86088	10192	21174	39948	67268	29938	32476
41	94456	66747	76922	87627	71834	57688	04878	78348	68970	60048
42	68359	75292	27710	86889	81678	79798	58360	39175	75667	65782
43	52393	31404	32584	06837	79762	13168	76055	54833	22841	98889
44	59565	91254	11847	20672	37625	41454	86861	55824	79793	74575
45	48185	11066	20162	38230	16043	48409	47421	21195	98008	57305
46	19230	12187	86659	12971	52204	76546	63272	19312	81662	96557
47	84327	21942	81727	68735	89190	58491	55329	96875	19465	89687
48	77430	71210	00591	50124	12030	50280	12358	76174	48353	09682
49	12462	19108	70512	53926	25595	97085	03833	59806	12351	64253
50	11684	06644	57816	10078	45021	47751	38285	73520	08434	65627

Bibliography

J. Banks, editor. *Handbook of Simulation – Principles, Methodology, Advances, Applications, and Practice.* Wiley, New York, 1998.

A. M. Law and W. D. Kelton. *Simulation Modeling and Analysis.* McGraw-Hill, New York, 3rd edition, 2000.

B. Page. *Diskrete Simulation – Eine Einführung mit Modula-2* ("Discrete Simulation – An Introduction with Modula-2", in German). Springer, Berlin, 1991.

O. Spaniol and S. Hoff. *Ereignisorientierte Simulation – Konzepte und Systemrealisierung* ("Event-Oriented Simulation – Concepts and System Implementation", in German). Thomson's Aktuelle Tutorien; 7. Thomson, Bonn, 1995.

Chapter 3

Object-Oriented System Development and Simulation

Wolfgang Kreutzer

Contents

3.1	Motivation and Overview	39
3.2	History & Core Concepts of Object-Orientation	42
	3.2.1 Some History	42
	3.2.2 Core Concepts	43
3.3	Object-Oriented Analysis and Design	49
3.4	Object-Oriented Programming Tools	53
3.5	Summary and Perspectives	54
	Further Reading	56
	Bibliography	57

3.1 Motivation and Overview

In the wake of rapid technological change, which replaced the shared mainframes of the 1960s and 1970s by today's powerful personal workstations, computer users have become increasingly intolerant of tools with arcane and cryptic interfaces. Although this has in many cases resulted in more accessible and user-friendlier applications, it has also greatly increased the complexity of system development. While hardware continues to become faster, smaller, and cheaper, the difficulty of developing effective and reliable programs now dominates the cost of software construction. The question of how to ease the effort required to guide and control the growth of large programs has therefore become a central focus of software research.

Object-oriented design and development, which claims to help master complexity, is now a well established part of a range of tools and techniques (e.g. visual languages, user-centered design, software agents) for solving the *software crisis*. This chapter looks at such claims from the perspective of simulation model development.

Chapter 3 Object-Oriented System Development and Simulation

Figure 3.1 presents programming as a process of human-computer communication, which requires a suitable tool – i.e. a programming language – to exchange information between a computing device and a user.

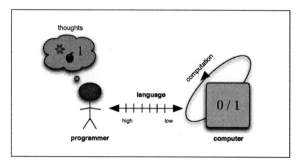

Figure 3.1: A model of programming as communication

From the viewpoint of *semiotics* (see Chandler 2000) all communication requires conventions regarding to the meaning of signs, and we must therefore decide which concepts to use to encode programs in. The closer such symbols correspond to a "familiar" context, the less work is needed for their encoding (program *design*) and decoding (*compilation* and *execution*). Of course, if "native" frameworks (i.e. familiarity) differ markedly between the parties involved (for example, if they come from much different cultures), an appropriate tradeoff must be made when deciding what language to use. In the early days of computing technology, computers were simple and very expensive. Data structures and algorithms supported by programming tools therefore closely reflected the capabilities of computer *hardware*. For this reason the first generation of tools (i.e. machine code and so-called assembly languages) are known as *low level languages*, simply because we consider the various forms of human communication as superior and "above" any such primitive means of expression. Since then the most general classification of programming tools has been based on this notion; i.e. a language is "higher" level if it supports a mode of communication which is closer to some mental framework which is familiar to a typical user. Much of the history of computing can in fact be described as an ongoing quest for reaching ever higher levels of human-computer communication, resulting in a vast number of so-called *high level languages* (e.g. Fortran, Algol, Lisp, Java) and *very high level languages* (e.g. Prolog, Miranda, Haskell) – with no end in sight. What is considered "familiar" will of course depend very much on the user. In the early days of computing, a small group of specialists had become so accustomed to writing machine code, that they eventually became very familiar and proficient with it. However, the relevant point is that humans have limited mental resources and that being forced to think at such low levels limits our capability to deal with complexity; i.e. it may severely constrain the range of what patterns of thought

3.1 Motivation and Overview

we can pursue. Together with hardware constraints the mental load on machine code programmers restricted the type of computer applications which could be built.

Irrespective of level all programming languages must offer a set of concepts through which computations can be described and cast into suitable linguistic abstractions. Although most programming tools are *"Turing complete"* (i.e. theoretically sufficient to describe any computable problem), in practice new languages offer new ways of viewing and thinking about particular aspects of the world – and not all are equally well suited to all types of applications. Thus we have programming languages which excel at numerical calculations (e.g. Fortran), business data processing (e.g. Cobol), systems programming (e.g. C), text (e.g. Snobol), symbol processing tasks (e.g. Lisp), and simulation modelling (e.g. GPSS, Simula, Simscript, DESMO-J). Of course, some languages are designed to be more "wide spectrum" than others (e.g. PL/1, Ada, or Java). Similar to the tools in a good craftman's toolkit, there are widely useful but relatively unsophisticated coding tools as well as highly specialized ones, which have been optimized for a narrow range of tasks.

Most early programming tools naturally sought to extend the framework suggested by classical computer architecture (i.e. the so-called "von Neumann machine"), making only relatively small changes to ease life for their programmers (e.g. symbolic references, procedures, more sophisticated operations, control structures, and data items). This has resulted in many variants of the so-called *imperative programming style*. Since then it has often been argued that other metaphors for describing a computation may give better support to human problem solving, and of the many alternative frameworks which have been explored three metaphors have achieved some degree of popularity. These are referred to as logic-based, functional, and object-oriented styles of programming. While research into conceptual foundations and effective implementation of functional, logic, and object-oriented programming styles has for many years been an ongoing activity, the wider computing community has only recently shown any interest. *Logic-based programming* became popular through its adoption by the Japanese "5th generation" effort (an ambitious attempt to build computers to support so-called *expert systems*). *Functional programming* offers advantages with regard to program verification, but it is still rarely used outside universities and research institutions. *Object-oriented programming*, however, has now become a dominant framework for building large software systems.

The state of software engineering today is reminiscent to what the science historian and philosopher Thomas Kuhn calls a *paradigm shift*, i.e. a time where established methodological frameworks (i.e. structured design and procedural programming) have been overthrown by a new one (like object-oriented design and programming). The main reason for this paradigm shift is grounded in a conviction that classical methods of program design do not offer much hope for solving software engineering's complexity problems. While object-orientation has many advantages in this regard, one must be careful not to overstate the capabilities of any new technology; a temptation which computing culture has always found difficult to resist. Object-orientation cannot be an

Chapter 3 Object-Oriented System Development and Simulation

answer to all of our problems (nor will any other single method), but it can be a useful tool for tackling software complexity. Since simulation model construction poses one of the most complex challenges to software design and implementation, object-oriented development methods have had a long history in this field.

3.2 History & Core Concepts of Object-Orientation

3.2.1 Some History

Object-oriented software development is not a new idea. When object-oriented programming became a main-stream technique in the mid-1980s, it already had a long and successful history of use in simulation model construction; a task for which it had proved to be particularly well suited. The term "object-orientation" was invented by Alan Kay, in connection with his design of the *Smalltalk* programming language in the early 1970s (see Kay 1977). Many of Smalltalk's foundations were directly derived from an early simulation language called *Simula* (see Dahl and Nygaard 1966).

Object-orientation's most central ideas (i.e. objects, classes, polymorphism, and inheritance) have an even more time-honoured history, reaching back to the classical Greek philosophers. In practice the object-oriented method fairly directly reflects what is widely known as the *"scientific method"* of problem solving. Given this pedigree it may seem rather surprising that it has been ignored by main-stream computing for so long. One of the reasons for this obscurity can be found in its relatively large computing and memory requirements, when compared to conventional programming techniques. If we remember that imperative programming styles grew quite directly out of the so-called "von Neumann style" of computer architecture, it should not be surprising that tools based on other formalisms will have performance penalties to pay. They have therefore always been seen as wasteful in terms of computing resources. Since human effectiveness was largely ignored until relatively recently, alternative programming styles were considered to be much too expensive for practical application. Their development and usage was therefore relegated to the research community. This perception only started to change in the mid-1980s, prompted by two factors which Balci and Nance (1988) call *applications pull* and *technology push*. The first term reflects the fact that applications had become so complicated that one needed all the help one could muster to successfully build them at all – never mind the expense. The second term stakes the claim that one could now "throw" more hardware at a problem than was economical possible just a few years before. Memory in particular had become much cheaper, a technological change which made a tremendous difference to the economics of user-friendlier interfaces and non-procedural styles of program development.

3.2 History & Core Concepts of Object-Orientation

3.2.2 Core Concepts

Object-orientation shares the conceptual bases of the "scientific method" mentioned already above. Both strategies seek to support the effective construction of models of reality. Since this perspective is obviously closely related to simulation, we will guide our discussion of object-orientation's core concepts along these lines.

Through the works of many philosophers and scientists we know that it is quite impossible to derive any objectively "correct" understanding of the world from our senses. As Dennett (1991, p. 101) rightly observes:

> "...Wherever there is a conscious mind there is a point of view. A conscious mind is an observer who takes in a limited subset of all the information there is..."

The elusive notion of understanding must therefore be viewed as a process of filtering and interpretation of information; relative to a taken point of view. If we accept the claim that we cannot help but use preconceived concepts to process raw sense impressions, it seems plausible to assume that a spatio-temporal network of objects and events serves as our minds' most basic frame of reference.

Coad and Yourdon (1991) express this succinctly:

> "Object-orientation is based upon concepts that we learned in Kindergarten: objects & attributes & behaviours, classes & members, wholes & parts..."

Abstraction, i.e. simplification, is a crucial foundation for model building. It helps us to keep models at manageable size. Figure 3.2 summarizes "reductionism", a modelling strategy built on abstraction.

Reductionism is a strategy for complexity reduction. Based on its success in science and technology it is now well established as *the* method of rational enquiry. In order to analyse complex phenomena, it asks us to identify and isolate a *system* as a collection of objects and events which are relevant to a given task and which are spatially, temporally, or causally related. Of course, by singling out any such objects from others we throw information away; which we justify by the often tacit assumption that it will not be "relevant" to the problem at hand. In building a simulation we make many such assumptions; we chose, for example, not to model weather conditions or social relationships between crew members in the container ship model of Section 5.2.3. Reduction is a recursive technique and can again be applied to each of the simpler objects we arrive at (i.e. by considering each of them as decomposable systems in their own right). Finally, a level is reached at which the elementary objects and their interactions seem simple enough for us to understand. Of course, the success of this strategy critically depends on an assumption that, in spite of our desire to simplify, we have not managed to

Chapter 3 Object-Oriented System Development and Simulation

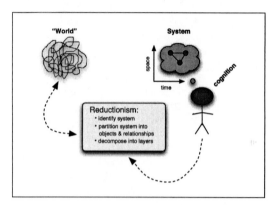

Figure 3.2: Applying reductionism to model construction

abstract the problem away; e.g. weather conditions may well be relevant for a container ship's travelling time and may therefore influence arrival patterns of vessels at a port. Problem reduction by recursive simplification therefore works best for simple systems, where only a few factors are seen as important. While less successful in the biological and social sciences, reductionism has long reigned unchallenged in the natural sciences and in engineering.

Object-oriented styles of systems analysis and program development support a reductionist model development strategy well. From this perspective writing a program asks us to build relevant models of task domains. Such models contain *objects*, *relationships* among objects, and processes in which *objects* engage in. In the container handling example from Section 5.2.3, ships, cranes, and containers are candidate objects, containers are carried by ships and handled by cranes (relationships), ships travel, and cranes load and unload (processes). Objects with similar properties and behaviours can be grouped into *classes*, whose descriptions encapsulate all properties and actions that we consider as relevant for our purpose. While there may be many ships in our model, all share common properties such as speed and loading capacity. *Ship* can therefore group all their descriptions. Relationships bind objects into structures, which can then play their role in a process. In our example all ships in a port can be considered a structural unit; e.g. a waiting line. Arrivals add ships to this structure, departures remove ships. Ships' travel and cranes' loading/unloading processes feed these events. Within a computational context processes are computations, as described by procedures framing a series of *messages* sent among objects; e.g. arrive, depart, load, unload. Viewed from a temporal perspective such computations unfold as a sequence of all participating objects' changes of state; e.g. ships may be "in port" or "travelling", cranes may be "idle" or "busy".

3.2 History & Core Concepts of Object-Orientation

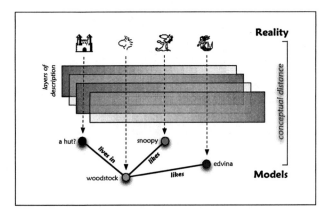

Figure 3.3: Crossing layers of description

While any programming tool can in principle be used to transform an object-oriented model into an executable program, the so-called *conceptual distance* (see Figure 3.3), defined as a measure of the mental difficulty of mapping one set of concepts into another, may become large if low level tools are employed (e.g. languages like Fortran, C, or Pascal) are employed for its implementation. To safely map models into a program, the conceptual distances need to be small; otherwise the complexity of the mapping may quickly become unmanageable. This means that the concepts used at the modelling and programming levels should not differ too widely; a requirement which calls for a tool which either already provides an appropriate set of abstractions, or which at least makes it easy for suitable high-level concepts to be defined on the fly. The second alternative is exactly what object-orientation provides in the form of a class library. In the example a modeller could cast his or her ship description into a suitable class definition and take advantage of a "crane" library class offering prepackaged property templates and loading/unloading behaviour.

To corroborate the analogy between model design and software construction, Figure 3.4 illustrates and associates the main phases of their development cycles.

In simulation modelling these phases are commonly referred to as *system identification, model design, model validation, model implementation, program verification*, and *experimentation*. The lifecycle of object-oriented software shows all of these phases as well. The names, however, have changed, and the literature typically distinguishes between *object-oriented analysis, object-oriented design, object-oriented programming*, and *verification and testing*.

It should be obvious from the discussion so far that *objects* form the core of object-oriented programs. They have an *identity*, some *properties*, and a set of *actions* which

45

Chapter 3 Object-Oriented System Development and Simulation

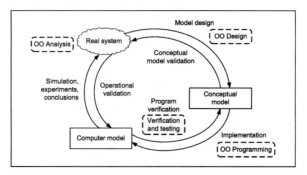

Figure 3.4: Analogies between model construction and software construction

they perform on request. A ship, for example, may be called Puddle Duck and have a loading capacity of 20,000 tons as well as sailing and docking procedures. Requests for triggering a behaviour are carried by *messages*; i.e. whenever we ask objects to perform actions we can think of entering into a "contract", the details of whose execution we need not worry about. This has the potential to reduce mental complexity by keeping information *local*, within an as tightly constrained context as possible. This notion is referred to as *encapsulation* and is again not a new one. In computing its merits have long been recognized and promoted under a variety of labels: e.g. abstract data types, working sets. By insisting on strict encapsulation of all information relevant to an object (i.e. state and behaviour), object-orientation carries this idea to its logical conclusion. Objects now become autonomous entities with which we communicate through messages specified by an interface or *signature*. Applying the principle of *information hiding* we can now limit complexity by keeping this interface as narrow as possible; separating an object's *specifications* (as defined by externally visible services) from its *implementation* (as described by internal properties and methods). In our example ships enter into loading and unloading contracts with cranes. Containers are passed through these interfaces, a process which may involve either or both of a ship's and a crane's actions. Only publicly accessible parts of their signatures need to become involved. Any resulting changes to non-public properties and delegations to internal procedures occur locally; i.e. within the two object's encapsulations.

Encapsulation also supports the concept of *polymorphism* (i.e. the effect of an action can take "many forms" depending on context) rather elegantly. We can now choose names for actions without undue concern about the context in which they may be applied; i.e. the kind of object to which messages are sent. This is achieved by delegating the binding of messages and a particular implementation to the receiver. For example, we can define a generic *show* message, which behaves differently over a wide range of objects (e.g. text, images, diagrams, movies, sound). While all of these objects'

3.2 History & Core Concepts of Object-Orientation

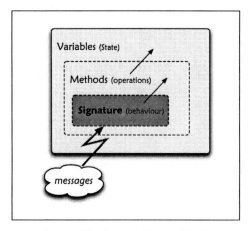

Figure 3.5: Encapsulating an object

responses will result in some kind of action for presenting themselves, the specific effect (i.e. what will appear on a screen, printer, or through a speaker) as well as the actual code to achieve this may differ widely. In an extended version of our container example, load and unload messages would result in different actions when sent to either a ship or a lorry.

Composition (i.e. assembling large structures from smaller ones) is another technique whose use for reducing complexity is well established. Object-orientation supports this idea by assembling a program in layers, where the components of complex objects are simpler composites themselves – ultimately grounded in a given language's linguistic abstractions (e.g. numbers, characters, booleans, arrays). Figure 3.6 shows an example decomposition of a "whole" car into some of its "parts".

This type of abstraction is well supported by most modern programming languages. In addition, however, object-oriented tools offer *classification* and *generalization* to foster abstraction; i.e. the removal and aggregation of superfluous detail. *Classes* are templates through which sets of similar objects can be described. Through their constructors they can also be used to create objects of a given category – e.g. an *account* class in a banking program could be made responsible for creating new account objects on request. Either *inheritance* or *delegation* can serve this purpose, but weaving classes into *inheritance hierarchies* is the most common strategy used by object-oriented programming tools. Inheritance capitalizes on the fact that some classes differ from others in only a few aspects. To improve flexibility and mental economy, we can therefore factor all commonalities into so-called "superclasses", from which they are then inherited by all variants. This method of multi-layered classification is prevalent in all sciences;

Chapter 3 Object-Oriented System Development and Simulation

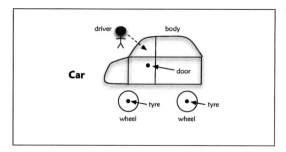

Figure 3.6: Wholes and parts

well known examples are Linne's systematization of the animal world or the periodic system of elements. While such schemas for classification are often arranged into hierarchies, they can also form lattices or networks. In object-oriented system development this leads to single or multiple inheritance structures. Because of semantic complexities (e.g. what to do when aspects with the same name are inherited along different paths?) multiple inheritance is only supported by few object-oriented programming languages. In anticipation of the notation described in detail in Section 4.3, Figure 3.7 shows an example where the concepts of apple tree and apple orchard are introduced as specializations of fruit tree and fruit orchard. Note how the notion of composition runs orthogonally to this – i.e. all orchards contain fruit trees and apple orchards are peculiar in that they must all be of the apple variety.

Returning to our container port example, we could populate a suitable model with abstract classes for vehicles and ships. The Vehicle class could store name and loading capacity, *inherited* by all kinds of ships, and act as a superclass to both Ship and Lorry. Ships could be specialized even further; e.g. as Tugboats and as Container Ships. Viewed from a different perspective container ships can be modelled as structures, one of whose properties stores a *composition* of containers. These can then be inserted and removed on demand; actions which would only ally to this class of ship. Another example for a composite structure is a discrete event monitor, as discussed in Section 2.3. There we compose a monitor from a clock and an event list, in addition to properties such as a reference to the next imminent event. Event lists in turn are composed of event notices, each of which stores at least an event time and a reference to a relevant event procedure or process phase. Potential inheritance structures in this context would be specialized discrete event and continuous simulation monitors, which share a system clock as a property and could therefore be viewed as subclasses of a more general Monitor class. Their scheduling behaviour (e.g. "process the next event" and "integrate over the next time interval") and the data structures required for performing these action would of course differ.

3.3 Object-Oriented Analysis and Design

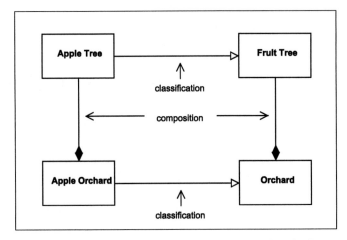

Figure 3.7: Composition and classification in an apple orchard

Both composition and inheritance have their specific advantages and disadvantages. Whole-part *decomposition* can be programmed quite easily; e.g. by using variables whose values are objects. This strategy has the advantage that such relationships are dynamic and can be changed on the fly; i.e. at program execution time. On the negative side, we need to mentally trace objects' histories to make sure what associations will currently hold. *Inheritance* is better suited to define more enduring and less dynamic relationships, which it makes easier to reason about. However, few general purpose programming languages can support it directly, and we trade ease of understanding against a loss in flexibility. On the positive side, inheritance provides us with an easy means of customizing objects by specializing and redefining canonical structures and behaviours, which is an important prerequisite for building reusable library classes. Both strategies impose a performance penalty caused by indirect references – i.e. on a path to an object we may need to traverse multiple segments. In order to empty container ships, for example, we cannot just set a *containers* property to *null*, but may need to ask a port object to ask one of its cranes, to ask the ship, to ask all of its containers (one by one) to let themselves be removed.

3.3 Object-Oriented Analysis and Design

In large scale program development object-oriented methods can no longer cater for the needs of a single user and more sophisticated tools to support analysis and design as well as strategies for managing teams of programmers are required. Object-oriented

Chapter 3 Object-Oriented System Development and Simulation

development does not sit well with classical methods of software construction and can be quite different from the recommendations given by the *Structured Programming* and *Structured Design* traditions which have dominated main stream computing in the 1960s and 1970s. Since 1980 these methods have been augmented by CASE (Computer Aided Software Engineering) tools and a whole industry has emerged to support their ideals. Unfortunately the tradition of *top-down functional design* has not been able to live up to all of its promises.

The ideal of this method is for a program and *proof* to evolve "hand in hand". Although the power of this style of *top-down* development has been convincingly advocated and demonstrated by well known computer scientists (using small and much cited examples), it is only suitable for problems whose properties are so well understood that invariant and rigorous specifications can be defined prior to coding. By asking us to avoid applications with ill-defined specifications and first to gain a precise understanding of the space of a problem's solutions *before* we embark on a program, this school of thought moves many problems beyond our reach. In areas characterized by a high degree of mental complexity, such as simulation modelling, there is often a dire need for some guidance on how to reach even an initial understanding of problem characteristics, and such an approach is therefore far too constraining and utterly unrealistic. A possible solution to this dilemma suggests itself when we look at how other disciplines (e.g. engineering or architecture) address a design. Often a *bottom-up* view of problem solving (i.e. by modifying solutions which are known to work) is prevalent there. In analogy to this strategy we would start from a collection of program components (e.g. a class library modelling logistics objects such as different types of vehicles and cranes) and compose a new model by combination and customization. This style fits object-oriented development well. Models are built from combinations of autonomous elements (i.e. classes), where each of these is an abstraction of interest to a chosen domain; in terms of its properties and behaviours.

Abstraction, encapsulation and layering can help us to master complexity, but we cannot rely on these methods alone. Finding the *right* representation for a problem (whose description may be quite fuzzy at the beginning) is a difficult task, and experimentation is often the only way to make progress. Tasks of this nature should be considered as *design problems* rather than implementation problems, and *program* and specification should evolve hand in hand. The method of *exploratory development* of prototypes recognizes this need and is therefore an indispensable tool for building complex pieces of software. Instead of following a waterfall model's prescription of strictly top-down decomposition, we proceed in two directions at once – from both top (e.g. by identifying relevant classes of objects to implement) and bottom (e.g. by adapting existing components which seem to be useful). This process is highly dynamic in nature and analysis, design, implementation, and experimentation with prototypes tend to be tightly coupled. While such *rapid prototyping* has sometimes been be-devilled as only a slightly respectable form of hacking, it has the potential for finding a working solution quite quickly. This can then be further refined and polished. Due to the complexity

3.3 Object-Oriented Analysis and Design

of its task domains, simulation model development and deployment often employs this technique.

Deciding what should be included in a conceptual model falls within the realm of *analysis*, while commitment to a particular kind of computer-based representation belongs to *design*. The results of design can then serve as *specifications* from which *implementation* can then proceed.

Typical problems which must be solved during *analysis* lead to questions such as:

1. What classes do we need? (e.g. identify relevant concepts which should be part of a model)
2. What functionality must be supported? (e.g. identify each class' responsibilities)
3. How should classes be related to each other? (e.g. describe compositions and generalizations)
4. How do objects cooperate in an application? (e.g. describe scenarios and trace events)

Returning once more to the port simulation example from Section 5.2.3, we could answer these questions for a particularly simple variant of this scenario as follows:

1. Relevant classes are: Port, Ship, and Crane. We will abstract from everything else; e.g. we will not consider tugboats, tides, lorries, dock workers, and innumerably many other aspects. Note that containers are not modelled as objects, but are just stored as counters attached to a ship. A number of ports, ships, and cranes need to be instantiated at the start of a simulation; populated with suitably initialised cranes and ships. Ports must then be told to start ships' unloading.

2. The Port class provides references to berthed ships and cranes. It can ask cranes to start unloading a ship, record ships' arrivals, and tell ships to leave.
   The Ship class stores information about loaded containers, routes for travelling from port to port in a specified sequence, and travel times between ports. It responds to queries for removing containers and whether a ship is currently empty. Ships also respond to requests to leave and, after travelling to a new port, inform the port of their arrival. When leaving a port, a ship's container load is reset to a specified value (i.e. we abstract from loading).
   Cranes unload containers. This activity is started by a port object and terminated by a ship reporting as empty.

3. While more elaborate versions of this model could require additional subclasses of an abstract Vehicle class, there are no class-subclass relationships in this model. However, the Port class contains lists of both ships and cranes as components. If more information about containers would be required, they could be modelled as a class of their own. Ship classes would then need a list of containers, with suitable access methods as attributes.

Chapter 3 Object-Oriented System Development and Simulation

4. Ports initiate the unloading of ships, using cranes. Cranes interact with ships to perform this activity. Relevant scenarios are: *ship arrives, ship departs, containers unloading*. Tracing each of these message sequences among relevant objects is left as an exercise to the reader.

Although some guidance on how to approach questions like these can be given, one must never forget to remember that the results of a modelling exercise depend strongly on the conceptual framework used by a modeller, and that different observers will classify reality in different ways. Finding good answers to the above questions requires experimentation and can greatly be aided by relevant experience. To answer the first two questions, it is often suggested that one should study the *language* of an application domain. This can be done by reading journals and textbooks, or by talking to experts. At the very least the outcome of this exercise should be an improved understanding and a *data dictionary* of key terms and phrases. The next step is *classification*, which demands that we find similarities, a task which presupposes choosing a point of view and level of abstraction from which we can group things that show common structure or behaviour. Creating a class can be justified when relevant data is complex (i.e. there is enough functionality and variation) or when there are opportunities for reuse and extension. For example, information about a vehicle's speed will rarely be elevated to classhood, but is normally better stored as a numerical attribute. Information about files (e.g. in a model of computer operating systems), however, will often have sufficiently variety to warrant a class of its own (see Mössenböck 1995, p. 278).

Protocol analysis (i.e. stepping through a collection of typical *use cases*) can be helpful and role playing has also been found productive. One particularly popular method was invented by Beck and Cunningham (1989). It uses what has since become known as *CRC cards*. This term stands for "Classes – Responsibilities – Collaborations" and indicates three types of information participants in a brainstorming session are expected to write on a set of index cards. During such sessions participants suggest and criticise proposals for classes, responsibilities, and collaborations, followed by actively playing the roles of such objects and simulating "what happens when..." types of questions. Clients (i.e. end users) as well as designers and implementers participate, so that the essential functionality and "look & feel" of an application can be tried and discussed. Often such sessions uncover inadequacies in design and may even suggest unanticipated patterns of usage. Eventually the information recorded on these cards will serve as a blueprint for an application's structure and can also help documenting the software later. Once we have decided what classes we may require, we arrange them into whole-part and generalization-specialization relationships. Typically the results are then cast into UML diagrams (see Chapter 4). Since they capture an application's structure, such use cases and class diagrams document what is known as the *static model* of an application. To specify an application's behaviour, we need to design a *dynamic model*. Again, many types of representations have been proposed for documenting dynamic models, ranging from simple event traces to UML's state and activity diagrams, lifecycle diagrams and Petri nets.

3.4 Object-Oriented Programming Tools

While the results of object-oriented analysis provide a conceptual model of the problem domain, this phase is followed by *object-oriented design*, which serves to answer more technology-specific and implementation-related questions. We might, for example, ask:

1. How many processes are needed to implement this model?
2. Do we need additional classes to support a user interface?
3. Do we need additional classes for database functionality?
4. Can we make use of existing class libraries?

At the end we should emerge with an appropriate and complete set of class descriptions for our application, arranged in a number of hierarchies. Higher levels of these hierarchies will refer to the classes identified during analysis (the so-called *domain classes*), while more implementation specific classes (e.g. so-called *interface classes*) will tend to populate lower levels.

Due to the mushrooming interest in object technology a large number of proprietary object-oriented analysis and design methods, ranging from fairly conventional modifications to traditional methods to much more radical proposals, appeared in the 1990s. More recently, however, many of them have converged on the *Unified Method* of Jacobson, Booch, and Rumbaugh (Quatrani 1997) – see Chapter 4.

3.4 Object-Oriented Programming Tools

Good notation should simplify and suggest rather than hinder expressing ideas. To foster this goal, a programming tool must express familiar concepts as directly and non-intrusively as possible. In Section 3.1 we have argued in favour of "higher level" and user-focussed tools. A perfect tool of this kind would be transparent, so that it would feel as if one were working directly on a problem. Unfortunately this remains an elusive goal, towards which today's programming languages still have a long way to travel. Novel ideas are only slowly accepted and make very gradual impacts on professional practice. As a result many commercial tools try to steer a difficult compromise between innovation and conservation, in that they regularly offer small chunks of modest improvements while trying their best to stay compatible with the horrors of the past. Unfortunately this often produces inelegant, baroque, and clumsy software, which rarely work well. Some object-oriented programming tools have fallen prey to this trend and their designers would do well to remember Antoine de Saint-Exupéry's words of caution:

> "Perfection is not reached when there is no longer anything to add, but when there is no longer anything to take away."

It is a common mistake to try learning a programming language in isolation, i.e. by studying only its syntax and semantics. Using a new tool while perpetuating old habits

Chapter 3 Object-Oriented System Development and Simulation

will invariably be disappointing, since history, programming environments, and typical idioms of usage deserve much attention. The widespread reluctance to invest in learning a whole new style can only partly be blamed on the time and effort this process requires. Often it also reflects an unwillingness to accept that hard-won skills may have become obsolete.

Based on its relatively long history object-oriented programming languages show a remarkably high degree of maturity. From a large number of competing designs a relatively small number of languages have emerged to dominate commercial practice today. Among these languages Common Lisp Object System (CLOS), Smalltalk, Eiffel, C++, C#, and Java have proved most successful; each catering for its own class of applications. CLOS (see Keene 1989) is most popular as a tool for programming artificial intelligence techniques (e.g. expert systems). Smalltalk (see Goldberg and Robson 1983) is an excellent prototyping language, particularly if user interfaces and graphical representations are involved. In addition it is also an excellent choice for learning and teaching good object-oriented style. While Eiffel (see Meyer 1992) is a good teaching tool, it is focussed on large projects where software reliability is of particular concern. Here it competes directly with C++ (see Stroustrup 1994), which is a much more pragmatic language with less solid formal foundations, but with particular strengths in supporting efficient "low level" implementation techniques; i.e. as a tool for writing programs "close to the hardware". Java's (see Arnold and Gosling 1996) popularity has been fuelled by its ability to make the World Wide Web come alive. C# (see Liberty 2003) is targeted at so-called *web applications* within the context of Microsoft's recent *.Net* initiative (see Chappel 2002). In terms of numbers of users, C++ still dominates all others, although Java has steadily risen in popularity. While a discussion of any particular tool's details is beyond the scope of this chapter, all of the above mentioned tools have so far survived, attracted a user community, and carved their own niches of application.

3.5 Summary and Perspectives

A programming metaphor's success – or lack of it – cannot be explained solely in terms of its technical merits. Many other factors have often more dominant roles to play. According to Gabriel (1998) we should bear in mind that programming metaphors and tools evolve in a social context, which is strongly influenced by prevalent values and habits. Successful languages must be seen as familiar and must have simple performance models and acceptable resource requirements. Few people will make the effort to learn how to use a new tool unless they run into problems with tools they are already familiar with (old habits are hard to break!). This tendency favours incremental over radical changes. While today's programmers are willing to tolerate tools with higher demands on resources, making a language very much bigger for little perceived gain will be unlikely to succeed. Promises of less change and large gains are much more attractive. This seems a major reason behind C++'s great success in the past and may bode less

3.5 Summary and Perspectives

well for more innovative tools. Of course, sometimes an old paradigm (e.g. imperative programming and functional decomposition) proves unable to cope with new problems. Once it collapses, a new framework is given a chance to take over. In the case of object-oriented software development, such a *paradigm shift* occurred in the 1990s and the technology has now established itself. As a new standard it can now be challenged by younger contenders.

In this chapter we have made a case for object-orientation's superiority in mastering the complexity of software design and implementation. To justify this claim, we identified three crucial properties:

1. *Object-orientation is a "natural" framework for modelling the world.*

   Its basic concepts suggest a strategy for model design based on the notions of *objects, classes, properties, actions,* and *messages*. Together with *whole-part and generalization-specialization* relationships these concepts can be used to build software in layers, while minimizing the conceptual gap between them. Employing this strategy can help us to ease understanding and explanation of programs and makes it much easier for end-users to become involved in a program's construction.

2. *Object-orientation tries to ensure that information is localized as tightly as possible.*

   During a model's and program's construction this strategy enables us to constrain our attention to small contexts, without any need for thinking about the effects of global states or "non-local" influences. Good object-oriented programs rarely need global variables and the use of abstract classes (i.e. classes which only act as repositories for shared functionality) ensures that "the same" information is kept in a single place. This eases understanding and change as well as the tracing of error conditions; which can in turn simplify maintenance and development. Object-oriented programs achieve their locality by *encapsulating* an object's state and behaviour in an entity which can only be accessed through a narrow interface. A beneficial side-effect of this is *Polymorphism*, which ensures that we can name methods independently of the type of object to which they apply. This can make models more readable and greatly eases the task of integrating them into new contexts (i.e. different programs).

3. *We gain flexibility compared to conventional procedures or module libraries.*

   Encapsulation, the fact that assemblies of objects can be composed and decomposed into whole-part relationships, and inheritance's support of *generalization and specialization* make it easier to build collections of *reusable components* (so-called *class libraries* and *frameworks*). Since hardly any global context need to be assumed, classes can simply be treated as black box components whose behaviour can be changed, restricted or extended by subclassing; without touching the original implementation. This incremental extensibility offers great advantages for the development of reusable software. The *patterns* community (Gabriel 1998) has made good use of these ideas.

Chapter 3 Object-Oriented System Development and Simulation

In summary there are good reasons why object-orientation has earned the popularity it enjoys. There are of course costs associated with using it, but in the light of technological advances these have become easier and easier to pay. After all, we need better tools to help us cope with the complexity of software construction, otherwise faster hardware will only allow us to make mistakes at a faster rate.

Ongoing research in this area focusses on formal foundations, the integration of object-oriented programming languages with other resources (e.g. databases and networks), better methods of analysis and design, the development and administration of class libraries and frameworks, and suitable techniques for managing teams of programmers working within this culture. Above all, we should hope that this new paradigm may trigger a shift in values. Current development is too narrowly focussed on short term gains. To gain the full benefits of an object-oriented approach, we need to adopt a more long-term and investment-based perspective. Design, construction, use, and refinement of a class library, for example, requires considerable effort; which will only pay for itself over time. In the longer term, however, the experiences gained, and the tools and components developed within this framework will make the design and implementation of future applications easier, faster, more reliable, and more productive. Using an object-oriented perspective and object-oriented development tools for building a simulation model is now firmly established. Within the discrete event simulation domain a number of class libraries cater for specific areas of application, such as manufacturing, logistics, computer systems, and communication networks. Chapter 9 briefly surveys two representative examples.

Further Reading

Two of the most readable and informative introductions to object-oriented development and programming are the textbooks by Budd and Meyer.

T. Budd's *An Introduction to Object-Oriented Programming* (2001) explains all key concepts and goes on to explore "whys" in a clear and understandable manner. Examples are chosen from a wide range of languages, including C++, Smalltalk, Objective C, Object Pascal, and Java. This approach is appropriate if you are trying to learn the principles of object-orientation, rather than just syntax and linguistic abstractions of a particular language. This book is equally useful if you have some experience in programming but wish to learn more about the reasons behind the much touted "object advantage", or as a companion when learning to use a particular object-oriented programming tool (e.g. Java, C#) for the first time.

In contrast to Budd, B. Meyer's *Object-Oriented Software Construction* (1997) discusses object-oriented software development with a specific programming tool; the Eiffel language designed by its author. Within this context Meyer offers a gentle but rigorous introduction to all the core concepts. He also tries to show how to employ object-orientation "well", and enumerates common mistakes and ways to avoid them. A comparison (with some bias towards Eiffel) of all key object-oriented languages, including Java, concludes the book.

There is now a vast body of literature on object-oriented analysis and design, with a particular emphasis on UML (see Chapter 4). A somewhat older, but still excellent, book which ranges quite widely, is P. Sully's *Modelling the World with Objects* (1993). Sully gives an insightful and readable introduction to the core issues of an object-centered point of view, and then takes an impartial look at the merits of different methodologies. The book is short, well illustrated and highly readable.

For those who yearn to learn more about object-orientation's contribution to the "software patterns movement", Richard Gabriel's *Patterns of Software: Tales from the Software Community* (1998) can be highly recommended. Although it is now a bit dated (it was first published in 1996), it is still one of the best books out there on the understanding of patterns. Starting with parallels to writing literature and Christopher Alexander's seminal insights on architectural design, Gabriel identifies several key ingredients of successful systems and tools, such as "habitability" and "piecemeal growth". Object-oriented development answers the corresponding plea for incremental software construction quite well. Although Gabriel is refreshingly sceptical about any "silver-bullets", he sees design patterns and domain specific programming frameworks (e.g. DESMO-J) as a useful first step in taming software complexity. The book is now available on the web; at http://www.dreamsongs.com/NewFiles/PatternsOfSoftware.pdf (the whole site is well worth browsing).

Bibliography

K. Arnold and J. Gosling. *The Java Programming Language*. Addison-Wesley, Reading, 1996.

O. Balci and R. E. Nance. *The Multidimensionality of the Computing Technology Pull.* Technical Report TR-88-26, Virginia Polytechnic Inst. and State University, November 1988.

K. Beck and W. Cunningham. A Laboratory for Teaching Object-Oriented Thinking. In *Proceedings of the OOPSLA '89 Conference on Object-Oriented Programming Systems, Languages, and Applications*, pages 1–6, October 1989.

T. Budd. *An Introduction to Object-Oriented Programming*. Addison-Wesley, Reading, 3rd edition, 2001.

D. Chandler. *Semiotics: The Basics*. Routledge, London, 2000.

D. Chappel. *Understanding .NET: A Tutorial and Analysis*. Addison-Wesley, Reading, 2002.

P. Coad and E. Yourdon. *Object-Oriented Analysis*. Prentice Hall, Englewood Cliffs, 1991.

O. Dahl and K. Nygaard. *SIMULA, an ALGOL-based simulation language*. Communications of the ACM, 9(9):671–678, September 1966.

D. C. Dennett. *Consciousness Explained*. Little, Brown & Co, Boston, 1991.

Bibliography

R. Gabriel. *Patterns of Software: Tales from the Software Community.* Oxford University, Oxford, 1998. [Online] http://www.dreamsongs.com/NewFiles/PatternsOfSoftware.pdf (in August 2005).

A. Goldberg and D. Robson. *Smalltalk-80 – The Language and its Implementation.* Addison-Wesley, Reading, 1983.

A. Kay. *Microelectronics and the Personal Computer.* Scientific American, pages 231–244, September 1977.

S. E. Keene. *Object-Oriented Programming in Common Lisp.* Addison-Wesley, Reading, 1989.

T. S. Kuhn. *The Structure of Scientific Revolutions.* Chicago University, Chicago, 2nd edition, 1970.

J. Liberty. *Programming C#.* O'Reilly, Cambridge, 2nd edition, 2003.

B. Meyer. *Eiffel: The Language.* Prentice Hall, Englewood Cliffs, 1992.

T. Meyer. *Object-Oriented Software Construction.* Prentice Hall, Englewood Cliffs, 2nd edition, 1997.

H. Mössenböck. *Object-Oriented Programming in Oberon-2.* Springer, New York, 1995.

T. Quatrani. *Visual Modeling with the UML: A Rational Approach.* Addison-Wesley, Reading, 1997.

B. Stroustrup. *The Design and Evolution of C++.* Addison-Wesley, Reading, 1994.

P. Sully. *Modelling the World with Objects.* Prentice Hall, Englewood Cliffs, 1993.

H. Züllighoven et al. *Object-Oriented Construction Handbook.* dpunkt/Morgan-Kaufmann, Amsterdam, 2004.

Chapter 4
Simulation Model Descriptions with UML 2

Nicolas Knaak, Ruth Meyer

Contents

4.1	Motivation and Overview	59
4.2	Introduction to the Unified Modelling Language	60
	4.2.1 The Road to UML 2	61
	4.2.2 Diagram Types and Design Principles of the UML	62
4.3	Modelling Static System Structures	65
4.4	Modelling Dynamic Behaviour	69
	4.4.1 Statecharts	70
	4.4.2 Activity Diagrams	77
4.5	Modelling Interactions	87
	4.5.1 Sequence Diagrams of Interaction Scenarios	88
	4.5.2 High Level Sequence Diagrams	90
	4.5.3 Timing Diagrams	92
	Further Reading	93
	Bibliography	93

4.1 Motivation and Overview

Constructing problem specific conceptual models from system descriptions, observations, data, hypotheses, and a-priori knowledge is one of the most crucial tasks of a simulation study (Page 1991, p. 13), whose importance was aptly emphasised by Paul Fishwick in a panel discussion at the 2003 Winter Simulation Conference: "Modelling is one of the primary components of simulation" (Barton et al. 2003, p. 2045). Good conceptual models must be transparent, valid, understandable, and preferably easy to map into computer implementations. In the history of computer simulation, a great deal of different notations and formalisms like event graphs, *Petri nets*, or *System Dynamics*

Chapter 4 Simulation Model Descriptions with UML 2

have been proposed and applied to conceptual modelling. In the object-oriented discrete simulation context described in this book it seems obvious to make use of today's standard graphical notation for object-oriented modelling: the Unified Modelling Language (UML). Using UML seems even more appropriate since its upcoming 2.0 version offers significant improvements in *dynamic behaviour modelling*, which is a key aspect in any discrete event simulation.

A scan of the computer science shelves of any good bookshop will quickly reveal that there is clearly no need for yet another introductory text on UML. The decision to include a chapter on UML-based modelling in this handbook was therefore not taken lightly and is justified on the basis that most general UML introductions are either very detailed and long (e.g. Jeckle et al. 2002) or focus strongly on structural modelling. They therefore do not discuss many of those aspects which are of particular importance to discrete event simulation, such as the treatment of time.

It is the goal of this chapter to offer students and practitioners of simulation a quick overview of those types of UML diagram that we consider most important in a simulation modelling context. These descriptions focus on simulation-specific applications and extensions of these diagrams and use examples from the gravel pit model presented in Chapter 2.

Section 4.2 starts with a general introduction to UML and sketches an overview of its diagram types as well as a short history up to its current version. The graphical language's meta-model and extension mechanisms, which we make use of for simulation specific extensions, are also addressed. Section 4.3 presents an example of using UML's structural modelling features with class- and object-diagrams in the simulation domain. The next two sections then cover the central topic of behavioural modelling. Section 4.4 focuses on state- and process-oriented behaviour descriptions of individual entities, while Section 4.5 looks at modelling interactions. Finally, a literature overview about UML modelling and its use in simulation is given.

The UML specific facts presented in this chapter are mostly based on the German textbooks *UML 2 Glasklar*[1] by Jeckle et al. (2002) and *Softwareentwicklung mit UML 2*[2] by Born et al. (2004).

4.2 Introduction to the Unified Modelling Language

Many texts on UML start with a definition of what UML is and – of equal importance – what it is not. According to the *UML reference manual*, it is "a general-purpose visual modelling language that is used to specify, visualize, construct, and document the artefacts of a software system" (Rumbaugh et al. 1999, p. 3). As Jeckle et al. (2002, p. 10) point out, UML is *not* "complete, not a programming language, not a formal

---

[1] The German title means "UML 2 made crystal-clear".
[2] "Software Development with UML 2".

4.2 Introduction to the Unified Modelling Language

language, not specialized to an application area and [...] first of all not a method or software process".

The latter quote stresses the fact that UML merely provides an application-independent graphical notation for object-oriented modelling and contains no directives for when and how to apply any of its diagrams in a software project. However, UML diagrams are intended to be general enough to apply to the specification of different software processes, as well as during the simulation modelling cycle presented in Section 1.5.

Though UML is indeed no formal or programming language, the semantics of certain diagram types can be defined in a formal way[3] and the so-called Model Driven Architecture (MDA) (Born et al. 2004, p. 273) attempts to make UML models completely executable. The generation of executable code from static and dynamic UML models provides an important means for narrowing the gap between conceptual and computer models in simulation (Klügl 2001, p. 80).

4.2.1 The Road to UML 2

As the term "Unified" in "UML" indicates, UML notation is an amalgamation of different object-oriented modelling methodologies that were popular in the beginning of the 1990s. During this time, object oriented (OO) programming languages gained increasing importance in industrial and business applications and the need for similarly powerful analysis and modelling tools became obvious. This led to a variety of OO modelling techniques that differed and contradicted each other in notation, terminology, method, and modelling focus, but were based on similar concepts and ideas (Rumbaugh et al. 1999, p. 5).

This era, which is often referred to as the "method wars" (see e.g. Born et al. 2004, p. 13), ended around the mid 1990s, when the authors of the most widely used OO modelling methods – OMT (Object Modelling Technique), OOSE (Object Oriented System Engineering), and the Booch method – James Rumbaugh, Ivar Jacobson, and Grady Booch, "began to adopt ideas from each other's methods" (Booch et al. 1999, p. xix). As a result of these efforts, the Unified Modelling Language version 0.9 was presented in 1996.

Jeckle et al. (2002, p. 12) list some additional milestones in the development of UML: The unification process was carried on to version 1.0 in 1997, which was then submitted as a standardized language proposal to the Object Management Group (OMG), an international standardization consortium. The following version (1.1) added an Object Constraint Language (OCL); i.e. a language for the formal specification of assertions and invariants in UML models. While publication of version 1.2 faltered on legal disputes in connection with transfer of copyrights to the OMG, version 1.3 was extended by adding an XML Metadata Interchange Format (XMI) as a means for representing UML models based on the Extensible Markup Language (XML).

---
[3]A formalization of UML state-charts is e.g. provided by Lilius and Paltor (1999)

Chapter 4 Simulation Model Descriptions with UML 2

Under the patronage of the OMG, the development was carried on to UML 1.5. Due to several drawbacks of the 1.x versions, a strongly revised version 2.0 has been proposed and recently adopted as the official UML version[4]. As hinted by the jump in version number, UML 2.0 adds many modifications and innovations. According to Jeckle et al. (2004) the new version intends to enhance the semantic precision of its graphical notation, thus making direct execution of models possible. The overly complex language specification is also redesigned to become smaller and more concise.

For simulation modelling it is of special importance that UML 2.0 contains numerous improvements to *dynamic behaviour modelling*. It introduces two new behaviour diagram types (timing diagrams and interaction overview diagrams), it strongly enhances the expressiveness and formal semantics of the existing diagram types (activity diagrams, interaction diagrams, and, to a lesser extent, state-charts), and it finally integrates the notion of time (Jeckle et al. 2004). A current drawback of adopting UML 2.0 is the fact that there is hardly any case tool or drawing software which supports the new version (Jeckle et al. 2002, p. 20).

4.2.2 Diagram Types and Design Principles of the UML

UML version 2.0 defines a total of 13 diagram types, which support different aspects of object-oriented modelling. According to Jeckle et al. (2002, p. 16) these diagrams can be broadly divided into three types:

❑ *Structural diagrams* serve to model the static structure of a system. Among these are *class diagrams, object diagrams, package diagrams, component diagrams, composition structure diagrams*, and *deployment diagrams*. In this book we will use class and object diagrams to depict entities and relations of a simulated system during the conceptual modelling phase. In Chapter 10 we also use package and class diagrams to display the structure of the DESMO-J simulation framework. Although component, composition structure, and deployment diagrams could be quite useful in component-based and distributed simulation[5], we will not cover these diagram types here. Interested readers should consult the additional literature listed after Section 4.5.

❑ *Behaviour diagrams* are used to display the dynamic behaviour of objects or components at different levels of detail. This includes *use case diagrams, activity diagrams, statechart diagrams*, and several types of *interaction diagrams*. Use case diagrams are often applied in requirements analyses, where they capture typical interactions between a software system and its potential users. Although they might be used to provide a broad overview of activities in a simulation model, the simplicity of our examples makes them unsuitable to demonstrate this diagram type. We will instead concentrate on detailed behaviour modelling of individual entities and events based on statecharts and activity diagrams.

---
[4]See http://www.uml.org.
[5]For an overview of this field see e.g. Bachmann (2003).

4.2 Introduction to the Unified Modelling Language

❑ *Interaction diagrams* are special behaviour diagrams that focus on interactions between two or more objects. Interaction diagrams can be divided into *sequence diagrams* and *timing diagrams*, *communication diagrams*, and *interaction overview diagrams*. *Timing diagrams* emphasise event orderings of interactions, while *communication diagrams* highlight the general structure of cooperations among the entities involved (Jeckle et al. 2002, p. 391). Since temporal aspects of interactions are of special importance in simulation, we will focus on sequence and timing diagrams in this book. The last (and possibly least used) interaction diagram type are *interaction overview diagrams*. These offer a mixture between activity diagrams and sequence diagrams, showing the causal and temporal interconnections among different interaction scenarios (Jeckle et al. 2002, p. 419).

Without diving into more details of the respective diagram types, it should be obvious that UML is a complex and voluminous visual language; incorporating a large number of different modelling techniques. Since complexity and partial inconsistency have been a major criticism against its 1.x versions (Jeckle et al. 2002, p. 13), the language definition for UML 2.0 follows general principles such as (Born et al. 2004, p. 10):

❑ hierarchical and object-oriented language design
❑ language definition by meta-modelling
❑ clean separation between the *models* themselves and the *diagrams* displaying them

Hierarchical language design follows the design of complex software systems by dividing UML into modules called *language packages*. These are broadly comparable to packages in the *Java* tradition. Different packages contain elements ranging from core modelling concepts (e.g. "classes", "properties", or "associations") to advanced and specialized diagram types (e.g. for state-based behaviour description). Basic object-oriented principles like classification, generalization, or information hiding are supported by all diagram types (Born et al. 2004, p. 10). They are also found in the language definition itself; as evidenced by the fact that UML diagram types are structured along a concept hierarchy similar to OO inheritance (e.g. "a sequence diagram is an interaction diagram, which is a specialized behaviour diagram...") (Jeckle et al. 2002, p. 16).

The use of OO vocabulary when talking about UML language concepts is due to the fact that there is no clear difference between building a model of a real-world domain (e.g. a harbour or a gravel pit) and defining an object-oriented visual language. As Born et al. (2004, p. 12) put it, the definition of UML concepts and diagrams is just another model and can therefore be expressed in terms of UML itself. This is exactly what the somewhat esoteric term "meta-modelling" means. In the same way that syntax, grammar, and semantics of a natural language are normally defined in the language itself the OMG specifies UML as an OO model in UML notation using mostly class and package diagrams (Born et al. 2004, p. 61).

To clarify this point, Figure 4.1 shows a small sample from the UML meta-model. This is essentially a UML class diagram (see Section 4.3) that explains the elements of

Chapter 4 Simulation Model Descriptions with UML 2

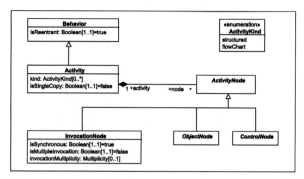

Figure 4.1: A sample from the UML 2 meta-model showing the elements of activity diagrams. Adopted with simplifications from OMG (2004, pp. 4–123)

UML activity diagrams (see Section 4.4.2) for modelling dynamic processes or activities. The rectangles depict classes (more precisely "meta-classes" of the meta-model) which represent UML elements for activity modelling. In this context an `Activity` is a specialized `Behaviour`. It consists of `ActivityNodes` that are divided into `InvocationNodes`, `ObjectNodes`, and `ControlNodes`. In the following sections we will explain activity diagrams and other UML diagram types in plain English in order to ease understanding. However, to understand the precise semantics of a UML element, a look at the meta-model can occasionally be useful.

As the reader might expect, the language definition in terms of an OO model makes extensions to UML easy. Similar to the way in which a software framework like DESMO-J provides a foundation for domain-specific simulation models UML concepts and diagrams can be customized and extended to cater more closely to special fields. Of course this can be done by extending the meta-model itself (Born et al. 2004, p. 245): A theoretician might, for example, want to add Petri nets to UML's repertoire of behaviour diagrams by deriving a new meta-class `PetriNet` from the `Behavior` meta-class.

For lightweight extensions UML offers the *stereotypes* mechanism. According to Jeckle et al. (2002, p. 95) a stereotype is "a class in the meta-model that is able to further specify other classes [...] by extension". Stereotypes can be expressed in UML notation by using an "extension" arrow with a filled arrowhead (Jeckle et al. 2002, p. 93).

Figure 4.2 demonstrates how stereotypes can be used to implement simulation specific extensions: In this example entity types and event classes are specified in terms of UML class diagram classes, by extending the meta-class `Class` with two stereotype <<entity>> and <<event>>.

4.3 Modelling Static System Structures

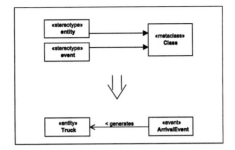

Figure 4.2: An example for simulation specific extensions of UML using the stereotype mechanism. These concepts can then be used by marking all relevant classes with a corresponding stereotype (in imitation of Jeckle et al. 2002, p. 94).

We follow Spaniol and Hoff (1995, p. 9) by saying that objects of classes tagged with the stereotype <<entity>> are "able to actively move forward in simulation time". When used in class diagrams entity classes can now be marked as entity types by attaching the word <<entity>> in angle brackets to the respective model elements. We will define event classes and further simulation specific extensions similarly in the following sections.

The last UML design principle mentioned above is the separation of models and diagrams. This is reminiscent of the well known "Model View Controller" (MVC) design pattern which suggests separation of model and view aspects in graphical software. A UML *model* is based on conceptual UML elements (e.g. classes), with the goal of finding a good set of abstractions for a real system. A UML *diagram*, on the other hand, shows a specific view of the model or certain parts of it (Born et al. 2004, p. 12). Different diagram types emphasise different aspects of the same model; such as its static structure, its interactions, or the behaviour of single entities.

4.3 Modelling Static System Structures

Object-oriented models of a system's static structure can be expressed in terms of UML *class diagrams*, which are a common notation for expressing the general concepts of object-orientation introduced in Section 3.2 (e.g. classes, inheritance...). As part of the conceptual modelling phase we can use class diagrams to understand, visualize, and communicate the structure of a system under analysis. For purposes of a model's implementation class diagrams can also display and document the architecture of relevant simulation programs, frameworks or tools.

In the remainder of this section, we will assume some understanding of OO programming concepts, terminology, and techniques. Read Chapter 3 if you feel rusty.

Chapter 4 Simulation Model Descriptions with UML 2

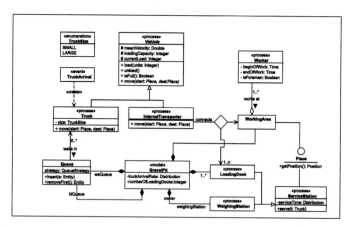

Figure 4.3: A class diagram of the gravel pit model serving as a continuing example

Figure 4.3 shows a class diagram of the structure of a gravel pit model, which was our first simulation example in Section 2.7 and will be used to introduce basic UML concepts here. This model is the result of system analysis and abstraction, similar to the "harbour" example from Section 3.3. During analysis system boundaries are identified, relevant objects classified, and important relationships between model entities are determined. The results of this phase can then be documented in a class diagram.

In the diagram, *classes* are depicted by rectangles divided into at most 3 compartments. The first compartment contains the class name and potential stereotypes. The class name can be set in italic to indicate an *abstract class* (see Section 3.3). The second and third compartment contain the class' *attributes* and *operations*. Depending on the respective modelling phase, these inscriptions can be stated informally, or (as shown in the example) in a UML syntax which is close to common OO programming languages. Stereotypes are employed to relate classes to notions from discrete event simulation. The stereotype <<process>> for example, identifies active entities with their own threads of control. Such process classes are needed in the process-interaction style of model specification introduced in Section 5.2.1. <<model>> tags the class representing the main simulation model, which aggregates all other model components. <<event>> marks an event class, such as the ones we need for event-scheduling styles of model specification (see Section 5.2.2). An <<enumeration>> is a standard UML 2 stereotype flagging simple enumeration types.

In the formal notation attributes are specified by a name, a type and an optional initial value. Operations are declared similarly to method signatures in *Java*; i.e. by giving a name, a parameter list and a return type. The visibility of attributes and

4.3 Modelling Static System Structures

operations is declared by using the symbols - (private), # (protected), ~ (package) and + (public). Abstract operations are set in italics. Class attributes and operations (also known as "static methods" in *Java*) are underlined. For type specifications one might either use the simple and structured types offered by UML (see Born et al. 2004, pp. 41), which ensures implementation independence, or types derived from an arbitrary programming language (in implementation-related diagrams).

The various arrow types in the diagram encode relations between classes. An important aspect of OO modelling is *generalization*, a concept expressed by a large blank arrowhead and describing an inheritance or "is-a" relation – where the class at the arrow's source specializes the class at its destination (e.g. "a truck is a special type of vehicle"). A related concept in OO programming is the implementation of *interfaces*, which are depicted by circles[6] in the class diagram (e.g. the interface Place defines a getPosition() operation). Classes implementing an interface (e.g. ServiceStation) are connected to the respective circle by a plain line.

The example shows further arrows describing *associations* between classes. Common associations for representing "whole-part" relationships are *aggregation* and *composition* (Jeckle et al. 2002, p. 84). Aggregations are shown by drawing a line with a blank diamond at the end between two classes. This connects parts to a whole and the arrow can be read as "consists of"; e.g. as in "a work area consists of several workers working in that area". Composition (shown with a filled diamond shape at its end) is a stronger form of aggregation, where the parts' individual existence depends on the whole ("no whole, no parts") and each part object can therefore only belong to a single whole object at a time (Jeckle et al. 2002, p. 85); see e.g. the relation between GravelPit and WorkingArea. Associations that are not aggregations (like the "waits in" relation between a truck and a queue) are indicated with plain lines or arrows without any diamond symbols.

If needed, further inscriptions can be added to associations: A textual label specifying the respective class' *role* can be attached to each end of an association line (e.g. the class GravelPit plays an "owner" role in a composition relationship with class WeighingStation). We can also indicate the *number* of objects taking part in a relationship; e.g. "a working area consists of an arbitrary number of workers, where each worker only works in one working area at a time". While most relationships in the example are binary, *n*-ary relations are also possible. There is one ternary association called "connects" between classes WorkingArea, LoadingDock, and InternalTransporter.

Associations in implementation-related class diagrams correspond roughly to references, and roles correspond to attribute names. The class WeighingStation, for example, has an attribute *owner* of type GravelPit. Relations that do not represent such links or references between model objects are called *dependencies* and are depicted by a dashed arrow (Born et al. 2004, p. 103). There are some predefined stereotypes specifying the type of dependency between two classes; e.g. <<creates>> (Born et al. 2004, p. 104).

---

[6]Alternatively interfaces can be depicted by a class symbol tagged with the stereotype <<interface>>.

Chapter 4 Simulation Model Descriptions with UML 2

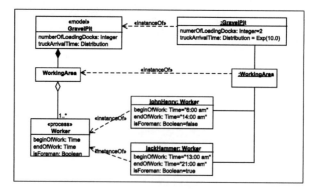

Figure 4.4: An example object diagram from the gravel pit model

In object-orientation classes represent templates for objects that are instantiated at runtime. UML expresses this relation in *object diagrams* (see Jeckle et al. 2002, p. 113), such as the one shown in Figure 4.4. An object diagram displays all objects that constitute a concrete instance of a class model. Objects are represented by rectangles with at most two compartments where the first compartment contains the (underlined) object name and type, and the second compartment lists the object's current attribute values. There are links between objects that instantiate associations specified in some class diagram. Classes and objects are related by the <<instanceOf>> dependency relationship.

The example therefore shows a gravel pit model instance with two workers working in its work area. Note that while the class diagram serves as general template for gravel pit models, the corresponding object diagram shows concrete snapshots of model instances at execution time.

The last static diagram type discussed in this chapter is called a *package diagram*. Package diagrams serve to display the modular structure of (software) systems (see Jeckle et al. 2002, p. 101). Figure 4.5 shows the package structure of an imaginary implementation of the gravel pit model in DESMO-J (see Section 10). As one might suspect, package diagrams are closely related to the package concept of the *Java* programming language.

The example shows a `gravelpit` package, which contains all classes within the gravel pit model. This package uses classes from the simulation framework's `desmoj.core` package and various of its subpackages. Note that packages can be described at various levels of detail: Here subpackages nested inside `desmoj.core` are explicitly shown. `desmoj.core.simulator` and `desmoj.core.dist` also show nested class diagrams depicting structural relationships between important classes within these packages. In

4.4 Modelling Dynamic Behaviour

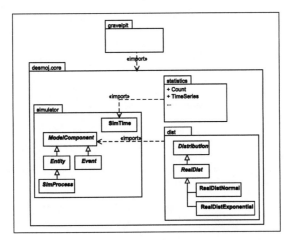

Figure 4.5: An example package diagram

contrast only visibility properties of classes within package desmoj.core.statistics are listed. An important relationship between packages is the <<import>> dependency. This concept corresponds roughly to import statements in Java. In UML imports can either be specified at package level, where a package imports all classes from another package, or at class level, where single classes are imported for use. A detailed description of package diagrams is found in Jeckle et al. (2002, Ch. 4).

4.4 Modelling Dynamic Behaviour

Since discrete event simulation models describe entities' changing states over time, UML's *behaviour diagrams* are of great importance for their description. UML 2 offers several behaviour diagram types, some of which are more appropriate for specifying the behaviour of single entities, while others focus on modelling interactions. As notations for modelling individual classes' behaviour, we will look at statecharts and activity diagrams here. Selected types of interaction diagrams are explained in the next section. All UML behaviour diagrams are built on top of an event-driven communication model quite similar to the basic ideas of discrete event simulation. Events occur at discrete points in time, where they are observed and processed by active entities. The UML specification distinguishes several event types that can occur in diverse situations; e.g. when a signal is sent or received by an entity, an operation is called, or a certain point in time has been reached. Please see Jeckle et al. (2002, p. 172) for a thorough discussion of how UML 2 models events.

Chapter 4 Simulation Model Descriptions with UML 2

4.4.1 Statecharts

UML's statechart notation is primarily based on the work of Harel (1987) and has only been subject to minor changes in version 2. Statecharts describe the behaviour of entity classes in terms of a finite state machine (FSM). An FSM consists of a finite set of states, which the object passes through during its lifecycle, and a set of event-driven changes in state. To make the notation more powerful, additional conditions can be attached to states and transitions. Description of hierarchically embedded and concurrent states is also supported. While statecharts are traditionally used in hardware and real-time system design, the formalism also fits state-based simulation approaches such as DEVS (see e.g. Zeigler et al. 2000, Ch. 4) quite well. In this book we will use statecharts predominantly in an early modelling phase to build an abstract conceptual model of the target system's state transitions. This state model is then refined into one or more activity diagrams that are closer to the respective event- or process-oriented simulation style (see Section 5.2).

Basic Elements of Statecharts

As an introduction to statecharts we will take a look at the familiar gravel pit model (see Sections 2.7 and 4.3). Figure 4.6 shows a diagram of a truck's states on its way through the gravel pit.

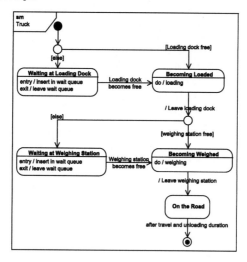

Figure 4.6: A statechart showing the lifecycle of trucks at a gravel pit

4.4 Modelling Dynamic Behaviour

Statecharts contain several state nodes (depicted by round rectangles) with a unique name in the upper segment of each. States are connected by directed edges, which represent event-driven transitions. At every moment in time the truck is in a given state and reacts to a specific set of events, causing it to change state. For example, when the truck is in state `Waiting at loading dock` and a signal `Loading dock becomes free` is received, its state changes to `Loading`.

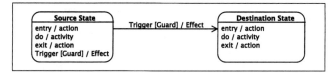

Figure 4.7: Summary of state and transition inscriptions in statecharts. Adopted with modifications from Jeckle et al. (2002, p. 275)

States and transitions can also contain miscellaneous inscriptions, as depicted in Figure 4.7. States can be assigned an *entry* and *exit action* (identified by the corresponding keywords). This action is executed each time a state is entered or left. The keyword *do* serves to initiate a (usually time consuming) activity that follows the *entry-action* as long as an object stays in the assigned state. Inscriptions attached to transitions have the general form `Trigger[Guard]/Effect`.

The *trigger* part names a class of events, which activate the transition and the *guard* is a Boolean expression describing what must be checked whenever a trigger event occurs. If the guard condition holds true, the active transition "fires" and changes from the current state to the transition's target state. The attached *effect* inscription specifies that an additional action is executed during the change; i.e. after the current state's exit action and before the target state's entry action is performed.

A transition with identical source and destination states is called a *self transition* and behaves exactly like any other transition; i.e. by leaving and re-entering the assigned state. Self transitions are distinguished from so-called *internal transitions*. These are denoted by state inscriptions of the form `Trigger[Guard]/Effect` and their firing does not trigger any state change with the execution of exit and entry actions.[7]

It should be obvious from the example in Figure 4.6 that all state and transition inscriptions are optional. A transition without trigger is called a *default transition*. Default transitions are triggered by the completion of a watched state's *do* activity; e.g. the outgoing transition from `Becoming Loaded` is triggered after completing the `Loading` activity. A default transition emanating from a state without a *do* activity is triggered immediately after execution of the *entry* action.

---

[7] An example of an internal transition is the reaction to the event `TruckArrival` in the state `Operating` of the statechart shown in Figure 4.9.

Chapter 4 Simulation Model Descriptions with UML 2

Another special case are *time triggered transitions*, which are activated whenever a certain time instant is reached. Time points can be either stated in absolute terms. Alternatively they can make use of the *after* keyword to specify time relative to the moment of entering the transition's source state.

Alongside states and transitions the truck example contains further statechart elements referred to as *pseudo states*. Pseudo states differ from "real" states in that the FSM doesn't stay in any of them for an extended period of time. Instead they connect and mark transitions in order to "display complex relations between states in a simple way" (Jeckle et al. 2002, p. 288).

An *initial state* is a pseudo state depicted by a filled in circle. It serves as a pointer to the state a modelled entity is in at the start of its lifecycle. The lifecycle is finished when the FSM reaches a *final state*, as shown by a circle with a black dot in the middle. Note that while an initial state is a pseudo state, a final state is considered to be a conventional one.

The initial state of the truck example is connected to another pseudo state called *choice*, which is denoted by a blank circle. Choices are used to introduce branching conditions in statecharts. They are connected to several guarded outgoing transitions, each of which represents an alternative execution path. Since choices are pseudo states, their outgoing transitions must not have any attached trigger events.

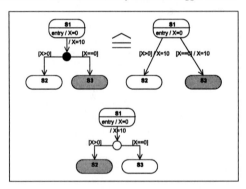

Figure 4.8: An example for the different semantics of junction and choice nodes, when applied to alternative execution paths in a statechart.
Adopted with modifications from Jeckle et al. (2002, p. 293)

Another kind of pseudo state that is very similar to a choice is called a *junction*. Junctions are shown as filled in circles (like initial states) and their semantics differ slightly from choice nodes. While a choice acts as an intermediate state between in-

4.4 Modelling Dynamic Behaviour

coming and outgoing transitions, a junction "builds a single overall transition from one or more [...] transition segments" (Rumbaugh et al. 1999, p. 320).

The example in Figure 4.8 hopefully helps to explain the subtle difference between junctions and choices. The junction in the upper left statechart serves merely as a transition connector. All transitions resulting from this connection are shown in the behaviourally equivalent upper right statechart. When an event E1 occurs, both transitions first check their guard conditions (X>0 or X=0 respectively). Since in state S1 the variable X is set to 0, the second condition holds true. The common effect X=10 is executed next and the FSM moves into state S3.

The semantics of the choice in the lower statechart of Figure 4.8 is closer to that of a standard state. When an event E1 occurs here, effect X=10 is executed first. The FSM depicted by the statechart then enters the choice node and checks its guard conditions, resulting in a transition to state S2.

Hierarchical and Concurrent Statecharts

In addition to the constructs shown so far, statecharts offer further possibilities for structuring an entity's state space via hierarchical state embedding. Figure 4.9 shows an example describing the behaviour of the gravel pit's loading dock. The loading dock's lifecycle starts in state Closed. At the begin of a working day, the FSM switches its state to Operating, which is a so-called *composite state* containing embedded *substates*. On entering a composite state, a number of activities are performed in fixed order:

- First the composite state's *entry* action is executed, causing the loading gear to be prepared in the example.
- Next the initial state of the embedded state machine is entered, which triggers execution of its respective entry action. The state machine representing the loading dock therefore enters its Idle state and waits for the next truck to arrive.
- *Do* activities of super- and substates are executed concurrently, where each activity is started after the corresponding *entry* action is finished.

The execution status of a hierarchical state machine is not represented in terms of a single "current state", but rather described by a so called *configuration*; i.e. a list containing all states the machine is currently in. When a new work day begins the example FSM moves into states Idle and Operating, which is justified by the commonsense fact that the loading dock is now ready for use and idle. We can therefore use a composite state's different substates (e.g. Idle and Loading) as a more precise and mutually exclusive specialization of the superstate's meaning. Of course, hierarchical embedding of states need not be limited to the two levels shown in this example.

Whenever an event occurs a hierarchical state machine searches its current configuration for a matching transition from "inside out". This means that the simple state

Chapter 4 Simulation Model Descriptions with UML 2

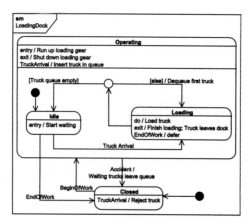

Figure 4.9: The gravel pit's loading dock modelled as a hierarchical state machine. The "emergency exit" behaviour shown here is a popular example for hierarchical state machines. It can, for example, be found in Köhler (1999, p. 38)

at the end of the state hierarchy (also called *leaf state*) is considered first. If this state cannot handle the event, search proceeds to its direct hierarchical predecessor.

Let the configuration in the example be [Operating, Idle]. On occurrence of a TruckArrival event, the state machine checks the leaf state Idle first. Finding a matching transition should move it into a Loading state. To accomplish this, the relevant transition fires and changes the FSM's configuration to [Operating, Loading]. In the model this corresponds to the loading dock starting to load the next truck.

Let us assume that another truck arrives while the state-machine is still Loading. Since the leaf state cannot handle this event search proceeds to its superstate Operating. This state has an internal transition that handles the arrival by inserting the truck into a queue. As soon as the current loading activity finishes, the loading dock checks this queue, removes the first truck and starts loading.

Notice that the "inside-out" nature of the search for matching transitions allows "overriding" of trigger events from superstates; just like methods from superclasses can be redefined in object-oriented programming. In the example the composite Operating state defines a default reaction to a TruckArrival event. This behaviour is "inherited" by the state Loading, but overridden and thereby specialized for the Idle state.

The event Accident is handled exclusively by the superstate and is not redefined in either Idle or Loading. When a gravel pit accident happens, the loading dock is closed for security reasons and the composite Operating state is left. This action is independent of state; i.e. it happens regardless of whether a loading dock is loading or idle. On

4.4 Modelling Dynamic Behaviour

leaving a composite state, the exit actions of all states in the current configuration are executed from inside out. When an Accident happens while the loading dock is busy (i.e. in configuration [Operating, Loading]). the loading dock first finishes loading (exit action of Loading) before shutting down (exit action of Operating).

While accidents cause the FSM to terminate operation regardless of state, an EndOfWork event can only be handled when the loading dock becomes idle after loading the last truck in the queue. This is indicated by an outgoing transition emanating directly from the Idle substate. Note that this transition also causes the loading dock to leave the Operating state and how this triggers the relevant exit action. Similar to such an *explicit exit* it is also possible to model *explicit entry* transitions pointing directly to a certain substate.

As mentioned before, the Loading state cannot handle EndOfWork events. However, it is still desirable not to discard this event when the loading dock happens to be active at the official end of the workday; otherwise it would simply keep operating forever. The Loading state therefore contains an internal transition, whose effect is labelled by the UML keyword **defer**. Deferring an event causes the state machine to buffer the event until its next change of state. Deferred events can then either be handled (as in state Idle), deferred further (as in state Loading) or simply discarded.

So far we have considered substates as "exclusive or" specializations of their superstates. Beyond this, UML statecharts are also capable of displaying concurrent behaviour modelled with so called *orthogonal regions*. The statechart in Figure 4.10 models the concurrent operation of a loading dock and a weighing station in the gravel pit example. In contrast to Figure 4.9 the Operating state has been extended to a composite state with two orthogonal regions, separated by a dashed line. The two subcharts embedded in those regions operate concurrently. The upper chart represents the loading dock and the lower chart models the weighing station.

Entries to the Operating state occur similarly as in our previous example. Operating's entry action is executed first, followed by concurrent execution of entry actions for both idle states; in parallel or in an unspecified order. Afterwards the FSM is in the Operating state and in both LoadingDockIdle and WeighingStationIdle substates at the same time. Note that, while we could represent the configuration of Figure 4.9's hierarchical statechart as a *list*, the configuration of a concurrent statechart is a *tree* with the topmost composite state (e.g. Operating) as its root and one leaf state from each region as leafs (e.g. LoadingDockIdle and WeighingStationIdle).

When an event occurs, the search for matching transitions starts from the leaf states and proceeds in an inverse breadth-first fashion. Let us assume that the state machine for our example is in configuration

[Operating,[WeighingStationIdle,LoadingDockIdle]].

On an EndOfWork event, the two leaf states of the FSM are searched for a transition first. Since one of them handles the event, the search does need proceed to the

Chapter 4 Simulation Model Descriptions with UML 2

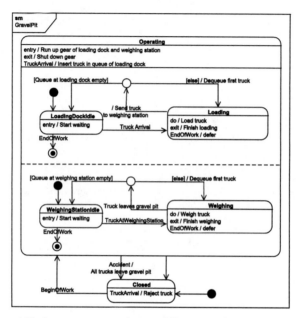

Figure 4.10: A concurrent statechart modelling a gravel pit with concurrent operations of loading dock and weighing station

superstate. In the example both concurrent substates can handle this event and the corresponding transitions are executed concurrently.

Outgoing default transitions of composite states are triggered when the subcharts in all orthogonal regions have reached a final state. When the composite state is exited, the exit actions of all active leaf states are executed before leaving the superstate. In our example the occurrence of an EndOfWork event causes the subcharts in both orthogonal regions to reach their final states. This then triggers the default transition emanating from the currently active superstate.

The subcharts of a concurrent statechart do not always work completely independently of each other. The loading dock and weighing station need some synchronization. A truck, for example, can only be weighed at the weighing station once it has been loaded at the loading dock. Synchronization between concurrent substates can be realized using signal events. When the loading dock leaves the Loading state after finishing the loading activity, it emits a signal TruckAtWeighingStation (implicitly by sending the truck to the weighing station). This signal triggers a transition from the weighing station, causing both subcharts to synchronize.

It should become obvious from the last example that UML statecharts are a very powerful notation for modelling complex event-driven behaviour. Since the occurrence of an event can lead to a large number of sequential and concurrent activities in a hierarchical statechart, the semantics of such models are not always easy to understand or implement in a simulation. In the next section we will encounter another type of UML behaviour diagram, which can be more directly related to the event- and process-oriented modelling perspectives discussed later in this book.

4.4.2 Activity Diagrams

According to Jeckle et al. (2002, p. 199) activity diagrams are the notation of choice for modelling processes. While this diagram type's main application in software engineering is the description of operations, use cases, or business processes (Jeckle et al. 2002, p. 199), activity diagrams are particularly well suited for modelling lifecycles of simulation processes in the process-interaction world view (see Section 5.2.1). Since they provide features such as concurrency, object flow and message-passing, they are convenient for showing the synchronization of two or more processes. They also find application in other tasks of a discrete event modelling project; e.g. for modelling event routines in event-oriented simulations.

Activity diagrams are the diagram type that has undergone most changes in the transition from UML version 1.x to 2.0. In UML 1.x activity diagrams were a special case of statecharts (see Section 4.4.1), emphasising synchronous control instead of asynchronous handling of events. The majority of states in an activity diagram were so-called action states, which could only be left via default transitions triggered by the completion of the states' activity. Action states were, however, sometimes mixed with normal states for handling asynchronous events.

In UML 2.0 the statechart-like event handling semantics of activity diagrams has been replaced by a Petri net-like token semantics. This makes this diagram type even more suitable for modelling concurrent processes. In the following we will learn how to use activity diagrams for describing the dynamics of discrete event simulation models. We start with basic features that allow us to use activity diagrams as simple flow charts, and explain their dynamics by means of the token semantics. After this, we proceed to more advanced concepts, such as object flow and concurrency. As before, the gravel pit model from Section 2.7 serves as a continuing example.

Using Activity Diagrams as Flowcharts: Basic Constructs

The basic purpose of activity diagrams is the description of activities; i.e. sequences of actions. According to UML semantics an *action* is the call of a behaviour or the processing of data that is not further divided in an activity (Jeckle et al. 2002, p. 212). Since

Chapter 4 Simulation Model Descriptions with UML 2

an action is an elementary indivisible step, it seems justified to additionally claim that in discrete event simulation no simulation time commences during an action's execution. Actions in an activity diagram are graphically shown by using rounded rectangles with a name or description attached (see Figure 4.11). We describe action sequences by connecting actions with directed *edges* indicating the activity's control flow. There are *start* and *end nodes* similar to those in statecharts, marking the beginning and end of an activity.

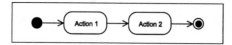

Figure 4.11: A simple activity diagram showing a sequence of actions

Most non-trivial activities do not proceed linearly, but have decision points where choices depend on conditions. Reminiscent of flowcharts, *decision nodes* in an activity diagram are depicted as diamond symbols with multiple outgoing edges. As in statecharts these edges might be watched by a guard, i.e. a Boolean expression describing the condition upon which control flows along this edge[8]. The keyword *else* denotes a "catch-all" case. The modeller should ensure that guards are mutually exclusive. If they are not, the behaviour described by the diagram is non-deterministic. Alternative courses of action emanating from a decision node can be rejoined using a *merge node*. Such nodes are also symbolized by a diamond shape (Jeckle et al. 2002, p. 234). Note that start, end, decision and merge nodes are not actions, but so-called *control nodes* – somewhat similar to pseudo states in a statechart.

Figure 4.12 shows how to use activity diagrams to represent state changes caused by events in event scheduling simulation. Our example event is the arrival of a truck at the gravel pit. The event routine is composed of elementary actions – like creation and modification of entities, or the scheduling of further events. Although understanding the behaviour described by such simple diagrams is straightforward, things can become quite difficult when several alternative or even concurrent trails of execution are possible. The dynamics of UML activity diagrams are therefore defined in a semi-formal way, using a so-called *token semantics*. This makes their operation more explicit.

While the token concept was originally introduced in the context of Petri nets, knowledge of Petri net theory is not required, but undoubtedly helpful, for its understanding and use in activity diagram.

A *token* is a small marker showing the current execution status of the diagram. When execution starts the token resides in the initial node. From there it is passed along the edges of the diagram. Whenever an action (e.g. "Create new truck entity") is executed, one can imagine that the corresponding action node "consumes" the token from its

---

[8]Different from statecharts, edges in an activity diagram cannot be associated with trigger and effect expressions.

4.4 Modelling Dynamic Behaviour

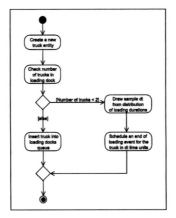

Figure 4.12: An example activity diagram describing actions performed for an "arrival of a truck in the gravel pit" event

incoming edge and produces a token on its outgoing edge. When the token reaches a decision node, it is propagated along any edge whose guard condition holds true. Every token that reaches a final state is removed from the diagram. Note that tokens are not allowed to reside in edges or control nodes (except for the initial node) (Jeckle et al. 2002), since these elements only serve to propagate the token from one action node to the next.

In order to understand or validate complex activity diagrams, it is sometimes helpful to follow their execution trails through an activity graph with real markers.[9] A Java applet for demonstrating token flow in an activity diagram is presented in Section 14.4.4.

Concurrency and Interactions

The diagrams shown so far were rather simple, largely because they contained only one thread of control represented by a single token. One of the most interesting features of UML activity diagrams, however, is their capability for modelling concurrency.

The most basic case of concurrency are truly concurrent activities that require no synchronization at all. We can model such activities by using multiple activity diagrams in parallel. Figure 4.13 shows a diagram of a worker and a clerk working independently at different locations (working area and office) of the gravel pit. Each actor has its

---
[9] A professor at Hamburg University prefers small screws or nuts to play this kind of "token game" in his lectures on Petri net theory.

Chapter 4 Simulation Model Descriptions with UML 2

own thread of control, represented by a token starting from the respective initial node. To improve the diagram's structure, there are two so-called *activity partitions*, with headings "Worker" and "Clerk". These show which actor the nested actions belong to. Although there are further reasons for partitioning activity diagrams, we will mostly use partitions to separate multiple actors in the way shown below.

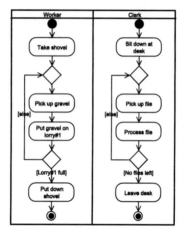

Figure 4.13: A worker and a clerk working concurrently in the gravel pit. No synchronization is required between them, since the clerk processes files at the gravel pit's office and the worker loads transporters in the working area.

Most real world processes – especially those that are interesting enough to simulate – are not independent; either because they compete for bounded resources or must collaborate to perform common tasks. In either case some kind of synchronization is required. One way to model synchronization in UML activity diagrams are so-called *fork* and *join nodes*, which are both symbolized by thick horizontal or vertical bars. Both node types share the same semantics and are therefore collectively referred to as *synchronization bars*. Control flow stops at a synchronization bar until tokens have arrived at all of its incoming edges. The node then "fires", consuming all tokens from its incoming edges and placing a token on each outgoing edge. Since this "AND"-semantics is also implemented by normal action nodes, it is allowed to omit synchronization bars and draw action nodes with multiple incoming and outgoing edges instead.[10]

Figure 4.14 shows different ways of splitting and merging control flow in activity diagrams. According to Jeckle et al. (2002, p. 237), a fork splits control flow from

---
[10] In contrast to this, the "OR"-semantics of decisions must *always* be made explicit by using decision and merge nodes.

4.4 Modelling Dynamic Behaviour

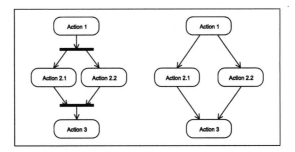

Figure 4.14: Explicit splitting and merging of control flow with fork and join nodes (left). Implicit splitting and merging of control flow by action nodes with multiple incoming or outgoing edges (right)

one incoming edge to multiple outgoing edges, while a join reunites it from multiple incoming edges to a single outgoing edge. Combinations of both cases are possible.

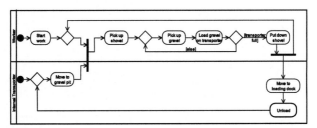

Figure 4.15: Synchronization of a worker and an internal transporter

A larger example of synchronization is shown in Figure 4.15. Here the actions of a worker have to be synchronized with the internal transport vehicle that the gravel is loaded on. Both activities start independently from their respective initial nodes. Synchronization is necessary because the worker might only load gravel onto the transporter when it is present at the gravel pit – and the transporter has to wait while being loaded. For security reasons the operator of the transporter will wait until the worker has put down his shovel after the loading is finished. He then drives his vehicle to the loading dock, where the gravel can be loaded onto a waiting truck.

Fork and join nodes can be used to show closely coupled concurrent activities synchronized by token flow. However, in discrete event modelling (and also many other disciplines like e.g. distributed systems) we often describe system dynamics from the perspective of individual actors, who communicate via messages or signals. Figure 4.16

81

Chapter 4 Simulation Model Descriptions with UML 2

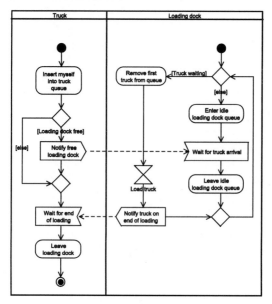

Figure 4.16: Synchronization of trucks and loading docks via sending and reception of signals

shows how an activity diagram description of this style of communication can be added to activity diagrams. In this example two process classes – trucks and (operators of) loading docks – synchronize their behaviour in response to signals which pass between them. The notation and modelling style is quite close to the *process-oriented simulation* world view described in detail in Section 5.2.1.

When a truck arrives at the loading dock, it joins a queue in the parking lot ("truck queue") first. If an idle loading dock is available the truck sends a signal to initiate loading. In the activity diagram this notification is expressed by a so-called *send signal action* (Jeckle et al. 2002, p. 214). The truck then remains passive until loading is finished. This is indicated by the *receive signal action* (Jeckle et al. 2002, p. 214) "wait for end of loading"[11]. In process oriented simulations all time consuming activities or wait states or modelled with receive signal actions[12], while no simulation time passes when executing a normal action node (see Section 5.2.1).

---

[11] Since token flow is explicitly delayed (thereby forcing the process to wait) until a matching signal has been received, the term "action" is somewhat misleading in this context.

[12] The time signal reception action explained below is regarded as a receive signal action as well.

4.4 Modelling Dynamic Behaviour

The loading dock cycles through an infinite loop serving arriving trucks. First it checks whether there are any waiting trucks in the truck queue. If so, it dequeues the first truck and performs some service operation which consumes simulation time. In our example the service's duration is determined *a priori*; e.g. by drawing a sample from a random distribution. While we use the standard form of a receive signal action for wait states without time constraints, delays with predefined duration are modelled using a *time signal reception action*, which is depicted by an hour glass symbol (Jeckle et al. 2002, p. 215). A time signal reception node delays incoming tokens for a specified duration. One might also imagine that the modelled process re-schedules itself by sending a "time signal" when the node is reached, and then waits for the relevant period (after which the signal will be received). In our example the service duration is stated implicitly. Besides naming the corresponding activity (e.g. "Load truck") we can also use keywords *after* and *when*, which we already discussed in the context of statecharts (see Section 4.4.1), for relative and absolute time specifications.

After finishing service, the loading dock operator notifies the waiting truck in order to leave the dock. Control then returns to the start of the loop. If no further truck is waiting, the loading dock inserts itself into a queue and waits for the next truck to arrive. Note that the dashed arrows between send and receive actions are not part of standard UML, but serve only to clarify the direction of signal flow between the processes here. In larger simulation models it is inadvisable to display all communicating processes in a single diagram. In that case we will draw a detailed activity diagram for each process and use sequence or timing diagrams (Section 4.5.3) to specify representative interactions. We will return to process modelling with activity diagrams in Section 5.2.1, where we will also define some signal stereotypes for process-oriented simulation.

Modelling Object Flow

While we have so far used activity diagrams only to model flow of control, they can also be used to show data flows. The main construct for modelling data flows is the *object node*, symbolized by a rectangle which is annotated with the type of objects which can be stored in the node. When the outgoing edge of an action is connected to an object node, firing the action creates a so-called *data token*[13] that contains an object representing the result of the execution. This data token is stored in the object node and might serve as input to another action whose incoming edge is connected to the object node. Although there are numerous ways to use and display object flows in UML 2 activity diagrams (see e.g. Jeckle et al. 2002, p. 218), we will only consider a quite restricted subset of these possibilities here.

A property of object nodes which is particularly useful for simulation modelling is their ability to buffer incoming data tokens. This allows us to use object nodes to model synchronization constructs like queues and resources. Figure 4.17 shows the interaction

---

[13] The semantics of object flow and data tokens in UML 2 activity diagrams is closely related to *coloured Petri nets* (Jensen 1992).

Chapter 4 Simulation Model Descriptions with UML 2

between trucks and the gravel pit's loading dock as a simple single server queueing system. A generator process creates truck objects at a certain arrival rate and inserts them into a queue, modelled as an object node. We use the <<queue>> stereotype to indicate that an object node serves as a queue in the model. The annotation "Trucks" prescribes which types of entities can be stored in the queue. The optional inscription in square brackets is a condition, which constrains the state all entities in this object node must be in.

Trucks are de-queued by the loading dock's "remove from queue" action. The semantics of the edge[14] connecting this action node to the queue are similar to standard edges in activity diagrams. When the queue node provides a data token (i.e. there is a truck waiting) and the standard edge above the action node provides a control token, the action node fires and removes one truck object from the queue. To indicate a "first in, first out" (FIFO) selection strategy, we also attach a note symbol with a <<selection>> stereotype to the edge. To simplify the remainder of the discussion, we will assume FIFO as a default queueing strategy, and will only add a selection note when a different strategy (e.g. shortest processing time) is used.

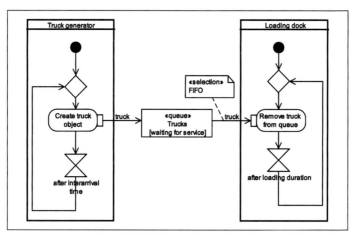

Figure 4.17: A queue modelled as an object node

---

[14]Note that edges do not connect action and object nodes directly. Instead a so called *pin* (depicted by a small rectangle) is inserted between the action node and the edge. The pin indicates that the action provides or consumes a data token (e.g. a truck object) as output or input respectively. However, our use of the pin notation is simplified and slightly different from the original UML semantics (see Jeckle et al. 2002, pp. 220).

4.4 Modelling Dynamic Behaviour

If no truck is present, the loading dock process waits for the arrival of the next one. Note that the queues we use in later examples of process-oriented simulations do not have these synchronization capabilities. In Section 5.2.3, for example, we must therefore explicitly check if any waiting objects have been filed into queues and synchronize processes explicitly by sending signals.

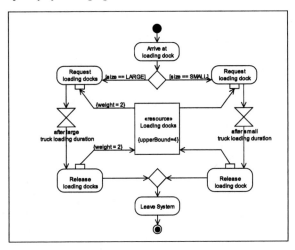

Figure 4.18: Interaction between trucks and loading docks modelled with a resource

Another use of object nodes in discrete event simulation models is shown in Figure 4.18, which depicts the lifecycle of a refined truck process. Trucks now come in two different sizes; large and small. To be loaded, large trucks need two of 4 available loading docks, while small trucks need only one. We abstract from loading docks as a separate process type but represent them as a resource with given capacity. The resource semantics of the object node is indicated by the <<resource>> stereotype. Again there is a condition which constrains the state of the available loading docks. As before, the truck process waits when there are too few resources for service. The maximum capacity of an object node can be specified by using an upperBound attribute, written in curly braces. Similarly, the number of tokens an edge consumes or produces is specified using a weight attribute, where the default weight of 1 needs not to be stated explicitly. We will return to resources and further modelling constructs based on UML object nodes when we discuss advanced modelling constructs in Section 5.3.

Chapter 4 Simulation Model Descriptions with UML 2

Advanced Concepts

UML 2 activity diagrams offer a number of advanced concepts such as nodes for structured programming similar to Nassi/Shneiderman diagrams (Jeckle et al. 2002, p. 210). Since most of them serve rather specialized needs and space is limited, we will only discuss two further modelling techniques here.

It might sometimes be useful to apply activity partitions not only to distinguish between different actors, but also between different places, responsibilities, or other properties. The activity diagram in Figure 4.19 shows a partition in 2 dimensions. The vertical separation indicates different processes (truck, operator of loading dock, and operator of weighing station) whereas the horizontal separation indicates different locations.

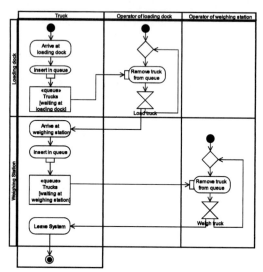

Figure 4.19: Using activity regions to distinguish between different actors and places in an activity diagram

Another important requirement of process oriented simulations is the ability to model *interrupts*. Figure 4.20 shows an example of a customer waiting in a queue; e.g. at a ticket booth. The customer's patience is limited. After waiting for an available teller for a specified period (e.g. 20 minutes) he will "balk" and leave the queue without being serviced. We can represent this behaviour in an activity diagram using an *interruptible activity region* , which is symbolized by a rounded rectangle with a dashed outline

(Jeckle et al. 2002, p. 241). The interruptible activity region contains a so-called interrupt edge, which is shaped like a "blizzard" (Jeckle et al. 2002, p. 242). When the customer reaches the teller station, he receives a *begin of service* signal which triggers the corresponding signal reception action. In the diagram this causes the interruptible activity region to be left, using the interrupt edge. In contrast to a standard edge, this step removes *all* tokens from the region, so that no further actions within the region (e.g. "swear loudly") will be executed.

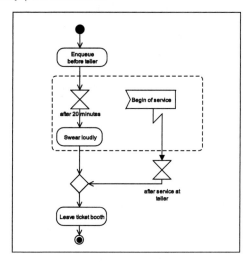

Figure 4.20: A customer with limited patience modelled with an interruptible activity region

4.5 Modelling Interactions

As shown in the previous sections, it is possible to model interactions between components of a simulation model by means of statecharts and activity diagrams. The main purpose of these diagrams, however, is the description of individual entities' behaviour. UML *interaction diagrams* are often better suited to model the interplay between multiple entities. The following discussion looks at sequence and timing diagrams, which focus on the temporal aspects of interactions. An in-depth treatment of UML interaction diagrams can be found in Jeckle et al. (2002, Ch. 12–14).

Chapter 4 Simulation Model Descriptions with UML 2

4.5.1 Sequence Diagrams of Interaction Scenarios

In its basic form, *sequence diagrams* display timely ordered message sequences describing an interaction scenario between two or more objects. Figure 4.21 shows an example for modelling interactions between a truck and a loading dock at the gravel pit. This example can be regarded as a possible execution sequence of the activity diagrams shown in Figure 4.16; i.e. it shows one possible case for a truck being serviced at the loading dock. In this particular scenario the loading dock is initially idle, and there are no other trucks waiting.

In sequence diagrams the different objects or roles taking part in an interaction are plotted along the horizontal axis, while the vertical axis represents time (Jeckle et al. 2002, p. 327). The main diagram elements are the *lifelines* of the interaction partners and what *messages* pass between them.

As in object diagrams (see Section 4.3), each interacting object is depicted by a rectangle and labelled by its class and (optional) object name. Underneath the object symbol is a dashed vertical *lifeline*, representing the object's life-span during the interaction. When the object's lifetime ends, this lifeline is truncated using an x-shaped termination symbol (see e.g. the `ArrivalEvent`'s lifeline in Figure 4.21).

During an interaction an object performs *action sequences* (represented as white boxes along the lifeline), sometimes *waits* in a passive state, and *communicates* with other objects via *messages*. As we know from Section 4.3, messages represent method calls to objects as well as the transmission of other communication signals in UML (see also Jeckle et al. 2002, p. 346).

In sequence diagrams each message is indicated by an arrow pointing from the sender's lifeline to the receiver's lifeline. The intersections between the lifelines and the message arrows represent *send* and *receive events*. The temporal order of these events is indicated by the arrow positions on the vertical time axis.

UML distinguishes several communication modes, each of which is symbolized by a different arrow-head (Jeckle et al. 2002, p. 346). A filled black arrowhead indicates a *synchronous* message, where the sender waits in its lifecycle until the message has been processed by the receiver. The receiver answers by sending a *response message*, represented by a dashed arrow with filled arrowhead. A typical example of synchronous communication are method calls in the Java programming language. When an object's method is called by a client, control passes to the object and only returns to the client after the method's execution. The client then receives a "response message" in the form of a return value. If there is no explicit return value (i.e. the method's return type is void) the response message might as well be omitted in the sequence diagram.

Asynchronous messages are symbolized by an open arrowhead. In asynchronous communication the sender continues its lifecycle *without* waiting for the message to be processed by the receiver. While synchronous communication can be compared to a telephone call, asynchronous messages correspond to E-Mail communications, where messages are answered only when the receiver has time to do so. Besides synchronous

4.5 Modelling Interactions

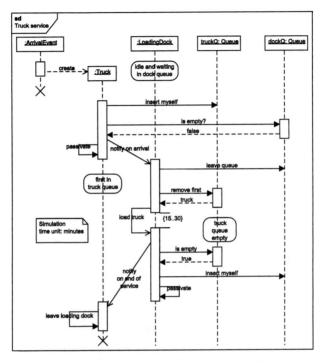

Figure 4.21: An example sequence diagram showing the service of an arriving truck at the loading dock

and asynchronous messages there are so-called *creation messages*. These are depicted by a dashed arrow with an open arrowhead. This message type is comparable to a constructor call initiating the creation of an object.

With this knowledge it should be possible to understand the diagram in Figure 4.21. The "truck service" interaction begins when a new truck is created by a truck arrival event. The event terminates immediately after that and the truck process begins its lifecycle with an action sequence. First it inserts itself into the loading dock's wait queue by synchronously calling a method of the truckQ object. Since this insert() method returns no result the response message can be omitted. Next the truck determines if a loading dock is available. This is the case if the idle loading dock queue is empty. In the example scenario, there is an idle dock and the corresponding method call returns true.

89

Chapter 4 Simulation Model Descriptions with UML 2

Conditions ensuring the correctness of a scenario (e.g. "loading dock idle") can be expressed by so-called *state invariants* (Jeckle et al. 2002, p. 356). State invariants are symbolized by using rounded rectangles which we already know as the UML symbol for states (from Section 4.4.1). State invariants are especially useful for the *verification* of interaction scenarios. They serve as post-conditions of the previous and pre-conditions of the following action sequence. A communication scenario is not implemented correctly if an object is not in a required state by the time its lifeline encounters a state invariant (Jeckle et al. 2002, p. 357).

Our example continues with the truck notifying the waiting loading dock process. Note that this notification is shown as an asynchronous message. The loading dock will not process it immediately, but only when the simulation scheduler selects it to become the next active process. Since there are only two processes present, this happens right after the truck has passivated itself and waits for the end of the service. In this book we will generally represent method calls as synchronous and process interactions as asynchronous messages.

The loading dock now leaves the idle queue and removes the truck from the head of the wait queue. Then it encounters a time constrained wait state, which represents the loading activity.[15] As an extension to standard UML notation we indicate this situation by a message arrow connecting two separate action sequences along the loading dock's lifeline.

There is an additional *time constraint* {15...30} shown in the example diagram. It states that a loading's duration will take from 15 to 30 minutes of simulation time. Such time constraints can be inserted at any place in the diagram where they are meaningful (Jeckle et al. 2002, p. 352). The notation used here is one of several possible forms for time constraints that are discussed in Jeckle et al. (2002, p. 352). In stochastic simulation it might be useful to specify time constraints based on probability distributions (e.g. $\{U(15, 30)\}$ for uniformly distributed loading duration).

At the end of our example scenario, the loading dock reactivates the truck and then checks the truck queue again. Since there are no more trucks to be loaded, it falls idle and the truck leaves the system.

4.5.2 High Level Sequence Diagrams

So far we have only dealt with elements that allow us to display sequence diagrams for single interaction scenarios. This restriction follows from the former UML 1.x notation. However, in UML 2 it is possible to represent alternative, optional, parallel, and repeated sequences of interaction. Furthermore, diagrams might contain references to other sequence diagrams that contain a refined description of particular interaction steps. Due to their derivation from so-called *High Level Message Sequence Charts* (Jeckle et al. 2002, p. 332), we will refer to this notation as "high level sequence diagrams".

---

[15] Remember the use of the hour glass symbol in Figure 4.16.

4.5 Modelling Interactions

Like activity diagrams and statecharts, high level sequence diagrams do not display a single scenario but rather a whole class of possible interaction sequences. A drawback of the extended notation is that such diagrams can become rather complex and difficult to understand. In particular, a high level sequence diagram does not represent a straightforward message sequence, where time proceeds along the vertical axis.

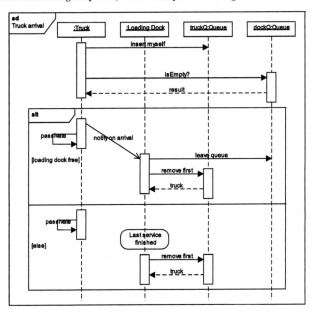

Figure 4.22: A high level sequence diagram containing an alternative

Figure 4.22 shows a high level sequence diagram displaying two alternative courses of an interaction modelling the arrival of a new truck at the gravel pit. As in our previous example, the scenario starts with a truck arriving at the loading dock and inserting itself into the truck queue. The idle loading dock queue is then checked to determine if a loading dock is available for immediate service.

Depending on the result of this check two alternative continuations of the scenario are possible. This is expressed in a so-called *interaction fragment*, using the keyword `alt` for "alternative". Each segment of the fragment box contains one possible alternative, which is taken when the corresponding guard holds true. When a free loading dock is available, it will therefore be notified by the truck on arrival, leave its wait queue and

Chapter 4 Simulation Model Descriptions with UML 2

de-queue the truck. Otherwise the truck just passivates itself to wait for a loading dock to be free.

Other operators influencing control flow (e.g. concurrency or loops) can also be represented by interaction fragments (see Jeckle et al. 2002, p. 359).

4.5.3 Timing Diagrams

Timing diagrams are the last diagram type we will employ to display interaction patterns in simulation models. They are exclusive to UML 2 and generally quite similar to sequence diagrams. Despite their name, there is not much a difference between timing and sequence diagrams in the representation of time constraints. However, timing diagrams are tailored to display how interaction partners change state over time (Jeckle et al. 2002, p. 403). This diagram type is therefore especially useful for illustrating interactions between entities modelled as statecharts.

UML provides two alternative notations for timing diagrams. The first one uses a so-called *state/condition timeline* (Jeckle et al. 2002, p. 411), reminiscent of signal diagrams from electrical engineering (Jeckle et al. 2002, p. 404). Since timing diagrams with many interaction partners and states are often difficult to read in this notation, we prefer an alternative form using *general value lifelines* (Jeckle et al. 2002, p. 416).

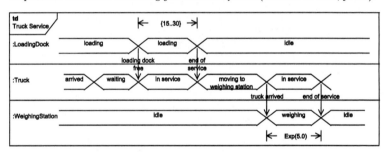

Figure 4.23: An example timing diagram showing the path of a truck through the gravel pit

The timing diagram in Figure 4.23 shows the sequence in which interactions occur during a truck's service at the gravel pit. This process has previously been modelled by using statecharts (e.g. in Figure 4.10). Different from sequence diagrams timing diagrams arrange interaction partners on the vertical axis, while time proceeds along the horizontal. Each interaction partner is assigned a *general value lifeline*, which traces its state changes over time. State changes are either self-induced (e.g. the truck's state changes from arrived to waiting) or triggered by *messages* symbolized with arrows pointing from sender to receiver.

4.5 Modelling Interactions

As in sequence diagrams, asynchronous, synchronous, and response messages are distinguished by the usual variations in arrow heads (Jeckle et al. 2002, p. 414). Time constraints can be stated similarly to sequence diagrams (as in Figure 4.23) or by using a timescale on the horizontal axis (see e.g. Jeckle et al. 2002, p. 416).

Further Reading

As mentioned before, there are a large number of UML 2 textbooks and manuals, with varying focus and level of detail. This chapter is based on a selection of material taken from the German textbooks *UML Glasklar* (Jeckle et al. 2002, *"UML 2 Made Crystal-Clear"*) and (fewer) *Softwareentwicklung mit UML 2* (Born et al. 2004, *"Software Design with UML 2"*). Both books give extensive and concise coverage of their topics. While Jeckle et al. (2002) focus on practical applications of UML diagrams, Born et al. (2004) treat theoretical aspects, such as UML's meta-model and extensibility, in more detail.

A well written English textbook of comparable scope is *UML 2 Toolkit* by Erikson et al. (2003). *UML distilled* by Fowler (2004) is a popular shorter introduction, which might be read in addition to this chapter. However, in our opinion it occasionally lacks precision. Although extremely voluminous and hard to read, the UML 2 specification (OMG 2004) available at the UML web site[16] might be consulted as a reference of last resort.

Considering that the idea of using UML as a modelling language for discrete event simulations is not new, there are still relatively few simulation textbooks which use it. *Object-Oriented Discrete-Event Simulation with Java* by Garrido (2001) is a notable exception. It applies UML 1.x class, use case, statechart, sequence, and collaboration diagrams[17] to the process interaction and activity scanning world views. Chapter 2 also contains a short introduction to these diagram types, written from a simulation modelling perspective.

Further applications of UML in discrete event simulation can be found in proceedings of conferences on simulation or related topics. For example, Oechslein et al. (2001) use extended UML 1.x activity diagrams as behaviour specifications in time-driven agent-based simulation models. These can be directly executed by the SeSam simulation tool[18]. Wet and Kritzinger (2004) report on an application of UML 2 component and activity diagrams in the performance analysis of network systems. While most papers on UML in simulation focus on single diagram types, Richter and März (2000) propose a standard process for using UML's class, sequence, and statechart diagrams in simulation model design.

---

[16]http://www.uml.org
[17]The former name of communication diagrams.
[18]http://www.simsesam.org

Bibliography

R. Bachmann. *Ein flexibler, CORBA-basierter Ansatz für die verteilte, komponentenbasierte Simulation* ("A Flexible CORBA-Based Approach of Distributed, Component-Based Simulation", in German). PhD Thesis, Faculty of Informatics, University of Hamburg, 2003.

R. R. Barton, P. A. Fishwick, J. O. Henriksen, R. G. Sargent, and J. M. Twomey. Panel: Simulation: Past, present and future. In S. Chick, P. J. Sanchez, D. Ferrin, and D. J. Morrice, editors, *Proceedings of the 2003 Winter Simulation Conference*, pages 2044–2050, 2003. [Online] http://www.wintersim.org/prog03.htm (in August 2005).

G. Booch, J. Rumbaugh, and I. Jacobson. *The Unified Modeling Language User Guide*. Object Technology Series. Addison-Wesley, Reading, 1999.

M. Born, E. Holz, and O. Kath. *Softwareentwicklung mit UML 2 – Die "neuen" Entwurfstechniken UML 2, MOF 2 und MDA* ("Software Design with UML 2 – The "new" Design Techniques UML 2, MOF 2, and MDA", in German). Programmer's Choice. Addison-Wesley, Munich, 2004.

H.-E. Erikson, M. Penker, B. Lyons, and D. Fado. *UML 2 Toolkit*. Wiley, Hoboken, 2003.

M. Fowler. *UML Distilled: A Brief Guide to the Standard Object Modeling Language*. Object Technology Series. Addison-Wesley, Reading, 3rd edition, 2004.

J. M. Garrido. *Object-Oriented Discrete-Event Simulation with Java – A Practical Introduction*. Series in Computer Systems. Kluwer Academic/Plenum, New York, 2001.

D. Harel. Statecharts: A visual approach to complex systems. *Science of Computer Programming*, 8:231–274, 1987.

M. Jeckle et al. *UML 2 glasklar* ("UML 2 Made Crystal-Clear", in German). Carl Hanser, Munich, 2002.

M. Jeckle et al. *UML 2.0: Evolution oder Degeneration* ("UML 2.0: Evolution or Degeneration", in German). *Objekt Spektrum*, (3):12–19, 2004.

K. Jensen. *Coloured Petri Nets: Basic Concepts, Analysis Methods and Practical Use*. Monographs in Theoretical Computer Science. Springer, Berlin, 1992.

F. Klügl. *Multiagentensimulation – Konzepte, Werkzeuge, Anwendung* ("Multi-Agent Simulation – Concepts, Tools, Application", in German). Agententechnologie. Addison-Wesley, Munich, 2001.

H. J. Köhler. *Code-Generierung für UML Kollaborations-, Sequenz- und Statechart-Diagramme* ("Code Generation for UML Collaboration-, Sequence-, and Statechart-Diagrams", in German). Diploma Thesis, University of Paderborn, 1999.

J. Lilius and I. P. Paltor. *The Semantics of UML State Machines*. Research Report 273, Turku Centre for Computer Science, 1999.

C. Oechslein, F. Klügl, R. Herrler, and F. Puppe. UML for Behaviour-Oriented Multi-Agent Simulations. In B. Dunin-Keplicz and E. Nawarecki, editors, *Proceedings of the CEEMAS*, number 2296 in Lecture Notes in Artificial Intelligence, pages 217–226, Springer, Berlin, 2001.

Bibliography

B. Oestereich. *Objektorientierte Softwareentwicklung – Analyse und Design mit der UML 2.0* ("Object-Oriented Software Development – Analysis and Design with the UML 2.0", in German). Oldenbourg, Munich, 2004.

OMG. *UML 2.0 Superstructure Specification.* OMG Document, Object Management Group, 10 2004. [Online] http://www.omg.org/cgi-bin/doc?ptc/2004-10-02 (in August 2005).

B. Page. *Diskrete Simulation – Eine Einführung mit Modula-2* ("Discrete Simulation – An Introduction with Modula-2", in German). Springer, Berlin, 1991.

H. Richter and L. März. Toward a Standard Process: The Use of UML for Designing Simulation Models. In J. A. Joines, R. R. Barton, K. Kang, and P. A. Fishwick, editors, *Proceedings of the 2000 Winter Simulation Conference*, pages 394–398, 2000. [Online] http://informs-cs.org/wsc00papers/prog00.html (in August 2005).

J. Rumbaugh, I. Jacobson, and G. Booch. *The Unified Modeling Language Reference Manual.* Object Technology Series. Addison-Wesley, Reading, 1999.

O. Spaniol and S. Hoff. *Ereignisorientierte Simulation – Konzepte und Systemrealisierung* ("Event-Oriented Simulation – Concepts and System Implementation", in German). Thomson's Aktuelle Tutorien; 7. Thomson, Bonn, 1995.

N. De Wet and P. Kritzinger. Using UML Models for the Performance Analysis of Network Systems. In *Proceedings of the Workshop on Integrated-reliability with Telecommunications and UML Languages (WITUL)*, Rennes, 2004.

T. Wiedemann. Simulation Application Service Providing. In B. A. Peters, J. S. Smith, D. J. Medeiros, and M. W. Rohrer, editors, *Proceedings of the 2001 Winter Simulation Conference*, pages 623–628, 2001. [Online] http://www.wintersim.org/prog01.htm (in August 2005).

B. P. Zeigler, H. Praehofer, and T. G. Kim. *Theory of Modeling and Simulation.* Academic Press, San Diego, 2000.

Chapter 5
Discrete Event Model Design

Bernd Page, Wolfgang Kreutzer

Contents

5.1	Motivation and Overview	97
5.2	Dominant Discrete Event Modelling Styles	98
	5.2.1 Process-Oriented Simulation Modelling	98
	5.2.2 Event-Oriented Simulation Modelling	108
	5.2.3 Comparison and Evaluation	117
5.3	Other Modelling Styles	129
	5.3.1 Transaction-Oriented Modelling	129
	5.3.2 Activity-Oriented Modelling	131
5.4	Object-Oriented Model Construction	133
5.5	Combined Modelling Styles	134
	5.5.1 Embedding Events in a Process-Oriented Model	134
	5.5.2 Example: A Combined Process/Event Model	135
Bibliography		140

5.1 Motivation and Overview

In this chapter we will learn how to model a discrete event system and which different modelling styles can be used in a simulation study. To demonstrate important ideas, we introduce a number of comprehensive examples, whose documentation makes good use of the UML diagram techniques presented in Chapter 4.

The most characteristic of computer-based discrete event simulation models is the representation of system states and their change over time; a requirement for which Section 5.2 highlights some commonly used strategies. Historically a small number of viewpoints, such as event- and process-based modelling styles, have been used for assembling a discrete event simulation. We will explain and demonstrate the two most dominant of these world views, i.e. process- and event-orientation, and compare their

Chapter 5 Discrete Event Model Design

effectiveness for different classes of problems (see Section 5.2.3). This section offers an in-depth comparison and evaluation of benefits and shortcomings of the two main modelling styles. As it turns out that their suitability is highly dependent on problem type, it is suggested that combining multiple viewpoints can sometimes be advantageous. This will be shown in Section 5.5. Other styles, such as transaction- and activity-based modelling, are discussed in Section 5.3. Object-oriented simulation can be seen as an extension of process-orientation and is summarized briefly in Section 5.4.

5.2 Dominant Discrete Event Modelling Styles

How to model the passage of time in between a state-changing method's invocation and its return is a major challenge for event-driven simulation frameworks. Following the lead of classic simulation programming tools (e.g. *Gasp*, *Simscript*, *Simula*) two strategies have become well established. These world views of event-based and process-based simulation offer alternative frameworks for modelling systems of entities and their interactions. This section will briefly survey the underlying ideas and their consequences. Less popular approaches like transaction-based (i.e. *GPSS*) or activity-oriented (e.g. *ECSL*) modelling styles will be mentioned only in passing. The popularity of object-oriented programming styles raises some additional issues and discussed in more detail in Chapter 3.

5.2.1 Process-Oriented Simulation Modelling

Concepts

Over the last 20 years the process interaction approach has established itself as the most commonly used discrete event simulation modelling framework. Its main distinguishing feature is that all activities "owned" by an entity are grouped into a process, which can then be viewed as that entity's *lifecycle*. Model time passes during such "active" entities' active phases; i.e. whenever a time delay is encountered. In our Java simulation software *DESMO-J* (see Chapter 10), for example, lifecycle descriptions are grouped in a `lifeCycle()` method. Conceptually, lifecycle processes execute in parallel (see Figure 5.1) and will pass control to the model's time management executive or "scheduler" whenever the model clock changes. Control then returns to the lifecycle process; either immediately or after some other processes' quasi-simultaneous state transformations have occurred. Viewed from an active entity's perspective, time passes while it acts. In practice such parallelism will, of course, most likely be mapped onto a uni-processor's sequential thread of execution; so this is another of the model executive's tasks.

During a process' active phases model state changes will occur. While the modelled activities or actions may ask for some model time to pass, the state transformations they cause are instantaneous (but will require some computation) at the model time level. A process can

5.2 Dominant Discrete Event Modelling Styles

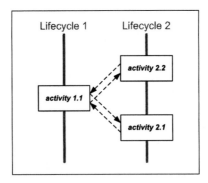

Figure 5.1: Transformations between lifecycles' active and passive phases

- modify entities' properties;
- generate new entities and their lifecycles;
- activate other entities at specified clock times;
- change or cancel active entities' active phases;
- deactivate itself and pass control to the model executive or to another entity's lifecycle; and
- terminate its own and other entities' lifecycles.

By updating the model clock, time passes during activities. During such phases a lifecycle can be considered inactive. There are two ways in which the passage of time can be described in this context; either by scheduling a delay of fixed duration (i.e. through hold()) or by falling into a passive state (i.e. through passivate()) from which a process must later be re-awoken (i.e. through activate()). After reactivation, an entity will move to the next phase in its lifecycle.

For example, to model the processing of some material by a machine during the interval Δt, we could define an active **machine** entity whose lifecycle process will deactivate itself after planning its own reactivation Δt time units in the future. The model executive (scheduler) will then reactivate this process at the time it requested; as long as the relevant event notice has not been cancelled or changed by some other process. In this way we model the concept of "processing" through the **machine** entity's inactive phases.

The *model executive* (scheduler) is the heart of any discrete event modelling tool. It ensures that state transformations are performed at the right time and in the right order. In a process-oriented framework the model scheduler considers each process to be in one of two states. It can be *active* and performs computations until it gives up

Chapter 5 Discrete Event Model Design

control, or it *passively* waits for events while some other process is active and in control. Figure 5.2 shows the transitions between a process' active and passive phases.

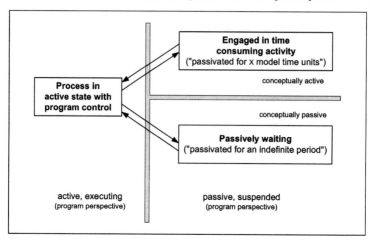

Figure 5.2: Transitions between a process' active and passive phases

The scheduler itself operates "behind the scenes"; i.e. it consumes no *model time*. However, to perform its tasks it needs to perform computations and consume *realtime* processor cycles.

The process-oriented world view allows the specification of arbitrarily many pseudo-parallel active entities (processes). Quasi-simultaneous events can occur whenever more then one process requests state transitions at the same model time instant. Such requests will need to be serialized by the scheduler, and the exact order in which they are executed may well have an impact on model logic. Simulation modelling tools typically offer a number of ways in which this order can be controlled (e.g. by pre-emption or through priority schemes).

If reactivation of processes are viewed as events, the processing patterns of process-based and event-based modelling views become very similar. Processes represent active entities' lifecycles, whose active phases (events) are recorded in an event list. As a minimum, each entry consists of a process reference and a time value. Entries are ordered by time, and – if any – by their priority. The scheduler (which is itself a process) repetitively chooses the entry at the head of its list of events, updates the model's clock to this event's time, and triggers the referenced process. The main difference to an event method is that a process does not need to start execution at its beginning, but will rather continue from the point at which it was last deactivated. This means that a

5.2 Dominant Discrete Event Modelling Styles

"reactivation point" as well as all attributes' values need to be stored in a process' state. This makes the implementation of process-oriented simulation with programming tools without good support for so-called *coroutines* more difficult than that of event-based frameworks. Because Java does not offer coroutines directly, Java-based tools such as DESMO-J often use Java's *thread* mechanism to meet this requirement although threads were designed to control real-time parallelism rather than the conceptual concurrency supported by process-oriented simulation frameworks.

A process-based model design should take an *object-oriented* perspective, identifying relevant entities, their properties, and behaviour. After documenting this high-level design with UML or some other convenient notation, attention should focus on the description of active entities' lifecycles as seen from the modelled entities own perspectives. This includes all relevant activities, the sequence in which they occur, and their relationships to other entities in the model. In the example of material processed by a machine, both machine and material would be viewed as entities. Further analysis may identify properties such as size and processing speed as important. Details of processing the material by the machine would be a candidate for an activity. In the simplest case this may be just mapped onto a time delay, but our model's purpose may also require more complex patterns of changes in both the material's and the machine's properties.

The following tasks are therefore required in a process-oriented simulation model design:

- identification of relevant objects
- identification of each object's relevant attributes
- identification of each object's relevant activities
- definition of model entity classes and process classes
- description of model entities' lifecycles (as viewed from the perspective of each modelled object)
- description of entity interactions
- identification and allocation of common tasks and responsibilities

What is *relevant* must, of course, always be decided by reference to a model's purpose. Even the simple example of processing manufacturing requests by a single machine shows that model descriptions will often not be canonic; i.e. different viewpoints can lead to different model structures. Since each transformation must be mapped into a lifecycle description, it must be attached to ("caused by") either machine or material entities. This choice will lead to a so-called *machine-oriented* or a *material-oriented* description. In this example the choice seems quite clear; real machines are active and we normally view materials as inert. In more complex situations the right choice may not be so clear. Any judgement on which perspective is the "better" one must always make sure to keep a model's purpose firmly in mind.

Chapter 5 Discrete Event Model Design

Application: Simulation of Queueing Systems

Since process-oriented modelling is particularly well suited for queueing systems, we will briefly review the basis of queueing/service system simulations here.

A queueing scenario's components model servers and service requests, where servers are often referred to as *resources* and service requests as *transactions*. Transactions require processing, for which they engage the servers. Servers have limited capacity and may be idle or busy. Successful engagement of servers requires at least as much free capacity as requested; otherwise a request will be *queued*. Queueing causes delays, whose duration we may want to measure. In so-called *open queueing systems*, transactions arrive from "outside" a model and disappear after processing. Models of a car wash or a post office may use this approach. *Closed queueing systems* have a fixed number of transactions, which cycle through various phases. Modelling a time sharing computer connected to a fixed number of terminals serves as an example.

Queueing scenarios can be employed for many purposes. To find, for example, an optimal strategy for allocating transactions to servers (e.g. *first come, first served, highest priority first, shortest time to completion first*), we may wish to obtain statistical measures such as server *utilizations*, transaction *waiting times*, system *response time* (average time from arrival to departure across all transactions), or system *throughput* (number of transactions served over a given time period). Such information can also help us to answer questions about minimum or maximum numbers of servers, how many servers would be needed to ensure minimal waiting times, or to decide which bottlenecks should best be removed if we have only a fixed amount of money to spend.

The following components are typically found in a queueing model:

- ❑ objects:
    - ❑ transactions (e.g. customers, materials, orders, requests) with properties like:
        - current state; e.g. *active* or *passive* (waiting)
        - service demands
        - priorities
        - preferences for particular servers
        - request sequence
        - statistical distribution for modelling arrival patterns (see Sections 7.2 and 7.3) and various statistical variables
    - ❑ servers (e.g. resources, machines, channels) with properties like:
        - capacity
        - current state; e.g. active or passive (waiting)
        - queue of transactions waiting for services
        - statistical distributions for modelling service activities and various statistical variables

5.2 Dominant Discrete Event Modelling Styles

- relationships:
    - synchronization of transactions and servers:
        - request/customer synchronization; e.g. waiting for service
        - concurrent processing of partial requests
        - resource/customer synchronization; e.g. processing a request
- activities:
    - service of specified duration
    - service whose duration is computed using both server and customer properties
- performance measures:
    - transaction delays:
        - waiting times
        - queue lengths
        - service duration (wait time plus service time)
    - system utilization:
        - server utilization (in %)
        - average number of transactions in system
    - degree of goal fulfilment:
        - satisfaction of preferences
        - probability of lost customers

Example: Modelling a Simple Computer Network

Problem Description: Simulating computer systems is an important technique in computer science and it can also serve as a good example for a queueing scenario with multiple server units and limited queueing space. This example models a decentralized computer laboratory in a university. The laboratory is run by a faculty and consists of multiple server machines with identical hard- and software, which are accessed by a number of client PCs via dial-in lines and modems. Students edit processor-intensive numerical programs (e.g. simulations) on the decentralized PC clients, after which they are sent to a server for processing. There are two different user groups (e.g. undergraduate and graduate students), whose programs differ in size and complexity. Processing requests also have different priorities dependent on which user group they originate from. Users have limited tolerance and will terminate a job when a maximum waiting time has been exceeded. We want to use simulation to determine the utilization of servers and dial-in lines, as well as estimate a user's waiting times during peak periods.

Chapter 5 Discrete Event Model Design

System Specification:
- There are 3 identical servers. No background processing needs to be considered; i.e. external jobs use only idle capacity.
- Requests from decentralized PCs arrive via dial-in lines. There are 10 dial-in lines and a buffer to store 7 waiting requests.
- There are 2 user classes with different priorities. 20 % of all requests come from graduate students (priority 1) and 80 % come from undergraduates (priority 2).
- Processing times of requests are described by the following distributions:
    - undergraduates: exponential with a mean of 1 minute
    - graduates: exponential with a mean of 5 minutes
- The willingness of students to wait is normally distributed with a mean of 6 and a deviation of 5 minutes. After this time, they will abort a request and leave.

Steps in Conceptual Model Design:
1. Draw diagrams of model states and transitions:
Figure 5.3 summarizes a service request's lifecycle.

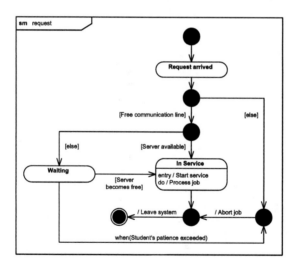

Figure 5.3: A UML state diagram of **requests**' lifecycles

104

5.2 Dominant Discrete Event Modelling Styles

2. Identify entity and process types:
   job and **server** are the model's two process types.
   - entity and process type job
     - temporary entity
     - properties: job type (graduate, undergraduate), priority
     - activities: request **server**, wait for processing
     - interaction with other processes: processing
       (active **server** processes passive job)
   - entity and process type **server**
     - permanent entity
     - properties: server number
     - activities: process a job
     - interaction with other processes: processing
       (active **server** processes passive job)
3. Draw UML activity diagrams:
   As mentioned in Section 4.4.2, UML activity diagrams fit the process interaction world view very well. Recall that process states with active program control are represented by actions (rounded rectangles) the execution of which does not consume simulation time. Passive wait states are expressed with the *signal reception* symbol that we will from now on mark with the stereotype <<passive>> for greater clearness. Conceptually active time consuming activities are depicted by the hourglass symbol that we mark with a <<hold>> stereotype, because it corresponds to the occurrence of a hold statement in the process lifecycle. Furthermore, we use the signal send action marked with the <<activate>> or <<interrupt>> stereotype to indicate that a process activates another waiting process or interrupts a conceptually active process respectively. An interrupt is handled by the receiver process with an *interruptible activity region* as shown in Figure 5.5. Figures 5.4 to 5.6 show lifecycles for **server**, **job**, and **job creation**.

Input Data:
- duration of simulation = 144,000 seconds (40 hours)
- Mean time between requests (exponentially distributed) = 30 seconds
- mean processing time of requests
  - made by undergraduates (exponentially distributed) = 60 seconds
  - made by graduates (exponentially distributed) = 300 seconds
- willingness to wait for a job's completion
  - mean (normally distributed) = 360 seconds
  - deviation (normally distributed) = 300 seconds

Chapter 5 Discrete Event Model Design

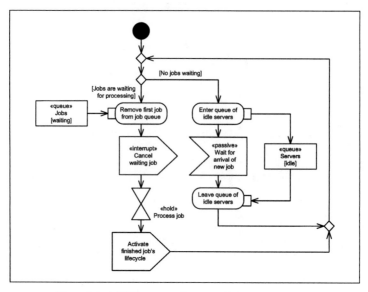

Figure 5.4: A UML activity diagram of the **server** process

Simulation Results:

- number of requests = 4,858
- completed requests = 3,406
- immediately processed requests = 814
- requests without processing (left by impatient students) = 695
- requests without a free dial-in line = 750
- requests in the system at simulation end = 10

- mean completion time of immediately processed requests = 101 seconds
- mean completion time of requests by undergraduates = 118 seconds with a deviation of = 131.2 seconds
- mean completion time of requests by graduates = 45.9 seconds with a deviation of = 67 seconds

- average queue length = 3.4
- server utilization = 91.5 %

5.2 Dominant Discrete Event Modelling Styles

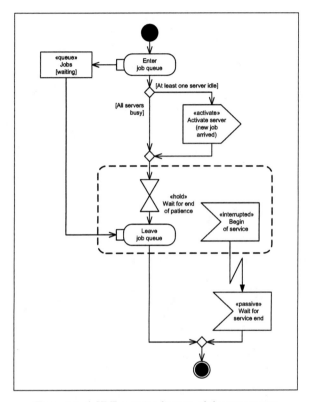

Figure 5.5: A UML activity diagram of the job process

Please note that these results are indicative only and should be viewed as exemplifying the order of magnitude of statistics one would expect when a model for this scenario were to be run. It should also be borne in mind that no efforts have been made to ensure the statistical significance of results.

Chapter 5 Discrete Event Model Design

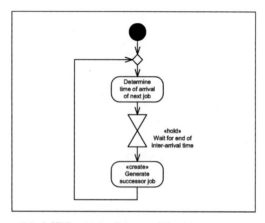

Figure 5.6: A UML activity diagram of the job creation process

5.2.2 Event-Oriented Simulation Modelling

Concepts

Event-oriented frameworks are older than process-orientation. This modelling style is sometimes also referred to as *event scheduling* simulation and focuses on the set of *all* transformations of *all* relevant entities at specified points in time. Instead of grouping chains of events into process descriptions, we cluster events based on their time of occurrence and model a system's behaviour in terms of a sequence of all temporally simultaneous but possibly causally unrelated events. Activities are not modelled directly. Rather they are implied by model clock's changes caused by scheduling statements. While real processor cycles are needed for computation, all state transformations happen without any changes in model time.

To build an event-based model, we must again identify all relevant objects and their properties. In contrast to a process-oriented viewpoint, however, a model designer must take a "birds eye view", from which s/he describes all states, events, and transformations of entities together with all interactions. All state changes, which are caused by events involving the same entities at the same times, can be grouped into an event class of a specified type. Descriptions can initially make use of textual or graphical (e.g. UML activity diagrams or classical flow charts) notations.

In contrast to the process-oriented viewpoint, where descriptions of system structure and behaviour are intertwined, an event-oriented modelling perspective allows clear separation between the specifications of system structure and behaviour. A model consists of:

5.2 Dominant Discrete Event Modelling Styles

- *Static components*; i.e. entities are data structures which model classes of objects and permanent individual objects (e.g. machines of a given type). Predefined attributes allow identification of individual entities and suggest and constrain possible state transformations.
- *Dynamic components*; i.e. all model events (e.g. start of processing of a piece of material) are cast into event classes and temporary entities (e.g. materials) whose dynamic creation and destruction during the course of a simulation is triggered by these events.

During implementation in a given programming language all state changes attached to a specified type of event will be mapped into *event routines* or event methods. These will then generate model behaviour by

- changing the values of attributes;
- creating and deleting temporary objects; and
- adding new events to and deleting existing events from the event list.

Just as in process-oriented modelling frameworks, there is a scheduler which processes the event list sequentially; i.e. in the right order, using a *next event* approach. As in process-oriented modelling frameworks, this means that model time "passing" in-between consecutive events is just skipped and the clock is jumped from one relevant event time to the next (see Figure 2.3).

Application: Simulating Inventory Systems

As shown in Figure 5.7, inventories serve as buffers between consumption and production. They are a popular area of application for simulation in management science. Since inventory simulations are typical candidates for an event-oriented modelling style, we will briefly look at the basic design.

Some of the most important goals of keeping inventories are:

- satisfying customer or in-house demand by keeping a high level of request fulfilment capability
- keeping the costs caused by out of stock items low
- keeping the cost of inventory low
- avoiding unnecessary capital investment
- taking advantage of low order costs

To meet these goals, the cost of keeping inventories must be balanced against the expected costs caused by out of stock items under specific inventory capacities and ordering strategies. In contrast to queueing systems, we now deal with consumable and renewable resources (stock) and the emphasis of analysis lies on being able to meet demand rather than ensuring efficient use of capacity-limited sets of resources. In this context typical state transitions are fluctuations in inventory levels; i.e. stock arrivals and departures. Minimizing a customer's waiting time while reducing inventory

Chapter 5 Discrete Event Model Design

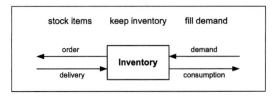

Figure 5.7: Structure of a classic inventory system

costs becomes the predominant goal. Inventory models can be combined with queueing scenarios – e.g. when modelling production facilities. Later, we will use a production system with both processing and inventory aspects as an example (see Section 5.5.2).

The following components are typically found in inventory models :

❏ objects:
  ❏ inventory (i.e. a set of products in stock) with properties such as:
    • inventory levels; e.g. *minimum, current,* and *desired* (waiting for stock)
    • list of orders which cannot be immediately filled
    • costs of keeping inventory, costs of ordering, and costs of being unable to meet demand
  ❏ customer request (i.e. sets of requests for stock) with properties such as:
    • arrival time distribution
    • items requested
    • willingness to wait for order fulfilment for a certain amount of time if necessary
    • priority of request
    • preferences; e.g. substitute products
  ❏ in-stock product delivered to customers
  ❏ orders sent to suppliers (i.e. requests for out-of-stock items) with properties such as:
    • temporal distribution: ordering cycle, fixed and variable ordering dates
    • quantity ordered: constant or variable
    • ordering costs: fixed and variable
    • priority
    • preferences; e.g. substitute products
  ❏ stock orders delivered to the inventory with properties such as:
    • temporal distribution (dependent on ordering dates with stochastic fluctuations)
    • costs (may be included in ordering costs)

5.2 Dominant Discrete Event Modelling Styles

- relationships:
  - customer requests cause product supply/order fulfilment from stock (possibly after delay)
  - orders sent to suppliers result in stock delivery (possibly after delay)
  - flow of resources:
    - supply of products and materials to customers leads to an inventory level reduction
    - delivery of stock to inventory increases inventory level
- activities:
  - placing an order for stock
    Examples for ordering policies:
    - (q,t)-ordering policy: order a constant quantity q for each item in fixed intervals t
    - (s,q)-ordering policy: order a constant quantity q for each item once its inventory falls below level s
    - (s,S)-ordering policy: order an item once its inventory falls below level s and raise the item's inventory level to a desired quantity S
  - continual checks of inventory levels (i.e. after each order fulfilment) or just at predetermined ordering times
- performance measures:
  - delivery capabilities (depending on capacity and ordering policies)
  - costs:
    - ... of inventory
    - ... of inability to fulfil an order (lost customer trust)
    - ... of ordering from a supplier

Example: Modelling a Single-Product Inventory System

Problem Description: The model represents a particular inventory system for a product. *Times between arrivals of customer requests* are independent, identically distributed random variables described by exponential distribution. *Delivery times* are given in days and follow a discrete uniform distribution. For reasons of simplification, *demand volumes* are fixed. The model uses a *(q,s)-ordering strategy*; i.e. we order a fixed amount q whenever the inventory level falls below a threshold s. If demand exceeds inventory, the inventory level will be 0 and pre-order volume is larger than 0. Whenever new stock arrives, open customer requests are fulfilled first; when necessary through partial deliveries. The *costs of being unable to fulfil an order* consist of the costs of additional order processing and the costs of free deliveries to customers. This is aggregated into an overall cost per item.

Chapter 5 Discrete Event Model Design

Average monthly inventory costs (IC) can be computed by $IC = \frac{ic}{n} * AI$, where ic stands for the monthly inventory costs per item. The total number of items processed is given by n, while AI denotes the time-weighted average of items held in inventory ($AI \leq n$).

Average monthly costs of being unable to fulfil demand (shortfall costs, SC) can be computed by $SC = \frac{sc}{m} * SI$, where sc stands for the shortfall costs per item and the number of months simulated is given by m. SI is the number of items for which demand outstripped supply.

The costs of ordering stock per month (OFC) are assumed to be fixed for each order.

System Specification: The modelled example has the following characteristics:
- There is 1 product type.
- The simulated time period is 1 year ($m = 12$ months or 240 working days).
- There are 100 customer requests per day (1 item per customer.)
- Delivery times are uniformly distributed between 3 to 5 days.
- Initial stock is 500 items.
- Initially there are no pre-orders.
- Fixed costs per order are 500 Euros.
- Monthly inventory costs are $ic = 30$ Euros per item.
- The minimal inventory level (s) is 300 items.
- Reorder quantity is 800 items.
- Costs of being unable to fill demand (shortfall costs) are $sc = 100$ Euros per item.

Modelling Goal: We want to simulate the model to determine optimal ordering quantities q (reorder quantity) and s (reordering threshold). This should yield the minimum sum of order, shortfall, and inventory costs.

Special Requirements of Inventory Models: A process-oriented viewpoint appears clumsy and unintuitive here since simulation objects are largely quantity levels (e.g. inventory level) and no modelling of time-consuming activities is required. Levels change instantaneously, in fixed intervals. *Active* objects, similar to transactions and servers in queueing scenarios, are difficult to identify. We might, for example, choose to model an inventory manager, who allocates deliveries to customers and places orders for stock, as a process *driving* the simulation. However, there is no real world correspondent to such a fictitious entity. It is arguably easier and more intuitive to describe state changes via events, and an event-oriented viewpoint seems therefore appropriate for modelling inventory systems.

5.2 Dominant Discrete Event Modelling Styles

Model Entities: We can recognize the following entities in the inventory model:
- customers with requests
- orders with quantities

Figures 5.8 and 5.9 show UML state charts for `customer request` and `order` entities in our example. The state diagrams help us to identify state transitions in the system, which are triggered by events. These events eventually represent the model events in the inventory system.

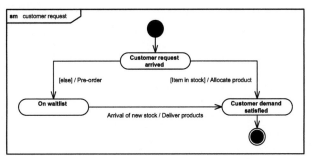

Figure 5.8: A UML state diagram of the lifecycle of a `customer request` entity

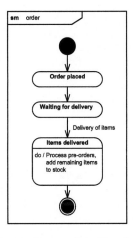

Figure 5.9: A UML state diagram of the lifecycle of an `order` entity

113

Chapter 5 Discrete Event Model Design

Types of Events: As we can see in the UML state diagrams the following event types are existent in the inventory model:

- Event `customer creation` generates a new customer and schedules a `customer request` event. It also creates and schedules the next `customer creation` event instance (see Figure 5.10).
- Event `customer request` reduces the inventory level (see Figure 5.11).
- Event `stock order` implements daily checks of inventory levels and initiates q product orders whenever inventory levels fall below quantity s (see Figure 5.12).
- Event `product delivery` reduces any pre-order quantities and increases the inventory level by the remaining amount (see Figure 5.13).
- Event `end simulation` terminates a simulation as soon as a requested duration was modelled.

Priorities of Events in Case of Simultaneous Event Occurrences: A sensible execution order for quasi-simultaneous events would be:

1. event `product delivery`
2. event `customer request`
3. event `end simulation`
4. event `customer creation`
5. event `stock order`

Overall it makes sense to only attend to events scheduled before a simulation terminates. Events scheduled to occur after the end of a simulation can be ignored.

UML Diagrams for Each Type of Event: As already mentioned Figures 5.10 to 5.13 show the structure of four of the model events. We use <<create>> and <<schedule>> stereotypes to mark some of the most common action types occurring in event routines (i.e. creation of entities and event scheduling). The `end simulation` event is so simple that it does not need to be shown.

Input Data:

- initial stock = 500
- inventory policy (q, s) = (800, 300)
- length of simulation = 240 working days (12 months)
- customer requests = exponentially distributed, with a mean of 100 items per day
- ordering times = once a day (delivery delay = 3 to 5 days, uniformly distributed)
- fixed order costs = 500 Euros
- inventory costs = 1 Euro per item, per day
- shortfall costs = 100 Euros per item

5.2 Dominant Discrete Event Modelling Styles

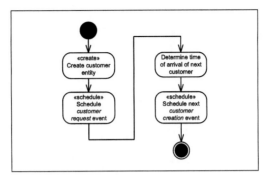

Figure 5.10: A UML activity diagram of the `customer creation` event

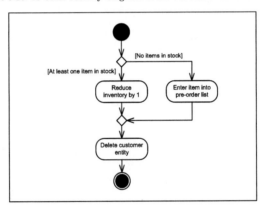

Figure 5.11: A UML activity diagram of the `customer request` event

Simulation Results:
- monthly customer demand = 1,913 items
- shortfall items (demand could not be met) = 529 items
- service level (% of demand fulfilment) = 72.3%
- average monthly costs
    - ... of inventory = 5,189 Euros
    - ... of ordering = 1,195 Euros
    - ... of shortfalls = 52,911 Euros

Chapter 5 Discrete Event Model Design

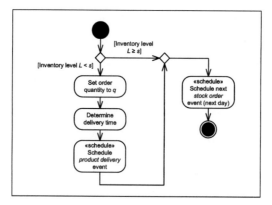

Figure 5.12: A UML activity diagram of the `stock order` event

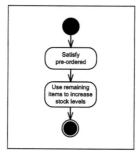

Figure 5.13: A UML activity diagram of the `product delivery` event

Again we must stress that these results should only be viewed as an example and that no claims with regard to statistical significance can be made.

5.2 Dominant Discrete Event Modelling Styles

5.2.3 Comparison and Evaluation

Process- versus Event-Orientation

There are many similarities between the model executives or schedulers for both process- and event-oriented modelling styles. Both use an event list and process events in a similar pattern. The main difference lies in the way in which state transformations are grouped into clusters. Event list elements in process-oriented modelling frameworks are processes together with their reactivation times. Event list elements in event-oriented modelling frameworks are events with a time of occurrence together with a reference to the involved entity. Since event-orientation is the more basic concept it is in fact not very difficult to map any process-based model into an equivalent event-based one. In spite of these similarities there is a number of differences in the way models should be assembled. While model description in process-oriented modelling styles stays very close to the properties of a modelled system, event-oriented modelling styles will reflect much more of a model's internal implementation; i.e. they reveal a model executive's operation (see Figure 2.2). This means that by using an event-oriented model design a designer must bridge a larger semantic gap than by taking a process-oriented point of view (see Figure 5.14).

Modelling a Logistics System: Container Shipment in the Baltic Sea

To provide a sound basis for a comparison of the two dominant modelling styles – event-oriented and process-oriented modelling – we will describe "the same" model using both styles. In the two model designs we can see the differences between the two styles in a more concrete manner.

For this purpose we have selected a model from the logistics application domain, where simulation is a widely used technique (which will be covered in more detail in Chapter 15). At first we give a general overview of simulating logistics systems before we turn to a specific example involving harbour logistics.

Background: Harbours are special, highly complex logistics centers, where cargoes are transferred from sea to land and vice versa. More than 90 % of all international goods pass through sea ports such as Singapore, Rotterdam, or Hamburg and more than 80 % of them are stored in containers.

The container terminal is therefore the largest and most important section of a typical sea port. We can view a container terminal as a facility for handling and controlling container flows from vessels to rail or road and vice versa. With this, a *terminal* is a physical link between sea transport and land-based modes of transport. The most important task of a container terminal is the turnover of several thousand containers passing between ship and land transportation (i.e. trucks and rail) per day.

We can differentiate between two separate traffic flows; export and import. *Export* describes the container flow from railway, roads, barges, or feeder vessels through a

Chapter 5 Discrete Event Model Design

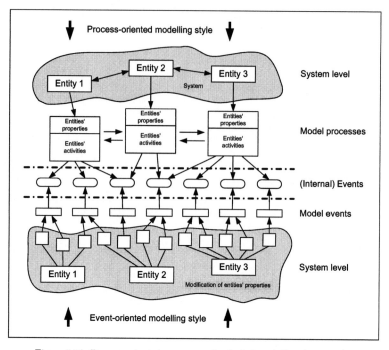

Figure 5.14: Process-oriented versus event-oriented modelling frameworks

terminal on to an overseas vessel. *Import* correspondingly refers to an opposite container movement; i.e. from overseas to domestic means of transportation.

Because of the high degree of competition between international sea ports, there is an ever increasing drive towards improved competitiveness and modern analysis techniques such as computer simulation, which can help to improve the quality of container turnaround in terms of speed, efficiency, and cost-effectiveness.

There is a number of reasons for employing simulation technology in harbour logistics:

- ❑ Changes of strategies and processes without major negative impacts are hard to find, and empirical experimentation is typically too disruptive and time consuming.
- ❑ Continual process control is a necessity.
- ❑ High costs of investment make high demands on planning quality.

5.2 Dominant Discrete Event Modelling Styles

- Simulation can assist both daily allocation and longer term planning decisions made by terminal managers.
- Simulations can generate statistical data to improve
  - container throughput;
  - vessel residence times;
  - utilization of personnel and machinery;
  - early detection of bottleneck potentials; and
  - results of capacity increases; e.g. in transport and loading facilities.

Within this context typical questions focus on

- utilization and availability of transport devices;
- effects of different strategies for maintenance and breakdowns; or
- strategies for allocation of personnel and transport devices; e.g.:
  - shift allocation
  - fixed versus job-based allocation of van carriers to container bridges
  - traffic control within terminals

When we look at harbour logistics from a modelling viewpoint, we will soon realize that they fit rather nicely into the queueing network scenario we introduced in Section 5.2.1. The reader may wish to return to this section to refresh his or her memory of this framework's characteristics in terms of typical objects, their relationships, activities, and performance measures. Harbour models may, in addition, deal with inventory aspects as well and Section 5.2.2 is therefore also of relevance.

Problem Description: Hamburg is Germany's principal seaport and largest overseas trade and transshipment centre. Here container bridges load a multitude of so-called *feeder ships* with containers for transport to overseas destinations; e.g. to ports within the Baltic Sea. These feeder ships travel different routes to supply several ports successively. In each of the visited ports, a different number of container bridges is available for unloading containers meant for this destination. From there the containers may be transported to the port's hinterland. The time needed for unloading a feeder ship depends on the number of containers it holds and can adequately be modelled by an exponential distribution with different means for each port.

Modelling Goal: The objective of simulating such a scenario is to gather information about bottlenecks among the container bridges (*cranes*) as well as the ships' waiting times in each port. For this purpose, statistical data about the number of containers unloaded in each port, the current number of ships in the model, the utilization of container bridges in each port, and the number of containers per ship are collected and reported at the end of a simulation run.

Chapter 5 Discrete Event Model Design

Model Specifications:
- The basic model time unit will be 1 hour.
- Ship arrivals in Hamburg (HH) follow an exponential distribution with a mean of 2.5 hours.
- Each feeder ship stops at several of the following ports and discharges containers:
  - Rostock-Warnemuende (RW)
  - Gdańsk (G)
  - Riga (R)
  - Tallinn (T)
  - St.Petersburg (StP)
  - Helsinki (H)
  - Stockholm (S)
  - Copenhagen (C)
- Each feeder ship travels along one of the following routes:
  - route 1: HH $\to$ RW $\to$ G $\to$ R $\to$ T $\to$ H (40 % of all feeder ships)
  - route 2: HH $\to$ C $\to$ S $\to$ H $\to$ StP $\to$ T (10 % of all feeder ships)
  - route 3: HH $\to$ G $\to$ S $\to$ C (20 % of all feeder ships)
  - route 4: HH $\to$ C $\to$ G $\to$ RW (30 % of all feeder ships)
- To determine the number of containers that are stored on a feeder ship destined for each of the Baltic seaports on its route, a random variable between 50 and 150 (uniformly distributed) is multiplied with the relevance of the seaport (shown in Table 5.1). This product is rounded if necessary. Since it seems irrelevant to the information we wish to obtain, we choose not to model this as a process but rather assign only the relevant numbers.
- Each port has a different number of container bridges (i.e. cranes) for unloading a feeder ship and a different mean time for unloading a single container, using one of the cranes (timings in hours). These numbers are given in Table 5.1, too.
- Table 5.2 shows the mean hours of travel from port to port. For simplicity we assume constant travel times here.

Table 5.1: Relevance, number of container bridges, and mean time for unloading a single container in each port

	RW	G	R	T	StP	H	S	C
Relevance	1.0	1.2	0.6	0.8	1.1	0.9	1.4	1.6
Bridges	6	11	3	6	2	4	4	7
Unloading time (h)	0.09	0.125	0.15	0.18	0.225	0.085	0.09	0.075

When simulating this model, we set the simulation time to 500 days. Principal statistics of interest are *crane utilization* at the different ports, *waiting times* and *queue lengths* for ships in a port, and overall travel times for the ships on each route. The

5.2 Dominant Discrete Event Modelling Styles

Table 5.2: Travel times between Baltic seaports (in hours)

	HH	RW	G	R	T	StP	H	S	C
HH	0.0	14.2	32.4	46.8	51.0	64.6	52.8	39.6	17.4
RW	14.2	0.0	20.4	36.6	40.8	54.4	42.6	29.4	7.2
G	32.4	20.4	0.0	24.0	28.8	40.8	30.6	22.8	20.4
R	46.8	36.6	24.0	0.0	14.4	26.4	16.2	14.4	34.8
T	51.0	40.8	28.8	14.4	0.0	14.2	4.0	15.0	39.0
StP	64.6	54.4	40.8	26.4	14.2	0.0	12.6	27.6	51.6
H	52.8	42.6	30.6	16.2	4.0	12.6	0.0	16.8	40.8
S	39.6	29.4	22.8	14.4	15.0	27.6	16.8	0.0	27.6
C	17.4	7.2	20.4	34.8	39.0	61.6	40.8	27.6	0.0

fact that we wish to determine these performance statistics again reinforces the appropriateness of a queueing model for this scenario.

A Process-Oriented Implementation: To assemble a process-oriented version of this model, we first identify relevant system objects; e.g. *container ships* as temporary and *cranes* in the ports as permanent entities. Containers are only of interest as quantities; i.e. their number determines the unloading time at a port. Again we use UML state diagrams to show model states and transitions. For example, ships cycle through the following states: waiting for unloading, being unloaded, sailing to the next port, and terminated (after service at last port on route). This cycle is shown in Figure 5.15. Because they just switch from idle to busy state vice versa, we will not show a state diagram for cranes.

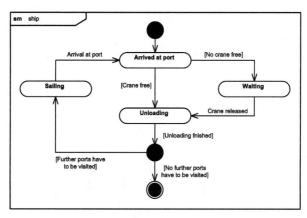

Figure 5.15: A UML state diagram of a **ship**'s states and transitions

Chapter 5 Discrete Event Model Design

For each of the two principal system object types (`ship` and `crane`) we define a process type; as suggested by our choice of a process-oriented modelling style. Beyond that it makes sense to add a `ship generator` process, because a temporary `ship` object needs to be dynamically created whenever a new ship enters the model (i.e. arrival at the Hamburg seaport) during a simulation run. We also need queues at each port for the ships waiting for service by the cranes, as well as for idle cranes. UML activity diagrams for this model's three process types are shown in Figures 5.16 to 5.18.

The `ship generator` process passivates itself for a predetermined time period, after which it awakens to create the next ship arrival. This delay's length is sampled from a distribution for ships' *inter-arrival times* (see Figure 5.16).

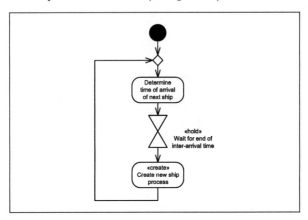

Figure 5.16: A UML activity diagram of the `ship generator`'s states and transitions

Our model's `ship` process represents feeder ships which supply Baltic ports with containers from Hamburg. Specifically it describes a feeder ship's journey from Hamburg to the last port on its route. Once a `ship` is created by the `ship generator` process it will be located in Hamburg, and we must decide how many containers will be loaded for each port on the ship's route. After suitable numbers are sampled from a discrete-valued statistical distribution, the ship visits all ports on its route in a fixed sequence. To model each journey from port to port, a `ship` releases control for a predetermined travel time (see Table 5.2). After such a delay, it "*arrives*" and inserts itself into the new port's queue of waiting ships (if any). Once at least one of the port's cranes is available, the ship proceeds to unloading containers destined for this port (which is carried out by the crane). While no `crane` is available, the `ship` passively waits in a queue until reactivated by another process; i.e. a crane in the ship's current port which has now become available. If there is at least one free `crane` in the current port (waiting

5.2 Dominant Discrete Event Modelling Styles

in the corresponding idle crane queue), the first **crane** is removed from this queue and starts unloading the feeder ship. During the unloading delay the **ship** remains passive (i.e. in *hold*), after which it is activated to sail to the next port on its route. The journey continues until we reach the last port on a route. After unloading there, the ship leaves the system; i.e. this **ship** process terminates (see Figure 5.17).

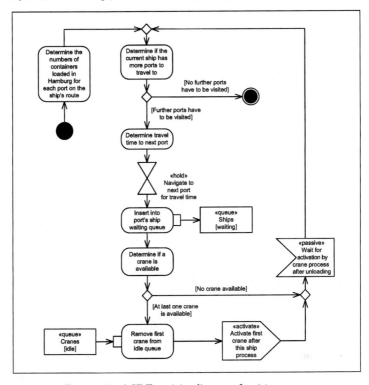

Figure 5.17: A UML activity diagram of a **ship** process

The **crane** process is simpler. Every time a **crane** is activated by another process, it checks if the port's **ship** queue contains any entries waiting for service: If there are ships to unload, the **crane** serves the first **ship** by removing it from the queue and by passivating itself for a predetermined loading time period. After unloading is finished, the **ship** is reactivated to continue on route. If there are no waiting ships, the **crane**

Chapter 5 Discrete Event Model Design

inserts itself into a queue of idle cranes (of the relevant port) and passivates itself until reactivated by a new ship arrival. Figure 5.18 shows the flow of this process.

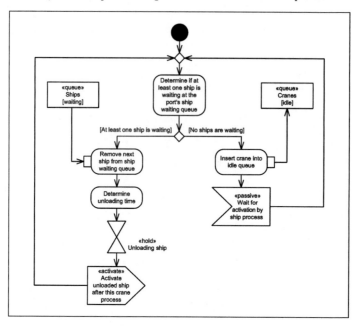

Figure 5.18: A UML activity diagram of a crane process

Please note the close correspondence between relevant real world objects and model entities (e.g. ships and cranes) in the process-oriented modelling style. Process descriptions also integrate model entities' attributes with their behaviour, which is defined via *lifecycles* as outlines in Section 5.2.1.

Our harbour model's crane entity encapsulates both the crane object's properties and its activities; i.e. the unloading of arriving ships over a time span. From the modeler's point of view this aggregation of object properties and behaviour simplifies model logic by narrowing the conceptual gap between system description and model design and allows us to map active and passive object phases (e.g. unloading a ship by an active crane, a ship's sailing, or idle cranes' waiting for ships to arrive) into a process-oriented model in a realistic manner. Interactions between objects are also easier to identify and represent than in an event-oriented modelling style.

5.2 Dominant Discrete Event Modelling Styles

An Event-Oriented Implementation: When modelling our shipping logistics example from an event-oriented point of view, we also identify all relevant entities first. As in the process-oriented version, there are two dominant objects; `ships` and `cranes`. These are still modelled as entity classes with properties. The `ship` entity's attributes include the number of containers for each harbour on route and `cranes` store a reference to their port. Instead of folding them into individual behaviour descriptions (processes), however, all state changes will now be modelled by global events.

In addition to the two dominant entities, our model includes two types of queues (i.e. ship queues and idle crane queues), where inactive entities are entered when they are idle. Closer analysis of model dynamics reveals some important changes of state in the model; e.g. when a new ship enters the system (i.e. Hamburg harbour), when a ship arrives at a port, or when an unloading process is complete. As a minimum, this suggests the specification of three corresponding types of events:

- event `ship creation`
- event `ship arrival at port`
- event `unloading completed`

Of course, to improve conceptual clarity, we could have used further events, at some loss in efficiency. For example, we could add both `start unloading` and `unloading completed` as well as `ship arrival` and `ship departure` events to the `ship creation` event. This would result in five types of events rather than three. However, a ship arrival will either immediately cause unloading to start – in which case an *unloading completed* event can be scheduled – or cause a ship to enter a queue – from which it will be removed by an idle crane and an `unloading completed` event can again be scheduled. Although it may well improve model clarity, no separate `start unloading` event is strictly needed. The same holds for `ship departure`, all of whose aspects can easily be bound to the `unloading completed` event since it will always follow it without delay. Three events therefore suffice to describe model logic.

Since it is triggered from *outside* the simulated system (Baltic ports), the `ship creation` event is referred to as an *external* event. It creates a new `ship` entity and places it at the first destination port (i.e. Hamburg harbour). A new event instance for modelling the details of a "ship arrival at its next port" is placed on the simulation's event list. By using the model's distribution for determining ships' inter-arrival times, the `ship creation` event then schedules a new `ship creation` event (see Figure 5.19).

The event `ship arrival at port` describes what happens if a `ship` is sailing into the next harbour along its route (see Figure 5.20). We first check at which harbour the ship has arrived. If this is Hamburg, we must decide how many containers for each port on the ship's route must be loaded. During this task all ports on the ship's route are accessed one after another and the number of containers for each destination is sampled from a statistical distribution. These container numbers are stored as a `ship` attribute; one per destination. Note that the container loading activity itself is not modelled at

125

Chapter 5 Discrete Event Model Design

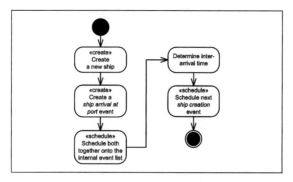

Figure 5.19: A UML activity diagram of the `ship creation` event

Hamburg. This reduces model complexity and can be justified by the fact that this omission makes no difference to the model statistics of interest.

After this initialisation, the `ship` sails to the first harbour on its route; i.e. a new `ship arrival at port` event is scheduled onto the simulation's event list. The time of this event is determined by accessing the relevant value in the model's sailing delays table (see Table 5.2). Remember that, for simplicity's sake, these values reflect constant travelling times. As soon as a `ship` arrives at a port on its route, it files itself into a queue and determines whether at least one of the port's cranes is waiting idle. If no crane is available, the `ship` remains in the queue until a freed crane removes it for processing. If at least one crane is available, the first in the cranes' idle queue is activated, the `ship` is removed from its queue, and unloading begins. The model time for this activity is determined and a corresponding event to finish unloading is placed on the simulation's event list. Unloading time delays are computed by multiplying unloading times for a single container with the number of containers to be unloaded in this port.

The last type of event, `unloading completed` (see Figure 5.21), describes what will happen after unloading containers is finished. We first check if there are any further ports to be visited on the ships route. If the ship has arrived at the last port on its route, it departs from the model, and its entity is deleted. If there are further ports to be visited, the next port on the current ship's route is selected, and a new `ship arrival at port` event is scheduled for this ship to occur after the sailing time delay.

After this, we must check if further unloading can now be performed. If there is at least one ship waiting in the current harbour, it is removed from its queue and a new `unloading completed` event is scheduled for it. Remember that unloading time is a random variable attached to a suitable distribution. If no further ships are waiting, the crane freed by this event is entered into the idle crane queue and waits for the next ship to arrive.

5.2 Dominant Discrete Event Modelling Styles

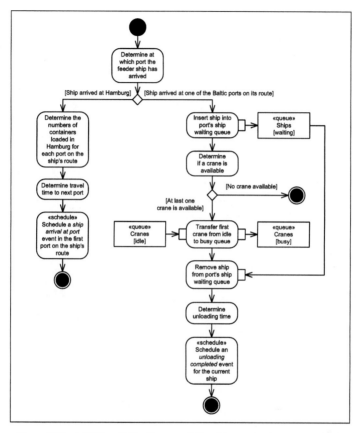

Figure 5.20: A UML activity diagram of the `ship arrival at port` event

From the discussion above it should be clear that an event-oriented viewpoint models dynamic system behaviour as event sequences. For each event a corresponding *event method* is tasked to carry out any desired system state changes. In the harbour logistics model we used three types of events: `ship generator`, `arrival at port`, and `unloading completed`. These events specify the model's dynamic behaviour. The model's structural description (e.g. ports, number of cranes, queues, distances) is completely separate from its dynamics (i.e. the event types). Time consuming activities

Chapter 5 Discrete Event Model Design

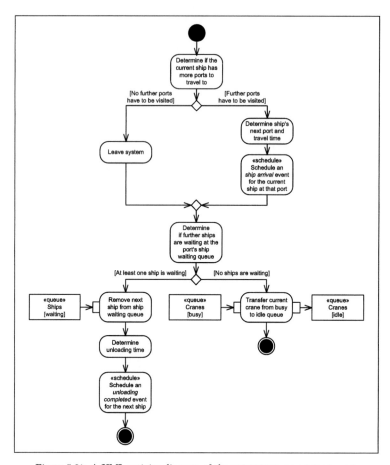

Figure 5.21: A UML activity diagram of the `unloading completed` event

such as unloading or sailing are not modelled explicitly. Their start and completion are only marked by events, which do not consume any model time themselves. The passage of model time is caused solely by the simulation monitor's actions; jumping the clock from one significant event time to the next.

5.3 Other Modelling Styles

In addition to the two dominant modelling styles mentioned above, simulation software may also support a *transaction-oriented* approach and an *activity-oriented* approach.

5.3.1 Transaction-Oriented Modelling

Transaction-oriented frameworks are special cases of process-oriented modelling styles. The transaction-based view is derived from the block diagrams widely used in systems analysis (see Page 1991, p. 32) and was first used in the GPSS simulation system. *Blocks* how actions performed by permanent and static system components, while *transactions* represent transient and dynamic model entities. Model dynamics are described in terms of the "flow" of transactions through blocks, where a transaction's state (i.e. its attributes) may be changed. Simple queueing scenarios map well into transaction-based models. Transactions, for example, may stand for materials in a jobshop simulation, where they are routed through (and processed by) blocks representing a variety of machinery.

We will use the harbour logistics model introduced in Section 5.2.3 to demonstrate the transaction-oriented modelling style in more detail. In this context we can view ships as transactions, while static system components (i.e. cranes) are modelled as blocks or resources. If we choose the resource approach (as in our Java-based DESMO-J simulation framework – see Chapter 10), we can model all *cranes* in a port as a pool of resources with given capacity (the number of cranes in the port). *Ships* now become transactions, which acquire one or more of these resources (i.e. cranes), use them for services (here for unloading), and release them after service completion. Resources are then made available to other processes. If a ship transaction cannot acquire the resource capacity it needs (here only a single crane), it must wait in a queue until sufficient capacity is released by other transactions.

A transaction can release its resources at any time. Whenever resources are returned to the pool, any associated queues are checked for blocked processes waiting for resources of the relevant type. When several resource pools are involved, it becomes possible to create *deadlock* conditions, where waiting entities are holding resources needed by other entities, which are holding resources required for the first kind of entities to proceed. A modeller needs to be aware of the possibility of such cyclic blocks. In a transaction-oriented model we no longer need any explicit queue for waiting ships. This function is subsumed by internal queues attached to resources and controlled by the model monitor, which also takes over all tasks to unblock waiting transactions as soon as sufficient capacity is made available. Since the cranes are now modelled as standard resources, we could even do without the whole crane process as well as the queue of idle cranes. This has the potential of making the model's structure much simpler.

On arriving at a Baltic seaport, feeder ships now try to engage a free crane by sending a *request* to the corresponding resource. If there are currently no free resource units

Chapter 5 Discrete Event Model Design

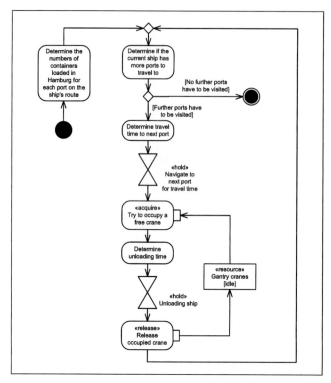

Figure 5.22: A UML activity diagram of a *transaction-oriented* version of the logistics model

available, they will be passivated and queued automatically. After successful acquisition of a crane, they will then switch into a hold-state for the unloading and release the occupied crane after it has been completed.

The UML activity diagram in Figure 5.22 summarizes this flow of transactions.

We have already mentioned that all process-oriented models can be reduced to models cast in the "lower level", event-based approach. By mapping transactions into entities and treating entry to and exit from blocks as events, this can also be done for transaction based models.

5.3 Other Modelling Styles

5.3.2 Activity-Oriented Modelling

Activity-oriented models, however, cannot be directly transformed to match an event-oriented world view. The core building blocks of activity-orientation are "activities", which may consume model time and start whenever a set of specified preconditions hold. While activity-oriented models may be easy to design, their implementation requires processor-intensive strategies which must check all preconditions of all possible activities at each change of state, as model time unfolds. Although intelligent implementation techniques can lighten some of this computational burden, this modelling world view's inherent inefficiencies have contributed to the rarity of activity-orientation's practical use (see Page 1991, p. 29).

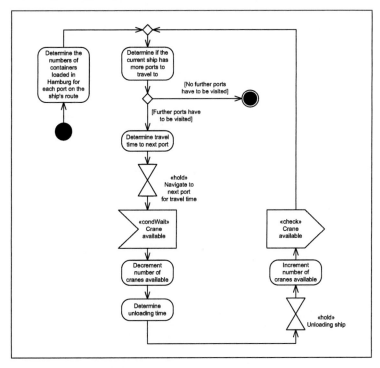

Figure 5.23: A UML activity diagram of a *activity-oriented* version of the logistics model

Chapter 5 Discrete Event Model Design

Again we refer to our model of harbour logistics and demonstrate how an activity-oriented model of this scenario could work. Active entities, modelled as processes, now must wait in a condition queue and are automatically passivated until a specified condition holds. Whenever a change occurs in the model, messages are sent to all queues whose conditions could possibly be affected by it. If, as a result, processes become unblocked, they are released from the queue and proceed on their lifecycles. It is the responsibility of the model designer to ensure that all relevant checks are performed, each time the model state changes. S/he must also formulate the relevant queues conditions, which are highly specific to each different model.

In the example the ships now invoke the condition queue's check on port arrival. They will be removed from the queue if a crane is available for unloading (condition). Otherwise they will be filed into or remain in the condition's queue until it eventually turns true. In this way a queue on condition `crane available` replaces the ships waiting queue of the previous version of this model. In the corresponding UML activity diagram (see Figure 5.23) this is indicated by a signal reception node marked with the stereotype `<<condWait>>`.

Beyond that cranes do not need to be modelled as processes of their own. Since only crane capacity is of interest to us, a simple variable storing the number of available cranes will suffice. This variable's value is part of the checked condition and will be decremented each time one of the port's cranes is acquired and incremented each time one is released. There is therefore no need for the original idle cranes queue in the process- or event-oriented versions.

After an unloading process has successfully been completed (and a further crane has thus become available), feeder ships will inform condition queues in each relevant port about this change. That condition queue is then automatically checked for ship entries which may be reactivated to successfully obtain the freed capacity. In this model all ships wait for the same condition (i.e. a free crane), so only the first item in a condition queue needs to be checked (indicated by an action with the stereotype `<<check>>`) in response to a message that a relevant crane has become available.

As we can see in the UML activity diagram in Figure 5.23, the activity-oriented version of this model is similarly as compact as the model using a transaction-oriented approach. Both model's sizes compare favourably to the process-oriented and the event-oriented model designs. It is, however, quite possible to develop higher level simulation constructs for both transaction-oriented and activity-oriented simulations, based on an underlying process-oriented implementation at a lower level of abstraction. An example of this approach is our simulation software DESMO-J (see Chapter 10).

5.4 Object-Oriented Model Construction

Object-orientation, which has recently emerged as a dominant feature in mainstream program development, has also become very popular in the discrete event simulation domain. In fact, the very idea of describing programs and models in terms of objects can be traced back to the simulation language *Simula*, whose development had begun as early as the nineteensixties. Simula as an early simulation programming language introduced concepts like classes and instances, encapsulation, inheritance, and process-based system description. Only much later did these ideas make any impact in main stream programming culture. Many aspects of the designs of the first general purpose object-oriented programming languages (e.g. *Smalltalk, Eiffel, C++*) were directly modelled on Simula.

The core idea of an object-oriented programming style is based on the perceived similarity notion between program development and execution and model design and simulation. From this viewpoint all program development becomes model construction. Many aspects of modern discrete event model development styles, in particular the process-oriented approach, can be viewed as a re-orientation towards Simulas's original ideas. Modern object-oriented simulation techniques go beyond this and support system representation with object-oriented design methods, object-oriented methods of implementation, and object-oriented programming tools. This more holistic approach makes object-oriented concepts useful for simulation at the design (e.g. with UML, see Chapter 4) as well as the implementation level (e.g. with DESMO-J, see Chapter 10). In contrast to conventional simulation where predefined language constructs offer only a limited degree of modifiability or extensibility, object-oriented simulation can provide fully reusable and extensible classes using inheritance hierarchies.

There is a number of specific advantages object-oriented simulation can offer:

- conceptual proximity to the problem domain
- reusabilty of models and model components
- unification of communication lines between components
- support of hierarchical modelling
- ease of simulation software development
- support for parallelization of simulation experiments
- support for distributed modelling techniques (e.g. using the Internet)

Based on its origins it should not be surprising that object-oriented simulation is closely related to the process-oriented modelling style, where we define a model in terms of entities with properties and lifecycles. Beyond this, however, object-oriented modelling styles offer additional features, such as inheritance, class hierarchies, and class composition. See Chapter 3 for object-oriented simulation covered in more detail.

Chapter 5 Discrete Event Model Design

5.5 Combined Modelling Styles

5.5.1 Embedding Events in a Process-Oriented Model

In spite of the fact that process-oriented designs dominate discrete event simulation models today, they are, however, not optimally suited for representing all of a system's aspects. For this reason it would be desirable to combine both approaches in the same model and use the best of them for each relevant system aspect. This includes the capability of using events in an otherwise process-oriented model; for example to represent a machine's maintenance or failure. While the machine itself may be modelled as a process, with an appropriate lifecycle, how to include a maintenance event seems somewhat unclear, and to create an abstract maintenance entity for this purpose seems artificial and constructed. An event-oriented viewpoint appears to be more appropriate for modelling this system aspect and permits a more direct and "natural" representation.

So-called jobshop models, where products are routed in different ways through a production facility, were one of the earliest applications of simulation technology and production systems are still one of the most important simulation domains. In particular, such models have many applications in management science.

The goal of such models is the identification and analysis of *bottlenecks*. Some typical aspects are machines or devices with specified performance characteristics, a set of production orders (with properties and types), service requests, arrival times, priorities, allocation of services to machines or devices, and different strategies for the sequencing of production orders (priority rules). While these characteristics fit well into a queueing network, there are often some aspects of inventory systems which must be considered.

Model Design: As an example, consider a production system with different groups of machines for assembling a product, stepwise processing of such production requests, and an inventory of raw materials. In addition, this model includes consideration of machine unavailability and reduced processing capability, repairs, and maintenance. Complex models may include all of these aspects and seek to analyse such a system's performance.

The following components are typically found in a production system models:

- objects:
    - production requests
    - machines, vehicles (for transportation), personnel
- relationships:
    - synchronization of production orders, machines, personnel

5.5 Combined Modelling Styles

- activities:
  - processing of orders with specified processing times
  - processing of orders whose processing times are computed from both resource and order attributes
- performance measures:
  - mean queue lengths in front of machines
  - mean processing times at machines
  - mean machine utilization
  - mean throughput (i.e. items processed per time unit)
  - mean time requests spend in the system

5.5.2 Example: A Combined Process/Event Model

This fictitious model has n *groups of machines*, each of which is served by a limited capacity *buffer*. Each arriving item of material is routed through these groups of machines in a fixed order. A machine group can consist of a number of identical servers (machines), each of which can operate on a single independent from the other servers of the same machine group. All arriving items enter the first machine group's buffer. Whenever a machine in a group becomes idle, it checks the group's buffer for items. If there are any, the first (FIFO) is removed, processed, and placed in the next machine group's buffer. All items which have been processed by the last group of machines leave the model. Figure 5.24 visualizes the model.

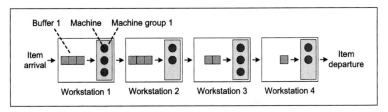

Figure 5.24: A *multi-stage production line* model

If a group of machines offers insufficient capacity over a longer period, unprocessed items will fill its buffer until it is full. This means that preceding machines cannot enter any more finished items and must wait until buffer capacity becomes available. This can drastically increase the production delays encountered by items. In addition, we assume that machines may require maintenance and therefore become unavailable for some time. This temporarily reduces a machine group's capacity.

Let us assume that there are $n = 4$ groups of machines. The processing times for items follow an exponential distribution with a mean of 20 minutes, 30 minutes, 12 min-

Chapter 5 Discrete Event Model Design

utes, and 5 minutes on machines of groups 1, 2, 3, and 4. We assume further that new items arrive every 10 minutes on the average. This inter-arrival time of the model's workload is also exponentially distributed. Due to preventive maintenance, machines ought to be switched off after an operating time of between 3 to 5 hours (uniformly distributed). After exactly one hour of maintenance time, such machines can be switched on again. For simplicity we assume that the owner of the machines acts shortsightedly by switching off only machines that are idle that moment; i.e. production of a machine will never be interrupted in favour of maintenance activities, which therefore are delayed (exceeding the recommended operating time mentioned above if necessary) until the machine becomes idle. Maintenance of a machine that has not processed at least one item since its last maintenance is delayed, too.

To evaluate system performance, we need to know that the cost of a machine is 25,000 Euros, the cost of a slot in buffer is 1,000 Euros, and that the return of each processed item is 200 Euros. Based on these costs and the model's simulation we aim to derive optimal buffer sizes. This motivation requires some balancing of conflicting goals, such as "maximize throughput", "avoid bottlenecks", "minimize costs for machines and buffers", and "minimize waiting and residence times".

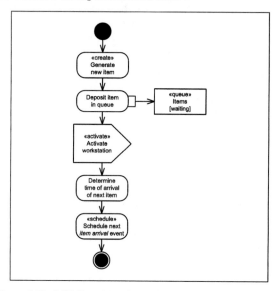

Figure 5.25: A UML activity diagram of the `item arrival` event

5.5 Combined Modelling Styles

Conceptual Model: To model this system, we cluster each group of machines and its buffer into a *workstation*. The process-oriented modelling style seems an obvious candidate for sketching the model's structure as a typical queueing system. However, since moments at which maintenance activities should be started occur at random (with stochastic uncertainty), they are best modelled through an event. Item arrivals from "*outside*" correspond to "external events" and will therefore fit better into an event-based style of description.

Workload items are modelled as simple and "*passive*" entities, which are routed through the model by the workstations' activities. Workstations themselves are modelled as processes. Item arrivals are described by an exponential distribution. After arrival, an item is deposited in the first buffer (represented as an unlimited queue), the associated workstation is activated, and the next item arrival is scheduled. Figure 5.25 shows this as a picture.

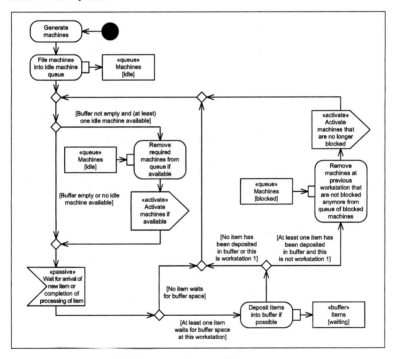

Figure 5.26: A UML activity diagram of the **workstation** process

Chapter 5 Discrete Event Model Design

Workstations (see Figure 5.26) are active entities, and each coordinates interactions between its machines and its buffer. A workstation remains passive until its buffer contains items for processing. Once this is the case, the workstation is activated and machines are allocated to tasks.

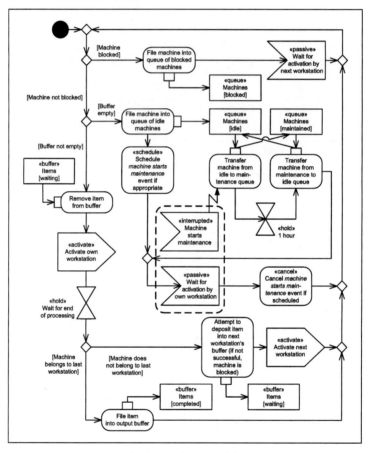

Figure 5.27: A UML activity diagram of the machine process

5.5 Combined Modelling Styles

Choosing machines uses a "longest idle time" strategy. If the machines of a preceding workstation are blocked because the buffer of the succeeding workstation was full, the succeeding workstation will unblock the machines of the preceding workstation once processing an item (and therefore its removal from the buffer) has started.

Machines (UML activity diagram shown in Figure 5.27) are components of workstations and are responsible for processing items. They can be in an "idle", "busy", "blocked", or "maintained" state. Until maintenance is necessary or workload items arrive for processing, machines will remain *idle*.

An *idle* machine that reaches its scheduled maintenance time (due to a *machine starts maintenance* event, which consists only of the interruption of an *idle* machine, see Figure 5.28) will become *maintained* and (after a constant delay of one hour) *idle* again. Note that after maintenance a machine has to process at least one item before it will be maintained again.

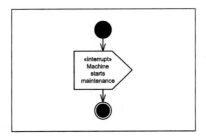

Figure 5.28: A UML activity diagram of the machine starts maintenance event

As soon as an item enters the buffer and is allocated to an *idle* machine, this machine removes the item, switches to *busy*, and starts processing. Processing items requires a *hold* command, as found in process-oriented modelling frameworks. Buffers are modelled as FIFO queues with limited waiting space (the buffer capacity).

After processing an item, a machine tries to deposit it into the succeeding workstation's buffer. If this is unsuccessful because that buffer is full, the machine becomes *blocked* and waits until suitable buffer space is available. If successful, the machine will start processing the next item from the workstation's buffer. If no such item is available, the machine becomes *idle* again and waits for a new item allocation or maintenance activities. Whether the deposition of the processed item into the the succeeding workstation's buffer or not, the machine activates the succeeding workstation and notifies it of the new item arrival. If a machine is part of the last workstation on an item's processing path, that item is made to leave the system after processing.

139

Bibliography

Simulation Results: Simulation experiments with different parameter settings for machine and buffer numbers were performed. Table 5.3 shows the "optimal" (i.e. maximum profit) solution. This was derived by combining the simulation with optimization tools based on genetic algorithms (see Section 13.5)

Table 5.3: Results of optimizing the multi-stage production system

	Machine group			
	1	2	3	4
Buffer size	1	5	3	5
Number of machines	5	5	4	4
Profit	2,252,800 Euros			
Items processed	13,584			
Costs machines/buffers	464,000 Euros			
Occupied buffers (mean)	0.99 of 1	2.32 of 5	0.35 of 3	0.26 of 5
Idle machines (mean)	0.01 of 5	0.29 of 5	1.20 of 4	2.75 of 4
Blocked machines (mean)	3.93 of 5	3.22 of 5	1.20 of 4	0.00 of 4

Discussion: This example highlights the need for modelling activities and interactions above a certain complexity threshold in a process-oriented style, whereas "unexpected" events, arrivals from "outside" of a model, and simple "autonomous" changes of state (e.g. rises and drops in inventory levels) may be more suited for event-oriented style. Such combination of modelling styles also favours reusability since it is not restrictive to only be able to combine sub-models in the same style for reuse in a different context.

To allow such a combination of modelling styles, simulation software must support it. In most simulation programming tools this is unfortunately not the case. It is one of the distinctive features of the DESMO-J simulation framework, discussed later in this book (see Chapter 10), that such a mixing of modelling styles is permitted.

Bibliography

J. Banks, editor. *Handbook of Simulation – Principles, Methodology, Advances, Applications, and Practice*. Wiley, New York, 1998.

D. Hill. *Object-Oriented Analysis and Simulation*. Addison-Wesley, Cambridge, 1996.

J. Košturiak and M. Gregor. *Simulation von Produktionssystemen* ("Simulation of Production Systems", in German). Springer, Vienna, 1995.

A. M. Law and W. D. Kelton. *Simulation Modeling and Analysis*. McGraw-Hill, New York, 3rd edition, 2000.

L. Oakshott. *Business Modelling and Simulation*. Pitman, London, 1997.

B. Page. *Diskrete Simulation – Eine Einführung mit Modula-2* ("Discrete Simulation – An Introduction with Modula-2", in German). Springer, Berlin, 1991.

Bibliography

B. Page, T. Lechler, and S. Claassen. *Objektorientierte Simulation in Java mit dem Framework DESMO-J* ("Object-Oriented Simulation in Java with the Framework DESMO-J", in German). Libri Book on Demand, Hamburg, 2000.

O. Spaniol and S. Hoff. *Ereignisorientierte Simulation – Konzepte und Systemrealisierung* ("Event-Oriented Simulation – Concepts and System Implementation", in German). Thomson's Aktuelle Tutorien; 7. Thomson, Bonn, 1995.

Chapter 6

First Steps in Simulation Programming

Bernd Page, Nicolas Knaak, Ruth Meyer

Contents

6.1	Motivation and Overview	143
6.2	Java as a "Simulation Language"	144
	6.2.1 General Requirements	144
	6.2.2 Simulation-Specific Requirements	146
	6.2.3 Advantages of Java as a Simulation Language	149
6.3	A Simple Java Class Library for Event-Oriented Simulation	149
	6.3.1 Event List	150
	6.3.2 Entities, Events, and Event Scheduling	152
	6.3.3 Distribution Sampling, Data Collection, and Queueing	153
	6.3.4 Example	156
	Further Reading	157
	Bibliography	157

6.1 Motivation and Overview

Simulation models must be implemented as simulation programs before they can be can used in computer-based simulation experiments. This requires a suitable programming tool, whose affordances and constraints (i.e. what seems or does not seem possible) may guide and inform both model and program structure. This chapter summarizes some general and specific requirements for discrete event simulation programming languages and comments on how Java meets each. At the end we will mention some further aspects which are relevant for both simulation and teaching. To support this discussion, we assemble a small and light-weight discrete event simulation library in a step-by-step fashion.

Knowledge of how to program in Java will be assumed. This requirement will surface again later when we discuss *DESMO-J*, a Java-based simulation framework, in

Chapter 6 First Steps in Simulation Programming

Chapter 10. Any attempts at teaching elementary Java programming would go well beyond the scope of this book. A multitude of specialized textbooks are available for this purpose, and we will list to a small number of useful ones at the end of this chapter.

6.2 Java as a "Simulation Language"

The flexibility of both a simulation model and its implementation in a simulation program can be strongly influenced by the capabilities of an implementation language. Choosing a popular programming tool will have the advantage of reaching a wide range of potential users, but not every programming language meets all of discrete event simulation's core requirements. *Java* is a highly popular modern programming language with many attractive features, whose suitability for discrete event simulation will be explored in this section.

6.2.1 General Requirements

Not all general purpose programming languages meet discrete event simulation's requirements for clear program structure, interactivity, modularity, run-time efficiency, and readability:

- ❏ **Interactivity**
  Simulation models require interaction at multiple levels. Error tracing and correction often requires following a model's execution step-by-step. To facilitate this activity, a programming tool or its development environment should, as a minimum, be able to show a variable's values during a simulation experiment. The freely available *JDK* (*Java Development Kit* – http://java.sun.com) from Sun Microsystems offers a suitable command line tool, and more convenient debugging systems are part of many commercial Java development environments. At the modelling level a programming language should at least allow interactive input of model parameters. Such model control should also be possible during a simulation experiment. Java offers a number of possibilities. Data can be read directly from the keyboard and standard component libraries such as *AWT* (*Abstract Windowing Toolkit*) and *Swing* (named after a style of dance band jazz) offer platform-independent foundations for window-based, mouse-driven graphical interfaces. Response times can be optimized by using concurrency for input and output; i.e. *threads*. All such convenience, however, comes at the price of increased development time and effort.

- ❏ **Modularity**
  In addition to component reuse, software modularity also supports cooperative styles of development. It provides the means for separating model- and simulation-specific functionality of a project; i.e. model design from experimental frames. In an early MODULA-based implementation of the DESMO-J frame-

6.2 Java as a "Simulation Language"

work, for example, it formed the foundation for separating simulation infrastructure from model specific components (see Page 1991, Chapter 7).
Java is a purely object-oriented language and uses classes to associate and encapsulate data (properties) with functions (methods). This is also the base for software reuse. A further level of modularisation is accomplished by the mapping of model components within the DESMO-J architecture. This allows reuse of entire models as components within more complex structures (see Chapter 10).

❏ **Efficiency**
Run-time efficiency is an important criterion for choosing a language to implement complex simulation experiments. The interpreted nature of Java, which is based on a platform-independent virtual machine, is a disadvantage in this regard. Run-time efficiency strongly depends on how well this virtual machine has been implemented for a particular family of computers. Modern Java implementations make use of a *JIT* ("just in time") strategy. This technique pre-fetches and translates the "next" code segment directly into machine code (bypassing the virtual machine) while the currently active block of code is still being executed. In this fashion a Java implementation can trade speed gains from native code again computations required for compilation. Where code is executed repetitively (e.g. in loops), this seems well worth the effort. Sun's "hot spot" technology even observes and profiles a routine's frequency of execution and uses this data to optimize frequently used code further. Speeds in excess of compiled C++ code have been reported as a result.

❏ **Structure and Readability**
Since semantic errors are notoriously difficult to track in badly structured and inadequately commented code, transparent structure and good readability are important requirements for understandable implementations of simulation models. Programming tools should be transparent; i.e. their syntax and semantics should support rather than hinder the expression of relevant ideas. This is of particular importance where analyses of alternative strategies require intensive manipulation of model code.
Java offers a number of advantages in this regard. The fact that its syntax is closely related to languages of the C family (e.g. C++) lessens the learning effort for C programmers. As in C++, identifiers can be chosen freely (as long as reserved words are respected). The *Javadoc* utility can extract comments from source code and cast them into an *HTML* page for each of a program's classes. This documentation is augmented with index pages for packages, classes, methods, and properties. Hyperlinks allow easy navigation between pages. The great advantage of this type of documentation is that it need not be separated from the source code itself, which minimizes the danger of inconsistencies. The following class library has been documented in just this fashion.

Chapter 6 First Steps in Simulation Programming

6.2.2 Simulation-Specific Requirements

A large range of discrete event simulation models show strong similarities in terms of structure and functionality of their implementation. Functions and data structures share common characteristics and interact in typical ways. A suitable implementation language for such models must provide concepts (i.e. data structures and methods) for their easy implementation. To emphasise this, we will list typical simulation model components, which must be mapped to software:

❏ **State Variables**

The model state is the set of all states across all model components. To represent the model state, a suitable programming tool must, as a minimum, offer numerical variables of different types.

Java offers basic numerical types, such as `int`, `long`, `float`, `double`, as well as `boolean` for *true/false* values. Classes allow the construction of arbitrary data structures and methods for their manipulation.

❏ **Simulation Clock**

Discrete event simulations uncouple model time from "real" time; i.e. the passage of model time is not directly related to and need not be proportional to the duration of any computation on the computer which is running the model. The *simulation clock* shows the currently relevant time in the model. This is a fictitious value which is determined each time an event is taken from the model's *event list* and executed (see Section 2.3). It should be noted that it does not make sense to decrement rather than increment the model clock's value. Since many model components will wish to have access to it, it is best stored in a global variable.

Java's object-oriented nature allows us to encapsulate model time as a protected attribute of a globally visible object; together with suitable methods for access. Beyond this we could define a new *Clock* data type, which e.g. does not allow time to run backwards.

❏ **Temporary Objects**

Many simulations create and delete transient entities at model execution time. In such cases dynamic storage management will be needed to dynamically allocate and de-allocate storage during a simulation experiment. A simple example for this is an *open* queueing scenario, where workload items ("customers") for a resource ("server") enter the model with a service request and leave after completion. In addition, the so-called event notices, which store details of future events, need to be dynamically created and deleted.

Java offers dynamic storage management. Memory can be reserved with the `new` operator and all non-reachable objects (i.e. those with no references) will periodically be *garbage collected* to free memory space. This is accomplished by a separate garbage collection process, running concurrently within the Java virtual machine. Because garbage collection needs to search through and compact

6.2 Java as a "Simulation Language"

storage locations, it will slow execution. However, Java will only do this when memory becomes tight.

❑ **Managing Future Events**
Planning and initiating event execution at the right point in model time is a central function of all discrete event simulation software. Information about each event scheduled to occur in the future is kept in an *event list*, which is ordered on model time. A *scheduler* process is responsible for processing this data structure and to execute all events in their correct temporal order, which includes updating the model clock to the next event's time. Model state will then change as required. Section 2.5 discusses this in more detail.

Within this context it should be noted that an empty event list will lead to a simulation run's termination. This may be intended (e.g. when simulating scenarios until all items are processed) or indicate a semantic modelling error (e.g. a process fails to correctly create successor events). Model initialisation must insure that at least one event is placed on the event list before a simulation is started and there must be provisions to generate the required stream of events during a run. Java' standard API (`java.util`) offers a `Collections` framework with suitable data structures for implementing an event list, which can be embedded in a *Scheduler* class with suitable methods for its manipulation.

❑ **Waiting Spaces and Waiting Lines**
Many models require the representation of waiting spaces and waiting lines (*queues*). Queueing scenarios, for example, are used to identify bottlenecks (e.g. servers with lengthy queues) and to study the effects of priority rules such as *LIFO* (last in, first out), *FIFO* (first in, first out), and others on waiting times. Often priority-driven queue ordering and searching for objects with specified attribute values is also required.

Java offers `Collections` classes to implement queues. As for event lists, these are best encapsulated in a suitable class guarding against illegal patterns of access.

❑ **Generating Random Numbers and Sampling from Distributions**
Random numbers, which generate random events (see Section 2.6), are an essential part of any stochastic simulation model. The standard Java library offers a class (`java.util.Random`) for creating such numbers algorithmically. This congruential generator has a word length of 48 bits and a maximum period of 2^{48}. It creates uniformly distributed numbers in the interval 0 to 1. Compared to a 32-bit generator it provides a much larger set of stochastically independent samples (by a factor of 2^{16}). Classes for representing specified distributions must apply suitable transformations to map their output into random variables (see Chapter 7).

❑ **Statistical Evaluations** Depending on the objectives of a simulation study, one or more model variables are of particular interest to a simulation experiment. Simulation software must offer the means to observe how such variables' values change over time and must be able to generate useful statistical informa-

Chapter 6 First Steps in Simulation Programming

tion. In addition to elementary measures like means, deviations, minima and maxima, time-weighted statistics are often needed to determine a model component's utilization.

Summary statistics are typically reported at the end of a simulation experiment. Modern simulation software, however, should also offer some means for observing how specified properties and measures change during model execution. This may, for example, guide changes at run time, which may in turn require a corresponding *reset* of statistical measures. Such interaction with a running model makes it possible to use *batch means*, where a long simulation is partitioned into a number of equal length segments ("batches") in order to sample each separately. Since no lengthy "warm up" periods need be repeated for each batch, this strategy can reduce execution time (see Page 1991, Section 4.4.3.3).

Object-oriented programming tools suggest the provision of suitable classes, which can be instantiated to provide different types of data collection objects. These objects store relevant data and provide methods to update, reset, compute, and display statistical measures on demand. Java's `java.util` API offers an `Observer` interface and an `Observable` class to facilitate their construction.

❏ **Reporting Results**

To allow for more thorough analysis, it should be possible to direct data onto the screen or into a file. Tables are the simplest kind of report, but more visual forms of data display have many cognitive advantages and are therefore commonly provided by modern simulation tools.

Java offers comprehensive support for platform independent graphic displays, as well as output to a text-based standard console. While there are no constraints for showing data on screen, access to the host's file system for writing data into a file is only possible if simulations run as applications rather than *applets*. This security constraint has been somewhat softened in newer versions of Java.

❏ **Interruptible Processes**

A process-oriented modelling style has many advantages (see Section 5.2.1), particularly if models consist of large numbers of interacting objects. At the implementation level this requires some means of interrupting and continuing an entity's lifecycle at any point. Such interruption and rescheduling of processes is controlled by a *scheduler*, in response to stepping through its list of events. Since "race conditions" could lead to invalid patterns of access to shared model variables, processes must be carefully synchronized and no more than one process must be allowed to be active at any given point in time.

Modula-2's *coroutines* were used to support this concept in the original DESMO framework (see Page 1991, Ch. 7). Unfortunately, Java offers no equivalent built-in component. *Threads* are provided to guide parallel execution, but these have been targeted at genuine parallelism (i.e. on multiple *physical* processors) rather than at supporting conceptual concurrency (i.e. through multiple *logical* processes). As a result, it becomes more difficult to prevent unwanted interactions

6.3 A Simple Java Class Library for Event-Oriented Simulation

caused by different speeds of a model's physical execution. Solving this problem in a safe and comprehensible manner played in important role in DESMO-J's design and development (see Chapter 10).

6.2.3 Advantages of Java as a Simulation Language

Java has been widely adopted as a teaching language in computer science curricula, a development which has also raised interest in the discrete simulation community. Since industrial applications of Java show a significant increase, we can assume that there will be a growing number of users for Java-based simulation tools.

An important reason for its growing popularity is Java's *platform independence*, which is based on a portable virtual machine, implemented on a wide range of platforms. This offers students the freedom of choice with regard to workstation type and tool vendors an opportunity for a much larger market. Java is also a very *robust* tool; in particular when compared with languages such as C++. Automatic memory management and the lack of free access to pointer variables makes faster and more reliable software development possible. Users of Java-based simulation class libraries need not concern themselves with issues of memory allocation or dangling pointers leading to mysterious program crashes at execution time. Even array access is guarded by suitable range checks.

Java owes its existence and its fast rise to prominence to the Internet. Its capability for developing *applets* as active components on web pages is also of interest for simulation since this offers much potential for the distributed execution of models and for using the Internet as a learning aid (see Chapter14).

6.3 A Simple Java Class Library for Event-Oriented Simulation

By identifying a number of essential requirements for all discrete event simulation projects, our previous discussion has laid the groundwork for taking a first step towards using Java as a simulation tool. In this we must keep reusability in mind so that we can repeatedly draw on a stable collection of foundational classes, which need only to be instantiated and slightly enhanced for each project. Java's object oriented nature permits the development of reusable class libraries. In this section we therefore discuss a step-by-step implementation of a class library for event-based discrete event simulations (see Section 5.2.2). Figure 6.1 shows a class diagram of the overall design of this *DES* ("discrete event simulation") library, which will be elaborated below. Note that a number of *abstract* classes are used to make the overall architecture more comprehensive and structured.

Implementation is broadly divided into three steps. The first of these implements an *event list*, all of whose operations are defined in an *interface*. This strategy supports easy replacement of implementations, which e.g. allows us to experiment with efficiency

Chapter 6 First Steps in Simulation Programming

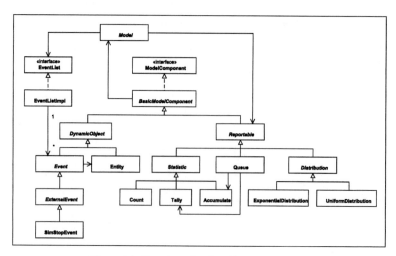

Figure 6.1: Overview of a class library to support event-based discrete event simulations

characteristics of different data structures. The event list forms the basis on which an implementation of event scheduling and processing can be built. This requires base classes for dynamic simulation objects (*events* and *entities*) as well as a *model* class, which aggregates all of a model's components. The simulation scheduler itself performs all the steps of the event processing loop known from the discussion in Section 2.5.

The third step of the framework's implementation is concerned with classes for random number generation, statistical data collection, and queueing. `Distribution` is an abstract base class for diverse streams of *random numbers*. To simplify matters, we will only consider uniform (`UniformDistribution`) and negative exponential (`ExponentialDistribution`) distributions. All *data collection* classes are derived from an abstract `Statistic` base class. These include a simple `Count` as well as two classes for simple or time-weighted aggregation of observations (`Tally` and `Accumulate`). The `Queue` class models a FIFO queue and employs tally and accumulate objects to track relevant statistics. All of these classes are derived from `Reportable`, which lets them contribute to a simulation report.

6.3.1 Event List

We have already learned that event lists are crucial to discrete event simulation. From a programming perspective they can be viewed as a FIFO queue with the most im-

6.3 A Simple Java Class Library for Event-Oriented Simulation

minent event always on top. Making the most frequent operations (e.g. `insert()` or `removeFirst()`) efficient would make an important contribution to minimize a simulation's run time. Since this may depend strongly on model structure, however, it is not immediately clear where insertions of new events may take place. Most implementations trade speed of removal against time for insertion and a *priority queue* therefore suggests itself as a suitable data structure. In spite of potential efficiency disadvantages many implementations make use of a simple ordered list.

Let us define the `EventList` interface first. It presupposes the existence of an `Event` class, which stores the numeric event time in a variable of type `double`. This value is set in `Event`'s constructor and cannot be changed later. Since we must be able to compare events based on event times, we must also implement Java's standard `Comparable` interface. `EventListImpl` in Figure 6.2 shows a proposed implementation for the `EventList` interface. Other structures are possible.

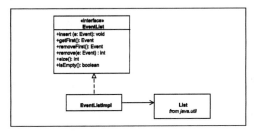

Figure 6.2: Interface and implementation for an `EventList`

Any indexed list structure from Java's collection classes (e.g. `java.util.Vector` or `java.util.ArrayList`) would be suitable for storing events in order of their occurrence. Searching for where to insert or delete an event is facilitated by binary search, which can either be implemented from scratch or by just using the default implementation of `binarySearch()` in `java.util.Collections`. Alternatively we could store the event list as a *heap* data structure. Heaps are ordered binary trees where the roots of each subtree stores the minimum or maximum value within that subtree. This means that a heap's minimum or maximum will be always on top and both insertions and root removal can be implemented in logarithmic time. Relevant algorithms are documented in most data structures and algorithms texts; e.g. Waite and Lafore (1998). A Java implementation suiting our purpose could again be based on an indexed list (e.g. `java.util.Vector` or `java.util.ArrayList`).

To test the proposed implementation, we can add a `main()` method to class `EventListImpl` in which we exercise *all* operations. For example, we can add 20 events with arbitrary event times between 0 and 100 and examine the resulting list. Java's standard `java.lang.Math.random()` method or the `java.util.Random` class can be called upon to provide suitable numbers. Note that in preparation for potential reuse

151

Chapter 6 First Steps in Simulation Programming

as well as for error detection it is very important to develop the habit of commenting code adequately. This includes *Javadoc* comments for describing a class as well as comments about the roles of all *public* and *protected* methods.

6.3.2 Entities, Events, and Event Scheduling

The next step in the development of our *DES* framework for event-based discrete event simulations implements classes for entities and events as well as a base class for simulation models. Figure 6.3 shows a relevant class diagram with interface definitions.

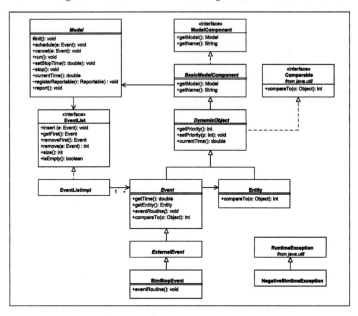

Figure 6.3: Basic functionality of the *DES* framework

The interface `ModelComponent` serves to represent model components in very general terms. Each model component has a name and a reference to the model in which it is used. This eases later reuse. `BasicModelComponent` is a simple implementation to derive concrete components from.

`Model` is a an abstract base class for simulation models. It includes an *event list*, a *simulation clock*, and a *scheduler* among its components. The `run()` method starts simulations. The abstract `init()` method must be implemented by all model sub-

6.3 A Simple Java Class Library for Event-Oriented Simulation

classes and is invoked at the start of each `run()` to schedule all required initial events for beginning a scheduling cycle. The methods `schedule()` and `cancel()` are used to insert and remove events from the event list. The `currentTime()` method always returns the current model time, which is set to 0 at the start of a simulation. The Method `setStopTime()` can schedule a simulation experiment's termination. The `stop()` method tells the scheduler to shut down (thereby terminating a simulation run). All other methods of `Model` are used for reporting results. These will be implemented in step 3.

`DynamicObject` provides an abstract base for temporary simulation objects, such as events and entities. All of these have a priority and own a reference to simulation time (mediated by the model). Implementation of dynamic objects' capability for being comparable must be deferred since this functionality differs between entities and events. If objects are created without priority, a default value is set to 100.

`Entity` is the base class for model entities. These can be compared with regard to priority, where higher priority counts as "smaller". This feature aids insertion into queues.

`Event` abstracts general functionality for events. All events store their time and a reference to the entity they are associated with. Both values are passed as parameters to the event's constructor function. Event times are relative; i.e. `new Event ("Arrival", customer, 10.0)` means that a new arrival event for the *customer* object should occur in 10 model time units. Trying to schedule events into a model's past (i.e. for a time smaller than the current value of the simulation clock) raises a `NegativeSimTimeException`. Events are ordered by event time (earlier event times are considered "smaller") and – if event times are equal – by priority (events with higher priority are considered "smaller"). The abstract `eventRoutine()` method must be implemented by the modeller in form of model specific subclasses for making all relevant changes of state. `getEntity()` can be used to refer to the entity with which the event is associated.

`ExternalEvent` is an abstract class for modelling *external* events; i.e. events whose conceptual creation lies outside the model and which are not associated with any entity. Its only difference to the `Event` class is that its creation refers to no entity and invoking the `getEntity()` method will raise a `java.lang.IllegalStateException`.

A `SimStopEvent` is used to tell the scheduler to terminate simulation runs.

A `NegativeSimTimeException` is raised whenever event times are smaller than the current value of the model clock. Some informative information should be provided when this exception is caught.

6.3.3 Distribution Sampling, Data Collection, and Queueing

This step extends the *DES* simulation library with class definitions catering for the generation of random numbers and variates, statistical data collection, and queueing scenarios. Figure 6.4 surveys a possible implementation:

Chapter 6 First Steps in Simulation Programming

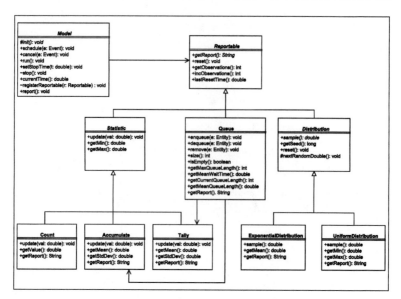

Figure 6.4: Class diagram for statistical distributions, data collection, and queueing

Reportable offers an abstract base class for all model components for which a report should be generated; e.g. random streams or statistical data collectors. Each object instantiated from one of its subclasses owns a counter for observations (e.g. number of random samples). This can be incremented with incObservations(), accessed with getObservations(), and reset to zero with reset(). A reset remembers its model time, which can be retrieved via lastResetTime(). The abstract method getReport() must be implemented by subclasses so that some text is returned. Reportable objects should register with their model after creation. The method registerReportable() serves this purpose.

Distribution is an abstract class which represents sources for random variates (i.e. samples from specified distributions). It encapsulates the random number generator of java.util.Random and uses that object's nextRandomDouble() method to create uniform random numbers over the [0,1] interval. The *seed* of this generator is passed as an argument to a distribution's constructor and can be read with getSeed(). The method reset() sets both number of observations to zero (e.g. to cater for "warm up" phases of simulation runs) and puts seeds back to their original values (to allow generating the same sequence of numbers again). The sample() method must be imple-

154

6.3 A Simple Java Class Library for Event-Oriented Simulation

mented as needed by each distribution subclass; e.g. a uniform, normal, or exponential distribution (see Section 7.2).

To generate suitable output, the Model class must be extended with some new properties and methods. Each model now keeps a list, which registerReportable() fills with reportable objects. When a report() is requested, a model uses this list to ask all of its reportable components for contributions.

Statistic is the abstract superclass of data collectors. These must all implement update() to record observations. The method update() is called whenever a model entity wants to provide a new value; e.g. when a queue changes its length. This value must be of type double. The functionality to record minima and maxima is implemented as part of Statistic.

While fully fledged discrete event simulation frameworks provide much more variety, here two classes for random variate generation, modelling *uniform* and a *negative exponential* distributions, are used to exemplify the structure of sampling objects.

- ❑ UniformDistribution is a distribution of values spread evenly over an interval bracketed by a lower and upper bound. These two boundary values (min and max) must be passed as arguments to its constructor and can be read via corresponding access methods. A UniformDistribution's report shows the distribution's parameters as well as the number of observations (observations), the time of the last reset (reset), and the seed of the generator (seed).

- ❑ ExponentialDistribution offers the means to sample an exponential distribution with a specified mean. As for the uniform distribution, this mean is passed its constructor at object creation time and can be queried. The information contained in an ExponentialDistribution's report is very similar to that in a UniformDistribution's report.

Distribution parameters passed to constructors are tested for plausibility (e.g. max > min). Any errors and inconsistencies raise an IllegalArgumentException, which should be caught and reported with suitable explanation.

Three classes are provided for data collection. All are implemented as subclasses of Statistic, which is itself derived from Reportable.

- ❑ A Count implements simple counters, which start at zero and can be incremented and decremented. update(double value) passes a value which will be added to a count's current value. Passing a negative value decrements counters. getValue() returns a counter's current state and getMin() and getMax() report minima and maxima since the last reset(). Counter reports should list current value, minimum, maximum, number of observations, and time of last reset. Resetting sets values to zero.

- ❑ A Tally records time series data. For this purpose it keeps a list of values (initially empty and of type double), for example of customer waiting times, which it uses to compute means, standard deviations, and minima and maxima on demand. update(double value) adds a new list value and increments the

Chapter 6 First Steps in Simulation Programming

number of observations. `getMin()`, `getMax()`, `getMean()`, and `getStdDev()` query the relevant statistics. Together with the number of observations and time of last reset these also form the contents of a tally's report.

❑ An `Accumulate` produces the same report and offers the same interface functionality as a tally. In contrast to a tally's statistics, however, an `Accumulate` observes *time-weighted* data; i.e. each value is tagged with the length of time over which it has been observed. This is, for example, needed to measure a utilization in terms of the percentage of the sum of all busy periods during a specified interval. Each invocation of `update(double value)` results in a tuple of (new value, time of change) to be stored. Time weighted means and standard variations can be computed from these tuples by multiplying each observation's value with its duration (time of next change minus time of current change).

Completion of the *DES* framework still needs an implementation for a FIFO *queue* of model entities. One possible structure encapsulates Java's internal `java.util.LinkedList` data structure for storing queued objects and offers public `enqueue()` and `dequeue()` methods for queue insertion and queued objects' removal. While `dequeue()` will always remove the queue's head in a FIFO fashion (or returns `null` when the queue should be empty), `remove()` can be used to remove a specified entity. This assumes that we hold a suitable reference and the entity is in fact a queue member. Otherwise `null` is returned. A simple and sometimes useful extension of basic queueing behaviour would allow priorities to be used as part of a queueing discipline.

Relevant statistics kept and reported by a `Queue` object include:

❑ maximum, mean, and current queue lengths
❑ mean wait times for all entities which have both entered and left the queue
❑ number of entities which immediately left the queue (with no delay)
❑ number of observations; i.e. number of entities which have both entered and left the queue

An `incObservation()` method should be provided to facilitate the recording of data for the last of these statistics. Internally `Count`, `Tally`, and `Accumulate` objects may be used for a queue's data collection, but, since queues produce reports of their own, these object's reports should be suppressed. A queue's priority rule (e.g. FIFO) and the time of its last reset should be included in its report and generic `reset()` functionality must be suitably redefined.

6.3.4 Example

It would be instructive to test the described *DES* class library by using it for a simple example. A simplified simulation of the shore operation of a container terminal can serve this purpose. Here we model the unloading of trucks with van-carriers, which are specialized transportation vehicles used in a port's container terminals. Let us assume that 2 van-carriers are available for unloading, which takes 3 to 7 minutes (uniformly distributed). Trucks which cannot find any available van-carrier after arrival must queue. This also holds for van-carriers. To facilitate the recording of suitable utilization statistics, we assume that they are filed into a line of either idle or busy van-carriers. Figure 6.5 shows this scenario.

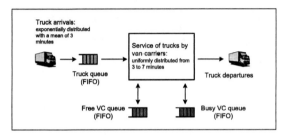

Figure 6.5: Conceptual diagram of a test model for the DES library

Further Reading

Today, many textbooks covering the Java programming language are available. Nevertheless, for many Java programmers and developers D. Flanagans's *Java in a Nutshell* (which once defined O'Reilly's "in a Nutshell"-series) is still the first resource: This book offers an introduction to the Java programming language and the key APIs and a Programmer's guide as well as a detailed package-by-package reference. The latest edition (2002) pays a great deal of attention to framework programming, and of course it includes an in-depth discussion of all changes Java 5.0 has undergone. The combination of practical advice, extensive reference, and (last but not least) a wealth of code examples illustrating the working of the APIs make this book an indispensable companion the programmer always keeps at his or her side.

Bibliography

D. J. Barnes and M. Kölling. *Objects first with Java. A practical Introduction using BLUEJ*. Prentice Hall, Harlow, 2003.

D. Flanagan. *Java in a Nutshell*. O'Reilly, Sebastopol, 5th edition, 2002.

B. Page. *Diskrete Simulation – Eine Einführung mit Modula-2* ("Discrete Simulation – An Introduction with Modula-2", in German). Springer, Berlin, 1991.

B. Page, T. Lechler, and S. Claassen. *Objektorientierte Simulation in Java mit dem Framework DESMO-J* ("Object-Oriented Simulation in Java with the Framework DESMO-J", in German). Libri Book on Demand, Hamburg, 2000.

Bibliography

O. Spaniol and S. Hoff. *Ereignisorientierte Simulation – Konzepte und Systemrealisierung* ("Event-Oriented Simulation – Concepts and System Implementation", in German). Thomson's Aktuelle Tutorien; 7. Thomson, Bonn, 1995.

Sun Microsystems. The Java Tutorial, 2004. [Online] `http://java.sun.com/docs/books/tutorial/index.html` (in August 2005).

M. Waite and R. Lafore. *Data Structures & Algorithms in Java*. O'Reilly, Corte Madera, 2nd edition, 1998.

Chapter 7

Simulation Statistics

Bernd Page, Julia Kuck, Johannes Göbel

Contents

7.1	Motivation and Overview		159
7.2	Creating Random Numbers		161
	7.2.1	General Approach	161
	7.2.2	The Java Random Number Generator	168
7.3	Estimating an Input Distribution		170
7.4	Analysing a Simulation Experiment		173
	7.4.1	Repeating a Simulation Run	173
	7.4.2	Stationary Model States	174
	7.4.3	Warm-up Phases and Steady States	174
	7.4.4	Analysing Simulation Results	179
7.5	Observing a Simulation Experiment		185
	7.5.1	Independent Replications	185
	7.5.2	Batch Means	186
	7.5.3	Terminating and Non-Stationary Systems	188
7.6	Sample Size and Simulation Experiments		188
7.7	Choosing Good Model Parameters		189
7.8	Conclusion		191
Further Reading			192
Bibliography			192

7.1 Motivation and Overview

Discrete event simulation models are characterized by stochastic components, which reflect random factors in a modelled system as much as abstractions from detail performed by the model's designer. Model *inputs*, in particular, are stochastic by their nature. Arrival times at a server, for example, may be represented by statistical distributions

Chapter 7 Simulation Statistics

whose shape and parameters were derived from empirical data. This implies that simulation *results* are also stochastic – i.e. they may differ from run to run – and that we must conduct careful statistical analyses at the end of each simulation experiment.

An adequate understanding of elementary statistics and probability theory is therefore a precondition for competent use of simulation techniques and is needed in many phases of model development and application, such as:

- data preparation and collection
- experimental design
- analysis of simulation results

The relevant methodologies cover a wide range and form a complex topic, which is discussed comprehensively in many simulation textbooks. While we agree on the importance of competent statistical analyses for the quality and success of a simulation study, we have chosen to emphasise model design and implementation issues in this handbook; an area whose treatment falls short in many other texts. However, some of the most important statistical design and analysis methods will be discussed in this chapter.

Although sound statistical designs and analyses are indeed important, one should also bear in mind that at today's state of technological development execution speed is much less of an issue than it was in the past and that it may therefore be counterproductive to invest too much effort in complex methods for run time reduction. An example for this are various variance reduction techniques, which we will therefore not cover at all. Instead, we will look only at "robust" methods which can be applied across a wide range of models.

Some knowledge of elementary statistical methods will be assumed. Readers without such a background should refer to a statistics text (e.g. Feller 1968) for more detail. The aim of this chapter is to foster an understanding of simulation runs as stochastic experiments, which must be based on sound empirical data and core competence in how to use elementary statistical methods in different phases of a simulation project.

To achieve this, the chapter covers a range of techniques. Section 7.2 teaches how to create random numbers, which are crucial for modelling a stochastic process. "Raw" random numbers must be transformed into samples from distributions, which may be empirically determined or specified by a standard formula. How to estimate theoretical distributions and their parameters from empirical data is the topic of Section 7.3. Since models with stochastic components will produce stochastic results, such results must be subject to statistical analyses. Section 7.4 looks at some of the most common techniques; e.g. replication of runs, "warm-up" phases and steady state detection, and the computation of confidence intervals to quantify a result's credibility. How to generate standard model instrumentation data (e.g. queue lengths, server utilization) is covered in Section 7.5. This is followed by a discussion of how many observations (sample size) will be needed to achieve a specified level of accuracy (in Section 7.6). Since simulation relies on sound experimentation and does not produce automatic optimizations, the

7.2 Creating Random Numbers

decision on what variations to explore is very important for its success. Section 7.7 therefore discusses how to choose good model parameters. Section 7.8 summarizes the chapter.

7.2 Creating Random Numbers

Simulation models with random components are categorized as stochastic. Most interesting discrete event models are of this type. In this context it is irrelevant whether this randomness is genuine (e.g. the decay of a radioactive particle) or just a reflection of our lack of understanding of an unknown and complex phenomenon, whose details we do not wish to investigate further. *External events*, whose causal roots lie outside a model's domain (e.g. order arrivals in a warehouse), are an example for the second case. Within a simulation we can represent such patterns through *stochastic variables*; i.e. variables whose values are determined by sampling a stream of random numbers. While this approach reduces both data collection and computational efforts considerably, we must bear in mind that it provides only an *approximation* to the modelled phenomena. How good an approximation is will depend on the accuracy of our observations, our knowledge about the modelled system, and the quality of the random numbers used to create sample streams.

This section first discusses general techniques for creating random number streams and then looks at how Java (i.e. java.util.Random) can be used for this task.

7.2.1 General Approach

A *random number generator* is a method for choosing a number from a set of numbers, with a specified probability for each possible choice. Normally, we formulate such probabilities in the form of a *statistical distribution*. Typical examples are the *discrete uniform* distribution, the *rectangular* distribution (or continuous uniform distribution), or the *exponential* distribution. In a discrete uniform distribution, all numbers from 1 to n inclusive have the same chance of being chosen, while all intervals of the same length are equally probable in a rectangular distribution. Exponential distributions are characterized by the distribution function

$$F(x) = \begin{cases} 0 & \text{for } x \leq 0 \\ 1 - e^{-\frac{1}{\mu}x} & \text{for } x > 0 \end{cases}, \quad (7.1)$$

where μ is the distribution's expected value.

Simulations typically require *streams* of random numbers instead of just single values. Orders by different customers during different periods of time are an example. It is important that numbers in such streams are *statistically independent* and that they do not repeat themselves in a cycle (or at least only in very long ones). Limit points must not occur unless predicted by the relevant distribution.

Chapter 7 Simulation Statistics

Since computers are deterministic and discrete state devices, it is obviously impossible to generate statistically independent random numbers by using any algorithmic method. We must therefore either use some external techniques (i.e. by referring to a stochastic device or by reading genuine random numbers from files) or be content with so-called *pseudo-randomness*. Even though the methods of generating pseudo-random numbers are deterministic, they can safely be used in place of "real" random numbers if they pass a set of relevant statistical tests for uniformity and independence. It is highly desirable that any method for generating such numbers has a long period; i.e. number sequences should not repeat themselves too quickly.

Methods for pseudo-random number generation typically consist of one or more mathematical operations, which are recursively applied to an expanding series of values. Performing these operations with the same starting value (*seed*) will repeat the same number sequence. Seeds should be chosen with care. While they could also be chosen "at random" (e.g. by sampling a computer's milliseconds clock), this usually proves to be inconvenient, since the reproducibility of the same random sequence by starting from a specified seed can be used to advantage during a model's debugging phase or for comparing two different strategies for the same scenario; e.g. for comparing different ordering rules while customer demand (a stochastic variable) remains the same.k,

While statistical independence and uniformity of pseudo-random number streams are of great importance, run time and storage aspects should also be considered when choosing a "good" generator. Since many simulations require long run times, during which they may consume long random streams, the effect of a faster generator on the duration of an experiment can be dramatic.

Another aspect of computers which an astute model designer must bear in mind is their limited numerical accuracy. Java, for example, offers two data types for floating point numbers: `float` and `double` (stored in either 4 or 8 bytes). This means that it is impossible to sample continuous distributions in any strict sense. We must instead be content with approximations; e.g. by generating integers distributed from 0 to some very large number n; division by n then returns an approximation to a rectangular distribution from 0 to 1 (so-called *normalized* random numbers). Conversely, we can multiply these numbers by n and then round up the result to compute integer samples from 1 to n; e.g. from 1 to 6 to model a die.

The quest for good random generators is almost as old as the digital computer itself. John von Neumann, a famous mathematician and the inventor of the stored program concept, proposed the *middle-square method* to serve this purpose already in 1946. This algorithm calculates number sequences by repetitively computing the squares of a number's n middle digits and using the result as a base for computing the next number. To generate a new 10 digit random number, for example, we would square the previous random number and screen out the result's ten middle digits. If 3,328,054,492 was the last number, we would compute

$$3,328,054,492^2 = 11,075,\underline{946,701,721},378,064 \qquad (7.2)$$

7.2 Creating Random Numbers

and the new random number would be 9,467,017,213. It quickly becomes apparent that one weakness of this method lies in the fact that once we start generating zeros they will stay part of all further results. Number sequences may therefore degenerate rather quickly. Another disadvantage is that some numbers (e.g. those with middle zeros) occur more frequently than others; a tendency which is confirmed by some simple statistical tests (see Section 7.3).

Congruential generators are a much more useful family of algorithms for creating discrete uniform random sequences, and the *linear congruential method* invented by Lehmer in 1948 is still the most widely used algorithm for this purpose today. In the **Random** class in Java's standard utilities library, this method is used (see Section 7.2.2).

Linear congruential generators can be customized through four parameters: the modulus m, a multiplier a, an additive constant c, and a seed value x_0. To create integers $(x_i)_{(i \in \mathbb{N})}$ from 0 to $m-1$, we evaluate the recursion

$$x_{n+1} = (a\,x_n + c) \bmod m \qquad (7.3)$$

The "quality" (i.e. its statistical randomness) of number sequences generated in this fashion critically depends on good choices for x_0, m, a, and c. If we choose $x_0 = 3$, $m = 10$, $a = 7$, and $c = 5$, we get: $3, 6, 7, 4, 3, 6, 7, 4, 3, 6, 7, 4, \ldots$ This is not a good sequence, since it has only a short period length of 4. Only 4 out of 10 possible digits (0 to 9) occur: 3, 4, 6, and 7. To achieve better coverage, we should have chosen better parameter values. Obviously the maximum period will be limited by m (the modulus), which we should therefore choose as large as possible. For efficiency it is also advantageous if m is 1 smaller than a power of 2, since its binary representation will then consist solely of ones and the modulo operation can simply be done with a logical AND. The additive constant c should be relative prime to m, which means that the greatest common divisor of both c and m will be 1. If $c = 0$, we talk of a *multiplicative* congruential generator, and we refer to a *mixed* multiplicative congruential generator if it is not. Other less obvious constraints on good parameter values are discussed in Knuth (1997, pp. 10–25) – a standard reference for this field. Knuth shows, for example, that for sequences to be able to reach their maximum period, $a - 1$ must be a multiple of every prime dividing m.

As mentioned, we can divide by n to map integers distributed uniformly between 0 and n to an approximation of a rectangular distribution of real numbers from 0 to 1. In practice, however, we must be able to generate samples from a wide variety of statistical distributions, with a wide range of parameters. Instead of inventing a new generator for each of these cases, we should look for more general transformations between distributions: If we can find a cumulative distribution function for a given distribution, we can use an inverse transformation. If, for example, values of $(u_i)_{(i \in \mathbb{N})}$ follow a rectangular distribution from 0 to 1, we can determine exponential distributed random numbers $(x_i)_{(i \in \mathbb{N})}$ with an expected value of μ by computing the inverse function of equation 7.1:

$$x_i = -\mu \ln(1 - u_i) \qquad (7.4)$$

Chapter 7 Simulation Statistics

Figure 7.1 visualizes the steps needed to compute this inverse transformation from rectangular random numbers distributed between 0 and n.

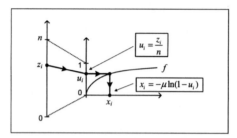

Figure 7.1: Generating exponentially distributed random numbers

Some distributions have no inverse transformation. In the case of the normal distribution for example, no closed form of its cumulative distribution function $\Phi(\frac{x-a}{\sigma})$ (see Table 7.1) exists. Therefore, we must resort to approximations, which must be customized for each distribution type. Sampling a normal distribution can use the polar technique described by Knuth (1997, p. 122). This method is also used by java.util.Random (see Section 7.2.2).

A number of theoretical distribution types are often derived from empirical data (see Section 7.3 and frequently used in simulation models. Tables 7.1 and 7.2 show parameters and typical applications for a number of these.

Note that $f(x)$ denotes the probability density function of each distribution. $F(x)$ refers to the cumulative distribution function for continuous distributions. EX is the expected value (mean) and $\text{Var}(X)$ the variance of a random variable X of the relevant distribution.

Nevertheless, not all empirical data can be described by one of these theoretical distributions. For example, we assume that the response times of a database server vary between 0 and 800 milliseconds (ms). Table 7.3 shows a possible distribution of measured response time data according to eight classes (0 to 100, 101 to 200, ..., 701 to 800). In the table each class is represented by its mean.

A graphical representation of this empirical distribution is shown by the bar chart on the left of Figure 7.2. Using this distribution for sampling requires some knowledge about the distribution of values in each of the classes. If the number of classes is large, we can avoid any significant errors if we assume a rectangular distribution. This assumption leads to the empirical continuous distribution function shown on the right in Figure 7.2.

We can apply the inverse transformation method again to generate a stream of appropriately distributed random samples. If the values of $(u_i)_{(i \in \mathbb{N})}$ are rectangularly

7.2 Creating Random Numbers

Table 7.1: Characteristics of important discrete statistical distributions

Discrete Distributions		
Fixed Value *a* fixed value	$f(a) = 1$	$\mathrm{E}\,X = a$ $\mathrm{Var}(X) = 0$
The fixed value distribution has only a single possible value. There is therefore no "randomness". In some cases this distribution can be very useful; e.g. for debugging and for comparisons of different distributions' effects on simulation results.		
Discrete Uniform *N* number of events	$f(k) = \frac{1}{N}$ for $1 \leq k \leq N$	$\mathrm{E}\,X = \frac{1}{2}(N+1)$ $\mathrm{Var}(X) = \frac{1}{12}(N^2 - 1)$
The discrete uniform (or *Laplace*) distribution assigns the same probability to each of *N* events. It is often used where no better estimates can be given.		
Bernoulli *p* event probability	$f(0) = 1 - p$ $f(1) = p$	$\mathrm{E}\,X = p$ $\mathrm{Var}(X) = p(1 - p)$
The Bernoulli distribution describes the pattern of randomness generated by two events with fixed probabilities. For example, whether a machine will produce a product within a given quality range.		
Binomial *p* event probability *N* number of attempts	$f(k) = \binom{N}{k} p^k (1-p)^{N-k}$ for $0 \leq k \leq N$	$\mathrm{E}\,X = Np$ $\mathrm{Var}(X) = Np(1 - p)$
The binomial distribution describes the effect of *N* replications of a Bernoulli experiment.		
Negative Binomial *p* event probability *r* number of desired successes	$f(k) = \binom{k-1}{r-1} p^r (1-p)^{k-r}$ for $r \leq k$	$\mathrm{E}\,X = \frac{r}{p}$ $\mathrm{Var}(X) = \frac{r(1-p)}{p^2}$
The negative binomial distribution captures the probability that *k* replications of a Bernoulli experiment will be needed to generate *r* successful samples. In analogy to the Bernoulli example, it can be used for characterizing the probability that a machine will need 5, 6, 7... attempts to produce a total of 5 products within a given quality range.		
Geometric *p* event probability	$f(k) = (1-p)^k p$ for $0 \leq k$	$\mathrm{E}\,X = \frac{1-p}{p}$ $\mathrm{Var}(X) = \frac{1-p}{p^2}$
The geometric distribution describes the probability that exactly *k* Bernoulli experiments will fail before the first success. For example, if a system allows only a single customer to arrive in each time interval (with fixed probability), the length of time between arrivals will be geometrically distributed.		
Poisson λ expected value of approximated binomial distribution	$f(k) = e^{-\lambda} \frac{\lambda^k}{k!}$ for $0 \leq k$	$\mathrm{E}\,X = \lambda$ $\mathrm{Var}(X) = \lambda$
A Poisson distribution approximates a binomial distribution well if *p* is small and *N* large. $\lambda = Np$ is the expected value of the approximated distribution. As long as the chosen interval is quite short, Poisson distributions can be successfully used to describe e.g. the number of arrivals of customer's telephone calls in a model.		

Chapter 7 Simulation Statistics

Table 7.2: Characteristics of important continuous statistical distributions

Continuous Distributions

Rectangular a lower bound b upper bound	$f(x) = \begin{cases} 0 & \text{for } x \leq a \\ \frac{1}{b-a} & \text{for } a < x < b \\ 0 & \text{for } b \leq x \end{cases}$	$F(x) = \begin{cases} 0 & \text{for } x \leq a \\ \frac{x-a}{b-a} & \text{for } a < x < b \\ 1 & \text{for } b \leq x \end{cases}$
	$\mathrm{E}\,X = \frac{1}{2}(a+b)$	$\mathrm{Var}(X) = \frac{1}{12}(b-a)^2$

Random numbers which follow a rectangular distribution (or continuous uniform distribution) are distributed over an interval $[a, b]$, whose subintervals all have the same probability of occurrence. While this type of distribution is rare in reality, it is useful where no better knowledge is available and cannot be obtained with acceptable effort. Rectangular distributions are also used in the inverse transformation method we have mentioned above.

Triangular a lower bound b upper bound c mode	$f(x) = \begin{cases} 0 & \text{for } x \leq a \\ \frac{2(x-a)}{(b-a)(c-a)} & \text{for } a < x \leq c \\ \frac{2(b-x)}{(b-a)(b-c)} & \text{for } c < x < b \\ 0 & \text{for } b \leq x \end{cases}$	$F(x) = \begin{cases} 0 & \text{for } x \leq a \\ \frac{(x-a)^2}{(b-a)(c-a)} & \text{for } a < x \leq c \\ 1 - \frac{(b-x)^2}{(b-a)(b-c)} & \text{for } c < x < b \\ 1 & \text{for } b \leq x \end{cases}$
	$\mathrm{E}\,X = \frac{1}{3}(a+b+c)$	$\mathrm{Var}(X) = \frac{1}{18}(a^2 + b^2 + c^2 + ab + ac + bc)$

In contrast to a rectangular distribution, in a triangular distribution values closer to the mode occur more probably than values near a or b. The sum of two independent rectangular distributions with equal interval length forms a triangular distribution. Triangularly distributed random numbers are also used where apart from other indications only knowledge about frequent values (in addition to lower and upper bounds) is available. Capacity estimates for natural resources like coal mines or oil wells are an example.

Exponential μ expected value	$f(x) = \begin{cases} 0 & \text{for } x \leq 0 \\ \frac{1}{\mu} e^{-\frac{1}{\mu}x} & \text{for } x > 0 \end{cases}$	$F(x) = \begin{cases} 0 & \text{for } x \leq 0 \\ 1 - e^{-\frac{1}{\mu}x} & \text{for } x > 0 \end{cases}$
	$\mathrm{E}\,X = \mu$	$\mathrm{Var}(X) = \mu^2$

The exponential distribution is the continuous counterpart of the geometric distribution. Inter-arrival times of customers or orders in systems without fixed time intervals follow exponential distributions.

Erlang μ expected value n distributions to add	$f(x) = \begin{cases} 0 & \text{for } x \leq 0 \\ \frac{x^{n-1} e^{-\frac{1}{\mu}x}}{\mu^n (n-1)!} & \text{for } x > 0 \end{cases}$	$F(x) = \begin{cases} 0 & \text{for } x \leq 0 \\ 1 - e^{-\frac{1}{\mu}x} \sum_{i=0}^{n-1} \frac{x^i}{\mu^i i!} & \text{for } x > 0 \end{cases}$
	$\mathrm{E}\,X = n\mu$	$\mathrm{Var}(X) = n\mu^2$

The Erlang distribution is created by a convolution of n independent exponential distributions. In practice this is done by adding n exponentially distributed random numbers for each sample. Erlang distributions describe waiting times in a queueing system. Characterizing the lifetime of products or the length of time between system failures are other common examples for their application.

Normal a expected value σ^2 variance	$f(x) = \frac{1}{\sqrt{2\pi}\sigma} e^{-\frac{(x-a)^2}{2\sigma^2}}$	$F(x) = \int_{-\infty}^{x} f(u)\,du =: \Phi(\frac{x-a}{\sigma})$
	$\mathrm{E}\,X = a$	$\mathrm{Var}(X) = \sigma^2$

The normal distribution is the continuous counterpart of the Binomial or Poisson distribution. The sum of "sufficiently" many Bernoulli or Poisson distributed random processes (e.g. the number of customer arrivals during a given time span) approximates a normal distribution. This is an implication of the *central limit theorem* (see 7.4.4). The sum of measurement errors or the number of order completions of a machine with stochastic processing times provide good examples for this.

7.2 Creating Random Numbers

Table 7.3: Empirical frequencies of response times for a database server (250 samples)

response time (ms)	50	150	250	350	450	550	650	750
number of samples	4	35	22	41	63	30	43	12
relative frequency	0.016	0.140	0.088	0.164	0.252	0.120	0.172	0.048
cumulative frequency	0.016	0.156	0.244	0.408	0.660	0.780	0.952	1.000

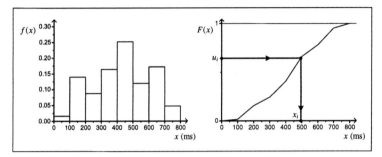

Figure 7.2: Relative frequency and distribution functions for the empirical distribution of Table 7.3

distributed between 0 and 1, we obtain a random sequence $(x_i)_{(i \in \mathbb{N})}$ following the relevant empirical distribution by using the transformation

$$x_i = x_i^{\downarrow} + (u_i - F(x_i^{\downarrow})) \frac{x_i^{\uparrow} - x_i^{\downarrow}}{F(x_i^{\uparrow}) - F(x_i^{\downarrow})}. \tag{7.5}$$

Here $x_i^{\downarrow}$ is the largest interval limit with $F(x_i^{\downarrow}) \leq u_i$ and $x_i^{\uparrow}$ is the smallest interval limit with $F(x_i^{\uparrow}) > u_i$. In this way we obtain e.g. for $u_i = 0.647$ that $x_i^{\downarrow} = 400$ and $x_i^{\uparrow} = 500$ (because of $F(400) = 0.408 \leq 0.647 < 0.660 = F(500)$) and therefore

$$x_i = 400 + (0.647 - 0.408) \frac{500 - 400}{0.660 - 0.408} \approx 495. \tag{7.6}$$

Random samples from discrete empirical distributions can be generated in a similar fashion. Table 7.4, for example, shows frequency measures for customer orders.

Table 7.4: Discrete frequencies of items per order

order volume (items)	1	2	3	4	5
relative frequency	0.32	0.14	0.11	0.38	0.05
cumulative frequency	0.32	0.46	0.57	0.95	1.00

Figure 7.3 displays them as a bar chart (left) and plots the corresponding distribution function (right). Note the stepped nature of the distribution function, which serves as

Chapter 7 Simulation Statistics

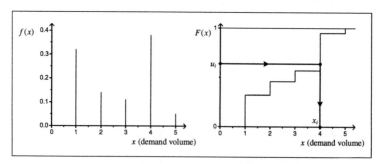

Figure 7.3: Relative frequency and distribution functions for the discrete distribution of Table 7.4

the base for an inverse transformation similar to the one we described for continuous distributions above. Here the transformation is particular simple, since the interval $[0, 1]$ must only be partitioned proportionally to the relative frequencies of events (i.e. order volumes). Table 7.5 shows the result; for $u_i = 0.647$ we would sample a value of $x_i = 4$.

Table 7.5: Partitioning the interval $[0, 1]$ according to table 7.4

random number $u_i \in$	$[0, 0.32)$	$[0.32, 0.46)$	$[0.46, 0.57)$	$[0.57, 0.95)$	$[0.95, 1]$
relative frequency	0.32	0.14	0.11	0.38	0.05
cumulative frequency	0.32	0.46	0.57	0.95	1.00
order volume (items)	1	2	3	4	5

We have already mentioned the need for testing the "randomness" of a generator in a statistical sense since biased random sequences can strongly influence the representativeness of a simulation's result. A test that serves this purpose is the *Chi-square test*, which we will look at in Section 7.3 in the context of input data distribution estimation. Since a model developer will hopefully only rely on well tested random generators (e.g. the ones offered by Java – see 7.2.2), there will rarely be any need to perform such tests directly. However, s/he should be aware of the importance of good random sequences and justified confidence in whatever off-the-shelf generator is being used.

7.2.2 The Java Random Number Generator

The Java Utility Package provides java.util.Random. This class, whose UML diagram is shown in Figure 7.4, encapsulates Java's random drawing facilities, which include sampling from discrete uniform distributions based on a linear congruential method.

Instances of java.util.Random can be created in two different ways:

7.2 Creating Random Numbers

```
        Random
       from java.util
#next(int bits): int
+nextBoolean(): boolean
+nextBytes(byte[] bytes): void
+nextDouble(): double
+nextFloat(): float
+nextGaussian(): double
+nextInt(): int
+nextInt(int n): int
+nextLong(): long
+setSeed(long seed): void
```

Figure 7.4: Class diagram of Java's class Random

- By using the Random(long seed) constructor. This method is passed a seed value (x_0), so that we can reproduce a sequence.
- By using the parameterless Random() constructor. In this case Java will sample the computer's millisecond clock to determine a seed "at random".

By sending a setSeed(long seed) message, seed values (which then take the place of the most recently generated number) can be altered at any time.

Internally random numbers are created by invoking the next(int bits) method, which returns a random sample of specified length (in bits, with a recommended maximum of 32 bits). This method uses a linear congruential generator with parameter values of $m = 25,214,903,917$, $a = 11$, and $d = 281,474,976,710,655$ $(= 2^{48} - 1)$. These settings allow maximum periods of 2^{48}. Only the most significant bits (as many as asked for) of each number are returned.

java.util.Random's protocol includes public methods nextBoolean(), nextDouble(), nextFloat(), nextInt(), and nextLong().

nextBoolean() returns *true* or *false* with equal probability, and the others return uniformly distributed random numbers across the whole range of the relevant data type. Since the binary representations of double and long require 64 bits, two consecutive random numbers (generated by calling next(int bits) twice) are concatenated for each returned value. float and double values will always lie between 0 and 1. These are obtained by using the method discussed in Section 7.2.1. nextByte(byte[] bytes) can be used to create random bytes in the same fashion, as long as the user passes a Byte array, which the method will then fill with random values.

nextInt(int n), the parametrized form of nextInt(), can be particularly useful. It returns an integer random number between 0 and $n-1$, which in essence it computes from the whole range of integers modulo n.

Chapter 7 Simulation Statistics

nextGaussian() generates random numbers which approximate a standard normal distribution (i.e. a normal distribution with mean 0 and standard deviation of 1). Its return type is double. The polar method described in Knuth (1997, p. 122) is used for this.

No class instantiations are needed if we only require a non-reproducible stream of type double, distributed between 0 and 1. In this case we can use class java.lang.Math's static random() method. Math.random() will automatically create an appropriate generator, using the computer's milliseconds clock to sample a seed.

7.3 Estimating an Input Distribution

In previous chapters we have seen that simulation input (e.g. inter-arrival times, demand volumes, transportation times, service, and processing times) is often stochastic in nature. This "randomness" makes simulation the only viable means of analysis for studying many complex dynamic systems. To support this task, we must estimate or derive suitable empirical and theoretical distributions from available data. While *empirical distributions* can faithfully reflect a real system's behaviour during a period of observation, *theoretical distributions* (e.g. normal, exponential, Erlang, binomial, or uniform distributions – see Tables 7.1 and 7.2) can be derived from empirical data, tempered with any additional insight a modeller may be able to contribute. Theoretical distributions are often simpler to handle and reduce a study's dependency on situation specific data. They can therefore give a more generalized view of the observed random processes.

The first step in determining a model's input distributions requires the identification of all relevant model parameters and the collection of data for those whose values we can quantify and observe. If such quantities are not deterministic and not known from any physical or technological context, we must record information about their behaviour by observing the system we wish to study. Time-varying stochastic measures in particular must be empirically collected and statistically analysed, a process which poses a number of practical problems (see Section 16.5).

To analyse the collected data, we often begin with a *descriptive analysis*, which is followed by some inductive statistical tests. Descriptive analyses include graphical representation. Frequency histograms (e.g. of customer inter-arrival times), for example, can offer high-level views of range, orientation, dispersion, and distribution types of an observed quantity. This can then be confirmed by applying more stringent tests of statistical fit.

Applying statistical tests, such as the Chi-square method, to empirical data can help us to answer the question of an input distribution's type and parameters (e.g. its mean). This *Goodness of Fit* test is also used to test the statistical quality of random sequences (i.e. their uniformity and independence).

7.3 Estimating an Input Distribution

Table 7.6 contains some raw data sampled from a computer-based system's response time (in hundredths of a second) to database queries. To confirm the hypothesis that the underlying random process can be accurately approximated by sampling a normal distribution, we will apply a *Chi-square* test (or χ^2 test) to this data. Note that the tested hypothesis may well have been inspired by a glance at the data's graphical representation.

Table 7.6: $n = 128$ response time measurements for a database query

44.0	42.8	40.8	41.4	44.4	43.9	42.8	44.0	42.2	44.8
43.3	42.5	43.5	44.7	45.8	42.0	45.2	41.1	43.8	43.8
42.9	43.7	45.8	41.4	42.6	45.0	44.5	41.6	44.3	43.5
43.8	44.4	43.2	42.3	42.0	41.2	44.1	45.5	43.0	39.8
43.2	44.9	42.6	40.1	43.2	43.0	42.7	43.5	44.0	44.8
44.5	44.0	42.7	44.0	42.3	44.2	44.8	41.7	43.7	42.4
43.5	44.3	43.7	45.4	44.6	42.4	45.5	40.8	44.3	43.7
44.1	46.1	45.3	43.6	43.0	46.8	44.8	42.9	45.3	44.1
43.8	42.5	46.0	44.4	42.0	45.4	44.0	45.3	42.0	42.9
44.2	43.9	43.5	42.1	44.2	44.2	43.8	41.7	46.5	43.5
44.5	44.8	45.2	43.6	42.3	43.5	43.5	46.0	43.6	44.0
42.0	41.1	43.4	45.0	44.2	42.8	42.0	46.1	43.4	42.6
46.7	44.5	44.0	44.8	43.3	42.7	43.1	43.8		

Since differences between the empirical data and theoretical expectations are highly likely, we employ a Chi-square test to choose between the following two mutually exclusive hypotheses:

- H_0: The response time frequencies in Table 7.6 are consistent with a normal distribution with a mean of 43.6 and a standard deviation of 1.4.
- H_1: The response time frequencies in Table 7.6 are not consistent with such a normal distribution.

To decide between these hypotheses, we need a *test statistic* which measures the deviation of observed *frequencies* f_i over a specified *range of values* (partitioned into equidistant *frequency classes*) from given theoretical expectations e_i; i.e. the expectation that it is indeed a normal distribution. If there are significant differences between actual and predicted frequencies, we will reject the so-called *null hypothesis* (H_0).

A popular test statistic for this purpose is

$$\chi^2 = \sum_{i=1}^{k} \frac{(f_i - e_i)^2}{e_i} \tag{7.7}$$

where χ^2 approximates the so-called χ^2 distribution (for $n \to \infty$) as introduced by Pearson.

Squaring the differences between observed and expected frequencies in the formula's numerator prevents positive differences from compensating for negative ones. It also

Chapter 7 Simulation Statistics

seems reasonable to normalize the expression with division by the theoretical expectation e_i; since a difference of e.g. $(1000 - 990)^2 = 100$ seems less significant than one of $(20 - 10)^2 = 100$.

The parameter f of the χ^2 distribution denotes its *degree of freedom*. This measure can be computed as 1 minus the number of frequency classes. We must reduce degrees of freedom if estimation of the theoretical distribution's parameters (e.g. its mean) is required. If there are k frequency classes and we must estimate m parameters, the degree of freedom becomes

$$f = k - m - 1. \tag{7.8}$$

If we chose e.g. 8 frequency classes ($k = 8$) and two parameters (mean and standard deviation), Formula 7.8 results in $f = 8 - 2 - 1 = 5$ degrees of freedom.

As a rule of thumb we assume that our approximation is adequate if a distribution is characterized by at least 50 observations and if all frequency classes are chosen so that they have at least 5 observations recorded (i.e. $e_i > 5$).

If empirical values differ too much from theoretical expectations, we must reject the hypothesis. This is reflected in too large a value for the χ^2 measure. If the null hypothesis H_0 is true, the χ^2 measure must asymptotically follow the χ^2 distribution with $f = 5$ degrees of freedom. A χ^2 table will tell us the critical value c, which our χ^2 measure must exceed to reject the H_0 hypothesis with a significance level of α. χ^2 tables can be consulted in any standard statistical text (e.g. Knuth 1997, p. 44). Of course, this will be automatically reported if a statistical software package is used. The critical value c is characterized by:

$$P(\chi^2 > c) = \alpha \tag{7.9}$$

This just means that we reject H_0 (e.g. the hypothesis that it is a normal distribution) if χ^2 is larger than c, and accept H_1 (e.g. the hypothesis that it is not a normal distribution) instead. How easily we reject or accept will depend on the chosen significance level. If, for example, we choose $\alpha = 0.05$, the probability for $\chi^2 > c$, if the empirical sample is taken from a normal distribution, becomes just 5 %. This measures the *type I* error, the *risk of rejecting H_0 erroneously*. With a maximum error of 5 %, we talk of a *significant* result. If the significance level were tightened to 1 %, we would talk of a *highly significant* result.

Since we are, however, more interested in confirming the normal distribution hypothesis H_0 and rejecting its negation H_1, we want to quantify the *risk of accepting H_0 erroneously*. Statistician's refer to this as a *type II error* (in contrast to the type I error we discussed before). In practical terms it is not all that important to quantify a type II error precisely. Since both error types are interdependent, it suffices if we do not set significance levels at too low a value (e.g. $\alpha = 0.3$). This will keep type II errors small.

Let us return to our example. If we choose $\alpha = 0.3$ and look up the value of c for 5 degrees of freedom, we get 6.06. If the χ^2 measure is smaller or equal to 6.06, we will therefore assume that our hypothesis that the empirical samples follow a normal distribution (with suitably estimated mean and variance) is correct. Shunning manual calculation and using a statistical software package, we obtain a χ^2 measure of 5.17, well within the acceptable range. We therefore assume that our normal distribution hypothesis with a mean of 43.6 and a deviation of 1.4 is correct and will use a corresponding theoretical distribution to represent this type of input within our model.

Provided the empirical sample is large enough, a Chi-square test can be applied to both discrete and continuous distributions. If sample sizes for a continuous distribution are small, the *Kolmogorov-Smirnov* test may be a better choice. It is also described in most statistical textbooks. Yet another method in this category is the *Poisson process* test.

In summary, we recommend a three step procedure for estimating a simulation models' input distributions. First we look at available empirical data and try to match it to a theoretical distribution (step 1). Kleijnen and van Groenendaal (1992, pp. 34–54) discuss a wide range of strategies and graphical data representation can be particularly helpful here. Once we suspect a specific distribution type, we must estimate relevant distribution parameters (step 2) and then test our hypothesis' goodness of fit; i.e. we must apply a statistical method to measure how closely the data matches our theoretical expectations (step 3).

7.4 Analysing a Simulation Experiment

Stochastic simulations generate large amounts of data, which must be presented in a clear and useful fashion. Since experiments with models containing stochastic components must be considered as random processes, suitable statistical evaluation plays a crucial role in this task. This section will therefore look at some possibilities for evaluating and analysing simulation results.

7.4.1 Repeating a Simulation Run

As stated, we must view all simulation experiments using random numbers as an exploration of state spaces defined by one or more stochastic processes. In this context we call a process $\{X_t | t \in \tau\}$ *stochastic* if it shows random behaviour over time. In that case we associate a random variable X_t with each instant t of time interval τ. Since they are all created by the same model, X's values (X_t) will likely be *autocorrelated* (i.e. they are algorithmically related) and will neither be independent nor identically distributed. Most standard statistical methods assume uncorrelated data, and evaluations of simulation results need to take this factor into account.

Simulation data analysis characterizes observed model behaviour by computing a number of measures. This computation can begin as soon as a simulation has terminated. If random generators are seeded with new starting values and a number of replications are used in place of a single simulation run, each replication provides an

Chapter 7 Simulation Statistics

estimate $\bar{X}_i$ for the "true" value of result parameter i. We must obtain a *sufficiently large* number of such estimates to gain confidence in the statistical representativeness of results. The more samples we take in this fashion, the better predictions about a model's probability space, i.e. its expected behaviour, we will be able to make. This is a general principle of *all* statistical methods.

7.4.2 Stationary Model States

In most cases we are interested in stationary stochastic processes and stationary phases of a simulation. We will refer to a process $\{X_t | t \in \tau\}$ as *stationary* if the probability of observation X_t does not depend on the value of t. Many stochastic processes converge to a stationary process over time. In such cases observing a model over a *sufficiently long* time interval would likely provide a relatively close approximation to its steady state behaviour. The time interval prior to reaching a stationary state is referred to as a "warm-up period", or initial transient, during whose duration observations cannot contribute to representative statistical measures. The simplest way to ensure that only significant data is analysed is to reset all statistical counters as soon as a steady state has been reached. Most simulation programming tools provide easy means for doing this.

Although most simulation studies are aimed at steady state analyses of a system, some *transient* effects may still be of interest. In a queueing model we may well wish to know what queue lengths occur from start-up until steady state is reached. This can, for example, help us to find a safe size for dimensioning waiting space.

Figure 7.5 shows a stochastic process' trajectory through its transient period towards a stationary state. Note that overestimation as well as underestimation of the initial period's duration can have a negative impact on the accuracy of a model's predictions. In the following sections we will therefore discuss some methods for dynamically (i.e. at run time) estimating an initial transient's length.

7.4.3 Warm-up Phases and Steady States

Since they may depend strongly on essentially arbitrary choices for initialising a model (e.g. stock levels and pending orders in an inventory model), no observation of model characteristics during a transient period must be included in any final statistical analyses. This means that we must find a way to detect when this phase is over and the model's stationary phase has begun. If we overestimate transient periods' length, we waste observations and lengthen run times due to a shorter stationary phase. Furthermore, we increase our estimates' variance, which will also increase run times if we require results at a specified confidence level. This is particularly undesirable if we need larger numbers of replications (see 7.5). If we, on the other hand, underestimate the initial transient's length, we may generate biased results. For this reason we must choose the length of a model's warm-up phase carefully, and we should make sure to

7.4 Analysing a Simulation Experiment

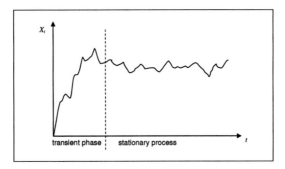

Figure 7.5: A *stationary* process and its initial transient phase

set its initial state close to the steady state we suspect. If this choice is made well, the model will likely reach steady state much more quickly.

There are 5 main categories of methods for steady state detection in simulation models:

- *Graphical methods* depend on visual inspection of data. Assuming a suitable representation for relevant time series, a model user may be able to detect stationary system states rather quickly.
- *Heuristic methods* are based on simple rules and are frequently customized for specific model classes; such as inventory models or queueing networks.
- *Statistical methods* use statistical tests to determine the end of a transient phase.
- Since a model's initial state can have a large impact on simulation results, it should be chosen to be both realistic and close to a steady state. This is of course not possible if such a state is unknown or if its discovery is itself the goal of the simulation. In such cases we can use a simulation's output to perform tests for estimating the *size of any initialisation error* step by step.
- *Hybrid methods* combine graphical, heuristic, and statistical analysis methods.

Although we only mention some particularly relevant and useful methods in this handbook, a much wider range of techniques is reported in the literature. Robinson (2002) gives a detailed survey and Pawlikowski (1990) presents 11 different rules for a stationary system states' detection.

Now we will look at three heuristic techniques and discuss some useful criteria. After that a statistical test for initialisation is presented.

Chapter 7 Simulation Statistics

Conway's Rule

Conway's simple rule tests for each value x_i of a stochastic sequence $x_1, \ldots, x_n$ whether it is a new minimum or maximum of the rest of the sequence $(x_{i+1}, \ldots, x_n)$. If this is the case, we assume that the value is part of the initial transient. Otherwise we explore the possibility that it indicates the start of a model's stationary state and apply further tests to confirm this hypothesis. Note that the observed sequence $x_1, \ldots, x_n$ need not contain single observations. Rather each value may itself be a mean computed from multiple observations.

We can modify Conway's rule if maxima or minima appear rather later in the series. Instead of looking at a value's successor, we can investigate its predecessor. In this case we start with x_n rather than x_1. If the predecessor x_{i-1} of a tested value (x_i) is neither a minimum nor maximum of the tested series $x_i, \ldots, x_n$, we suspect a stationary process. In this fashion we can apply the minimum/maximum test to all members in reverse order, until a minimum or maximum is detected. This then becomes the end of the initial transient phase. Figure 7.6 shows where the Conway rule and its modification finds the start of a stationary phase for a short series of 10 observations.

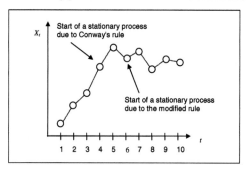

Figure 7.6: Comparing *Conway's rule* to its modification

Crossing the Mean

The method of crossing the mean uses a sequence of n observations $x_1, \ldots, x_n$. For each x_i it computes the sample mean of $x_1, \ldots, x_i$:

$$\bar{x}(i) = \frac{1}{i} \sum_{j=1}^{i} x_j \qquad (7.10)$$

We then test how often the series $x_1, \ldots, x_{i-1}$ crosses this mean and declare a process to be stationary if its values circle around it. As a rule, 3 to 5 crossings are considered

7.4 Analysing a Simulation Experiment

to offer sufficient support for the stationarity assumption. Figure 7.7 shows a 10 item sequence for which stationarity is suspected after 3 crossings.

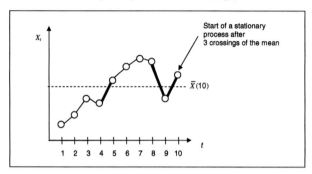

Figure 7.7: Detecting stationarity by *Crossing the Mean*

The Marginal Standard Error Rule

The *marginal standard error rule* (MSER) was discovered by J. K. Preston White (see White 1997) and can be used to estimate an initial transient's length. MSER defines the end of an initial transient, so that it minimizes the width of the marginal *confidence interval* (see Section 7.4.4) around the remaining series' mean. If $x_1, \ldots, x_n$ is a simulation's observation trajectory, the optimal endpoint (i) of the transient period can be computed as

$$i = \arg\min_{0 \leq i \ll n} \left[\frac{S^2}{n-i} \right]. \qquad (7.11)$$

In this formula S^2 is the sample variance of observed values $x_{i+1}, \ldots, x_n$:

$$S^2 = \frac{1}{n-i-1} \sum_{j=i+1}^{n} (x_j - \bar{x}_{n,i})^2 \text{ with } \bar{x}_{n,i} = \frac{1}{n-i} \sum_{j=i+1}^{n} x_j \qquad (7.12)$$

The series' remainder $x_{i+1}, \ldots, x_n$ is then assumed to be stationary, and the minimal marginal confidence interval $mser_i$ is computed from:

$$mser_i = \left[\bar{x}_{n,i} - \frac{S^2}{n-i}, \bar{x}_{n,i} + \frac{S^2}{n-i} \right] \qquad (7.13)$$

Since MSER assumes that the stationary sequence $x_{i+1}, \ldots, x_n$ is considerably longer than the initial transient ($i \ll n$), the test requires a sufficient number of observations.

Chapter 7 Simulation Statistics

If we therefore compute a minimum i which is not markedly smaller than n, we must lengthen the observation period and reapply the MSER test to a now longer sequence.

It must further be noted that the fact that the marginal confidence interval of an autocorrelated sample is not a valid estimator for the remaining sequence's mean is irrelevant for an MSER test's success.

The MSER method's efficiency can profit from the following two modifications as a rule of thumb, described in Kuck (2004):

- To compute an optimal terminator i for the initial transient of a sequence $x_1, \ldots, x_n$, we can rewrite the formula

$$i = \arg\min_{0 \leq i \ll n} \left[\frac{S^2}{n-i} \right] \qquad (7.14)$$

as

$$i = \arg\min_{0 \leq i \leq \frac{4}{5}n} \left[\frac{S^2}{n-i} \right]. \qquad (7.15)$$

- We then specify a lower bound of, for example, 0.05. If x_i is the first value of $x_1, \ldots, x_{4n/5}$ for which $mser_i$ is the minimum, or for which $mser_i < 0.05$ holds, we can take i as the initial transient's optimal endpoint (as long as $i \ll n$ holds).

These two modifications ensure that a value whose marginal confidence interval is not minimal but lies below a 0.05 threshold will still be chosen as the initial transient's endpoint. This can provide an efficient and still sufficiently accurate estimation.

The Batch Mean Test

In contrast to the heuristic nature of the techniques discussed above, the *Batch Mean Test* is a *statistical* method. It partitions a series of n observations $x_1, \ldots, x_n$ so that $n = bm$ holds. The sample mean $\bar{x}_i(m)$ of observations over the interval $i \in [1, 2, \ldots, b]$ and the estimator S^2_{BM} of the observations' variance can be computed as

$$\bar{x}_i(m) = \frac{1}{m} \sum_{j=1}^{m} x_{(i-1)m+j}, \qquad (7.16)$$

$$S^2_{BM} = \frac{m}{b-1} \sum_{i=1}^{b} \left(\bar{x}_i(m) - \frac{1}{b} \sum_{j=1}^{b} \bar{x}_j(m) \right)^2. \qquad (7.17)$$

We can now partition the sample means into two groups – not necessarily of the same size. The first b' means belong to the first group, and the remaining $b - b'$ means to the second. $S^2_{BM,1}$ is now a variance estimator computed over the first group's values by applying Formula 7.17, and $S^2_{BM,2}$ is a variance estimator computed over the second

7.4 Analysing a Simulation Experiment

group's values. We can now test for an initialisation error using an F-distribution statistic. If no such error is present, the fraction $S^2_{BM,1}/S^2_{BM,2}$ will approximate a random variable following the F-distribution – with a suitable degree of freedom. Depending on the probability of error α, we must, however, assume an initialisation error if

$$S^2_{BM,1}/S^2_{BM,2} > F_{1-\alpha, b'-1, b-b'-1} \qquad (7.18)$$

holds. In this case the end of the initial transient is unknown. To find it, we can use the above method to successively test two groups with $b = 1$ to $b = \lfloor n/2 \rfloor$. The first value for which

$$S^2_{BM,1}/S^2_{BM,2} \leq F_{1-\alpha, b'-1, b-b'-1} \qquad (7.19)$$

holds starts the *stationary* phase.

Since this method only offers a stepwise approximation and cannot guarantee any better precision in detecting a series of observation's steady state than the heuristics we have discussed before, we may as well opt for one or more of the heuristic techniques mentioned before. White and Spratt (2000) discusses a number of heuristics for detecting initial transients, including the Conway test, MSER, and the Batch Means method, whose behaviour and results are experimentally analysed and compared.

Hybrid methods, which pair a heuristic technique with e.g. visual inspection of simulation results' graphical representations, offer another promising approach for determining initial transients.

7.4.4 Analysing Simulation Results

Experiments with stochastic simulation models generate large data sets, which must be statistically processed to present clear and informative results. The following sections summarize some relevant statistical concepts and present a number of suitable methods for analysing a simulation's output data.

Statistical Estimators

When we analyse random values, such as a simulation experiment's results, in an empirical fashion, we often would like to draw some conclusions about a random variate's distribution. Because of a model's stochastic nature we must treat all observations as random samples. The larger the sample size (i.e. the more observations we make), the more precise our statistical analyses and estimations can be. In practice we are constrained to finite numbers of samples and finite numbers of replications, which must be characterized by suitable statistical *estimators*. In simulation as well as in other applications of statistical methodology, a time series' mean and variance are of particular interest.

Chapter 7 Simulation Statistics

We can compute an unbiased estimator for the expected value EX of a random variable X for a given sample $x_1, \ldots x_n$ by computing the *sample mean*

$$\bar{x} = \frac{1}{n} \sum_{i=1}^{n} x_i. \tag{7.20}$$

A corresponding estimator for X's variance can be obtained from the *sample's variance*

$$S^2 = \frac{1}{n-1} \sum_{i=1}^{n} (x_i - \bar{x})^2. \tag{7.21}$$

See Schickinger and Steger (2001, p. 139) for more detail.

An estimator U for random variable X is called *unbiased* if the expected value of estimator EU is equal to the estimated parameter ϑ; i.e. $EU = \vartheta$.

Computing Confidence Intervals

Beyond the fact that their accuracy rises proportionally to increases in sample size we do not know much about estimators. One relevant question is how large a sample size needs to be, to assure a desired level of precision. *Confidence intervals* offer an answer. In place of a single estimator (U) for the ϑ parameter, two estimators $(U_1$ and $U_2)$ are used. These are chosen so that

$$P(U_1 \leq \vartheta \leq U_2) = 1 - \alpha \tag{7.22}$$

holds. The probability $1 - \alpha$ is referred to as a *confidence level*, which can be chosen based on the precision we wish to obtain. Once we've sampled the U_1 and U_2 estimators we are assured that for $\vartheta \in [U1, U2]$ the probability of erroneous conclusions will be at most α. Here $[U1, U2]$ is the confidence interval, and $1 - \alpha$ is the probability with which the true value ϑ will be found in this interval. Often a symmetric confidence interval (i.e. $U_1 := U - d$ and $U_2 := U + d$) is derived from a single value (U). In this case d is the half length of the interval $[U - d, U + d]$. Figure 7.8 exemplifies confidence intervals taken from 10 samples for a distribution's mean value μ. Confidence intervals which include the expected value are *valid*. All others are *invalid*. In Figure 7.8 valid intervals make up 80 % of the ones shown.

In summary, a confidence level of $1-\alpha$ means that we can expect that for $100*(1-\alpha)$ % of all real or imagined samples the confidence interval will contain ϑ, while for $100*\alpha$ % it will not.

Choosing a confidence level $1 - \alpha$ is not a mathematical problem. Model designers must instead ponder what level of risk a possibly wrong prediction can bear. Asking for high levels of precision widens the corresponding confidence intervals, which we must then successively shorten by obtaining additional samples.

7.4 Analysing a Simulation Experiment

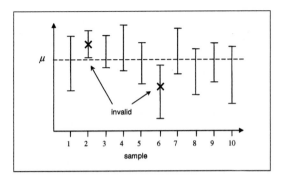

Figure 7.8: Valid and invalid confidence intervals for a mean value μ

So far this section has shown what a confidence interval is and what it is used for, but not how to compute it. Computing a confidence interval is strongly dependent on what parameters are known, and there are a number of well established techniques for determining confidence intervals for a range of distributions and their parameters. For example, there are standard methods for computing an estimator for a normal distribution's mean, with known and unknown variance. Since, however, we often don't know distribution types prior to simulation experiments (e.g. if this is what the experiment tries to determine), we need a more general method, which will work with *unknown* distribution types. For this reason we aim to compute confidence intervals for expected *means* of unknown distributions, which we are often most interested in and whose derivation requires significantly smaller sample sizes than estimates for distribution *variances*.

Based on a series of samples produced by a simulation run we can use the following method to compute confidence intervals for the mean μ of an unknown distribution. It assumes that a number of properties hold for $X = X_1 + \cdots + X_n$ independent random variables with identical mean μ and variance σ^2 (Kreyszig 1998):

1. X has an expected mean of $n\mu$ and a variance of $n\sigma^2$.
2. X is normally distributed if variables $X_1, \ldots, X_n$ are normally distributed.
3. If variables $X_1, \ldots, X_n$ are not normally distributed, then X will still be normally distributed for large values of n (central limit theorem).

The central limit theorem mentioned in (3) is an important cornerstone of probability theory.

Chapter 7 Simulation Statistics

> **Central limit Theorem:**
> Let $X_1, \ldots, X_n, \ldots$ be independent random variables with identical distribution functions, identical mean μ and identical variance σ^2. Also, let $Y_n = X_1 + \cdots + X_n$. The random variable Z_n
>
> $$Z_n = \frac{Y_n - n\mu}{\sigma\sqrt{n}} \qquad (7.23)$$
>
> will then be asymptotically normally distributed, with mean 0 and variance 1 so that the following relation will hold for all $x \in \mathbb{R}$ and Z_n's distribution function $F_n(x)$ (Kreyszig 1998, p. 201):
>
> $$\lim_{n \to \infty} F_n(x) = \Phi(x) = \frac{1}{\sqrt{2\pi}} \int_{-\infty}^{x} e^{-\frac{u^2}{2}} du \qquad (7.24)$$
>
> Normal distributions with a mean of 0 and a standard deviation of 1 are called standard normal distributions ($N(0,1)$), so that we conclude: The Z_n distribution converges towards a standard normal distribution for $n \to \infty$.

Let us return to constructing a symmetric confidence interval for mean μ of an unknown distribution $\bar{X}$ from a given sample stream; where $\bar{X} = \frac{1}{n}(X_1 + \cdots + X_n)$. In this case $X = X_1 + \cdots + X_n$ applies and the random variables $X_1, \ldots, X_n$ are independent, with identical means μ and variances σ^2. This means that properties (1), (2), and (3) hold for X and that $X \sim N(n\mu, n\sigma^2)$ holds for large n. Also, $\bar{X} = \frac{1}{n}(X_1 + \cdots + X_n) = \frac{1}{n}X$ holds. If sample size n is large, the random variable $\bar{X}$ will be approximately normally distributed, i.e. $\bar{X} \sim N(\mu, \frac{\sigma^2}{n})$, according to the theorem of a linear transformation of a normal distribution.

> **Theorem: Linear Transformation of a Normal Distribution:**
> Let V be a normally distributed random variable with $V \sim N(\mu, \sigma^2)$. Then, for any $a \in \mathbb{R} \setminus \{0\}$ and $b \in \mathbb{R}$, $Y = aV + b$ is normally distributed with $Y \sim N(a\mu + b, a^2\sigma^2)$ (Schickinger and Steger 2001, p. 107).

In practice the expected variance σ^2 will rarely be known. In this case we can use the sample's variance S^2 as an estimator for σ^2. Note, however, that for unknown variances we cannot work with standard normal distributions, but must use the random variable

$$T = \sqrt{n}\frac{\bar{X} - \mu}{S} \qquad (7.25)$$

whose distribution function corresponds to a t-distribution with $n-1$ degrees of freedom. The symmetric $1 - \alpha$ confidence interval for the mean μ now becomes

$$\left[\bar{X} - \frac{t_{n-1, 1-\alpha/2} * S}{\sqrt{n}}, \bar{X} + \frac{t_{n-1, 1-\alpha/2} * S}{\sqrt{n}} \right], \qquad (7.26)$$

where $t_{n-1, 1-\alpha/2}$ is the $1 - \alpha/2$ quantile of a t-distribution with $n-1$ degrees of freedom.

7.4 Analysing a Simulation Experiment

> **Definition: Quantile:**
> Let X be a continuous random variable distributed according to F_X. A number x_γ with
> $$F_X(x_\gamma) = \gamma \qquad (7.27)$$
> is called the γ-quantile of X and its distribution F_X. For standard normal distributions the γ-quantile is denoted by z_γ (Schickinger and Steger 2001, p. 33).

Figure 7.9 shows a graphical representation of a standard normal distribution's q-quantile z_q and the interval bracketing all values with probability $1 - \alpha$.

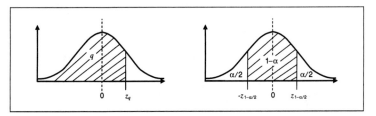

Figure 7.9: q-Quantile of a standard normal distribution and its $1 - \alpha$ interval

No closed form expressions are known for either the normal or the t-distribution. Their values and quantiles must therefore be computed numerically or retrieved from tables in statistical textbooks.

The t-distribution has a higher variance than the normal distribution, and it therefore also requires a wider confidence interval. At higher degrees of freedom the t-distribution, however, approximates the standard normal distribution. This is convenient, since it justifies focussing on the normal distribution for large sample sizes. A commonly used threshold for value in simulations is 30; i.e. we use normal distributions in place of t-distributions when more than 30 observations are available. If a distribution is "not too unsymmetric", this sample size produces satisfactorily precise confidence intervals for expected means of unknown distributions with unknown variance.

In general the width of a confidence interval for expected value estimations (and in analogy for stochastic simulation experiments) hinges on thee factors:

1. The variance σ^2. The less variation in observations there is, the more precisely we can predict.
2. The sample size n. The larger the sample size, the smaller the confidence interval needs to be.
3. The required confidence level $1 - \alpha$. The higher statistical confidence requirements are, the wider the corresponding confidence intervals must become.

183

Chapter 7 Simulation Statistics

Simulation experiments collect samples of relevant statistical measures during a single run or over a number of replications. In this context a *replication* i is a simulation run which differs from other replications by using a different random number seed. The sample mean of a series of such a replication's observations can serve as an estimator for the relevant statistical measure's expected value, and can be viewed as a random value of the stochastic variable $\bar{Y}$. For larger sample sizes and as long as each replication is independent (assured by using different random streams), the central limit theorem ensures that $\bar{Y}$ will be approximately normally distributed. If we run w replications to generate w independent random samples for variables $\bar{Y}_1, \ldots, \bar{Y}_w$, we obtain w expected means for the observed variable. Note that we treat each replication as an independent sample, for which we can estimate mean and standard deviation and compute a confidence interval (see first part of Section 7.4.4).

This section has shown how simulation models can derive estimates for means and variances of simulation results and has introduced confidence intervals as a means for exploring the accuracy of such estimators. So far we have assumed that a simulation traces the values of only a single result. If more than a single variable is of interest, we must deal with *simultaneous confidence intervals*.

Simultaneous Confidence Intervals

Models are often designed to support flexible explorations of problems' state spaces. For this purpose we typically wish to observe multiple instead of just single variables. We have seen how simulation allows us to estimate expected means and deviations for streams of stochastic values. However, if these values have not been collected in separate simulation runs or independently initialised segments of simulation runs, these will be *cross-correlated* as well as *autocorrelated*. Confidence intervals for cross-correlated data are referred to as *simultaneous confidence intervals* and must be cautiously handled. Because of such cross connections the likelihood that confidence intervals contain "true" expectations decreases as the number of observed variables increases. This is of course undesirable, and we should strive to make sure that *all* simultaneous confidence intervals contain *all* true expectations. Fortunately there is a simple, accurate, and easily understandable method to achieve this.

> **Method of Bonferroni:**
> If we compute k simultaneous confidence intervals with confidence levels $1 - \alpha_1, \ldots, 1 - \alpha_k$, then the probability that each interval contains its parameter is at least
> $$1 - \sum_{i=1}^{k} \alpha_i \qquad (7.28)$$

For an example of two observed measures with confidence levels of 0.975 the *Bonferroni method* therefore deduces that there will be at least a 95 % probability that both intervals will contain their parameters. Or, if we wish to assure a 90 % probability that confidence intervals will include all parameters for 5 different streams of observation, the Bonferroni method tells us that this requirement will force us to compute each of the corresponding five confidence intervals to a confidence level of 0.98.

7.5 Observing a Simulation Experiment

In Section 7.4.4 we looked at techniques for analysing existing simulation data. We will now discuss how such data can be obtained; e.g. by combining techniques for data collection with analysis methods.

There are two common techniques for data collection in stationary simulation processes. The first of these requires *independent replications* of simulation runs (as mentioned in 7.4.4). The second assumes very long runs, which can be partitioned for *batch mean* collection. We will look at both of these.

If processes terminate or are not stationary, we must use different methods – a problem we will return to at this section's end.

7.5.1 Independent Replications

The method of *Independent Replications* requires a sufficient number of simulation runs (replications) for each model parameter constellation. Replications may differ only in their random seeds and will collect a fixed number of observations for each relevant measure. We assume that these observations are taken in steady (stationary) state and that any initial bias has been removed (see Section 7.4.4). Means are computed for each of the time series observed by each replication, which we assume to be stochastically independent and identically distributed (see Pawlikowski 1990, p. 131). Remember that these means are themselves samples for a particular measure, whose mean can in turn be used as an estimator for that measure's expected value. To make this estimator more informative, we can also compute a confidence interval at a chosen confidence level.

If we sample a measure m times per replication, we generate the following values for k replications:

$$(x_{11}, x_{12}, \ldots, x_{1m}), (x_{21}, x_{22}, \ldots, x_{2m}), \ldots, (x_{k1}, x_{k2}, \ldots, x_{km}) \qquad (7.29)$$

In this context x_{ij} is the measure's j-th value during the i-th replication. During each replication we should make at least 100 observations for each measure.

The sample mean for a replication $\bar{x}_1(m), \bar{x}_2(m), \ldots, \bar{x}_k(m)$ can be computed as

$$\bar{x}_i(m) = \frac{1}{m} \sum_{j=1}^{m} x_{ij} \qquad (7.30)$$

Chapter 7 Simulation Statistics

and we can estimate its expected value μ as

$$\bar{\bar{x}}(k,m) = \frac{1}{k}\sum_{i=1}^{k} \bar{x}_i(m). \qquad (7.31)$$

To derive a confidence interval, we then need an estimate for the sample variance

$$S^2[\bar{\bar{x}}(k,m)] = \sum_{i=1}^{k} \frac{(\bar{x}_i(m) - \bar{\bar{x}}(k,m))^2}{k-1} \qquad (7.32)$$

and the interval for the estimator's confidence level is computed as:

$$\bar{\bar{x}}(k,m) \pm t_{k-1, 1-\alpha/2} \frac{S[\bar{\bar{x}}(k,m)]}{\sqrt{k}} \qquad (7.33)$$

Figure 7.10 shows three replications of a stochastic process with initial transients. To ensure our results' accuracy, we must truncate all observations during the process' warm-up periods. In terms of computing time long initial transients are therefore a liability and the method of Independent Replications is most effective when transient periods are short. Compared to a single long simulation it has the advantage of higher precision for estimates.

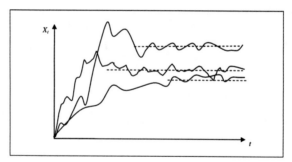

Figure 7.10: Three replications of a stationary process

7.5.2 Batch Means

In contrast to Independent Replications, the method of *Batch Means* needs only a single long simulation run. This run is split into segments, which are then analysed as if they were separate replications. Figure 7.11 visualizes this technique.

Generally we assume that temporally distant segments are only weakly related; i.e. that they have low *autocorrelation*. The longer the run, the more realistic this

7.5 Observing a Simulation Experiment

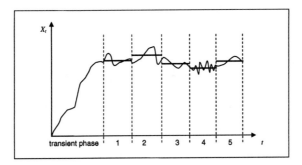

Figure 7.11: Batch means in a segmented simulation run ($k = 5$)

assumption will be. If there is an initial transient, it must be detected and truncated before segmentation.

Any sufficiently long run with k segments of length m will have a total number of $n = k * m$ simulated values. Assuming long enough and therefore approximately uncorrelated segments, we can compute a confidence interval for the measure's expected value. For each segment i with $i = 1, \ldots, k$ we compute the sample means $\bar{x}_i(m)$, which are then aggregated to a mean of means, to predict the expected value for the observed measure:

$$\bar{\bar{x}}(k, m) = \frac{1}{k} \sum_{i=1}^{k} \bar{x}_i(m) \qquad (7.34)$$

This value is used as an estimator for μ, whose accuracy we can bracket by using the samples' variance

$$S^2[\bar{\bar{x}}(k, m)] = \sum_{i=1}^{k} \frac{(\bar{x}_i(m) - \bar{\bar{x}}(k, m))^2}{k - 1} \qquad (7.35)$$

to compute a confidence interval for it:

$$\bar{\bar{x}}(k, m) \pm t_{k-1, 1-\alpha/2} \frac{S[\bar{\bar{x}}(k, m)]}{\sqrt{k}} \qquad (7.36)$$

To ensure unbiased results, *tests for autocorrelation* should be applied to each of the segments. If correlations are high, we must lengthen the simulation (and therefore each segment) and test again – until an acceptably low level of correlation is reached (Page 1991, p. 132, Pawlikowski 1990, p. 132).

In practice we recommend that at least 10 segments with approximately identically and independently distributed sample means are used to compute the confidence interval. More than at most 30 are typically not required (Pawlikowski 1990, p. 133).

7.5.3 Terminating and Non-Stationary Systems

Discrete event simulations most often concentrate on studying the behaviour of stationary processes, for which suitable long simulation runs can be performed. Models of terminating systems, however, can only be simulated until they terminate; i.e. their run length is limited. For such processes stationary behaviour is an exception rather than the rule. In this context we often wish to study a system's *transient* phase; e.g. to determine the first overflow of a waiting space in a queueing model. Statistical analysis of non-stationary systems differs substantially from that of stationary ones. On the one hand, no initial transient needs to be removed, and we therefore also need not concern ourselves with shortening of transients through suitably chosen initial conditions. Instead, we can start simulations in an empty state. On the other hand, we find that we cannot improve estimators' precision by lengthening simulation runs beyond the terminal state. Observations also tend to be highly autocorrelated, so that the batch means method (which assumes independent means for each segment) cannot be applied.

What remains is the possibility for multiple runs until termination, the means of each of those observations can be aggregated. How many such replications we need will depend on the modelled system's variability (i.e. its means' standard deviation) as well as on the required confidence levels and precision. Often we will wish to predict the length of the time interval until termination, rather than any variable values. A significant number of replications (e.g. > 30) may be required to compute an acceptable confidence interval for the observed model characteristic (e.g. the time until the first waiting space overflows).

A practical example may illustrate these issues. A discrete event simulation model for predicting effects of people moving around an aircraft cabin has been developed in *DESMO-J* (see Chapter 10) in cooperation with the German branch of the Airbus corporation (see Czogalla and Matzen 2003). With this model we can e.g. study the impact of cabin layouts on boarding times for Airbus aircrafts, where *boarding time* is a quantity whose value is estimated by each simulation run. Only sufficiently many replications will produce sufficiently reliable estimates for this measure.

7.6 Sample Size and Simulation Experiments

Similar to conventional statistical methods simulation experiments must decide on a sample size n; i.e. the number of observations of relevant output values a simulation will be expected to generate. This *sample size n* must be large enough to minimize estimation errors in computing confidence intervals based on normality assumptions suggested by the central limit theorem. A sample size of $n = 30$ is often considered sufficient for this. We also, however, wish to attach an acceptable degree of precision to our results, which means that the relevant confidence intervals should not exceed certain widths. This depends on a measure's unknown standard deviation as much as on sample size (see Section 7.4.4, Formula 7.26). All these considerations require that we settle on a maximum width for the confidence interval and a specific confidence level prior to the start of a simulation run. These choices reflect our need for precision and will let us derive an appropriate sample size.

If we modify Formula 7.26 for computing a confidence interval accordingly and set half the length of the confidence interval to δ, we obtain:

$$\delta = \frac{zs}{\sqrt{n}} \Rightarrow n = \frac{z^2 s^2}{\delta^2} \tag{7.37}$$

which shows that we must first estimate the standard deviation S of the sample. This can then be used in a stepwise procedure for estimating a simulation experiment's sample size. The first step gathers n_1 independent samples from simulation runs (e.g. $n_1 = 30$). The statistical credibility of each of these must be assured by Independent Replications or Batch Means (see Section 7.5). Any initial transients must have been removed.

The results of this process then allow us to compute estimators and confidence intervals for the expected values μ of relevant simulation statistics. Once these are at an acceptable confidence level we can terminate the experiment, otherwise we must use estimators for the standard deviation to compute the required number of runs (i.e. replications or batch means, respectively) from Formula 7.21. The difference $n_2 = n - n_1$ between the required and current number of runs indicates what number of additional samples (n_2) we need.

Since our model generates a stochastic process we must repeat the above procedure until the required statistical precision is reached; i.e. until the width of the desired confidence interval is not exceeded. Simulation software can automatically perform such computations "in the background" and terminate a run as soon as a specified precision is reached.

Since longer runs increase output quality, but may also require substantially more computation, model users must often make compromises between adequate precision and acceptable runtimes. Prior pilot experiments may yield preliminary estimates for precision and sample size and may be of help for deciding what confidence levels are needed.

7.7 Choosing Good Model Parameters

In contrast to analytical optimization (e.g. linear programming or queueing theory), simulations are descriptive in nature. By simulating long chains of relevant state transitions described by the model's logic they estimate measures of system performance under given initial conditions and constraints. Systematic experimentation and comparison of results for different parameter sets and model structures drives the discovery of good solutions for a given problem. No optimality guarantees can be given.

Chapter 7 Simulation Statistics

If we would try to simulate *all* possible settings of *all* controllable parameters to circumvent this limitation, we would quickly reach the limits of computability. To determine solutions for event, a relatively small number of controllable factors with discrete value sets needs prodigious amounts of processor time; particularly if we must replicate long runs to assure high levels of statistical credibility. Since it grows exponentially with the number of parameters we must consider, the number of possible scenarios is in most cases far too large to enumerate completely. It may not even be finite. For this reason simulation developers must try to minimize the number of relevant scenarios; i.e. the parameter combinations a model is meant to explore.

Classical experimental techniques such as 2^k *factorial design* can be used in this context. This is a simple method for gaining some feeling for the influence of model parameters on model outputs. In place of all possible scenarios, only a small number of skilfully chosen model configurations is explored. The results of these explorations, however, can give us a good indication for which parameters are more relevant than others. 2^k factorial designs are a well established technique which is also used in real life physical experiments. They are based on the idea of choosing only two representative levels, which must differ significantly from each other, for each controllable parameter's value. Since this decision requires good judgment, it is hard to automate and must be done individually for each parameter by the model's user. Model configurations based on these parameter settings can then be simulated and their results can be analysed with regard to the parameter values' sensitivity and their effects on output measures.

For example, if a model has k controllable parameters and we choose two representative but different settings for each of them, 2^k model configurations must be simulated and simulation results must then be analysed to decide which "direction" to explore any further. Table 7.7 shows a design matrix for a 2^k factorial design for 3 model parameters. Plus and minus signs indicate the two contrasting (i.e. "representative and different") parameter values.

Table 7.7: Design matrix for a 2^k factorial design

Run(i)	Parameter 1	Parameter 2	Parameter 3	Result
1	−	−	−	R_1
2	−	−	+	R_2
3	−	+	−	R_3
4	−	+	+	R_4
5	+	−	−	R_5
6	+	−	+	R_6
7	+	+	−	R_7
8	+	+	+	R_8

Coupling a simulation to an *optimization method* offers alternative ways for avoiding computation of all possible combinations of model parameters. *Operations research* offers many techniques, which typically assume a goal function for which an optimum – i.e. a minimum or maximum – is to be found. In place of precisely computed and ex-

7.8 Conclusion

actly reproducible values and for a limited combination of model parameters, stochastic results from a simulation model can take the role of this function.

A search for optimal parameter constellations with simulation will typically first explore the neighbourhood of the model parameters' starting values. The model must be run for each value combination we wish to investigate, often for a considerable time or number of replications. Results must then be compared to previous ones. In this fashion we will explore modifications to either just one or to multiple parameter values simultaneously. The method of *steepest ascent*, for example, proceeds by looking most closely at values whose modification yields the largest (steepest) contribution to the model objective expressed by the goal function we mentioned above. The search terminates if no further improvements can be made, a strategy which of course holds the danger of getting trapped in a *local* optimum. However, since aspirations of simulation studies are usually satisfied by just finding a significantly "better" instead of an optimal solution, this is not normally much of a problem.

Compared to analytical methods an obvious disadvantage of simulation-based optimization lies in the computational effort associated with each single step; i.e. for simulating each data point. In addition we must bear in mind that simulation is a stochastic technique and that a stochastic variable's random deviations can lead to an optimum to be discarded in favour of a neighbouring point which shows just a "random" improvement. *Variance reduction* techniques and identically initialised replications of random streams can reduce stochastic variation and thereby minimize this risk.

Chapter 13 will return to the question of how simulation models can be optimized, using heuristic techniques such as *genetic programming* to estimate optimal parameter values.

7.8 Conclusion

This chapter has offered a brief introduction to the use of some relevant statistical methods in the context of simulation experiments. Simulated scenarios differ from physical ones in that their output values are typically *not* independent, and many statistical methods must therefore be modified to take this aspect into account. While this difficult topic is often covered extensively in many discrete event simulation textbooks, we have not emphasised it in this handbook. Even though thorough statistical analyses are indispensable for credible simulation results, we can ensure this with relatively few robust techniques if we are willing to accept somewhat longer execution times in experiments. The dramatic increase in processing power of modern computer systems makes this an acceptable price to pay in return for a less complex design of our models and the experiments they serve to perform. What remains important is that we systematically collect and evaluate data so that we can

- ❑ create an *adequate database* for our simulation studies;
- ❑ use goodness of fit tests to derive suitable *input distributions*;

Chapter 7 Simulation Statistics

- provide statistically valid *random number streams* for all relevant distributions;
- detect and discard *initial transients* prior to gathering output data; and
- perform *clean evaluations* of data collected during an experiment's stationary phase, based on either a single long simulation run or multiple independent replications.

Statistical evaluations include computation of *measures* such as mean, minimum and maximum, as well as the estimation of *confidence intervals* at specified confidence levels. Without such confidence estimates simulation results will largely be useless. Precision requirements also determine the *length of a simulation run*; i.e. how many observations of output variables we must create to bracket predictions by given confidence intervals.

To brush up their statistical skills, diligent readers are referred to one of the many statistics textbooks. Searching e.g. a university library's catalogue or the Amazon site (see http://www.amazon.com) will yield a large bounty. The section on "further reading" makes some recommendations to get you started.

Further Reading

While mathematically exact, *Diskrete Strukturen – Wahrscheinlichkeitstheorie und Statistik* (Schickinger and Steger 2001, "Discrete Structures – Probability Theory and Statistics", in German) presents an intuitive and readable introduction to probability theory and statistics. It can be used to lay a foundation for beginners as well as for a reference text for more advanced readers. The first two chapters cover discrete probability spaces and continuous random variables with density functions. The most important distribution types are described. Chapter 3 then looks at applications of statistical methods and includes a detailed introduction to estimators and confidence intervals. Some statistical tests, such as the Chi-square method for testing goodness of fit, are also presented. Chapter 4 analyses random processes, and Chapter 5 surveys randomized algorithms.

Volume 1 of the textbook *An Introduction to Probability Theory and its Applications* (Feller 1968) offers an equivalent introduction to probability theory and statistics for English speaking readers. While heavy going at times, there are many examples. The approach in *Simulation: A Statistical Perspective* (Kleijnen 1992) is different: This advanced textbook covers statistical techniques from the viewpoint of simulation. Very comprehensive, but not for the faint of heart. *Simulation Modeling and Analysis* (Law and Kelton 2000) is a standard introductory simulation textbook with an emphasis on statistical methods. Very readable and a good choice for beginners.

Finally, Chapter 3 of *The Art of Computer Programming – Seminumerical Algorithms* (Knuth 1997) is the standard reference for everything about generating and testing random numbers.

Bibliography

R. Czogalla and B. Matzen. *Agentenbasierte Simulation von Personenbewegungen in kontinuierlichem Raum* ("Agent-Based Simulation of Pedestrian Movement in Continuous Space", in German). Diploma Thesis, Faculty of Informatics, University of Hamburg, December 2003.

W. Feller. *An Introduction to Probability Theory and its Applications*. Wiley, New York, 3rd edition, 1968.

J. P. C. Kleijnen. *Statistical Techniques in Simulation*. Dekker, New York, 1992.

J. P. C. Kleijnen. Simulation: A Statistical Perspective. In J. Banks, editor, *Handbook of Simulation – Principles, Methodology, Advances, Applications, and Practice*, pages 55–306. Wiley, New York, 1998. Chapters 3–8.

J. P. C. Kleijnen and W. van Groenendaal. *Simulation: A Statistical Perspective*. Wiley, Chichester, 1992.

D. E. Knuth. *The Art of Computer Programming – Seminumerical Algorithms*, volume 2. Addison-Wesley, Reading, 3rd edition, 1997. Chapters 3.2.1 and 3.3.1.

E. Kreyszig. *Statistische Methoden und ihre Anwendung* ("Statistical Methods and their Application", in German). Vandenhoeck & Ruprecht, Göttingen, 7th edition, 1998.

J. Kuck. *Automatisierte Auswertung und Terminierung von Simulationsexperimenten mittels statistischer Verfahren* ("Automated Evaluation and Termination of Simulation Experiments Using Statistical Methods", in German). Diploma Thesis, Faculty of Informatics, University of Hamburg, December 2004.

A. M. Law and W. D. Kelton. *Simulation Modeling and Analysis*. McGraw-Hill, New York, 3rd edition, 2000. Chapters 4, 6, 7, 8, 9, and 10.

B. Page. *Diskrete Simulation – Eine Einführung mit Modula-2* ("Discrete Simulation – An Introduction with Modula-2", in German). Springer, Berlin, 1991. Chapter 1.

K. Pawlikowski. Steady-state simulation of queuing processes: a survey of problems and solutions. *ACM Computing Surveys*, 22(2), June 1990.

K. Pawlikowski, H.-D. Joshua Jeong, and J.-S. Ruth Lee. On Credibility of Simulation Studies of Telecommunication Networks. *IEEE Communications Magazine*, pages 132–139, January 2002.

S. Robinson. A statistical process control approach for estimating the warm-up period. In E. Yücesan, C.-H. Chen, J. L. Snowdon, and J. M. Charnes, editors, *Proceedings of the 2002 Winter Simulation Conference*, 2002. [Online] http://informs-cs.org/wsc02papers/prog02.html (in August 2005).

T. Sauerbier. *Theorie und Praxis von Simulationssystemen* ("Theory and Practice of Simulation Systems", in German). Vieweg, Brunswick/Wiesbaden, 1999. Chapter 8.

T. Schickinger and A. Steger. *Diskrete Strukturen – Wahrscheinlichkeitstheorie und Statistik* ("Discrete Structures – Probability Theory and Statistics", in German), volume 2. Springer, Berlin, 2001.

R. Sedgewick. *Algorithms*. Addison-Wesley, Reading, 2nd edition, 1992.

J. K. P. White. An effective truncation heuristic for bias reduction in simulation output. *Simulation*, 69(6):323–334, 1997.

Bibliography

J. K. P. White and S. C. Spratt. A comparison of five steady-state truncation heuristics for simulation. In J. A. Joines, R. R. Barton, K. Kang, and P. A. Fishwick, editors, *Proceedings of the 2000 Winter Simulation Conference*, 2000. [Online] http://informs-cs.org/wsc00papers/prog00.html (in August 2005).

Chapter 8

Validation, Verification, and Testing of Simulation Models

Nicolas Knaak, Bernd Page, Wolfgang Kreutzer

Contents

8.1	Motivation and Overview	195
8.2	Foundations of Model Validation	197
	8.2.1 Basic Terms	197
	8.2.2 The Validation Process	199
	8.2.3 A Philosophical View of Model Validation	203
	8.2.4 Principles and Guidelines for Model Validation	205
	8.2.5 Classification of Validation Techniques	210
8.3	Selected Validation Techniques	211
	8.3.1 Conceptual Model Validation	212
	8.3.2 Model Verification and Testing	215
	8.3.3 Operational Validation of Model Behaviour	221
8.4	Summary	230
	Further Reading	231
	Bibliography	231

8.1 Motivation and Overview

Simulation models have become important tools for supporting decision makers in science, engineering, and business; a role for which close correspondences between simulation results and a modelled system's behaviour are an essential requirement (Page 1991, p. 147).

In practical terms this means that a model must offer sufficiently close and valid representations of a "real" system under investigation, at least with regard to the goals of the study in question. Although models are necessarily always abstractions of reality

Chapter 8 Validation, Verification, and Testing of Simulation Models

(see Chapter 1), a close correspondence to all "relevant" aspects of their target systems (which may or may not yet exist) is a crucial prerequisite for their usefulness. Otherwise – as sometimes has been said – modelling may just become science fiction. But even in purely fictious models, such as a computer game which simulates spaceships, a model must exhibit "valid" behaviour; i.e. it must meet user expectations or must at least not violate them in any implausible way.

From daily experience we are used to the fact that computer systems and their software contain errors, whose consequences may reach from mere nuisance (e.g. figures which "magically" disappear in a document) to utter disaster (e.g. the explosion putting an end to the maiden flight of the Ariane 5 rocket only 40 seconds after liftoff[1]). Computer models and the simulation programs by which they are implemented are unfortunately just as error-prone as any other complex piece of software. Indeed, since large simulation models are often rather complex programs, establishing their correctness is a particularly important concern and awareness of this issue should therefore permeate all phases of a simulation study; from system analysis to the interpretation of data obtained from simulation runs. Building and using models whose validity has not been established "[contributes] nothing to the understanding of the system being simulated" (Naylor and Finger 1967, pp. B-92).

To illustrate the extent of the problem, Barton and Szczerbicka (2000, pp. 387) identify typical errors, which result in invalid models whose use leads to invalid conclusions:

❏ Relevant components or functionalities of the system are wrongly or too drastically simplified, or not implemented correctly.

❏ Missing data forces experts to give imprecise estimates for characteristic model parameter values.

❏ The model is driven by input data derived from invalid or insufficiently accurate approximations of a real system's behaviour.

❏ Errors are introduced during the transformation of a conceptual model into a program.

Following Page (1991, pp. 146), we should ideally accept model validity as one of the most important criteria for judging model quality. Establishing a model's validity is often a challenging task, and the wide range of literature on this topic reflects its importance. There are numerous papers and textbooks, which emphasise different aspects, such as practical techniques (e.g. Balci 1998), statistical methodology (e.g. Kleijnen 1999), or the many similarities between the core problems of validation and the verification of theories in the philosophy of science (e.g. Naylor and Finger 1967).

Other disciplines, such as software engineering, theoretical computer science, or statistics, have developed approaches to verification, validation, and testing, which are also relevant for simulation. Kleindorfer and Ganeshan (1993, p. 50) emphasise the "eclectic" character of validation in this regard, an aspect that also dominates the approach presented in a seminal paper by Naylor and Finger (1967).

---
[1] See e.g. http://www.cs.unibo.it/~laneve/papers/ariane5rep.html

This chapter gives an overview of the state-of-the-art in simulation model validation. After an introduction to general terms, principles, and the limits of validation, we analyse some modern validation techniques. In this context our selection of topics is influenced by relevant practices in various domains, such as data analysis, software testing, and real-time system verification. We will classify these techniques, examine their applicability to the model-building process, and discuss some tools to support them.

Due to the chapter's limited scope, we cannot aim for completeness. To guide readers who are interested in learning more, we will conclude with some pointers to relevant literature. Generally, one should be aware that good model validation – maybe even more than model building itself – requires much background knowledge and highly specialized skills. In spite of increasing support by analysis, verification, and testing tools, the application of validation techniques and the interpretation of their results remains more an art than a science or craft. There is no adequate substitute for the insights and intuitions gained by experience and practice.

8.2 Foundations of Model Validation

The literature on model validation and verification contains a number of basic terms, which are not always used in a consistent manner (see also Barton and Szczerbicka 2000, p. 390) and whose meaning varies between different subdisciplines of computer science. Sometimes a term's meaning may even depend on an author's native language; e.g. the meaning of the French "verification" corresponds to the English "validation", and vice versa.

To dispel some of this babylonic confusion, we will briefly discuss proper use of the terms *validation*, *verification*, and *test* within computer simulation and its neighbouring fields. Based on this review we will then settle on definitions to use in the rest of this book.

8.2.1 Basic Terms

Although definitions for these terms can be found in practically all simulation textbooks, the inconsistent use of "validation" and "verification" often causes confusion. Balci (1998, p. 336), for example, defines and distinguishes these terms as follows:

> "*Model Validation* is substantiating that the model within its domain of applicability behaves with satisfactory accuracy consistent with the study objectives. [...] *Model Verification* is substantiating that the model is transformed from one form into another [...] with sufficient accuracy".

From this follows that the main difference between model validation and verification is that for validation the structure and behaviour of the model is compared to a *real*

Chapter 8 Validation, Verification, and Testing of Simulation Models

system. The goal is to determine if the model represents the real system closely enough to give reliable answers to relevant questions. Verification, on the other hand, refers to the relationship between different model representations; e.g. a conceptual UML model and the corresponding computer implementation.

While more informal, the often cited definition by Boehm (1979) also makes this distinction; claiming that model validation deals with "building the *right model*[2]" (see Balci 1998, p. 336). In model verification different model representations, such as a conceptual UML model or a computer model implemented in Java, are compared to each other and checked for consistency. Boehm therefore claims that "model verification deals with building the *model right*" (Balci 1998, p. 336).

Brade (2003) offers an interesting twist by separating validation and verification activities using the terms *suitability* and *correctness*. Validation then focuses on the question of whether a model is a "suitable representation of the real system with respect to an intended purpose of the model's application" (Brade 2003, p. 16). In contrast, verification requires checking if "the model is correctly represented and was correctly transformed from one representation into another" (Brade 2003, p. 14).

Page (1991, p. 16) (as well as some other authors) constrains the meaning of model verification to the two most important artifacts created during a simulation study and therefore defines it as the process of checking if a computerized model is a "correct implementation of the (formal) conceptual model".

Any quality assurance for simulation models must take account of both the external world and the model's intended purpose (Brade 2003, p. 15). Verification simply refers to the equivalence of different model representations, while validations are always conducted with regard to the original system and the goals for whose pursuit a model is to be used. We should, however, note that in theoretical computer science and software engineering these terms are used in a more rigorous way. There, only exhaustive formal proofs of model correctness are accepted as verification.

Let us now summarize the reviewed definitions and add the notion of *testing* as an important verification technique. The following formulations are mostly adopted with extensions from Brade (2003, Ch. 1.5):

❑ *Model validation* is the activity of establishing that a model is a suitable substitute for a real system with regard to the goals of a simulation study. In this book the term *validation* is also occasionally used as an umbrella term for all quality assurance activities (i.e. all of model validation, verification, and testing).

❑ *Model verification in the wider sense* is the activity of establishing that a model is correctly represented and consistently transformed from one form of representation into another; e.g. from a conceptual model into a program. *Model verification in the narrower sense* is the activity of formally proving the cor-

---

[2]Since his definition is directed towards software engineering in general, Boehm uses the term "product" in place of "model".

8.2 Foundations of Model Validation

rectness of model representations and their transformations – relative to some canonical reference model (e.g. a formal specification).

❏ *Model testing* is the activity of executing a computerized simulation model in order to corroborate that it correctly implements its corresponding conceptual model. In this book testing is regarded as an important technique for model verification in the wider sense.

8.2.2 The Validation Process

Because of the importance of model validity for the success of a simulation study, validation activities play an important role in all process models for modelling and simulation. We will call the part of the process model that determines how to connect validation activities to certain phases of model development a *validation process*. Brade (2003, p. 41) uses this term in a similar way.

Let us briefly investigate the different roles and responsibilities of the parties involved in simulation modelling. Many authors (e.g. Drougoul et al. 2002, p. 5; Sargent 2001, p. 107) distinguish three typical roles that we might call *model user*, *model designer*, and *model implementer*. The latter two roles can be subsumed under the notion of *model developers*. Often an additional role for conducting independent verification and validation is involved (see Sargent 2001, p. 107 and Section 8.2.4), which we call the *validation agent*.

The *model user* commissions a simulation study and frames the questions it is intended to answer. Often (though not always) model users have a deep understanding of the target system, but relatively poor knowledge of modelling, implementation, and simulation techniques. The *model designer* builds a model based on the model user's system descriptions. In doing so, s/he may employ some semi-formal notation, such as UML. The model designer needs simulation modelling skills, both in general terms and in specific domains. Although model designers often have some degree of programming experience, such skills are not strictly required. Instead, model implementation is the domain of the *model implementer*, whose task it is to transform model designer's specifications into executable programs.

Note that, due to different backgrounds, vocabulary, and expectations, communication between people filling these roles is often awkward. Since "an important aspect of model validation is the close collaboration with potential model users" (Page 1991, p. 148), model designers must mediate between model users and implementers (Drougoul et al. 2002, p. 6). Shared problem understanding and a common language are crucial prerequisites for a project's success.

Many authors, e.g. Page (1991, p. 16) and Sargent (2001, p. 108), differentiate between three validation phases:

1. *Conceptual model validation* is performed during the conceptual modelling phase. It aims to ensure that the model is a plausible representation of the real system; i.e. suitable to answer all questions raised by the problem definition.

Chapter 8 Validation, Verification, and Testing of Simulation Models

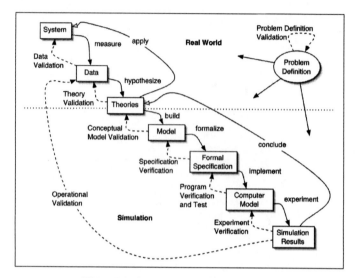

Figure 8.1: A view of the validation process
(adopted with modifications from Balci 1998, p. 337 and Sargent 2001, p. 109)

2. *Model verification* (in the wider sense) is performed during the implementation phase and seeks to establish that the computerized model implements the conceptual model correctly.

3. *Operational model validation* is conducted before and during simulation experiments. Its aim is to determine how closely a model's behaviour resembles the real system's behaviour. This correspondence must at least be sufficient to allow simulation experiments to reliably answer the questions framed in the project's original goals. To achieve this, data collected during model execution is compared with corresponding data gathered during the real system's operation.

These three phases constitute a basic validation template, which Sargent (2001, p. 107) calls "the paradigm of the simple way". Further refinements can add further detail.

Figure 8.1 shows our view of this template, which has been strongly influenced by Sargent (2001, p. 109), Balci (1998, p. 337), and the "V&V triangle" (standing for validation and verification) presented in Brade (2003, p. 62). In the following sections we will use this pattern to discuss general validation principles.

In Figure 8.1 the *problem definition* is placed in the center, resembling a "sun" which illuminates the whole modelling process. This placement highlights the fact that "a sim-

8.2 Foundations of Model Validation

ulation model is built with respect to the study's objectives and its credibility is judged with respect to those objectives" (Balci 1998, p. 346). Validation, no matter how thoroughly it may be performed, can never guarantee "absolute" model validity. Just like empirical corroboration of scientific theories it can only improve models' credibility for answering certain questions about the modelled system by means of certain simulation experiments. Zeigler et al. (2000, p. 369) refer to this endeavour as an "experimental frame". A valid model has to be re-validated whenever the experimental frame changes in any significant way; i.e. validation can only be *relative* to a set of experiments and the set of questions which these are meant to answer (Balci 1998, p. 348).

Since the initial problem framed by customers and other stakeholders at a study's beginning, is "rarely sufficiently clear, specific, or organized" to "enable specific research action", Balci (1998, p. 338) notes that validation of the *problem definition* itself is also required. This is plausible, since the accuracy with which a problem can be described will affect the assessment of acceptability and credibility for simulation's results (Balci 1998, p. 354).

Another important aspect of validation, as shown in Figure 8.1, is that "validation should be conducted throughout the whole modelling cycle" (Page 1991, p. 148). This request asks that every phase must be accompanied by an associated validation activity; i.e.:

1. Data collected from the *real system* must be validated to determine its quality. This can be accomplished by investigating the measured data as well as the measurement process itself, using common empirical research techniques (e.g. statistical techniques or comparison with existing theories).
2. Collected data and existing hypotheses are abstracted into theories about the real system's structure and behaviour. These *theories* must be validated by comparing them to existing data as well as to other relevant theories and hypotheses.
3. Any informal *conceptual model* derived from theories and observations about some relevant aspect of the target system must also be validated against data and other relevant theories. This is normally done using qualitative methods, such as discussions of model structure among model developers and users.
4. The correctness of every *transformation* during the formal design of a conceptual model and its implementation must be verified. Figure 8.1 refers to the comparison of a computerized model and its formal specification. Verification of formal and computer models can be accomplished with formal verification techniques, or, more commonly, with test and review methods frequently used in software engineering.
5. *"Pilot runs"* must be conducted for operational model validation before the start of experiments. These should ensure that model behaviour is checked for plausibility and compared to available data about the real system's behaviour. In this context we can choose between many operational validation techniques, some of which are presented below. Since model results rarely fit real system behaviour

Chapter 8 Validation, Verification, and Testing of Simulation Models

after the first iteration, *model calibration* becomes an important aspect of operational validation; i.e. we must adjust model parameters "whose proper values are unknown" (Zeigler et al. 2000, p. 388) and thereby improve the fit between a model's predictions and the real system's empirical data.

6. Experiments to answer problem relevant questions can be conducted *after* successful model validation. As in any empirical science, the design of such experiments and the methods applied to analyze and interpret their results must be questioned and verified, to ensure that only valid conclusions are drawn.

Although the process shown in Figure 8.1 is somehow reminiscent of software engineering's classical waterfall model, it must be stressed that model building is a strongly iterative activity. On the one hand, every modelling phase has a complementary validation phase, which might lead to revision of whatever artifact it returns. On the other hand, any invalid results may necessitate revisions of earlier phases. If, for example, some unexpected behaviour is detected during attempts to verify a model's computer implementation, the cause may be an implementation error or, just as likely, an undiscovered mistake in the model's specifications, which was not exposed prior to model execution. If this is the case, we must return to and modify the specification. In the context of his "V&V triangle", Brade (2003, Ch. 4.7) emphasises that every modelling artifact must in principle be checked for internal consistency, as well as compared to every other artifact produced in earlier phases of a modelling project.

Participatory and iterative process models from software engineering (see e.g. Pomberger and Blaschek 1996, Ch. 3.1) are well suited to increase model validity in simulation projects. Techniques such as prototyping offer useful support for user participation in simulation. While early availability of a preliminary operational prototype can help to uncover false expectations about a simulation's contribution to solving the model users' problems, it also documents the developers' current understanding of the target system, and thereby enhances communication between model users and developers.

Another recent trend in software engineering are so-called "agile", i.e. lightweight and code-centric, software processes; such as *eXtreme Programming* (XP) (Beck and Andres 2005). XP techniques include test-driven development (see Section 8.3.2) and Pair Programming, which are good strategies for enhancing the quality of simulation model implementations. A drawback of using XP for simulation, however, is that it intentionally neglects the conceptual modelling phase in order to produce executable software early and to avoid inconsistencies between conceptual models and their implementations. There have been some attempts to apply the principles of the XP approach to the modelling phase, but such "eXtreme Modelling" (Boger et al. 2000) is still in its infancy. Further progress in this area relies heavily on future development of tools for testing and building executable conceptual models.

8.2 Foundations of Model Validation

8.2.3 A Philosophical View of Model Validation

Complementary to its technical aspects, the problem of model validation raises interesting issues in a much wider context. As Cantú-Paz et al. (2004, p. 1) point out, "computer simulations are increasingly being seen as the third mode of science, complementing theory and experiments". If we regard simulation models as "miniature scientific theories" (Kleindorfer and Ganeshan 1993, p. 50), it becomes obvious that there is a close correspondence between validation of simulation models and the more general problem of validating a scientific theory (see Troitzsch 2004, p. 5 cited in Küppers and Lenhard 2004, p. 2). The latter problem traditionally belongs to the domain of the *philosophy of science* and has been studied extensively.

Critical rationalism is arguably still the most dominant theory in this area. Popper (see e.g. 2004, p. 118), its chief proponent, views scientific progress as a continuing process of "trial and error", leading to theories with increasing explanatory power. Although we will never be able to prove this, critical rationalists hope that these theories will eventually converge towards "truth". This evolutionary process of framing and corroborating a sequence of theories can be summarized in a 4 step cycle, repeating in a potentially infinite manner (Popper 2005, p. 32):

1. Identification of an initial (practical or theoretical) problem.
2. Formulation of preliminary theories in order to solve the problem. Such theories are "often erroneous [...] and will remain hypotheses or conjectures forever" (Popper 2005, p. 21).
3. Elimination of erroneous theories by "critical discussion, including experimental analysis" (i.e. comparison with empirical observations).
4. Identification of new problems that emerge from the critical analysis of the erroneous theories and lead to the formulation of revised theories in repetition of step (2).

The main characteristic of the so-called "scientific method" lies in the third step, which demands that we make every effort to *falsify* the preliminary theories. In this context falsification is superior to verification[3], since inductions from facts (i.e. empirical observations) to theories can never be justified on logical grounds alone, and theories can therefore never be empirically *verified* (Popper 1982, p. 198). We can, however, use empirical observations to falsify a theory. A single wrong prediction suffices. A putative theory should be refuted if it significantly contradicts observations, since it then seems an inadequate description of reality and a better theory should be sought.

Popper sees the falsifiability of theories as the primary criterion for distinguishing scientific from non-scientific (e.g. theistic) explanations. To ensure falsifiability, a scientist should *always* ask: "Under what circumstances would I conclude that my theory

---

[3] As the astute reader might have noticed, the "verification of theories" is in fact a "validation" according to our definitions. However, in the philosophy of science we traditionally speak of "theory verification".

Chapter 8 Validation, Verification, and Testing of Simulation Models

is false?" (Popper 2004, p. 48). From this principle it also follows that the theory with the highest degree of testability ought to be preferred whenever alternative theories compete for attention. Although it may at first glance seem rather straightforward, this *scientific* approach poses a number of methodological (e.g. what criteria to use, what counts as "valid" observations, what degree of precision should be used for the test), as well as psychological issues; e.g. it may not be easy to rigorously criticise one's own creations.

Before using Popper's aforementioned prescriptions to extract general principles for practical model validation, let us summarize some suggestions for how to "conduct scientific inquiries" (Shannon 1975, p. 212) and how these could contribute to model validation.[4]

Rationalism, Empiricism, and Critical Rationalism

To explain the functioning of an observed system, *rationalists* "postulate the way elements of a system interact and then try to discover whether the facts fit their hypothesis. [...] Their effort is usually directed toward developing a mathematically expressible hypothesis devised to fit the observed facts, subsequently applying the rules of formal logic to deduce various consequences" (Shannon 1975, p. 212). An extreme variant of rationalism is the "pure rationalism" of Kant, according to which theories should be exclusively based on obvious everyday premises, whose validity can be trusted without any need for controllable experiments (Shannon 1975, p. 212).

The methodological opposite of rationalism is *empiricism*, which "regards empirical science, and not mathematics, as the ideal form of knowledge" (Naylor and Finger 1967, pp. B-94). Or, as Shannon (1975, p. 214) puts it, "in its purest form, empiricism asks that we begin with proven or verifiable facts, not assumptions".

As mentioned above, Popper (1982, p. 198) considers the inductive formulation and verification of general theories on the basis of specific observations as logically impossible. Furthermore, he points out that theory formulation never starts from observations, because the selection of what we observe can never be "theory-free", but is always influenced by what theories we have to make sense of the world and what problems we are trying to solve (starting with the problem of survival in a hostile environment). Popper's *critical rationalism* therefore stresses the importance of empirical data and falsification, as well as the rationalist view that theory formation is a *deductive* process, starting from *problems*, rather than an *inductive* process, generalizing from *observations*.

---

[4]Similar treatments are found in Shannon (1975, p. 212), Naylor and Finger (1967, pp. B-93), and Kleindorfer and Ganeshan (1993).

8.2 Foundations of Model Validation

Instrumentalist and Utilitarian Approaches

Although philosophical questions such as "Is modelling a deductive or inductive process?" or "How can the correspondence between a theory's assumptions and reality be established?" lay an important foundation for model validation, their requirements may be too demanding for practical model building in science, business, or industry. In his "essays in positive economics", Friedman (1953) "emphasises that success in economic prediction is the criterion to be used in judging a theory, and not the assumptions themselves" (Kleindorfer and Ganeshan 1993, p. 53).

This instrumentalist or *pragmatist* view suggests an approach to modelling and validation that stresses a theory's ability to serve a purpose over any abstract correspondences with reality (Shannon 1975, p. 214). A theory is seen as a black box that can adequately predict certain aspects of the described system's behaviour, without any need for a "deeper" explanation. Of course, it is exactly this lack of insisting on explanations which raises concerns that "it leaves one without an understanding of the reasons for the exemptions" (Koopmans 1957, p. 139 cited in Naylor and Finger 1967, p. B-95).

Another practical viewpoint, proposed by Naylor and Finger (1967, pp. B-95), takes a "utilitarian" view of validation, with a mixture of rationalist, empiricist, and pragmatist aspects. The corresponding methodology proceeds in 3 simple steps:

1. *Rationalist step*: assessment of intuitive plausibility of model structure. By following the rationalist approach, i.e. criticising a model based on well-founded a-priori knowledge, this step seeks to eliminate obviously erroneous assumptions.
2. *Empiricist step*: detailed empirical validation of those assumptions that have "survived" the first step.
3. *Pragmatist step*: validation of model behaviour by comparing model output to corresponding output obtained from the target system (if available). In this step the model's ability to predict the real system's behaviour is tested. Passing such tests strengthens our confidence that the model can serve its purpose.

Using the terminology introduced in Section 8.3.1, steps 1 and 2 are concerned with conceptual model validation. Step 3 views the model as a "black box" and corresponds to what we have called operational validation before.

Note that step 1 serves as a "filter" for step 2; i.e. if we can make confident a-priori judgements that an assumption is not valid, it makes no sense to engage in often complex attempts of empirical validation.

8.2.4 Principles and Guidelines for Model Validation

Let us now pause and reflect on what can be learned from our brief excursion into philosophy. A number of principles for guiding a validation effort can be derived. In the following discussion we refer to Page (1991, Ch. 5.2) and Balci (1998, Ch. 10.3) for similar and partly complementary discussions.

Chapter 8 Validation, Verification, and Testing of Simulation Models

Degrees of Model Validity

In Section 8.2.3 we learned that *rationalists* and *empiricists* are interested in models that explain the behaviour of systems in terms of their structure. In contrast to this, *pragmatists* simply view systems as black boxes and rate model quality solely on the basis of a model's predictive power. No attempts are made at explaining *why* certain inputs cause certain outputs. Only system *behaviour* is seen as accessible to analysis. In the simulation domain these two perspectives have led to the definition of different degrees of model validity, which Bossel (1989, p. 14) summarizes as follows (cited from Martelli 1999, pp. 88):

1. *Structural validity*: The model represents all structural relations of the system with relevance for the simulation study's purpose in a suitable way.
2. *Behavioural validity*: The model exhibits the same behaviour as the real system for all inputs and initial conditions that are possible in reality.
3. *Empirical validity*: The empirical results of the model are suitably similar to those of the real system, with respect to the relevant range of system behaviours.
4. *Application validity*: The model serves the purpose of the simulation study and produces useful information.

Due to the need to consider *all possible* system inputs, behavioural validity is a rather strong requirement hardly ever met in practical simulation studies. We will therefore mostly restrict ourselves to assessing a model's *empirical* validity. If no suitable empirical results are available, model results can at least be checked for plausibility.

Scope and Effort of Model Validation

Popper's aforementioned claim of the impossibility of empirical theory verification strongly suggests that the establishment of "absolute" model validity is also a logical impossibility. This belief is confirmed by many other results in science and mathematics, including the limits to formalization explored by Goedel and Turing (see e.g. Gruska 1997, Ch. 6). Since all models are abstracted and idealized approximations with respect to the problem-relevant aspects of a system under investigation, *no* model can claim universal validity. From this observation Balci (1998, Ch. 10.3) deduces a number of important practical principles for validation:

- The outcome of simulation model validation, verification, and testing should not be considered a binary variable, where a model is either absolutely correct or absolutely incorrect. There are many shades of grey.
- A simulation model is built with respect to the study's objectives and its credibility is judged according to those objectives.
- Simulation model credibility can be claimed only for the conditions for which the model has been validated or tested.
- Exhaustive testing of simulation models is an impossibility.

8.2 Foundations of Model Validation

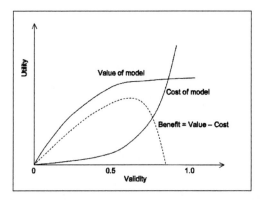

Figure 8.2: Estimation of cost, value, and benefit in model validation (adopted with modifications from Shannon 1975, p. 209)

Despite the immense theoretical and practical importance of model validity, Shannon (1975, pp. 208) stresses the need for an "economic" approach to validation activities. The pseudo-quantitative estimation in Figure 8.2 shows that value and cost of a model do not increase in a linear fashion with the model's validity.

Instead, as can be seen in the figure, a model's benefit often reaches its maximum at a "medium" level of accuracy. In several cases simple but suitably accurate models are better than extremely detailed ones, whose complexity and data requirements quickly become intractable. This is another example of the principle of "Occam's Razor", which in this case claims that a simpler theory with fewer parameters should be preferred over a more complex one, based on its easier testability (Popper 2004, p. 188).

Developer's Bias and Independent V&V

Popper's claim that model validation should always be based on falsification instead of verification leads to practical consequences regarding the question of how and by whom validation should be conducted.

The main problem is that a model developer "needs to be objective, but the way s/he makes progress is through following up subjective insights" (Blyth 1973 cited in Shannon 1975, p. 212). To resolve this conflict, Shannon (1975, p. 212) proposes to split roles in model development into a subjective part, i.e. the model developer with his or her intuitions and ideas of how the real system might work, and an objective one, i.e. the validation agent who applies tests to expose errors in model structure and behaviour. To avoid biased results, the model developer and validation agent should not be the same person. The term *developer's bias* (Balci 1998, p. 347) is often used in this

Chapter 8 Validation, Verification, and Testing of Simulation Models

context. It refers to the phenomenon that developers of programs, models, or scientific theories, may find it hard or even impossible to effectively question the validity of their own creations. If model development and validation are conducted by the same person, s/he must endeavour to act as in a kind of "split personality" mode, constantly switching between a developer's and a tester's perspective. To ensure effective validation, a tester must not seek to "prove", but should rather try hard to question and refute a model's validity. Myers (2004, p. 7) therefore stresses that *successful* tests are not those that programs or models "pass", but rather those that detect serious errors instead.

The "Human Factor"

In critical domains such as model validation, people often call for increased formality, automation, and tool-support in order to compensate for human fallibility. However, according to Page (1991, p. 147), "the application of mathematical and statistical methods in model validation is limited" and such methods typically impose strong restrictions on model representation and complexity. Metrics for model quality which hold promise for automated validation techniques, like those presented in Barton and Szczerbicka (2000, pp. 308), only cover a narrow aspect of model validity.

Brade (2003, p. 90) concludes that "although automated computer-based validation techniques are more objective, more efficient, more likely to be repeatable, and even more reliable than human review, the human reviewer plays an extremely important role for the V&V of models and simulation results". Irrespective of any future advances in automation, model validation will therefore always require a high degree of subjective and human-centered analysis, such as result visualization, model animation, and expert reviews. In recognition of this, proponents of formal and automated techniques should seek to develop tools whose primary focus is the support and augmentation of human modelling and validation activities.

Importance of Documentation

Although not a validation method in its own right, documentation is an extremely important means for enhancing model quality and credibility. According to Page (1991, p. 147), "all steps of the [modelling and] validation process should be precisely documented. Only the transparency of the whole simulation study establishes model credibility". The requirement for documenting all assumptions flowing into a simulation model can be traced back directly to the need for falsifiability we have argued for in the previous section. Different documentation techniques can be used, depending on the phase of the simulation study and its associated artifacts.

The conceptual modelling phase is often documented by diagrams in a graphical modelling language, such as UML. However, it might be impossible to document *all* model assumptions by using a graphical notation. Often additional textual documentation is

8.2 Foundations of Model Validation

therefore required. To assist in this task, UML offers a "note" symbol which lets model developers attach comments to any model element.

Code documentation is an important and often neglected task during the implementation phase. Many modern programming languages try to support the programmer's "documentation ethics" by means of powerful source documentation systems. Java, for example, offers the *Javadoc* tool, which generates program documentations in the form of linked HTML pages directly from source code. The *Javadoc* system documents packages, classes, attributes, and methods, together with their parameter lists and return values. It thereby helps us to keep documentation consistent with code. In addition, some of the verification techniques presented in Section 8.3.2 (e.g. assertions and unit tests) can also be regarded as "program documentation".

Further documentation should be produced during all steps of the validation process. Premises and results of simulation runs, as well as known model limits and preconditions need concise documentation as well. However, there are hardly any standards and tools which support model documentation beyond the coding level. This drawback has been denounced by several simulation researchers (see e.g. Brade 2003, p. 105) and some domain-specific model documentation systems, such as ECOBAS for ecological modelling (Benz et al. 2001), have since been proposed.

We conclude this section with a catalog of *requirements for model documentation*:

- a meaningful and descriptive model name
- name and contact information of one or more model designer(s) and implementer(s)
- goals of the simulation study
- data and data sources used for model building
- premises and assumptions underlying the model
- methods applied in model building (e.g. simulation world view)
- concise description of all validation steps
- graphical representation of the conceptual model (e.g. UML diagrams)
- source code and program documentation
- technical details and prerequisites of the simulation (hardware requirements, integration methods used in continuous simulations, etc.)
- input and output for examples of simulation runs (parameter settings, trace files, simulation reports)
- interpretation of model results with detailed documentation of all analysis steps and premisses
- range and limits of model applicability
- comparison with similar models (if available)
- list of literature used for the simulation study

Chapter 8 Validation, Verification, and Testing of Simulation Models

8.2.5 Classification of Validation Techniques

The simulation literature offers more (e.g. Balci 1998) or less (e.g. Garrido 2001) exhaustive listings of model validation techniques. Many of the large number of proposals originate in different fields, such as theoretical computer science, software engineering, or theoretical computer science. To bring some structure to this "chaos", many authors propose their own schemes for classifying validation techniques.

Balci (1998, p. 355) classifies validation techniques as informal, static, dynamic, and formal. Garrido (2001, p. 216) distinguishes black box validation techniques for checking behavioural validity by comparison of results from white box validations for checking structural validity. As mentioned above, Page (1991, p. 16) classifies validation techniques by their location in the model building cycle. He therefore distinguishes between conceptual validation, verification, and operational validation techniques.

In contrary Brade (2003, p. 56) points out that it "does not seem to be reasonable to classify V&V techniques as methods for either model verification or validation. Most techniques can be used for both validation or verification". He then goes on to distinguish between (Brade 2003, p. 56)

- symbolic model analysis techniques;
- input analysis, output analysis, and embedded data analysis techniques; and
- development and evaluation techniques for high yield test cases.

To integrate these different schemes into a coherent classification, we will in this book arrange validation techniques along the following dimensions (see also Figure 8.3):

- *Approach*: We separate exploratory from confirmatory validation techniques. *Exploratory* techniques are applied to gather more knowledge about a model's structural or behavioural features, while *confirmatory* techniques serve to test some pre-established hypotheses.

- *Phase in model building cycle*: This dimension describes whether a validation technique is mainly used for conceptual model validation, model verification, or operational validation; or one of the phases attached to a more sophisticated validation process.

- *Degree of formality*: Along this dimension we differentiate between qualitative informal, quantitative formal, and symbolic formal validation methods. Qualitative methods rely exclusively on human judgement and are of great value to validation. Quantitative methods typically use statistical techniques for result analysis, while symbolic techniques are used in attempts at formal verification.

- *System view*: This dimension refers to the perspective which characterizes a validation technique. Here, we mainly distinguish between techniques for the static validation of system structure and the dynamic validation of system behaviour. However, dynamic validation techniques might themselves focus on specific system views, such as the dynamic behaviour of single entities, interactions between multiple entities, or structures emerging from these interactions.

8.3 Selected Validation Techniques

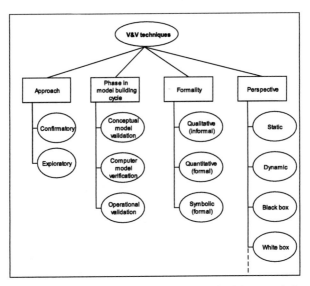

Figure 8.3: Dimensions used for the classification of validation techniques

8.3 Selected Validation Techniques

This section explores a number of selected validation and verification strategies we consider important. Due to the already mentioned eclectic character of model validation (Kleindorfer and Ganeshan 1993, p. 50), this list is far from "complete". More comprehensive treatment would require a textbook of its own. A more extensive list containing about 75 different validation techniques can be found in Balci (1998, Ch. 10.4).

Our discussion is based on the classification we presented above. The model building phase is used as the main criterion, which also determines the predominant system view (see Figure 8.4). Conceptual model validation is mainly static, while operational validation is by definition dynamic. The sections on conceptual validation and verification are further partitioned by the presented techniques' degree of formality. Finally, particular attention is paid to validation techniques and tools that are applicable in the context of object-oriented simulation with UML and Java.

The section on operational validation is further divided into the complementary approaches of exploratory and confirmatory validation. While many texts strongly focus on statistical techniques, we will try to present a representative cross-section of methods from statistics, software engineering, artificial intelligence as well as formal analysis.

211

Chapter 8 Validation, Verification, and Testing of Simulation Models

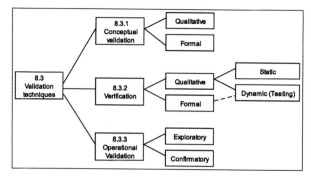

Figure 8.4: Structure of the presentation of validation techniques in this chapter

We include "classical" methods such as statistical hypothesis tests, as well as innovative techniques such as model-based trace checking (Howard et al. 2003) or the application of data mining techniques to validation (Remondino and Correndo 2005).

8.3.1 Conceptual Model Validation

The applicability of conceptual validation methods obviously will depend strongly on the form of representation we choose to use for the conceptual model. Usually a conceptual model will contain one or more of the following components:

1. A *textual* description of the system under study. This description provides an abstracted view of the real system and is influenced by the simulation's goals, hypotheses, and assumptions.
2. A *diagrammatic* semi-formal description of the model's structure and dynamic behaviour (e.g. Petri nets or UML).
3. Measured or estimated *values* for model parameters and input distributions. These are typically abstracted from the available data.

In the following we first review qualitative validation methods, and then show how quantitative and formal methods can be applied in an early modelling phase. The astute reader will recognize this structure as reminiscent of the first two steps of the "utilitarian" validation process (Naylor and Finger 1967, pp. B-95) presented in Section 8.2.3.

Qualitative Validation Techniques

Before proceeding to detailed quantitative and formal validation, we should always perform a qualitative conceptual model validation in order to establish a model's so-

8.3 Selected Validation Techniques

called "face validity". The goal is to eliminate obvious errors in model structure and to ensure that the model seems plausible to domain experts "at first glance". The range of possible qualitative conceptual validation techniques is quite limited, since most of them rather obviously depend on expert reviews of several model aspects. The following list of techniques has been compiled from Page (1991, Ch. 5.3.1) and Balci (1998, pp. 358):

Expert Reviews are applied in checking model assumptions and hypotheses, as well as data quality and model structure. In cooperation with domain experts the model developer should ensure that the assumptions flowing into the model are consistent with existing theories, that the applied abstractions are feasible, and that the underlying empirical data is representative (Page 1991, p. 149).

Structural model validation is based on graphical representations, such as UML diagrams, and should be performed by model designers as well as external experts (Page 1991, p. 149). The cautious application of graphical modelling languages helps to communicate even detailed descriptions of the model's structure and dynamics to domain experts. An internal consistency check of the model's structure should be performed by the model designers. A number of guidelines for avoiding syntactic and semantic errors in several UML diagram types are presented by Jeckle et al. (2002). As an example, non-final states in a statechart should always have at least one outgoing transition (Jeckle et al. 2002, p. 322).

Conceptual model animation is a technique for the early validation of model dynamics. Although conceptual validation traditionally focuses on model structure, developers and users should strive to obtain an impression of the model's behaviour as soon as possible. This principle is derived from the benefits of software prototyping mentioned in Section 8.2.2.

Graphical modelling tools often contain simulators that allow the execution and animation of conceptual models. "Manual" animations of dynamic diagrams are also possible. By means of a manual "token game" (see Section 4.4.2) Petri nets and UML activity diagrams allow vivid animations of control flow, object flow, concurrency, and synchronization. The manual and computer animation of UML models supports many of the validation techniques presented in Balci (1998, pp. 359), such as concurrent process analysis, control flow analysis, state transition analysis, and data flow analysis.

Dependency graphs: Many semi-formal conceptual validation techniques are based on directed graphs, which show dependencies between model elements. Among these techniques, Balci (1998, pp. 359) discusses *cause-effect graphing* and *data dependency analysis*.

Cause-effect graphing assists in finding out "what causes what in a model representation" (Balci 1998, p. 359). The causes and effects identified in the model are first checked for consistency with the real system. Then a dependency graph showing their interconnections is built. From this graph a "decision table is created by tracing back through the graph in order to determine combinations of causes resulting in each effect" (Balci 1998, p. 359). The attachment of probabilities to cause-effect graphs leads to Bayesian networks (see e.g. Pearl 2001, pp. 13).

Chapter 8 Validation, Verification, and Testing of Simulation Models

Data dependency analysis is conducted in order to determine "what variables depend on what other variables" (Dunn 1984 as cited in Balci 1998, p. 360). It can be performed with the aid of dependency graphs similar to those known from *System Dynamics* (Bossel 1994, p. 213).

Formal Validation Techniques

Although formal methods have only limited applicability to model validation, some techniques have been successfully used to verify a conceptual model.

Dynamic system behaviour, for example, can be conveniently captured with Petri nets or finite state machines (FSM). *Petri nets* in particular offer a powerful formalism to rigorously analyse system properties like e.g. lifeness. They can also be used in formal studies of synchronization properties, such as mutual exclusion (see e.g. Jessen and Valk 1997, pp. 128). An advantage of UML as a conceptual modelling language is that dynamic diagram types like statecharts and activity diagrams can be easily mapped onto FSMs or Petri nets.

Finite state machines offer a suitable base for *model checking*, a formal verification technique that has gained some practical relevance in several applications; e.g. protocol analysis (Holzmann 1991, Ch. 11). The core idea of model checking is to give a specification of expected model behaviour in a logical language, and then apply a "model checker" tool to verify if the finite state model's behaviour conforms to this specification.

Since we are interested in *dynamic* model behaviour, a *temporal logic* is chosen as specification language. Temporal logics are extensions of propositional or predicate logic with temporal operators, such as "until" and "next". Temporal logics allow us to specify properties for feasible state sequences of a FSM. The most basic form of temporal logic is *Propositional Linear Temporal Logic* (PLTL). It extends propositional logic with the following operators (modified citation from Brade 2003, p. 83):

- X (Next): If p is a logical formula, then Xp means that p will hold in the next state of the state sequence.
- U (Until): If p and q are logical formulae, then pUq means that p holds until the step in the state sequence where q first holds.
- F (Future): If p is a logical formula, then Fp means that p will hold in *some* future state of the state sequence.
- G (Globally or Generally): If p is a logical formula, then Gp means that p holds in *all* future states of the state sequence.

In PLTL we can specify properties of finite state machines, such as "state S_i is not reached until state S_j has been reached" or to give a more concrete example: "In the gravel pit model, every truck that has left the loading dock must next enter the weighing station". This specification translates to the PLTL formula

$$G(LeaveLoadingDock \Rightarrow XEnterWeighingStation).$$

8.3 Selected Validation Techniques

A number of model checking tools can be applied to conceptual simulation model verification. SPIN (Holzmann 1997) is a popular model checker for Linear Temporal Logic (LTL). An important advantage of model checking compared to nearly all other operational validation techniques is that it provides *exhaustive* verification: This means that it can verify that a specification holds *for all possible state sequences*. This advantage is a consequence of the finite state property of the input model.

8.3.2 Model Verification and Testing

There are several complementary methods for verification of simulation models, most of which are rooted in software engineering. The following techniques can be of help to assess and ensure correspondences between formal models and their computer-based implementations:

- Software engineering techniques that support the creation of comprehensible and maintainable program code. This includes suitable programming languages, object-orientation programming styles, relevant design-patterns, mature simulation frameworks or systems, etc.
- Model-driven development and code-generation techniques which can reduce the gap between specification and program.
- Consistent and informative documentation of models and code which is updated regularly.
- Qualitative techniques, such as code reviews or pair-programming.
- Software testing, debugging, and logging, for which several programming languages (including Java) offer excellent tools.
- Software metrics for numerical "measurement" of code quality.
- Early use of formal verification (see above).

Producing High-Quality Code

Establishing model correctness does not just begin with the verification phase, since it largely depends on the way formal specifications and code are developed. Comprehensibility and maintainability of computer models is strongly influenced by the software on which they are based. As described in Section 9.4, several different classes of software support the development of simulation models; i.e. general programming languages, simulation languages, simulation packages or frameworks, parametrized models, and simulation systems.

A *programming language* influences code quality mainly through factors such as readability, security, complexity, appropriateness, and the linguistic abstractions it offers. Modern languages like Java support the creation of readable and secure code with numerous concepts, such as block-structure, strong typing, encapsulation, and automatic garbage collection. However, all good concepts are wasted if they are not used ap-

Chapter 8 Validation, Verification, and Testing of Simulation Models

propriately by a programmer. As in all software projects, model implementers should therefore take great care to follow established general and project-specific coding conventions, such as the use of meaningful identifiers, proper code formatting, avoidance of obscure programming constructs (e.g. the infamous GOTO statement), etc. Consult Bloch (2001) for a more detailed overview on good Java programming style.

Another important language property which influences the quality of simulation code is the availability of simulation specific abstractions. Since simulation models implemented with general purpose languages "include many implementation details that can obscure the underlying model" (Overstreet 2002, pp. 641), the use of *simulation specific languages* or *packages* is often preferred. In this case, however, important details of simulation code, such as the scheduler's operation, might be encapsulated and not available to a model implementer (Overstreet 2002, pp. 642). Their correct operation must therefore be taken on trust.

Especially where the package's source code is available (as for so-called "open source" software), simulation packages based on general purpose programming languages offer a reasonable trade-off between generality, understandability, and testability of simulation code. These criteria can be met even better by using established design and implementation patterns; e.g. those presented in Gamma et al. (1995). The "Java Simulation Handbook" describes the DESMO-J simulation framework, which is a Java-based open source tool and contains several design patterns, such as *Observer* for statistical data collection and *Composite* for hierarchical modelling.

Another means for enhancing the quality of code is the use of visual programming and automatic code generation. Since it narrows the gap between a conceptual model and its implementation (Klügl 2001, p. 86), visual and interactive modelling tools have a long-standing tradition in the simulation community. In the ideal case such interfaces have the potential to reduce the cost of code verification substantially. Stimulated by model-driven program design and UML, visual programming styles are currently enjoying anew attention within the software engineering community. However, efficient model-driven design relies heavily on adequate tool support; i.e. for model building, code generation, and for keeping alternative representations consistent.

Qualitative Verification

Qualitative verification requires structured discussions of model specifications and code among model developers and other stakeholders. Balci (1998, pp. 356) distinguishes several forms, which differ in team composition and organization:

Audits (Balci 1998, p. 356) are performed periodically by management staff to ensure that model developers closely adhere to "established plans, policies, procedures, standards, and guidelines".

Documentation checking (Balci 1998, p. 356) is needed to confirm that the code's and other forms of model documentation are both complete and consistent.

8.3 Selected Validation Techniques

Inspections (Balci 1998, pp. 356) are a type of structured discussion between team members playing several roles. A *moderator* leads the discussion, a *reader* presents the design to be discussed, and a *recorder* documents any errors which occur. A member of each of the design, programming, and quality assurance teams should also be present. Note that not only specification and code, but *all* artifacts produced in the simulation study are subject to inspection. A quite similar but less extensive technique with different team composition and organization is often referred to as a *walkthrough* (Balci 1998, p. 358). If managers and users participate, inspections and walkthroughs are called a *review* (Balci 1998, p. 357).

Desk Checking (Balci 1998, p. 356) affirms an implementer's constant vigilance in detecting syntactic and semantic program errors, deviations from specifications or violations of coding standards as early as possible. To avoid developer's bias, team members should regularly check the work of each other. An efficient approach to ensure this is "Pair Programming", which has recently been popularized by the eXtreme Programming (XP) movement (Beck and Andres 2005, pp. 42). In Pair Programming two developers share a common workstation. One operates the computer and enters code, while the other comments and corrects work where needed. To provide fresh perspectives, these roles are constantly switched.

At first sight Pair Programming seems an expensive technique, since suitable workplaces must be set up and only one of the implementers actually "hacks code" at any time. However, empirical studies of Pair Programming have shown it to be quite efficient: The cooperation of implementers with similar levels of experience improves code quality, and teams can quickly incorporate less experienced developers by pairing them with more experienced staff (Lippert et al. 2002, p. 86).

Software Testing and Debugging

Testing is a dynamic code verification technique, where parts of a model's code are run and observed to detect deviations from specifications. According to Popper's falsification principle it is testing's goal to detect as many and as drastic failures as possible, "while not increasing costs too much" (Andrews 2004, p. 1). Software engineers identify a number of testing phases, which apply to the testing of simulations as well (see Pomberger and Blaschek 1996, pp. 147; Balci 1998, pp. 345):

- *Unit (or sub-model) testing*: In unit testing the functionality of isolated components or sub-models is checked for conformance with their specifications. Unit testing is often performed during programming, by the implementer himself, but it can also be delegated to independent testers. The technical requirements include an object under test (OUT) (Link 2002, p. 322), a test driver checking the OUT's export interface (Link 2002, p. 324), and several so-called "dummy objects" which satisfy the OUT's import specification (Link 2002, p. 92).
- *Integration testing*: An integration test checks interactions between multiple components that have already passed unit tests. According to Balci (1998, p. 346)

Chapter 8 Validation, Verification, and Testing of Simulation Models

the "objective is to substantiate that no inconsistencies in interfaces and communication between the submodels exist when [...they] are combined to form the model".

- *System (or model) testing*: System testing is performed to ensure that the model as a whole behaves as expected.
- *Acceptance testing*: Acceptance testing requires the participation of model users. "Its objective is to establish [...] credibility of the simulation model so that its result can be accepted [...] by the sponsor" (Balci 1998, p. 346).
- *Regression testing*: Regression testing (Balci 1998, p. 370) is needed where a model must be extended or refactored without changing its original functionality. It consists of repeating a number of test cases the model has already passed during unit, integration, and system tests.

Complementary to these phases we distinguish two further types of tests which we already encountered in our discussion of *utilitarian* validation schemes in Section 8.2.3 (Pomberger and Blaschek 1996, pp. 151): In *black box testing* we assume that no knowledge of the internal structure of the OUT is available, and proceed to check only correctness of input-output-transformations. For efficient black box testing we must therefore be able to draw on a reasonable number of cases, which ideally should cause the OUT to exhibit a wide range of behaviour.

In *white box testing* our knowledge about the OUT's internal structure (e.g. the programming logic) influences test case selection. The goal is to develop test cases that lead to execution of as many paths through a model's code as possible. Software engineers distinguish between different degrees of code coverage, ranging from the requirement that every code statement is executed at least once, to the often unrealistic demand that all possible execution paths must be tested (Pomberger and Blaschek 1996, p. 152).

The creation of "high yield test cases" (Brade 2003, p. 56) is one of the hardest problems in software testing. Some basic approaches to meet this demand are (Balci 1998, pp. 370):

- *Equivalence partitioning testing*: Input data is partitioned into equivalence classes; i.e. sets of values that produce "similar" outputs with regard to the test unit's behaviour. One value from each equivalence class is then chosen for testing.
- *Extreme input testing*: Extremes (e.g. highest and lowest values) of the input domain are used as test inputs.
- *Invalid input testing*: This test ensures that the test unit handles *invalid* input data in a controlled and predictable fashion. In a Java program we might, for example, test that relevant error conditions raise the expected exceptions.

Because of the importance and complexity of software testing a large number of support tools are available to automate some of its aspects. A popular example is *JUnit*[5], a

---
[5]http://www.junit.org

8.3 Selected Validation Techniques

lightweight framework for automated unit and regression tests of Java programs (Link 2002). With *JUnit* we can assign a test case to each class that checks its methods' functionality by means of assertion statements. Multiple test cases can be arranged in suites, which are executed and controlled through a graphical interface. Although JUnit is a relatively simple tool, it enjoys great popularity among Java developers and can be integrated into many development environments, such as *Eclipse*[6].

The assertion construct which has recently been added to Java also offers an opportunity for improving a program's reliability. *Assertions* can be inserted into Java programs to check input data correctness and program invariants during execution. They are based on the notion of "programming by contract" (Züllighoven et al. 2004, pp. 44); i.e. a class "commits itself" to generate correct output data for a restricted domain of correct input data. Violations are reported with user-defined messages.

The availability of powerful test automation tools has stimulated new approaches to software development, which are also well suited to verify simulations. The "test first" approach mandated by eXtreme Programming (Beck and Andres 2005, p. 50), for example, requires that *every* functionality of a production code[7] unit (e.g. a Java class) must be tested and that these tests should be written prior to the tested code itself. This "upside down" approach yields a number of practical advantages (Link 2002, pp. 15):

- The programmer receives instant and often motivating feedback about the quality of his or her code from the test automation tool.
- The test-suite serves as a further documentation of how and under what conditions the production code should be used.
- The development of a test case prior to implementation forces the programmer to think more deeply about the production code's functionality and interface. Software developed from a test-driven perspective is often designed more systematically and is less feature-laden than software produced by conventional development styles.

So far we have discussed testing of simulation models from a purely software engineering perspective. However, according to Overstreet (2002, p. 641) "testing simulations often raises issues that occur infrequently in other types of software [... and] many [...] characteristics that [...] occur in simulation code are exactly those that the software testing community has identified as making testing challenging". Some of these characteristics are listed below (Overstreet 2002, pp. 642):

- Only few components of a simulation model (e.g. a route planner in a traffic simulation) can be sensibly tested using the functional unit test approach. Most model components do not adhere to the simple paradigm where a single input

---

[6]http://www.eclipse.org
[7]In software testing we refer to the code of the actual software system under development as *production code* as opposed to *test code* used to test this system (see e.g. Link 2002, p. 15).

Chapter 8 Validation, Verification, and Testing of Simulation Models

causes a single output, but rather exhibit more complex behaviour in execution; i.e. during a simulation run.
- In many simulations, e.g. those using the process interaction approach, concurrent processes are the core model components. Unfortunately, "testing of parallel [...] code is significantly more complex than sequential code [...] due in part to the many possible execution orders" (Overstreet 2002, p. 643).
- Simulation models often contain stochastic elements. Although deterministic behaviour can usually be enforced by using a fixed random seed, input-output-tests of simulation models must consider a significant range of stochastic behaviour and apply statistical analysis to report meaningful outputs.

The analysis of a simulation model's dynamics can be supported by techniques such as debugging and logging (also known as *tracing*). A debugger is a tool that allows the stepwise execution of programs and the inspection of data at runtime. While most modern programming languages and development environments include powerful debuggers, tailor-made debugging tools, which incorporate time series analyses and graphical animation, have been proposed as extensions for simulation (see e.g. Grimm 2002).

Logging is a simple technique, whose use for program debugging has a long standing tradition. So-called log-statements that list changes in relevant information (e.g. the values of observed state variables) during a program's execution are displayed on the console, or written into a log file.

Logging can easily be implemented using a programming language's standard output commands; e.g. `System.err.println` in Java. There are, however, also specialized "logging frameworks", such as the *Java logging API* or the Apache project's *Log4J*[8], which distribute logging messages to several different output channels (including SQL data bases), support different log entry formats, and offer extensive configuration possibilities.

Some simulation software, like DESMO-J, contain a specialized logger for the creation of *simulation traces*. Since logging generates large masses of data, the analysis of log-files is a challenging task, for which we suggest some support in Section 8.3.3 on operational validation.

Quantitative and Formal Verification Techniques

Due to the complexity of simulation models the applicability of formal verification techniques to simulation programs remains rather limited. While the application of model checking (see Section 8.3.1) to simulation programs has sometimes been successful, the fact that exhaustive model checking relies on a system description cast in the form of a finite state model remains a major disincentive to its wider use. Even the simplest of simulations contains state variables that can in principle range over an infinite set

---

[8] http://logging.apache.org

8.3 Selected Validation Techniques

of values. Two solutions, each with specific advantages and disadvantages, have been proposed to tackle this problem:

Program abstraction (Visser et al. 2003) is based on the idea that we can derive a finite state model from a program that exhibits *at least* all erroneous behaviour of the original code. The derivation of this model could be performed manually, which is in itself a complex and error-prone task. Alternatively, Visser et al. (2003) propose a tool for the automatic abstraction of Java programs, named *Java PathFinder*. However, this approach only works on a restricted subset of Java, and its practical applicability is therefore limited.

Model-based trace checking [9] (Howard et al. 2003) applies the concept of model checking to log-file analysis. As in "traditional" model checking the expected dynamic behaviour is described in terms of a temporal logic. However, instead of a finite state model, a trace of a single simulation run is checked for correspondence with its specification. Model-based trace checking is easier to perform than program abstraction and will, in principle, work for arbitrarily complex models.

A drawback to model-based trace checking is that it offers no exhaustive behaviour verification, but rather checks a single simulation trajectory. In order to gain reasonable levels of confidence in the correctness of stochastic simulations we must therefore consider traces for several independent simulation runs. Brade (2003, pp. 81) has developed a tool called *Violade* for assisting in model checking of simulation traces on the basis of Propositional Linear Temporal Logic (PLTL).

Let us conclude this section with a brief comment on quantitative verification techniques. Software engineering research has long tried to measure the quality of code as well as other aspect of software development, using quantitative *software metrics*. Very basic examples for such metrics are the lines of code a program contains or the number of dependencies between its modules (coupling). A wide range of software metrics and measurement tools is now available (see e.g. Kan 2003). However, as with all quantitative approaches, often hidden assumptions abound, and users of software metrics must always be vigilant and very careful to derive valid interpretations from numbers produced in this fashion.

8.3.3 Operational Validation of Model Behaviour

Operational model validations seek to ensure that a model's dynamic behaviour and the results of corresponding simulation runs are "sufficiently close" to the modelled system's responses. Two major scenarios can be distinguished:

1. Matchable output data from the real system is available. In this case the task is to show that output data from model and system do not differ significantly at a required level of accuracy.

---

[9]Trace-based model checking would be as good a name for this technique.

Chapter 8 Validation, Verification, and Testing of Simulation Models

2. No matchable output data from the real system is available; either because no "real" instance of the modelled system exists, or because no useful data about it can be obtained. In this case we can only check model outputs for plausibility or compare it to outputs of similar models which have been successfully validated. This is sometimes called *model-to-model analysis* (Hales et al. 2003).

Techniques for operational validation can be broadly divided into *exploratory* and *confirmatory* analysis methods. Exploratory techniques seek to *understand* aspects of the model's behaviour, such as the model's reaction to parameter changes. In contrast to this, confirmatory techniques are content to simply *substantiate* or *refute* given hypotheses about model behaviour. For this they will use techniques such as model-based trace checking (see Section 8.3.2) or statistical tests of model output.

Exploratory Validation Techniques

Calibration and Sensitivity Analysis: Most models contain *free parameters*, for which appropriate values are not known at the start of a simulation run. Reasons for this may be that the real-world correspondences of these values could not be measured with sufficient accuracy, or that parameters have no readily identifiable real-world correspondences and are merely abstract artifacts which have been introduced for reasons of modelling convenience. A first task for model exploration during operational validation is therefore to *calibrate* the model; i.e. to find appropriate values for such parameters.

The goal of calibration is to estimate model parameters so that a model's behaviour becomes as realistic as possible. Usually this is done according to the following simple algorithm:

1. Choose plausible parameter settings from within the domain of feasible inputs.
2. Run a simulation with these settings and compare the resulting model outputs with all available and corresponding real data. Note that we must perform several independent replications and consider arithmetic means, confidence intervals, or other statistical aggregations of outputs for models containing stochastic components.
3. If the results are sufficiently accurate, the process terminates. Otherwise we change the parameter settings in order to minimize any observed deviations and return to step 2.

Unfortunately, this deceptively simple procedure raises a number of difficult problems:

1. It is always possible to misuse calibration for "tuning" a model's performance by varying parameter values in order to cover errors in model structure. Such practices certainly do not increase model credibility, and Page (1991, p. 153) therefore demands that we use calibration with care, and only on those parameters which are stable according to sensitivity analysis.
2. It is often unclear how to proceed if settings are rejected during step 3. The calibration of a complex (e.g. agent-based) model with several interdependent

8.3 Selected Validation Techniques

parameters might lead to a lengthy sequence of "trials and errors" (Klügl 2001, p. 83), particularly if dependencies between free parameters and results are insufficiently well understood. This problem can either be tackled with systematic experimental designs (see e.g. Law and Kelton 2000, Ch. 12), or through simulation-based optimization (see below).

3. It is often hard to decide if model and system output are "sufficiently similar", particularly if models contain stochastic components and the simulations' results are complex; e.g. spatial patterns in multi-agent-based simulations.

Some support for calibration is offered by simulation-based optimization tools. In general terms calibration can be viewed as a multi-criteria optimization problem (Drougoul et al. 2002, p. 12), whose goal is to minimize deviations between model and system output (Klügl 2001, p. 213). Using suitable weights, multiple criteria for model validity can be collapsed into a single objective function G (Zitzler 1999). In an (often too) simplistic approach, G computes a weighted sum of all deviations between relevant model and system outputs:

$$G(\mathbf{x}) = \min\left(\sum_{i=1}^{n} w_i \cdot |F_i(\mathbf{x}) - y_i|\right).$$

In the above equation F_i is the i-th output variable that the model computes from a vector $\mathbf{x}$ of input parameters, while y_i is the corresponding empirical output quantity measured from the real system. A major challenge is the appropriate choice of weighting factors w_i for output quantities with different dimensions. The collapse of multiple complex validity criteria into a single number may also require invalid simplifications. These difficulties might be resolved by delegating responsibility for evaluating results to the users and feedback *their* ratings into the optimization's attempts at improving parameter settings. An example for such an approach are the interactive genetic algorithms proposed by Boschetti (1995). Automatic simulation-based optimization has occasionally been applied to the calibration of real world simulation models, e.g. to the simulation of a tailplane rudder by Barton and Szczerbicka (2000) and to an agent-based simulation of city courier services by Bachmann et al. (2004).

The analysis of a model's sensitivity to parameter changes is another important step in the exploration of a model's operational validity. Like calibration, sensitivity analysis can also be performed by systematic variation of settings for model parameters, but the result analysis differs: A well-known approach is presented by Page (1991, p. 151). Here *sensitivity coefficients*, which relate the variation ΔX_i of an input parameter X_i to the change ΔY_i of an output variable Y_i, are computed as:

$$S_{ij} = \frac{\Delta Y_i/Y_i}{\Delta X_j/X_j}.$$

Values of S_{ij} which are close to 0 indicate low sensitivity of an input parameter X_j. The parameter can therefore be varied more confidently in calibrations or, if the value is very low, can even be omitted to simplify the model. Large values of S_{ij} indicate

Chapter 8 Validation, Verification, and Testing of Simulation Models

instable or even chaotic model behaviour. This may point to errors in model structure. The results of sensitivity analysis influence model calibration as well as the conclusions we can draw from a model experiment. They should therefore always be documented in detail.

Meta-Modelling Meta-modelling is yet another technique to increase a modeller's insight into a model's response to parameter variations. Simply put, meta-modelling is about building a more abstract or, as Zeigler et al. (2000, p. 32) call it, "lumped" model, which exhibits similar relevant behaviour as the original. Note that this definition does neither restrict the representational form of the meta-model, nor does it prescribe whether the meta-model should be built algorithmically or in a "manual" fashion.

A common technique used in meta-modelling is to derive mathematical approximations of input-output functions computed by the original model. In this approach model parameters are again systematically varied within given ranges, and the corresponding results are sampled. From these samples a *reaction surface* is computed, using an interpolation technique such as polynomial fitting or neural networks (Kilmer et al. 1997).

There are applications of meta-modelling in validation which go beyond explorations of the original model's response surface. For example, we can use the comparison of meta-models as a quantitative operational validation technique. In this approach two polynomial meta-models are derived from both model and real system or from an already validated reference model. Validation is then performed by checking the coefficients of both meta-models for similarity. Another technique, presented in Barton and Szczerbicka (2000) and Remondino and Correndo (2005), derives meta-models using symbolic machine-learning techniques instead of function interpolation. Such "interpretable" meta-models can help users understand dependencies between model components. In some cases they can even serve as guides to automatic calibration.

Visual Simulation Output and Trace Analysis: A popular German proverb states that "a picture tells more than a thousand words". With some limitations this often holds true for simulation analysis and validation, and visualizations and animations of simulation results are therefore among the most commonly used validation techniques:

- ❑ Often statistical methods such as hypothesis tests or confidence intervals (see Sections 7.3 and 7.4) cannot be used due to overly restrictive statistical assumptions or the lack of comparable system data (Sargent 2001, p. 110).
- ❑ Given a descriptive representation of model dynamics, human experts can often detect faults more quickly and more reliably than even the most sophisticated computer-aided analysis methods.
- ❑ Visualization and animation help model developers to detect obvious errors during design and implementation. It also helps to improve communication with model users.

8.3 Selected Validation Techniques

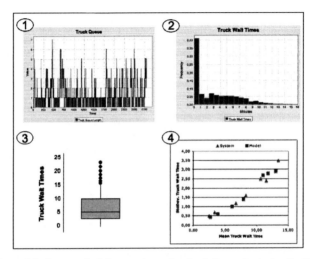

Figure 8.5: Some typical diagram types for simulation output visualization: Time series (1), histogram (2), box plot (3), and behaviour graph (4). The Diagrams 1 and 2 stem from a simple simulation of a container terminal model in the DESMO-J tutorial. The Diagrams 3 and 4 were adopted with modifications from Sargent (2001, pp. 111).

Unfortunately, visualizations also have a number of important disadvantages. For example, since it is only a single snapshot which might show completely untypical random behaviour, one must be very careful not to draw overly general conclusions from the animation of single stochastic simulation trajectories. This is a particular concern if such animations are (mis)used as the sole basis for making decisions. In addition, visual analysis of simulation results is largely subjective and must draw on expert knowledge which cannot be readily automated or objectified.

According to Sargent (2001, pp. 111) common diagrams for visualizing numerical results include time series plots, behaviour graphs, histograms, and box-plots (see Figure 8.5).

Time-series plots show the temporal evolution of model variables. In validation they are often used to visually check simulation results' plausibility or to compare results to corresponding real-world data – which should ideally be plotted in the same diagram (Oechslein et al. 1999, p. 6).

Behaviour graphs use scatter-plots to picture "comparisons [...] between different behaviour relationships in the simulation model and [...] in the system" (Sargent

225

Chapter 8 Validation, Verification, and Testing of Simulation Models

2001, pp. 112). These show a relevant model and system quantity (e.g. mean truck wait time vs. standard deviation of truck wait times in the gravel pit model) on each axis of their coordinate system. Validation is then performed by visual comparison of the relevant functional relations. Sargent (2001, p. 112) emphasises that "there are no specific statistical assumptions required of the data used in behaviour graphs".

Histograms and box plots can be used to depict the statistical distribution of observed model variables (e.g. the mean residence time of trucks in the gravel pit), which are collected in one or more simulation runs. Sargent (2001, p. 110) points out that "the data used in histograms and box plots needs only to be identically distributed [and ...] may be the observations themselves or some function [...] of the collected information".

Histograms display the absolute or relative frequency of observed values, which can easily be compared to corresponding histograms of real system data or visually scanned for similarities with some assumed theoretical probability density (e.g. the exponential distribution of an arrival process). A drawback of histograms is that they require a large number of observations (Sargent 2001, p. 110). *Box plots* provide an alternative view of an output quantity's statistical variations, and "generally require less data points than histograms" (Sargent 2001, p. 110).

While visualizations of model outputs offer an aggregate overview of one or more simulation runs' results, detailed understanding of model components' behaviour is better achieved through trace-analysis, trace-visualization, and trace-animation. Simulation models usually generate large masses of log-file data. Manual analysis of such traces is often a daunting task. Since log-file analysis is a problem that simulation shares with numerous other disciplines, such as distributed or multi-agent systems, a large number of suggestions for better support can be found in the literature. The following techniques seem appropriate for simulation validation:

- *Filtering* of trace entries can focus the modeller's interest on particularly relevant processes, events, or entities in the model. Powerful filtering techniques are made possible by storing trace entries in a relational or XML data-base, retrieving them when required by using a database query (e.g. in SQL).
- The behaviour of one or more entities can be graphically displayed using numerous *trace visualization* techniques. We will discuss some of these below.
- *Model-based trace checking* (see Section 8.3.2) can verify a trace's adherence to specific behavioural requirements. However, trace checking is a confirmative technique that only supports falsification of given assumptions. It cannot make any contribution to increase knowledge about the causes of model behaviour.
- *Data and process mining techniques* can discover temporal or causal patterns in simulation traces. Although still in its infancy, this method has occasionally been used in simulation studies and is described in some detail below.

In spite of some attempts at automating trace analyses, *trace visualization* still remains the most important means for exploring a models behaviour in detail. Some complementary methods for displaying trace information are (see also Figure 8.6):

8.3 Selected Validation Techniques

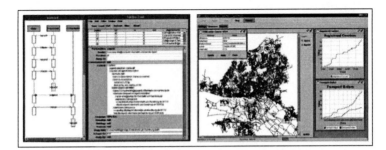

Figure 8.6: Some techniques for the visualization of simulation traces. Left: Sequence diagram of a communication trace in an agent-based simulation of the "Settler" game running on the Mulan agent platform (see Section 11.4.5). Right: Visualization of the movement of simulated city couriers within a model of Hamburg's road network.

- ❑ *UML sequence diagrams* of message exchanges, which can show interactions between multiple entities (see Section 4.5.1). This approach is, for example, supported by several platforms for multi-agent-based simulation such as JADE and Mulan/Capa (see Section 11.4.5).
- ❑ *UML timing diagrams* or similar notations can show the state changes an entity passes through over time (see Section 4.5.3).
- ❑ *Displays of entities' movement in a spatial environment* can show the behaviour of entities in spatially explicit models; e.g. models of production systems or agent-based models.

Further techniques for trace visualization in simulation are presented by Tolujew (1999). Independent of which visualization technique is being used, there are two general approaches for trace visualization (see Section 9.6):

- ❑ A trace can be animated *online*; i.e. while a simulation is running. One advantage of online animation is that the observer can terminate a possibly lengthy simulation run immediately after detecting invalid behaviour.
- ❑ However, since online animation significantly slows down simulator performance, many simulation tools only provide *offline* trace animations, shown *after* completion of simulation runs. An important advantage of this technique is the capability to replay an animation, as well as the possibility for leisurely examination of details.

Supporting Validation through Data Mining: Due to the superiority of human insight, opportunities for computer support in exploratory model analysis and validation are limited. However, tracing complex simulation models and running lengthy series

Chapter 8 Validation, Verification, and Testing of Simulation Models

of experiments has the potential to generate vast amounts of data, which will quickly exceed the capacity of human analysts trying to make sense of such "data mountains". As a result, important relationships (or even errors) in simulation results may remain unnoticed.

A relatively novel approach for tackling this problem is occasionally mentioned in the simulation literature. It draws on the application of data mining techniques to model analysis and validation. *Data mining* is "the automated analysis of large or complex data sets in order to discover significant patterns or trends that would otherwise go unrecognized" (Woods and Kyral 1997, p. 6 cited in Köster 2002, p. 54).

The goals of data mining are quite similar to those of traditional exploratory statistics, but the technique focuses more strongly on algorithms that automatically abstract complex hypotheses (i.e. models) from large sets of data. These algorithms are an eclectic mixture of methods from machine learning, soft computing, and pattern recognition. Popular examples are neural networks, decision-tree learning, and clustering algorithms.

Although the application of data mining to model validation is not well established, some promising work has been reported. Generally, models and algorithms from data mining can be useful to the analysis and comparison of a real system and its models (Remondino and Correndo 2005, p. 378). In closing this section we will therefore briefly mention some selected applications of data mining to the validation of simulation models:

❑ Cantú-Paz et al. (2004) use pattern recognition techniques to validate spatial patterns in a simulation of fluid mixing behaviour.
❑ Köster (2002) uses genetic algorithms to mine operator trees representing functional dependencies between several model variables in microscopic epidemiological models and flight training simulations.
❑ Barton and Szczerbicka (2000) use interpretable meta-models (see above) in the form of association rules to guide the automatic calibration of a tailplane rudder.
❑ Remondino and Correndo (2005) recommend data mining as a suitable validation technique for agent-based simulations.
❑ Jacobs et al. (1998) apply inductive logic programming to synthesize rule-based models of agent behaviour from simulated football games.

Confirmatory Techniques

After this brief survey of the state-of-the-art in *exploratory* model validation, we will now look at more established techniques for *confirmatory* validation. In contrast to the goals of exploratory validation, which seeks to improve a modeller's insight into model's dynamics, the focus of confirmatory validation centers on falsification of a-priori hypotheses about model behaviour. Confirmatory validation of stochastic simulation models is often supported by formal methods; either numerical or symbolic.

8.3 Selected Validation Techniques

Statistical Techniques for Output Analysis: A classical technique for confirmatory output analysis are statistical hypothesis tests and confidence intervals (see Section 7.3). Using output analysis, we seek to falsify the hypothesis that there is no significant difference between model output and real system behaviour; the so-called "null hypothesis" H_0. Following Page (1991, pp. 151), a number of statistical methods can be applied to operational validation.

Correspondences between model and system outputs can be established by comparing statistical parameters, such as arithmetic mean, median or variance over the output set. For models containing stochastic components such comparisons must utilize methods like the t-test or rank tests (see Section 7.4.4).

The distribution of relevant outputs produced by a model and the corresponding data obtained from the system under investigation can be compared with goodness of fit tests, such as the (two sample) χ^2-square test (see Section 7.3). Tool support for statistical tests and distribution fitting is provided by common statistical software, such as SPSS[10].

A confidence interval (see Section 7.4.4) can be computed over the difference between model and system output. If the interval contains the the point predicted by the null hypothesis H_0 (i.e. a negligible difference; e.g. of value 0), we can conclude that there is no significant difference. However, Page (1991, p. 152) notes that "even larger deviations can be tolerated if they do not lead to different conclusions and decisions". An unfortunate drawback of this approach is the "multiple response problem" (Balci 1998, pp. 351). This effect occurs when analysis is extended to include confidence intervals over multiple output variables.

Since numerous simulation textbooks describe statistical methods for validation in much detail, we will not delve any further into this topic, but rather refer interested readers to Law and Kelton (2000, Ch. 5), Balci (1998, pp. 372), and Shannon (1975, Ch. 6). Let us instead finish the validation chapter by relating confirmatory operational validation to software engineering's test-driven development approach, followed by some suggestions for suitable tools.

Model-based Validation of Simulation Results: In Section 8.3.2 we lauded the benefits of using eXtreme Programming's "test first" approach for computer model verification. The core idea there is that we must write formal specifications of expected behaviour (e.g. a unit test) *prior* to implementation. During implementation we then use a test automation tool such as *JUnit* to constantly re-check all implemented behaviours against these specifications. Since most test tools only support functional unit tests, this approach is only of limited use to simulation.

However, the "test first" approach can still contribute to dynamic model verification and operational validation if we can draw on suitable tool support for automatically checking simulation results. For this the following proposals are found in the literature:

---

[10]http://www.spss.com

Chapter 8 Validation, Verification, and Testing of Simulation Models

- As already mentioned, model-based trace checking can determine if a simulation trace conforms to a specification in temporal logic (see e.g. Brade 2003, Ch. 5.3). As in regression tests, this check must be repeated whenever the model is extended or refactored.
- Birta and Özmizrak (1996) propose a knowledge-based system for automatic result validation. The user can define several kinds of numerical validity criteria, such as required causal dependencies of input and output quantities or so-called "change-in-value relationships". The latter represent statements of the type "if the value of the input parameter *mean loading dock service time* is increased by a given amount, the value of the output variable *mean loading dock queue length* should increase correspondingly". The system can automatically check if the output of a single simulation run or the aggregate output of several runs adhere to their specifications.

8.4 Summary

This chapter has surveyed the philosophy, basic concepts, techniques, and tools for validating a simulation model. Based on the literature, we have reviewed basic terms of model validation, sketched a validation process, and identified several roles involved in this process.

We have then related model validation to the philosophy of science and derived several validation principles commonly found in the literature from the notions of critical rationalism and falsification.

Finally, we have developed a four-dimensional classification scheme for validation techniques containing the dimensions *approach*, *phase in model building cycle*, *degree of formality*, and *system perspective*. We have presented several practical verification and validation techniques within this framework.

Let us conclude the chapter by recapitulating those validation techniques that we consider as the most important in Table 8.1. Each technique is classified along the aforementioned four dimensions. Naturally this classification is sometimes ambiguous. The table also contains page numbers that specify where a certain validation technique is described in this chapter.

8.4 Summary

Table 8.1: Validation techniques

Validation Technique	Approach	Phase	Formality	Perspective	Page
Structural model validation	E, C	C	I	S	213
Conceptual model animation	E	C	I	D	213
Dependency graphs	E	C	Q, S	S	213
Model checking	C	C, V, O	S	D	214
Audit	E, C	C, V	I	S	216
Documentation checking	E, C	C, V, O	I	S	216
Inspection	E, C	C, V, O	I	S	216
Desk checking	C	C, V, O	I	S, D	217
Testing	C	V	I	D	217
Debugging	E	V, O	I	D	220
Software metrics	E	V	Q	S	221
Calibration	E	O	I, Q	D	222
Sensitivity analysis	E	O	I, Q	D	223
Meta-modelling	E	O	I, Q, S	D	224
Output visualization	E	V, O	I	D	225
Log file analysis	E	V, O	I, S	D	226
Animation/Trace visualization	E	V, O	I	D	226
Data mining	E	V, O	Q, S	D	227
Hypothesis tests	C	O	Q	D	229
Confidence intervals	C	O	Q	D	229
Model-based validation	C	O	Q, S	D	229

Approach: Confirmatory (C), Exploratory (E)
Phase: Conceptual validation (C), Verification (V), Operational validation (O)
Formality: Informal (I), Quantitative (Q), Symbolic (S)
Perspective: Static (S), Dynamic (D)

Further Reading

The contents of this chapter is largely based on textbook introductions by Balci (1998) and Page (1991). A more thorough treatment of the current state of the art in validation processes and techniques can be found in the dissertation by Brade (2003), who also discusses a tool for and its application to model-based checking of simulation traces.

Our presentation of validation processes and visual validation techniques has also been guided by Sargent (2001), whose paper gives a comprehensive overview of this field. Relations between simulation model validation and the philosophy of science are presented in Shannon (1975) and, more recently, Küppers and Lenhard (2004). A practical introduction to eXtreme Programming and software testing with the JUnit framework can, for example, be found in Beck and Andres (2005) and Link (2002). Some recent advances in the application of artificial intelligence based techniques such as meta-modelling and data mining to the validation of simulation models are reported in Szczerbicka and Uthmann (2000).

Bibliography

J. H. Andrews. Relevant Empirical Testing Research: Challenges and Responses. In S. Andradottir, K. J. Healy, D. H. Withers, and B. L. Nelson, editors, *Workshop on Empirical Research in Software Testing (WERST) at the International Symposium on Software Testing and Analysis*, Boston, July 2004.

R. Bachmann, B. Gehlsen, and N. Knaak. Werkzeuggestützte Kalibrierung agentenbasierter Simulationsmodelle ("Tool-Supported Calibration of Agent-Based Simulation Models", in German). In T. Schulze, S. Schlechtweg, and V. Hinz, editors, *Simulation und Visualisierung 2004*, pages 115–126, SCS-Europe, Magdeburg, March 2004.

O. Balci. Verification, Validation and Testing. In J. Banks, editor, *Handbook of Simulation – Principles, Methodology, Advances, Applications, and Practice*, pages 335–393. Wiley, New York, 1998. Chapter 10.

R. Barton and H. Szczerbicka. Maschinelles Lernen zur Validation von Simulationsmodellen ("Machine Learning Applied to the Validation of Simulation Models", in German). In H. Szczerbicka and T. Uthmann, editors, *Modellierung, Simulation und Künstliche Intelligenz* ("Modelling, Simulation, and Artificial Intelligence", in German), pages 387–416. SCS-Europe, 2000.

K. Beck and C. Andres. *Extreme Programming Explained: Embrace Change*. Addison-Wesley, Boston, 2005.

J. Benz, R. Hoch, and T. Legovic. ECOBAS – Modelling and Documentation. *Ecological Modelling*, (138):3–15, 2001.

L. G. Birta and F. N. Özmizrak. A Knowledge-Based Approach for the Validation of Simulation Models: The Foundations. *ACM Transactions on Modeling and Computer Simulation*, 6(1):76–98, January 1996.

J. Bloch. *Effective Java – Programming Language Guide*. The Java Programming Series. Addison-Wesley, Boston, 2001.

C. R. Blyth. Subjective vs. Objective Methods in Statistics. *The American Statistician*, 26(3), June 1973.

B. W. Boehm. Software Engineering: R & D Trends and Defense Needs. In P. Wegner, editor, *Research Directions in Software Technology*, chapter 22, pages 1–9. MIT, Cambridge, 1979.

M. Boger, T. Baier, F. Wienberg, and W. Lamersdorf. Extreme Modeling. In *Extreme Programming and Flexible Processes in Software Engineering – XP2000*. Addison-Wesley, 6 2000.

F. Boschetti. *Application of Genetic Algorithms to the Inversion of Geophysical Data*. Research Report, University of Western Australia, 1995.

H. Bossel. *Simulation dynamischer Systeme – Grundwissen, Methoden, Programme* ("Simulation of Dynamic Systems – Foundations, Methods and Programs", in German). Vieweg, Brunswick, 1989.

H. Bossel. *Modeling and Simulation*. Peters, Wellesley, 1994.

Bibliography

D. Brade. *A Generalized Approach for the Verification and Validation of Models and Simulation Results*. PhD Thesis, University of the Federal Armed Forces Munich, October 2003.

E. Cantú-Paz, S.-C. Cheung, and C. Kamath. Retrieval of Similar Objects in Simulation Data Using Machine Learning Techniques. In *Image Processing: Algorithms and Systems III. SPIE Electronic Imaging*, San Jose, January 2004.

A. Drogoul, D. Vanbergue, and T. Meurisse. Multi-agent Based Simulation: Where are the Agents. In J. Simao Sichman, F. Bousquet, and P. Davidsson, editors, *Multi-Agent-Based Simulation II*, pages 2–15, Springer, Berlin, 2002.

R. H. Dunn. *Software Defect Removal*. McGraw-Hill, New York, 1984.

M. Friedman. *Essays in Positive Economics*. University of Chicago, Chicago, 1953.

E. Gamma, R. Helm, R. Johnson, and R. Vlissides. *Design Patterns: Elements of Reusable Object-Oriented Software*. Addison-Wesley, Reading, 1995.

J. M. Garrido. *Object-Oriented Discrete-Event Simulation with Java – A Practical Introduction*. Series in Computer Systems. Kluwer Academic/Plenum, New York, 2001.

V. Grimm. Visual Debugging: A Way of Analyzing, Understanding, and Communicating Bottom-Up Simulation Models in Ecology. *Natural Resource Modeling*, (15): 23–28, 2002.

J. Gruska. *Foundations of Computing*. International Thomson Computer Press, London, 1997.

D. Hales, J. Rouchier, and B. Edmonds. Model-to-Model Analysis. *Journal of Artificial Societies and Social Simulation*, 6(4), 2003. [Online] http://jasss.soc.surrey.ac.uk/6/4/5.html (in August 2005).

G. J. Holzmann. *Design and Validation of Computer Protocols*. Software Series. Prentice Hall, Englewood Cliffs, 1991.

G. J. Holzmann. The Model Checker SPIN. *IEEE Transactions on Software Engineering*, 23(5):279–295, May 1997.

Y. Howard, S. Gruner, A. M. Gravell, C. Ferreira, and J. C. Augusto. Model-Based Trace-Checking. In *Proceedings of UK Software Testing Research II*, University of York, York, 2003.

N. Jacobs, K. Driessens, and L. De Raedt. Inductive Verification and Validation of Multi Agents Systems. In *Workshop on Validation and Verification of Knowledge Based Systems*, pages 10–18, August 1998.

M. Jeckle et al. *UML 2 glasklar* ("UML 2 Made Crystal-Clear", in German). Carl Hanser, Munich, 2002.

E. Jessen and R. Valk. *Rechensysteme: Grundlagen der Modellbildung* ("Computer Systems: Foundations of Model Building", in German). Studienreihe Informatik. Springer, Berlin, 1997.

S. H. Kan. *Metrics and Models in Software Quality Engineering*. Addison-Wesley, Boston, 2003.

R. A. Kilmer, A. Smith, and L. J. Shuman. An Emergency Department Simulation and Neural Network Metamodel. *Journal of the society for health systems*, 5(3):63–79,

Bibliography

1997.
J. P. C. Kleijnen. Validation of Models: Statistical Techniques and Data Availability. In P. A. Farrington, H. B. Nembhard, D. T. Sturrock, and G. W. Evans, editors, *Proceedings of the 1999 Winter Simulation Conference*, pages 647–654, 1999. [Online] http://www.wintersim.org/prog99.htm (in August 2005).

G. B. Kleindorfer and R. Ganeshan. The Philosophy of Science and Validation in Simulation. In G. W. Evans, M. Mollaghasemi, E. C. Russell, and W. E. Biles, editors, *Proceedings of the 1993 Winter Simulation Conference*, pages 50–57, 1993.

F. Klügl. *Multiagentensimulation – Konzepte, Werkzeuge, Anwendung* ("Multi-Agent Simulation – Concepts, Tools, Application", in German). Agententechnologie. Addison-Wesley, Munich, 2001.

T. C. Koopmans. *Three Essays on the State of Economic Science*. McGraw-Hill, New York, 1957.

F. Köster. *Analyse von Simulationsmodellen mit Methoden des Knowledge Discovery in Databases* ("Analysis of Simulation Models by Means of Knowledge Discovery in Databases", in German). Research Report, Department für Informatik, Carl von Ossietzky University of Oldenburg, 2002.

G. Küppers and J. Lenhard. *Validation of Simulation – Patterns in the Social and Natural Sciences*. Research Report, University of Bielefeld, 2004.

A. M. Law and W. D. Kelton. *Simulation Modeling and Analysis*. McGraw-Hill, New York, 3rd edition, 2000. Chapters 4, 6, 7, 8, 9, and 10.

J. Link. *Unit Tests mit Java* ("Unit Tests with Java", in German). dpunkt, Heidelberg, 2002.

M. Lippert, S. Roock, and H. Wolf. *Software entwickeln mit Extreme Programming* ("Developing Software with Extreme Programming", in German). dpunkt, Heidelberg, 2002.

B. Martelli. *Leitlinien einer Methodik zur Validierung und zum Vergleich von kognitionswissenschaftlichen Modellen am Beispiel der Helligkeitswahrnehmung* ("Guidelines for a Methodology to Validate and Compare Models in Cognitive Science", in German). Dr. Kovac, Hamburg, 1999.

G. J. Myers. *The Art of Software Testing*. Wiley, Hoboken, 2nd edition, 2004.

T. H. Naylor and J. M. Finger. Verification of Computer Simulation Models. *Management Science*, 14(2):B/92–106, Fall 1967.

C. Oechslein, F. Klügl, and F. Puppe. Kalibrierung von Multiagentenmodellen ("Calibration of Multi-Agent Models", in German). In *13. Workshop der ASIM-Fachgruppe Simulation und Künstliche Intelligenz, Chemnitzer Informatik-Berichte (CSR-99-03)*, Chemnitz, 1999.

C. M. Overstreet. Model Testing: Is it only a Special Case of Software Testing. In E. Yücesan, C.-H. Chen, J. L. Snowdon, and J. M. Charnes, editors, *Proceedings of the 2002 Winter Simulation Conference*, pages 641–647, 2002. [Online] http://www.wintersim.org/prog02.htm (in August 2005).

B. Page. *Diskrete Simulation – Eine Einführung mit Modula-2* ("Discrete Simulation – An Introduction with Modula-2", in German). Springer, Berlin, 1991.

Bibliography

J. Pearl. *Causality*. Cambridge University, Cambridge, 2001.

G. Pomberger and G. Blaschek. *Software Engineering: Prototyping und objektorientierte Software-Entwicklung* ("Software Engineering: Prototyping and Object-Oriented Software Development", in German). Hanser, Munich, 2nd edition, 1996.

K. R. Popper. *Logik der Forschung* ("The Logic of Scientific Discovery", in German). Mohr, Tübingen, 7th edition, 1982.

K. R. Popper. *Ausgangspunkte* ("Unended Quest – An Intellectual Autobiography", in German). Piper, Munich, 2004.

K. R. Popper. *Alles Leben ist Problemlösen* ("All Life is Problem Solving", in German). Piper, Munich, 2nd edition, 2005.

M. Remondino and G. Correndo. Data Mining Applied to Agent Based Simulation. In Y. Merkuryev, R. Zobel, and E. Kerckhoffs, editors, *Proceedings of the 19th European Conference on Modelling and Simulation*, pages 374–380, SCS-Europe, Riga, June 2005.

R. G. Sargent. Some Approaches and Paradigms for Verifying and Validating Simulation Models. In B. A. Peters, J. S. Smith, D. J. Medeiros, and M. W. Rohrer, editors, *Proceedings of the 2001 Winter Simulation Conference*, pages 106–114, 2001. [Online] http://www.wintersim.org/prog01.htm (in August 2005).

R. E. Shannon. *Systems Simulation – The Art and Science*. Prentice Hall, Englewood Cliffs, 1975.

H. Szczerbicka and T. Uthmann, editors. *Modellierung, Simulation und Künstliche Intelligenz* ("Modelling, Simulation, and Artificial Intelligence", in German), 2000. SCS-Europe.

J. Tolujew. Untersuchung und Visualisierung der in den Tracefiles aufgezeichneten Prozesse ("Analysis and Visualization of Processes Recorded in Trace Files", in German). In O. Deussen, V. Hinz, and P. Lorenz, editors, *Proceedings Simulation und Visualisierung '99*, pages 261–274, SCS-Europe, Magdeburg, 1999.

K. G. Troitzsch. Validating Simulation Models. In G. Horton, editor, *Proceedings of the 18th European Simulation Multiconference*, SCS-Europe, Magdeburg, June 2004.

W. Visser, K. Havelund, G. Brat, S. Park, and F. Lerda. Model Checking Programs. *Automated Software Engineering Journal*, 10(2), April 2003.

E. Woods and E. Kyral. *Ovum Evaluates: Data Mining*. Ovum, 1997.

B. P. Zeigler, H. Praehofer, and T. G. Kim. *Theory of Modeling and Simulation*. Academic Press, San Diego, 2000.

E. Zitzler. *Evolutionary Algorithms for Multiobjective Optimization: Methods and Applications*. PhD Thesis, Swiss Federal Institute of Technology Zurich, 1999.

H. Züllighoven et al. *Object-Oriented Construction Handbook*. dpunkt/Morgan-Kaufmann, Amsterdam, 2004.

Part II

Software

Chapter 9

Simulation Software

Bernd Page, Wolfgang Kreutzer, Volker Wohlgemuth

Contents

9.1	Motivation and Overview	239
9.2	Requirements	240
	9.2.1 General Requirements	240
	9.2.2 Simulation-Specific Requirements	241
9.3	Some History	243
9.4	Classification	247
9.5	Examples	251
	9.5.1 Extend	252
	9.5.2 eM-Plant	254
9.6	The Role of Animation	257
9.7	Criteria for Choosing Simulation Software in Practice	259
9.8	Commercial Discrete Event Modelling Tools	260
	Bibliography	261

9.1 Motivation and Overview

Choosing a programming tool for model implementation and simulation is a far reaching decision, which must be based on sound criteria, such as:

❏ Should customized simulation programming environments and tools be chosen, or should the model be built with a general purpose tool?

❏ Which general purpose programming language has appropriate capabilities for this task? This topic has already been discussed in Chapters 3 and 6 in the context of *Java*.

❏ What requirements need to be met by a customized simulation programming system?

Chapter 9 Simulation Software

- What aspects should be considered when selecting a commercial simulation development tool?

Building programming tools for specific classes of applications is a core competence of computer science research, and many such tools have been targeted at a wide range of simulation metaphors catering for different levels of user experience and skills. This chapter surveys, analyses, and discusses the use of customized programming tools for building discrete event simulation models. It aims to provide a sound understanding of simulation software's requirements, an awareness of different classes of modelling tools and their strengths and weaknesses, as well as a summary of what one should look for when a tool must be chosen.

9.2 Requirements

9.2.1 General Requirements

In addition to simulation's specific needs, simulation software tools must also offer all *general* capabilities we now demand from modern programming tools. This includes aspects such as correctness, reliability, user friendliness, maintainability, efficiency, and portability. Since Chapter 6 has already discussed these in a Java-based context, we will not dwell on them at any length here. We will, however, briefly comment on those we consider of particular importance for convenient model construction (see Law and Kelton 2000, pp. 208–210 or Oakshott 1997, pp. 326–327):

- **User friendliness and interactivity**
  Usability is an important indicator for the effectiveness of any tool. This includes ease of learning as well as quick and convenient model construction and support for simulation experiments. Graphical interfaces based on a suitable metaphor for direct interaction with symbolic models can help meet the requirements. Being able to interact with a model at different levels of description is also an important characteristic of user friendly simulation software. At model initialisation time parameters should, for example, be entered interactively, and the modeller should be able to stop simulations, change states, and request step-by-step execution at runtime.

- **Flexibility and reusability**
  Flexibility often requires user-directed extension of concepts and services offered by simulation tools. This feature can potentially support applications which fall outside the range of domains at which a tool has been targeted, and it also provides the means for assembling libraries of customized components. Depending on a tool's level of abstraction and the nature of the required change, this can be a relatively easy or very difficult task. Many *high-level* tools require the use of a scripting language for all *major* changes; asking the modeller to step down from a user-friendly metaphor to a more abstract coding level. Ideally, such culture

9.2 Requirements

shocks should be avoided and *simple* extensions should be possible through the same high-level interfaces offered for other modelling tasks. As long as they fall within a range of allowed modifications, changes can indeed often be made in this way. Simple parameter adjustments or changes to mathematical formulas and functions are some examples (see Law and Kelton 2000, p. 208). However, once a modeller wishes to shape a tool in unforeseen ways, graphical interfaces typically fail to offer suitably flexible abstractions. While this whole issue is subject to further research, such lack of flexibility seems an inherent property of high-level interfaces, and the definition of reusable components may require quite abstract descriptions. Developing user friendlier interfaces for supporting this task remains a challenge.

❏ **Structure and readability**
Understanding a model and its programmed representations is much helped by clear structure, clean layout, and good naming practices. These aspects aid readability, documentation, correctness, reliability, and reusability. As a result, they play an important role in ensuring safe and successful transformations of models and programs from one conceptual layer to another; i.e. from a *high-level* symbolic representation to *low-level* code.

9.2.2 Simulation-Specific Requirements

In order to justify the development and use of customized tools, simulation models of a domain must have common characteristics whose representation must be both important and difficult. Chapter 6 has already discussed many of discrete event simulation's specific requirements and has demonstrated the complexity of software solutions with which these can be met. To support all phases of a simulation model's design, implementation, and execution, a number of essential services must therefore be provided by any effective simulation modelling tool (see Košturiak and Gregor 1995, pp. 156–159; Law and Kelton 2000, pp. 208–215; Oakshott 1997, pp. 326–329):

❏ **Support for data collection**
Simulation tools must assist users with data collection and entry. At the very least it must be possible to read input from files; so that data values need not to be entered by hand. Tools for further processing and aggregation of inputs (e.g. for statistical analyses) should also be available, and interfaces to CAD systems will allow input of layouts and symbols for animations. Utilities for testing a data set (e.g. the parameters of distributions) for completeness (are all needed values provided?) and correctness (do values violate any constraints?) can also be helpful.

Chapter 9 Simulation Software

❑ **Support for model construction**
A good modelling tool should permit easy and fast model construction. This is aided by a wide range of prefabricated model components, whose specific properties and behaviours can be customized quickly. Graphical interfaces should support model assembly by selecting, clicking, dragging, and dropping easily understandable symbols and their connections. Hierarchical organization of model components in libraries supports reusability, which also needs good and accessible documentation; e.g. through tool tips and hyperlinks. Extensibility from within and outside (e.g. via plugins) of the modelling tool is desirable. This should allow modifications to a process' flow of control as well as its structure, properties, and actions. Some of these changes may require the use of an internal scripting language or even linking to externally compiled procedures (e.g. written in C). For some applications mixing discrete event and quasi-continuous modelling styles may be useful, and such *hybrid* viewpoints should be supported by the modelling tool.

❑ **Support for simulation experiments**
In preparation for simulation experiments relevant parameters, such as duration or other criteria for terminating a simulation run, must be easy to enter. The simulation software should take care of all details when multiple runs with systematic parameter variations are needed. This includes the initialisation of separate streams of random variates, any resets of statistical counters at the right times, and all details of model initialisation in general. It should be possible to request that simple statistical evaluations (see Section 7.4) are performed for each simulation run, and that suitable *warm-up periods* are initiated, monitored, and terminated by the simulation software; resetting statistical counters as needed. User interaction during a simulation should permit interactive debugging, tracing of model behaviour, and changing of state variables. Ideally, this should allow users to "force" a model into any desired state. Visualization and animation of relevant state changes can help to identify interesting patterns. Since speed of execution is an important aspect of many simulation studies it should be possible to dynamically switch interaction and animation features on or off. For more extensive animations an *offline* animation tool, which can be used to visualize model behaviour after a simulation has terminated, should be available. Finally, deploying a model as a decision making tool for domain specialists can be facilitated by offering runtime-only versions, in which parameter variations can be experimented with, but the core model logic cannot be changed.

❑ **Support for analysing simulation results**
When assembling a model, simulation development tools should provide for some default standard statistics (e.g. events, utilizations, queue lengths, residence times, frequencies, throughputs) that are collected and displayed automatically. These can be attached to components. Simulation results should be available in a range of formats and visualizations; e.g. counters, means, time series, his-

tograms, chronological graphs, pie charts. It should also be possible to store statistical data in internal or external files and databases and to show the results of multiple runs in the same diagram. Interfaces to popular spreadsheet and graphic programs (e.g. Excel) can be used to provide more specialized analyses and displays. Similar interfaces should be available for common mathematical and statistical packages.

Since no tool can hope to offer all features potential users may ever want, it should be possible to extend a tool's capabilities without undue difficulties. This can be attempted in different ways; e.g. via scripting languages or interfaces to plug-ins and externally compiled procedures. One must, however, always be aware that the development, maintenance, and support of such interfaces puts a significant burden on tool developers, and that the depth of understanding required for using them competently often expects much training and experience on the part of the user.

9.3 Some History

Schmidt (1987) already proposed a scheme for partitioning the development of simulation software into generations, each spanning approximately a decade. We can update this scheme, starting in the late 1960s and continuing into the 21st century, and identify and characterize five such generations. Each of these can then be characterized by its most relevant characteristics:

- ❏ **1st generation (1960s): Simulation using general purpose programming languages**
  This period is characterized by the use of general purpose programming tools for assembling a simulation model. In line with what was available at the time modelling projects commonly used assembly languages, Fortran or Algol. Since none of these programming tools offered any simulation specific features, each simulation model and its runtime control system had to be built from scratch. Strategies for generating random numbers, processing event lists, and event scheduling were reinvented, re-implemented, and re-debugged over and over again. While this took advantage of the developers' existing programming skills, allowed easy tailoring of the software for specific requirements, made all details of a simulation's operation transparent to the developers, and incurred no additional costs for purchasing new tools, a high price was paid in terms of model reliability and development time and effort. Model implementation required considerable programming skills, and models written in such individual fashion tended to be hard to reuse and difficult to understand and modify by anyone other than the original programmers.
  While much progress has been made since those times, and general purpose programming tools are rarely seen as a viable option for complex model development, writing a simulation from scratch using Pascal, Modula, C, C++, Delphi, Java

Chapter 9 Simulation Software

etc. is still far from uncommon. This is due to a misguided belief that learning new tools can never be as cost effective as sticking to skills one already has; a misapprehension which completely ignores the considerable effort of re-implementing and sometimes reinventing many well known techniques, and wrestling with inadequate tools to represent patterns of structures and processes which they have not been designed to support; e.g. list processing and coroutines.

❏ **2nd generation (1970s): First simulation packages and simulation languages**
This period is characterized by a growing recognition that a small set of patterns for random sampling, data collection and display, event list processing, numerical integration, and runtime control can be observed to occur over and over again; in different classes of simulations (e.g. discrete event and quasi-continuous frameworks). These patterns were therefore packaged as subroutines or procedures and offered as part of so-called *simulation packages*. While most popular simulation packages (e.g. GASP, GASPL/1, SLAM) were based on Fortran, Algol, or Pl/1, some Pascal- and Modula-based packages (e.g. SimPas, ModSim) were developed at academic institutions. Using C and Java as hosts came much later.

Simulation packages were available for discrete event simulation as well as quasi-continuous simulation modelling styles, but there were also some hybrid systems which could be used to combine these world views in a single model. This often allowed more realistic representation of complex systems. Models were either based on a discrete event metaphor with quasi-continuous submodels, or they were driven by a quasi-continuous process and coupled to discrete event submodels through *time events* or *state events*.

Discrete event simulation packages were typically based on an *event-oriented* framework. Some early attempts at offering the means for *process* description were made (e.g. in SLAM), but, due to limitations on the expressiveness of their base languages (which offered no *coroutine* or *task* abstractions) these often proved to be far too clumsy to use.

Simulation packages are the simplest means of pre-packaging repetitive tasks. In comparison to fully fledged simulation languages, they retain the full flexibility of their base languages and knowledgeable users can extend package functionality quite easily. Although new concepts (i.e. those offered by the package's functionality) need to be learned, all prior skills in using the base language are transferable and can be built on.

A short time after the first simulation packages appeared, the first proper self-contained simulation languages were developed. Many of them were initially implemented as *pre-compilers*; i.e. their translators generated a Fortran or Algol program instead of mapping models directly into machine code. This made such systems more portable, but required a two step translation (e.g. model to Fortran, Fortran to machine code). Examples for some of such early simulation languages were Simula, Simscript, GPSS, and Dynamo. These languages offered

9.3 Some History

customized linguistic abstractions to describe simulation models of a given category; e.g. discrete event models, queueing scenarios, or system dynamics. This allowed use of higher-level building blocks, such as servers with integrated FIFO (first in, first out) queues or even special components such as disks and processors in computer models. At the back of the coin, however, such highly customized linguistic abstractions also constrained the range of applications these tools could support.

In contrast to simulation packages the first self-contained *simulation languages* supported metaphors for describing event sequences more conveniently than through event-orientation. Simula is an example for an early *process-oriented* language, while ECLS offered an *activity-oriented* modelling perspective.

Overall, special purpose simulation packages and languages reduced implementation effort considerably. This was paid for by the need to adhere to a pre-structured modelling framework and learning the relevant concepts. Either a library of customized data structures and procedures or a simulation language compiler had to be purchased. While building a model had become an easier, faster, and more reliable task, considerable programming skills were still needed in addition to a solid grounding in the respective methodologies.

❏ **3rd generation (1980s): Application-specific simulation tools**
The 1980s saw the development of many software tools for modelling specialized applications in areas such as manufacturing systems, material flow and queueing systems, computer systems, and automatic control. These programming systems were often deployed on personal workstations and offered increasingly sophisticated interactivity and animation features. This facilitated quicker and more convenient model construction, while the increasing specialization of tools led to ever more problem specific libraries. Their building blocks were targeted for use by application experts with little programming and general simulation knowledge. In terms of model validity this development turned out to be a two-edged sword, and it often resulted in low flexibility, low execution efficiency (i.e. long runtimes) and high software costs. ARENA, DOSIMIS-3, NETWORK, SEE WHY, SIMFACTORY, WITNESS are relevant examples.

❏ **4th generation (1990s): Integrated simulation systems**
The fourth generation of simulation programming tools more and more aimed to support *all* phases of the simulation modelling cycle. As a result, software solutions for data management and processing, model specification, hierarchical model assembly from comprehensive component libraries, experimental design and support, statistical processing of simulation results, and graphical model instrumentation, assembly, display, and animation were made available through increasingly sophisticated interfaces. This went along with a trend towards object-oriented styles of description and the provision of access to databases, spreadsheet programs, graphics, and statistics packages. CREATE!, eM-Plant, Extend, and Simplex III are prominent simulation development tools of this era.

Chapter 9 Simulation Software

Advantages gained were e.g.:
- increased user friendliness through comprehensive project support in a single uniform framework
- a shift of developer concerns from programming to modelling issues (at least as long nothing went wrong)
- openness towards services offered by standard software
- better potential for customizing and extending both the tools' functions and their component libraries

On the negative side, learning how to use such complex software skilfully and appropriately became an ever more challenging task. Futhermore, some of the most prominent systems were rather costly, and claims of "automatic modelling" often served only to hide the dangers of misuse by users with inadequate methodological knowledge and experience.

- **5th generation (since 2000): Adding new methods and technologies**
The newest methodological and technological trends focus on better reusability of model libraries based on object-oriented application frameworks; where frameworks are viewed as task-focussed component collections with predefined patterns of cooperation. Frameworks therefore provide classes, interfaces, and whole models and sub-models. Patterns of cooperation seek integration into CORBA, JavaBeans, EJB, Microsoft .NET, and other emerging standards. Coupling simulations to optimization tools, better support for distributed simulations and effective means for offering web services are among many other areas of research. The DISMO-Package and the simulation package MILAN are examples for these developments.

Table 9.1 summarizes the five generations' most important characteristics.

Modern simulation systems fall into two classes: universal simulation systems and application-specific model development tools. Universal simulation systems evolved from high-level programming tools and general purpose simulation languages. They offer a wide range of applicability, but require a high degree of programming competence. Modern application-specific simulation tools, on the other hand, have been derived from programming and simulation tools for specific purposes. While their flexibility is limited and their range of application can be rather narrow, they offer efficient modelling frameworks with a high degree of familiarity for application experts.

Although giving context to a more detailed discussion, the above historical review of simulation software is rather idealized and simplified. Most modern simulation software straddles some generations, has been extended with new features numerous times, and may offer interfaces to separate component libraries and other high-level general purpose programming and modelling tools. There is now a definite trend towards embedding universal tools within integrated development environments, which are based on an object-oriented software design and whose capabilities can easily be extended through a hierarchy of specialized libraries of components.

Table 9.1: Five generations of simulation development tools

Generation	Period	Characteristics	Examples
1st	1960s	Use of general purpose programming languages. Event-oriented modelling.	Fortran, Algol
2nd	1970s	First simulation packages and simulation languages. Process-oriented modelling. Simulation languages for *combined* discrete/continuous simulation	GASP, ACSL GPSS, Simscript, Simula
3rd	1980s	Application specific simulators. First component libraries. First graphical modelling tools. First integration of animation tools.	SEE WHY, SIMFACTORY, WITNESS
4th	1990s	Integrated development environments. Object-oriented modelling. Comprehensive support for 2D and 3D graphics and animation.	CREATE!, Extend, eM-Plant, SIMPLEX III
5th	Since 2000	Component-based simulation libraries. Integration of simulations with optimization tools. Web-based simulation.	MILAN, DISMO

9.4 Classification

We can classify simulation tools in a number of ways; e.g. according to:
- their level of application
- the type of system and conceptual framework they support
- their underlying modelling (resp., simulation) concept
- their degree of specialization

The *level of application* (see Page 1991, p. 157) refers to the level of abstraction at which a tool must be used. Here we can e.g. distinguish between the levels of a programming language, an existing parametrized model, or a comprehensive simulation tool. Figure 9.1 illustrates this classification.

If simulation tools operate at the *package* or *language level*, their users must have experience in using a programming language. Modelling support is given via pre-packaged procedures or built-in linguistic abstractions for simulation-specific tasks; e.g. for process control, model time management, and statistical evaluation. This class of software can be hosted through a procedure package or implemented as a translator for a self-contained simulation programming language. It supports only the implementation phase of a simulation project.

If a simulation tool operates at the level of a *parametrized model*, users are constrained to customize and experiment with an *existing* model. Typically they will be able to experience the visualization of relevant aspects through a graphical in-

Chapter 9 Simulation Software

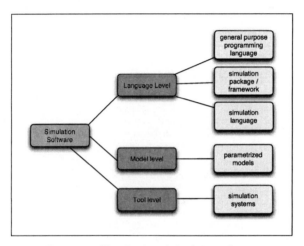

Figure 9.1: Classification of simulation software

terface. Examples for such modelling tools are flight simulators or strategic modelling games; e.g. SimCity (see http://www.simcity.ea.com) or Railroad Tycoon (see http://www.railroadtycoon.com). The models need not be programmed by the user, who therefore needs only minimal computer skills. However, only a limited range of actions and modifications are possible. More heavily parametrized simulation models may offer somewhat more flexibility, but they are still closed systems whose functionality and semantics are predetermined. Simple didactic demonstrations in teaching software (e.g. a model of human blood circulation – see Oxsoft Heart – http://www.cellmc.com) can be seen as examples.

Modern integrated simulation development tools often operate at the level of *comprehensive simulation systems*; i.e. they aim to support *all* phases of a simulation project, such as system identification, model design, model implementation, model experimentation, and the analysis of results. A user should be able to work completely within such an environment, without any need to "step outside". An additional motivation of such environments is their support of domain experts with relatively low levels of computer skills. In particular, no assumption of programming skills should be made (see Häuslein 1993, p. 68). This goal is facilitated by comprehensive libraries of components, which can be browsed, customized, and reused in a transparent and convenient fashion. In analogy to databases the term *model base* has been used to refer to this concept. Examples for such functionality can be found in ARENA, Extend, or SIMPLEX III (see Law and Kelton 2000, p. 215).

9.4 Classification

Using *system type* as a means to classify simulation tools distinguishes between alternative ways in which *state transformations* are specified. Different means of implementing time sequencing and runtime control are required to implement discrete or quasi-continuous simulation models. Some *hybrid* tools (e.g. GPSS-Fortran or SLAM II) allow both world views to be used alongside each other.

In the context of different discrete event *simulation world views*, we can distinguish between modelling frameworks such as event-, process-, and activity-orientation (see Chapter 5), as well as between different modelling perspectives. For example, a discrete event scenario can be modelled from either a material- or a machine-oriented point of view. This terminology traces back to the simulation of different allocation and routing strategies of machines and materials in so-called *jobshops*; one of the earliest applications of discrete event simulation.

While *material-orientation* describes model dynamics from the perspective of transient workload items, *machine-orientation* focusses on describing the lifecycles of permanent model entities. In some modern simulation tools this distinction is hidden at an internal level of implementation, which need not be referenced by a model designer – who operates at a higher level.

Classifying a simulation tool according to *modelling concept* distinguishes between different styles of textual, graphical, or mixed modes of model representation. Although we list some popular alternatives here, it should be noted that these will rarely be found in pure form and that mixing types of representation is common (see Noche and Wenzel 1990, p. 7 or Košturiak and Gregor 1995, p. 148):

❏ **Building block representation of models**
Choosing from a collection of prefabricated components (building blocks), which are connected by different types of "flows", is the most common style in which modern simulation tools support model construction. Building blocks range from those representing very general concepts (e.g. a model scheduler, various distributions, and data collectors) to components for modelling highly specific task domains (e.g. different vehicle types for simulating logistics problems). If components are well chosen and a problem fits the supported framework well, models can be quickly constructed by a domain expert himself and no deeper methodological knowledge or higher computer skills are required. This is, of course, paid for by a loss in flexibility. If problems do not fit the framework's assumptions, either more flexible tools (e.g. a programming language) must be used, or the framework must be extended. To cater for this eventuality, tool vendors often try to provide means for customizing existing building blocks or construct new components of a user's own choosing. Invariably, this requires deeper knowledge of a tool's internal operation, as well as programming skills. The building block approach combines well with other techniques, such as Petri nets or queueing scenarios.

Chapter 9 Simulation Software

❑ **Object-oriented representation of models**
The characteristics, strengths, and weaknesses of object-oriented styles of description have been discussed in Chapter 3. Object-orientation can be found at all levels of a system's representation; e.g. in languages, models, and tools. There are many similarities to the building block concept, in that building blocks or components can be viewed as classes which encapsulate prefabricated states and behaviour. Placing and linking them into a model instantiates them as objects, which interact with each other and initiate actions through messages passed during a model's execution. Object-orientation, however, supports far more flexible patterns than just simple component libraries. eM-Plant (see http://www.emplant.com), for example, combines the flexibility of object-oriented description with a building block approach, and DESMO-J supports object-orientation at the language level.

❑ **Representation of models as queueing scenarios**
Queueing scenarios can be used to model any system which includes capacity constrained resources. The above mentioned building block approach fits this class of model well. Customization leads to three classes of model components: transactions, servers, and queues. *Transactions* can represent messages, orders, or customers. Their creation times are drawn from suitable distributions, after which they step through a cycle of actions which include requests for the servers' services. *Servers* fill a transaction's requests, but have limited capacity. *Queues* act as buffer for transactions whose service requests are delayed by a server's lack of availability. Fishwick (1996) describes an example scenario set in the context of modelling a computer system.

❑ **Representation of models as Petri nets**
Petri nets are a methodology for analysing the interaction of complex processes. Their use of graphical representation is motivated by a desire to offer an intuitively understandable tool for studying concurrency and interactions in non-deterministic systems. Formally, a Petri net is a directed graph with two types of nodes called *places* and *transitions*. Edges can only connect two nodes of different type. In addition to this static structure, a Petri net's model dynamics is captured by moving *tokens* along its edges; according to rules attached to transitions. Petri nets are well suited to answer questions such as reachability of states and the possibility of deadlocks; i.e. states in which none of a set of mutually dependent processes can proceed. In the context of simulation, so-called *timed* and *coloured Petri nets* have been used to model communication networks, computer systems, and workflows in organizations. Examples of relevant tools are PACE (see http://www.ibepace.com), Design/CPN (see http://www.daiml.au.dk/designCPN), or Renew (using an object-oriented approach – see http:/www.renew.de).

9.5 Examples

❏ **Representations based on automata theory**
Automata theory can be a powerful tool for modelling systems where elements of an input set I are recognized, transformed, and mapped into an output set O. Its variations span a wide range, from finite automata to general Turing machines. An example of a simulation modelling tool based on this theoretical framework is ATMOS (see Noche and Wenzel 1990).

❏ **Tools augmented with knowledge-based systems**
Some interesting simulation systems have evolved within programming environments traditionally used for research into artificial intelligence. These frameworks are typically coupled to knowledge-based systems and therefore well suited to offer expert support to a model developer. This can be helpful in both model design and the analysis of simulation runs. Examples for simulation development tools supported by knowledge bases are DYNAMIS (see Häuslein 1993) and PLATO-SIM (see Hartenberger 1993).

Classing a simulation tool according to its *degree of specialization* asks if the tool is universally applicable across a wide range of model types, or if it supports relatively narrow groups of application. If it is specialized, it can still be quite widely applicable (e.g. for modelling production or logistic problems), or it can be very focussed (e.g. concentrating on just automatic guided vehicle systems or inventory models). Specialized simulation tools are generally highly tuned for fast and effective representation of their chosen domains and targeted at application experts rather than computer professionals. Their flexibility and range can be correspondingly low. Universal simulation tools, on the other hand, can be employed very widely, but application to a specific problem will require considerable methodological and programming skills in addition to the relevant application knowledge. Model development will also require more time than if specialized tools are used.

Figure 9.2 summarizes these classifications in a *morphological box*. Morphological boxes are two-dimensional schemata, which depict classifying properties in columns and their realizations in rows. Colouring the relevant cells for each class of tool yields a tool's profile (see e.g. Figure 9.5).

9.5 Examples

Today simulation analysts can choose from many powerful modelling tools and environments. The two examples we will look at in this section were chosen because each reflects one of two major philosophies; i.e. a universal simulation systems (*Extend*) and a specialized tool for modelling a specific application domain (*eM-Plant* – targeted at production and manufacturing problems). Another reason for choosing *Extend* and *eM-Plant* as examples is the experience we have gained in their use at the Faculty of Informatics of the University of Hamburg. Law and Kelton (2000) give a good summary of modern simulation systems and Banks et al. (1999) survey specialized

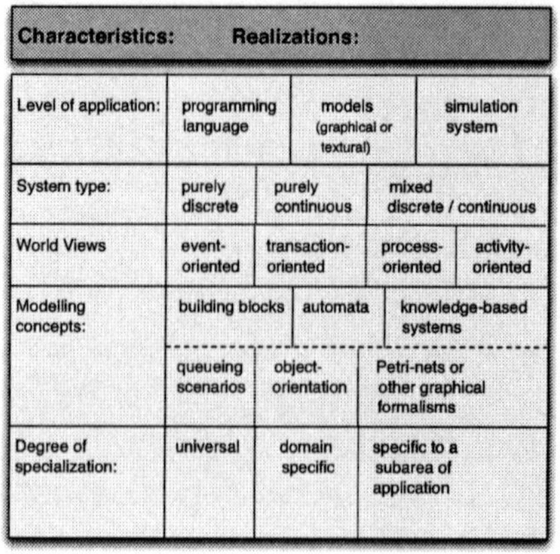

Chapter 9 Simulation Software

Characteristics:	Realizations:			
Level of application:	programming language	models (graphical or textural)	simulation system	
System type:	purely discrete	purely continuous	mixed discrete / continuous	
World Views	event-oriented	transaction-oriented	process-oriented	activity-oriented
Modelling concepts:	building blocks	automata	knowledge-based systems	
	queueing scenarios	object-orientation	Petri-nets or other graphical formalisms	
Degree of specialization:	universal	domain specific	specific to a subarea of application	

Figure 9.2: Morphological box for classifying a simulation tool

tools for modelling production and manufacturing problems. Searching the Internet (e.g. at http://www.lionhrtpub.com/orms/surveys/Simulation/Simulation.html or http://www.wior.uni-karlsruhe.de/bibliothek/Simulation) will yield more up-to-date snapshots of the state of the art. Many interesting applications can be found in the annual *Winter Simulation Conference* proceedings or the German language series *Fortschritte der Simulationstechnik*.

Simulation modelling tools have developed quite rapidly over recent years, and there seems to be no end in sight. Our descriptions therefore cannot claim to reflect all of the latest developments and are only intended to exemplify general principles and ideas.

9.5.1 Extend

Extend (see http://www.imaginethatinc.com) is a modern universal simulation environment which aims to support a model developer during model design and implementation, as well as the execution of simulation runs and the display and statistical evaluation of their results (see Krahl 2002). Since it provides a rich repertoire of functionality for both discrete event and quasi-continuous simulation, it can substantially reduce the effort of model construction and use.

Extend models consist of blocks (components) which are chosen from libraries and then inserted and linked into a flowchart-like diagram (see Figure 9.3). Blocks describe processes, which specify computations or steps associated with changes in model state as well as selection from alternative paths. Functionality prepackaged in different types

9.5 Examples

of blocks can be used to e.g. represent machines, evaluate expressions, or display data in various forms. Blocks are connected by lines, which represent two different types of relationships. One type prescribes "flows" of transient model components (e.g. customers, orders, and messages) while the other probes model entities' (e.g. servers, queues, and data collectors) states. Probing an entity's state produces numerical data, which can be routed to blocks using it for computation or display. The appearance of each block can be changed in an editor, which also allows the specification of relevant parameters and the documentation of a block's functions and purposes.

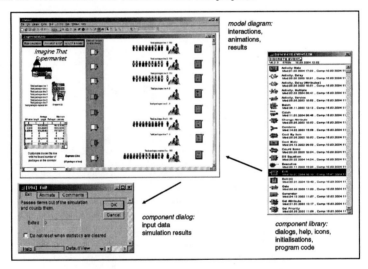

Figure 9.3: Basic structure of an Extend model

Extend models can consist of multiple layers, which are processed in a top-down hierarchical fashion; i.e. blocks can themselves be described via diagrams. This recursive evaluation stops at the level of built-in primitives. In this way Extend's users can add their own types of blocks to the library. A C-like scripting language called *ModL* must be used if deeper changes of functionality are required. For experienced programmers with good knowledge of Extend's internal operation this offers the opportunity for wide ranging changes to both appearance and behaviour of model components. In this way whole new libraries, catering for very specialized applications, can be added to Extend's core. The tool vendor itself (ImagineThat) as well as third parties offer such extensions commercially.

Simulation results can be displayed as time series, histograms, chronological graphs etc. and Extend's blocks also offer many functions for two-dimensional animations,

Chapter 9 Simulation Software

showing both static entities' states and dynamic entities' flows. These can be modified in the same way as mentioned above. More sophisticated 3D animations can be constructed by using an interface to third party software. There are also methods for performing simple automatic sensitivity analyses of model results. Data displays and the appearance of model interfaces can be highly customized using input fields, buttons, and sliders.

Although *ModL*'s scripting capabilities allow us to communicate with and control other applications, many important data processing tools are already built into the system. For example, there is an integrated relational database for persistent storage of models' inputs and outputs for later analyses. Estimating distribution shapes and parameters from empirical data is also supported. There are even some tools for optimization based on guiding the design of multiple simulation runs. Finally, Extend's costs are considerably lower than comparable systems with similar functionality. Other examples of modern universal simulation development systems are Simul8, Micro Saint, AweSim, and MODSIM III (see Law and Kelton 2000, pp. 225).

9.5.2 eM-Plant

eM-Plant is a commercial tool for modelling, simulating, and animating production and material flows in manufacturing systems. It is derived from an earlier system called Simple++ and is marketed by Tecnomatics Technologies (see http://www.emplant.com). All interaction with eM-Plant during the phases of model design, experimentation, and analysis occurs through an integrated graphical interface. Since even its most basic version offers a rich repertoire for representation of its chosen domain, it can be classed as an *application specific* modelling tool; in contrast to Extend, which gains its domain specific functionality only through its component libraries.

eM-Plant offers special building blocks for modelling information flows. Assembling a model occurs in a point, click, drag and drop fashion similar to Extend. eM-Plant's libraries have a hierarchical structure and eM-Plant's models can be assembled hierarchically. There is a dialogue editor for customizing interactions with model users. This allows the deployment of models in multilingual environments. eM-Plant combines a component-based approach with strict object-orientation. New building blocks can inherit from other building blocks and can add and redefine properties and behaviour. A *sensor-actor* technique is used to connect components. Sensors are attached to both entries and exits of building blocks to register dynamic entities' arrivals and departures. A scripting language called *SimTalk* is available to define any specialized actions triggered by such events. *SimTalk* can also be used to interface with other programming tools and eM-Plant offers a comprehensive debugger for error tracing. Figure 9.4 shows eM-Plant's user interface.

Controlling the execution of simulation runs is the responsibility of an event scheduler. A model's initial state must be initialised at the start of a simulation run and changes of state and model dynamics can be animated using two-dimensional or three-dimensional

9.5 Examples

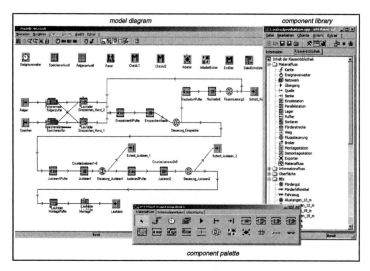

Figure 9.4: eM-Plant's user interface

representations. As in Extend, eM-Plant's animation support is connected to blocks. Many statistical values are collected and computed automatically. A profiler is available to analyse and optimize a model's runtime performance. It shows which components use how much processor time and indicates how often they are invoked.

eM-Plant provides a range of graphical representations for data displays, such as digital and analogue counters, bar charts, pie charts, and chronological graphs. These can either be updated during or at the end of a simulation run. A specialized notation (so-called *Sankey diagrams*) is used to show mass-proportional displays of material flows.

eM-Plant also offers many interfaces for entering data and to communicate with external programs and processes. There are text, ASCII, ActiveX, COM, DDE, HTML, and VRML2 interfaces, many of which, however, are only available as extra and costly add-ons.

Additional commercial extension packages are available for further specialized applications; e.g. to model driver-less transportation systems, conveyor belts, and assembly systems. There are also extension packages for specific industries, such as car assembly and body painting.

Generally, eM-Plant offers a wealth of useful functionality, but its purchase price is quite high. AutoMod, ProModel, WITNESS, Taylor Enterprise Dynamics, QUEST,

255

Chapter 9 Simulation Software

and DOSIMIS-3 are other examples of specialized simulation environments for manufacturing and material flow systems (see Law and Kelton 2000, pp. 672). Figure 9.5 uses the morphological box shown in Figure 9.2 to characterize and compare eM-Plant with Extend. If a tool meets a certain characteristic, this is indicated by a grey accentuation within the morphological box.

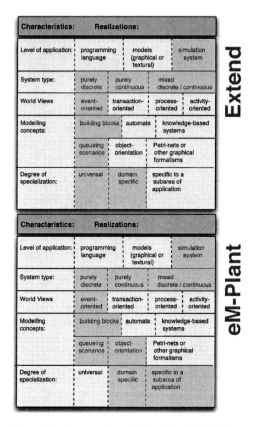

Figure 9.5: A comparison of *Extend* and *eM-Plant*

9.6 The Role of Animation

Driven by rapid improvements in graphic capabilities of personal workstations and a graphical representation's obvious attractiveness to computer users, model and data visualizations have become an increasingly important part of commercial development tools. By visualizing changes in both space and time, animations carry this trend towards more and more concrete presentation of a model's behaviour one step further. Particularly from a marketing perspective animation has now become an irreplaceable part of modern simulation tools. *Animating* a model means visualizing dynamic processes through suitably chosen displays of relevant events and state changes. Some common reasons for animating a model are

- better model validation through easier identification of erroneous or implausible model behaviour and eventually even model structures difficult to understand;
- better communication of functionality and logic to model users;
- more comprehensible and visual presentation of simulation states; e.g. to detect inconsistencies and bottlenecks.

Animations can be performed *online* or *offline*; i.e. they can occur while a simulation is running or can be replayed as a separate process once a simulation has terminated (see Košturiak and Gregor 1995, pp. 159–160). Online animation may require an intentional slow-down of execution speed, to help people observe how events unfold. Since animations consume processor resources, involuntary and undesired slow-downs of model execution may well be unavoidable. Offline animations, on the other hand, only require that relevant data has to be written into a trace file, from which an animation at suitable speed of display can be constructed later. While this precludes any interactions with a "live" model, it has the advantage that animations can be watched multiple times and at different speeds.

Simulation tools can automate building an animation in different ways. Often animation facilities are integrated in model components; e.g. in DOSIMIS-3, eM-Plant (see Figure 9.6), or SIMFACTORY II.5. Alternatively, simulation systems can offer specialized animation editing tools, which may be able to import graphical data from external image editors or CAD systems. Siman and Cinema are examples for such a tool. Yet another possibility is to use external animation tools, which obtain data through suitable interfaces to the simulation, as, for example, PROOF Animation in the context of GPSS/4.

Modern commercial simulation development tools typically offer the following features for defining and running an animation:

- completely graphical definition of both static and dynamic animation components, such as:
  - backgrounds
  - moving items
  - different colours and/or symbols for indicating different states

Chapter 9 Simulation Software

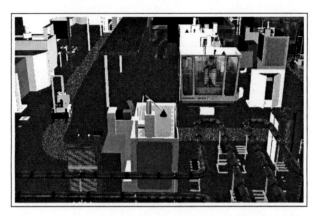

Figure 9.6: An eM-Plant animation (http://www.emplant.com)

- multiple animation windows to show different parts of a model
- stepwise adjustment of animation speed and views (e.g. through zooming and panning)
- optional online and real-time animation
- graphical animation libraries, populated with standard and user-defined symbols
- CAD interfaces; e.g. DFX, IGES
- optional offline playback of animations:
  - automatic recording and replay
  - options to move animations forward and backwards, as well as rewind without rerunning a simulation
- interactive control over:
  - turning animations on or off
  - stepping through animations
  - taking snapshots of system states

In summary, animations can be a valuable tool for presenting a model's results to a non-technical audience and they can play a useful role in validation. They also offer an excellent base for discussions with domain experts. Animation can, however, also tempt us to jump to premature conclusions on the basis of insufficient evidence, and they should therefore be no substitute for more carefully reasoned analyses.

9.7 Criteria for Choosing Simulation Software in Practice

At the start of the third millennium, we find a large range of commercial simulation software; well over 200 products, of which 50 % are targeted at modelling manufacturing systems. Therefore it has become increasingly difficult to choose the most suitable tool for a job. However, we have discussed a number of factors which suggest themselves as a basis for such decisions:

- ❏ Does the tool support relevant modelling concepts?
    - ❏ discrete versus quasi-continuous modelling frameworks
    - ❏ event, activity, or process-based metaphors for discrete event simulations
    - ❏ material or machine-oriented modelling perspectives for discrete event simulations
    - ❏ numerical integration methods for quasi-continuous modelling styles
    - ❏ hierarchical model structures
    - ❏ component libraries with suitable building blocks for chosen model types
    - ❏ object-orientation
    - ❏ ease of model construction through graphical interface
    - ❏ ease of understanding model results through animation
- ❏ Does the tool support the relevant area(s) of application?
    - ❏ manufacturing, material flows, logistics...
    - ❏ information flows
- ❏ Does the tool offer all needed functionality?
    - ❏ How does it model components and their properties?
    - ❏ How does it model distributions and other statistical aspects?
    - ❏ What support is available for experimentation?
    - ❏ What error tracing and correction support is provided?
- ❏ Does the tool offer a convenient user interface?
    - ❏ multiple windows, graphical model construction, context-sensitive help...
- ❏ What are the requirements for the tool's use?
    - ❏ knowledge of simulation methodology
    - ❏ special programming and software skills
    - ❏ time required for learning how to use the tool
- ❏ What are the tool's price and costs of operation?
    - ❏ costs of software acquisition; can range from less than 1,000 to more than 75,000 Euros
    - ❏ platform-dependent cost differences (mainframes, Unix workstations, PCs)
    - ❏ training costs
    - ❏ cost of operation (may be higher than purchase price)

Chapter 9 Simulation Software

- What are the tool's hardware and software requirements?
  - platform, operating system, screen resolution, GUI standard...
- How can the tool present simulation results?
  - statistical instrumentation, graphical displays, output to files...
- What types of animation does the tool support?
  - online, offline
  - 2D, 3D
- What interfaces to external programs are available?
  - CAD, ASCII, SQL, spreadsheet programs, external C++ or Java programs...
- Miscellaneous aspects:
  - documentation, maintenance, number of installations
    between 10 and 100 installations of most tools, while well established ones (e.g. SIMAN, SLAM) may boast 1,000 to 10,000 (including free installations at educational institutions)
  - user training and support
  - reviews, testimonials, and references in the press and from other users
  - availability of test versions and demos

Košturiak and Gregor (1995, pp. 164–166) offer a detailed checklist for choosing a simulation tool.

9.8 Commercial Discrete Event Modelling Tools

The most detailed and up-to-date market review of simulation software has been produced by the American Institute for Operations Research and the Management Sciences, which publishes a comprehensive survey of discrete-event simulation software on an biannual basis. In 2003 the sixth of these surveys was published in the *OR/MS Today*. It is available as a download from: http://www.lionhrtpub.com/orms/surveys/Simulation/Simulation.html.

The survey is based on a questionnaire sent to almost 50 simulation vendors. Questions include the following:

- vendor
- typical applications of the software
- primary markets at which the software is targeted
- system requirements: RAM, operating systems
- model building:
  - graphical model construction (icons, drag-and-drop...)
  - model building through predefined modules

Bibliography

- ❏ runtime debugging tools
- ❏ input distribution fitting
- ❏ output analysis support
- ❏ batch runs
- ❏ support for experimental designs
- ❏ support for optimization
- ❏ code reuse (e.g. objects, templates)
- ❏ model packaging (e.g., can a completed model be shared with others who might lack the software to develop their own models?)
- ❏ animation:
  - ❏ real-time displays
  - ❏ animation export (e.g., MPEG version that can be run independently of a simulation)
  - ❏ compatible animation software
- ❏ prices:
  - ❏ standard version, student version, cost of add-ons...
- ❏ major new features (since last survey)
- ❏ general vendor comments
- ❏ how to contact the vendor

Bibliography

J. Banks, J. S. Carson, and B. L. Nelson. *Discrete-Event System Simulation*. Prentice Hall, Upper Saddle River, 1999.

P. A. Fishwick. Web-based Simulation: Some Personal Observations. In D. T. Brunner, J. J. Swain, J. M. Charnes, and D. J. Morrice, editors, *Proceedings of the 1996 Winter Simulation Conference*, pages 100–103, 1996. [Online] http://www.wintersim.org/prog96.htm (in August 2005).

H. Hartenberger. *Wissensbasierte Simulation komplexer Produktionssysteme* ("Knowledge-Based Simulation of Complex Production Systems", in German), volume 32 of *Institut für Werkzeugmaschinen und Betriebswissenschaften der Technischen Universität München (iwb), Forschungsberichte*. Peter Lang, Frankfurt, 1993.

A. Häuslein. *Wissensbasierte Unterstützung der Modellbildung und Simulation im Umweltbereich: Konzeption und prototypische Realisierung eines Simulationssystems* ("Knowledge-Based Support of Modelling and Simulation in Environmental Science: Conception and Prototypical Realization of a Simulation System", in German), volume 12 of *Europäische Hochschulschriften, Reihe XLI*. Peter Lang, Frankfurt, 1993.

J. Košturiak and M. Gregor. *Simulation von Produktionssystemen* ("Simulation of Production Systems", in German). Springer, Vienna, 1995.

Bibliography

D. Krahl. The Extend Simulation Environment. In E. Yücesan, C.-H. Chen, J. L. Snowdon, and J. M. Charnes, editors, *Proceedings of the 2002 Winter Simulation Conference*, pages 205–213, 2002. [Online] http://www.wintersim.org/prog02.htm (in August 2005).

A. M. Law and W. D. Kelton. *Simulation Modeling and Analysis*. McGraw-Hill, New York, 3rd edition, 2000.

B. Noche and S. Wenzel. *Marktspiegel Simulationstechnik in Produktion und Logistik* ("Mirror of the Market of Simulation Engineering in Produktion and Logistics", in German). TÜV Rheinland, Cologne, 1990.

L. Oakshott. *Business Modelling and Simulation*. Pitman, London, 1997.

B. Page. *Diskrete Simulation – Eine Einführung mit Modula-2* ("Discrete Simulation – An Introduction with Modula-2", in German). Springer, Berlin, 1991.

B. Page, T. Lechler, and S. Claassen. *Objektorientierte Simulation in Java mit dem Framework DESMO-J* ("Object-Oriented Simulation in Java with the Framework DESMO-J", in German). Libri Book on Demand, Hamburg, 2000.

B. Schmidt. Simulation von Produktionssystemen ("Simulation of Production Systems", in German). In *Fachtagung - Rechnerintegrierte Simulationssysteme*, pages 237–277, Erlangen/Nuremberg, 1987.

J. J. Swain. *Power Tools for Visualization and Decision Making*. OR/MS Today, 28 (1):52–63, 2001.

J. J. Swain. *2003 Simulation Software Survey*. OR/MS Today, 30(4):46–57, 2003. [Online] http://www.lionhrtpub.com/orms/surveys/Simulation/Simulation.html (in August 2005).

T. W. Tewoldeberhan, A. Verbraeck, E. Valentin, and G. Bardonnet. An Evaluation and Selection Methodology for Discrete-Event Simulation Software. In E. Yücesan, C.-H. Chen, J. L. Snowdon, and J. M. Charnes, editors, *Proceedings of the 2002 Winter Simulation Conference*, pages 67–75, 2002. [Online] http://www.wintersim.org/prog02.htm (in August 2005).

T. Witte, P. Feil, and M. A. Grzybowski. *LASIM - Ein interaktives Lagerhaltungssimulationssystem* ("LASIM – An Interactive Stockkeeping Simulation System", in German). Beiträge des Fachbereichs Wirtschaftswissenschaften, University of Osnabrück, 1988.

Chapter 10

DESMO-J – A Framework for Discrete Event Modelling & Simulation

Ruth Meyer, Bernd Page, Wolfgang Kreutzer, Nicolas Knaak, Tim Lechler

Contents

10.1 Motivation and Overview	263
10.2 Simulation with DESMO-J	266
10.2.1 The Event-Oriented World View	268
10.2.2 The Process-Oriented World View	273
10.2.3 Combining Events and Processes in a Single Model	274
10.2.4 Some Core Model Components	276
10.3 Experimentation with DESMO-J	280
10.4 Advanced Concepts	284
10.4.1 Higher-Level Modelling Constructs	284
10.4.2 Hierarchical Modelling Constructs	291
10.4.3 Graphical Interfaces	293
10.5 Example: Modelling Container Traffic in the Baltic Sea	293
10.5.1 Model Description	293
10.5.2 An Event-Oriented Implementation	294
10.5.3 A Process-Oriented Implementation	307
10.5.4 Using Higher-Level Modelling Constructs	314
10.6 Development and Evaluation	334
Bibliography	335

10.1 Motivation and Overview

DESMO-J (for "Discrete-Event Simulation Modelling in Java") is an object-oriented software development framework for discrete event simulation; i.e. it offers a collection

Chapter 10 DESMO-J — A Framework for Discrete Event Modelling & Simulation

of software components to support this specific range of tasks. By scaffolding an application's architecture and pre-packaging suitable components for its implementation, frameworks ease model construction. Before the software design pattern movement (see Gamma et al. 1995) reached its current popularity, they were often been referred to as "packages".

Using a simulation framework consists of selecting, connecting, and customizing prepackaged model components and patterns of interaction. When necessary these can be endowed with additional functionality and supplemented by hand-crafted modules. Using a so-called *black box* framework requires only suitable instantiation of predefined off-the-shelf components. Modifications are restricted to simple parameter changes. *White box* frameworks, on the other hand, offer more abstract classes, which must be adapted and customized to serve a model's specific needs. DESMO-J extends the general purpose programming language Java with a mixture of black box and white box components for modelling discrete event scenarios.

Figure 9.1 has already shown how simulation software can support simulation studies at different levels of abstraction; trading between the conflicting demands of usability and flexibility and catering for the needs of different classes of users.

Frameworks are bound at the *language-level*; i.e. they assume programming skills. Model- and tool-level software does not require that users are able to program. An ability to edit text files and change the parameters of pre-packaged models suffices. *Black box* frameworks offer "closed" constructs, whose linguistic abstractions are close to a model design. This makes them easy to use and act as appropriate tools for domain experts with basic programming skills. *White box* frameworks, on the other hand, are firmly embedded in a programming language and often distributed as libraries for general purpose languages (e.g. Java or C++) or special purpose simulation programming tools (e.g. Simula). This makes white box frameworks more flexible and applicable to a wider range of domains, but their competent use also requires highly developed coding skills. They are therefore often a tool of choice for software professionals. DESMO-J offers a mixture of black box and white box components and is therefore targeted both at simulation experts with coding skills and software developers with basic knowledge of discrete event simulation. Indeed, the framework was originally designed to help teaching discrete event simulation concepts. How much programming skill is required for its successful deployment strongly depends on a model's complexity. Section 10.5 shows some examples.

DESMO-J follows the tradition that simulation frameworks rarely support all phases of the software development cycle and typically restrict themselves to the implementation and (to a lesser extent) experimentation phases.

To support discrete event simulation model development, frameworks must offer components and suitable linguistic abstractions to capture the following concepts:

- *entities*, which model real-world scenarios in terms of objects and their properties, behaviour, and relationships

10.1 Motivation and Overview

- stochastic *distributions* to model random behaviour
- *data collectors* to record statistical data for later analysis
- a *clock* entity to track model time
- an *event list* to store pending events or process activations
- a *scheduler* entity to control model execution; i.e. to simulate interactions between conceptually concurrently active entities

DESMO-J's black box components therefore provide:

- A discrete event simulation's infrastructure (i.e. event list, simulation clock, event scheduler). This functionality is part of a Model class.
- A means for recording and storing simulation result and protocol data in files (i.e. reports, event traces, debugging information, and errors). This functionality is encapsulated in an Experiment class.
- Constructs for modelling queues and random processes.
- Constructs or collecting statistical data.

DESMO-J's white box features extend this core functionality to model-specific entity types with active behaviour. To meet their requirements, DESMO-J offers generic Model, Entity, Event, and SimProcess objects, whose functionality must be subclassed as needed.

DESMO-J strictly separates modelling aspects from simulation experiments. Model properties include declarations and descriptions of entities, events, processes, queues, distributions, and data collectors, while black box components like scheduler, event list, and model clock are encapsulated by an Experiment class. Figure 10.1 shows a snapshot of DESMO-J's class hierarchy. Note that the term "hot spot" has been attached to those classes whose behaviour needs to be detailed by a model designer (i.e. white box components), while black box components only need to be instantiated and their parameters set. In the figure white box (or "hot-spot") classes are shaded more lightly than black box classes.

DESMO-J distinguishes between *schedulable* and *reportable* objects. Dynamic entities, events, and processes can all be scheduled to change model state at specified model time instants. The abstract Entity, Event ExternalEvent, and SimProcess classes grant this capability to their subclasses. From a modeller's viewpoint, instances of Reportable and its subclasses are static; i.e. no explicit descriptions of state changing actions need to be attached. Statistical performance measures are automatically collected and reported at the end of a simulation run. Classes Model, Distribution, QueueBased, and StatisticalObject offer this functionality.

Following the class hierarchy in Figure 10.1, Figure 10.2 shows how DESMO-J chunks its functionality's implementation into a number of Java packages, with simulator, dist, statistic, report, and exception at its core. Packages extensions, gui, and util cater for application specific extensions (e.g. harbour logistics), graphical interfaces, and internal utility functions.

Chapter 10 DESMO-J – A Framework for Discrete Event Modelling & Simulation

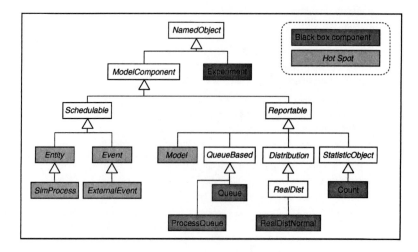

Figure 10.1: A snapshot of DESMO-J's class hierarchy

10.2 Simulation with DESMO-J

DESMO-J can host many different modelling styles; e.g. event-orientation, process-orientation, combined event/process-orientation, activity-orientation, and transaction-based modelling. Since their descriptive levels are "higher", activity-, and transaction-based scenarios use DESMO-J's higher-level modelling constructs, but are ultimately based on an event- or process-oriented model.

DESMO-J model construction can be split into a number of tasks:

- Selection of any required "black box" components, such as data collectors (e.g. `Histogram`), statistical distributions (e.g. `RealDistExponential`), and queues (e.g. `Queue`)
- Implementation of lifecycles for dynamic "white box" components by customizing suitable "hot spot" classes: `SimProcess, Entity,` and `Event`
- Implementation of top level functionality – e.g. instantiation and parametrization of model components, scheduling of active entities' processes – as part of the `Model` entity's lifecycle. Note that `Model` is a singleton class; i.e. each DESMO-J model must have exactly one instance.

10.2 Simulation with DESMO-J

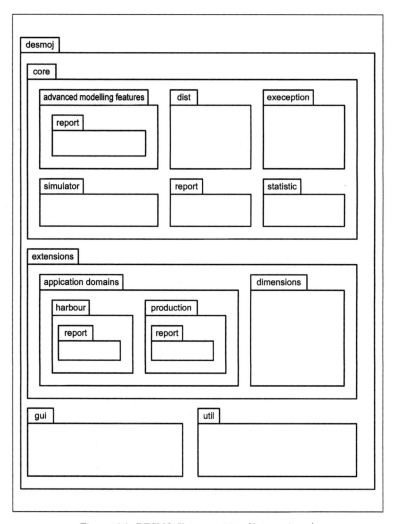

Figure 10.2: DESMO-J's composition (Java packages)

Chapter 10 DESMO-J – A Framework for Discrete Event Modelling & Simulation

10.2.1 The Event-Oriented World View

Event-oriented modelling styles chunk states into entities' properties and describe transformations in terms of events. To implement such scenarios in DESMO-J, a model builder must specialize "hot spot" classes `Entity` and `Event`; i.e. subclasses of `Entity` are extended by suitable attributes and subclasses of `Event` or `ExternalEvent` describe model-specific behaviour patterns in their `eventRoutine()` methods. While the simulation scheduler itself is attached to the `Experiment` class, DESMO-J grants scheduling capabilities for storing events in its event list to abstract `Entity`, `Event`, and `ExternalEvent` classes. Specific models derive specific subclasses from them. This means that dynamic entities, events, and external events can schedule themselves and have no need to access the scheduler object directly.

All objects for which lifecycles are described must ultimately be subclasses of the abstract `Entity` class. This allows entity manipulation by a given event (see below) to be planned for specific model time instants; also assignment of a priority (i.e. an integer whose higher values indicate higher urgency) to an entitiy is possible. Inherited scheduling methods include `schedule(Event what, SimTime when)` and `cancel()`; both can be applied to events and phases in entity lifecycles. DESMO-J offers comparison methods for priorities and a model builder can add further attributes and methods (e.g. for reading and writing such attributes) to the standard methods and properties inherited from class `Entity`. Entities can also be members in one or more queues (simultaneously). All data structures and methods required to provide this functionality are inherited from the `Entity` superclass.

In an event-oriented model algorithmic descriptions of dynamic behaviour must be encapsulated in subclasses of the `Event` and `ExternalEvent` classes. Multiple subclasses can cater for multiple types of events, which give different implementations for the abstract `eventRoutine(Entity who)` method. Each event in a simulation run is then instantiated from these classes, will be processed by the model's scheduler, and its memory allocation will eventually be "garbage collected" – once it has served its purpose and is free of all references.

Class `Schedulable` grants the following scheduling methods to all of its subclasses:

- ❏ `schedule(Entity who, SimTime when)` plans an event involving the referenced entity to occur *at* the specified model time.

- ❏ `scheduleAfter(Schedulable after, Entity who)` plans an event involving the referenced entity to happen *after* an event involving the specified schedulable object has occurred.

- ❏ `scheduleBefore(Schedulable before, Entity who)` plans an event involving the referenced entity to happen *before* an event involving the specified schedulable object has occurred.

Note that DESMO-J only allows placing a single reference to each entity on its event list, which means that the above schedules are unique (i.e. there must be a single before and after).

10.2 Simulation with DESMO-J

Currently active events or entities can be referred to by using the global variables `currentEntity`, `currentEvent`, and `currentSchedulable`. Movement through a simulated time dimension is a defining property of all types of time-dynamic simulations, and the representation of model time is therefore of great importance. DESMO-J's designers considered two different strategies for providing this functionality. Storing time in a simple variable (e.g. of type `double`) would reap the benefits of simplicity. No special time objects would need to be generated, storage requirements would be low, arithmetic operations and comparisons on time values could be performed in a direct and straightforward fashion, and implementation would have been easy. Storing time as a special time object, on the other hand, would require a special class and its usage would be less convenient. The advantages of special time objects would be conceptual clarity (e.g. they help documentation in interface definitions) and better error control (e.g. one can allow only positive values for random delays). Ultimately DESMO-J's designers decided to use `SimTime` objects for all model time references, where this class encapsulates a `double` value and various methods for model time access.

Internally (i.e. as part of its black box aspects) DESMO-J keeps track of events with an event list, consisting of so-called event notices. Each event notice holds references to three objects:

❑ an `Entity` instance, which specifies who is to be changed
❑ an `Event` instance, which describes what the change will involve
❑ a `SimTime` instance, which prescribes the time instant at which the change will occur

DESMO-J's event list is ordered by model time; i.e. the most imminent events are always in front. There is also a time object's property `NOW`, whose use can ensure that a new event will be inserted in the front-most event list position (see Figure 10.7).

Figures 10.3 shows an event list's initial state and Figures 10.4 to 10.7 demonstrate the effects of different scheduling statements on DESMO-J's event list.

Entity	Event	SimTime
Entity1	Event1	1.5
Entity4	Event4	2.7
Entity3	Event3	5.2
Entity2	Event2	8.3

Figure 10.3: Event list at model time 1.1

Chapter 10 DESMO-J – A Framework for Discrete Event Modelling & Simulation

Let us assume that the scheduling statement

`event5.schedule(entity5, new SimTime(8.1));`

plans a new event to occur 8.1 model time units into the model's future. This causes the scheduler to compute this event's time of occurrence (1.1 + 8.1 = 9.2) and then generate a suitable event notice. This event notice is placed at its appropriate place in the event list (here, at the back). Figure 10.4 shows the result.

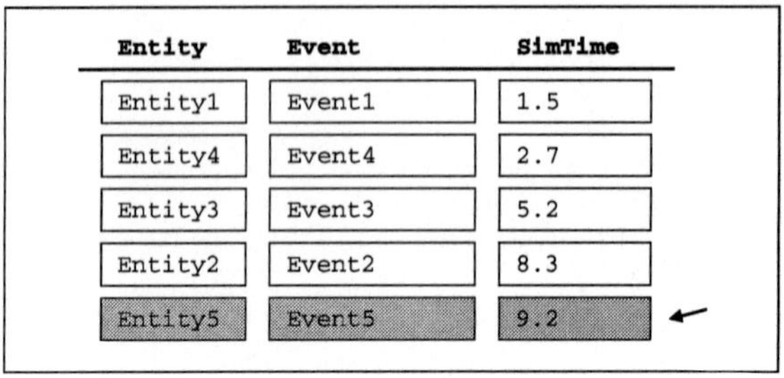

Entity	Event	SimTime
Entity1	Event1	1.5
Entity4	Event4	2.7
Entity3	Event3	5.2
Entity2	Event2	8.3
Entity5	Event5	9.2

Figure 10.4: Event list at model time 1.1 after
`event5.schedule(entity5, new SimTime(8.1))`

At this point we schedule a further event

`event6.scheduleAfter(event4, entity6);`

which the scheduler packages into an event notice and files behind **event4**. Note that this new event now shares its time of occurrence with **event4**, but – since all events must be serialized at execution time (at least on a single processor machine) – will happen after **event4** has occurred. Figure 10.5 shows the result.

Now

`event7.scheduleBefore(entity4, entity7);`

creates an event immediately prior to the event involving **entity4** (i.e. **event4**). This new event again takes the time aspect of the event it precedes (and will happen before it), see Figure 10.6.

The example shows that `scheduleAfter()` and `scheduleBefore()` can take either a reference to some successor or predecessor event, or can be given an entity reference (here **entity4**). For DESMO-J the second case requires that, in order to ensure unique identification of relevant events when given an entity reference, each entity can have only *one* event scheduled at any given point in time. This restriction simplifies event list operations as well as the signatures of the `cancel()`, `reSchedule()`, and `schedule()` methods.

10.2 Simulation with DESMO-J

Entity	Event	SimTime
Entity1	Event1	1.5
Entity4	Event4	2.7
Entity6	Event6	2.7
Entity3	Event3	5.2
Entity2	Event2	8.3
Entity5	Event5	9.2

Figure 10.5: Event list at model time 1.1 after
event6.scheduleAfter(entity4, entity6)

Entity	Event	SimTime
Entity1	Event1	1.5
Entity7	Event7	2.7
Entity4	Event4	2.7
Entity6	Event6	2.7
Entity3	Event3	5.2
Entity2	Event2	8.3
Entity5	Event5	9.2

Figure 10.6: Event list at model time 1.1 after
event7.scheduleBefore(entity4, entity7)

Our final scheduling example

event8.schedule(entity8, SimTime.NOW)

is functionally equivalent to event8.scheduleAfter(this, entity8), where the this pseudo variable refers to the currently executing event routine. The reference to SimTime.NOW ensures that the event will be executed immediately (at the current clock time); i.e. as soon as the currently processed event has finished. Figure 10.7 therefore shows event8 at the head of the event list. Note that in order to immediately execute any event scheduled with the NOW predicate in a *process*-oriented scenario, the currently executing process will be interrupted and rescheduled. Since events cannot involve time

271

Chapter 10 DESMO-J – A Framework for Discrete Event Modelling & Simulation

delays (they must all be explicitly scheduled), such pre-emption will never be needed in an event-oriented scenario.

Entity	Event	SimTime
Entity8	Event8	1.1
Entity1	Event1	1.5
Entity7	Event7	2.7
Entity4	Event4	2.7
Entity6	Event6	2.7
Entity3	Event3	5.2
Entity2	Event2	8.3
Entity5	Event5	9.2

Figure 10.7: Event list at model time 1.1 after
event8.schedule (entity8, SimTime.NOW)

In summary, implementing an event-oriented model in DESMO-J requires derivation of subclasses of Entity for each of the model's entity types. These must then be enriched with suitable properties and given constructor methods to pass relevant arguments like a reference to the model it is part of (necessary in order to facilitate communication with the scheduler and the model itself) and various reporting options to their superclass.

We must also define a subclass of Event for each type of event in the model. All these need implementations for the abstract eventRoutine(Entity who) method, in which state changing actions can be described. Such actions may include changes which are instantaneous in terms of model time; e.g. changing property values, filing entities into and removing them from lists or waiting lines. Any model time consuming activities must be mapped into scheduling statements; e.g. using schedule() or one of its variants. "External" events, i.e. those whose occurrence is determined by actions outside of a model's scope, can be derived from an ExternalEvent class. Both internal and external events require constructors to pass arguments to their respective superclasses.

10.2 Simulation with DESMO-J

10.2.2 The Process-Oriented World View

Processes are conceptually active entities which package both properties and behaviour. Properties are declared as data structures of suitable type and behaviour is described in lifecycles, whose passive phases model delays and whose active phases prescribe changes in state. In contrast to event-oriented scenarios, processes can be interrupted and continued at will. Process definition in DESMO-J requires specialization of a SimProcess class, whose subclasses are extended with model specific properties and must implement lifeCycle() methods. SimProcess grants scheduling features to all its subclasses. Figure 10.8 reviews (see Chapter 5, Figure 5.2) how hold(), passivate(), and activate() can be used to interleave active and passive process phases.

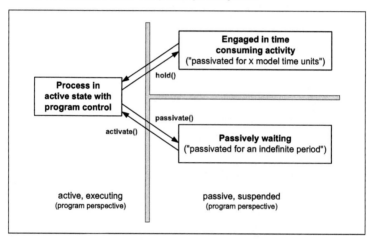

Figure 10.8: Transitions between active and passive phases in a process-oriented DESMO-J model

hold(SimTime dt) stops and delays processes for dt model time units, after which they will be reactivated. passivate() interrupts execution for an indefinite time period. activate(SimTime dt) awakens a passive process after a specified dt delay (i.e. relative to the current model time). activateAfter(Schedulable after) and activateBefore(Schedulable before) are used to establish scheduling relationships with other processes, and reActivate(SimTime dt) reschedules a process' next active phase to a model time instant computed by adding an interval dt to the current value of model time.

Note how activate(), activateAfter(), and activateBefore() correspond to the event-based methods schedule(), scheduleAfter(), and scheduleBefore(). The

Chapter 10 DESMO-J – A Framework for Discrete Event Modelling & Simulation

main difference lies in the fact that process references replace event references and that all processes must remember the point in their execution where they last relinquish control. A suitable data structure (e.g. a "coroutine") is needed to implement this and DESMO-J augments Java with a coroutine feature based on *secure threads* for this purpose.

In contrast to the event-oriented perspective we discussed in Section 10.2.1, a process description's `lifeCycle()` method permits any number of interruptions and changes in who has control. It therefore encapsulates *all* of a process' behavioural aspects in a single snippet of code. Event-oriented scenarios cannot deliver such a degree of descriptive flexibility and all `eventRoutine()` methods attached to events must run to completion each time they are called. This means that only *simultaneous* changes can be clustered into the code representing events and that all time delays map into scheduling networks.

In an event-oriented model design, methods such as `passivate()` or `hold()` relinquish control to the model's scheduler, which in turn passes control to the next imminent event on the event list. Control does not return to the modules which issued this transfer. In a process-oriented scenario, however, a `lifeCycle()` method can have any number of entry and exit points, and while `passivate()` or `hold()` also prompt the model scheduler to activate the next pending process' next active phase, control may eventually return to the module (lifecycle) which initiated these transfers.

To summarize the key features of process-oriented model development, we note that a separate subclass of `SimProcess` must be defined for each conceptually active entity in a model. Each of these must implement their own version of a `lifeCycle()` method and may provide any number of additional attributes. Lifecycles should describe how entities change state, how they enter and leave lists or waiting lines, and how active and passive process phases are interleaved. As long as relevant references are available, these descriptions can refer to the currently active process as well as to other entities in the model. As always, subclasses of `SimProcess` need to provide a constructor method which passes relevant information, such as a model reference and reporting options, to their superclass.

10.2.3 Combining Events and Processes in a Single Model

Both event-oriented and process-oriented viewpoints can be used in the same DESMO-J model. Such mixed world views can result from choosing the best modelling perspective for different aspects and may also help foster greater sub-model reusability.

To mix process with event-based specifications, the model scheduler must be able to distinguish and process both lifecycle and event references stored in event notices. Since DESMO-J's class hierarchy ultimately derives both the `SimProcess` and `Event` classes from `Schedulable` (see Figure 10.1), this seems unproblematic. However, while all processes are also subclasses of `Entity`, events are not. They have therefore no easy

10.2 Simulation with DESMO-J

means of accessing **Model** properties and must own separate references to all entities which they involve.

In mixed models the model scheduler encounters three types of event notices on its event list:

- a "normal" event, with references to entities it involves
- an "external" event, with no entity references
- a process activation, whose state changing actions may operate on the process' own attributes or those of additional "known" entities

Figure 10.9 shows an event list snapshot with two "normal" events, one external event (fourth from the top), and three process events.

Entity	Event	SimTime
Entity1	Event1	1.5
Entity3	Event3	2.7
Process1	-	5.2
-	Event2	8.3
Process2	-	9.2
Process3	Event4	9.4

Figure 10.9: An event list with "normal" events, external events, and pending process activations

The first two entries refer to both entities and events. The third and fifth entry only refer to the relevant process, and the fourth entry only points to an event. Since this is an external event, it need not refer to any entity. For example, it could represent a customer arrival, where there is yet no data structure for holding this customer's state information. The sixth entry is a "normal" event, which refers to **Event4**'s code and passes **Process3** as a parameter. This allows the event to process this process; for example a process' execution could be interrupted through an event such as machine breakdown.

The model scheduler will act according to the type of event notice; i.e. it will call an event routine with or without passing an entity as a parameter, resume a process' lifecycle etc.

Chapter 10 DESMO-J – A Framework for Discrete Event Modelling & Simulation

10.2.4 Some Core Model Components

A simulation framework's black box components offer frequently used functionality, such as:

- queues to help synchronize model entities' behaviour
- stochastic distributions, based on pseudo-random samples
- statistical data collectors, which record data for later analysis

All of these predefined model components are implemented as "passive" data structures; i.e. they must be manipulated by other entities (e.g. processes and events). DESMO-J wraps them into a number of packages; i.e.:

- queues in `desmoj.core.simulator`
- distributions in `desmoj.core.dist`
- data collectors in `desmoj.core.statistic`

Queues

In discrete event scenarios queues are a frequently used and important classes of model components. They are particularly essential for modelling systems involving capacity constrained resources. DESMO-J provides classes `Queue` and `ProcessQueue`. Both are derived from class `QueueBased`, which is itself a subclass of `Reportable`. This means that queues' automatic data collection can make use of `Reportable`'s reporting facilities to display standard statistical measures.

Although not strictly necessary, DESMO-J distinguishes "ordinary" queues from queues which contain processes. The difference between these two classes shows only in the declaration of parameter types. No type transformations between members of either class of queue are needed.

Queues own methods for insertion and removal of entities. `insert(Entity e)` adds an entity to the tail of a queue, using a FIFO (first in, first out) strategy. Entities' priorities are also taken into account. `remove(Entity e)` removes entities from a queue's head. Entities can be inserted relative to another entity's queueing position, using `insertAfter(Entity e, Entity after)` and `insertBefore(Entity e, Entity before)`. This, however, can destroy the queue's order; i.e it may not remain a priority-sequenced FIFO queue afterwards.

Queues also provide a number of methods for testing for emptiness (`isEmpty()`) and for referring to entities in prominent positions. References to a queue's first and last members are returned by `first()` and `last()`, while successors and predecessors of entities can be retrieved with `succ(Entity e)` and `pred(Entity e)`.

As an example, Figure 10.10 shows the state of a queue after 6 entities with respective priorities (in brackets) have been entered. The numbers in these entities' names reflect their insertion order. Queueing discipline is higher-priority first, then FIFO.

10.2 Simulation with DESMO-J

Pos.	Entity
1	Entity6 (2)
2	Entity2 (0)
3	Entity4 (0)
4	Entity5 (0)
5	Entity3 (-1)
6	Entity1 (-2)

Figure 10.10: A priority-based FIFO queue

DESMO-J also endows queues with typical performance instrumentation, to record measures like average queue length, average waiting times, current queue length, maximum and minimum queue lengths, maximum and minimum waiting times, etc. These statistics are maintained automatically and suitable access methods are provided. In addition, there is a `zeroWaits()` method for retrieving the number of entities which did not encounter any delays, and a `reset()` method for wiping all statistical counters. The latter functionality is particularly useful for furnishing simulation experiments with a "warm-up" period.

Queues can be searched for entities which meet specified conditions. This functionality requires derivation of a suitable subclass of DESMO-J's `Condition` class and instantiation of a condition object of that class. This object is then passed to queue methods as a parameter, guiding the search. For example, `first(Condition c)` looks for the first entity in a queue for which the given condition is met, while `last(Condition c)` searches the queue from its tail to find the last matching entry. `pred(Entity e, Condition c)` and `succ(Entity e, Condition c)` can be used to identify the first relevant predecessor or successor of a queued entity. Together these methods offer much flexibility in processing queue members and can be used to implement queueing strategies which are less common than FIFO.

Random Numbers

DESMO-J's distribution objects are based on `java.util.Random` in Java's standard utilities library. This class provides a linear congruential random generator with a maximum cycle of 2^{48} (see Section 7.2). A better random class can be substituted, as long as it implements the `UniformRandomGenerator` interface and implements the `nextDouble()` method for drawing a random number as well as `setSeed()` for growing sequences from specified seeds.

277

Chapter 10 DESMO-J – A Framework for Discrete Event Modelling & Simulation

An abstract `Distribution` class is used to bundle common properties and methods, whose subclasses represent different types of distributions. Random streams are not shared among distributions; all instances of all distribution classes have their own random generator components.

The `Distribution` class offers generic means for seeding a random stream (using `setSeed()` or `reset()`) and for generating reports; it makes use of reporting functionality inherited from class `Reportable` and creates a separate `Reporter` object for each of a model's distributions. Reported results include distribution type, parameters, seed values, and number of samples.

To facilitate typing of sampling results, DESMO-J uses intermediary classes `RealDist`, `IntDist`, and `BoolDist` (all subclasses of `Distribution`) to derive `RealDistExponential`, `RealDistNormal`, `RealDistErlang`, `RealDistUniform`, `RealDistEmpirical`, `IntDistPoisson`, `IntDistUniform`, `IntDistEmpirical`, `BoolDistBernoulli`, and some others. All instances of these respond to a `sample()` method, which returns a randomly sampled value; taken from the specified range according to the relevant distribution's shape. For testing purposes DESMO-J also provides `RealDistConstant`, `IntDistConstant`, and `BoolDistConstant`. Instances of these three classes always return the same value.

Statistical Data Collectors

Data collectors are used to collect, evaluate, and report simulation results which are not automatically collected by one of DESMO-J's black box components (e.g. by queues or resources). All data collector classes inherit display capabilities from class `Reportable` and can simply be updated (with `update()`) or serve as the basis for implementing observer patterns mediated by instances of the `ValueSupplier` class. Data collectors implement the `java.util.Observer` interface in support of the second case. In addition to `update()`, all data collectors own a `reset()` for setting statistical counters to zero and the times of last change to the current clock time.

DESMO-J's data collectors include `Tally`, `Accumulate`, `Histogram`, `TimeSeries`, and `Regression` classes. Figure 10.11 shows the relevant part of their class hierarchy (in package `desmoj.core.statistic`).

Counters (i.e. instances of class `Count`) can be used to record occurrences of events; e.g. number of customer arrivals or orders in progress. As for all data collection objects, the `update()` method is used for this. Note that updating a counter may provide no argument, in which case it is simply incremented by one. If values other than one or negative increments are required, the `update(long n)` variant can be used. Reports on counters list number of observations, their current values and minima and maxima.

Tallies (i.e. instances of class `Tally`) record a time series' mean and standard deviation. Each observation carries the same weight; i.e. no account is taken of the length of a state's duration. Computing the average time customers spent in a model segment is a task for a tally. Tallies are updated, using `update(double val)`, each time a new

10.2 Simulation with DESMO-J

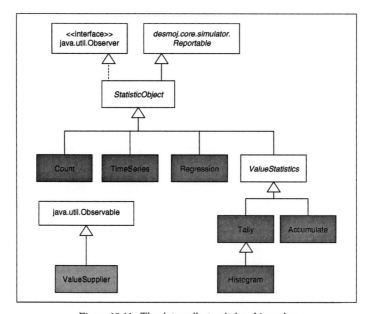

Figure 10.11: The data collectors' class hierarchy

value must be recorded. A report, listing observations, mean, and standard deviations, is produced on demand or at the end of a simulation run. getMean() and getStdDev() can be used to retrieve these two values at any time.

Accumulates (i.e. instances of class Accumulate) also record a time series' mean and standard deviation. In contrast to tallies, however, each observation is weighed by the interval during which a state has endured. To keep track of a state's value's interval, DESMO-J records the instant of the observed value's last change (in attribute lastTime). The relevant reports and getMean() and getStdDev() therefore return time-weighted statistics. Observing the utilization of capacity-constrained resources (servers) is an example for when the time-weighted updates associated with an accumulate will be needed.

If we require immediate updates of an accumulate – to provide accurate measures at any model time instant – we can enlist cooperation of a ValueSupplier and set the accumulate's automatic parameter to true.

DESMO-J's implementation of data collectors is based on the *Observer* design pattern (see Gamma et al. 1995). Whenever an observed object (i.e. an instance of interface

279

Chapter 10 DESMO-J – A Framework for Discrete Event Modelling & Simulation

java.util.Observable) changes its state, an observer object (a subclass instance of java.util.Observer) is notified. In our context data collectors observe model objects to derive relevant statistical measures about their performance. The abstract ValueSupplier class is a white box ("hot spot") component which offers basic functionality to support this pattern; e.g. registering and de-registering of observers. How to provide the data itself must be specified in suitable subclasses by a model designer.

The Model Class

DESMO-J's Model class is responsible for administering all model components, initialising the experiment's event list prior to the start of a simulation run, and for automatic creation of simulation reports.

It is an abstract class, whose abstract methods must be implemented in its subclasses. Model builders must define Model subclasses and provide method bodies for:

- init() to initialise all model components
- doInitialSchedules() to provide events for an experiment's start
- description() to give a brief model documentation (e.g. domain, purpose, author)

10.3 Experimentation with DESMO-J

Since it offers an interface to all of DESMO-J's infrastructure, the Experiment class is the largest class in the simulation framework. It provides a *Facade* in the sense of the Gamma et al.'s design pattern of the same name (see Gamma et al. 1995) and generates and administers all of a simulation's infrastructure (e.g. model clock, event list). Model builders need only to know the Experiment class' interface and have no direct access to infrastructure components. This eases the modelling effort and also permits changes to important aspects of the DESMO-J framework's design without the need for a model's components to change. Experiment and a simulation's infrastructure are therefore black box components, whose internal details are only relevant for framework developers. No modifications by model designers are expected.

This architecture facilitates clean separation of models from experiments a modeller may wish to perform. The class diagram in Figure 10.12 summarizes this interplay of a model and its experiments. Here the user-defined white box ("hot spot") classes are more darkly coloured than the Experiment class. The Experiment class serves as an interface to the model's infrastructure; i.e. to

- the *model scheduler*;
- the *event list*; with event notices ordered by time (most imminent events listed first); or
- the *simulation clock* (SimClock); a SimTime object holding the current model time.

10.3 Experimentation with DESMO-J

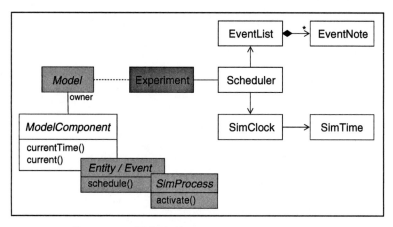

Figure 10.12: DESMO-J's Model and Experiment classes
(with some of their components)

DESMO-J uses connectToExperiment() to associate a model with its experiments. This lets the model request services from the simulation infrastructure.

Each model component is part of a Model and owns (via property owner) a reference to it. This means that model components have indirect access to any experiments they participate in. DESMO-J's white box components (instances of "hot spot" classes) can also directly access the following methods:

❑ currentTime() returns the current value of SimClock.

❑ current() refers to the currently active model component.

Since these are inherited from class ModelComponent, they are available to all model objects.

In order to move simulations through time, conceptually active components (i.e. events or processes) use

❑ schedule() for putting a suitable event on the event list; and

❑ activate() for putting a suitable process activation on the event list.

To set up a new experiment, a model builder must provide an implementation for the abstract main() method, which is contained in a suitable Model subclass. main() always starts a model's execution and is responsible for instantiating both model and experiment objects. The sequence in which these two objects are created is unimportant, but they must eventually be linked; i.e. we either create a model, then create an experiment, then link the model to the experiment, or we create an experiment, then

Chapter 10 DESMO-J - A Framework for Discrete Event Modelling & Simulation

create a model, and then link the experiment to the model. Listing 10.1 shows how a simple model may attend to these tasks.

```
public static void main(String[] args) {

    // create model and experiment
    MyModelClass model = new MyModelClass();
    Experiment exp = new Experiment("MyExperiment");

    // and link them
    model.connectToExperiment(exp);

    // initialise experiments parameters
    exp.setShowProgressBar(true);
    exp.tracePeriod(new SimTime(0.0), new SimTime(100.0));
    exp.debugPeriod(new SimTime(10.0), new SimTime(50.0));
    exp.stop(new SimTime(480.0);

    // start experiment
    exp.start();

    // generate report and shut everything down
    exp.report();
    exp.finish();

} // end of main method
```

Listing 10.1: A DESMO-J model shell

This code first creates both model and experiment (lines 4 and 5). Although there are none needed here, some models may require some arguments. This also holds for experiments. As a minimum we must name them, so that DESMO-J can label the experiment's output files. Note that this means that an experiment's name must be compatible with any naming restrictions a particular operating system may have. connectToExperiment() links the experiment to the model (line 8). This will implicitly call init(), whose execution initialises all model components.

At this point further parameters of an experiment can be set. For example, we can request that a progress bar is shown during the simulation run (setShowProgressBar(true) in line 11). We can also determine the degree of data collection (e.g. for tracing and debugging purposes). The relevant intervals can be chosen freely. Lines 12 and 13 request a trace from 0 to 100 and a debugging phase from 10 to 50 (all in terms of model time). The stop() statement shown in line 14 is needed to plan the end of the simulation run. Here we request a duration of 480 model time units. Note that it is up to the modeller to decide how model time is mapped onto real time. Depending on context the 480 model time units could represent milliseconds, minutes, days, or years.

10.3 Experimentation with DESMO-J

The phrase `exp.start()` in line 17 begins a simulation. This implicitly calls `doInitialSchedules()`, which schedules the first event(s) and starts the model scheduler, which is then tasked with moving the model through time.

At the end of a simulation, control returns to the `main()` method. This is often the right time and place to show a report and ensure that all open files are closed and all active processes (threads) terminated. The statements in lines 20 and 21 take care of this.

Each DESMO-J experiment is equipped with four standard output channels: `Report`, `Debug`, `Trace`, and `Error`. These are associated with HTML-files whose names are composed of both experiment name and report type. Experiment results are automatically recorded and computed. They are stored in file

`<experiment name>_report.html`.

Within that file they are sorted by object classes and list all measures provided by the relevant `Reporter` objects. If an execution trace had been requested, an

`<experiment name>_trace.html`

file presents a sequence of (model time, event, entity, action) tuples. This includes all event list entries and all queueing operations within the specified model time interval. Traces can be requested by using `Experiment`'s `tracePeriod()` method. Traces should be used sparingly, since they slow an experiment's execution and have the potential to generate large masses of data. Annotations can be sent to a trace file by using `sendTraceNote(String description)`.

Spawned by `Experiment`'s `debugPeriod()` method and a `debugOn()` message in at least one dynamic model component, the file

`<experiment name>_debug.html`

holds additional information about scheduling and queueing operations; together with snapshots of the relevant list's states. Each line reports model name, time, object, and message. `sendDebugNote(String description)` can be used for additional annotations. Any error conditions encountered during a simulation run are stored in an

`<experiment name>_error.html`

file, in which each error is reported in terms of description, location, reason, and prevention. A model designer can write to this file by using the `sendWarning(String description, String location, String reason, String prevention)` method.

Chapter 10 DESMO-J – A Framework for Discrete Event Modelling & Simulation

10.4 Advanced Concepts

10.4.1 Higher-Level Modelling Constructs

Many discrete event simulation models use queues to synchronize entities which are conceptually acting concurrently. As seen above, patterns of interaction among such entities can be described from either an event-based or a process-based perspective. *Higher-level modelling constructs* enable a model designer to cast these descriptions in more problem relevant terms. The expression of typical patterns of processes waiting for different types of events are supported in terms of suitable linguistic abstractions; e.g.:

- waiting for completion of services
- waiting for shared resources to become available
- waiting for other processes within common actions
- waiting for specific events

To reduce the cognitive load on a model designer, DESMO-J's implementations of higher-level constructs for serving these needs share a number of features:

- They are all based on queues (i.e. lists).
- Entities or processes are automatically filed into queues.
- When leaving a queue, events, or processes are automatically activated.
- Relevant statistical measures are automatically recorded and reported.

As shown in Figure 10.13, DESMO-J supports four different patterns of synchronization:

- Capacity constrained resources (class `Res`) and processes competing for their acquisition. Processes wait until sufficient resource capacity is available to proceed.
- Producer/consumer relationships with unlimited capacity buffers (classes `Bin` and `Stock`). Any number of producers and consumers may share a bin or stock and bottlenecks will occur if consumption exceeds production or production exceeds a capacity limit (for stocks).
- Conditional waiting until a specified model state has occurred (class `CondQueue`). Any number of processes can wait for the same condition, in which case a priority-led FIFO discipline is enforced to serialize execution.
- Direct process cooperation in the form of asymmetric master-slave relationships (class `WaitQueue`). This pattern allows shared strands of execution in which activities are described in terms of cooperation objects.

The light shading of the five higher-level process synchronization classes in Figure 10.13 flags their status as black box components; i.e. a model designer needs only to instantiate them, furnish suitable parameters, and ensure that relevant messages are sent. All implementation details can be kept hidden (in package `desmoj.core.advancedModellingFeatures`). The figure also shows that these constructs are derived

10.4 Advanced Concepts

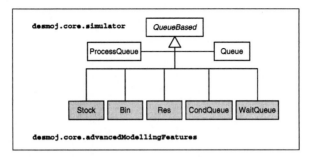

Figure 10.13: DESMO-J's process synchronization classes

from the abstract `QueueBased` class, whose functionality is also inherited by the event-oriented `Queue` and process-oriented `ProcessQueue` constructs.

Resources (Class Res)

DESMO-J's `Res` entities model pools of non-distinguishable resources. They own a `capacity` attribute, whose units can be requested by sending a `provide(int n)` message. Resources own a queue of waiting processes. If insufficient capacity is available to fill a request, the requesting process is passivated and queued automatically. It will only be awakened when its request can be filled. Capacity units can be returned via a `takeBack(int n)` message. Sending `getAvail()` queries resource availability, so that a process can decide whether to queue or to take alternative action. Figure 10.14 shows a `Res`' operation.

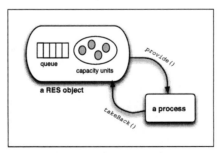

Figure 10.14: A `Res`' operation

Chapter 10 DESMO-J — A Framework for Discrete Event Modelling & Simulation

Res objects automatically record their utilization as well as various waiting times and queue length statistics. Although it remains the modeller's responsibility to ensure that capacity is requested and returned in a safe manner, DESMO-J offers some help with deadlock detection. A number of consistency checks also gives warnings in case of requests less than 0, requests higher than the resource's maximum capacity, returns greater than what has been requested so far, and attempts at resource initialisations with capacity less than 0.

Models of production facilities are good examples for where Res objects are useful. Here groups of identical machinery (servers) with specified capacities process batches of orders with different sequencing constraints and different processing times on each server. Such servers can easily be modelled with Res objects, which are acquired for a processing activity's duration and released once it is finished. The lifecycle of an order within such a "jobshop" model would therefore request a server by sending provide(1), simulate processing via hold(serviceTime), and return the requested capacity unit by sending a takeBack(1) message upon completion. If the provide(1) request cannot be filled, the order would queue automatically; until enough capacity has become available.

Containers (Class Bin and Class Stock)

Bins represent unlimited capacity containers holding non-distinguishable goods, whose number is maintained by a counter. Bin objects can model producer-consumer scenarios, where some processes (producers) deposit items while other processes (consumers) remove them. Consumers must wait if there are not enough items available. Bins can be asked to deliver(int n) items to a consumer and to store(int n) items by a producer. They also automatically queue each consumer whose request can currently not be filled. Figure 10.15 shows a bin's operation.

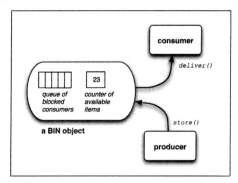

Figure 10.15: A Bin's operation

10.4 Advanced Concepts

Stock objects vary a bin's functionality in that they set a capacity limit. Similarly to bins they model containers of non-distinguishable goods. Consumers retrieve(int n) and producers store(int n) items. Both methods block requests if a capacity limit is reached and stocks must therefore provide *two* internal queues; one for waiting consumers and one for waiting producers. Figure 10.16 pictures this change.

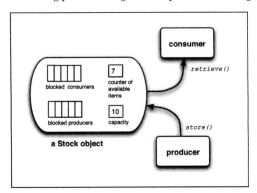

Figure 10.16: A Stock's operation

Both bins and stocks return the number of stored units in response to getAvail(). This means that processes can first check for delays and then take appropriate action. Automatic statistics include initial, current, maximum, and average numbers of units held, as well as the standard statistics for each queue (one for bins and two for stocks).

Although bins and stocks use a priority-led FIFO rule for their queue management, they offer a setPassBy(true) method to allow processes whose requests can be filled to pass processes which remain blocked.

Conditional Waiting (Class CondQueue)

Condition queues are the most flexible of DESMO-J's process synchronization constructs and all other synchronizations can in principle be expressed by them (at a lower level). Condition queues model processes waiting for given events; i.e. a process awakens when some other process changes the system's state in an interesting way.

DESMO-J models condition queues in terms of its CondQueue and Condition classes. Processes request synchronization and pass the relevant system state (i.e. the condition) by sending a waitUntil(Condition cond) message. A CondQueue will then block any such process until its condition evaluates to "true". There is no delay if the condition already holds when a process enters the CondQueue.

Chapter 10 DESMO-J – A Framework for Discrete Event Modelling & Simulation

DESMO-J's implementation of `CondQueue` uses a strategy in which state changing processes must signal each `CondQueue` to which any of the changes they make may be of significance. The message `signal()` is used to accomplish this. A model designer must ensure that this message is sent where appropriate. An alternative to this scheme, which would arguably be less burdensome to the modeller, requires "active" waiting. It has been implemented by simulation languages such as GPSS, but burdens the model executive with a large overhead. All conditions of all blocked processes will need to be checked each time *any* state change occurs. DESMO-J's solution avoids this execution time penalty. Only when signal messages are received by a condition queue, waiting processes will be tested to see if they can now proceed. Unless the condition queue's `checkAll` property is set to "true", it is even assumed that all processes wait for the same condition and only the first waiting process condition needs to be looked at.

DESMO-J's `Condition` class is used to encapsulate state descriptions. It is a white box ("hot spot") class for which implementations of `check()` and `check(Entity e)` must be given.

Master-Slave Process Cooperation (class `WaitQueue`)

DESMO-J's `WaitQueues` offer an elegant means to describe asymmetric rendezvous-type synchronizations between processes, where one acts as an active master while others remain passive (slaves).

Classes `WaitQueue` and `ProcessCoop` implement this functionality, which requires that wait-queues maintain two waiting lines of delayed processes – one each for slaves and masters. Which process is master or slave is determined by their behaviour. Processes acting as masters send `cooperate(ProcessCoop coop)` and intending slaves send `waitOnCoop()` messages. Within the same model relationships can easily be reversed in a different synchronization; i.e former slaves can now become masters and vice versa. Slave processes hold references to their current masters, which they recognize with a `getMaster()` method. Sending a `canCooperate()` message determines if a process already cooperates with a master.

Different from other discrete event modelling frameworks (e.g. Demos) common actions performed by both master and slave are described in a separate instance of a subclass of class `ProcessCoop`, where class `ProcessCoop` is a white box ("hot spot") class whose subclasses need implementations for `cooperation(SimProcess master, SimProcess slave)`.

The UML sequence diagrams in Figures 10.17 and 10.18 trace cooperations between a `WaitQueue`, a slave, and a master process by showing the order in which messages must be sent and received. In the first case no suitable master is available and the propsective slave must be queued. In the second case a waiting process is successfully enslaved by its master.

Figure 10.17's sequence diagram shows three involved entities. The slave process calls `waitOnCoop()`, which causes the `WaitQueue` to insert it in its slave queue, return

10.4 Advanced Concepts

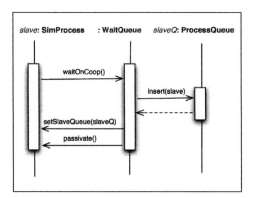

Figure 10.17: WaitQueue – a willing slave must wait for a master

a reference to the slave (so that it knows where it sleeps), and then passivate it. If at least one master were waiting, that process would be activated. Since there is none, the synchronization stops here; i.e. with one more slave waiting in limbo.

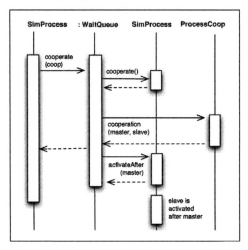

Figure 10.18: WaitQueue – a master engages a waiting slave

289

Chapter 10 DESMO-J – A Framework for Discrete Event Modelling & Simulation

Figure 10.18's UML sequence diagram shows what happens when a master process seeks to enslave and waiting slaves are available. In this case a master process, a `WaitQueue` instance, a slave process, and a `ProcessCoop` object become involved. The master sends a `cooperate()` message to the `WaitQueue` object and also passes a `ProcessCoop` object describing the common activities it wishes a slave to engage in. In response to this message the `WaitQueue` object looks for a slave (in its slave queue) and, if available, removes it from the queue and informs it about the cooperation. This is accomplished by sending `cooperate()`, a method owned by all simulation processes, which provides the slave with a reference to its new master. The passed `ProcessCoop`'s `cooperation()` method specifies the common activity to be performed. After cooperation has ceased, control returns to the master and the slave is scheduled for reactivation.

If there had been no waiting slave when the master process sent the `cooperate()` message or if other aspiring masters were already waiting for cooperations, the inquiring master process would be passivated and queued in a master queue (separate from the slaves).

Interrupting a Process' Execution (Method `interrupt` in Class `SimProcess`)

Class `SimProcess`' protocol includes the method `interrupt(InterruptCode interruptReason)`, which allows interruption of active processes' execution. This simple form of direct process communication can be sent by any active process to another; either passive or active. The interrupt message passes a reason in terms of an `InterruptCode` object and interrupted processes can choose to react according to the provisions made by the model designer in their `lifeCycle()` methods. A SimProcess' interrupt status can be tested with `isInterrupted()` and `getInterruptCode()` and can be reset by sending `clearInterruptCode()`. Any attempts to interrupt blocked or already interrupted processes are simply ignored (with a warning).

Interrupt messages pass `InterruptCode` objects as arguments, stating an interrupt's reason. Although this is often simply an integer, a modeller may choose to use more descriptive names. Figure 10.19 shows the relevant protocol.

Many server and queueing scenarios offer a typical usage example for interrupts; i.e. by higher-priority orders pre-empting lower-priority ones during an ongoing service activity. In this case the higher-priority process sends `interrupt()` to a lower-priority process, which may be somewhere inside a `hold()` interval. If successful, the lower-priority process' activity is interrupted, causing it to be rescheduled for restart and continuation for the remaining delay time, after the interrupting process' completion. The higher-priority process' lifecycle is then continued to initiate any requested delays.

Modelling interrupts imposes some effort on the model designer. All interruptible processes must implement suitable reactions to each valid `InterruptCode` and must explicitly test for interrupts and their reasons after *each* inactive phase. A suitable reaction to a priority server request, for example, must make provision to

10.4 Advanced Concepts

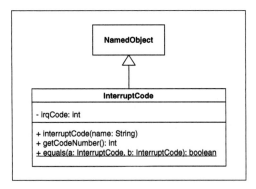

Figure 10.19: An `InterruptCode`'s protocol

- pre-empt and reschedule the lower priority process' execution;
- attend to the higher-priority process' request; and
- continue the remaining lower-priority process' execution after the higher-priority one has finished.

Listing 10.2 (next page) shows an example for how interrupted processes must be coded to facilitate the above strategy. Here we see how a process checks for an interrupt after each `hold()`, which really means that it tests if an interrupt arrived during the hold. If this was the case, the reason is found in the `InterruptCode`, as returned by `getInterruptCode()`. If, for example, the reason is a request from a higher-priority job (line 11), suitable actions are taken. This is not shown explicitly here, but may involve filing the interrupted job back into the queue (to request to be processed again) and starting to process the higher-priority one. If the reason for interruption is something else, e.g. a machine failure (line 16), a repair process can be triggered. Normal processing will continue if there was no interrupt (line 24).

10.4.2 Hierarchical Modelling Constructs

Hierarchical modelling constructs allow models to act as components of other models. Since they can be obtained and adjusted from a generic model library, such sub-models facilitate reusability.

Chapter 10 DESMO-J – A Framework for Discrete Event Modelling & Simulation

```
public void lifeCycle() {

    ...
    hold(new SimTime(serviceDuration));

    // check for interrupt
    if (isInterrupted()) {

        // test and react according to interrupt code
        Int erruptCode reason = getInterruptCode();
        if (reason.equals(highPriorityJob)) {

            // preempt current job and start serving high priority job
            ...

        } else if (reason.equals(machineFailure)) {

            ...

        } // end else branch

    } // end of testing interrupt codes

    else {

        // not interrupted, carry on...
        ...

    } // end else branch
    ...
}// end of lifecycle method
```

Listing 10.2: Interrupting a process' execution

DESMO-J supports this idea through the inheritance relationship between a `Model` and its `ModelComponent` classes. A Composite design pattern (see Gamma et al. 1995) can be established by instantiating all submodels in the owning model's `init()` method (as any other model component) and requiring all submodels to `register(Model submodel)` with their owners. Since each model component, including each submodel, is owned by a single model, this establishes a tree structure in which only a root model instance needs to be attached to experiments. `isMainModel()` can be used to hunt for such roots and the model hierarchy relationship itself is used for grouping an experiment's results in a suitable fashion.

10.4.3 Graphical Interfaces

DESMO-J offers user-friendly graphical interfaces to parametrize models and their experiments. Sets of parameters can be stored and reused, experiments can be started and interrupted, and visual representations of some statistical measures (time series, histograms) can be displayed. Since XML is used for report presentation, displays of results can be easily customized. This functionality is contained in an `ExperimentStarter` class, instances of which can run either as browser-embedded applets or stand-alone applications. The screenshot in Figure 10.20 shows an example.

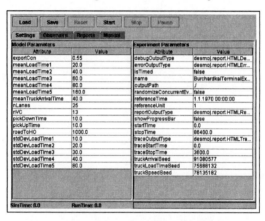

Figure 10.20: A DESMO-J interface

10.5 Example: Modelling Container Traffic in the Baltic Sea

10.5.1 Model Description

In this example we return to the Baltic sea logistics model we used to demonstrate different simulation world views in Sections 5.2.3 and 5.3. This model is well suited to show how models are mapped into DESMO-J's concepts and it also highlights the usefulness of higher-level synchronization patterns for processes.

All detail of model structure and parameter values has been given in Section 5.2.3. The model's purpose is to gather information about container ships' travel and waiting times to and in each of a number of Baltic seaports. This serves to identify bottlenecks among container bridges used for ships' loading and unloading. Statistical data about the number of containers unloaded in each port, the current number of ships in the

Chapter 10 DESMO-J — A Framework for Discrete Event Modelling & Simulation

model, the utilization of container bridges in each port, and the number of containers per ship are collected and reported at the end of a simulation run.

Sections 10.5.2 to 10.5.4 give multiple implementations of this model in different modelling styles. To illustrate only a model's essential features, brief excerpts of relevant code are presented and the complete source code can be downloaded from the book's web site.

10.5.2 An Event-Oriented Implementation

The event-oriented model implementation of this model uses two main entity types:

- container ships, whose properties store routing details and the number of containers delivered to each port on route
- container bridges (cranes), which hold references to the ports in which they are located

Three classes of events are necessary:

- ship creation, where new ship objects (i.e. instances of the Ship class) enter the model, are initialised and sent on their routes
- ship arrivals in a new port, where they are unloaded (if cranes are available) or must queue (if no crane is idle)
- end of unloading events, where ships are sent to sail on, and cranes attend to the next waiting ship or must queue until one arrives

Figure 10.21 shows a skeleton of this model design. Note that the model is a singleton class; i.e. there must be exactly one instance of it. Any number of ships and cranes can be instantiated and any number of ship creation, ship arrival and unloading finished events can occur. Note also how the model class starts a simulation by scheduling the first ship creation event within its doInitialSchedules() method. This event then serves to generate and schedule all other ships; until the model shuts down.

Each model component can be represented by a suitable Entity or Event subclass. Relevant properties are stored as attributes. For example, container ships' ports are encoded as integer numbers, which enables us to store route information in an array. Entity instances are created by their classes' constructors. These methods first need to invoke the constructor of their respective superclass (via a super() call) and set parameter values (e.g. model reference, entity name, trace flags). Model specific methods are added to the subclasses' descriptions. For example, ship entities provide getCurrentHarbour() and getNumberOfContainers(); for retrieving the next port to visit and the number of containers to be unloaded there. Listing 10.3 shows the DESMO-J code for a Ship's definition. Note that we do not show code details for initialising route and container numbers here (below line 17). This can be done with reference to suitable distribution objects, as defined in the Model class.

10.5 Example: Modelling Container Traffic in the Baltic Sea

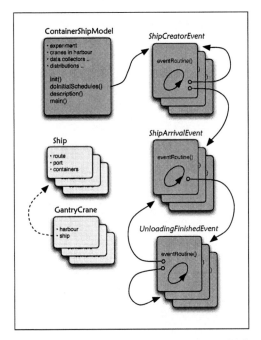

Figure 10.21: Class skeleton for an event-oriented model design

```
1  import desmoj.core.simulator.*;
2
3  public class Ship extends Entity {
4
5      // number of route the ship serves
6      int route;
7      // index of port the ship currently sailed to
8      int routeIndex;
9      // number of containers for each port (loaded in Hamburg)
10     int[] numberOfContainers;
11     // model time instant at which the ship appeared
12     double startTime;
13
14     /** constructor method */
15     public Ship(ContainerShipmentModel owner) {
16
17         super(owner, "ship", true);
```

Chapter 10 DESMO-J – A Framework for Discrete Event Modelling & Simulation

```
18      // initialise attributes: assign route
19      ...
20      // determine number of containers loaded in Hamburg for each port
21      ...
22      // record time of arrival (used in statistical computations)
23      startTime = currentTime().getTimeValue();
24
25   }  // end of constructor
26
27   public int getNumberOfContainers(int harbour) {
28      return numberOfContainers[harbour];
29   }
30
31   public int getCurrentHarbour() {
32      return model.routes[this.route][this.routeIndex];
33   }
34
35 }  // end of class Ship
```

Listing 10.3: Class **Ship**

In this model container bridges (cranes) are passive entities, for whose definition we need only some properties and a constructor (see Listing 10.4).

```
1  import desmoj.core.simulator.*;
2
3  public class Crane extends Entity {
4
5     // port this crane is located in
6     private int harbour;
7     // ship this crane is currently unloading
8     private Ship ship;
9
10    /** constructor method */
11    public Crane(ContainerShipmentModel owner, int harbour) {
12
13       super(owner, "crane at " + owner.nameOfHarbour[harbour], true);
14
15       // initialise attributes
16       this.harbour = harbour;
17       this.ship = null;
18
19    }  // end of constructor method
20
21 }  // end of class Crane
```

Listing 10.4: Class **Crane**

10.5 Example: Modelling Container Traffic in the Baltic Sea

This model variant must describe model dynamics in terms of three types of event:
- `ShipArrivalEvent`, at which a ship reaches a port on its route. Unloading will start if a container bridge (crane) is available. Otherwise the ship will wait. Unloading a ship will be modelled by sampling a suitable distribution and scheduling a "ship has been unloaded" event.
- `UnloadingFinishedEvent`. This event occurs once a ship's unloading has finished and travel to the next port en-route can commence. Initiating a ship's onward travel must again sample a distribution and schedule the relevant "ship arrival" event. Since termination of unloading activities releases a crane, we must also check if there are any ships waiting in port and start their unloading; i.e. schedule another "ship has been unloaded" event. The released crane will wait if no ships are waiting.
- `ShipGeneratorEvent`, through which new ships enter the model (always in Hamburg), are loaded and allocated to their routes. Ships then travel to the first port on that route. Since this activity consumes model time, the creation event ends with an arrival event being scheduled at a suitable time in the future.

In DESMO-J each event can be represented as an `Event` subclass. Since ship creation can be considered to happen "outside" the model, we will use an `ExternalEvent` to derive that event. Code for event definitions requires
- a constructor method, which uses `super()` to pass a class reference, the event's name and a trace flag as arguments to its superclass' constructor;
- an `eventRoutine()` method describing all changes in model state associated with this event; for example, ships entering and leaving waiting lines, scheduling ship arrival events, and endings of unloading activities.

This model needs two queues in each harbour; one for waiting ships and one for idle cranes, These can simply be instantiated from DESMO-J's `Queue` construct (a black box component) and initialised in the top-level class representing the model. This model class also takes responsibility for instantiating and initialising suitable distributions to model duration of ship travel and unloading activities, as well as container numbers destined for each port. Note that we make the assumption that no new containers are loaded at any port other than Hamburg and that, once finished sailing along an assigned route, ships disappear (from the model). This simplification reduces the number of types of events to consider.

In this scenario automatic queueing statistics include mean waiting times and queue lengths for each of the harbours. We will, however, need to define data collectors for measuring:
- Utilization of cranes in each port; for which `Accumulate` objects are used and updated each time an event involving a crane has occurred.
- The overall time ships spent completing deliveries along their assigned routes. If we update it by travel time whenever a ship leaves the model, a global instance

Chapter 10 DESMO-J – A Framework for Discrete Event Modelling & Simulation

of the `Tally` class can gather this information. To make this strategy work, ships must hold their creation time as an attribute (see line 23 in Listing 10.3), so that journey times can be measured by subtracting that value from the model clock time when they leave.

- The number of ship journeys simulated by a given experiment. This number can simply by recorded by updating a `Counter` each time a new ship is created. Note that this counts ship arrivals rather than journey completions. To derive the latter measure we must deduct the number of ships still in the model when a simulation shuts down.

Listing 10.5 shows the DESMO-J code for ship arrival events.

```
import desmoj.core.simulator.*;

public class ShipArrivalEvent extends Event {

    /** constructor method */
    public ShipArrivalEvent(ContainerShipmentModel owner) {

        super(owner, "ship arrival event", true);

    } // end of constructor method

    /** event routine: what happens when a ship arrives in a port */
    public void eventRoutine(Entity e) {

        // get a reference to the model, relevant ship, and relevant port
        ContainerShipmentModel model = (ContainerShipmentModel)getModel();

        Ship ship = (Ship)e;
        int harbour = ship.getCurrentHarbour();

        // on arrival at a port the ship joins a queue of
        // waiting ships
        model.shipQueue[harbour].insert(ship);

        // check if a crane is free
        if (!model.idleCraneQueue[harbour].isEmpty()) {

            // at least one crane is idle:
            // remove first crane from queue of idle cranes
            Crane crane =
                (Crane)model.idleCraneQueue[harbour].first();
            model.idleCraneQueue[harbour].remove(crane);

            // update statistics
            model.craneUtil[harbour].update(1 -
                model.idleCraneQueue[harbour].length() /
                (double)model.numberOfCranesInHarbour[harbour]);
```

10.5 Example: Modelling Container Traffic in the Baltic Sea

```
38          // remove ship from queue
39          model.shipQueue[harbour].remove(ship);
40
41          // give crane a reference to the unloading ship
42          crane.ship = ship;
43
44          // compute duration for unloading, based on number of
45          // containers to unload and quality of service in this port
46          double unloadingDuration;
47          ...
48
49          // create a new event to end the unloading and schedule it
50          UnloadingFinishedEvent event =
51              new UnloadingFinishedEvent(model);
52          event.schedule (crane, new SimTime(unloadingDuration));
53
54      } // end of if (idle cranes)
55
56    } // end of eventRoutine method
57
58 } // end of class ShipArrivalEvent
```

Listing 10.5: Event class `ShipArrivalEvent`

References to ships are passed to the `eventRoutine(Entity e)` method as generic entity references. These are then cast into ships; i.e. `Ship ship = (Ship)e` (line 17).

The top-level `Model` class defines all static model components (queues, distributions, data collectors) and we use `getModel()` to access them. Since `getModel()` returns references of the generic `Model` type, we must also cast these to the subclass our model defines; e.g. line 16:

`ContainerShipmentModel model = (ContainerShipmentModel) getModel();`

Note that arriving ships always enter a waiting ships queue. The event routine will immediately remove them again if cranes are available; otherwise they continue to wait. In model statistics such "zero entries" are shown as a separate category.

During unloading a new event is created to determine the end of this activity. Its duration is sampled from a suitable distribution. Note that the scheduling reference is relative; i.e. to determine the time the "finish unloading" event will occur, the scheduler adds its duration to the current clock time.

We must update the port's utilization statistics each time cranes become busy or idle. This is done by sending an `update()` message to the relevant `Accumulate` object. This update's argument is the ratio of busy cranes computed from 1 minus ratio of idle cranes (i.e 1 minus number of free cranes in that port divided by the total number of cranes in that port.

Chapter 10 DESMO-J – A Framework for Discrete Event Modelling & Simulation

```java
import desmoj.core.simulator.*;

public class UnloadingFinishedEvent extends Event {

  /** constructor method */
  public UnloadingFinishedEvent(ContainerShipmentModel owner) {

    super(owner, "unloading finished event", true);

  } // end of constructor method

  /** event routine: crane finishes unloading a ship */
  public void eventRoutine(Entity e) {

    // get a reference to the model, relevant ship, crane and port
    ContainerShipmentModel model = (ContainerShipmentModel)getModel();
    Crane crane = (Crane)e;
    Ship ship = crane.ship;
    int harbour = ship.getCurrentHarbour();

    // the ship leaves the port and continues on route
    ship.routeIndex++;

    // check route is completed
    if (ship.routeIndex >= ship.route.length) {

      // leave model and update statistics
      model.residenceTime[ship.route].update
         (currentTime().getTimeValue() - ship.startTime);
      model.numberOfShipsInSystem.update(-1);

    } // end of route finished branch

    else {

      // route not completed
      // travel to the next port and schedule the ships arrival
         there
      ShipArrivalEvent newShipArrival = new ShipArrivalEvent(model);
      newShipArrival.schedule(ship,
          new SimTime(model.getTravelTimes(harbour,
          ship.getCurrentHarbour())));

      // crane starts unloading next waiting ship (if any)
      crane.ship = null;

    } // end else (travel to the next port)

    // check if further ships are waiting in port
    if (!model.shipQueue[harbour].isEmpty()) {
```

10.5 Example: Modelling Container Traffic in the Baltic Sea

```
51      // at least one ship is waiting, remove from queue
52      ship = (Ship)model.shipQueue[harbour].first();
53      model.shipQueue[currentHarbour].remove(ship);
54
55      // let crane keep a reference to ships it is unloading
56      crane.ship = ship;
57
58      // compute duration for unloading, based on number of
59      // containers to unload and quality of service in this port
60      double unloadingDuration;
61      ...
62
63      // create a new event to end the unloading and schedule it
64      UnloadingFinishedEvent event
65          = new UnloadingFinishedEvent(model);
66      event.schedule(crane, new SimTime(unloadingDuration));
67
68    } // end of if (further ships waiting)
69
70    else {
71
72      // no ships are waiting; return crane to idle queue
73      model.idleCraneQueue[currentHarbour].insert(crane);
74
75      // update statistics
76      model.craneUtil[currentHarbour].update(1
77          model.idleCraneQueue[currentHarbour].length() /
78          model.numberOfCranesInHarbour[currentHarbour]);
79
80    } // end else (no more ships waiting)
81
82  } // end of eventRoutine method
83
84 } //end of UnloadingFinishedEvent class
```

Listing 10.6: Event class UnloadingFinishedEvent

The UnloadingFinishedEvent refers to two entities; a ship and the crane used for unloading. Since DESMO-J restricts events to a single entity reference, we must decide which entity will be associated directly and which will be linked through a reference. In this model we pass the crane as the dominant and conceptually active entity to the eventRoutine(Entity e) method. The crane will in turn keep a ship reference for use in both "ship arrival" and "unloading finished" events. This reference is created in line 18 of Listing 10.6. Two entities' lifecycles are touched by this event:

❑ Ships leave and travel to the next port on their route. This requires that a new "ship arrival" is scheduled (line 17). If this port was the last on the ship's route some statistics must be recorded instead. In this case a counter is decremented by one (line 30) and the tally of ships' travel times is updated (line 28). Since

Chapter 10 DESMO-J – A Framework for Discrete Event Modelling & Simulation

DESMO-J's tally requires numbers instead of `SimTimes`, we must first extract this information; i.e. by using `currentTime().getTimeValue()`.

❑ If one is waiting, cranes can now start to unload the next ship (line 44). This requires scheduling a new incarnation of the "finish unloading" event (lines 64 and 66). If there are no waiting ships, then the crane can be sent to retire at the end of the ports idle crane queue (line 73) and the cranes' utilization `Accumulate` for the port must again be updated (line 76).

As foreshadowed, ship creation is modelled in a subclass of `ExternalEvent` (see Listing 10.7). Since there are no existing entities to refer to, the `eventRoutine()` method needs no parameters.

```
1   import desmoj.core.simulator.*;
2
3   public class ShipGeneratorEvent extends ExternalEvent {
4
5     /** constructor method */
6     public ShipGeneratorEvent(ContainerShipmentModel owner) {
7
8       super(owner, "ship generator event", true);
9
10    } // end of constructor method
11
12    /** event routine: a new ship enters the model */
13    public void eventRoutine() {
14
15      // get model reference
16      ContainerShipmentModel model = (ContainerShipmentModel)getModel();
17
18      // create a new ship in Hamburg
19      Ship ship = new Ship(model);
20
21      // update statistics: new ship enters the model
22      model.numberOfShipsInSystem.update(1);
23
24      // send ship to first harbour on its route
25      // create and schedule arrival event
26      ShipArrivalEvent arrival = new ShipArrivalEvent(model);
27      arrival.schedule(ship, new SimTime(model.getTravelTimes(0,
28        ship.getCurrentHarbour())));
29
30      // wait until its time for the next ship to enter the model
31      // event schedules itself for the next ships arrival
32      schedule(new SimTime(model.arrivalStream.sample()));
33
34    } // end of eventRoutine method
35
36  } // end of ShipGeneratorEvent class
```

Listing 10.7: External event class `ShipGeneratorEvent`

10.5 Example: Modelling Container Traffic in the Baltic Sea

Note how the ShipGeneratorEvent refers to two future events:
- an event for the ship's arrival at the first port on its route (lines 26 and 27)
- an event for the next ship's creation (line 32)

Both events' time of occurrence is sampled from suitable distributions in the top-level model; e.g. as in new SimTime(model.arrivalStream.sample()).

A top-level ContainerShipmentModel (Listing 10.8) is needed to complete the event-based variant of our example. This class defines some global parameters, all data collection components, all distributions and all queues. Its init() method instantiates and initialises all global components, including the cranes for each port. It also enters these objects into their relevant queues. In our model ships are transient components. Although they are created and initialised by external ShipGeneratorEvents, the model must schedule the first of these within its doInitialSchedules() method. Note that ShipGeneratorEvents are also responsible for planning a ship's arrival in its first port, after which UnloadingFinishedEvents pass them along their route.

```
1  import desmoj.core.simulator.*;
2  import desmoj.core.dist.*;
3  import desmoj.core.statistic.*;
4
5  public class ContainerShipmentModel extends Model {
6
7    /** model parameters, e.g. the ports, routes, number of cranes
8     in each port */
9    static int NUM_HARBOURS = 9;
10   static int NUM_ROUTES = 4;
11   String[] harbourNames;
12   int[][] routes;
13   int[] numberOfCranesInHarbour;
14   ...
15
16   /** static components: queues, distributions, data collectors */
17   // queue of ships waiting to be unloaded (one for each harbour)
18   Queue[] shipQueue;
19   // queue of idle cranes (one in each harbour)
20   Queue[] idleCraneQueue;
21   // distribution of inter-arrival times for new ships
22   RealDistExponential arrivalStream;
23   // distribution of service times in each port
24   RealDistExponential[] serviceTimeStream;
25   // distribution of sailing times between ports
26   RealDistExponential[][] travelTimes;
27   ...
28   // counter of ships in the model
29   Count numberOfShipsInSystem;
30   // accumulation of utilization of cranes in each port
31   Accumulate[] craneUtil;
32   // tally of average model residence times across ships
33   Tally[] residenceTime;
```

Chapter 10 DESMO-J – A Framework for Discrete Event Modelling & Simulation

```
34      /** constructor method */
35      public ContainerShipmentModel() {
36
37         super (null, "Container Shipment in the Baltic Sea" +
38            "(Event-Oriented Model)", true, false);
39
40         // initialise model parameters
41         nameOfHarbour
42            = new String[] {"Hamburg", "Rostock-Warnemuende", "Gdansk",
43              "Riga", "Tallinn", "St.Petersburg", "Helsinki", "Stockholm",
44              "Copenhagen" };
45         numberOfCranesInHarbour
46            = new int[] {0, 6, 11, 3, 6, 2, 4, 4, 7};
47         routes = new int[NUM_ROUTES][];
48
49         // route Hamburg -> Rostock-Warnemuende -> Gdansk -> Riga ->
50         // Tallinn -> Helsinki
51         routes[0] = new int[] {1, 2, 3, 4, 6};
52
53         // route Hamburg -> Copenhagen -> Stockholm -> Helsinki ->
54         // St.Petersburg -> Tallinn
55         routes[1] = new int[] {8, 7, 6, 5, 4};
56
57         // route Hamburg -> Gdansk -> Stockholm -> Copenhagen
58         routes[2] = new int[] {2, 7, 8};
59
60         // route Hamburg -> Copenhagen -> Gdansk -> Rostock-Warnemuende
61         routes[3] = new int[] { 8, 2, 1};
62
63         ...
64
65      } // end of constructor method
66
67      //** initialisation of static model components */
68      public void init() {
69
70         // queues for ships and idle cranes in each Baltic Sea harbour
71         shipQueue = new Queue[NUM_HARBOURS];
72         idleCraneQueue = new Queue[NUM_HARBOURS];
73         for (int i = 1; i < NUM_HARBOURS; i++) {
74            shipQueue[i] = new Queue(this,
75               "ships waiting in " + nameOfHarbour[i], true, true);
76            idleCraneQueue[i] = new Queue(this,
77               "idle cranes in " + nameOfHarbour[i], true, true);
78         } // end of loop
79
80         // distribution of inter-arrival times for new ships
81         arrivalStream = new RealDistExponential(this,
82            "inter-arrival time of ships", 2.5, true, false);
83
84         // distribution of service times (one for each harbour)
85         serviceTimeStream = new RealDistExponential[NUM_HARBOURS];
```

10.5 Example: Modelling Container Traffic in the Baltic Sea

```
86      for (int i = 1; i < NUMBER_OF_HARBOURS; i++) {
87        servicetimestream[i] = new RealDistExponential(this,
88          "service time for one container in " +
89          nameOfHarbour[i], meanServiceTime[i], true, false);
90      } // end of loop
91
92      // distributions for sampling travel times between ports
93      travelTimes = new RealDistExponential[NUM_HARBOURS][NUM_HARBOURS];
94      for (int i = 0; i < NUM_HARBOURS; i++) {
95        for (int j = 0; j < NUMB_HARBOURS; j++) {
96          travelTimes[i][j] = new RealDistExponential(this,
97            "travel times from " + nameOfHarbour[i] + " to " +
98            nameOfHarbour[j], meanTravelTime[i][j], true, false);
99        } // end of inner loop
100     } // end of outer loop
101
102     ...
103
104     // counter for number of ships in the model
105     numberOfShipsInSystem = new Count(this,
106       "number of ships in system", true, false, true);
107
108     // accumulates for the utilization of cranes in each harbour
109     craneUtil = new Accumulate[NUM_HARBOURS];
110     for (int i = 1; i < NUM_HARBOURS; i++) {
111       craneUtil[i] = new Accumulate(this,
112         "crane utilization in " + nameOfHarbour[i], true, false);
113     } // end of loop
114
115     // tallies for residence times across ships (one for each route)
116     residenceTime = new Tally[NUM_ROUTES];
117     for (int i= 0; i < NUM_ROUTES; i++) {
118       residenceTime[i] = new Tally(this,
119         "residence time for route " + i, true, false);
120     } // end of loop
121
122     // create cranes and insert them into idle queues for each harbour
123     for (int i = 1; i < NUM_HARBOURS; i++) {
124       for (int k = 1; k <= numberOfCranesInHarbour[i]; k++) {
125         Crane crane = new Crane(this, i);
126         this.idleCraneQueue[i].insert(crane);
127       } // end of inner loop
128     } // end of outer loop
129
130   } // end of init method
131
132
133   /** activates dynamic components by scheduling first event(s) */
134   public void doInitialSchedules() {
135
```

305

Chapter 10 DESMO-J – A Framework for Discrete Event Modelling & Simulation

```
136         // create and schedule a ship arrival to start the simulation
137         new ShipGeneratorEvent(this).schedule(new SimTime(0.0));
138
139     } // end of doInitialSchedules method
140
141
142     /** return a model description for statistics reports */
143     public String description() {
144         return "This is an event-oriented implementation of ...";
145     }
146
147     /** run the model */
148     public static void main(String[] args) {
149
150         // create model and experiment
151         Experiment experiment = new Experiment("ContainerShipmentEvents");
152         ContainerShipmentModel model = new ContainerShipmentModel();
153
154         // and link them to each other
155         model.connectToExperiment(experiment);
156
157         // set experiment parameters
158         experiment.tracePeriod(new SimTime(0.0), new SimTime(100.0));
159
160         // initiate warm-up period
161         // simulate experiment for 25 (model) days (600 hours)
162         // reset statisticial data collectors
163         experiment.stop(new SimTime(600));
164         experiment.start();
165         model.reset();
166
167         // perform the rest of the simulation experiment
168         experiment.stop(new SimTime(LENGTH_OF_SIMULATION_RUN *
169             HOURS_PER_DAY));
170         experiment.start();
171         experiment.report();
172         experiment.finish();
173
174     } // end of main method
175
176     /** sample from the travel times random variate stream */
177     public double getTravelTimes(int from, int to) {
178         return travelTimes[from][to].sample();
179     }
180
181 } // end of class ContainerShipmentModel
```

Listing 10.8: Class `ContainerShipmentModel`

10.5 Example: Modelling Container Traffic in the Baltic Sea

10.5.3 A Process-Oriented Implementation

Although their model structures are largely similar, a process-oriented implementation of this example would take a somewhat different approach. Ships, cranes, and a ship generator can now all be modelled as active objects:

- A **Ship** class steps through a lifecycle of sailing along from port to port on its route and delivering a specified number of containers in each:
  - After arrival, it queues and tests the port's crane queue for availability.
  - If cranes are available, it leaves the ship queue, grabs the first crane, and activates it.
  - If no crane is free, it passivates itself at the tail of the waiting ships queue.
  - If a crane has been acquired and activated, the ship passivates itself; to wait for unloading to finish.
  - Once unloading is finished, the crane will reactivate the waiting ship, which accesses travelling time information to the next port and then leaves; i.e. it passivates itself via hold() for a crossing's duration.
- **Cranes** know the ports they are working in and unload one ship after the other:
  - If the port's queue of waiting ships is not empty, a crane grabs the first ship, determines unloading time and holds for the duration. The ship remains passive throughout this activity.
  - Once unloading is finished, the crane notifies (i.e. schedules) the relevant ship and cruises the waiting ship queue for work.
  - If no waiting ships can be found, a crane files into the port's crane queue and passivates (to wait for a ship's arrival).
- Just as in the event-oriented scenario we treat ship arrivals as caused by forces outside of the model. Instead of using external events, however, we define a **ShipGenerator** entity, whose lifecycle generates ship after ship; placing, initialising, and activating each of them in Hamburg. This cycle is driven by hold()s in a loop, which terminates once the simulation is stopped.

Figure 10.22 shows the core aspects of this design. Note that the model class remains much as it was in the event-oriented model variant. The **ShipGenerator** is now a process, but behaves fairly similar to the way it did before. Ships and cranes now group both structural and behavioural descriptions together. They become processes, with suitable properties and lifecycles. No separate event descriptions are needed, all state changing actions are described within ships' and cranes' lifecycles. Note also that ships and cranes can activate each other directly, as well as model delays using the hold() command. This leads to a cleaner model structure, with a model class and three active types of entities in addition to a number of global black box components (queues, data collectors, and distributions).

In DESMO-J the three entity types are derived from the **SimProcess** class. Their properties are mapped into suitable attributes and their lifecycles are captured within

Chapter 10 DESMO-J — A Framework for Discrete Event Modelling & Simulation

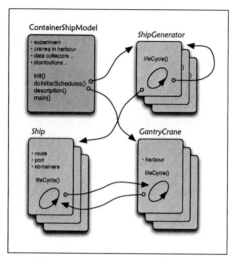

Figure 10.22: Class skeleton for a process-oriented model design

each of the classes' implementation of their lifeCycle() method. Listings 10.9 to 10.12 show these three classes as well as the top-level model description.

As before, Ships (see Listing 10.9) are temporary entities, which are created (by a ShipGenerator), sail along a route and exit the model. Their lifecycle is therefore a sequence of:

1. sail to next harbour
2. queue
3. wait for a crane to begin to unload (with or without delay)
4. wait for unloading to finish

This pattern is easily captured in a do-while loop.

```
import desmoj.core.simulator.*;

public class Ship extends SimProcess {

    // number of route the ship serves
    int route;
    // index of port the ship currently sailed to
    int routeIndex;
```

10.5 Example: Modelling Container Traffic in the Baltic Sea

```
 9      // number of containers for each port (loaded in Hamburg)
10      int[] numberOfContainers;
11
12      /** constructor method */
13      public Ship(ContainerShipmentModel owner) {
14
15          super(owner, "ship", true);
16
17          // initialise attributes: assign route, initialise number of
18          // containers for each destination on route (loaded in Hamburg)
19          ...
20
21      } // end of constructor method
22
23      /** the ship's lifecycle */
24      public void lifeCycle() {
25
26          // get model reference
27          ContainerShipmentModel model = (ContainerShipmentModel)getModel();
28
29          // update statistics: another ship enters the model
30          model.numberOfShipsInSystem.update(1);
31
32          // record start time
33          double startTime = currentTime().getTimeValue();
34
35          // each ship starts at Hamburg
36          int harbourOfDeparture = 0;
37
38          do {
39
40              // determine port to sail to and start sailing
41              int currentHarbour = model.routes[this.route][this.routeIndex];
42              hold(new SimTime(model.getTravelTimes
43                  (harbourOfDeparture, currentHarbour)));
44
45              // queue ship on arrival in port
46              model.shipQueue[currentHarbour].insert(this);
47
48              // check for free crane
49              if (!model.idleCraneQueue[currentHarbour].isEmpty()) {
50
51                  // at least one crane is idle, remove first one
52                  Crane crane = (Crane)model.idleCraneQueue
53                      [currentHarbour].first();
54                  model.idleCraneQueue[currentHarbour].remove(Crane);
55
56                  // update statistics: utilization of cranes in this port
57                  model.craneUtil[currentHarbour].update(1 -
58                      model.idleCraneQueue[currentHarbour].length() /
59                      (double)model.numberOfCranesInHarbour
60                      [currentHarbour]);
```

Chapter 10 DESMO-J – A Framework for Discrete Event Modelling & Simulation

```
61         // activate crane
62         crane.activateAfter(this);
63
64       } // end if crane is free ...
65
66       // wait until unloading is finished
67       passivate();
68
69       // prepare to sail to next port
70       harbourOfDeparture = currentHarbour;
71       this.routeIndex++;
72
73     } while (this.routeIndex < model.routes[this.route].length);
74
75     // all ports have been visited - update statistics and leave
76     model.numberOfShipsInSystem.update(-1);
77     model.residenceTime[route].update(currentTime().getTimeValue() -
78         startTime);
79
80   } // end of lifecycle method
81
82 } // end of class Ship
```

Listing 10.9: Process class Ship

In this model we treat cranes (see Listing 10.10) as permanent model components; i.e. we instantiate, place, and schedule them when a simulation starts (in the model's init() and doInitialSchedules() methods) and do not add or remove any later. However, this is just due to our model's purpose and time horizon. Different questions and modelling perspectives may well wish to add and remove cranes as part of a model's dynamics. Cranes' lifecycles are simple; they loop though a monotonous sequence of unloading activities, resting only while waiting for ships to arrive.

```
1  import desmoj.core.simulator.*;
2
3  public class Crane extends SimProcess {
4
5    // harbour this crane works in
6    private int harbour;
7
8    /** constructor method */
9    public Crane(ContainerShipmentModel owner, int harbour) {
10
11     super(owner, "crane␣at␣" + owner.nameOfHarbour[harbour], true);
12     this.harbour = harbour;
13
14   } // end of constructor method
```

310

10.5 Example: Modelling Container Traffic in the Baltic Sea

```java
/** the crane's lifecycle */
public void lifeCycle() {

    // get a model reference
    ContainerShipmentModel model = (ContainerShipmentModel)getModel();

    // cycle indefinitely through unloading and waiting for ships
    while (true) {

        // check if ships are waiting
        if (model.shipQueue[harbour].isEmpty()) {

            // no ship is waiting  insert crane into queue
            model.idleCraneQueue[harbour].insert(this);

            // update crane utilization in this port
            model.craneUtil[harbour].update
                (1 - model.idleCraneQueue[harbour].length()/
                (double)model.numberOfCranesInHarbour[harbour]);

            // wait for a ship to arrive
            passivate();

        } // end if (no ships are waiting)

        else {

            // at least one ship is waiting — remove from its queue
            Ship ship = (Ship)model.shipQueue[this.harbour].first();
            model.shipQueue[this.harbour].remove(ship);

            // compute duration for unloading, based on number of
            // containers to unload and quality of service in this port
            double unloadingDuration;
            ...

            // unload ship
            hold(new SimTime(unloadingDuration));

            // unloading is finished; activate ship
            ship.activate(new SimTime(0.0));

        } // end of else (ships to unload)

    } // end of loop

} // end of lifecycle

} // end of class Crane
```

Listing 10.10: Process class `Crane`

Chapter 10 DESMO-J – A Framework for Discrete Event Modelling & Simulation

Although it is now a process class, the ship generator (Listing 10.11) works much as the ship creation event did before. It simply loops through a sequence of ship creations. As before, each ship is placed in Hamburg, assigned a route, filled with containers and set to sail. Inter-arrival times between ships are determined by sampling a global distribution, whose value is then used for putting the process to sleep (i.e. by sending hold()).

```
import desmoj.core.simulator.*;

public class ShipGenerator extends SimProcess {

    /** constructor method */
    public ShipGenerator(ContainerShipmentModel owner) {

        super(owner, "ship generator", true);

    } // end of constructor method

    public void lifeCycle() {

        // get model reference
        ContainerShipmentModel model = (ContainerShipmentModel)getModel();

        while (true) {

            // create and activate a new ship
            new Ship(model).activateAfter(this);

            // wait for the next ship to enter
            hold(new SimTime(model.getArrivalStream()));

        } // end of loop

    } // end of lifecycle

} // end of class ShipGenerator
```

Listing 10.11: Process class `ShipGenerator`

As foreshadowed, the main model class (see Listing 10.12) is very similar to its event-oriented incarnation. The only significant differences are that all waiting lines must now be instances of `ProcessQueue` instead of `Queue` and that the `doInitialSchedules()` method now needs to create and activate all cranes in addition to the process for ship generation.

10.5 Example: Modelling Container Traffic in the Baltic Sea

```
import desmoj.core.simulator.*;
import desmoj.core.dist.*;
import desmoj.core.statistic.*;

public class ContainerShipmentModel extends Model {

    // initialise ports, routes, number of cranes
    // in each port etc. (as before)
    ...

    // instantiate static model components: queues, distributions,
    // data collectors etc. (as before)
    ...

    /** queue for ships waiting to be unloaded (one for each harbour) */
    ProcessQueue[] shipQueue;

    /** queue for idle cranes (one for each harbour) */
    ProcessQueue[] idleCraneQueue;
    ...

    /** constructor method */
    public ContainerShipmentModel() {

        super (null, "Container Shipment in the Baltic Sea " +
            "(Process-Oriented Model)", true, false);

        // initialise model parameters
        ...

    } // end of constructor method

    /** initialise static model components */
    public void init() {

        // queues for ships and idle cranes in each port
        shipQueue = new ProcessQueue[NUM_HARBOURS];
        idleCraneQueue = new ProcessQueue[NUM_HARBOURS];
        for (int i = 1; i < NUM_HARBOURS; i++) {
            shipQueue[i] = new ProcessQueue(this, "ships waiting in " +
                nameOfHarbour[i], true, true);
            idleCraneQueue[i] = new ProcessQueue(this,
                "idle cranes in " + nameOfHarbour[i], true, true);
        } // end of loop

        // distributions and data collectors
        ...

    } // end of init method

    /** activates dynamic model components */
    public void doInitialSchedules() {
```

Chapter 10 DESMO-J – A Framework for Discrete Event Modelling & Simulation

```
53      // create and activate ship generator
54      new ShipGenerator(this).activate(new SimTime(0.0));
55
56      // create and activate cranes for each port
57      for (int i = 1; i < NUM_HARBOURS; i++) {
58          for (int j = 0; j < numberOfCranesInHarbour[i]; j++) {
59              new Crane(this, i).activate(new SimTime(0.0));
60          } // end of inner loop
61      } // end of outer loop
62
63      } // end of doInitialSchedules method
64
65      /** return a model description for statistics reports */
66      public String description() {
67          return "This is an process-oriented implementation of...";
68      }
69
70      ...
71
72  } // end of class ContainerShipmentModel
```

Listing 10.12: The top-level `ContainerShipmentModel` class

10.5.4 Using Higher-Level Modelling Constructs

In this section we will demonstrate how DESMO-J's high-level modelling constructs can simplify model design.

Parts of Listings that are left out stay the same as in the process-oriented version of this model (see Section 10.5.3).

Resources (Class `Res`)

If we take a transaction-oriented perspective, we can describe the example in terms of transactions (ships) which are routed through a network of servers (harbours). In each harbour ships acquire resources (cranes), use them for specified model time intervals (unloading), and return them once finished.

In this scenario we can therefore model all cranes as a pool of resources that are not distinguishable (i.e. `Res` instances) with specified capacity (number of cranes) for each harbour. Ships remain active processes, which in each port will now grab crane resources, model unloading with `hold()`, and release cranes again. All relevant queueing mechanics are handled by DESMO-J's `Res` objects. This means that we do not need any global queues for modelling waiting ships and cranes. Since `Res` objects also collect and report standard utilization statistics, we do not need to collect these "by hand", and the `Accumulate` we used for this purpose becomes obsolete. The process-oriented version of the `ShipGenerator` entity can be used as it is.

10.5 Example: Modelling Container Traffic in the Baltic Sea

Overall, this perspective leads to the most compact model representation (see the following Listing 10.13).

```java
import desmoj.core.simulator.*;

public class Ship extends SimProcess {

    // attributes and constructor remain as in the
    // process-oriented version

    /** the ship's lifecycle */
    public void lifeCycle() {

        ...

        do {

            // determine port to sail to and start sailing
            int currentHarbour = model.routes[this.route][this.routeIndex];
            hold(new SimTime(model.getTravelTimes
                (harbourOfDeparture, currentHarbour)));

            // request crane on arrival
            model.cranes[currentHarbour].provide(1);

            // compute duration for unloading, based on number of
            // containers to unload and quality of service in this port
            double unloadingDuration;
            ...

            // unload ship
            hold(new SimTime(unloadingDuration));

            // release crane again
            model.cranes[currentHarbour].takeBack(1);

            // prepare to sail to next port
            harbourOfDeparture = currentHarbour;
            this.routeIndex++;

        } while (this.routeIndex < model.routes[this.route].length);

        // all ports on route have been visited -
        // update statistics and leave
        model.numberOfShipsInSystem.update(-1);
        model.residenceTime[route].update(currentTime().getTimeValue()
            startTime);

    } // end of lifecycle method

} // end of class Ship
```

Chapter 10 DESMO-J – A Framework for Discrete Event Modelling & Simulation

```
50  import desmoj.core.simulator.*;
51  import desmoj.core.dist.*;
52  import desmoj.core.statistic.*;
53
54  public class ContainerShipmentModel extends Model {
55
56      // initialise ports, routes, number of cranes
57      // in each port etc. (as before)
58      ...
59
60      // instantiate static model components: queues, distributions,
61      // data collectors etc.
62      // (but not the Accumulate we used for utilization statistics)
63      ...
64
65      /** one pool of resources cranes) for each harbour */
66      Res[] cranes;
67
68      /** constructor method */
69      public ContainerShipmentModel() {
70
71          super (null, "Container Shipment in the Baltic Sea " +
72              "(Transaction-Oriented)", true, false);
73
74          // initialise model parameters
75          ...
76
77      } // end of constructor method
78
79      /** initialise static model components */
80      public void init() {
81
82          // resources cranes) for each harbour
83          cranes = new Res[NUM_HARBOURS];
84          for (int i = 1; i < NUM_HARBOURS; i++) {
85              cranes[i] = new Res(this, "cranes in " +
86                  nameOfHarbour[i], numberOfCranesInHarbour[i],
87                  true, true);
88          } // end of loop
89
90          // distributions and data collectors
91          ...
92
93      } // end of init method
94
95      /** activates dynamic model components */
96      public void doInitialSchedules() {
97
98          // create and activate ship generator
99          new ShipGenerator(this).activate(new SimTime(0.0));
100
101     } // end of doInitialSchedules method
```

10.5 Example: Modelling Container Traffic in the Baltic Sea

```
102     /** return a model description for statistics reports */
103     public String description() {
104         return "This is a transaction-oriented implementation of...";
105     }
106
107     ...
108
109 } // end of class ContainerShipModel
```
Listing 10.13: Classes using resources

Conditional Waiting (Class `CondQueue`)

From an activity-oriented viewpoint models can be described as sets of activities, each of which is guarded by a condition under which it may occur. DESMO-J's `CondQueue` construct supports model designs in this flavour.

In the example of Listing 10.14 below ships stay as they are; i.e. the are still modelled as processes. What changes is that we attach a `CondQueue` to each port, whose condition will test whether a crane is available or blocks ships to wait. DESMO-J requires that we wrap such conditions in a `Condition` subclass with suitable instantiation. Cranes can now be modelled by a simple "available cranes" counter for each of the ports, since they cease to be responsible for access control and queue management.

Remember that DESMO-J's implementation of passive waiting requires that condition queues are signalled each time a relevant change in a state has occurred, so that waiting processes' conditions can be re-tested. Since all ships are waiting on the same condition (an idle crane), we can leave the condition queue's `checkAll` property at its default setting (test only the first waiting process).

Since utilization statistics for `CondQueues` are not automatically recorded, we have to commission an `Accumulate` data collector for this task; as we did in the raw event- and process-oriented model versions.

```
1  import desmoj.core.simulator.*;
2
3  public class Ship extends SimProcess {
4
5      // attributes and constructor remain as in the
6      // process-oriented version
7
8      /** the ship's lifecycle */
9      public void lifeCycle() {
10
11         ...
12         do {
13
14             // determine port to sail to and start sailing
15             ...
```

317

Chapter 10 DESMO-J – A Framework for Discrete Event Modelling & Simulation

```
16        // upon arrival, enter condition queue to wait for a free crane
17        model.shipQueue.waitUntil(model.condition);
18
19        // grab crane
20        model.availableCranes[currentHarbour]--;
21
22        // update statistics
23        model.craneUtil[harbour].update
24        (1 - model.idleCraneQueue[harbour].length()/
25        (double)model.numberOfCranesInHarbour[harbour]);
26
27        // compute duration for unloading, based on number of
28        // containers to unload and quality of service in this port
29        double unloadingDuration;
30        ...
31
32        // unload ship
33        hold(new SimTime(unloadingDuration));
34
35        // release crane
36        model.availableCranes[currentHarbour]++;
37
38        // update statistics
39        model.craneUtil[harbour].update
40        (1 - model.idleCraneQueue[harbour].length()/
41        (double)model.numberOfCranesInHarbour[harbour]);
42
43        // notify other waiting ships that a crane is available
44        model.shipQueue[currentHarbour].signal();
45
46        // prepare to sail to next port
47        harbourOfDeparture = currentHarbour;
48        this.routeIndex++;
49
50        } while (this.routeIndex < model.routes[this.route].length);
51
52        // all ports on route have been visited —
53        // update statistics and leave
54        ...
55
56     } // end of lifecycle
57
58 } // end of class Ship
59
60
61 import desmoj.core.simulator.*;
62
63 public class CraneIsFreeCondition extends Condition {
64
65     /** constructor method */
66     public CraneIsFreeCondition (ContainerShipmentModel owner) {
67
```

10.5 Example: Modelling Container Traffic in the Baltic Sea

```
68          super(owner, "crane is free condition", false);
69
70      } // end of constructor method
71
72      /** checks if there is at least one available crane */
73      public boolean check(Entity e) {
74
75          ContainerShipmentModel model = (ContainerShipmentModel)getModel();
76          Ship ship = (Ship) e;
77          return (model.availableCranes[ship.getCurrentHarbour()] > 0);
78
79      }
80
81      // this method will never be called in this model; return false
82      public boolean check() {
83          return false;
84      }
85
86  } // end of class CraneFreeCondition
87
```

```
88
89  import desmoj.core.simulator.*;
90  import desmoj.core.dist.*;
91  import desmoj.core.statistic.*;
92
93  public class ContainerShipmentModel extends Model {
94
95      // initialise ports, routes, number of cranes
96      // in each port etc. (as before)
97      ...
98
99      // instantiate static model components: queues, distributions,
100     // data collectors etc.
101     ...
102
103     /** condition queue for ships waiting for a crane
104     (one for each port) */
105     CondQueue[] shipQueue;
106
107     /** condition the ships wait on (same for each ship and each port) */
108     CraneIsFreeCondition condition;
109
110     /** cranes are simply modelled as numbers */
111     int[] availableCranes;
112
113     /** constructor method */
114     public ContainerShipmentModel() {
115
116         super (null, "Container Shipment in the Baltic Sea " +
117             "(Activity-Oriented)", true, false);
118
119         // initialise model parameters
```

319

Chapter 10 DESMO-J – A Framework for Discrete Event Modelling & Simulation

```
120        ...
121
122        } // end of constructor method
123
124        /** initialise static model components */
125        public void init() {
126
127            // one condition queues for each harbour
128            shipQueue = new CondQueue[NUM_HARBOURS];
129            for (int i = 1; i < NUM_HARBOURS; i++) {
130                shipQueue[i] = new CondQueue(this, "ships waiting in " +
131                    nameOfHarbour[i], true, true);
132            } // end of loop
133
134            // the condition
135            condition = new CraneIsFreeCondition(this);
136
137            // distributions and data collectors
138            ...
139
140        } // end of init method
141
142        /** activates dynamic model components */
143        public void doInitialSchedules() {
144
145            // create and activate ship generator
146            new ShipGenerator(this).activate(new SimTime(0.0));
147
148        } // end of doInitialSchedules method
149
150        /** return a model description for statistics reports */
151        public String description() {
152            return "This is an activity-oriented implementation of...";
153        }
154
155        ...
156
157  } // end of class ContainerShipModel
```

Listing 10.14: Classes for `CondQueue` model

Master-Slave Process Cooperation (Class `WaitQueue`)

If we use DESMO-J's `WaitQueue` component for synchronization during unloading, we can view cranes as masters and ships as slaves. Both ships and cranes are still processes and unloading is modelled as a cooperation between them. To group common activities, we can derive an `Unloading` class (from `ProcessCoop`). Each port is furnished with an off-the-shelf `WaitQueue` object, with internal queues for both slaves (waiting ships)

10.5 Example: Modelling Container Traffic in the Baltic Sea

and masters (waiting cranes). This architecture fits our example well and no additional waiting line objects are needed.

For data collection purposes we again need an `Accumulate` to record and report utilization statistics across all the cranes in each port.

Listing 10.15 shows the main parts of this variant.

```
import desmoj.core.simulator.*;

public class Ship extends SimProcess {

    // attributes and constructor remain as in the
    // process-oriented version

    /** the ship's lifecycle */
    public void lifeCycle() {

        ...
        do {

            // determine port to sail to and start sailing
            ...

            // upon arrival, enter the wait queue as a slave;
            // will be reactivated after cooperation (unloading)
            // is finished
            model.waitQueue[currentHarbour].waitOnCoop();

            // prepare to sail to next port
            harbourOfDeparture = currentHarbour;
            this.routeIndex++;

        } while (this.routeIndex < model.routes[this.route].length);

        // all ports on route have been visited -
        // update statistics and leave
        ...

    } // end of lifecycle

} // end of class Ship

import desmoj.core.simulator.*;

public class Crane extends SimProcess {

    // attributes and constructor remain as in the
    // process-oriented version
```

321

Chapter 10 DESMO-J – A Framework for Discrete Event Modelling & Simulation

```
/** the crane's lifecycle */
public void lifeCycle() {

    // get a model reference
    ContainerShipmentModel model = (ContainerShipmentModel)getModel();

    // cycle indefinitely through unloading and waiting for ships to
    // unload
    while (true) {

        // enter the wait queue as a master.
        // reactivate after cooperation (unloading) is finished
        model.waitQueue[harbour].cooperate(model.unloading);

    } // end of loop

} // end of lifecycle
```

```
import desmoj.core.simulator.*;

public class Unloading extends ProcessCoop {

    /** constructor method */
    public Unloading(ContainerShipmentModel owner) {

        super(owner, "unloading", false);

    } // end of constructor method

    /** implements unloading of ship */
    public void cooperation(SimProcess master, SimProcess slave) {

        // get references to model, crane, ship, and current port
        ContainerShipmentModel model = (ContainerShipmentModel)getModel();
        Crane crane = (Crane)master;
        Ship feederShip = (Ship)slave;
        int harbour = crane.harbour;

        // update utilization statistics
        model.craneUtil[harbour].update
        (1 - model.waitQueue[harbour].mLength()/
        (double)model.numberOfCranesInHarbour[harbour]);

        // compute duration for unloading, based on number of
        // containers to unload and quality of service in this port
        double unloadingDuration;
        ...

        // unload ship
        hold(new SimTime(unloadingDuration));
```

10.5 Example: Modelling Container Traffic in the Baltic Sea

```
            // update utilization statistics
            model.craneUtil[harbour].update
               (1 - (model.waitQueue[harbour].mLength() + 1) /
               (double)model.numberOfCranesInHarbour[harbour]);

            // Note: The crane will insert itself back into the
            // port's wait queue after this method completes
            // "manually" add 1 to the current master queue length
            // (waitQueue[harbour].mLength()) for computing the utilization

        } // end of unloading method

} // end of class Unloading


import desmoj.core.simulator.*;
import desmoj.core.dist.*;
import desmoj.core.statistic.*;

public class ContainerShipmentModel extends Model {

    // initialise ports, routes, number of cranes
    // in each port etc. (as before)
    ...

    // instantiate static model components: queues, distributions,
    // data collectors etc.
    ...

    /** a wait queue for ships and cranes waiting for cooperation
    (for each port) */
    WaitQueue[] waitQueue;

    /** cooperation (unloading) between a crane and a ship */
    Unloading unloading;

    /** constructor method */
    public ContainerShipmentModel() {

        super (null, "Container Shipment in the Baltic Sea " +
           "(Direct Process Cooperation Model)", true, false);

        // initialise model parameters
        ...

    } // end of constructor method

    /** initialise static model components */
    public void init() {

        // wait queues for each harbour
        waitQueue = new WaitQueue[NUM_HARBOURS];
```

323

Chapter 10 DESMO-J — A Framework for Discrete Event Modelling & Simulation

```
147         for (int i = 1; i < NUM_HARBOURS; i++) {
148             waitQueue[i] = new WaitQueue(this, "wait queue in " +
149                 nameOfHarbour[i], true, true);
150         } // end of loop
151
152         // the cooperation
153         unloading = new Unloading(this);
154
155         // distributions and data collectors
156         ...
157
158     } // end of init method
159
160     /** activates dynamic model components */
161     public void doInitialSchedules() {
162
163         // create and activate ship generator
164         new ShipGenerator(this).activate(new SimTime(0.0));
165
166         // create and activate cranes in each harbour
167         for (int i = 1; i < NUM_HARBOURS; i++) {
168             for (int j = 0; j < numberOfCranesInHarbour[i]; j++) {
169                 new Crane(this, i).activate(new SimTime(0.0));
170             } // end of inner loop
171         } // end of outer loop
172
173     } // end of doInitialSchedules method
174
175     /** return a model description for statistics reports */
176     public String description() {
177         return "This implementation uses direct process cooperation.";
178     }
179
180     ...
181
182 } // end of class ContainerShipmentModel
```

Listing 10.15: Classes for WaitQueue model

Extending the Model with Interrupts and Priorities

Attaching priorities to a process, so that it can interrupt less important processes, is useful for modelling many server-based systems; ranging as widely as "jobshop" models or simulating data communication protocols and computer operating systems.

Although DESMO-J does support **Interrupts** as one of its black box components, it still requires substantial programming effort for implementation. To demonstrate the basic ideas, we will extend our example accordingly and introduce high-priority ships, which should be processed in preference to others. In fact, when such a ship arrives in

10.5 Example: Modelling Container Traffic in the Baltic Sea

a port in which no free cranes are available and ships with lower priority are unloading, one of the lower priority ships' unloading activity should be interrupted and its crane assigned to the higher-priority ship. After the higher-priority ship has been unloaded, processing of the pre-empted lower priority ship should then continue.

To implement this scenario, we must ensure that higher-priority ships are in front of lower priority ones in all queues and that interrupted ships are re-queued, so that their unloading can continue at a later time.

DESMO-J allocates a default priority of zero with all processes. This value can be changed by the modeller. Queues are already ordered according to a priority based FIFO rule; i.e. all higher-priority items queue in front of all lower priority ones. To unload higher-priority ships more quickly, we need to add interrupt handling code to the `Crane`'s lifecycle. Since unloading is modelled by `hold()` and it would be difficult and computationally very expensive to break holding time into small chunks to test for priority ship arrivals during unloading, we fudge reality somewhat and test for priority tasks *at the end* of each hold. If an interrupt has occurred (tested for by `isInterrupted()`) the remaining processing interval for the interrupted process is determined (finish time minus interrupt time), its priority is temporarily raised (so that it is at the head of the queue when the priority process is finished), and the pre-empted crane is allocated to the higher-priority process.

For simplicity's sake we assume that higher-priority ships otherwise behave just like lower priority ones. No separate classes with different behaviour are needed. However, if, after arrival in port, no free cranes are available, a slight variation in ships' lifecycles now causes them to look for a crane which is currently unloading a lower priority ship. To facilitate this strategy, we must add a queue of busy cranes (`busyCraneQueue`) to the ship and idle cranes queues at each port. We must also provide a condition to use as a filter; i.e. an instance of a new class `LowPriorityShipCondition`. Execution of

`model.busyCrane[harbour].first(model.lowPriorityCondition);`

returns the first crane which is busy unloading a lower priority ship; or null, if none can be found.

Look carefully at Listing 10.16 below and try to understand how these classes interact.

```
import desmoj.core.simulator.*;

public class Ship extends SimProcess {

    ...

    // constants to specify priorities
    static final int HIGH = 2;
    static final int RAISED = 1;

    protected SimTime startUnloading;
```

Chapter 10 DESMO-J – A Framework for Discrete Event Modelling & Simulation

```
12      /** remaining time for unloading in current harbour */
13      protected SimTime remainingTime;
14
15      /** constructor method */
16      public Ship(ContainerShipmentModel owner) {
17
18          super(owner, "ship", true);
19
20          // set priority
21          if (owner.shipPriorityStream.sample()) {
22              setPriority(HIGH);
23          }
24
25          // initialise attributes: assign route, initialise number of
26          // containers for each desitnation en route (loaded in Hamburg)
27          ...
28
29      } // end of constructor method
30
31      /** the ship's lifecycle */
32      public void lifeCycle() {
33
34          ...
35          do {
36
37              // determine port to sail to and start sailing
38              ...
39
40              // queue ship on arrival in port
41              model.shipQueue[currentHarbour].insert(this);
42
43              // check for free crane
44              if (!model.idleCraneQueue[currentHarbour].isEmpty()) {
45
46                  // grab first one and activate it
47                  ...
48
49              } else if (getPriority() == HIGH) {
50
51                  // high priority ship searches for a crane
52                  // (interrupting a low priority one)
53                  Crane crane =
54                      model.busyCranes[currentHarbour].first
55                      (model.lowPriorityShipCondition);
56
57                  if (crane != null) {
58
59                      // found one - interrupt it
60                      crane.interrupt(model.interruptCode);
61
62                  }
63              }
```

10.5 Example: Modelling Container Traffic in the Baltic Sea

```
         // wait until unloading is finished
         passivate();

         // if this ship has been interrupted,
         // its priority must be reset
         if (getPriority() == RAISED) {
           setPriority(0);
         }

         // prepare to sail to next port
         harbourOfDeparture = currentHarbour;
         this.routeIndex++;

       } while (this.routeIndex < model.routes[this.route].length);

       // all ports on route have been visited -
       // update statistics and leave
       ...

     } // end of lifecycle method

} // end of class Ship


import desmoj.core.simulator.*;

public class Crane extends SimProcess {

  // reference to currently served ship
  protected ShipProcess currentShip;
  ...

  /** the crane's lifecycle */
  public void lifeCycle() {

    // get a model reference
    ContainerShipmentModel model = (ContainerShipmentModel)getModel();

    // cycle indefinitely through unloading and waiting for ships
    while (true) {

      // check if ships are waiting
      if (model.shipQueue[harbour].isEmpty()) {

        // no ship is waiting  insert crane into queue
        ...

      } else {

        // at least one ship is waiting - remove from its queue
        currentShip = (Ship)model.shipQueue[this.harbour].first();
        model.shipQueue[this.harbour].remove(ship);
```

Chapter 10 DESMO-J – A Framework for Discrete Event Modelling & Simulation

```
            // insert self into queue of busy cranes
            model.busyCranes[harbour].insert(this);

            // unload ship
            if (currentShip.remainingTime == null) {

                // ship has just arrived - compute duration for unloading
                double unloadingDuration;
                ...
                currentShip.remainingTime =
                    new SimTime(unloadingDuration);

            } // end if (ship just arrived)

            // wait until unloading is finished
            currentShip.startUnloading = currentTime();
            hold(currentShip.remainingTime);

            // check if unloading was interrupted
            if (isInterrupted()) {

                // determine remaining time for unloading
                currentShip.remainingTime =
                    SimTime.diff(currentShip.remainingTime,
                    SimTime.diff(model.currentTime(),
                    currentShip.startTime));

                // raise ship's priority and re-insert into queue
                currentShip.setPriority(Ship.RAISED);
                model.shipQueue[harbour].insert(currentShip);

                // clear interrupt code
                clearInterruptCode();

            } else {

                // unloading completed - notify ship
                currentShip.remainingTime = null;
                currentShip.activate(new SimTime(0.0));

            } // end of else (unloading completed)

            currentShip = null;

        } // end of else (one ship waiting)

    } // end of while loop

  } // end of lifecycle

} // end of class Crane
```

328

10.5 Example: Modelling Container Traffic in the Baltic Sea

```
168  import desmoj.core.simulator.*;
169  public class LowPriorityShipCondition extends Condition {
170
171      /** constructor method */
172      public LowPriorityShipCondition(ContainerShipmentModel model) {
173
174          super(model, "low priority ship condition", false);
175
176      } // end of constructor method
177
178
179      /** checks if the crane is unloading a low priority ship */
180      public boolean check(Entity e) {
181
182          CraneProcess crane = (CraneProcess)e;
183          return crane.currentShip.getPriority() < Ship.HIGH;
184
185      }
186
187      // this method will never be called in this model; return false
188      public boolean check() {
189          return false;
190      }
191
192  } // end of class LowPriorityShipCondition
193
194
195  import desmoj.core.simulator.*;
196  import desmoj.core.dist.*;
197  import desmoj.core.statistic.*;
198
199  public class ContainerShipmentModel extends Model {
200
201      // initialise ports, routes, number of cranes
202      // in each port etc. (as before)
203      ...
204
205      // instantiate static model components: queues, distributions,
206      // data collectors etc.
207      ...
208
209      /** a queue for busy cranes in each port */
210      ProcessQueue[] busyCraneQueue;
211
212      /** a distribution to determine if a ship has a high priority */
213      BoolDist shipPriorityStream;
214
215      /** condition to use to filter the busy crane queue */
216      LowPriorityShipCondition lowPriorityShipCondition;
217
218      /** the interrupt code */
219      InterruptCode interruptCode;
```

329

Chapter 10 DESMO-J – A Framework for Discrete Event Modelling & Simulation

```java
    /** constructor method */
    public ContainerShipmentModel() {

        super (null, "Container Shipment in the Baltic Sea " +
            "(Model with Priorities and Interrupts)", true, false);

        // initialise model parameters
        ...

    } // end of constructor method


    /** initialise static model components */
    public void init() {

        // queues for each harbour
        busyCraneQueue = new ProcessQueue[NUM_HARBOURS];
        for (int i = 1; i < NUM_HARBOURS; i++) {
            busyCraneQueue[i] = new ProcessQueue(this,
                "busy cranes in " + nameOfHarbour[i], true, true);
        } // end of loop

        // distributions and data collectors
        ...

        shipPriorityStream = new BoolDistBernoulli(this,
            "priority ships", 0.2, true, false);   // 20% important ships

        // the filter condition
        lowPriorityShipCondition = new LowPriorityShipCondition(this);

        // the interrupt code
        interruptCode = new InterruptCode("priority ship arrived");

    } // end of init method

    ...

    /** return a model description for statistics reports */
    public String description() {
        return "This implementation uses priorities and interrupts.";
    }

    ...

} // end of class ContainerShipmentModel
```

Listing 10.16: Classes for **Interrupt** model

10.5 Example: Modelling Container Traffic in the Baltic Sea

Extending the Model with Capacity Limits on Buffers (class `Stock`)

Our last model extension shows how `Stock` objects are used to represent buffers. Remember that `Stocks`, in contrast to `Bins`, have both lower (i.e. nothing can be taken if they are empty) *and* upper (i.e. nothing can be added if they are full) limits.

To demonstrate stocks, we assume that containers will be loaded on newly created ships in Hamburg; before they set out on their journeys. For this we equip Hamburg harbour with a crane and limited buffer capacity; i.e. only a limited number of containers can reside in a staging area close to the crane. A new entity, `VanCarrier`, is used to transport containers from a yard to the crane's staging areas. Van carriers therefore `store()` what the crane will `retrieve()`. Blockages may lead to queueing for either the crane (no container to retrieve) or a van carrier (no space to store more containers).

Listing 10.17 below is again based on the process-oriented model, but has been extended by class definitions for van carriers and a crane in Hamburg.

To ensure proper instantiation, initialisation, and scheduling, parts of the `Model` class also have changed.

We forebear from listing the `ship` class since ships remain passive partners for both unloading and loading; i.e. they only need to take into account that they must now first be loaded in Hamburg before they can sail.

```
import desmoj.core.simulator.*;

public class VanCarrier extends SimProcess {

   /** id of the crane this van carrier is assigned to */
   private int id;

   /** constructor method */
   public VanCarrier(ContainerShipmentModel owner, int id) {

      super(owner, "van carrier", true);
      this.id = id;

   } // end of constructor method

   /** the van carrier's lifecycle */
   public void lifeCycle() {

      // store one container after another into the
      // crane's stock
      while (true) {

         // fetch a container from the yard
         hold(new SimTime(model.transportTimes.sample()));

```

Chapter 10 DESMO-J – A Framework for Discrete Event Modelling & Simulation

```
26              // place container into stock
27              model.buffers[id].store(1);
28
29          } // end of while loop
30
31      } // end of lifecycle
32
33  } // end of class VanCarrier
34
35
36  import desmoj.core.simulator.*;
37
38  public class CraneProcessInHamburg extends SimProcess {
39
40      /** the crane's id */
41      int id;
42
43      /** constructor method */
44      public CraneProcessInHamburg
45          (ContainerShipmentModel owner, int id) {
46
47          super(owner, "crane in Hamburg ", true);
48          this.id = id;
49
50      } // end of constructor method
51
52      /** the crane's lifecycle */
53      public void lifeCycle() {
54
55          // get a model reference
56          ContainerShipmentModel model = (ContainerShipmentModel)getModel();
57
58          // cycle indefinitely through unloading and waiting for ships'
59          // activities
60          while (true) {
61
62              // check if ships are waiting
63              if (model.shipQueue[0].isEmpty()) {
64
65                  // no ship is waiting  insert crane into queue
66                  ...
67
68              } // end if (no ships are waiting)
69
70              else {
71
72                  // at least one ship is waiting – remove from its queue
73
74                  Ship ship = (Ship)model.shipQueue[0].first();
75                  model.shipQueue[0].remove(ship);
76
```

10.5 Example: Modelling Container Traffic in the Baltic Sea

```
             // load containers
             for (int i = 0; i < ship.size; i++) {
                 model.buffers[this.id].retrieve(1);
                 hold(new SimTime(model.getServiceStream(0)));
             }

             // loading is completed; activate ship
             ship.activate(new SimTime(0.0));

        } // end of else (ships to load)

    } // end of loop

  } // end of lifecycle

} // end of class CraneProcessingInHamburg
```
```
import desmoj.core.simulator.*;
import desmoj.core.dist.*;
import desmoj.core.statistic.*;

public class ContainerShipmentModel extends Model {

    // initialise ports, routes, number of cranes
    // in each port etc. (as before)
    ...

    // instantiate static model components: queues, distributions,
    // data collectors etc.
    ...

    /** distribution for the time it takes a van carrier to fetch
     a container from the yard*/
    RealDistExponential transportTimes;

    /** constructor method */
    public ContainerShipmentModel() {

        super (null, "Container Shipment in the Baltic Sea " +
           "(Process-Oriented Model with Stock)", true, false);

        // initialise model parameters
        ...

    } // end of constructor method

    /** initialise static model components */
    public void init() {

        // queues for ships and idle cranes in each harbour and Hamburg
        ...
```

Chapter 10 DESMO-J – A Framework for Discrete Event Modelling & Simulation

```
129      // distributions and data collectors
130      transportTimes = new RealDistExponential(this,
131         "transport time for a container", 0.08, true, false);
132
133    } // end of init method
134
135    /** activates dynamic model components */
136    public void doInitialSchedules() {
137
138      // create and activate ship generator
139      new ShipGenerator(this).activate(new SimTime(0.0));
140
141      // create and activate cranes in each harbour
142      ...
143
144      // create and activate the van carriers
145      for (int i = 0; i < numberOfCranesInHarbour[0]; i++) {
146        for (int j = 0; j < numberOfVCs[i]; j++) {
147          new VanCarrier(this, i).activate(new SimTime(0.0));
148        }
149      }
150
151    } // end of doInitialSchedules method
152
153    /** return a model description for statistics reports */
154    public String description() {
155      return "This implementation uses a stock.";
156    }
157
158    ...
159
160  } // end of class ContainerShipmentModel
```

Listing 10.17: Classes for model with **Stock**

10.6 Development and Evaluation

DESMO (previous version of DESMO-J) was developed at the Faculty of Informatics of the University of Hamburg (Germany). Its design has been inspired by Graham Birtwistle's Simula-based *Demos* framework, which had been constructed at the Universities of Leeds (UK) and Calgary (Canada) in the late 1970s and early 1980s. DESMO's first implementation by Boelckow et al. used Modula-2 (see Page 1991, Ch. 7). This was followed by partial implementations in Smalltalk, Oberon, and C++.

Current versions of the simulation framework are now available in Java and Delphi. Lechler and Claassen implemented a first Java-based version, DESMO-J, in 1999 (Page et al. 2000) and this was refactored and re-implemented as DESMO-J 2.0 in 2004.

In addition to its core framework classes, DESMO-J also offers some domain-specific extensions; for example, to model production systems and harbour logistics.

The DESMO-J framework is a discrete event simulation package and library of highly flexible and reusable classes. It aims to support easy model implementation and offers support for simulation experiments. Its object-oriented design makes it easy to extend towards specific applications and minimizes potential errors through encapsulation and a clean separation of specification and implementation.

DESMO-J supports a number of modelling styles, such as event-orientation and process-orientation, which can be freely mixed within the same model. Its CondQueue component even allows a limited form of activity-oriented model design. DESMO's higher-level modelling features include black box constructs for easy implementation of resources and master-slave and producer-consumer synchronization. Some support for interrupt-driven modelling patterns is also provided. When compared to other discrete event simulation frameworks some distinguishing features of DESMO-J are

- its emphasis on component reusability and hierarchical modelling styles;
- the clean separation of model and experiment, which allows multiple experiments with the same model without any complex restart procedures; and
- its rich libraries of application-specific model components.

Finally, in line with the original goals of the framework's design, DESMO-J offers an excellent didactical tool for teaching and learning about discrete event simulation concepts.

Download of DESMO-J

At http://www.desmoj.de DESMO-J's compiled classes (desmoj_all.jar) are available for download. The source code, API documentation, and a tutorial can be found there, too. Note that the sources require libraries (desmoj_libs.jar) that have to be downloaded as well.

Bibliography

E. Gamma, R. Helm, R. Johnson, and R. Vlissides. *Design Patterns: Elements of Reusable Object-Oriented Software*. Addison-Wesley, Reading, 1995.

B. Page. *Diskrete Simulation – Eine Einführung mit Modula-2* ("Discrete Simulation – An Introduction with Modula-2", in German). Springer, Berlin, 1991.

B. Page, T. Lechler, and S. Claassen. *Objektorientierte Simulation in Java mit dem Framework DESMO-J* ("Object-Oriented Simulation in Java with the Framework DESMO-J", in German). Libri Book on Demand, Hamburg, 2000.

University of Hamburg – Faculty of Informatics. DESMO-J, 2004. [Online] http://www.desmoj.de (in August 2005).

Part III

Advanced Methodology

Chapter 11

Multi-Agent-Based Simulation (MABS)

Nicolas Knaak, Wolfgang Kreutzer, Bernd Page

Contents

11.1 Motivation and Overview 339
11.2 Multi-Agent Systems 340
    11.2.1 The Agent Metaphor 340
    11.2.2 Characteristics of MAS 341
    11.2.3 Architectures for Agent Design 342
11.3 Different Views of Agent-Oriented Simulation 347
11.4 Foundations of Multi-Agent-Based Simulation 348
    11.4.1 Applications of MABS 349
    11.4.2 Comparison of Agent-Based and Classical World Views 351
    11.4.3 Components of Multi-Agent-Based Simulation Models 353
    11.4.4 Conceptual Modelling Methods 357
    11.4.5 Tools for Agent-Based Simulation 360
11.5 Conclusion: Potentials, Limitations, and Prospects for MABS 365
Further Reading 367
Bibliography 368

11.1 Motivation and Overview

Throughout the last decade computer science has shown increasing interest in software designs based on *multi-agent systems* (MAS); i.e. a range of techniques whose common bond is that they describe systems in terms of aggregations of goal-oriented, interacting, and autonomous entities, placed in a shared environment. Such entities are referred to as "agents" and, since no or only minor central control is imposed, global system behaviour emerges solely from their cooperation or interactions. In addition to applications in the social and life sciences, where it originated, this framework has now also become popular

Chapter 11 Multi-Agent-Based Simulation (MABS)

in several subareas of computer science; e.g. software engineering, distributed systems, and robotics.

There are many connections between MAS and simulation. Though there are differences, the metaphor of interacting autonomous agents is closely related to object-oriented system design and offers convenient cognitive scaffolding for human decision makers' views of the world. Since MAS can be used to analyse how global phenomena can emerge from local interactions, they have proved of particular use in the social sciences and in modelling patterns of behaviour in economics and biology. Although model validation often remains problematic, simulations can lend much support to the formation and corroboration of theories in these fields.

This chapter draws on a number of sources (mainly Klügl 2001; Wooldridge 2003; Ferber 1995; Uhrmacher 2000) and gives a brief overview of core concepts of MAS and their application to simulation.

11.2 Multi-Agent Systems

11.2.1 The Agent Metaphor

Multi-agent systems have become an important metaphor for model construction in disciplines as diverse as computer science, sociology, economics, or biology. Unfortunately, no agreement on exact definitions of terms (e.g. *agent*) and what distinguishes agency from related concepts (e.g. *objects*) has so far been reached. As a result, ambiguous usage of terms remains a concern for MAS research. To address this concern and retain enough flexibility to capture all the diversity of the subject, some authors resort to very general and abstract definitions. An often cited example for this is the following characterization of *agent* by Franklin and Graesser (1997, p. 25):

> "An autonomous agent is a system situated within and a part of an environment that senses that environment and acts on it, over time, in pursuit of its own agenda and so as to effect what it senses in the future."

Wooldridge (2003, p. 15) points out that nearly every entity inhabiting an environment and capable of autonomously reacting to changes within it, *can* be regarded as an agent. Whether a trivial device (such as e.g. a thermostat) should be viewed in this way will solely depend on how much benefit a modeller can derive from this view (Wooldridge 2003, p. 16).

Another prominent and slightly more concrete approach is the definition of agents by means of a set of properties, all or some of which a prospective agent must possess (see e.g. Klügl 2001, pp. 14, Ferber 1995, p. 10, and numerous other sources):

❏ *Autonomy*: An agent is able to fulfil its tasks without or with only minor interventions by other entities.

11.2 Multi-Agent Systems

- *Situatedness*: An agent inhabits some environment that it can sense and act upon.
- *Reactivity*: An agent is able to respond to changes in its environment in a timely fashion.
- *Goal-orientation*: An agent does not merely react to environmental stimuli, but can act pro-actively – according to a set of persistent goals. To meet these goals, it is able to execute plans over time.
- *Sociality*: In order to reach its goals an agent communicates and interacts with other agents in a cooperative or competitive manner.
- *Adaptivity*: An agent can adapt its future behaviour based on past experiences; i.e. it can learn.
- *Mobility*: An agent is able to change its location within a physical or virtual environment (e.g. a computer network).

11.2.2 Characteristics of MAS

A straightforward definition of *multi-agent systems* (MAS) views them as systems in Section 1.2's sense. MAS' defining property is that its components are sets of agents, located and cooperating in a shared environment (Wooldridge 2003, pp. 105).

Typical attributes of MAS are that they require no (or only minor) central control and that the agents operate with incomplete information (Jennings et al. 1998 cited in Klügl 2001, p. 17). They often place restrictions on an agent's sensory capabilities and range of action. MAS also lend themselves to distributed data management and processing.

We can classify MAS in a number of different ways (see e.g. Klügl 2001, pp. 31; Ferber 1995, pp. 12):

- *Number and complexity of agents*: We often find that systems have either a few complex agents (e.g. in process control problems) or many simple agents (e.g. in experiments with artificial life).
- *Type of communication*: Communication can be implicit through shared environments (e.g. ants communicating with pheromones) or explicit through messages.
- *Heterogeneity of agents*: Different agent architectures can be combined in the same MAS. By using standard communication protocols such as those proposed by FIPA (see Section 11.4.5) and computer networks, agents that were designed by different developers and may run on different machines can all contribute to the goals of a MAS. Of course, heterogeneous and open MAS tend to be more complex than homogeneous ones.
- *Pattern of interaction*: Agents can compete to pursue their own goals, or they can cooperate with each other to solve common problems (distributed problem solvers). In either case coherent global behaviour can emerge.

Chapter 11 Multi-Agent-Based Simulation (MABS)

❏ *"Substance"* of agents and their environments (see Klügl 2001, p. 71; Franklin and Graesser 1997, p. 31): Physical MAS may consist of robots or real life agents. Virtual MAS can be placed in either a "real" (e.g. the Internet) or a simulated virtual environment (e.g. a simulation model).

❏ *Environmental complexity*: The complexity of shared environments determines the complexity of agent architectures and patterns of cooperation. See the classification by Russel and Norvig (2003, pp. 40) for details.

While often used in the context of MAS, the notion of *emergence* is still very vague. Its underlying idea has been inspired by *Gestalt Psychology's* and *General System Theory (GST)'s* belief that a "whole" may have "emergent" properties which cannot be derived from simple aggregation of properties of its parts; i.e. "the whole is greater than the sum of its parts" (Holland 1998 cited in Klügl 2001, p. 82). This concept is closely related to the idea of self-organization, which has often been referred to as *computational emergence*; i.e. "complex global forms can arise from local computational interactions" (Cariani 1991 cited in Jones 2003, p. 418). There is a "mysterious" quality to the way in which emergent properties of wholes relate to the behaviour of their parts, and such processes are often described in terms such as novelty, unpredictability, self-maintenance, and downward causation (Jones 2003, p. 419). One of the goals of agent-based simulations is to help reaching a better understanding of such phenomena.

11.2.3 Architectures for Agent Design

Figure 11.1 shows the general architecture of agent objects. While there are many variations on this theme, the idea that agents have sensors, effectors, and capabilities for internal information processing and decision making is very common. Agents can therefore be viewed as "situated control systems" (Wooldridge 2003, p. 16), which react to and manipulate their environments through positive (amplifying) or negative (dampening) feedback techniques.

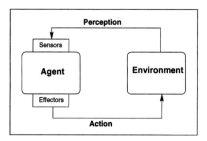

Figure 11.1: An agent's basic architecture (adopted from Wooldridge 2003, p. 16)

11.2 Multi-Agent Systems

Particularly useful classifications of different agent architectures are offered by Klügl (2001, pp. 19) and Müller (1996, Ch. 2). In recapitulation of those classification schemes, we can identify the following different types of agent architectures: Subsymbolic, reactive (or subcognitive[1]), and deliberative architectures. The characteristics of these architecture types are described below with the aid of some typical examples.

Subsymbolic Architectures

These are architectures with their roots in "Soft Computing" and non-symbolic Artificial Intelligence (AI). In such architectures there is no explicit symbol processing and complex behaviour emerges from interactions between simple patterns (Klügl 2001, p. 22).

A typical example for subsymbolic agent control are *connectionist architectures* or *neural networks* (Ferber 1995, pp. 137). Neural networks (NN) were inspired by information processing in biological systems and are often used for simulating models from this domain.

A *neural network* consists of a multitude of simple and identical computational elements, so-called *formal neurons*, which are linked together. Each neuron computes its activity level (output) as the weighted sum of all of its input values. If a threshold is crossed, the neuron will "fire". This event passes its activity level to other neurons as shown in Figure 11.2. Most neural networks have multiple *layers*, where level n outputs serve as inputs for level $n + 1$. When such multi-layered networks are used to guide agents (e.g. robots), all input layers will be connected to the agent's sensors and output layers will control the effectors. By aggregating and propagating partial numeric results, intermediate layers can form "abstractions" representing an agent's decision procedures (see Figure 11.3).

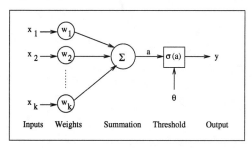

Figure 11.2: Functionality of a formal neuron (from Haykin 1999, p. 11)

---

[1]Though the name "reactive agent" is more common for these types of architectures, Klügl (2001, p. 24) argues that "subcognitive agent" is a more appropriate term since subsymbolic and deliberative agents can exhibit *reactive* behaviour as well.

Chapter 11 Multi-Agent-Based Simulation (MABS)

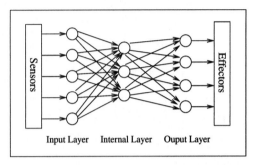

Figure 11.3: A Multi-layered neural net for agent control (from Ferber 1995, p. 137)

What action an agent chooses is determined by the weights of its neurons' connections. These weights can be adjusted whenever computed outputs differ from what is expected; i.e. the network can "learn". The so-called *backpropagation* algorithm is the most common strategy for pursuing this goal (Ferber 1995, p. 138).

Many NN architectures have been based on this simple *multi-layer perceptron* design or other neural processing approaches. The textbook by Haykin (1999) offers a survey.

Subcognitive or Reactive Architectures

These architectures are model-based, i.e. they assume "meaningful" symbols to represent the state of the agent and its environment. However, no dynamic planning or mental concepts are involved in their interpretation (Klügl 2001, p. 24).

Subsumption designs are a well known subcognitive architecture for building reactive agents. This method was proposed by Brooks (1999, p. 10), who used it to model simple "social" robots.

Subsumption designs consist of multiple modules, each of which is responsible for a particular behaviour pattern. Such modules are based on simple stimulus-response networks or finite automata. Processing is hierarchical; i.e. activities of low-level modules block activities at higher levels. In biological terms this means that reflexes for survival are given higher priority than exploration and goal-directed behaviour. For example, the cognitive capabilities of the ore mining robot shown in Figure 11.4 (example adopted with modifications from Ferber 1995, pp. 131) are usually engaged in exploring and mapping geographical areas. Whenever ore deposits are encountered, these activities are pre-empted by the higher priority process of mining. Even higher priorities are attached to collision avoidance and refuelling, since these tasks are crucial to the robot's survival.

11.2 Multi-Agent Systems

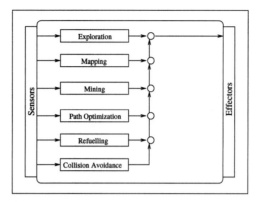

Figure 11.4: Schematic representation of a subsumption design for controlling an ore mining robot (adopted with modifications from Ferber 1995, pp. 132)

Ferber and Drougoul's *competitive tasks* architecture (Ferber 1995, pp. 132) also assigns alternative behaviour descriptions (*tasks*) to agents. Each of these tasks, of which only one can be active, corresponds to a relevant activity; e.g. *acquire energy* or *mine ore*. Each activity is in turn grounded in a programming tool's linguistic abstractions; e.g. *move robot arm* (examples adopted with modifications from Ferber 1995, p. 133). All tasks receive the same signals from the agent's sensors, which they then use to compute activation strengths for an activity, based on specified weights. The signal *ore sighted*, for example, is highly weighted by the *mine ore* task.

A supervisory module allocates control over agent behaviour to the task with the highest activation strength at that time. Both negative and positive feedback is used in this process: Task completions dampen a relevant signal's intensity and the most frequent tasks' signals will adjust their connection weights (positive feedback) and thereby increase activation strengths over time.

Deliberative Architectures

In these architectures an agents' behaviour *is* based on "mental concepts", such as beliefs, desires, and intentions. Some researchers differentiate further between deliberative, cognitive (Klügl 2001, pp. 25), and hybrid (Müller 1996, Ch. 2.6) architectures. These are nearly the same, but cognitive architectures are based on cognitive theories, while deliberative architectures are designed from a purely engineering point of view. Hybrid architectures contain different layers for, at a minimum, reactive and deliberative behaviour. Examples for cognitive architectures are BDI (Rao and Georgeff 1995)

Chapter 11 Multi-Agent-Based Simulation (MABS)

and PECS (Urban 1997), while InterRap (Müller 1996, Ch. 3) is a well-known hybrid architecture.

The BDI (Belief, Desire, Intention) framework was proposed (among others) by Rao and Georgeff (1995) and is derived from a formalization of philosophical theories of intentional actions (see e.g. Bratman 1987); i.e. questions about how people develop intentions and how they map these into actions.

Any BDI agent can be viewed as a knowledge-based system, whose state is described by three components (Klügl 2001, p. 27):

1. The current *beliefs* of the agent about itself and its environment.
2. The *desires* or goals of the agent. At this stage these can still show contradictions.
3. The agent's specific *intentions*, i.e. a contradiction-free subset of the agent's goals.

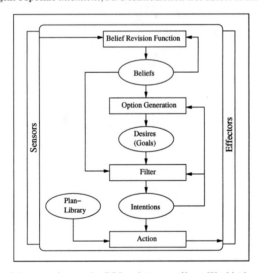

Figure 11.5: Schematic design of a BDI architecture (from Wooldridge 1999, p. 58)

Figure 11.5 shows the dynamic behaviour of a BDI agent (see also Wooldridge 1999, pp. 58): *Beliefs* are cast into symbolic form and stored in a knowledge base. A *belief revision function* is responsible for keeping the knowledge base up-to-date. This function is triggered by incoming sensor data. In response an agent derives all possible *desires* which can be pursued within the current constraints of the world (*option generation*) and selects those as *intentions* whose pursuit would not cause any contradictions (*filtering*). Each intention is associated with a plan, stored in a *plan library*. Executing a plan will further the associated intentions. If, however, the agent believes that a

346

relevant goal cannot be reached, or that it has ceased to be relevant, a plan's execution will be aborted.

It should be noted that the *option generation* phase captures both an agent's assumptions and its intentions (Wooldridge 1999, p. 59). These two factors together determine an agent's goals. Abstract intentions (e.g. "go on holiday") trigger the pursuit of more concrete goals (e.g. "apply for leave" or "visit a travel agent"). The option generation phase therefore composes plan hierarchies in a recursive fashion. Singh et al. (1999) propose a formal representation for the BDI architecture in terms of a modal logic and its realization in terms of a BDI interpreter. This proposal has subsequently been used as a basis for different implementations.

11.3 Different Views of Agent-Oriented Simulation

The relationship between agent technology and simulation can be viewed and exploited in a number of different ways (Uhrmacher 2000, p. 16):

1. Due to the complexity of agents' internal processes and interactions, software systems based on an agent metaphor are often hard to validate and test. While formal verification methods are only of limited use, simulation provides an important tool for the operational validation of MAS (Moss 2004, p. 2). Simulated environments for testing software or hardware agents are often called *agent testbeds*. Ören (2000, p. 1758) refers to this application of simulation to agent technology as *agent simulation*.

2. The MAS metaphor brings an additional modelling perspective to simulation. MAS theory offers a framework for improving both understanding and modelling of systems consisting of multiple, autonomous, and goal-oriented actors. This agent-based modelling perspective has been referred to as *multi-agent-based simulation (MABS)* and is most frequently used to simulate social, biological, and economic systems. However, in MABS, agent concepts are often employed exclusively at the conceptual modelling level, while the corresponding computer models are implemented in a more or less conventional object-oriented style (Drougoul et al. 2002, p. 11).

3. Simulation software can be designed and implemented using agent technology. According to Uhrmacher (2000, p. 16), such agent-based simulation tools can enhance distribution and interoperability (see Chapter 12). Software agents employing AI techniques, such as data mining, can offer support for experimentation in knowledge-intensive domains; e.g. simulation data analysis, validation, parameter calibration, or experiment planning. Ören (2000, p. 1758) calls this application of agent technology to simulation *agent-supported simulation*.

Note that all three views of agent-oriented simulation are closely related. Agent simulation and MABS only differ in that software agents populating a software engineering

Chapter 11 Multi-Agent-Based Simulation (MABS)

model are usually destined to function in a "real" environment later, whereas simulated agents in MABS models do not exist outside the model.

Finally, due to the inherent complexity of data analysis in agent-based models (Sanchez and Lucas 2002, p. 117), simulation tools built on the agent metaphor may occasionally even be helpful during an agent-based model's design and analysis (Drougoul et al. 2002, pp. 10). This book, however, describes the classical use of simulation as a tool for analysing "real" systems. While many aspects may apply to other viewpoints as well, further discussion in this chapter focuses on *multi-agent-based simulation* in the sense of the second alternative of the above classification.

11.4 Foundations of Multi-Agent-Based Simulation

A microscopic model maps relevant system components to entities and studies their dynamic behaviour by means of algorithmical simulation. Autonomous actors with complex behaviour, such as individuals in economic or sociological models, or animals in predator-prey scenarios, often form an important part of such models. Section 11.2 showed that autonomous actors can be suitably represented as agents, and societies of such actors as MAS.

The entities of a MABS model will therefore be agents, which interact (i.e. cooperate and compete) in a simulated environment. The spectrum of possible implementations extends from scenarios in which all entities are agents to those where agents model only some entities; e.g. people (Klügl 2001, p. 67). In the second case, other model components and their behaviour can be described in a different modelling framework; e.g. an event-oriented or equation-based viewpoint. The following aspects, however, form a common bond for all MABS models (see Klügl 2001, pp. 67; Ferber 1995, p. 37):

1. *Agent-orientation*: The majority of system components are modelled as agents, which interact among themselves and with their simulated environments.

2. *Local behaviour modelling:* Behaviour modelling is largely local; i.e. it is described from an agents's point of view. To ensure autonomy, each agent encapsulates its behaviour as well as its state. All state changes are performed by the agent itself. External events serve only as triggers.

3. *Behavioural complexity*: An agent's range of behaviour is complex and can be described via "goals" (Klügl 2001, p. 67). There are few restrictions on the behaviour and control patterns that can be modelled. This fexibility gives support to a large number of methodological alternatives.

4. *Environment- and space-orientation*: Simulated agents act in a simulated environment, which they can sense and change. There may be constraints on the spatial range of perceptions and actions. A model may also represent some dynamic effects independently of agents; e.g. the weather and other natural or man-made factors. Agents may have spatial location and may be able to move about.

11.4 Foundations of Multi-Agent-Based Simulation

5. *Interaction and organization*: MABS models focus on analysing properties and interactions of single agents, as well as any macro-phenomena they may generate at the system level. In addition to modelling real world multi-agent systems, they are therefore particularly well suited for simulating emergent phenomena and local patterns of organization in multi-agent societies.

11.4.1 Applications of MABS

Biology and the social Sciences are primary areas of application for MABS models. We will discuss some examples from these domains in the following and then extend our view to other application areas.

Applications in Biology

Biological models support exploration of animal behaviour, cognitive processes, and learning, as well as complex cooperation in swarms and packs such as the social organization of insect colonies. While focusing more closely on general principles of living organisms, models for so-called "artificial life" explorations fall also into this context (Klügl 2001, p. 69).

A well-known example for a biologically inspired MABS model is the *MANTA* model (Modelling Anthill Activity) of Drogoul and Ferber (see Ferber 1995, pp. 389). This model simulates the emergence of social structures in ant colonies founded by a new queen. MANTA represents individual ants as agents, which move through the nest's local environment. They are motivated by the need to preserve the nest and perform relevant tasks to achieve this goal; e.g. they forage for food and care for the young.

As often in "real life", interactions are caused by indirect stimuli (i.e. *pheromone trails*) rather than direct exchanges of messages. This creates gradient fields of stimuli in the environment, which serve to guide ants along their steepest ascent; e.g. food. Stimuli are not solely created and placed by ants. Environmental factors such as light, temperature, and moisture, which may sometimes themselves be modelled as agents, are also taken into account.

MANTA controls ant behaviour by using a *competitive tasks* architecture (see Section 11.2.3). This pattern selects whatever task is triggered by the strongest stimulus during a given time interval. Functional specialization of individuals (e.g. worker, soldier) is achieved via activation thresholds for common tasks.

The MANTA model has been used to simulate and explore many social scenarios, including the low probability with which a queen will successfully establish a new colony (Ferber 1995, p. 395).

Chapter 11 Multi-Agent-Based Simulation (MABS)

Applications in the Social Sciences

In the *social sciences* models which track individual entities' lifecycles, have successfully been used for some time. They are often called on to explain social structures as emergent phenomena of human behaviour and have led to the conclusion that if even simple patterns of interaction are replicated often enough, they may suffice to create complex social structures. Similar investigations have also confirmed the conjecture that most social systems are non-linear and therefore not easily amenable to analytical study (Gilbert 1996). Simulation offers a means to experiment and is therefore employed as a method of last resort.

MABS models offer concrete representations of human decision making in heterogeneous societies. The "Socionics" research program, for example, aims to operationalize and demonstrate sociological theories and models, using Petri nets (von Lüde et al. 2003).

Another focus of social research is the investigation of so-called *Artificial Societies*; i.e. the simulation of collections of agents which need not to have correspondences in reality. Studying such societies can help to isolate and uncover social patterns, which can then be generalized and help understand interactions in real world contexts.

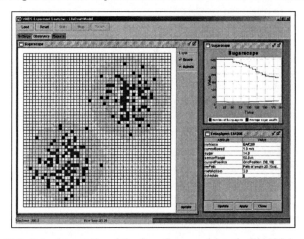

Figure 11.6: Reimplementation of the *SugarScape* model in the FAMOS framework

The *SugarScape* model of Epstein and Axtell (1996), shown in Figure 11.6, is maybe the best known example of this model type. It describes a society of simple agents which move across fields of squares. Each square is modelled as a cell in a cellular automaton and contains different quantities of a renewable resource; e.g. "sugar". This

11.4 Foundations of Multi-Agent-Based Simulation

can be harvested and is needed for agents to survive. The variants of this model described by Epstein and Axtell have different levels of complexity. For example, they investigate survival of agents with different "genetic" dispositions regarding their depth of perception, as well as the sugar levels they need to survive. More complex variants introduce a second resource ("spice") and allow trade among agents.

Other Application Areas

Other productive applications of MABS models can be found in domains which are characterized by distributed decision making and multi-dimensional goals, e.g. in *economics*, *ecology*, and *logistics*. Economic decisions, for example, often involve social and ecological constraints as well as profits. In this context the simulation group at Hamburg University has used MABS models of courier services for studying the economic, ecological, and social effects of introducing new logistic strategies based on strategically located transfer points (Knaak et al. 2003).

11.4.2 Comparison of Agent-Based and Classical World Views

MABS is characterized by a micro-perspective; i.e. a system is modelled from the viewpoints of participating autonomous actors. Although this modelling style is closely related to popular modelling world views for discrete event simulation, there are differences that justify MABS's classification as a modelling style of its own. Klügl (2001, p. 70) even regards agent-based simulation as a more general superset of classical simulation methods. In the following we will briefly compare MABS to some other popular simulation world views (and thereby extend and complement the similar treatment in Klügl 2001, pp. 70):

Agent-Based versus Event-Oriented Modelling

At first glance the idea of agent autonomy and behaviour encapsulation seems to contradict event-oriented modelling styles' need for global behaviour definitions; i.e. its use of event routines and their application to passive entity structures (see Section 5.2.2).

Some authors like Spaniol and Hoff (1995), however, view event-orientation differently, and attach no event routines to events. Instead, events are processed by *active entities*, which contain the event's relevant actions. Each entity groups state changing actions for all events in which it participates and performs these on demand; i.e. whenever relevant events occur. This viewpoint matches agent-based modelling frameworks much better. It offers an efficient base for controlling a set of simulated agents' behaviour and is instantiated in some software systems, such as *Swarm* (see Section 11.4.5). It should be noted that in this context agents act only if an external event occurs, or if a relevant event has been triggered by the agent itself. Between events the agents' states remain constant.

Chapter 11 Multi-Agent-Based Simulation (MABS)

Agent-Based versus Process-Oriented Modelling

A simulation *process* is an active and persistent entity, whose behaviour is described from a local perspective (see Section 5.2.1). Although the agent concept is somewhat more general, it fits a process-based simulation's world view quite well (Klügl 2001, p. 94). Inter-process communications occur either through direct or indirect synchronizations; i.e. processes are delayed in their lifecycles and must wait until reactivated, or they must queue for a resource. Patterns of communication in agent-based models can be richer. Some MABS models may even require negotiations according to complex protocols.

The behavioural flexibility of simulation processes, in whose lifecycles a linear sequence of actions unfolds in a synchronous fashion, also falls short of some MABS models' requirements. Agents may be placed in highly dynamic environments and must react quickly to asynchronous events. Different from the process interaction world view, spatial location often also plays an important role in MABS. Simulation processes should therefore be viewed as particularly simple, pro-active agents, with limited capabilities for communication and movement.

Agent-Based versus Object-Oriented Modelling

Any comparison of agent-based and object-oriented simulation must necessarily reflect the more general issue of distinguishing between MAS and object-oriented system. Since both technologies map to a set of communicating objects at implementation level, a clear distinction can be difficult to draw. Since *agents* are a more abstract concept than *objects*, there are, however, some conceptual differences.

Objects are defined through their interfaces; i.e. the services they can perform on demand. Their implementation must therefore ensure that all methods are correctly implemented and that expected results are returned (Ferber 1995, p. 57). This viewpoint clashes with the requirement for agent autonomy, which leaves agents free to pursue their own goals. Agents can, for example, refuse a request if it would cause conflict or if some information is currently unavailable (Ferber 1995, p. 58).

The important point of distinction is that such decisions are based on the perceived state of an environment, as well as the state of the agent's internal knowledge base. The same request can therefore lead to different reactions at different times. In a typical implementation this results in an additional *filtering* level, which mediates between service requests and internal agent processes (see Figure 11.7). In this way agents themselves retain tight control over their own behaviour.

In spite of these differences many similarities between object-oriented and multi-agent systems remain (Ferber 1995, p. 58): Agents can be viewed as an extended object type with goal-directed behaviour, and objects can be viewed as "degenerate" agents whose communication competence is limited to reactions to method calls, and whose goal is simply to execute orders.

11.4 Foundations of Multi-Agent-Based Simulation

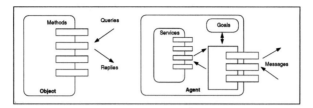

Figure 11.7: Conceptual distinction between objects and agents
(adopted from Ferber 1995, p. 58)

Object-oriented software architectures offer a good base for MAS implementation. This also holds true in the simulation domain, where MABS can be built using object-oriented simulation frameworks (Klügl 2001, p. 96).

11.4.3 Components of Multi-Agent-Based Simulation Models

Figure 11.8 shows a much simplified view of a MABS model's components. Agents encapsulate state and behaviour and are coupled to an environment. The interaction among agents and between agents and their environment creates macro phenomena, such as spatial and social organization or global dynamic processes. The following description of main MABS components is based on Klügl (2001, Ch. 3.3–3.5).

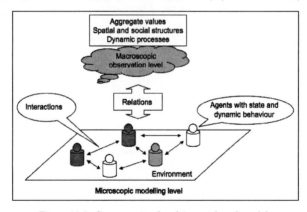

Figure 11.8: Components of multi-agent-based models

353

Chapter 11 Multi-Agent-Based Simulation (MABS)

Scheduling and Time Advance

Scheduling in MABS can be both time- or event-driven. For models with few complex agents, which communicate via messages, event-driven scheduling is often the better choice. Conversely, time-driven control may be preferable where models consist of large numbers of agents with similar behaviour, and where every agent is activated in every simulation cycle and similar actions are executed in a regularly fashion.

Execution order of agents is an important aspect in time-driven, and to a lesser extent in event-driven scheduling strategies. While conceptually agents will act in parallel, the serialization of actions required to execute on a single processor may introduce so-called "artifacts" into the model.[2] The execution order of agents in time-driven models is therefore often randomized at each simulation step (Klügl 2001, p. 157).

Agents and their Behaviour

Agents are the most important part of a MABS model. Similar to any MAS, MABS differ in both number and complexity of agents. Artificial life models and social simulations often contain many agents, each of which may be very simple. Socio-technical models and agent testbeds (e.g. for exploring logistics or manufacturing control), on the other hand, may only be populated by few agents with relatively complex patterns of behaviour. In general, simple models are used much more frequently, since they are easier to design and have lower computational and data requirements.

All agent architectures we have described can in principle be used to implement MABS. Which pattern is chosen should depend on a model's purpose. Deliberative architectures, for example, are well suited to represent human actors, while reactive architectures excel at modelling social animals. Finally, adaptive agents and evolutionary algorithms are often chosen to model self-organising systems.

Communication and Organizational Structures

Agents can interact either by direct communication (i.e. via messages) or indirectly through changes to shared environments (Ferber 1995, p. 13). In scenarios without any explicit environment, such as some economic or sociological models, message passing becomes the only possible mode of interaction. These models are most often used to study patterns of cooperation, negotiation, or competition, and may contain complex interaction languages and protocols. Biological models with situated agents which only affect their environments (e.g. by depositing pheromone trails) are at the other side of the spectrum. It is, of course, also possible to use both means of communication within the same model.

---

[2] In particular such "model-artifacts" are artificial causal dependencies due to the serialization of originally concurrent actions.

11.4 Foundations of Multi-Agent-Based Simulation

If communication is to be message-based, a model must offer a suitable infrastructure for message reception and transmission. This is a trivial task if message transmission is instantaneous and error-free. If, however, message delays and error sources are to be modelled, all communication infrastructure (i.e. source, carrier, and destination) must be explicitly represented. Such representations may also need to make provisions for *multicast* techniques, which route messages to multiple destinations.

Modelling the organizational structures of MABS is an important aspect of agent-based model design. In this context the term *organization* refers to sets of objects which form a unified whole, show subordination relationships and pursue common goals (Ferber 1995, p. 88). Organizational structures control and order their agents' patterns of interaction. Within MABS models such structures can be defined in two different ways (Ferber 1995, p. 114):

1. They can be set *a priori* by the model designer. For example, this is a sensible approach for modelling institutions or companies in which individuals and groups are involved in ritual negotiations.

2. They can emerge *a posteriori* during a simulation. Such phenomena may occur whenever reactive agents without predetermined organizational structures interact and communicate over time.

Modelling fixed organizational structures benefits from constructs which cluster agents with common properties, such as groups and roles. Ferber's *Agent-Group-Role* (AGR) model considers such groupings as central features of all agent-based organization (Ferber and Gutknecht 1998). In this context hierarchical structures can be used to both reflect real hierarchies and to support *hierarchical agent-based modelling styles*. The second of these possibilities suggests a view under which groups of agents are themselves modelled as agents, which can then represent and control interactions between their members at some "higher" level (see e.g. Ferber 1995, p. 90).

Environments

Depending on model type and architecture, environment specifications may differ widely. In the simplest case an environment will contain only agents, but it may also include passive components and have both spatial and temporal aspects.

A simple way in which environments can be modelled is discussed by Klügl (2001, p. 93), who suggests using an *"environment agent"* for this task. This technique fosters reuse of suitable agent functionality, but may lead to inelegant modelling constructs and awkward implementations. Overall it may be better to invest in customized interfaces between agents and their environment (Klügl 2001, p. 93).

Figures 11.9 and 11.10 show how MABS can model space and movement. In the first case, a simulated ant wanders through a field of pheromone markers. As soon as it finds a relevant stimulus, it follows its gradient; i.e. it moves in the direction of increasing

Chapter 11 Multi-Agent-Based Simulation (MABS)

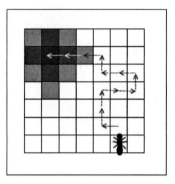

Figure 11.9: Modelling space and movement: a simulated ant's random walk through a square neighbourhood on a grid-based spatial model

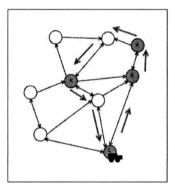

Figure 11.10: Modelling space and movement: a transport vehicle's shortest roundtrip between a warehouse (L) and three customers (K) on a graph-based spatial model

signal strength. In the second case, a transport vehicle seeks shortest routes in a road network modelled as a directed graph.

Environments with spatial extension must be mapped to models with spatial aspects. Choosing regular *grids* for this purpose, whose cells may differ in shape, size, and neighbour relations, is the most popular choice. Two-dimensional grids with square cells are particularly common. Other designs, e.g. three-dimensional grids or hexagonal cells, are used occasionally. Neighbourhood relationships guide agents' movements and reachability. Strongly non-homogeneous spaces, like road networks in traffic simula-

11.4 Foundations of Multi-Agent-Based Simulation

tions, require irregular grids and are best mapped onto graphs. Although graphs offer more flexibility than grids, they are also more complex to implement and potentially less efficient.

Patterns of agent movement are another important aspect for the explicit modelling of space. Again, different strategies cater for different requirements. Biological models, for example, often suggest *random walks* or movements which *follow a gradient*. In contrast to this, models in the logistics or robotics domains guide agents along carefully planned trajectories, while striving to avoid obstacles. The modelled environment itself may also have spatial dynamics of its own, as we have seen in the form of distributed pheromones in *MANTA*, or consumable resources in *SugarScape* (see Section 11.4.1). Although such effects are most often modelled as cellular automata (Klügl 2001, p. 58), they can also be represented with other methods, such as simulation events and processes.

11.4.4 Conceptual Modelling Methods

Declarative Modelling

While declarative descriptions based on rule-based production systems are a traditional tool for constructing expert systems in AI, they can also be useful for modelling agent behaviour. The relevant methodological spectrum ranges from simple stimulus-response models to symbolic knowledge bases processed by complex interpreters. This description of declarative modelling is mainly based on (Klügl 2001, pp. 60).

The central idea of declarative modelling is a strict separation of knowledge from the way it is processed. Declarative models define relevant properties and their values rather than strategies for solution (Klügl 2001, p. 60). A declarative model of agent behaviour therefore contains rules which map perceptions to actions. Control aspects, which specify in which order rules should be tried and in which order "simultaneous" state changes should occur, are not part of an agent's *knowledge base* and must be resolved by the implementation's rule interpreter.

Rules consist of conditions and actions. In our context conditions may refer to the internal states and sense perceptions of agents. The form of conditions and actions may vary from binary strings to complex symbolic expressions. If all its conditions hold true, a rule may "fire"; i.e. the agent performs the specified actions.

Declarative specifications differ from procedural prescriptions in execution semantics. In contrast to the imperative programming paradigm's temporal chain of sequential execution of commands, rules give time-independent descriptions of what is to happen whenever particular states will occur. Rules are conceptually active and may be triggered at any time. This is why early AI systems referred to a similar concept as "demon procedures" (i.e. they lurk and pounce unpredictably). Rule application occurs under control of a rule interpreter, whose execution cycle can be described by three steps (see Luger 2002, p. 172; Klügl 2001, p. 64):

❑ *Rule selection*: All rules whose conditions are "true" are selected.

Chapter 11 Multi-Agent-Based Simulation (MABS)

- *Conflict resolution*: This step determines which of the previously selected rules will fire. A range of strategies can be used to prioritize.
- *Rule execution*: All actions associates with the selected rule are performed.

Generally there are two fundamentally different strategies on which rule interpreters can be based (Luger 2002, p. 182; Klügl 2001, p. 63): *Forward chaining* is data driven. In our context it would add new perceptions and deductions to an agent's knowledge base at each step in its operating cycle. When rules apply, their actions are performed and cause changes in state as well as possibly changes in agents' knowledge bases. In contrast to this strategy *backward chaining* uses a goal-driven approach, which works well for state-based planning. Goals are incrementally added to agents' knowledge bases and the interpreter scans for rules through whose actions these goals may be reached. Such rules' conditions are inserted as new goals in the knowledge base. This process continues until all conditions of relevant rules are met. The resulting rule sequence can then be used as a feasible plan for reaching the original goal.

MABS models must couple rule application to simulation time. Forward chaining makes this quite easy (see also Klügl 2001, p. 63). In a time-driven model each cycle either activates all agents once, or it triggers as many activations as needed to reach a state where no rule can fire. The first case applies if agents can perform at most one action per cycle, while the second strategy can cope with any pattern of interaction. Event-driven models activate their rule interpreter only if an agent becomes involved in external or internally generated events. In this case the knowledge base is updated and one or more scanning cycles result. Since we must consider interactions between plan generation (by recursing through goals) and rule execution (by cycling through rule applications), the relation to simulation time management becomes much more complex in backward chaining.

The aforementioned independence of the rules is one of the central advantages of declarative modelling. However, this aspect can also be viewed as a disadvantage (see Klügl 2001, pp. 65): Since no rule directly invokes any other, causally connected action sequences are difficult to determine. Instead, rules determine conditions under which other rules may become active. Any such indirect causal connections may be quite hard to understand and predict .

This is a particular problem in models with large numbers of rules, where the lack of explicit structure quickly leads to scenarios whose validity becomes difficult to establish and hard to maintain. It will also reduce execution efficiency, since many rules must be scanned multiple times (until none can fire) for each cycle. Partitioning an agent's rule set can help ameliorate these effects and Klügl (2001, p. 119) claims that models with forward chaining may profit considerably from grouping rules based on common parts in conditions. The resulting model structure then becomes similar to an automaton and can be documented in UML-like diagrams (see Oechslein et al. 2001).

11.4 Foundations of Multi-Agent-Based Simulation

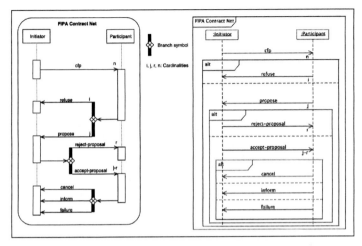

Figure 11.11: An example for modelling agent interaction protocols with with AUML (left) and UML 2 (right). Both diagrams show the popular *Contract Net* protocol for distributed task allocation (adopted with modifications from Bauer and Odell 2004, p. 16).

UML and AgentUML

Because of the numerous similarities between agent-based and object-oriented modelling, UML (see Chapter 4) can be used for modelling and documentation of MAS as well. In its pure form UML offers no special support for modelling agent concepts like goals and beliefs, but specialized notations like *AgentUML* (AUML) offer suitable extensions. In our opinion, the following diagram types of UML are most appropriate for modelling MAS:

- ❑ *Class diagrams* can be employed to model agent organizations and ontologies; i.e. the domain-dependent parts of an agent communication language (Bauer and Odell 2004, p. 5). AUML extends UML class diagrams in a way that agents can be modelled as classes with additional "mental" properties such as goals and beliefs.

- ❑ *Interaction diagrams*: While sequence diagrams can be used for modelling simple agent interactions, communication diagrams are needed to represent general communication relationships among agents (i.e. social networks). AUML interaction diagrams are extended sequence diagrams offering roles and additional control structures for modelling branches, loops, concurrency, and multicast-

Chapter 11 Multi-Agent-Based Simulation (MABS)

communication (Bauer and Odell 2004, p. 15). In doing so, AUML anticipates many features of UML 2 sequence diagrams. Figure 11.11 shows a comparison of the UML 2 and AUML notation. In our opinion, the readability of the AUML diagram is slightly superior to UML 2 due to the more explicit display of control flow.

- *Statecharts*: UML state charts can be used to model reactive agents' state-dependent responses to message or signal reception. They are also used occasionally to represent protocols or agents' reactive plans (Bauer and Odell 2004, p. 14). The statechart notation is supported by many agent platforms and MABS tools, such as JADE (Griss et al. 2002), SeSAM (Oechslein et al. 2001), and FAMOS (Knaak et al. 2002). Since they focus on how agents react to asynchronous events, statecharts might be better suited for modelling reactive agents than activity diagrams.
- *Activity diagrams*: Activity diagrams model an agent's tasks; i.e. its plans or protocols (Bauer and Odell 2004, p. 13). Patterns of synchronization between concurrent tasks performed by different agents, or within the same agent, can be modelled using synchronization bars or send and receive signal actions.

11.4.5 Tools for Agent-Based Simulation

This section surveys a range of tools which can be used to build and support MABS.

Agent Platforms and Testbeds

An agent platform is "a software environment agents live in"; i.e. a runtime environment for agent-based software (Rölke 2004, p. 159). Most available platforms are based on Java and follow the *FIPA* (Foundation for Intelligent Physical Agents) standard. This standard defines an agent communication language (ACL), as well as a platform architecture consisting of an agent communication channel (ACC) and two special agents called AMS (Agent Management System) and DF (Directory Facilitator) (see e.g. Rölke 2004, pp. 87). By registering and de-registering agents with a unique identifier, the AMS provides so-called "white page services". The DF manages the agents' service descriptions ("yellow page services"). The internal agent architecture is not part of the FIPA standard.

Agent platforms can be employed to build MABS as well. This offers a number of advantages:

- Agent platforms often come with powerful frameworks for modelling complex agents (e.g. those of the BDI architecture, see Section 11.2.3), which are rarely available in pure simulation environments.
- Since agent platforms are usually designed as distributed systems, the distributed execution of complex models is supported in a natural way. Platform interoperability is ensured by the FIPA standard.

11.4 Foundations of Multi-Agent-Based Simulation

❑ Agents interacting with a simulated environment on an agent platform can be easily deployed in their "real" environment after the testing phase.

Since simulation is not an application domain most agent platforms were originally designed for, there are also disadvantages to their use:

❑ Often there is no simulation scheduler for managing simulation time, and for synchronizing agents with simulated environments.

❑ Typical simulation tasks like stochastic modelling, planning experiments, data collection, and statistical data analysis are usually not directly supported.

❑ Agents running on typical agent platforms are often quite "heavy-weight" objects, with one or more concurrent threads of control. This might cause performance problems in models with many such agents.

There are, however, a number of agent platforms which make simulation support available as an integral part of their architecture or as an add-on.

JADE: The *Java Agent DEvelopment Framework*[3] (Bellifemine et al. 2001) is a widely used open source agent platform, which follows to the FIPA standard. JADE offers a distributed agent runtime environment, an extensible framework for behaviour modelling, and some graphical agent management and debugging tools; e.g. a so-called "sniffer agent" which constructs simple UML sequence diagrams tracing agent communications. An agent's dynamic behaviour is composed of so-called *behaviour objects*, each of which represents a single agent task. Since these tasks can be added to and removed from an agent dynamically at runtime, the architecture offers a powerful base for defining complex behaviour. There are extension packages for behaviour modelling with hierarchical UML statecharts (Griss et al. 2002) or the Jadex BDI architecture (Pokahr et al. 2003). Some graphical modelling tools are also available.

JADE has not been specifically designed to support MABS, but a so-called *time service*, i.e. a process-oriented simulation scheduler encapsulated in a JADE agent, has been developed as an add-on package by Braubach et al. (2003). While JADE does not directly support systematic experimentation, data collection and statistical analysis of simulation results, it provides some interesting tools for analysing agent behaviour based on ACL message traces. In addition to the above mentioned "sniffer agent", a tool called *ACLAnalyser* (Botía et al. 2004) can be used to aggregate message traces into social networks at different levels of detail. JADE has occasionally been applied in MABS; e.g. for the agent-based simulation of supply chains (Ahn and Park 2004).

Mulan/Capa (Rölke 2004; Duvigneau 2003) is a FIPA compliant agent platform built on top of the Java-based Petri net simulator *Renew* (Reference Net Workshop, Kummer 2002). The system was developed by the theoretical foundations group at the Faculty of Informatics of the University of Hamburg. It is worth noting that both the *Mulan*

---
[3]http://jade.tilab.org

Chapter 11 Multi-Agent-Based Simulation (MABS)

MAS architecture and the FIPA compliant *Capa* platform are themselves modelled as executable reference nets with Java inscriptions. While this approach leads to reduced performance in model execution, it provides an explicit and easily understandable architecture for both platform and agent models.

Important concepts of the Mulan architecture are MAS, platforms, agents and protocols. Each Mulan agent consists of a knowledge base and a number of protocols; i.e. task templates which control its communication with other agents. Graphical modelling support for agents and their protocols uses both *AUML* interaction diagrams and Petri nets.

In the conceptual modelling phase a model designer draws interaction diagrams of relevant agent communications. Interaction diagrams are then automatically mapped into protocol templates for the communication's participants, which are represented as Petri nets. To implement an executable agent, the user fills templates with Java code for elementary agent actions. Since the Mulan system is still in a prototype stage, agent modelling suffers from some inconveniences, but the overall approach seems very promising.

Since Mulan's Petri net simulator Renew supports execution of timed Petri nets, simulation scheduler functionality is available. Further built-in simulation support, e.g. for experimental planning, data collection, or result analysis, is currently not offered. However, prototypical data analysis tools, which help in using Renew for discrete and agent-based simulations, have been developed (Strümpel 2003), and several agent-based simulation models, e.g. a simple predator-prey model and an agent-based version of the "Settlers of Catan" parlour game, have been implemented as Mulan models in courses on agent-based software engineering.

Object-Oriented Simulation Frameworks

Swarm and RePast: *Swarm*[4] (Minar et al. 1996) is a MABS framework originally developed at the Santa Fe Institute. Due to a sizeable number of applications and re-implementations it has since become a standard tool for MABS. Swarm offers a discrete simulation framework written in Objective-C. It is particularly suitable for implementing networks of simple reactive agents. Within this context it provides a small number of orthogonal constructs, which can be combined freely. Swarm also contains powerful libraries for tasks such as data collection, random number generation, and graphical instrumentation.

Agents, swarms, and *schedules* are the fundamental building blocks of a Swarm model. Agents serve as simple entities which encapsulate properties and methods, but not behaviour. Instead, behaviour is modelled by allocating agents to swarms and schedules. Swarms in turn are collections of agents whose behaviour they control by invoking their methods at relevant moments in simulation time. To support this strategy, each swarm

---
[4] http://www.swarm.org

11.4 Foundations of Multi-Agent-Based Simulation

owns an event list (schedule), which is ordered on time. Schedules are usually static and cyclic, which maps easily into a fixed-interval time advance strategy. However, it is also possible to schedule method calls dynamically, which can be used to support event-oriented modelling styles.

Its hierarchical structure is one of the strengths of a Swarm model. Swarms can contain other swarms as well as individual agents. In such cases the simulation architecture combines schedules automatically and ensures that events happen in the right sequence. Swarms can therefore be viewed as conceptually concurrent constructs, whose behaviour and interaction generates the overall system dynamics.

The notion of "virtual laboratories" is the basis for experimentation with Swarm. Like DESMO-J, this concept cleanly separates models from simulation experiments. Each simulation program is controlled by a so-called *model swarm*, which may contain hierarchical swarm collections, and *observer swarms*, which encapsulate all observers and data collectors, together with their graphical instrumentation. Observer swarms collect data by either using a separate schedule (time-driven) or under control of events in the model (event-driven). Other responsibilities of observer swarms are the provision of parameters and input data to models. *Graphical observer swarms* provide graphical interfaces, while *batch observer swarms* simply execute and record scripted experiments. *Probes*, which offer a unified interface for reading and writing attribute values, support data collection. This permits model instantiation through generic dialogues and data collection using generic collection objects.

Swarm offers two-dimensional grids for modelling space, as well as support for their graphical display. The framework seems to be well suited for efficient simulation of interactions in large assemblies of simple individuals, which often arise in *Artificial Life* applications. It seems less useful where autonomous agents with high levels of internal complexity must be modelled.

RePast is a Java reimplementation of the core concepts from the Swarm framework that is characterized by its developers as follows[5]:

> "The Recursive Porous Agent Simulation Toolkit (RePast) borrows many concepts from Swarm but has since evolved into an independent simulation package with built-in adaptive features such as genetic algorithms and regression."

FAMOS: The *Framework for Agent-based MOdelling and Simulation* (Knaak et al. 2002) is a DESMO-J extension for MABS. Agents in FAMOS are active DESMO-J entities with an internal schedule of "signals", which they use to communicate with other agents and for turning intentions to action; i.e. as a base for modelling reactive and pro-active behaviour. Agents are based on DESMO-J entities and are implemented as lightweight objects without threads. The handling of signals is delegated to a special

---

[5]See http://repast.sourceforge.net

Chapter 11 Multi-Agent-Based Simulation (MABS)

behaviour object, whose interface serves as a basis for different behaviour modelling techniques (see Figure 11.12). This design is a simplified version of the behaviour modelling architectures found in agent platforms like JADE (see Section 11.4.5) or Madkit[6].

A graphical UML state chart editor eases behaviour description, and declarative modelling styles are supported by integration with the JESS[7] expert system shell. Beyond this, FAMOS can be used with both simple event-driven and process-oriented modelling styles, and seeks to offer a goal-driven architecture for dynamic planning applications (Czogalla and Matzen 2003, pp. 100). Agent organization can be modelled by an extended version of Ferber's AGR model (see Section 11.4.3), which allows hierarchical and spatially defined groups.

FAMOS also provides an extensible framework for spatial modelling (Meyer 2001). Spatial models can be defined in terms of discrete regular grids (as in Swarm), non-rectangular and irregular grids, graphs (e.g. for road networks), or continuous representations with so-called "obstructed planes". Different patterns of movement, such as random walks, following gradients, or route planning, are provided for all spatial models. Agent and model attributes can be observed using probes, similar to Swarm. FAMOS has been used to support funded research projects for modelling city courier services (Knaak et al. 2003) and passenger movement in planes (Czogalla and Matzen 2003).

Simulation Systems for MABS

SeSAm: The *ShEll for Simulated Agent SysteMs*[8] (Klügl 2001) has been developed at Würzburg University. The original implementation in CLOS, an object-oriented extension to Common Lisp, has recently been replaced by a platform independent Java version.

SeSAm offers a visual framework for modelling agent behaviour, as well as a time-slice-based simulator, two-dimensional grids for representing environments, and a graphical interface for controlling experiments and their evaluation. Behaviour descriptions are rule-driven. Agents choose activities based on what rules will apply to a given state of environment and then perform the prescribed sequence of primitive actions. This means that agents need not to test all, but only a subset of rules which are relevant to its current activity. SeSam refers to this innovation as an *activity automaton*. By embedding activity automata as states in other automata, hierarchical styles of behaviour modelling become possible.

The SeSAm interface asks model designers to specify rules by filling a form and choose from prepackaged predicates and primitive sensor and effector actions. Addi-

---

[6] http://www.madkit.org
[7] http://herzberg.ca.sandia.gov/jess
[8] http://www.simsesam.de

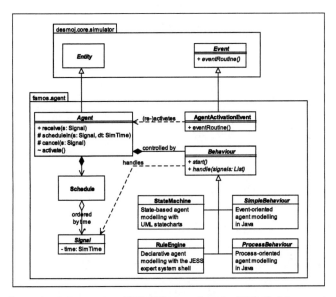

Figure 11.12: Integration of FAMOS agents into the DESMO-J framework (adopted with modifications from Knaak et al. 2002)

tional dialogues allow combinations of predicates and actions to form "higher level" abstractions.

SeSAm also provides graphical editors for designing activity automata in a notation resembling UML activity diagrams, and for placing agents in grids. Its graphical interface for experimentation offers animation as well as interactive control over model execution and the design of experiments. Simple statistics and diagrams are created from *trace data* collected during a model's simulation run. SeSAm has recently been extended for interaction with the FIPA compliant JADE agent platform.

11.5 Conclusion: Potentials, Limitations, and Prospects for MABS

Much of the following summary of multi-agent-based simulation's potential and limits is taken from Klügl (2001, Ch. 3.6), while some prospects have been added concerning the validation of such models in particular.

Chapter 11 Multi-Agent-Based Simulation (MABS)

The MABS metaphor offers a natural perspective for many systems composed of autonomous actors. It allows detailed models of heterogeneous agent societies to be built in an intuitive way, with only a few restrictions concerning agent behaviour, patterns of interaction, and the representation of space. This makes it superior to other formalisms, such as cellular automata or process-oriented simulation models. When a common communication language is used, agents with different complexity and architecture can be combined easily in the same model. While MABS are a natural extension of object-oriented simulations, they add more complex interaction protocols and AI methods like planning and learning. MABS therefore contribute useful functionality to simulation methodology, while simulation technology adds an important model validation technique to agent-based software engineering (Moss 2004).

Limitations of MABS include the difficulty of finding the right level of modelling detail (Klügl 2001, p. 83). While this is a common concern for all types of simulation technologies, the pronounced lack of restrictions on agent-based modelling styles makes it a particularly worrying issue here. Detailed models with complex agents are difficult to design and implement. They are often computationally very complex and hard to validate. On the other hand, simple models like SugarScape (see Section 11.4.1) are often too abstract to draw valid and useful conclusions for any real-life model they may correspond to.

Another problem which MABS shares with other types of simulation is that not enough "real" data may be available to model complex agent behaviour in a valid fashion. Agent-based models take micro-level modelling perspectives, which makes them difficult to calibrate where the intended macro-level behaviour of a reference system cannot easily be reproduced (Klügl 2001, p. 83). Due to the large amounts of data observed at the micro-level, even simple MABS models require complex output analyses (Sanchez and Lucas 2002). The behaviour of MABS is also often nonlinear or chaotic; i.e. small changes in initial conditions can lead to large fluctuations in simulation trajectories (Rand et al. 2003). This makes reliable input data and good parameter calibration a particularly crucial requirement.

At the implementation level of MABS, agent concepts are rarely used (Drougoul et al. 2002). Since MABS and classical discrete simulation each have their own user communities with their own specific concerns, there have been many "reinventions of the wheel". Better communication between fields could do much to help avoid such undesirable duplication of effort.

While agent-based simulation techniques have come a long way from their simple beginnings in trying to simulate the emergence of "life", and have migrated into many other areas of application, further development is continuing. Some key prospects for future improvements to MABS are:

❑ *Better validation methods*: Pattern-based validation (Rand et al. 2003) asks that certain macroscopic patterns that valid models must reproduce are defined before models are built, and then requires them to be present in the model. Trace

11.5 Conclusion: Potentials, Limitations, and Prospects for MABS

analysis and visualization can help to improve understanding of agent behaviour at the micro-level.

❑ *Tool support for analysis and validation*: An example for this is the application of data mining tools to detect cause-effect relationships in MABS as proposed by Remondino and Correndo (2005).

❑ *Tool support for calibration*: The calibration of individual level parameters remains one of the hardest problems in MABS (Oechslein et al. 1999, p. 1). Simulation-based optimization in the sense of Chapter 13 might be a promising approach to support this. For a case study see e.g. (Bachmann et al. 2004).

❑ *Participatory simulation* (Drougoul et al. 2002): Complex behaviour of human-like actors might be modelled by providing agents with the ability to "learn" behaviour by observing live actors.

❑ *Better documentation of models and their assumptions*. There is an urgent need for improvements in this area if better reuse is to be made of existing models and frameworks. Better documentation would also improve communication and cooperation among MABS researchers (Edmonds 2000).

Further Reading

Much of the material and structure of this chapter has been derived from a German textbook; i.e. *Multiagentensimulation* by Klügl (2001, "Multi-Agent Simulation"). At the time of writing this was, to our knowledge, the only text dealing exclusively with multi-agent-based simulation.

A chapter on using MABS in the context of social simulations can also be found in Troitzsch's *Simulation for the Social Scientist* (Gilbert and Troitzsch 1999), and Adele Uhrmacher (2000) has written an introductory article on agent-oriented simulation in which she discusses the three views described in Section 11.3.

Good introductions to the more general field of multi-agent systems, which make a few references to multi-agent-based simulation, are offered by Wooldridge (2003) and Ferber (1995). Finally, many insights into current MABS research are to be found in the proceedings of the *MABS conferences*, which have been published in Springer's *Lecture Notes in Artificial Intelligence* (LNAI) since 1998.

A free source for current information on research using agent-based social simulation is the web-based magazine *JASSS* at http://jasss.soc.surrey.ac.uk.

Bibliography

H. J. Ahn and S. J. Park. A Multi-Agent System using JADE for Simulation of Supply Chains. In *4th Asian Business Workshop*, Chengu, August 2004. [Online] http://www.ebiz.uestc.edu.cn/documents/ppt_pdf/session 3/3-1 ahn,hyung jun.pdf (in August 2005).

R. Bachmann, B. Gehlsen, and N. Knaak. Werkzeuggestützte Kalibrierung agentenbasierter Simulationsmodelle ("Tool-Supported Calibration of Agent-Based Simulation Models", in German). In T. Schulze, S. Schlechtweg, and V. Hinz, editors, *Proceedings Simulation und Visualisierung 2004*, pages 115–126, SCS-Europe, Magdeburg, March 2004.

B. Bauer and J. Odell. *UML 2.0 and Agents: How to Build Agent-based Systems with the new UML Standard*. Research Report, University of Augsburg, 2004.

F. Bellifemine, A. Poggi, and G. Rimassa. Developing Multi-Agent-Systems with JADE. In C. Castelfranchi and Y. Lesperance, editors, *Intelligent Agents VII*, pages 89–103, Springer, Berlin, 2001.

J. A. Botía, A. López-Acosta, and A. F. Gómez-Skarmeta. ACLAnalyser: A Tool for Debugging Multi-Agent Systems. In R. López de Mántaras and L. Saitta, editors, *Proceedings of the 16th Eureopean Conference on Artificial Intelligence*, pages 967–968, IOS, Valencia, 2004.

M. Bratman. *Intention, Plans and Practical Reason*. Harvard University, Cambridge, 1987.

L. Braubach, A. Pokahr, W. Lamersdorf, K.-H. Krempels, and P.-O. Woelk. Time Synchronization for Process Flows in Multi-Agent Systems. In *Second Seminar on Advanced Research in Electronic Business (EBR03)*, 2003.

R. Brooks. *Cambrian Intelligence – A Short History of the New AI*. MIT, Cambridge, 1999.

P. Cariani. Emergence and Artificial Life. In C. G. Langton, C. Taylor, J. D. Farmer, and S. Rasmussen, editors, *Artificial Life II*, Addison-Wesley, Reading, 1991.

R. Czogalla and B. Matzen. *Agentenbasierte Simulation von Personenbewegungen in kontinuierlichem Raum* ("Agent-Based Simulation of Pedestrian Movement in Continuous Space", in German). Diploma Thesis, Faculty of Informatics, University of Hamburg, December 2003.

A. Drougoul, D. Vanbergue, and T. Meurisse. Multi-Agent-Based Simulation: Where are the Agents. In J. Simao Sichman, F. Bousquet, and P. Davidsson, editors, *Multi-Agent-Based Simulation II*, pages 2–15, Springer, Berlin, 2002.

M. Duvignau. *Bereitstellung einer Agentenplattform für petrinetzbasierte Agenten* ("An Agent-Platform for Petri Net-Based Agents", in German). Diploma Thesis, Faculty of Informatics, University of Hamburg, 2003.

B. Edmonds. The Use of Models – making MABS more informative. In S. Moss and P. Davidson, editors, *Multi Agent Based Simulation 2000*, pages 15–32, Springer, Berlin, 2000.

Bibliography

J. M. Epstein and R. Axtell. *Growing Artificial Societies – Social Science from the Bottom Up.* MIT, Cambridge, 1996.

J. Ferber. *Multi-Agent Systems.* Addison-Wesley, Harlow, 1995.

J. Ferber and O. Gutknecht. A Meta-Model for the Analysis and Design of Organizations in Multi-Agent Systems. In *Third International Conference on Multi-Agent Systems (ICMAS '98) Proceedings.* IEEE Computer Society, 1998.

S. Franklin and A. Graesser. Is it an Agent or just a Program? A Taxonomy for Autonomous Agents. In *Proceedings of the Third International Workshop on Agent Theories, Architectures, and Languages,* published as *Intelligent Agents III,* pages 21–35, Springer, New York, 1997.

N. Gilbert. Simulation: An Emergent Perspective. In *Conference on New Technologies in the Social Sciences,* Bournemouth, 1996.

N. Gilbert and K. G. Troitzsch. *Simulation for the Social Scientist.* Open University, Buckingham, 1999.

M. L. Griss, S. Fonseca, D. Cowan, and R. Kessler. Using UML State Machine Models for More Precise and Flexible JADE Agent Behaviors. In F. Giunchiglia, J. Odell, and G. Weiss, editors, *Agent-Oriented Software Engineering III: Third International Workshop 2002 in Bologna,* pages 113–125, Springer, Berlin, 2002.

S. Haykin. *Neural Networks – A Comprehensive Foundation.* Prentice Hall, Upper Saddle River, 2nd edition, 1999.

J. Holland. *Emergence.* Helix, 1998.

N. R. Jennings, K. Sycara, and M. Wooldridge. A Roadmap of Agent Research and Development. *Autonomous Agents and Multi-Agent Systems,* 1(1):7–38, 1998.

S. Jones. Organizing Relations and Emergence. In R. K. Standish, M. A. Bedau, and H. A. Abbass, editors, *Artificial Life VIII,* pages 418–422, MIT, Cambridge, 2003.

F. Klügl. *Multiagentensimulation – Konzepte, Werkzeuge, Anwendung* ("Multi-Agent Simulation – Concepts, Tools, Application", in German). Agententechnologie. Addison-Wesley, Munich, 2001.

N. Knaak, R. Meyer, and B. Page. Agentenbasierte Simulation mit einem objektorientierten Framework in Java ("Agent-Based Simulation with an Object-Oriented Framework in Java", in German). In D. Tavangarian and R. Grützner, editors, *Frontiers in Simulation (12),* Rostock, September 2002.

N. Knaak, R. Meyer, and B. Page. Agent-Based Simulation of Sustainable Logistic Concepts for Large City Courier Services. In A. Gnauck and R. Heinrich, editors, *Proceedings of the EnviroInfo 2003 – 17th. International Conference Informatics for Environmental Protection,* pages 318–325, Metropolis, Marburg, September 2003.

O. Kummer. *Referenznetze* ("Reference Nets", in German). PhD Thesis, Faculty of Informatics, University of Hamburg, 2002.

G. F. Luger. *Artificial Intelligence – Structures and Strategies for Complex Problem Solving.* Addison-Wesley, Reading, 4th edition, 2002.

R. Meyer. Bewegungsgraphen – Ein Konzept für die räumliche Modellierung der Umgebung in der individuen- und agenten-basierten Simulation ("Movement Graphs – A Concept for Spatial Environment Modelling in Individual- and Agent-Based Simula-

Bibliography

tion", in German). In J. Wittman and L. Bernard, editors, *Simulation in Umwelt- und Geowissenschaften – Workshop Münster*, pages 47–60, Shaker, Aachen, 2001.

N. Minar et al. *The Swarm Simulation System: A Toolkit for Building Multi-Agent Simulations*. Research Report, Santa Fe Institute, 1996.

S. Moss. *Intuition and Observation in the Design of Multi Agent Systems*. Research Report, Centre for Policy Modelling, Manchester Metropolitan University Business School, 2004.

J. P. Müller. *The Design of Intelligent Agents – A Layered Approach*. Springer, Berlin, 1996.

C. Oechslein, F. Klügl, R. Herrler, and F. Puppe. UML for Behaviour-Oriented Multi-Agent Simulations. In B. Dunin-Keplicz and E. Nawarecki, editors, *Proceedings of the CEEMAS*, number 2296 in Lecture Notes in Artificial Intelligence, pages 217–226, Springer, Berlin, 2001.

C. Oechslein, F. Klügl, and F. Puppe. Kalibrierung von Multiagentenmodellen ("Calibration of Multi-Agent Models", in German). In *13. Workshop der ASIM-Fachgruppe Simulation und Künstliche Intelligenz, Chemnitzer Informatik-Berichte (CSR-99-03)*, Chemnitz, 1999.

T. I. Ören. Agent-Directed Simulation – Challenges to Meet Defense and Civilian Requirements. In J. A. Joines, R. R. Barton, K. Kang, and P. A. Fishwick, editors, *Proceedings of the 2000 Winter Simulation Conference*, pages 1757–1762, 2000. [Online] http://informs-cs.org/wsc00papers/prog00.html (in August 2005).

A. Pokahr, L. Braubach, and W. Lamersdorf. *Jadex: Implementing a BDI-Infrastructure for JADE Agents. EXP – in search of innovation (Special Issue on JADE)*, 3(3):76–85, 9 2003.

W. Rand et al. Statistical validation of spatial patterns in agent-based models. In *Agent-Based Simulation 4*, Montpellier, 2003.

A. S. Rao and M. P. Georgeff. BDI Agents: From Theory to Practice. In V. Lesser, editor, *Proceedings of the First International Conference on Multi-Agent Systems*, pages 312–319. MIT, 1995.

M. Remondino and G. Correndo. Data Mining Applied to Agent Based Simulation. In Y. Merkuryev, R. Zobel, and E. Kerckhoffs, editors, *Proceedings of the 19th European Conference on Modelling and Simulation*, pages 374–380, SCS-Europe, Riga, June 2005.

H. Rölke. *Modellierung von Agenten und Multiagentensystemen: Grundlagen und Anwendungen* ("Modelling Agents and Multi-Agent Systems: Foundations and Applications", in German). PhD Thesis, Faculty of Informatics, University of Hamburg, 2004.

S. Russel and P. Norvig. *Artificial Intelligence – A Modern Approach*. Prentice Hall, Upper Saddle River, 2nd edition, 2003.

S. M. Sanchez and T. W. Lucas. Exploring the World of Agent-Based Simulations: Simple Models, Complex Analyses. In E. Yücesan, C.-H. Chen, J. L. Snowdon, and J. M. Charnes, editors, *Proceedings of the 2002 Winter Simulation Conference*, pages 116–126, 2002. [Online] http://www.wintersim.org/prog02.htm (in August 2005).

Bibliography

M. P. Singh, A. S. Rao, and M. P. Georgeff. Intelligent Agents. In G. Weiss, editor, *Multiagent Systems*, chapter 8. MIT, Cambridge, 1999.

O. Spaniol and S. Hoff. *Ereignisorientierte Simulation – Konzepte und Systemrealisierung* ("Event-Oriented Simulation – Concepts and System Implementation", in German). Thomson's Aktuelle Tutorien; 7. Thomson, Bonn, 1995.

F. Strümpel. *Simulation zeitdiskreter Modelle mit Referenznetzen* ("Simulation of Time-Discrete Models with Reference Nets", in German). Diploma Thesis, Faculty of Informatics, University of Hamburg, 2003.

A. M. Uhrmacher. Agentenorientierte Simulation ("Agent-Oriented Simulation", in German). In H. Szczerbicka and T. Uthmann, editors, *Modellierung, Simulation und Künstliche Intelligenz ("Modelling, Simulation, and Artificial Intelligence", in German)*, pages 15–45, SCS-Europe, Ghent, 2000.

C. Urban. Entwicklung und Einsatz eines Referenzmodells für Multiagentensysteme ("development and application of a reference model for multi-agent systems", in german). In A. Kuhn and S. Wenzel, editors, *Simulationstechnik – 11. Symposium in Dortmund*, number 10 in Fortschritte in der Simulationstechnik, Wiesbaden, November 1997.

R. von Lüde, D. Moldt, R. Valk, and M. Köhler. *Sozionik – Modellierung soziologischer Theorie* ("Socionics – Modelling Sociological Theory", in German). Lit, Münster, 2003.

M. Wooldridge. Intelligent Agents. In G. Weiss, editor, *Multiagent Systems*, chapter 1. MIT, Cambridge, 1999.

M. Wooldridge. *An Introduction to Multiagent Systems*. Wiley, West Sussex, 2003.

Chapter 12

Parallel and Distributed Simulation

Björn Gehlsen, Bernd Page

Contents

12.1 Motivation and Overview	373
12.2 Synchronization	374
12.3 Modes of Distribution	376
12.3.1 Parallel Simulation	377
12.3.2 Component-Based Simulation	378
12.3.3 Web-Based Simulation	380
Further Reading	382
Bibliography	383

12.1 Motivation and Overview

Statistical arguments often suggest multiple replications of simulation runs and can lead to experimental designs which result in very long computations. This computational load increases even further whenever attempts at optimization (see Chapter 13) are made. For this reason the use of special purpose hardware and multiprocessors to speed-up a simulation run has long been attractive. Aided by further advances in hardware and middleware technologies, the allocation of workloads to different processors or machines, and the parallel execution of independent tasks now holds much promise for large scale simulations.

The increased integration and interconnection of computers within the research community and easy access to the Internet as a global communication resource favour the use of distributed computation. Both simulation-specific and general computational tasks can be distributed across networks of standard PCs and workstations which would otherwise run idle. Modern distributed systems technology offers transparent access to distributed resources and mediates convenient interfaces to special applications. Distributed systems have therefore become an important tool for pursuing computationally

Chapter 12 Parallel and Distributed Simulation

intensive goals, such as the simulation of complex systems and simulation-based optimization.

Both the development and operation of distributed systems produce additional costs. However, the ability to use remote resources offers sufficient advantages to justify this expenditure. Primary among these are the *run time* reductions provided by parallel execution. Such efficiency improvements are particularly important for time-critical tasks. In addition, we may gain from the possibility of integrating resources by different manufacturers and across different hardware and software boundaries. In this way *interoperability* of legacy systems, single applications, or component-based partial solutions can be obtained without re-implementation. Provided they are constructed in a way which allows quick replacement of individual processors or system components when they malfunction, distributed systems also exhibit a higher degree of *fault tolerance*.

In view of these benefits one can almost neglect the effects of communication errors caused by data transmissions. If a distributed system can be suitably partitioned, even delays induced by longer transmission times play a minor role only. What is important, is that patterns of synchronization between distributed processes can guarantee the correctness of simulation results. This section therefore first looks at some relevant synchronization techniques. Later, the potential of using distributed systems technology for simulation is surveyed more fully.

12.2 Synchronization

Whenever computing tasks are dispatched on distributed systems, the exact order in which individual steps are performed becomes dependent on a number of external factors (e.g. transmission delays) and is therefore hard to control. Since producing the same results as a serial process is an important requirement for any successful parallelization, we must take great care to synchronize parallel processes at all relevant points in their life cycles. A number of different *synchronization strategies* have been designed to attend to this task.

Preserving "real world" causality in a model requires that all its events must occur before all of their direct or indirect consequences. Processes operate on events by changing status and process variables, and by scheduling new events engaging themselves and others. If, as in parallel simulation runs, events must be processed concurrently, it must be assured that all *causality constraints* are attended to. This means, for example, that an event E may be processed only after all other events by which it could be affected have happened. No cyclic causal dependencies (e.g. E depends on D, which depends on E) can be allowed.

Sequential execution on a single processor preserves causality constraints by using a single event list. Scheduled events in this list are sorted by their event times. When using multiprocessor systems or distributed computations, a maximum speed increase is

12.2 Synchronization

obtained by striving for as high a degree of parallelism as possible. This requires that the event list is skilfully partitioned and that the events' execution is cleverly delegated to processors. In this context dependencies between events executed on different processors must receive particularly careful attention.

Processes in a real system are represented by logical processes in a model. The model's state variables are partitioned among the processes such that each logical process influences only a subset of all possible state variables. State variables of other logical processes can only be accessed by sending a message. Assuming sufficient resources, the simplest parallelization would assign separate processors to each of the logical processes. If all local causality constraints can be preserved, it can also be shown that the model's causality as a whole is assured. However, a process may also attend to events of whose needs it is notified by a message sent by another process. In a distributed context there is unfortunately no absolute and global simulation time across all model processes, since their progress may depend on effectively unpredictable conditions at remote sites. To demand that all processes always advance in synchronized steps would negate any speed-ups we hope to gain from parallelization. In distributed simulations therefore no shared model clock or common event list exists (see Coulouris et al. 1994, pp. 288–289 or Law and Kelton 2000, p. 82).

Although these constraints make parallel execution of interacting processes a challenging task, a number of patterns have been found to assure "safe" synchronizations. A common distinction is drawn between so-called "conservative" and so-called "optimistic" techniques. While conservative synchronizations take great care to avoid the occurrence of causality violations, optimistic strategies may only take notice once they have happened – causing a "rollback" of all actions which have been performed prematurely (Praehofer and Reisinger 2000, p. 90). Whether to be conservative or optimistic hinges on how much and what types of interaction a model's processes generate. If synchronizations occur only rarely, it seems attractive to let all processors run at "full speed" and pay the price for a (rare) rollback when needed. If process synchronizations are frequent, however, any parallelization speed-ups we gain may well be negated by frequent rollbacks' computational expense.

Conservative synchronization strategies (Fujimoto 2000, p. 51) avoid causality violations by guaranteeing for each process that an event E is processed only if no other events are scheduled prior to it in the same process. In addition they require that in every other process all events which might impact on E must also be processed completely before E can happen. This raises the question of how to detect other processes' progress. One possible solution uses signals for synchronization. For example, sending a *null message* with time stamp T can signal that the sender will not schedule any events with a time of occurrence prior to T. Under the assumption that all processes continually send and receive such messages to and from their peers (i.e. other processes), a given process can conclude that events scheduled for T (or earlier) can safely proceed if all other processes have sent null messages with time stamp T (or later).

Chapter 12 Parallel and Distributed Simulation

Cyclic dependencies of scheduled events in the event lists of different processes carry the risk of a *deadlock*. Deadlocks must either be avoided, or recognized and resolved. This also needs the implementation of suitable strategies. For example, a process could broadcast a message telling all others that it will not generate any events for some short future time interval (lookahead time). The success of this method will of course depend on choosing the right length of this lookahead interval, and its appropriate choice requires detailed knowledge of model semantics.

In contrast to conservative strategies, *optimistic strategies* do not attempt to preserve causality while distributed processes process events (Fujimoto 2000, p. 97). Instead, the possibility of causality violations is accepted in return for gains in execution efficiency. If eventually causality violations occur, they are recognized and dealt with; i.e. all state changing actions which were processed too early will be revoked (*rollback*). In addition, all effects of these actions elsewhere in the model must also be cancelled. The concept of "anti messages" allows a process to ask other processes to recursively cancel all state transitions and messages which occurred after the time it "rolls back" to. Sufficiently detailed state information must be kept to recover model states prior to a causality violation. The whole process has been compared to a "time warp".

The advantages of conservative strategies include smaller storage requirement and easier implementation. No information for rollbacks needs to be monitored and stored. This must be weighed against the cost of delaying processes (and processors) waiting for notifications that it is now safe to proceed. Optimistic strategies do not delay processes (and processors) in this manner. For models with a low rate of synchronization, execution can therefore be faster. If there are many synchronization points, however, the computational efforts associated with state logging and rollbacks will cause significant slowdown and will quickly negate this advantage.

As a result, conservative strategies are better suited for models with a relatively high level of process interaction, which would require the effort of numerous rollbacks in the case of optimistic strategies. On the other hand, optimistic strategies excel where processes are largely independent and require infrequent synchronizations. Praehofer and Reisinger (2000, p. 97) discuss a number of different hybrid synchronization schemes. Any decision whether and which form of parallelization to use should be made early; i.e. at the time a model is designed. Individual subsystems can then be described in whatever style maximizes process independence and minimizes synchronization overhead as much as possible.

12.3 Modes of Distribution

The term *distributed simulation* describes the execution of simulation models on several processors. Distributed simulations can be categorized into *parallel simulations*, which focus on delegation of workloads to remote machines, *component-based simulations*, which emphasise interoperability of independently developed simulation functionality,

12.3 Modes of Distribution

and *web-based simulations*, which concentrate on accessing remote services using Internet technology, especially the WWW. In this context remote services include simulation specific (e.g. random number generation, synchronization techniques) as well as application specific tasks (e.g. customer requests, order data, current weather or traffic information). Since hybrid models combine aspects, this classification cannot always be precise.

12.3.1 Parallel Simulation

Simulation experiments often cause long computations. *Parallel simulation* is a special form of distributed simulation which aims to reduce a simulation's duration (i.e. its run time) by parallel execution of multiple tasks.

We can further distinguish between parallel execution of independent experiments with a single model and the concurrent execution of several processes in a model on different processors (i.e. as part of a single experiment). In the latter case causality must be preserved by careful process synchronization (see above).

This need for synchronization poses a challenge for any distributed execution of processes. To preserve local causality, individual logical processes may make no use of shared variables. Their allocation to different processors therefore partitions the state space (space parallel simulation). Similarly it is also feasible to parallelize long simulation runs by partitioning their time axis (time parallel simulation). Following (Fujimoto 2000, p. 178) the two techniques are contrasted in Figure 12.1. Here the time axis is partitioned into non-overlapping intervals $[T_0, T_1), [T_1, T_2), \ldots, [T_{n-1}, T_n]$, with a single logical process assigned to each.

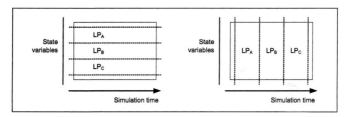

Figure 12.1: Space parallel simulation and time parallel simulation

An advantage of time parallel simulations is their high degree of parallelism during long simulation runs. If logical processes are independent, no synchronization is needed once a simulation has started.

However, because system state at the start of the $i + 1$-th interval cannot readily be computed without knowing the final state during the i-th interval, a "state matching problem" occurs. Methods to solve this problem are described in Fujimoto (2000,

Chapter 12 Parallel and Distributed Simulation

p. 179). The main drawback of all of them is the need for special knowledge of application semantics. No general claims can therefore be made for different types of application. Also, the question regarding optimal partitioning points for the time axis can only be answered heuristically; i.e. no guarantees for a solution's quality can be given. Time parallel simulations are therefore not considered as robust (Fujimoto 2000, p. 190). In spite of these cautions, improvements over conventional execution can be achieved in special cases; e.g. for processes with cyclic activity, well-known periods, and recurring or easily predictable conditions at the start of each cycle.

12.3.2 Component-Based Simulation

In recent years there has been a growing shift of interest away from parallel execution of independent simulation runs towards distributed execution of individual model components on separate processors. Spatially distributed and heterogeneous systems are most often involved in this type of distributed simulation, which we should more accurately refer to as component-based simulation.

Component-based simulations are implemented as assemblies of cooperating components, solving a common simulation task. This includes parallel simulation as a special case (see Section 12.3.1). The main objective of component-based simulation is not run time acceleration through parallel computation, but rather the integration of distributed services and the use of different heterogeneous resources to accomplish a common goal. Its focus is on the reusability of simulation functionality in different contexts, and on avoiding repeated implementation expenditure. For example, consider a component which provides random numbers drawn from a specified distribution. Such functionality will be useful for a majority of all simulation projects and could therefore be made available as a remote service.

In contrast to the parallel simulation approach, component-based simulations usually suffer from reduced speed, caused by the need to overcome the heterogeneity of its components and any additional overhead required to cross system borders. However, this is rewarded with faster model implementation; at least as long as suitable components are available. Although some speed up can be obtained by concurrent execution of replicated individual components, component-based simulation's primary goal remains the interoperability of heterogeneous simulation models and the reusability of simulation-specific services in different contexts. This cooperation of software modules across different hardware platforms, operating systems, and programming languages, which would not be feasible otherwise, opens many new areas to the application of simulation techniques.

The *Common Object Request Broker Architecture* (CORBA) is an established communication standard for distributed objects, which was developed by the members of the Object Management Group (OMG). It offers a suitable software base for component-based simulations. Several public domain (free) and commercial implementations of the CORBA standard are available. The so-called "High level Architecture (HLA)"

12.3 Modes of Distribution

has been developed since 1995 as an initiative of the Defense Modeling and Simulation Office (DMSO); an institution attached to the US-American Department of Defense (DoD). HLA's objective is to guarantee interoperability of existing and new simulation components developed or funded by the DoD (Fujimoto 1998). To meet this goal, HLA augments CORBA with simulation-specific functionality (called "federates"), such as techniques for component synchronization.

As many civilian applications of HLA outside the American military exist (Schulze et al. 1999), it has now established itself as a distributed simulation standard. Because of the lengthy time periods associated with any standardization effort[1], many simulation models which where developed in parallel with the ongoing standardization do not fully conform with all its requirements. In such cases interoperability must still be established by "manual" means.

In Zeigler et al. (2000, pp. 142, 261) a formalization of parallel simulation is framed in terms of DEVS (discrete event simulation system specification). This proposal aims to provide a general methodology for parallelizing discrete event systems, with particular emphasis on component-based simulations. Praehofer and Reisinger (2000, p. 96) also discusses a parallel simulator based on DEVS, which is targeted at parallel computers and models containing only few processes.

The MOBILE research project at Hamburg University assumes that partitioning a model's functionality into separate components offers a solid foundation for their distributed execution, and that this can also improve the reusability of components developed by others. The interface description language MSL (MOBILE Script Language, see Mügge and Meyer 1996 and Hilty et al. 1998) was designed to support this. MSL permits the description of communications between model components, of which more complex models can be composed later. Alongside its purpose to find and reuse models as "higher-level" components in others (Mügge et al. 1997, p. 388), such descriptions include definitions of the compound systems' structure.

Bachmann (2003) also presents a proposal for partitioning simulation systems, which he calls CoSim (Component Based Distributed Simulation). CoSim supports the interoperability of simulation components by acting as an automatic "adapter generator". CAGE (CoSim Adapter Generator) is CoSim's Java-based incarnation. It automatically generates adapter classes which allow the use of existing models as distributed components in HLA-style federations. This facilitates the cooperation of heterogeneous building blocks in a distributed simulation environment, without the need for re-implementation.

---

[1] OMG and IEEE came to a provisional agreement on this standard in 2000.

Chapter 12 Parallel and Distributed Simulation

12.3.3 Web-Based Simulation

The term "web-based simulation" has been applied to many diverse concepts and systems. At an extreme end of this spectrum, even a tutorial for a simulator accessed via the WWW could be referred to as "web-based simulation" (Neidhardt 2000). Web-based simulation services in a broader sense are also exemplified by projects which support web-based cooperation between partners who simply use simulation tools; e.g. through electronic manuals (as in Straßburger and Schulze 2001, p. 173).

More appropriate uses of the term "web-based simulation" refer to the execution of simulation models in a web-based environment. Such simulations often follow a client/server pattern; i.e. a client uses the services offered by a simulation server (Straßburger and Schulze 2001, p. 170). This is in contrast to the predominantly peer-to-peer architecture of the distributed simulations we have discussed so far. While there is a control component – which is mainly responsible for discovering what services are available – web-based simulations in this narrower sense are meant to orchestrate collaborations between different components at the same hierarchy level.

"Batch-oriented" can be distinguished from interactive tools, based on the services they provide on remote or local computers. In the first case (batch-orientation), a remote computer is used as an application server; e.g. it implements Java Servlets. In the second case (interactivity), a local computer acts as a file server for mobile code; e.g. it embeds Java applets in a web browser.

The basic idea and main objective of web-based simulation is to make use of the location-independence and platform transparency of the WWW in order to offer simulation services in terms of either code or data. Model re-implementations may be required to meet this goal. This is acceptable, since web-based simulations do not focus on interoperability of services in the same way as component-based simulations do.

So far remote simulation services are not common and have generally remained limited to rather unique contexts. There are examples of models embedded in browsers, which, when supplied with appropriate inputs over the Internet, trigger remote simulations, whose results they receive and display. Since complex models are usually well adapted for the needs of their specific context of application, it is a difficult task to find existing models whose characteristics meet given problem specifications. Although such models serve some well defined purposes well, a set of customizable model components and web services can clearly offer more flexibility and reusability than CORBA, HLA, and RMI[2] can provide.

By means of web services simulation-specific or user-specific functionality can be made available over the web. Data requirements and interfaces can be described using extensible markup language (XML) and the Internet can take on the role of a globally accessible medium of transportation. Web services also allow composition of models from distributed parts, a task for which directory services (repositories) help in locating suitable components. Because of user inertia, missing standards, and tools, however,

---
[2]Remote Method Invocation

12.3 Modes of Distribution

web services have proved to be difficult to establish. Due to web services' profits this will certainly change in the near future.

Flexible delegation of simulation tasks over the Internet has now become possible. This means that web-based simulation services can be offered, as proposed in Wiedemann (2001) and Wiedemann and Krug (2002), where concepts for a simulation-oriented application service (ASP) are presented. While modelling services can still be provided in the same way we referred to above, externally developed remote components can also be integrated into models which have been developed locally. The resulting ease of model construction is particularly attractive for small and medium-sized enterprises (SME), for which conventional modelling styles represent a very large obstacle. By interfacing with web-based simulation models or by using remotely provided components, they can make use of simulation technologies in a much easier and faster way.

One of the highest hurdles for increasing the popularity of web based simulations lies in the field of data's security and the difficulty of billing for services. Since customers are often asked to provide sensitive data for driving a model, trust and security are essential prerequisites for acceptance, and without any reliable means of billing for services there is no or only low motivation to develop and offer components for commercial use. If this new technology is to "take off", a critical mass of industry-wide and simulation-specific web-services will be required. The military and automobile industry are encouraging examples for sectors where simulation technology has steadily gained in importance.

It is far from trivial to retrieve and customize model components obtained from the web or from special collections. Fishwick (1997) suggests distributed model repositories, which document models and model fragments and make them available web-wide. In 1997, he suggested a formalization of model-relevant meta information in the IDF (independent definition file) format. Such a uniform means of description and keyword indexing of models and model components would be of great help to browsing and searching. Results of a search could then even be returned in a form which would make easy access to relevant models and model components available (e.g. a URL-like address model://my_Model_Component.models.desmo.de).

Miller et al. (1997) demands that web-based simulation must ensure that models as well as simulation results are just as simple to access and combine as other web documents. For example, it is relatively easy to aggregate different HTML documents into a single web site, even if they reside on different computers and were developed by different authors. Coupling of models, however, is a much more complicated task, since it requires component-based model structures and the capability of embedding simulations into a larger system.

The automated use of simulation-relevant resources, which are globally accessible over the WWW, is also the focus of Seila and Miller (1999). In addition to models and data sources, it discusses tools for supporting scenario management, including experimental designs and control, as well as statistical techniques for the aggregation of simulation results and automatic steady state detection (see Chapter 7).

Chapter 12 Parallel and Distributed Simulation

To help a decision support system to run simulations in the background of other tasks, models should be implemented as "thin clients", which delegate most simulation-specific computations to a remote server.

Finally, as suggested in Chandrasekaran et al. (2002, p. 606), there is a duality between web services and simulation. The development and deployment of services and their compositions can be supported by simulation; both before implementation and before introduction to market. Expected behaviours can be derived and quantified. Such information can be essential for E-commerce applications, which often fail if they are not available immediately after publicity campaigns and if they don't work as expected under full load after a very short introduction phase. On the other hand, web services can provide building blocks for distributed simulation environments. Here we can distinguish three distinct service types. A web service can offer complete models for evaluating scenarios whose parameters are obtained through message- or form-driven interfaces. Commercial services of this nature may charge for each use, or may offer some form of renewable time-based contract (Chandrasekaran et al. 2002, p. 612).

Another possibility is to distribute common simulation infrastructure components over the web. The more easily a component can be separated from the simulation itself, the more feasible it becomes. Offering components in this way can increase flexibility and cash flow, since they are much more widely applicable than a more specialized model. Candidates for such types of distribution include database services, which are needed before the start and after the end of a simulation run; e.g. to provide inputs and to (temporarily) store simulation results. Visualizations, which display simulation results from different perspectives, are also quite independent from the simulation itself. Services concerning statistical preparation of required input data or providing result analysis and statistical measures can also be thought of. The same holds for experimental controllers, with or without functionality for optimization. These can be used to automate experimentation (Gehlsen 2004), see Chapter 13.

The possibility of supporting model federates in the HLA sense (see above) as a web service should also not be overlooked. This becomes particularly attractive if only few interactions between different services are needed. In this case the advantage gained from increased interoperability will easily outweigh the additional costs associated with distribution and the preservation of causality (see above). Extending web services with transaction properties can also be considered (Wiedemann and Krug 2002).

Further Reading

The interested reader is referred to the "Bible" of parallel and distributed simulation, *Parallel and Distributed Simulation Systems* (Fujimoto 2000). The author offers an in-depth survey of discrete event simulation on different hardware platforms using multiple processors. The text is divided into three parts. The first part gives an introduction to the field and describes typical applications for the technology. Discussed hardware ranges from multiprocessor computers and grids of workstations to spatially distributed systems, including web-based configurations. The second part's emphasis is on using multiple processors to speed simulation analyses. Both conservative and optimistic synchronization is covered in detail. The third part is concerned with distributed virtual environments and interactive simulations. These applications – either for training or education – require real-time performance, as well as collaborations between models residing on specialized machines. Thus, remote access via the High Level Architecture (HLA) is discussed in this context.

Bibliography

R. Bachmann. *Ein flexibler, CORBA-basierter Ansatz für die verteilte, komponentenbasierte Simulation* ("A Flexible CORBA-Based Approach of Distributed, Component-Based Simulation", in German). PhD Thesis, Faculty of Informatics, University of Hamburg, 2003.

S. Chandrasekaran, G. Silver, J. A. Miller, J. Cardoso, and A. P. Sheth. Web Service Technologies and their Synergy with Simulation. In E. Yücesan, C.-H. Chen, J. L. Snowdon, and J. M. Charnes, editors, *Proceedings of the 2002 Winter Simulation Conference*, pages 606–615, 2002. [Online] http://www.wintersim.org/prog02.htm (in August 2005).

G. Coulouris, J. Dollimore, and T. Kindberg. *Distributed Systems – Concept and Design*. Addison-Wesley, Wokingham, 1994.

P. A. Fishwick. Web-Based Simulation. In S. Andradóttir, K. J. Healy, D. H. Withers, and B. L. Nelson, editors, *Proceedings of the 1997 Winter Simulation Conference*, pages 100–103, 1997. [Online] http://www.wintersim.org/prog97.htm (in August 2005).

R. Fujimoto. Time Management in the High Level Architecture. *Simulation*, 71(6):388–400, 1998. [Online] http://www.cc.gatech.edu/computing/pads/PAPERS/Time_mgmt_High_Level_Arch.pdf (in August 2005).

R. Fujimoto. *Parallel and Distributed Simulation Systems*. Wiley, New York, 2000.

B. Gehlsen. *Automatisierte Experimentplanung im Rahmen von Simulationsstudien – Konzeption und Realisierung eines verteilten simulationsbasierten Optimierungssystems* ("Automated Experiment Planning within the Scope of Simulation Studies – Conception and Realization of a Distributed, Simulation-Based Optimization System", in German). PhD Thesis, Faculty of Informatics, University of Hamburg, 2004.

L. M. Hilty, B. Page, R. Meyer, H. Mügge, H. Deeecke, C. Reick, B. Gehlsen, M. Hupf, O. Becken, M. Bosselmann, M. Neumann, M. Poll, T. Lechler, and T. Böttger. Instrumente für die ökologische Bewertung und Gestaltung von Verkehrs- und Logistiksystemen ("Instruments for Ecological Assessment and Design of Transportation and Logistics Systems", in German). In C. Ranze, A. Tuma, H.-D. Haasis, and O. Herzog, editors, *Abschlussbericht des Forschungsprojektes MOBILE* ("Final Report on

Bibliography

the MOBILE Research Project", in German). Faculty of Informatics, University of Hamburg, 1998.

A. M. Law and W. D. Kelton. *Simulation Modeling and Analysis*. McGraw-Hill, New York, 3rd edition, 2000.

J. Miller, A. Seila, and X. Xiang. The JSIM Web-Based-Simulation Environment. *Future Generation Computer Systems*, 15, 1997. [Online] http://orion.cs.uga.edu:5080/~jam/jsim (in August 2005).

H. Mügge and R. Meyer. Eine Modell- und Experimentbeschreibungssprache ("A Model and Experiment Description Language", in German). In C. Ranze, A. Tuma, L. M. Hilty, H.-D. Haasis, and O. Herzog, editors, *Intelligente Methoden zur Verarbeitung von Umweltinformationen* ("Intelligent Methods for Processing Ambient Information, in German), pages 165–180, 2. Bremer KI-Pfingstworkshop, Metropolis, Marburg, 1996.

H. Mügge, R. Meyer, L. M. Hilty, and B. Page. Object-Orientated Specification of Models and Experiments in Traffic Simulation. In R. Denzer, D. A. Swayne, and G. Schimak, editors, *Environmental Software Systems*, volume 2, pages 335–342, 11th International Symposium on Environmental Software Systems (ISESS97), Chapman & Hall, London, 1997.

O. Neidhardt. *Erstellung eines WWW basierten Tutorials und Evaluation eines Frameworks zur zeitdiskreten Simulation in JAVA* ("Development of a WWW-Based Tutorial and Evaluation of a Framework for Discrete Event Simulation in JAVA", in German). Diploma Thesis, Faculty of Informatics, University of Hamburg, 2000.

H. Praehofer and G. Reisinger. Komponentenbasierte parallele Simulation unter objektorientierter Realisierung ("Component-Based Parallel Simulation with Object-Oriented Realization", in German). In H. Szczerbicka and T. Uthmann, editors, *Modellierung, Simulation und Künstliche Intelligenz* ("Modelling, Simulation, and Artificial Intelligence", in German), pages 75–109. SCS-Europe, Ghent, 2000.

T. Schulze, S. Straßburger, and U. Klein. *Migration of HLA into Civil Domains: Solutions and Prototypes for Transportation Applications. Simulation*, 73(5):296–303, 1999.

A. F. Seila and J. A. Miller. Web-Based Simulation. In P. A. Farrington, H. B. Nembhard, D. T. Sturrock, and G. W. Evans, editors, *Proceedings of the 1999 Winter Simulation Conference*, pages 1430–1437, 1999. [Online] http://www.wintersim.org/prog99.htm (in August 2005).

S. Straßburger and T. Schulze. Verteilte und Web-basierte Simulation: Gemeinsamkeiten und Unterschiede ("Distributed and Web-Based Simulation: Things in Common and Differences", in German). In K. Panreck and F. Dörrscheidt, editors, *Simulationstechnik* ("Simulation Engineering", in German), pages 168–174, 15. Symposium, SCS-Europe, Ghent, 2001.

T. Wiedemann. Simulation Application Service Providing. In B. A. Peters, J. S. Smith, D. J. Medeiros, and M. W. Rohrer, editors, *Proceedings of the 2001 Winter Simulation Conference*, pages 623–628, 2001. [Online] http://www.wintersim.org/prog01.htm (in August 2005).

Bibliography

T. Wiedemann and W. Krug. Simulation Application Service Providing im webbasierten Umfeld zur simulationsbasierten optimierten Produktionsplanung ("Simulation Application Service Providing in a Web-Based Environment for Simulation-Based, Optimized Production Planning", in German). In D. Tavangarian and R. Grützner, editors, *Simulationstechnik* ("Simulation Engineering", in German), pages 119–124, 16. Symposium, SCS-Europe, Ghent, 2002.

B. Zeigler, H. Praehofer, and T. Kim. *Theory of Modeling and Simulation.* Academic Press, San Diego, 2nd edition, 2000.

Chapter 13

Simulation-Based Optimization

Björn Gehlsen, Johannes Göbel

Contents

13.1 Motivation and Overview	387
13.2 Integration of Simulation and Optimization	388
13.3 A Formal Model for Simulation-Based Optimization Problems	391
13.4 Characteristics of Simulation-Based Objective Functions	392
13.5 Genetic Algorithms	394
13.5.1 Terminology	395
13.5.2 General Strategy	395
13.5.3 Parallelization	397
Further Reading	397
Bibliography	398

13.1 Motivation and Overview

In Chapter 1, this handbook's introduction describes simulation as a method for analysing properties and behaviour of existing systems as well as a tool for studying any system that does not yet exist. Relevant aspects of the modelled system are explored in a series of experiments, also called simulation runs. Varying model parameters within specified bounds leads to better understanding of system behaviour, while well chosen objective functions can quantify the results. Unfortunately, however, simulation is only a descriptive (i.e. it lets us ask "what if" questions) rather than an optimization technique which can answer "how to" questions. The effectiveness of simulation therefore hinges largely on a user's skill in choosing which model parameters to explore. This in turn might require relevant but still not existing experience with the system under consideration.

Optimization techniques guide total or partial analyses of parameter sets. Each of these parameter sets (vectors) represents a scenario, i.e. specified parameter settings under which the system is observed. From the point of view of optimization, these parameter vectors are candidate solutions which are searched for the most favourable behaviour for reaching a given goal, i.e. optimizing an appropriate objective function. If the parameter vector specifies a scenario which violates the system's constraints, it has to be treated as an infeasible solution. While evaluation of each candidate solution can be quite easy, maybe competent decisions on which candidates to evaluate and which to ignore are required because searching the complete solution space in acceptable time is impossible in most cases of practical relevance.

This chapter focuses on the integration of simulation and optimization concepts and the requirements which a simulation-based optimization must meet. In this context we will also look briefly at how genetic algorithms can be used to combine simulation-based optimization with distributed simulation (see Chapter 12).

13.2 Integration of Simulation and Optimization

Attempts to combine simulation with optimization are motivated by the desire to benefit from advantages and avoid disadvantages of both methodologies. Optimization of real-life problems typically requires a large number of simplifying and restrictive assumptions, while simulation can explore only a few of a large space of potential solutions. Searching for (heuristic) optima is therefore not the primary idea of simulation since computational constraints make this infeasible in all but the simplest of cases.

Given this background, integration of simulation and optimization seems a worthwhile attempt to help optimize complex systems that cannot be evaluated analytically. To achieve this, the two methods must be combined in a way which allows more focussed and efficient searches for parameter values which satisfy a specific goal. Since exhaustive search of solution spaces to find optimal scenarios is practically always impossible in acceptable time, solution space searching must rely on heuristic procedures.

The combination of simulation experiments and optimization methods is the subject of *simulation optimization*. In addition to well designed models, simulation studies seeking to optimize system parameters require some quantitative measure of system performance; i.e. an objective function. Based on such objective functions, optimization methods can iteratively generate parameter assignments for possible system configurations, which are then passed to a simulation model as inputs. A typical simulation study performs many such experiments, possibly with multiple replications, whose aggregated results are ranked by the objective function. Such analyses of model configurations measure the "quality" of a range of alternative scenarios and help to find new parameter settings which promise even better results. The ultimate goal of this process is to find system configurations which perform as well as possible; i.e. those with the highest contribution to the objective function's value.

Figure 13.1 can be seen as an extension of Figures 1.6 and 3.4 and shows how to integrate optimization into a simulation study. New parameter assignments for model

13.2 Integration of Simulation and Optimization

configurations which describe relevant system aspects are iteratively proposed by the optimization method. Model behaviour for these settings is then investigated through simulations, whose aggregated results serve as objective function values for the parameter settings. The next iteration of optimization uses these values as a base for further improvements.

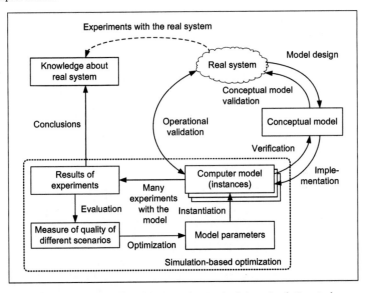

Figure 13.1: Integration of optimization methods in a simulation study

Simulation and optimization often use different terms to refer to related concepts. The most important of these are opposingly listed in Table 13.1.

Table 13.1: Corresponding terms from the simulation and optimization domains

Modelling and simulation	Mathematical optimization
Simulation study (aiming at optimization)	Optimization problem
System configuration / Scenario	Candidate solution
Set of all alternative system configurations	Solution space
Practical realizability	Permissibility (restrictions are met)
Measure of decision quality	Objective function
(Series of) experiments	Calculation of objective function's values
Model parameters	Vector elements of candidate solution

Chapter 13 Simulation-Based Optimization

Figure 13.2 shows interaction between simulation and optimization. Quality measures (i.e. objective functions) are derived from practical applications within a simulation study's domain. Instantiation of experiments is controlled locally. Optimization methods help to determine new assignments for all model parameters which are influenced by results from a previous iteration and explored in further experiments. In distributed simulations each experiment can be delegated to a remote server.

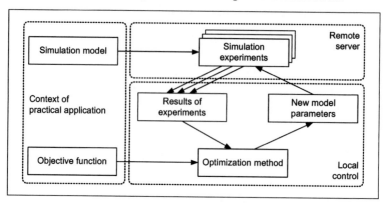

Figure 13.2: Interaction of simulation and optimization by embedding simulation experiments in an iterative optimization process

Optimization and simulation can also be combined in a different way; i.e. optimization can be used *within* simulation models. One context in which this is useful is where a modelled system's behaviour depends on the results of an optimization process. An example is given by the short-distance transportation service examined in Meyer et al. (1998), which describes the simulation of a courier service. Every modelled courier tries to minimize the length of his routes from a shipment's start to its destination. In this case optimization becomes an integral part of the simulated behaviour.

Due to statistical considerations, simulation experiments often need to be replicated many times. This highlights the importance of deciding on parameter values in as simply a fashion as possible and suggests that approximation techniques should be explored. In the above mentioned short-distance transportation service, the shortest path between two locations must be computed repeatedly. For some decisions (e.g. delivery time), however, it suffices to know just the length of the path; a measure which can be determined by approximation. Thus, for these decisions there is no need to find an exact path.

13.3 A Formal Model for Simulation-Based Optimization Problems

Formal definitions of system specification (i.e. a model) and optimization can be combined into a scientifically sound foundation for simulation-based optimization. Using the simplified definition of a discrete system proposed by Hammel and Bäck (2000, p. 303), the relations established by a simulation model Ψ can be described as a (stochastic) function

$$\Psi : S \times X \times T \to Y,$$

which maps a vector of input parameters $x \in X$ to a vector of model outputs depending on the system state $s \in S$ and the observation time $t \in T$. The stochastic nature is introduced by many experiment replications differing only in the seed data for their random numbers. Each simulation experiment then computes the (stochastic) function

$$\Psi(s_0, x, t) \text{ with } s_0 = s(t_0) \in S, t, t_0 \in T,$$

whose vector of output parameter values $y \in Y$ is the result of a series of transformations on the model's initial state $s_0 \in S$ (i.e. the model state at initial time $t_0 \in t$) after $t \in T$ time units, using a vector of input parameters $x \in X$. Since this function can normally not be expressed in closed form (otherwise simulation would not be needed) and analytical computation of $\Psi(s_0, x, t)$ is therefore not possible, each $y \in Y$ value must be determined by simulation.

In a similar way we can define an optimization problem Π as a tuple

$$\Pi = \{L, f, \text{GOAL}\}.$$

It consists of a search space L, which contains all possible solutions to the problem description (normally this includes restrictions that have to be met by all members of the solution space), an objective function $f : L \to \mathbb{R}$, which assigns a scalar value to each candidate solution, and the optimization's goal $\text{GOAL} \in \{\max, \min\}$, which indicates whether maximization or minimization of the objective function is sought. An *optimal solution* to an optimization problem is a candidate solution whose contribution to the objective is rated equal or better than that of all other candidates. A typical example for an optimization problem is discussed in this handbook's introduction (see 1.4).

The integration of simulation with optimization is achieved by an objective function with evaluates the simulation model's multi-dimensional output by mapping it on a scalar value. The objective function for simulation-based optimization can be given as

$$\tilde{f} = \tilde{f}(\Psi), \quad \tilde{f} : Y \to \mathbb{R}.$$

Given a simulation scenario (s, x) which consists of a fixed initial state s and inputs x, which are used to initialise or influence all variable parameters during the experiment, optimizing the system specified by model Ψ can be described as the problem

Chapter 13 Simulation-Based Optimization

$$\Pi_{Sim} = \{(s_0, x), \tilde{f}(\Psi), \text{GOAL}\}.$$

The solution space of this optimization problem corresponds to the set of all scenarios with initial state $s_0 \in S$ and input $x \in X$. If required, every candidate solution must be evaluated by performing multiple simulation experiments, each of which results in computing the model function $\Psi(s_0, x, t)$ (i.e. all changes in state) for simulation time t.

13.4 Characteristics of Simulation-Based Objective Functions

From an optimization perspective a model can be viewed as a *black box*; i.e. no details about the way it produces results need to be known, as long as these can serve as quantitative measures for assessing a candidate solution's "quality". Such one-dimensional quality measures are derived from an objective function, whose properties are discussed in this section.

Just as the credibility of simulation results is contingent on careful validation, practical relevance of optimization results also depends strongly on the validity of their objective function, which must closely reflect the intentions and values of the decision maker. All aspects of the relevant application domain must be taken into account and need to be corroborated by reliable data.

Thus, formal derivation of objective functions for simulation studies is a task far from trivial. Since it strongly influences the topology of a search space, a carelessly chosen objective function can easily misguide a corresponding optimization process in such a way that the optimization of the system under consideration becomes erroneous or even impossible.

The results of a simulation experiment typically include a number of relevant quantities. For each experiment we therefore can give partial orderings only, so that it may not always be possible to choose deterministically between two alternatives. For the purpose of optimization it has to be ensured that one can always decide which of two alternatives is to be preferred or that both alternatives are indifferent with respect to the optimization criteria. Therefore, objective functions for optimization impose total orderings on all points (i.e. sets of parameter values) in a solution space.

In contrast to optimization techniques, simulation is normally used for system analyses for which *no* explicit objective function can be derived. No analytical expressions to characterize system behavior can be given. Instead, simulation results are algorithmically computed and generally provide no analytically useful information about a solution space's structure. In the general case no gradients or partial derivations offer hints regarding a search space's topology, which could be employed to give goal-directed guidance towards optimal or promising regions of the search space. This means that only *direct* optimization methods which work on the basis of individual evaluations by simulation experiments are of any use to a simulation study.

13.4 Characteristics of Simulation-Based Objective Functions

While the long duration of typical simulation runs poses no general mathematical problems, it adds to the length of each candidate solution's evaluation. This makes simulation a computationally expensive technique. We must also take into account that simulations often contain stochastic components, which require multiple replications of runs to attain specified levels of statistical credibility. This adds further to the computational burden and makes use of parallel and distributed computer systems very attractive.

The results of a stochastic model's multiple replications also contain "stochastic noise", and probabilistic techniques are used to reduce this to expected values and confidence intervals. Optimizations that employ simulation must take into account such uncertainties.

A solution space's dimension is defined by the number of model parameters. Since simulation models typically have a set of many variable parameters, the size of their search space can be very large. This favours heuristic over exact optimization, for which the number of possibilities can quickly become much too large. Since a model will also impose problem-specific constraints, each potential solution must also be tested for permissibility; i.e. to ensure that all the model constraints are met. If this is not the case, a potential solution is infeasible and must be rejected or at least be treated as representing a non realizable scenario; e.g. the objective function could be modified to include penal costs in order to guide the optimization process to feasible solutions only.

Unlike mathematical optimization, objective functions for simulation models cannot be directly used to rank elements of a solution space. Instead, evaluation by running experiments and aggregation of their results must be performed before an objective function can be applied. Just as in real life, realistic problem results will also be plagued by non-linearity and discontinuities. These effects create a multi-modal objective function's surface with many peaks and local optima. In a simulation context we are often content with finding a number of good solutions, none of which may yield a global optimum but which are approximately equivalent and reasonably close to it. Since optimality can rarely be guaranteed, informed evaluations of good scenarios by the model analyst become particularly important. In some cases optimization results can serve as a basis for experimentation with more detailed models. Practicability of nearly equivalent solutions can be discussed with a larger circle of domain experts, and this may well lead to some solutions being preferred or discarded.

Multi-criteria objective functions are prevalent in simulation-based optimization. In this context contradictory subgoals are quite common. To serve as a base for an optimization, all subgoals must be weighed or prioritized, where prioritization can be seen as a special case of assigning a weight. Without any one-dimensional quality measure no global optimum can be determined and a set of Pareto-optimal solutions may be the only alternative. A Pareto-optimal solution is a solution of a multi-criteria optimization problem which can only be improved with respect to a certain subgoal at the cost of being downgraded instantaneously with respect to at least one other subgoal. Michalewicz (1999, p. 171) reports that Pareto-optima are highly regarded in practice, since they provide understandable and transparent decision support. Compared to the Pareto-optimal solutions of multi-criteria optimization, however, using artificially aggregated quality measures to characterize a whole model's merits is difficult to justify and often fails to gain user acceptance. We refer to Michalewicz (1999, p. 168) for more detail on multi-modal and multi-criteria optimization.

13.5 Genetic Algorithms

Simulation's lack of a closed form objective function requires the use of *direct* optimizations; i.e. techniques that need no more information than an objective function measure for each candidate solution. In this context *genetic algorithms* (GA), which generate and perpetuate implicit knowledge about a solution space's structure along a series of "generations", have been proven particularly useful. Genetic algorithms' potential for parallelization is a further attractive characteristic. Zitzler (1999) therefore proposes the use of genetic algorithms for multi-criteria optimization and discusses suitable methods for their solution.

In this section we will give a brief overview of genetic algorithms. Readers who wish to apply this technique will require additional detail and should consult the literature section at the end of this chapter.

Genetic algorithms are a class of easily adaptable techniques which can be used for discrete optimization in a wide range of context. They differ from classical optimization in that they:

- *Directly use evaluations of candidate solutions.* No derivations, analytical information, or problem specific knowledge is needed. This property makes them particularly well suited for simulation-based optimization, where no closed form expression is known and quantitative results must be obtained by model-based experimentation.

- *Work at each iteration not just on a single solution*, but on a whole *population*; i.e. a *set* of solution space elements. This aspect allows straightforward parallelization of evaluations for each candidate solution, a property that becomes particularly advantageous if series of processor intensive simulation runs are needed to evaluate each candidate.

- *Use probabilistic strategies to generate new candidate solutions from a previous generation.* Since probabilities governing propagation of properties are linked to a candidate solution's evaluation (i.e. the higher the evaluation, the more probable it becomes that a property will be passed on), these strategies hopefully lead to successively better solutions.

- *Work with encodings of decision parameters* instead of their direct manipulation. These problem-specific encodings allow application of general genetic operators that represent universal meta-heuristics.

13.5 Genetic Algorithms

13.5.1 Terminology

Genetic algorithms are derived from evolutionary principles that govern genetic structures in natural organisms. This has led practitioners to adopt a biologically inspired terminology.

Genetic algorithms work on *candidate solutions* referred to as *individuals*. A set of such individuals forms a *population* and every iteration of the algorithm creates a new *generation* of individuals. Individuals in a population (*phenotypes*) are represented by *genotypes* to which genetic operators can be applied. Genetic operators iteratively compute new generations by simulating biological mechanisms for *selection* and *reproduction*. Their proper choice leads to improvements in generation "quality", i.e. its *population fitness*. Problem specific encoding ensures unique mappings from phenotypes to genotypes, eases adaption to specific problems, and makes the genetic operators independent of a particular application.

13.5.2 General Strategy

The strategy employed by genetic algorithms is referred to as a *meta-heuristic* and follows a number of steps. Based on a given or randomly generated population new generations of candidate solutions are created iteratively. This process involves genetic operations for selection, recombination, and mutation of genotypes. Particularly promising candidates of the initial populations are selected and some of their parts are combined to create new solution candidates for an intermediate population. After this step, the worst candidates from both initial and intermediate populations are removed with highest probability, to ensure that population size remains constant over time. Genetic operators use random strategies that are, however, biased in favour of candidates with "better" evaluations. These have higher probabilities of being selected for recombination and mutation. Since candidate solutions with "weaker" evaluations have correspondingly lower probabilities, they are likely to gradually disappear from a population.

Note that genetic operators must be implemented according to a chosen encoding. Working with encodings of decision parameters instead of their direct manipulation allows for the application of general genetic operators which make up the universal meta-heuristic. The pseudo-code in Table 13.2 on next page Hammel and Bäck (2000) demonstrates this technique.

Selection distinguishes between *pre-selection*, of individuals for recombination or mutation and later *deselection* of individuals that should be removed from a population. Variation of pre-selected individuals involves recombination of pairs, followed by mutations of single individuals. Depending on implementation, parents (i.e. members of previous generations) may participate in this. At the end of every iteration, the required number of individuals are deselected to keep population size constant.

Chapter 13 Simulation-Based Optimization

Table 13.2: Pseudo-code for a genetic algorithm:

```
initialise population;
evaluate population;
while NOT termination condition fulfilled        // iterative process
do
    select-mates from population;                // selection of "best"
    recombine mates (form 2 new individuals from 2 already existing ones);
    mutate mates (random change of selected single individuals);
    evaluate resulting population;               // evaluation
    select-best from old and intermediate population;  // deselection of "worst"
    start next iteration;
od
```

While genetic algorithms are probabilistic, they do more than only random choices. Since good candidate solutions are favoured over weaker ones, they offer a high probability of reaching promising regions of a solution space, thus being random-based rather than random.

To adapt this scheme to a specific problem, a number of steps are required prior to or during an implementation:

❏ *Choosing encodings.* Binary encodings are always possible, but vectors of numerical parameters can also be used. In this case it must be ensured that recombination operators or the algorithm itself can react on infeasible solutions eventually produced.

❏ *Defining a fitness function.* In contrast to objective functions, which are *absolute* quality measures for individuals (i.e. they are ranked independently), this function determines the *relative* suitability of individuals in a population.

❏ *Choosing genetic operators* and possibly their implementation details.

❏ *Choosing domain-specific parameters* for the genetic algorithm and its operators, such as population size, probabilities for operator selection, and generation gap (how many individuals in each generation should be replaced).

❏ *Determining methods for initialisation and termination.* In this context we can create the first generation out of randomly generated individuals or seed the model with solutions whose superior quality is already known.

Since a more thorough introduction would go well beyond the scope of this handbook, we refer interested readers to the literature section at the end of this chapter.

13.5 Genetic Algorithms

13.5.3 Parallelization

The population-based architecture of genetic algorithms, which allows individuals to be computed in isolation, hints at easy gains from parallelization techniques. In a simulation context optimizations must perform simulation experiments for each individual. This is computationally expensive, and parallel evaluation on separate computers can significantly reduce waiting times for statistically reliable results. This is exacerbated by the need for multiple replications, whose number may depend on the required level of the results' statistical confidence.

There are four ways in which genetic algorithms can be parallelized (Cantú-Paz 2000):

- globally parallel GA (master-slave GA)
- coarse grained GA
- fine grained GA
- hierarchical hybrids

Here we will only look briefly at *globally parallel GA*, where a central computer (a *master*) administers the complete population, applies the genetic operators, and distributes individuals to be processed by a collection of slaves. For obvious reasons this strategy is also referred to as *master-slave* parallelization. Overall responsibility for the optimization remains with the master while slaves work on all details. Parallelizing a simulation-based optimization in this manner is easy and yields good performance. Using this strategy to parallelize individual model components would require much more synchronization overhead.

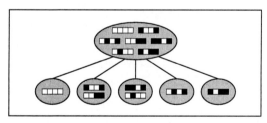

Figure 13.3: Globally parallel GA (master-slave) evaluates individuals on distributed computers (slaves). Control and synchronization remains with a master.

Further Reading

Simulation-based optimization combines ideas from different fields of research, and in-depth treatments must therefore refer to a wealth of sources. Some relevant items are listed below (without any claims for completeness).

Bibliography

The "Bible" of genetic algorithms, which summarizes both historical and current lines of research, is *Genetic Algorithms in Search, Optimization, and Machine Learning* (Goldberg 1989). The text ranges widely and is still cited in nearly every paper about genetic algorithms. *Genetic Algorithms + Data Structures = Evolution Programs* (Michalewicz 1999) is a more recent book in which evolutionary programming is emphasised. Another excellent source for the latest information on genetic algorithms (always worth a click) is the web site of the *Illinois Genetic Algorithms Laboratory* (IlliGAL) at http://www.illigal.org. Finally, aspects of multi-objective optimization are surveyed in *Evolutionary Algorithms for Multiobjective Optimization: Methods and Applications* (Zitzler 1999), while *Efficient and Accurate Parallel Genetic Algorithms* (Cantú-Paz 2000) focuses on genetic algorithms' potential for efficient parallelization.

Bibliography

E. Cantú-Paz. *Efficient and Accurate Parallel Genetic Algorithms*. Kluwer, Boston, 2000.

D. E. Goldberg. *Genetic Algorithms in Search, Optimization, and Machine Learning*. Addison-Wesley, Reading, 1989.

U. Hammel and T. Bäck. Optimierung in der Simulation: Evolutionäre Algorithmen ("Optimization in Simulation: Evolutionary Algorithms", in German). In H. Szczerbicka and T. Uthmann, editors, *Modellierung, Simulation und Künstliche Intelligenz* ("Modelling, Simulation, and Artificial Intelligence", in German), pages 303–331. SCS-Europe, Ghent, 2000.

R. Meyer, C. Reick, B. Gehlsen, L. Hilty, H. Deecke, and B. Page. Modellierung eines Stadtkurierdienstes im Hinblick auf ökologische Effizienz und soziale Verträglichkeit ("Modelling a City Courier Service with Respect to Ecological Efficiency and Social Compatibility", in German). In *Vernetzte Strukturen in Informatik, Umwelt und Wirtschaft* ("Networked Structures in Computer Science, Environment, and Economy", in German), pages 266–279, EnviroInfo 1998 – 12th. International Conference Informatics for Environmental Protection, Metropolis, Marburg, September 1998.

Z. Michalewicz. *Genetic Algorithms + Data Structures = Evolution Programs*. Springer, Berlin, 3rd edition, 1999.

E. Zitzler. *Evolutionary Algorithms for Multiobjective Optimization: Methods and Applications*. PhD Thesis, Swiss Federal Institute of Technology Zurich, 1999.

Part IV

Applications

Chapter 14

Simulation and E-Learning

Gaby Neumann, Bernd Page, Wolfgang Kreutzer, Gunnar Kiesel, Ruth Meyer

Contents

14.1 Motivation and Overview	401
14.2 E-Learning Foundations	403
14.2.1 Definition	403
14.2.2 Technological Development	404
14.2.3 Three Theories of Learning	407
14.2.4 Requirements for the Design and Implementation of E-Learning	410
14.3 Computer Simulation to Improve E-Learning	412
14.3.1 Simulation and Learning	412
14.3.2 Simulation and E-Learning	413
14.3.3 Simulation-Based Learning in LogEduGate	415
14.4 E-Learning to Support Simulation Learning	419
14.4.1 Using DESMO-J to Teach Simulation Courses	420
14.4.2 The DESMO-J Web Tutorial	421
14.4.3 The DESMO-J Internet Laboratory	422
14.4.4 Using Java Applets to Demonstrate Key Simulation Concepts	424
14.5 A Web Platform for Cooperative Teaching and Learning	427
14.6 Conclusions	429
Further Reading	430
Bibliography	431

14.1 Motivation and Overview

When discussing the link between computer simulation and learning in general we have to distinguish the learning by use of simulation from the learning about simulation:

Chapter 14 Simulation and E-Learning

- In *simulation-based learning*, computer simulation (usually in combination with animation or any other visualization technique) is used as a means of supporting learning in a particular field such as logistics or computing. Here, simulation models assist explanation and understanding of complex processes, illustrate abstract knowledge, demonstrate connections or interdependencies, and allow experiential learning or situated knowledge application. For example, aircraft simulators or models of medical procedures are used for training aspiring pilots or doctors.
- In *simulation-focussed learning*, computer simulation is the subject of learning. I.e. modelling concepts, simulation methodology and software tools for modelling and simulation are introduced, explained, and practised to enable a student to apply computer simulation for solving practical problems either in general or specific to a particular application area such as logistics.

This differentiation also applies when talking about cross-connections between simulation and e-learning, i.e. learning assisted by electronic media; both to augment conventional educational programs and by supporting new distance teaching initiatives:

- Computer simulations might be integral parts of interactive or even gaming-like environments. Students use them eventually not being aware of simulation methodology and not necessarily having any theoretical simulation background.
- Simulation methodology is purposefully and consciously applied to a particular context within specialized experimentation environments.
- Education and training of core simulation concepts themselves can make use of electronic technologies including the use of simulations for simulation learning.

In general, the term *e-learning* describes a relatively new phenomenon whose potential for forging a "global knowledge society" and for facilitating "lifelong learning" has been greeted with much hope and enthusiasm (see Bentlage et al. 2002, p. 7). Technological progress was the key driver of this development initiating also some rethinking about educational theory and research on appropriate didactic concepts. Critical discussion about the effects of using multimedia, providing navigational diversity, or enabling access to learning anywhere and at anytime led to more thoughtful and responsible design of technology-based learning.

Against this background this chapter looks at those aspects of e-learning which are relevant to simulation modelling. Some foundational issues of e-learning are presented in Section 14.2, which provides definitions and discusses technologies in their historical setting. This sets the stage for a survey of different types of e-learning. Competing educational theories are analysed with regard to their relevance to e-learning. The discussion concludes with presuming about requirements for designing highly-motivating, attractive and effective e-learning.

Section 14.3 takes a closer look at the connections between learning (e-learning) and computer simulation with particular emphasis on using simulation models as learning tools. *LogEduGate* (for "Logistics Education Gate"), a virtual learning environment

14.2 E-Learning Foundations

for logistics, is used as example to illustrate how integration of simulation can improve e-learning within a simulation-based learning scenario.

Some e-learning materials developed to support simulation-focussed learning are briefly presented in Section 14.4. This includes Java applets for teaching general simulation concepts as discussed in the previous chapters of this textbook (e.g. how event lists work, see Chapter 2) as well as more specialized software for teaching how to use the DESMO-J simulation framework; i.e. a web tutorial and an Internet-based simulation laboratory.

Reflecting the social dimension of learning and teaching, i.e. the strong need for learner-learner, learner-teacher, and teacher-teacher communication, collaboration, and exchange *CommSy* (for "Community System"), an Internet platform for cooperative teaching and learning, is presented in Section 14.5. In addition to its role as a repository for electronic learning materials, CommSy supports cooperative learning styles and has been used in this way in a large number of courses at the University of Hamburg and at many other universities. Readers of this textbook can access a CommSy project, where additional learning materials are available for browsing and download.

Chapter 14 ends with some conclusions, recommendations for further reading, and references to relevant literature.

14.2 E-Learning Foundations

This section briefly introduces into e-learning; i.e. learning assisted by electronic media. After giving a definition, we will survey different types of e-learning and the educational theories on which they are based, before we will derive requirements for how simulation-based and simulation-focussed e-learning should be designed.

14.2.1 Definition

There have been many terms to describe the use of technology for learning, but most are either antiquated or no longer appropriate for a digital world. Nowadays, *e-learning* is the term used to describe web-based learning scenarios enabling anyone to learn anywhere at anytime. It refers to the use of Internet technologies to deliver a broad array of solutions that enhance knowledge and performance (see Rosenberg 2001, p. 28). More specifically Rosenberg (2001) identifies three fundamental criteria e-learning is based upon:

- ❏ E-learning is networked, which makes it capable of instant updating, storage/retrieval, distribution, and sharing of instruction or information.
- ❏ E-learning is delivered to the end-user via a computer using standard Internet technology.
- ❏ E-learning focuses on the broadest view of learning solutions that go beyond the traditional paradigms of training.

Chapter 14 Simulation and E-Learning

So, in some kind of common understanding e-learning appears to be characterized by the exploitation of web-based technologies to create learning materials and for course delivery accessed via a browser with some form of online learner support. It is adapting to universities, industry, corporate bodies, and government departments at an ever-increasing speed. E-learning is widely expected to revolutionize education and training. Compared to today's pedagogical approaches e-learning is said to be the chance for providing education in a way more likely to

- focus on the needs of the learner instead of those of the teacher or institution,
- take advantage of the today's sophisticated technological possibilities such as the availability of the Internet anywhere and anytime,
- bring together people to collaborate and learn,
- personalize content (e.g. by combining learning objects on the fly),
- offer alternative learning methods, or
- incorporate administrative functions such as registration, payment, monitoring learner progress, testing, or maintaining records.

The fact that Internet-based learning materials can be accessed at any time and from nearly anywhere is seen as an important prerequisite for lifelong learning, since it gives individual learners the freedom to autonomously decide when and where to consult needed materials. These technologies therefore promise both qualitative and quantitative improvements and augmentation of traditional learning styles. Multimedia materials lend themselves to highly motivating and attractive styles of presentation. Contents can be shown in different ways, involving many senses. As a result, students' interaction with learning materials can last longer and may be more intensive (see Bentlage et al. 2002, p. 18).

In addition, material on the Internet can be delivered to a potentially very large audience and can be updated and changed very quickly. But for delivery and distribution of e-learning materials a variety of media other than the Internet might be used as well: CD-ROM and DVD, for example, still have a significant role to play. But as useful as CD-ROMs and DVDs are for instruction and information delivery, especially for rich media-based simulations, they lack the networkability that enables information and instruction to be distributed and updated instantly. So while CD-ROMs contain indeed technology-based learning systems, they should not be classified as e-learning (see Rosenberg 2001, p. 28).

14.2.2 Technological Development

Although ideas for how to improve knowledge acquisition and learning are nearly as old as mankind, the history of technology-based learning practically does not start until the first computers were introduced. In an attempt to make learning more transportable and visually engaging, but also to exploit the cost benefits of student-led learning, programs were employed in teaching vocational skills. These *Computer-Based Training*

14.2 E-Learning Foundations

(CBT) courses delivered on CD-ROM facilitate a limited form of autonomous learning through computer-led presentation of teaching materials and automated feedback for simple exercises (see Dittler 2002, p. 15). Interfaces and interaction styles of early CBT systems were rather crude and mechanical, but further technological development soon enabled and encouraged an extensive use of multimedia in the design of more attractive CBTs. Despite these improvements CBTs still lacked instructor interaction and dynamic presentations – making the experience slower and less engaging for students.

Along with the Internet's rapid rise Computer-Based Training evolved into *Web-Based Training* (WBT), *Online Learning*, and finally *E-Learning*. The advent of e-mail, web browsers, HTML, media players, low-fidelity streamed audio/video, and simple Java began to change the face of multimedia learning. Basic mentoring via e-mail, Intranet CBT with text and simple graphics, and Web-Based Training with low-quality intermittent-delivery web casts emerged. Technological advances – including Java/IP network applications, rich streaming media, high-bandwidth access, and advanced web site design – created new opportunities for the design of learning. In addition to what CBT had to offer, e-learning now supported *cooperative* learning styles, involving two or more participants. Learning software played the roles of both facilitator and arbiter. The Internet as distribution medium of the learning nearly automatically supported goals like ubiquity (i.e. "use anywhere and at any time"), almost unbounded numbers of potential participants, or increased ease and speed of updating materials. All of these characteristics are now considered important prerequisites for effective learning.

The ultimate motivation for attempting to computerize teaching and learning can be traced to an increasingly popular view of knowledge as a commercial commodity and as a "tradable" good (see Bentlage et al. 2002, p. 7). This new perspective led universities and large corporations to vie with each other in developing more convenient and more effective means of access to and transmission of knowledge. New teaching styles and their supporting technologies were seen as vital means for survival in such a competitive environment, and much hope was pinned on e-learning for fitting the bill. E-learning eases global distribution of learning materials, fuels ambitions to cater for increasing numbers of students at low marginal costs, and promises a short "time-to-market". If material is skilfully packaged, it lends support to the vision of individualized learning; i.e. the tailoring of content and presentation to the needs of a particular student, whose preferred learning styles can also be taken into account.

To help distribution of e-learning materials and provide ubiquitous access to learning, *Learning Management Systems*, or LMS, such as Blackboard, WebCT, Moodle have been developed. In contrast to a collection of teaching scripts or educational presentations on a web server, LMSs are designed to support the management of teaching and learning processes and to automate the administration of learning events. For this, an LMS manages the log-in, registration, and access rights of users, manages course catalogues, records data from learners, and provides reports to management. Furthermore, applications track student training, support different communication methods, and provide functionality to display course content, learning objects, and educational media

Chapter 14 Simulation and E-Learning

in a web browser (see Schulmeister 2003). In addition to this (see brandon-hall.com 2005), an LMS may or may not include further functions such as:
- authoring
- classroom management
- competency management
- knowledge
- certification or compliance training
- personalization
- mentoring

Alternatively, those functions can also be provided separately to the LMS by external tools. Especially for multimedia authoring a large number and variety of editors and *authoring tools*, i.e. software applications for use by non-programmers that uses a metaphor (book, flow chart) to create online courses, is available.

Corresponding to the ever-increasing amount of learning objects and course material *Learning Content Management Systems*, or LCMSs, emerged. An LCMS is an environment where developers can store, reuse, manage, and deliver learning content from a central object repository, usually a database. LCMSs generally work with content that is based on a learning object model. These systems usually have good search capabilities, allowing developers to quickly find the text or media needed to build training content. Learning content management systems often strive to achieve a separation of content – which is often tagged in XML – from presentation. This allows many LCMSs to publish to a wide range of formats, platforms, or devices such as print, web, and even wireless information devices (WID) like Palm and Windows CE hand-helds, all from the same source material (see brandon-hall.com 2005).

Latest developments with regard to technology-based learning made e-learning going mobile. In the near future we might expect that everyone and everything is connected from everywhere by a mobile network being able to support voice, image, and video. Because of this, future communication will mostly be wireless; e-learning will at least partially be moved into *m-learning*. But for this, mobile multimedia will require new content types that allow information retrieval on the first glance: reminders and alerts, communications with peers and coaches, memory joggers and tips of the day, full text of materials, glossary information, specific search functionality, course registration.

Despite all technological progress, there are still handicaps that need to be taken into consideration when thinking of introducing and using e-learning scenarios. On one hand not yet everybody is equipped with technology enabling high-speed Internet connections and acceptable data transfer rates. In such cases long response times and slow download processes fail to motivate the e-learner. On the other hand not everybody really wants to learn anywhere and at anytime but wishes to meet people and have personal contacts instead. Therefore, a hybrid delivery of learning, which is often referred to as *blended learning*, combining remote components with face-to-face settings, is an appropriate

14.2 E-Learning Foundations

way of making use of educational technology according to individual possibilities and needs. It allows

- to be as flexible as different technological standards, personal attitudes, and pedagogical scenarios require, and also
- to continuously adapt learning environments to changing needs from the content, technological and pedagogical points of view.

The challenge consists in deciding what to deliver best in which way by use of which medium.

Rapidly developing information and communication technology will provide an ever-increasing variety of e-learning scenarios. To let those virtual learning environments really enable high-quality learning processes, a fundamental change of pedagogic paradigms and a wide-span cultural shift are required in all fields of knowledge and at all levels of education and training. With this it is necessary to understand (and accept) that more is expected of students and teachers operating virtually than within a traditional distance regime and this does not always suit all participants (Ryan and Woodward 1998). So, it is extremely important to introduce students and teachers to this new way (culture) of learning and teaching, including how to learn and teach within a virtual environment.

14.2.3 Three Theories of Learning

Media didactics distinguishes between three fundamentally different theories of how students learn. These are referred to *behaviourism*, *cognitivism*, and *constructivism* (see Coenen 2002, p. 28):

- **Behaviourism** views learners as "black boxes", for who only inputs and outputs can be directly observed. It assumes that there is *some* connection between input, observed behaviour, and a desired outcome, but it refuses to speculate about what it might be. Any attempts at defining causal connections between input (stimulus) and output (response) is seen as "unscientific", since these cannot be directly observed and measured. To achieve desired outcomes (e.g. a learning goal), we simply reward desirable and punish undesirable behaviours. This process is referred to as *conditioning* and has been popularized by Pavlov's proverbial dog. According to this viewpoint, behaviours which lead to punishments or have no interesting consequences will diminish in frequency over time and the desired behaviour will successively take over.

  The approach of *programmed learning* as created by Skinner to manage human learning under controlled conditions formed the foundation of a number of computer-based teaching programs in the 1960s still referred to as *Drill & Practice* software. Typically, the computer presents the material to be learned in a series of very small steps, after each of which simple questions are asked.

Chapter 14 Simulation and E-Learning

Students' answers then cause either a positive or a negative response from the program and lead to new information or a repetition of the previous ones.

❏ **Cognitivism** is based on a much richer model of learners' goals and aspirations. In place of "black boxes" they view learners as active information processors, who strive to integrate new information with what they already know. Knowledge acquisition is therefore strongly dependent on what previous knowledge a learner can bring to bear. Acceptance of this thesis implies that any self-guided learning must either adapt automatically to a learner's model of (part of) the world and his or her learning style (which would be difficult), or it must support free and effective navigation through choice from wide ranges of alternative learning materials. Kolb (1975) suggests that this style of knowledge acquisition requires an experiential learning circle, which consists of four phases: (i) concrete experience; (ii) observation and reflection; (iii) forming abstract concepts; and (iv) testing in new situations. Cycling through each of these phases encourages the generalization of learned problem solutions and their transference to new problem types. Content development based on cognitivist theories must therefore ensure all four learning phases are visited. Project-based work with concrete examples or real-life problems fits this style well.

Cognitivism aims at conceptual learning and development of problem solving ability; discovering problem solving methods through exploratory learning is of more importance than reproducing facts. Educational technology developed upon this basis is, for example, the class of *Intelligent Tutoring Systems* (ITS). These are learning systems adapting to different users to provide individual support and offer personalized alternatives in *problem-based learning*. With this, ITSs try to simulate the behaviour of a tutor who accompanies and guides the student through the learning process.

❏ **Constructivism** postulates that learners actively create individualized and subjective knowledge structures and that they integrate learning materials into existing conceptual frameworks. Since different learners own different conceptual frameworks, their use of "the same" material may well result in different knowledge structures. Different from cognitivism, constructivist learning theories suggest that students generate and solve their own rather than work on established problems. This demand encourages students to develop ability for creating their own problem solving techniques; a skill which they can then bring to bear on new challenges and in unfamiliar settings. In this style of learning, teachers play the roles of mediators and coaches instead of authority figures and experts. Their task is to create the right environment for self-directed constructive learning to occur, and to motivate and assist students along the way. Relevant approaches of constructivism are known as *situated learning, goal-based learning, case-based learning*, and *problem-based learning*. Constructivist learning aims at developing competence, instead of acquiring knowledge (in cognitivism) or achieving perfor-

14.2 E-Learning Foundations

mance (in behaviourism). Therefore, implementing constructivist learning into an e-learning environment is a quite challenging task.

Table 14.1: Paradigms of learning and teaching software
(adapted from Baumgartner and Payr 1994, p. 110)

	Behaviourism	Cognitivism	Constructivism
First approaches originated from...	1913	1920	1945
Important representatives were...	Pavlov, Skinner	Piaget, Gagné	Maturana, Varela
The learning paradigm is...	stimulus-response	problem solving	construction
The teaching strategy is...	chalk-teaching	helping	coaching
Focus is on...	reflection	cognition	interaction
Problem solving is...	task-centred	solution-centred	process-centred
Teachers are...	authority figures	tutors	coaches, trainers
Learning goals are...	producing correct answers	discovering correct methods for finding answers	coping with complex problems
Examination focuses on...	reproducing learning content	active problem solving	checking comprehensive understanding
Students are expected to work...	on their own (individually)	together with other students (couple)	interactively in a group of students (team)
The human brain is...	a passive knowledge container	a linear information processor	a closed information system
Students are assessed with regard to...	performance (questioning of facts)	knowledge (examination of concepts)	competence (identifying the general problem)
Learning material is presented in...	small portions	complex environments	unstructured reality
Feedback is...	externally given	externally modelled	internally modelled
Knowledge is...	objective	objective	subjective
Knowledge can be...	stored	processed	constructed
Human-computer interaction is...	rigidly structured	dynamically dependent on an external model	self-referential, circular, autonomous
Software characteristics are...	rigid sequence, quantitative time and answer statistics	dynamic sequence, prepackaged problems, answer analysis	dynamic sequence, knowledge networks, no prepackaged problems
The software paradigm is...	mechanical teaching machines	artificial intelligence	socio-technological environments
"Ideal" software would use...	drill & practice, tutorial systems	CBT, adaptive systems, intelligent tutoring systems	simulations, microworlds, hypermedia

Chapter 14 Simulation and E-Learning

The whole question of how students learn seems to be a highly complex one, which is also very context-dependent. None of these educational theories can be called right or wrong, and which to choose as a base for a learning tool largely depends on what goals should be served. Table 14.1 offers some guidance.

E-learning applications must always be based on *didactic concepts* which are appropriate for both learner and problem. We have seen how specific choices depend strongly on relevant goals. In the context of "lifelong learning" initiatives, cognitivism and constructivism offer much more appropriate foundations for learning frameworks and learning software than behaviourist theories. Instead of requiring the memorization of masses of facts, modern society places great value on the ability to acquire relevant information and skills "just-in-time" (see Bentlage et al. 2002, p. 9). This ability is fostered by both cognitivist and constructivist learning styles. Behaviourist techniques, on the other hand, can only be justified for teaching factual knowledge and largely mechanical skills and possibly as components in more sophisticated learning environments.

14.2.4 Requirements for the Design and Implementation of E-Learning

E-learning is still in its infancy. Despite the great efforts undertaken to establish e-learning in larger scale, it is not yet achieving the gains expected. Major reasons for this are the traditional attitudes towards learning and education, the lack of proper e-learning solutions, and above all constraints in administration:

- ❑ The methods of instruction that dominate the e-learning market look more like the classroom than an interactive immerse learning environment. Text predominates; lecturing, reading, and test taking still prevail.
- ❑ The rich use of graphics, simulations, animations, embedded assessment, people-to-people connection, and just-in-time personalization can hardly be found in e-learning, but still belong to massive multi-user gaming only.
- ❑ The traditional educational institutions are not capable to deal with the digital economy. Institutions of the future need to be new kinds of knowledge incubators, where you have research, industry, school all happening in the same place.

As Wittmann and Möller (2003) point out, attitudes and deeply ingrained habits of trainers, teachers, and lecturers must change. They need to adapt to exploit opportunities and take into consideration constraints associated with new technologies. But for this a "cultural shift" will be needed – a shift away from a focus on teaching to a greater focus on learning. This has to be understood as the overall challenge in today's education raising a number of issues – including the attitudes and perceptions of a number of stakeholders in learning and teaching, such as ICT[1] skills required to operate efficiently, ownership and control of learning and teaching, respective roles, and relationships etc. – and has implications for institutions, the curriculum, staff, and students. Unfortunately, tools and materials to make this easier are still badly lacking.

---
[1] Information and Communication Technologies

14.2 E-Learning Foundations

This holds particularly strongly for the difficult task of developing contents for e-learning courses in suitable form (see Schulmeister 2003, p. 151). But what form and properties e-learning congruent contents should have? Publications written for conventional paper-based media and merely mapped into online form without any substantial changes to their original (e.g. sequential) style cannot just be quickly and mechanically turned into e-learning materials. Adoption of cognitivist and constructivist educational theories as bases for modern e-learning environments asks that such systems must go beyond merely presenting and querying facts. Instead, they must support discovery-based learning styles (cognitivism) and provide motivating learning environments; e.g. a simulated company (constructivism). While not every type of contents lends itself to such styles of presentation, Schulmeister (see 2003, p. 160) lists a number of promising candidates:

- simulated companies, business process simulations, stock market games, business games, project planning
- virtual laboratories for avoidance of bottlenecks in queueing scenarios
- models and simulations in architecture, mathematics, natural science, medicine, economics, and business studies
- processes involving computer participation; e.g. computer science models, automata
- problem-oriented teaching in areas where experimental subjects are rare and expensive, or where experiments may be dangerous; e.g. experiments with animals, some medical procedures
- pre- and post-analyses of real-world learning activities; e.g. geological excursions
- storage and transmission of teaching events which cannot be observed sufficiently frequently or in the right place; e.g. bedside teaching

This also meets the criticism by Jonassen (2001) describing nowadays e-learning solutions as being information delivery systems only. But information as such does not guarantee learning and so, one of the biggest obstacles on the way to more effective learning are people's conceptions what learning is and what it should be. Technology needs to be used for creating learning-by-doing and perceptual environments for problem-based learning, where you are immersed in making rapid fire decisions, rushing to gain new information, utilizing the expertise of colleagues, and relying on your ability to create and store useful knowledge that will allow you to innovate and get your products to market way before your competitor. To enable this, gaming-like environments are needed where objects are interoperable and where tools from any domain can interact. Those new kinds of learning environments are hardly yet available, but the Internet provides us with the platform to achieve this goal.

Though, further development of e-learning will be a very dynamic process touching all aspects: pedagogy, technology, and content.

Chapter 14 Simulation and E-Learning

14.3 Computer Simulation to Improve E-Learning

This section focuses on simulation-based learning, i.e. the use of computer simulation to assist learning in a variety of domains. Simulation and animation are ideal tools for supporting knowledge acquisition or informative knowledge retrieval by illustrative enlargement of lexical functions, for example. Prepared scenarios, processes, and models are mainly used. In principle, two fields of application are to be distinguished for simulation and animation: either simulation is hidden to the user, for example if simulation is only a tool for the generation of animations and visualizations of any duration. Or the learner is consciously using simulation for experiments to figure out sensitivities or identify specifics.

After taking a closer look at the cross-connections between computer simulation and learning in general, we move our discussion towards the use of computer simulation to improve e-learning, before we illustrate opportunities for this by use of LogEduGate, an e-learning environment tailor-made to support logistics learning.

14.3.1 Simulation and Learning

The spectrum of learning applications is as wide as the range of different types of simulation which can profitably support them. We can use, for example:

- flight simulators for pilot training (see http://www.lufthansa-pilot.de)
- ship simulators for maritime education (see http://www.sf.hs-wismar.de)
- computerized building construction to train students of Architecture (see Post 2002)
- simulations of complex data communication systems (see Tranter 1997)
- simulations of medical laboratories (see Bach et al. 2003)
- simulation in manufacturing (i.e. production facilities and their material flows) and logistics (see Standridge 2001 and Neumann 2003)
- sociological simulations of behaviour patterns in a society (see Epstein and Axtell 1996)

In spite of the fact that these are just a few examples for applying computer simulation to learning, it should be apparent that simulation models are not only used in those disciplines in which they are well established (e.g. computer science, engineering, logistics, or natural sciences), but that they have also become increasingly popular in non-traditional fields; such as marine sciences, architecture, medicine, economics, and sociology. Within these disciplines simulations are used for a wide range of purposes. They can help to train practical skills (e.g. flight and ship simulators), explore complex relationships (e.g. interactions in multi-layered production systems), or demonstrate implications of theories (e.g. in sociological models). While these applications differ in many respects from each other, a common bond is that they strive to provide an improved understanding of the simulated system or process.

14.3 Computer Simulation to Improve E-Learning

What are the reasons why so many different disciplines employ computer simulation techniques in their education and training? A general answer to this question is given by the advantages of modelling and simulation as discussed in Section 1.7.1. More specifically, simulation can be considered an almost ideal learning tool. In many fields, such as aeronautics or medicine, it is almost unimaginable to train students with real subjects. The risks which would be involved in this become obvious when behaviour in extreme situations is meant to be taught; e.g. the treatment of heart attacks or the failure of aircraft engines during landing. Simulation makes it possible to demonstrate and practice appropriate responses to such events. Another reason for training by use of a model in place of a real system is the costs of, for example, constructing a building or manufacturing electronic circuits in reality instead of virtuality. Some training scenarios which simulations can model in vivid detail, such as city planning or inventory management, would not even be possible to create and explore in reality. Speeding or slowing the temporal evolution of processes is another of simulation's capabilities which can be put to good use in an educational setting. We can easily model the long term effects of various events (e.g. pollution) on an ecosystem (e.g. a lake) or observe the details of an almost instantaneous chemical reaction in slow motion. Simulation's ability to improve understanding of complex interactions among processes can also be a great boon. Many real life systems are so complicated that they can hardly be understood as a whole. For students it is often much simpler to study partial aspects in isolation, whose insights can then contribute to a more holistic view later. Different forms of goal-driven abstraction can be of much use, and simulation can help us explore such alternative points of view. Studying ecosystems or communication networks are two examples which profit greatly from such an approach.

As implied by the chosen examples, there are many overlaps between application areas and many of the positive aspects of simulation technology may apply to them all.

14.3.2 Simulation and E-Learning

In the previous section we have looked at the use of computer simulation in teaching and learning. This section narrows the view and investigates simulation itself as a tool to improve e-learning. E-learning and simulation both use the computer as their *central* medium, which makes their combination particularly convenient. No change of context or any additional tool is required.

With regard to learning theory as discussed in Section 14.2.3, we can state that simulation is an important tool for developing e-learning contents based on cognitivism and constructivism (see Table 14.2).

To facilitate cognitivist learning, students with specific knowledge might use simulation models with specific learning goals to acquire knowledge by linking new information with what they already know. In constructivist learning we must stimulate problem generation and strategies for solution discovery by the student him- or herself. Good tools must therefore offer exploratory contexts conducive to such an endeavour, a task

Chapter 14 Simulation and E-Learning

Table 14.2: Simulation and educational theories

Educational Theory	Applications of Simulation
Behaviourism	none
Cognitivism	use models with fixed learning goals
Constructivism	use models without fixed learning goals, but which stimulate exploration

which simulation is more than well-suited for (see Blumstengel 1998). In a behaviourist inspired context, however, models and simulations make little sense.

To integrate simulation and animation into e-learning, Neumann and Ziems (1994) identified five different cases:

- ❏ The content of animation sequences can be fixed by defined trace files if animation is used only for a comprehensible and vivid representation of knowledge to be imparted, for example, to illustrate processes and calculation algorithms. In this case animation data can be generated outside the e-learning environment in advance. Then neither the generation process itself nor all means and methods used in it are available to the user and do not need to be so; the student directly starts the animation sequence.

- ❏ This procedure is also suitable if, for example, alternative process variants are to be represented for comparison. But before dynamically visualizing any process, the student must be able to select a variant to be represented.

- ❏ If knowledge acquisition may be supported by the independent planning, running, and analysis of experiments, the student must know and purposefully use the simulation method. Here, animation is one of several possible forms for presenting simulation results. If experiments are based on a manageable quantity of pre-set parameters and/or model variations, respective simulations could be run externally. Analogous to the presentation of process alternatives, one trace file, which is the basis for animation of processes, is generated for each possible combination between a model and a set of experimental parameters. But because of the psychology of learning the student should seemingly start a simulation run.

- ❏ As soon as a user can optionally input experimental parameters, a previous simulation is no longer possible. Starting the simulation run really causes its execution inside the e-learning environment and simulation results for visualization are simultaneously collected.

- ❏ The highest degree of freedom for designing simulation experiments is reached when the user can describe own models. In this case a valid operational simulation model has to be generated from user-own specifications before the simulation run. Phases of model generation and simulation could be started together.

Integration of simulation into an e-learning environment (especially in the latter two cases) causes specific demands referring to possibilities for guiding the student and for enabling student interaction. Comfortable guidance and support in the course

14.3 Computer Simulation to Improve E-Learning

of simulation experiments avoid problems which can directly derive from the use of particular simulation software.

Those challenges are typically related to

- selecting or specifying model variations, experimental parameters, and forms of representation of result;
- comparing results within a series of experiments;
- influencing the ability to reproduce simulation results.

Following Chapman (2005) online simulations have been touted as the next big wave in e-learning. Learners generally prefer them because they offer complexity, realism, and an opportunity to practise new skills in a risk-free environment. Administrators like them because they result in more motivated students and (perhaps most importantly) higher retention rates. In the past, simulations were often extremely expensive and time-consuming to create. Now, however, there are powerful and easy to use simulation-authoring tools available for use on desktop or laptop computer and serving the following instructional categories to push beyond typical page-turning learning systems:

- software simulations (e.g. SAP tutor)
- soft skills simulations, such as role-play, business skills, business modelling/analytical, story-problem, scenario-based, sales process simulators, etc.
- hard skills/technical simulations, including trouble-shooting, diagnostic, procedural walk-through, simulating physical systems, simulating concepts, emergency response, virtual worlds/spatial relationships, etc.

But in an e-learning context it is often not satisfactory to just integrate an existing simulation into a learning activity. The dynamic and interactivity aspects of simulation models make them very attractive for use in e-learning and Schulmeister (see 2003, p. 160) therefore mentions gaming, virtual laboratories, and simulation as particularly appropriate techniques to support e-learning activities in a wide variety of subjects.

14.3.3 Simulation-Based Learning in LogEduGate

LogEduGate[2] (http://www.logedugate.de) is a new kind of a logistics e-learning environment that is tailor-made to the specific needs of this complicated, complex, interdisciplinary field of knowledge. This Logistics Education Gate is a web-based learning, information, and communication platform enabling to support wide-scale and multimedia education and training in logistics in both modes, face-to-face and distance learning. For this it interlinks a large number of knowledge units covering different aspects of logistics from engineering and business points of view at the same time and especially

---

[2]LogEduGate has been jointly developed by the Universities of Dortmund, Magdeburg, and Stuttgart, which are the leading universities in logistics education in Germany. From 2001 to 2004 the project was funded by the German Ministry of Education and Research within its Investing into Future Program "New Media in Education".

Chapter 14 Simulation and E-Learning

provides functionality to strengthen competencies in problem solving, decision making, organizing, designing etc.

The technological basis of LogEduGate is formed by the learning management system (see Section 14.2.2) WebCT Campus Edition 4.0 (http://www.webct.com). Following the underlying concept of WebCT, course-based access to learning material is the basic principle of LogEduGate as well. But the didactic concept of LogEduGate goes far beyond this to enable and encourage a holistic approach to learning. The idea is to offer a variety of access points and access paths to and through content units. Precondition for this was a consequent modular structuring of content into units and a clear separation of learning modules, information modules, and project modules.

Learning modules are designed to encourage, support, and guide learning. They represent a particular bit of declarative, conceptual, or procedural knowledge in a comprehensive way and are oriented towards a clearly specified learning goal. Interactive components support knowledge acquisition and deepening. Here, simulation-based exercises play a prominent role.

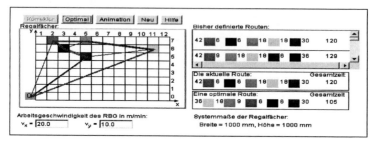

Figure 14.1: Java applet for solving routing problems (in German)

Figure 14.1 shows the example of a "playground" implemented as Java applet which allows solving routing problems for randomly selected locations in a rack and adjustable moving and lifting speeds of the rack-serving unit. By clicking on the locations in the desired sequence the student defines a particular route for which the total moving time is calculated and displayed. After this, the student might describe an alternative route linking the same locations and compare its moving time with the one of the previous trial. The objective consists, for example, in identifying the fastest route. To achieve this goal, the student might run some more trials until s/he concludes to have found the solution and asks the system to show the optimal route for comparing it with the own one. Finally, an animation illustrates the real movement of an object which results from the combination of the rack serving unit's moving and lifting operations. Due to the fact that the Java applet contains the experimental space only, whereas the problem or task to be solved is separately provided to the student, further questions, e.g. for the

14.3 Computer Simulation to Improve E-Learning

influence of a changing moving/lifting speed ratio on the average total moving time, might be addressed and easily be added to the learning environment.

Information modules represent knowledge in a well-structured way but without any link to a specific learning goal or learning process. They might be used as a pool of knowledge resources or as a library providing access to additional information in the course of the learning process. Small simulations and animations illustrate, for example, elementary material flow operations (see Figure 14.2) or more complex logistics processes within the respective library.

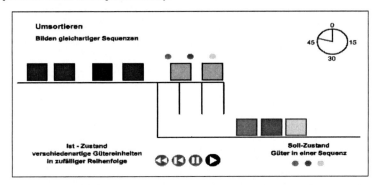

Figure 14.2: Flash animation to illustrate re-sequencing of objects (in German)

Project modules enable and initiate individual problem solving and decision making inside or outside learning processes. They themselves do not include a learning goal, but require a certain level of competence with the student. The results of this kind of competence scanning might serve self-identification of gaps and lacks to be the focus of further learning. This problem-based access to learning, where learning is encouraged and driven by a problem the learner wants to or is asked to solve within one of the project modules, directly meets the constructivist paradigm of learning. The student has access to all learning and information modules currently available in LogEduGate, but whether s/he makes use of them and to what extent directly depends on his or her individual need for support throughout the problem-solving process. For implementing this mode of providing access to material and learning, LogEduGate uses an office-like metaphor to enable, encourage, and support project work (see Figure 14.3).

In this *virtual project workspace*, students find a variety of communication and information functionality, a logistics knowledge map linked to all knowledge units, a library of knowledge units and elements in alphabetical order, and a folder containing general information about all projects available for being selected and solved. Depending on individual desires and intentions the student chooses one of these projects, registers for the team, and starts working. Since projects are of very different nature, they might

417

Chapter 14 Simulation and E-Learning

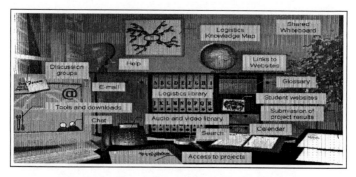

Figure 14.3: Virtual project workspace in LogEduGate

require the use of special tools for developing solutions. These tools are offered for download if copyrights are not violated. Within this working environment students gain all information necessary for solving the problem and finalizing the project. They can organize project work in there, upload files, collaborate, and finally submit project results as requested. A (human) tutor or trainer can coach working groups, discuss with students, and provide feedback.

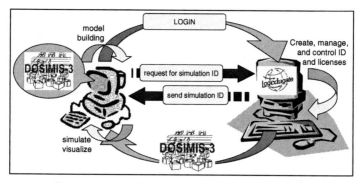

Figure 14.4: Embedding a commercial simulation package into a virtual learning environment

One of the projects that are offered to the students via the virtual project workspace in LogEduGate contains a simulation study. For integration into the LogEduGate environment, DOSIMIS-3 (see Section 15.3.2) is used as simulation tool. As shown in Figure 14.4, DOSIMIS-3 is available for download in LogEduGate. Everybody with ac-

14.4 E-Learning to Support Simulation Learning

cess to the virtual project workspace can download this simulation package and install it on the own computer. After that and without any further add-ons, the simulator automatically comes up with its demo mode enabling to build and run small simulation models which do not consist of more than 15 elements. For dealing with more complex problems and building larger models an additional, personalized simulation ID is required that is centrally created and provided on demand. This ID is valid for a certain period of time according to the time scale of the simulation project. During this period the complete functionality of the package is available, whereas after the expiry date has passed by the software automatically returns to demo mode again. In this way, the learner needs to be online for downloading the package, requesting for and receiving the simulation ID and submitting simulation results or making use of other information and communication functionality. All more time-consuming activities, like model building, validation, running experiments, watching animation, or monitoring and analyzing results, take place in offline mode. With this, the simulator works and can be used exactly in the same way as it would happen in an industry setting. There is no loss of speed and performance; online costs are reduced to a minimum once the package has been downloaded. The management and control of licenses that are in use at a particular period of time lies with the central instance which could be either the administrator of the entire platform or a person who takes responsibility for this particular piece of software.

Learning processes initiated on such basis usually show a high level of (ongoing) motivation with the learner. To transfer these excellent preconditions into learning success, long-lasting effects, and best benefit with respect to all three elements of competence – knowledge, abilities, and skills – that is the challenge a successful and attractive learning environment has to face, no matter if it is a real or a virtual one. Amongst others, this requires to integrate the "real" tools, i.e. those of the real world and not just academic toys, into the learning process and make them available to the learner for individual training and personal gaining of experience. An improved integration of simulation method and real-life simulation projects into a logistics e-learning environment is a decisive factor for its acceptance with educational institutions, trainers, and learners.

14.4 E-Learning to Support Simulation Learning

Whereas the previous section linked computer simulation and e-learning to enable simulation-based learning, i.e. learning about other subjects such as logistics by use of simulation, we will now discuss to what extend e-learning can support simulation-focussed learning processes. In general, simulation learning might address two different goals: learning about simulation methodology and applying this knowledge to practical problem solving or learning about how to use a particular simulation tool for model implementation and experimentation. The first requires some sophisticated learning material covering all aspects that have been subject to the previous chapters of this

Chapter 14 Simulation and E-Learning

book, including targeted knowledge presentation and interactive elements for training concepts and applying knowledge. The latter needs to be designed in the form of an interactive tutorial specifically dedicated to understand and master particular simulation software, and, for this, closely linked to it – ideally within the e-learning environment.

To understand constraints primarily related to this, it is necessary to bring back to our minds that in all of the common learning management systems, i.e. those tools forming the standard platform for any e-learning, however, one looks in vain for any convenient means of integrating simulation models into learning materials. Unfortunately this places all responsibility for connecting content to models on the course authors' shoulders, a burden which frequently leads to the development of e-learning in which learning management and simulation tools run simply alongside each other and do not show much integration or interaction. A symptom for this is the frequent change of context initiated by rapid switches among overlapping windows. The example of integrating DOSIMIS-3 into LogEduGate as discussed in Section 14.3.3 gives proof of this dilemma, although the intention of making students familiar with a commercial simulation package widely deployed in practical application even produced an additional challenge.

Against this background, this section shows how learning a simulation tool, i.e. the DESMO-J framework (see Chapter 10), can be supported by e-learning material. A brief recapitulation of DESMO-J's merits for teaching discrete event simulation is followed by a presentation of e-learning concepts and materials which were developed for this purpose at the Faculty of Informatics of the University of Hamburg. This includes an introductory web tutorial for DESMO-J, an Internet-based laboratory with many relevant examples and exercises, and some Java applets for demonstrating some of the key simulation concepts explained in the previous chapters of this book.

14.4.1 Using DESMO-J to Teach Simulation Courses

One of the main motivations for the development of the DESMO-J simulation framework (see Chapter 10) has been the need for a tool to teach simulation to computer science and information systems students at the University of Hamburg. DESMO-J has since been successfully used for this purpose; i.e. for supporting an introduction to and practical experimentation with the design and implementation of discrete event system models not only at the University of Hamburg, but at many other universities around the world as well.

DESMO-J is based on Java. Although we also gain some technical advantages by using Java as a base language for a simulation tool (see Section 6.2.3), this decision was largely motivated by Java's widespread adoption as a programming language in undergraduate computer science curricula.

The name DESMO-J refers to a whole simulation framework rather than simply a simulation language. In contrast to other tools of this kind, whose users often do not venture beyond what can be expressed with rather simplistic graphical interfaces, this

14.4 E-Learning to Support Simulation Learning

means that a skilled user may need to dig deeper, down to DESMO-J's programming layer and class library. To assist learning the relevant skills, we provide both a web-based tutorial (see Section 14.4.2) and a laboratory (see Section 14.4.3). These e-learning components are meant to augment more conventional learning materials (e.g. this book) as well as the students' own experimentation. Some simulation knowledge is needed to use these two web-based tools. This will typically be acquired by attending a series of lectures or by reading a book such as this one. However, experience shows that true understanding of theory is not possible without practice. This corroborates the credo of cognitivist educational theories (see Section 14.2.3). DESMO-J is an excellent tool for such discovery-driven learning, in particular if the student already has good programming skills.

To build their first models, students must understand DESMO-J's core concepts. Here s/he encounters some of discrete event simulation's most elementary ideas: event lists, event classes and methods, different types of statistical distributions, model instrumentation etc. Customizing a model by programming DESMO-J's so-called "hot spot" classes uses a familiar tool; i.e. Java. Since we assume that students are already competent Java programmers, they can therefore concentrate solely on learning the relevant simulation concepts, which will be new to them. A further advantage of DESMO-J in this context is that it supports both event-based and process-based model description, which allows experiments with these alternative world views within the same software (see Section 5.2). Experience shows that students who have used DESMO-J in such a discovery-driven style will generally develop a deeper understanding of key discrete event simulation concepts than users of other modelling tools.

14.4.2 The DESMO-J Web Tutorial

The DESMO-J web tutorial is part of the e-learning materials meant to support a blended learning style of knowledge transmission. It augments this book as well as traditional lecture-based courses at university level.

The web tutorial helps students to learn how to use DESMO-J. We assume that they are already familiar with object-oriented programming in Java and that they have a basic understanding what discrete event simulation is all about.

Figure 14.5 shows how the tutorial is organized in a number of separate sections. The ones on the left-hand side deal with general issues of DESMO-J's usage. This includes a brief overview of its functionality (DESMO-J in a nutshell), a demonstration of what a simulation with DESMO-J looks like (DESMO-J at work), and a concise guide to building a DESMO-J model (DESMO-J distilled). The right-hand side sections provide more in-depth treatments of different parts of the framework; i.e. statistical data collectors, stochastic distributions, advanced modelling features, and extensions for special application domains such as harbour logistics.

As mentioned above DESMO-J supports both the process-oriented and the event-oriented modelling style. The tutorial offers a step-by-step introduction to how to use

Chapter 14 Simulation and E-Learning

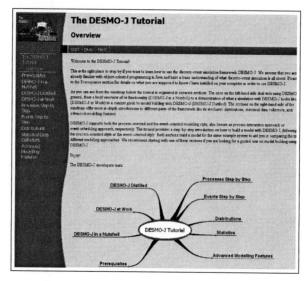

Figure 14.5: Entry page to the DESMO-J tutorial

DESMO-J in either of these two styles. To help compare the two modelling paradigms, the tutorial uses the same example for this. For a guided tour on simulation modelling with DESMO-J we recommend starting with one of these sections.

It should also be noted that a student can always refer to the API[3] documentation for details on each class and each package within the DESMO-J framework.

14.4.3 The DESMO-J Internet Laboratory

DESMO-J's Internet laboratory (see Figure 14.6) is part of the DESMO-J e-learning framework and provides a large collection of DESMO-J models. Models include problem specifications and further model specific materials, as well as all functionality for experimentation. The laboratory has three main components (Bentz and Rave 2004):

- a model presentation component
- an extension component with additional models and exercises
- an administration component with user and rights management features

---
[3] Application Programming Interface

14.4 E-Learning to Support Simulation Learning

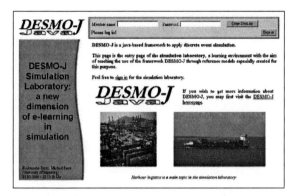

Figure 14.6: Entry page to the DESMO-J Internet laboratory

The main goal of the laboratory is to enable a student to work with examples and learn about simulation techniques and how they can be applied in DESMO-J. This style of learning is supported by the model presentation component, which for each model allows access to information of different kind:

- model description or problem specification
- "supplementary materials"; e.g. background information on areas of application, images, external links to additional information
- "conceptual model" in terms of UML 2 activity diagrams (see Section 4.4.2)
- "recommended procedure"; e.g. details for using DESMO-J classes and methods, hints about difficult programming details, explanations of event and process methods
- source code in DESMO-J or Java respectively
- reports and traces as generated by DESMO-J runs

The second laboratory component allows learners to add their own models without any knowledge of the laboratories internal structure. Since many users are university teachers who use the laboratory to deploy graded exercises, it was necessary to introduce layers of access rights to the models or model components. A Role-Based-Access-Control-Concept (RBAC) is used to administer these rights. Individual identification and passwords with different access rights for different user groups support this idea.

The teaching materials stored in this laboratory contain many DESMO-J models, which can be used for discovery-led learning of various modelling and simulation concepts, in the style suggested by constructivist learning theory (see Section 14.2.3). Since uploading new models is easy, this collection can be easily extended. Currently it contains models taken from different application areas (e.g. harbour logistics, production

Chapter 14 Simulation and E-Learning

systems) and for illustrating different modelling concepts (e.g. Monte Carlo simulations, i.e. random experiments without time dependency, event-oriented simulations, process-oriented simulations, different patterns of process synchronization). The harbour logistics model (see Sections 5.2.3, 5.3 and 10.5) plays a special role, since it is implemented in different variants. This reference model is particularly well suited to give students a wide ranging overview of DESMO-J's functionality in relatively compact form. It can also be used as a guideline for implementing a student's own models.

Authorized users can enter the laboratory from DESMO-J's homepage (http://www.desmoj.de).

14.4.4 Using Java Applets to Demonstrate Key Simulation Concepts

While both web tutorial and Internet laboratory are stand-alone modules, Java applets are meant to be used as components in web-based presentations. In this context the term *applet* means "[...]an embedded Java application, which executes in an applet viewer such as a web browser" (see Niemeyer and Knudsen 2000, p. 654). By embedding such applets in web pages, e-learning software augments and enriches presentations with highly visual and interactive demonstrations and explanations. The DESMO-J tutorial, for example, contains a web page where learners can interact with a "live" simulation model by means of an applet.

The DESMO-J e-learning package distinguishes between two kinds of applet whose purpose can be *simulation* or *documentation* (see Kiesel 2004).

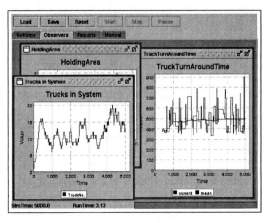

Figure 14.7: Results of a container terminal simulation as shown by an applet

14.4 E-Learning to Support Simulation Learning

Simulation applets allow students to configure models, run simulations, and analyse the results directly from a web page. Such applets can be implemented completely within the DESMO-J framework itself. Figure 14.7 shows the results of an applet-based simulation of a simplified model of a container terminal.

DESMO-J supports implementation of simulation applets with the provision of a `gui.ExperimentStarterApplet` class (see Section 10.4.3). Once we insert one of its instances into a web page, page's visitors gain control over a linked simulation model via a graphical interface. For example, they can change a model's parameters, its initial state, and its output formats. No direct changes to model code are required. This is an important prerequisite to make experimentation with models accessible to a wide range of users and purposes.

Simulation applets can be used for reference models as well as for exercises in simulation and statistical analysis.

Documentation applets are the second type of applet type we provide[4]. They help to present content with an assembly of images, sound, and text. Web site visitors can view step-by-step animations, which can be interrupted and rewound at any time.

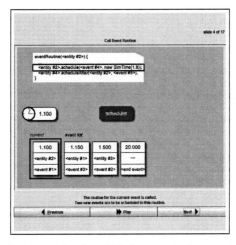

Figure 14.8: A Java animation which demonstrates how event lists work

---

[4]Documentation applets were developed as part of "E-Learning and Multimedia in College" project of the Federal State of Hamburg's Department of Science and Technology (2003-2005)

Chapter 14 Simulation and E-Learning

Each animation step is accompanied by explanatory text as audio to ensure minimal distraction from following the visual presentation. We will look at two such documentation applets in more detail.

The *"Scheduler-Demo"* applet explains how a discrete event simulator executes simulations. Its particular goal is to help to understand how *event lists* are processed (see Section 2.5). To this end it shows how DESMO-J inserts (i.e. schedules) events into this list and how the list is used to determine what event or process should next gain control. The intricacies of this fairly abstract topic are often hard to understand by beginners and the combination of verbal description and visual animation improves comprehension. Since it is part of a *web application*, the demonstration can be accessed and watched by a student at any time and as often as desired (see Figure 14.8).

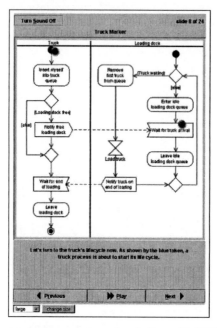

Figure 14.9: An applet showing process synchronizations with UML activity diagrams

The applet *"Process-Synchronization in UML 2"* (see Figure 14.9) uses a simple queueing scenario to show patterns of synchronization in process-oriented model descriptions (see Section 5.2.1). Within this context two activity diagrams, one for client and one for server processes, are presented in UML 2 notation. Animation then uses

14.5 A Web Platform for Cooperative Teaching and Learning

Petri net style movements of tokens to illustrate changes in process states. Process actions like *activate*, *passivate*, and *hold*, which are hard to describe textually, can now be explained in a more lively and comprehensible fashion.

Some additional applets can be found in the CommSy area (see Section 14.5) for this book (accessible by http://www.desmoj.de).

14.5 A Web Platform for Cooperative Teaching and Learning

CommSy (short for: "community system") is a web-based environment for cooperative teaching and learning. It was designed at the University of Hamburg, Faculty of Informatics, to support asynchronous styles of communication in teaching projects at educational institutions. For this CommSy offers access to innovative educational media (e.g. web-based tutorials – see Section 14.4.2, web-based laboratories – see Section 14.4.3, and applets for interactive explorations of concepts – see Section 14.4.4) used alongside classical learning tools (e.g. conventional lectures and laboratories, this textbook) to meet our intention of blended learning.

CommSy's key concepts are so-called "project rooms", which are established for each course or project, and to which only participants can be admitted. Such project rooms can be used to announce relevant news and dates, to give access to relevant working and reference materials, and to discuss topics of interest. In addition, participants can provide personal information on individual web pages and present details of any subgroups they may have formed. Figure 14.10 shows an entry page to the CommSy platform.

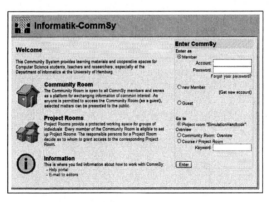

Figure 14.10: Entry page of a project room in the CommSy platform

Chapter 14 Simulation and E-Learning

Rooms for individual projects are embedded in a room serving the whole CommSy community (e.g. a department). This offers a commonly accessible place where, for example, courses can be announced and entry to project rooms can be gained. If desired, CommSy-wide access to teaching materials and research activities can be granted, and selected contents can be exposed to guests and therefore to all of the WWW community.

CommSy uses freely available Internet technologies. Only a web browser is required to access it. No provisions for cookies, JavaScript, Java, or specialized plug-ins (e.g. Flash) need to be made. On the server side CommSy is supported by MySQL and PHP[5] scripting. Its source code is freely available under the GNU Lesser GPL [6].

CommSy is less a learning management system (see Section 14.2.2), but more a computer-supported cooperative learning (CSCL) system. Its design is based on three core principles:

- *Simplicity.* This principle is particularly important in learning environments and suggests that learning contents must not be overshadowed by technical aspects. To guarantee this, CommSy has a simple and easily memorable architecture, a concise functionality range which is not overloaded with features of marginal utility, and a pleasing but simple layout.
- *Responsible usage.* This principle constrains CommSy's use to transparent and well-defined communities and discourages anonymous postings or "spyware". A "minimal rights" feature ensures that all members of a group can view and do the same things. The community character of CommSy is also reflected in the fact that information cannot be individualized, but can only be adapted to a group or community as a whole.
- *Coherent media mixes.* To honour this principle, CommSy fails to support inappropriate combinations of media. The vision of CommSy's designers has been to cater for media competent users who are able to choose suitable means of representation. A universal tool supporting all types of communication was seen as unrealistic and undesirable goal.

Table 14.3 shows CommSy's attributes and functionality from the different viewpoints of individual participants, a learning community, and the organization in which the learning takes place (e.g. a university).

A CommSy community room named *"The Java Simulation Handbook"* has been allocated to readers of this textbook. It serves as a repository for additional electronic materials and can either be accessed from DESMO-J's home page (`http://www.desmoj.de`) or directly via the CommSy server (`http://commsy.informatik.uni-hamburg.de`). Authorized users can access the DESMO-J web laboratory (with exercises and their solutions) from there and can also communicate with the authors and other readers.

---

[5]Personal Home Page (originally); today officially as recursive acronym "PHP Hypertext Preprocessor"
[6]GNU Lesser General Public Licence; see http://www.gnu.org/copyleft/lesser.html

Table 14.3: Different perspectives on *CommSy*'s attributes and functionality

Participants	Learning community	Organization
❏ interaction, discussion, and scientific exchange ❏ clarification and discussion of individual goals and items of work ❏ location and time independent access to information and resources ❏ publication of own materials	❏ virtual room with protected access ❏ support for communication and cooperation among project participants ❏ visible group structure ❏ effective administration of materials ❏ centralized presentation of relevant news ❏ centralized announcement of relevant dates	❏ overview of how content is organized ❏ centralized display of contents structure ❏ central repository for all internal and external contacts

14.6 Conclusions

E-learning technologies are well suited to augment and improve classical learning styles. From the viewpoint of educational theory such *blended learning* environments facilitate cooperative knowledge construction within communities in which learning activities can be made independent of temporal and physical limitations and can take better account of individual capabilities. Students can learn at their own speed anywhere and at any time. Knowledge acquisition is not seen as a static result (i.e. a *state*), but rather as a *dynamic process* which continually adds to and changes what has already been learned. *Cognitivist* and *constructivist* approaches to learning are well suited to this and electronic media can support such learning styles very effectively; e.g. by showing different views of a topic and by offering opportunities to work collaboratively. By adding electronic collaborative learning features, such as the ones offered by the web-based environment for cooperative teaching and learning *CommSy*, to conventional teaching events (e.g. lectures and group meetings) learning communities gain additional opportunities to present and exchange relevant information and materials.

The symbiosis of e-learning and simulation brings many advantages to both fields. Computer simulations greatly help in the presentation of abstract ideas and processes whose details and implications would otherwise be very hard to understand (e.g. illustrations and exercises related to logistics in LogEduGate). On the other hand, e-learning also serves well in support of teaching simulation techniques (e.g. the web tutorial for programming simulation models in DESMO-J).

Chapter 14 Simulation and E-Learning

Further Reading

Written for both e-learning consumers and designers, R. C. Clark and R. E. Mayer's (2002) *e-Learning and the Science of Instruction: Proven Guidelines for Consumers and Designers of Multimedia Learning* shows how to select and design effective e-learning courseware. Three types of e-learning are used to illustrate how the principles can be applied to diverse types of multimedia, namely e-learning of information, e-learning of procedural skills, and e-learning of problem-solving skills. Based on scientific theory of how people learn the book discusses the best use of texts, visuals, and audio resources as well as the best use of collaborative communication tools; such as chat rooms and discussion boards. Each chapter includes examples drawn from Internet sites and CD-ROM courseware.

The textbook *Learning Theories: An Educational Perspective* (Schunk 2003) surveys theories, principles, and research relevant for human learning; with emphasis on specific examples of their application in a variety of educational settings. It is written in easy-understanding language and features clear explanations and overviews of current behavioural, cognitive, and developmental theories. The book is well suited for self-study.

Course Management Systems for Learning by P. McGee, C. Carmean, and A. Jafari (2005) gives a comprehensive overview of standards, practices, and possibilities of course management systems (CMS) in higher education. It summarizes what the current knowledge is (best practices, research, standards, and implementations), surveys the history of CMS, and discusses how innovative practices in CMS design are informed by pedagogical theories.

Online Simulations 2005: A KnowledgeBase of 35+ Custom Developers, 300+ Off-the-Shelf Simulation Courses, and 40+ Simulation Authoring Tools (Chapman 2005) is designed to help inform learning specialists, software purchasers, and decision-makers about the tools and resources that exist in the simulation marketplace. It is packed with information about simulation products and services, with handy at-a-glance charts, online tools for comparing products and services side-by-side, screen shot examples, and meta-data that examines how these tools can be used to create effective simulations. Partly a reference guide to compare simulation authoring tools feature-by-feature, partly a breakdown of the off-the-shelf courseware choices that are out there, and partly an examination of the most innovative custom simulation service providers, this research covers all things simulation.

Bibliography

M. Bach, J. Himstedt, and J. Wittmann. *Einbindung von Simulationen in computergestützte Lernumgebungen auf der Basis einer Client/Server-Architektur in HALE – Dokumentation des Status Quo* ("Integration of Simulation into Computer-Based Learning Environments Using a Client/Server-Architecture in HALE – Documentation of Status Quo", in German). Research Report, Faculty of Informatics, University of Hamburg, 2003.

M. Bank, V. Tsingouz, and J. Gavan. *Computer Based Training: On-line Simulation Model as Teaching Strategy.* Research Report, Department of Communications Engineering, Holon Institute of Arts and Science, 1999.

P. Baumgartner and S. Payr. *Lernen mit Software* ("Learning with Software", in German), volume 1 of *Digitales Lernen*. Österreichischer Studien Verlag, Innsbruck, 1994.

U. Bentlage, P. Glotz, I. Hamm, and J. Hummel. *E-Learning – Märkte, Geschäftsmodelle, Perspektiven* ("E-Learning – Markets, Business Models, Perspectives", in German). Bertelsmann Stiftung, Gütersloh, 2002.

A. Bentz and M. Rave. *Konzeption und Realisierung eines Simulationslabors auf einer E-Learning-Plattform* ("Conception and Realization of a Simulation Lab on an E-Learning Plattform", in German). Diploma Thesis, Faculty of Informatics, University of Hamburg, 2004.

A. Blumstengel. *Entwicklung hypermedialer Lernsysteme* ("Development of Hyper-Medial Learning Systems", in German). PhD Thesis, Department of Computer Science, University of Paderborn, 1998. [Online] http://dsor.uni-paderborn.de/de/forschung/publikationen/blumstengel-diss/ (in August 2005).

brandon-hall.com – Glossary, 2005. [Online] http://www.brandonhall.com/public/glossary/ (in August 2005).

B. Chapman. *Online Simulations 2005: A KnowledgeBase of 35+ Custom Developers, 300+ Off-the-Shelf Simulation Courses, and 40+ Simulation Authoring Tools.* brandon-hall.com, Sunnyvale, 2005.

L. Chwif and M. R. P. Barretto. *Simulation models as an aid for the teaching and learning process in operations management.* CEPI Unifico, São Paulo, 2003.

C. Clark and R. E. Mayer. *e-Learning and the Science of Instruction: Proven Guidelines for Consumers and Designers of Multimedia Learning.* Pfeiffer, San Francisco, 2002.

O. Coenen. *E-Learning-Architektur für universitäre Lehr- und Lernprozesse* ("E-Learning Architecture for Teaching and Learning Processes at a University", in German). Josef Eul, Lohmar, 2002.

U. Dittler. *E-Learning – Erfolgsfaktoren und Einsatzkonzepte mit interaktiven Medien* ("E-Learning – Success Factors and Application Concepts Using Interactive Media", in German). Oldenbourg, Munich, 2002.

J. M. Epstein and R. Axtell. *Growing Artificial Societies – Social Science from the Bottom Up.* MIT, Cambridge, 1996.

Bibliography

D. Jonassen. *E-Learning to Solve Problems. Keynote of ED-MEDIA World Conference on Educational Multimedia and Hypermedia.* Tampere, 2001.

G. Kiesel. *Einsatz von Computersimulationen im Kontext von E-Learning-Umgebungen unter Verwendung des Frameworks DESMO-J* ("Application of Computer Simulation in the Context of E-Learning Environments Using the Framework DESMO-J", in German). Diploma Thesis, Faculty of Informatics, University of Hamburg, 2004.

D. A. Kolb. Toward an applied theory of experiential learning (together with R. Fry). In C. Cooper, editor, *Theories of Group Process.* Wiley, London, 1975.

P. McGee, C. Carmean, and A. Jafari, editors. *Course Management Systems for Learning: Beyond Accidental Pedagogy.* Idea Group, Hershey, 2005.

R. Meyer, A. Möller, and B. Page. *Modellierungswerkzeuge zur Simulation umweltökonomischer Systeme – Interaktives Modul im Rahmen der universitären Präsenzlehre der Angewandten Informatik und der betrieblichen Fortbildung* ("Modelling Tools for Simulation of Environmental-Economic Systems – An Interactive Module within the Scope of Presence Teaching in Applied Computer Science and Corporate Advanced Training at a University", in German). Final Project Report, E-Learning Consortium Hamburg (ELCH)-Project, Faculty of Informatics, University of Hamburg, 2005.

G. Neumann. Simulation in a problem-based e-learning environment for logistics. In Y. Merkuryev, A. Bruzzone, G. Merkuryeva, L. Novitsky, and E. Williams, editors, *Proceedings of HMS 2003 – The International Workshop on Harbour, Maritime & Multimodal Logistics Modelling and Simulation,* pages 268–276, Riga, 2003.

G. Neumann and D. Ziems. *Einbindung von Simulation und Animation in Logistik-Teachware* ("Integration of Simulation and Animation in Logistics Tearchware", in German). *ASIM-Mitteilungen,* (42):277–288, 1994.

P. Niemeyer and J. Knudsen. *Learning Java.* O'Reilly, Sepastopol, 2000.

K. Patrick. *Simulation as a tool for learning.* EPI Group RMIT University, Melbourne, 1999.

J. D. Post. *Simulationssysteme in der Architekturausbildung* ("Simulation Systems in Architecture Education", in German). imlab.de, Wismar, 2002.

M. J. Rosenberg. *E-Learning. Strategies for Delivering Knowledge in the Digital Age.* McGraw-Hill, New York, 2001.

M. Ryan and L. Woodward. Impact of Computer Mediated Communication (CMC) on Distance Tutoring. In *Proceedings of ED-MEDIA World Conference on Educational Multimedia and Hypermedia 1998,* pages 1203–1207, Association for the Advancement of Computing in Education, Charlottesville, 1998.

R. Schulmeister. *Lernplattformen für das virtuelle Lernen* ("Learning Plattfoms for Virtual Learning", in German). Oldenbourg, Munich, 2003.

D. H. Schunk. *Learning Theories: An Educational Perspective.* Prentice Hall, Upper Saddle River, 4th edition, 2003.

C. R. Standridge. Teaching manufacturing systems simulation in a computer aided teaching studio. In B. A. Peters, J. S. Smith, D. J. Medeiros, and M. W. Rohrer, editors, *Proceedings of the 2001 Winter Simulation Conference,* pages 1613–1618,

Bibliography

2001. [Online] http://www.wintersim.org/prog01.htm (in August 2005).

W. H. Tranter. *The Role of Simulation in the Teaching of Communications.* Research Report, Department of Electrical Engineering, University of Missouri-Rolla, 1997.

J. Wittmann and D. P. F. Möller. *Demands for flexibility in authoring and e-learning platforms under the aspect of integrating simulation models.* Research Report, Faculty of Informatics, University of Hamburg, 2003.

Chapter 15

Simulation and Logistics

Gaby Neumann

Contents

- 15.1 Motivation and Overview 436
- 15.2 Introduction to Logistics 436
- 15.3 Modelling and Simulation in Logistics 440
  - 15.3.1 Application of Simulation in Logistics 440
  - 15.3.2 Logistics Simulation Tools 442
  - 15.3.3 Simulation Experiments in Logistics Problem Solving 443
- 15.4 Knowledge Acquisition and Knowledge Sharing in Logistics Simulation . . 446
  - 15.4.1 Logistics Simulation Knowledge.................. 446
  - 15.4.2 Cooperative Knowledge Sharing in Logistics Simulation Projects . 448
  - 15.4.3 Simulation Model as Knowledge Repository 450
  - 15.4.4 Experiment-Based Knowledge Creation 451
  - 15.4.5 Knowledge Management and Logistics Simulation 452
- 15.5 Cases in Logistics Simulation 453
  - 15.5.1 Simulation to Support Logistics Planning:
    The Case of a Paper Store 453
  - 15.5.2 Simulation to Support Modification:
    The Case of a Pallet Flow System 458
  - 15.5.3 Simulation to Support Logistics Operation:
    The Case of an Order Picking System 461
- 15.6 Conclusions 465
- Further Reading 467
- Bibliography 468

Chapter 15 Simulation and Logistics

15.1 Motivation and Overview

Logistics is one of the most relevant application areas of discrete event simulation. In logistics, discrete event simulation has widely been accepted as an appropriate method and tool for the support of the planning, implementation, and operation of logistics systems and processes. Logistics simulation is to be understood as the application of simulation methodology to the field of logistics. Following VDI (1993) we define *logistics simulation* as the representation of an existing or planned logistics system and its dynamic logistics processes by an executable model in order to obtain findings and conclusions which can be transferred to reality.

This chapter will

- ❑ explain the chances and challenges simulation methodology provides for logistics;
- ❑ illustrate logistics simulation projects as problem-solving processes, as a collaborative approach and as both knowledge acquisition and knowledge sharing processes;
- ❑ highlight some trends in logistics simulation; and
- ❑ summarize lessons learned, guidelines and recommendations.

After reading the chapter, a student will understand the need to apply modelling and simulation to logistics, have an idea about the specifics of logistics simulation projects, have seen some examples, and know about future trends in logistics simulation. Many references to other chapters of this book allow links to be made to more detailed knowledge on certain aspects of simulation methodology.

Special emphasis is placed on relating logistics simulation to knowledge flows and knowledge management. Knowledge gained in the course of a simulation project quite often remains in the heads of the people involved in the project. It is not sufficiently externalized because documentation tasks are time-consuming, seen as an add-on to the real problem-solving process and poorly supported. As a result, project-specific knowledge about assumptions, decisions, modelling philosophy, implementation, experiments, and results is not kept but lost, even if it is retained by the people involved. As a contribution to overcoming this problem, logistics simulation knowledge is identified and processes of knowledge sharing, creation, and acquisition in the course of a logistics simulation project are analysed. Although closely related to logistics simulation, the methods proposed are easily adapted to other application areas of simulation – and should be applied to them as well.

15.2 Introduction to Logistics

Logistics is defined by the European Logistics Association (2004) as the planning, execution, and control of the movement and placement of people and/or goods and of the support strategies related to such activity within a system organized to achieve specific

15.2 Introduction to Logistics

objectives. Logistics aims to provide the right goods of the right quality in the right quantity at the right costs and under the right ecological conditions at the right place and the right time. For this it is not enough to focus on logistics operations to bridge space and time only. Instead, logistics has to be understood as a coordination function for the comprehensive design of effective and efficient material flows and, further, as a management concept for the design of object flows in process chains and value-adding networks. These changing views on logistics have mainly been driven by the globalization of economies and by improvements in information and communication as well as material-handling technology. As a result logistics processes and systems are characterized by an increasing level of complexity that needs to be managed in order to provide the required logistics service.

In general, a *process* considered in the field of logistics is formed by a series of interrelated actions and/or activities that transform a particular input (information and/or material, components, work, energy etc.) into a particular output (new information and/or products). In logistics there are two main types of process depending on the object transformed:

- *Material flow processes* are chains of activity for acquiring, working on, processing, or distributing goods (materials or products). This covers all transportation and storage processes including related loading or unloading operations, storage or retrieval, and order picking.
- The *information flow process* comprises a set of activities for acquiring, transferring, processing, storing and providing information which initiate, precede, accompany, or conclude material flows.

Both types of processes are closely interconnected and jointly form the *logistics process*.

The *logistics system* carries a logistics process and enables it to provide the required logistics service. Consequently, it consists of a material flow system and an information flow system, each of which is formed by all those components or elements and relations between them that are necessary purposefully to transform the respective objects.

A logistics system may interact with its environment through sources and sinks (see Figure 15.1):

- *Sources* represent all influences external to the logistics system providing it with physical or logical input: i.e. the system load, in the form of arriving materials or goods to be handled, arriving trucks, pallets or containers to be loaded and incoming customer orders to be fulfilled, or information to be used for managing or controlling physical operations.
- *Sinks* represent the exit points of the logistics system, providing its output to the environment. They can either be open any time or work on a demand-driven basis.

With regard to system theory (see Chapter 1.2) logistics systems can generally be considered *open systems*. Nevertheless, there are sub-processes and sub-systems deal-

Chapter 15 Simulation and Logistics

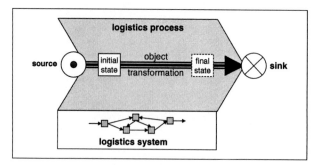

Figure 15.1: The logistics world

ing, for example, with the flow of reusable or system-specific pallets which stay inside the system all the time. In this case the (sub-)system is characterized by a missing interaction with the environment and is therefore to be called a *closed system* without any sources and sinks.

Logistics key performance indicators are a comprehensive but limited set of measurements against a standard or norm that provide feedback on the progress of the logistics plans and the execution of the main functions concerned in the management of the goods flow (marketing/sales, manufacturing, and logistics) and that identify the need for investigation and corrective action where there is a shortfall (European Logistics Association 2004). There are quantitative and qualitative performance indicators in logistics:

- *Qualitative characteristics* such as customer satisfaction describe a company's logistics performance in a more general, non-quantitative way. They do not provide absolute measures, but allow the derivation of comparable (soft) benchmarks for the demonstration of developments and the identification of the need for modifications or changes in the logistics process.
- *Quantitative measures* such as throughput, storage/retrieval rate, turnover, service level, stock level, or utilization of resources specify certain aspects of a company's logistics performance that produce exact figures intended as part of a business report or used as hard benchmarks.

Logistics planning aims at the planning of logistics processes and systems in general and on both levels, the strategic and the operational. Whereas logistics planning on a strategic level results in the purposeful design and needs-related development of the logistics solution based upon long-term decisions to prepare for investment, logistics planning on an operational level comprises all activities needed to operate the logistics system to run the logistics process according to requirement in the most efficient and effective way. The latter is also referred to as *logistics operation*, aimed at executing all

15.2 Introduction to Logistics

activities necessary for performing and managing a certain logistics process and system mainly based upon short-term decisions.

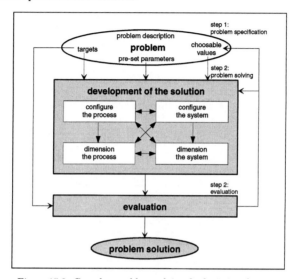

Figure 15.2: Complex problem solving for logistics planning

Due to the complicated structure of potential solutions, logistics problems in planning and operation but also corresponding problem-solving processes are of complex nature. They are subject to a variety of influences, demands, and circumstances entailing steps to configure, dimension, or evaluate according to what is given and what has to be defined. As shown in Figure 15.2, *logistics problem solving* can be characterized as a phased process of loops, as a process developing variants for and versions of both the logistics process and the logistics system. Analysing steps and creative, evaluating steps for synthesis with partially changing cognitive problems and views take turns. As a rule searching for appropriate and suitable components for solving the problem comes first. After that, the defined components must be rendered consistent with one another in order for the overall functionality as given in the problem specification to be realized. Methods available for this process are many and diverse; they are selected according to the type of planning problem (i.e. design, decision-making, parameter-setting, selection, and evaluation), the current state-of-the-solution and available input data and information. The stock of methods includes simple deterministic as well as complicated stochastic calculation models in the form of analytical formulae and extends as far as simulation models. Furthermore, logistics problem solving is embedded

Chapter 15 Simulation and Logistics

in a dynamically changing environment. Time pressure and limited resources define restrictions to be taken into consideration. Even at an early planning stage and on the basis of only a little information, a maximum of reliability and quality must be reached with minimal effort and in minimal time. In the end the challenge does not usually consist of searching for the optimal solution in theory, but of searching for an appropriate, practicable, and realizable one that solves the identified problem properly and efficiently. Within these constraints simulation is in many cases an appropriate method and tool.

15.3 Modelling and Simulation in Logistics

Due to the complexity of its systems and processes, logistics is a prominent application area of discrete event simulation allowing the chronological reproduction of real processes and systems realistically and accurately in any detail. Processes can safely be shown and speeded up; they are as repeatable and variable as desired. Precondition for this is an appropriate, valid simulation model representing an existing or planned logistics solution at the required level of detail. It finally results from the model-building process explained in Chapter 1. Input data such as time parameters, other quantitative parameters, or process rules are either obtained from analysing real systems (for modelling an existing system) or derived from settings and expert assumptions (when modelling a planned system). Purposeful experimentation with the model produces a wide variety of output data that need to be transferred into results by context-sensitive and problem-specific interpretation on the basis of statistical compression and graphical representations. Additionally, results can clearly be visualized by means of animation which supports model validation, experimentation, understanding of output, and presentation of results to the same extent.

Simulation methodology is to be applied to logistics problem solving whenever in reality not (yet) existent logistics systems or contexts are to be investigated, cause-effect chains are highly complex in nature, future or visionary scenarios are to be observed, alternative design variants are to be analysed, or a long-term analysis of system behaviour needs to be run.

15.3.1 Application of Simulation in Logistics

Modelling, simulation, and visualization are approved methods for the support of logistics planning and operation to

- ❑ effectively and efficiently design logistics services;
- ❑ trustfully test and evaluate not yet existent logistics systems for their functionality and performance;
- ❑ analyse and modify already existing logistics systems and processes with respect to changing loads or scenarios;

15.3 Modelling and Simulation in Logistics

- identify and remove bottle necks;
- evaluate, compare, or test control strategies and algorithms;
- look ahead in logistics process operation for trouble shooting;
- document, illustrate, and communicate logistics planning results and operation strategies/decisions.

Furthermore, simulation models of logistics systems are used as test beds for process control algorithms and software. Here the model replaces an existing or even just planned real system and communicates with the implemented control system instead. This way many simple and more serious bugs in the logic and implementation of the control algorithm can be identified and removed in the developmental lab before working with the real system. As a result physical implementation times are reduced, customer satisfaction is increased and working conditions for the team of developers are improved.

Typical application areas of simulation in logistics practice are related to material flows in manufacturing systems, warehouses and distribution centres, sea ports and container terminals, transportation systems etc., but also to the activities of human resources in material flows as well as to more fundamentally oriented investigations such as analysis of sensitivities or breakdowns. Figure 15.3 provides an overview of typical fields in which discrete event simulation is applied in logistics and links them to the lifecycle of a logistics system covering all three phases of planning, implementation, and operation individually, but also comprehensively.

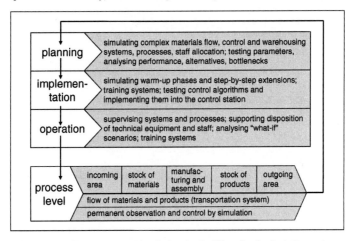

Figure 15.3: Discrete event simulation in the lifecycle of a logistics system (adapted from Arnold et al. 2002, p. A2-A3)

Chapter 15 Simulation and Logistics

Before this background the *general objectives* of applying simulation to logistics consist in:

- improving system performance with respect to more cost-effective solutions
- supporting decision making in the system's design and selection of appropriate alternatives
- checking hypotheses
- approving planning results
- illustrating complexity
- supporting logistics learning processes

15.3.2 Logistics Simulation Tools

As already pointed out in Chapter 9, the selection of an appropriate simulation tool for a particular subject and goal of investigation strongly influences the quality of simulation results, the flexibility in model design and modification as well as the efforts to be spent on model implementation, experimentation and retrieving relevant output data. For application to logistics simulation representatives of each class or generation of simulation software are in principle suitable and used. Nevertheless, most commonly used packages in this particular application area are application-specific simulation tools and integrated simulation systems (e.g. eM-Plant – see Chapter 9) with different underlying modelling concepts. To bring model building and simulation closer to the experts in an application area – in our case material flows and logistics – eventually enabling them to implement and use a simulation model themselves, a variety of tools using building blocks for model representation emerged.

DOSIMIS-3 (http://www.sdz.de) is one of these simulation packages. It specializes in the answering of questions related to functionality and performance measures of logistics systems and processes. It is widely deployed in industry as well as logistics education and training in German-speaking countries. DOSIMIS-3 provides an extensive library of components (i.e. building blocks – see Figure 15.4) from the material flow and logistics world, enabling model-building by a few clicks on the basis of a well-structured conceptual model. The simulation model then consists of the selected components specified by respective sets of technical, geometrical, topological, and strategic parameters which are placed in a work area and logically linked to each other by so-called nodes, i.e. directed arrows free of any further information. The tool's interactive graphical user interface provides functionality to support modelling, validation, experimentation, and presentation of results, enabling logistics experts with a certain understanding of simulation methodology to make use of it in standard situations eventually as quickly and easily as a calculator. But there is also a programming interface (C++) for tailoring building-block functionality to specific requirements. With this, DOSIMIS-3 addresses both types of user, the logistics planner or decision-maker on the one hand and simulation experts with programming know-how on the other.

15.3 Modelling and Simulation in Logistics

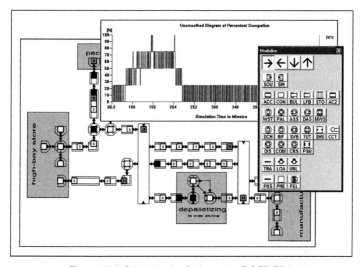

Figure 15.4: Logistics simulation using DOSIMIS-3

Despite the ever-increasing variety, power, and functionality of simulation tools dedicated to or suitable for logistics simulation, the careful selection of the tool ultimately to be used for solving a particular problem remains crucial. Here, the experience, knowledge, ability, skill and personal preference of the simulation expert – no matter if s/he is a logistics or a programming person – is of the same relevance as the subject and goal of the simulation. Depending on the particular problem to be solved and the current focus of a specific problem-solving step, different methods and tools might even apply. This eventually leads to the need for the purposeful changing between tools in the course of a project, always aiming to use the most appropriate method and tool within a given context.

15.3.3 Simulation Experiments in Logistics Problem Solving

Simulation experiments to support logistics planning and operation might be oriented towards modifications in either functionality or structure or parameters of a model and its components or even in a combination of those variations leading to more complex fields of experiments. Experimentation efforts are directly related to the type of variation required. The latter depends on the specific design of the simulation model resulting from the underlying modelling concept of the simulation tool and the design of the conceptual model by its developer.

Chapter 15 Simulation and Logistics

Functional variations are aimed at the systematic modification of physical or logical functionality implemented in particular model components, well-defined sub-models, or even the entire model. Examples are studies related to analysing the influence of varying control strategies at different levels of hierarchy, such as the sequencing of orders and their allocation to material handling technology, on a system's performance. For this, the extent of changes to the model might range from simply switching between standard strategies such as "first in, first out" (FIFO) or "shortest distance" to re-implementing complex strategies at global level.

Structural variations are those non-parametric experimentation strategies which lead to the modified placement of single components in the model structure or changed arrangement of groups of components in relation to other model components. This kind of variation is typically required when using building-block representations of the model, because here model structure is defined and changed in a graphical way. For example, increasing or decreasing the number of machines or other stationary components in the system can only be implemented in the model by adding or removing the corresponding building blocks (including their physical and logical links to the existing model). However, modification effort for this kind of variation might eventually be quite high. Of course, the same extent of changes would take much less effort if the number of equal model components were defined by parameters. In this case only modifications in the respective parameters would be required.

Parameter variations are limited to changing the value of certain parameters within specific model components. The opportunity for implementing changes to the model by modifying parameters only depends again on the underlying model-building philosophy. If, for example, buffering functionality is represented by one model component, the number of places in the buffer (its capacity) usually can be changed via parameters. Where separate model components represent the single places of a buffer instead, modification of the buffer's capacity is not subject to parameter variation anymore, but requires more laborious variation of the model structure.

Consequently, the objectives of a simulation and the questions to be answered by experiments should already be taken into consideration when designing the conceptual model. Specific opportunities and features offered by the selected simulation tool then influence transformation of the conceptual model into the computer model when it comes to model implementation. The clearer the concept, the less the effort that needs to be spent on model modifications for experimentation purposes. Within this context, it is worth thinking in more detail about what a simulation customer (the logistics expert) might look for when analysing the outcome of simulation experiments:

- ❑ **Typical events.** The logistics expert specifically looks for moments at which a defined situation occurs. This kind of query can be related, for example, to the point in time at which the first or last or a specific object enters or leaves the system as a whole or an element in particular. Other enquiry might be oriented towards identifying the moment when a particular state or combination of states is reached or conditions change as defined.

15.3 Modelling and Simulation in Logistics

❏ **Typical phases.** The logistics expert is especially interested in periods characterized by a particular situation. In this case s/he asks for the duration of the warm-up period, for the period of time the system, an element or object is in a particular state, or how long a change of state takes.

❏ **Statements.** The logistics expert looks for the global characteristics of processes, system dynamics, or object flows such as process type (e.g. steady-state, seasonal changes, terminating/non-terminating), performance parameters of resources (e.g. throughput, utilization, availability), parameters of object flows (e.g. mix of sorts, inter-arrival times, processing times). This information is usually based on statistics resulting from trace file analysis and replies to either a specific or more general enquiry by the user.

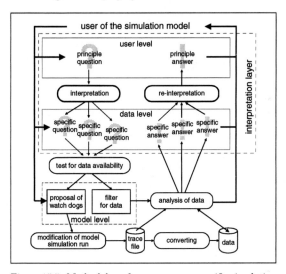

Figure 15.5: Methodology for a more user-specific simulation

When the potential interests of a simulation customer are compared, one significant difference emerges: whereas the first two aspects need specific questions formulated by the logistics expert directly at data level, the last aspect is characterized by usually fuzzy questions of principle from the more global user's point of view. Before these questions of principle can be answered, they have to be transferred to the data level by explaining them in detail and putting them in terms of concrete data (see Figure 15.5). As result of this process of interpretation a set of specific questions is defined, each of them providing a specific part of the overall answer in which the user is interested.

Questions at data level correspond to results that can be delivered directly by the simulation even if minor modifications to the simulation model should be required (see Tolujew 1997). To derive an answer in principle to a question of principle the respective set of specific answers needs to be processed further. These steps of additional analysis and condensing can be understood as a process of re-interpretation to transfer results from data to user level.

All steps of interpretation and re-interpretation aim to link the user's (logistics expert's) point of view to that of the simulation expert. They not only require an appropriate procedure, but, even more importantly, an interpretative model representing the application area in which simulation takes place. This model needs to be based on knowledge and rules expressed in the user's individual expertise, but also in generalized knowledge of the (logistics) organization regarding design constraints or system behaviour and the experience of the simulation expert derived from prior simulations.

15.4 Knowledge Acquisition and Knowledge Sharing in Logistics Simulation

One of today's challenges consists in seeing simulation in the context of human-centred processes. This requires understanding simulation as a complex problem-solving, knowledge-generation, and learning process but simultaneously as a tool to support teaching and as the subject of knowledge application. Hence this section draws links between simulation methodology and knowledge management approaches both to enable human resources involved in a simulation project to act properly as knowledge stakeholders and knowledge users to the benefit of the project; and also to strengthen the other role of simulation – to be a very valuable methodology and tool for the acquisition and storage of knowledge about the structure and organization of logistics systems and about processes of lasting effect for running, maintaining, or even re-designing them. Exemplary concepts will illustrate specific ways to achieve these objectives on the basis of strengthening collaboration and exchange in a simulation project as well as encouraging reflection on what happens in the course of a simulation project anyway.

15.4.1 Logistics Simulation Knowledge

Knowledge is generally defined by Beckman (1999) as reasoning about information and data to actively enable performance, problem solving, decision making, learning, and teaching. In logistics simulation as in any other kind of problem solving this knowledge is to be related to both the subject of the simulation study and the procedure of the simulation project. In general, *logistics simulation knowledge* can be described as entirety of specific or generalized theoretical or experienced knowledge about the simulation problem and its solution (subject-related knowledge), but also about the procedure and organization of the simulation project (procedure-related knowledge)

15.4 Knowledge Acquisition and Knowledge Sharing in Logistics Simulation

that either explicitly or implicitly exists or is created in the course of the simulation project.

Subject-related logistics simulation knowledge

- *Domain-specific knowledge* necessary to clearly understand the specifics and constraints of the application area. In our case this refers to general knowledge about logistics and material flows on the one hand, and complementary knowledge from related fields such as material-handling technology, automation and control technology, ergonomics, or economics and management on the other.
- *Problem-specific knowledge* unambiguously characterizing the specific problem to be solved in this particular simulation project. In logistics simulation this includes knowledge about
  - the logistics system (e.g. structure, layout, technical or geometric parameters) and the logistics process (e.g. activities, flows) to be investigated,
  - logistics objects (i.e. goods, pallets, possibly trucks or other moving entities) effected by them, and
  - interfaces with or links to the system's environment (e.g. sources, sinks, incoming/outgoing flows, system load) to be taken into consideration,

  but also knowledge about
  - the question, goals, and constraints of the simulation.

  Usually this knowledge comes with the tender specification for the simulation project or is to be identified and generated in the problem definition and data collection phases of the simulation as described in Chapter 1.
- *Solution-specific knowledge* describing the outcomes of the simulation project. This covers all knowledge that explains how the given or identified problem might be solved. Depending on the current stage of the problem-solving process and phase of the simulation project it exists in two forms. Hypotheses on what a possible solution to the given problem might look like can refer to an appropriate system/process design, the resultant system behaviour, maximum system performance, or any other relevant target characteristics. Output data or results in the form of system characteristics (e.g. performance indicators – see Section 15.2) and recommended designs or modifications of a planned or existing logistics system and process evolve in the course of the simulation project to answer all questions directed to the simulation.

Procedure-related logistics simulation knowledge

- *Methodological knowledge* necessary to run a logistics simulation project. This refers to simulation knowledge such as modelling and discrete event simulation methodology, experimental design techniques, validation methods, or simulation

Chapter 15 Simulation and Logistics

tools, but also to underlying concepts from problem solving and decision making, mathematics and statistics, and queueing theory.

❑ *Management knowledge* covering all aspects of the strategic and operative management of the simulation project such as project organization, team building, roles and responsibilities in the simulation project, or knowledge sources/stakeholders (see Chapter 16).

As shown in Figure 15.6 logistics simulation knowledge combines aspects from a wide variety of subjects and logistics simulation projects require a related collection of interdisciplinary expertise. Furthermore, logistics simulation knowledge is dynamic and always evolves in the course of a project. Techniques like structured documentation, continuous exchange, or ongoing reflection and generalization help to cope with this and to master complexity and dynamics to the benefit of both a logistics simulation project in particular and logistics simulation methodology in general.

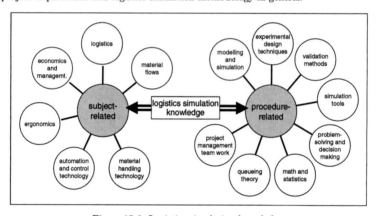

Figure 15.6: Logistics simulation knowledge

15.4.2 Cooperative Knowledge Sharing in Logistics Simulation Projects

As in any other field (see Chapter 16), simulation projects in the field of logistics are organized in the form of a service involving both simulation experts and logistics experts with individual knowledge to be of use at certain stages in the project (Neumann and Ziems 1997). Simulation experts are primarily responsible for model building and implementation, whereas logistics experts mainly provide application-specific knowledge for problem description, identification of input data, and evaluation of results. To bridge the gap between both worlds of knowledge and experience permanent communication must be organized (see Figure 15.7): at the beginning of the simulation project only

15.4 Knowledge Acquisition and Knowledge Sharing in Logistics Simulation

the logistics expert planning or operating a logistics system – the potential simulation customer – specifically knows the processes and their problems. Unfortunately, this knowledge is mainly of an internal nature (existing inside the brains and experience of people directly involved) and is externalized very poorly in any kind of document or file. For this reason, additional time and patience are spent by the logistics expert on the explanation of what the simulation model should reproduce. Eventually s/he is even asked to produce additional documentation to make the simulation expert familiar with the concept underlying the solution, the functionality of the technical system as well as the logic of the processes in such detail and completeness as is required for developing an executable simulation model meeting the intentions. This procedure is normally seen as an additional and unpleasant load, although it may be of benefit to the logistics expert as well. The simulation expert, who is going to become involved as simulation service-provider for solving these problems, inevitably has to work on his or her own understanding of the situation and problem right from the beginning by using techniques for systematic analysis and abstraction. This newly created knowledge on the part of the simulation expert needs to be matched against that of the simulation customer or even against reality for the purposes of validation and evaluation. In this way knowledge is created at an initial level that could have been acquired much more easily from the knowledge sources of the customer organization if known and accessible.

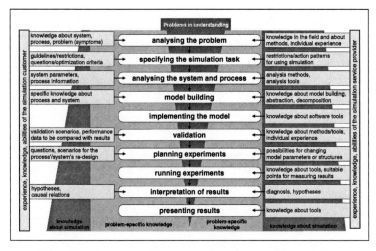

Figure 15.7: Customer and service provider as knowledge stakeholders in a simulation project

Chapter 15 Simulation and Logistics

A simulation expert typically does not have a level of subject-specific knowledge and terminology comparable to that of the logistics expert. Because of this the process of communication and improving understanding becomes increasingly important as a process of checking and harmonisation. From this, a joint glossary including the definition of terms and a well-documented description of the simulation model can result, if this knowledge is systematically recorded. Consequently, the model-building process should be seen by both sides as an important phase of collecting, evaluating, and structuring information. With this, really new knowledge is accordingly created with both the logistics expert and the simulation expert. The logistics expert learns about the methodology, steps, and tools of simulation; the simulation expert gains enhanced knowledge and experience of the application area and its specific problems from the joint developmental process (see Figure 15.7). This process continuously reduces the gap in knowledge between both sides and increases understanding and acceptance. However, for these achievements to be lastingly effective, both the knowledge itself and the process of knowledge-creation and exchange need to be described, recorded, and stored in well-structured documents which are easily understood and open to purposeful access by future logistics operators, planners, or simulation service providers. This finally would also form the basis for increased confidence in the results of a simulation project and acceptance of its outcomes.

15.4.3 Simulation Model as Knowledge Repository

Often modelling and model implementation are quite superficially aimed at running simulation experiments and case studies. Here the simulation model is just a tool necessary to achieve certain objectives of experimentation and cognition. This understanding is undoubtedly right, but covers only one side of the potential offered by a simulation project. If one considers the whole picture, the simulation model is more than an executable reproduction of the real or planned logistics world to be analysed. In the course of a simulation project the simulation model is developed, modified, used, evaluated and extended within an ongoing process. Therefore, the simulation model is also a kind of dynamic repository containing knowledge about parameters, causal relations, and decision rules gathered through purposeful experiments. In the end, knowledge stored in the simulation model can be considered proven, independently of whether it was developed by the domain expert him- or herself or by a consultant simulation expert. Usually this knowledge is not very well documented and therefore exists implicitly only inside the simulation model. To be used when the results of the simulation project are put into practice, it needs to be explained in such a way as to be accessible to the simulation customer as domain expert (e.g. in the field of logistics) in the subject-specific terminology and to be applicable without any loss of information or misrepresentation. Otherwise the technical or organizational solution in the real world cannot be expected to work in the way demonstrated by the respective simulation model.

15.4 Knowledge Acquisition and Knowledge Sharing in Logistics Simulation

To this day the translation of simulation knowledge into the domain expert's terminology or even directly into the source code of, for example, a control system or a control station remains an unsolved problem. Thus one continues to find a break and discontinuity in applying simulation results. Knowledge important for the realization of simulated functionality is lost and needs to be redeveloped by renewed implementation and testing.

To overcome this unpleasant situation consistent, up-to-date knowledge about the simulation model and its developmental process needs to be gathered directly from and continuously during the simulation project. To achieve this, all participants in a logistics simulation project, i.e. simulation experts and logistics experts, need to be encouraged (and supported) permanently to provide background knowledge about his or her motivation for going in one rather than the other direction, for changing the model structure or parameters in a certain way, for keeping a particular type of possible solution and abandoning others, for looking for information, knowledge, and support from one source instead of another. This procedure will only work if directly integrated into the "normal" simulation activities – with no or little extra effort.

15.4.4 Experiment-Based Knowledge Creation

In principle simulation runs provide results which are admittedly subject to randomness, but as discussed in Chapter 7 their statistical reliability can be increased to the desired extent by an appropriately large number of replications (samples). With this, guaranteed (abstract) knowledge about quantitative dependencies, times etc. can be gained that has now to be related to the real application. Here, initial settings, experimental scenarios, and modelling constraints (e.g.: What has been reproduced at what level of detail and what has deliberately been ignored when building the model?) need to be considered very critically to determine to what extent the findings are valid. The modification of structures and parameters such as initial states, resources (capacities and assignments), control strategies, or external influences enables one, for example, to check hypotheses or carry out comparative studies on the scope of validity (see Chapter 8), sensitivities etc. In the end deepened, readily generalized knowledge about dynamic behaviour, relations, and dependencies is produced. In addition, the logistics expert can directly test his or her intentions and draft solutions according to logical and functional criteria by experimenting with the simulation model. In this way simulation systematically "creates" knowledge based on the systematic design of experiments (including a meaningful definition of parameters and strategies) and the intelligent interpretation of results. This feature benefits not only scientific investigation but also, for example, case-based learning processes or the instruction and training of operators, enabling them to run systems and processes as planned.

Chapter 15 Simulation and Logistics

15.4.5 Knowledge Management and Logistics Simulation

Human resources involved in a simulation project are the key factors for its success and efficiency. As discussed in the previous sections, the different background knowledge and expertise of the simulation and domain experts who jointly run the project produces a considerable need for cooperation (see also Chapter 16) and with this for communication and explanation as well as mediation, moderation, and translation. The basis for successful collaboration is an ongoing, well-defined, and well-structured documentation of both simulation model and simulation runs and of the simulation project with all its assumptions, agreements, and decisions. Procedures, e.g. on the basis of so-called viewpoint descriptions as introduced into model validation by Helms and Strothotte (1992), help to identify who knows what about the system and the process, but also about the simulation project behind it, why something was decided in which way, which system configuration and which set of parameters work well together, what is in the simulation model, and what the limitations of its validity and usability are.

With this the process of a simulation project becomes a process of knowledge creation and acquisition at the same time without too much additional effort for all involved (see Figure 15.8). The clue to the successful implementation of those knowledge management procedures is often an appropriate (supporting) environment and climate in the organization. Concerning this, there is a greater need for a cultural shift than for additional software tools and IT solutions.

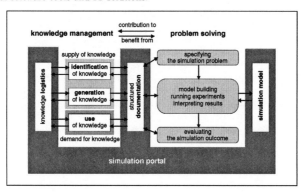

Figure 15.8: Problem solving and knowledge acquisition in a simulation project

15.5 Cases in Logistics Simulation

This section contains three examples illustrating the application of discrete event simulation to logistics, its benefits, and the related challenges. The cases were selected from projects actually run for companies on a consulting basis to investigate material flow solutions with different main focuses. In particular they aimed at:

- analysing material flows, system configuration, and process design to identify bottlenecks and propose effective measures and activities for improving the logistics performance
- investigating a material flow system's performance to determine the system load limit and derive conclusions regarding the system's ability to cope with future loads
- proposing strategies for the best allocation of a minimum number of workers to a certain number of picking zones

The cases represent typical application areas and questions related to logistics simulation as discussed in Section 15.3.1; DOSIMIS-3, introduced in Section 15.3.2, was used as a simulation tool in all three examples. All cases are presented in the same way. The chosen structure of the description allows the reader to follow the evolutionary process of each case from the problem and simulation task via the simulation model to the results and proposed changes and hence can easily be related to the general simulation modelling cycle (see Chapter 1). At the same time the necessity for the closer linking of logistics simulation and knowledge management as encouraged in Section 15.4 will become obvious and the need to really embed simulation into logistics planning and operation will be strengthened.

15.5.1 Simulation to Support Logistics Planning: The Case of a Paper Store

Logistics planning problem and simulation tasks: In a printing house printing machines need to be provided with rolls of paper in such way that the flow of paper is not interrupted during the printing process. To achieve this, a logistics system was implemented which handles the rolls automatically (see Figure 15.9):

- Packaged rolls of paper are delivered by trucks in an upright position. After unloading the rolls are moved into horizontal position and forwarded to the entry point of the store.
- Rolls of paper are horizontally stored in a single layer on the floor. The store is operated by an automatic bridge crane and forms the central part of the logistics system linking incoming area, work area, and printing area. A second crane of the same type and parameters is used merely as backup in case the other crane breaks down.

Chapter 15 Simulation and Logistics

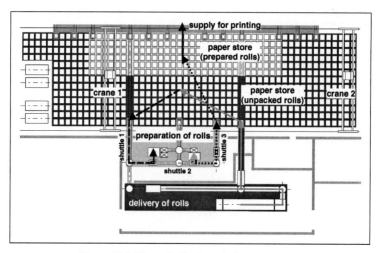

Figure 15.9: Flow of rolls through the paper store

- All rolls of paper need to be prepared for printing. For this the crane moves packaged rolls as required to the work area. Here, rolls are transported, by automatic shuttles, to the unpacking and preparation process as well as back to the store.
- Prepared rolls ready for use in printing are stored in a separate area. On demand they are forwarded by the crane to the printing area where another system of shuttles supplies the printing machines with them.

After implementation final performance tests showed that this newly built, fully automated logistics system did not perform as expected and required. The planning process had not been supported by simulation; practical experiments with the implemented material flow and control solutions did not result in the desired effects. Observation suggested the automatic crane was the bottleneck in the system. Against this background a simulation project was launched to analyse the implemented solution with regard to the performance of the logistics system as a whole and of all its components individually, but especially to propose measures and activities for considerable improvement in the situation with as little modification and re-implementation effort as possible.

Simulation model: Although various data as well as a clear hypothesis about the bottleneck element in the system were provided by the customer, the project started with a plausibility check and deterministic analysis based upon given information as

15.5 Cases in Logistics Simulation

well as impressions and data gained from observing the system in operation. After eliminating some simple, but serious planning errors the crane's average working-cycle times were recalculated. These new, but valid data provided immediate proof of the insufficient performance of the crane. Figure 15.10 shows an extract from a respective Gantt chart[1] illustrating the different working phases of relevant system elements. Very soon after the process started crane 1 is busy nearly all the time providing packaged rolls to the work area or removing prepared rolls from the work area. Even without an additional load initiated by arriving rolls (shuttle A is idle) this leads to waiting times for the loaded shuttle 3 which moves rolls from machine 2 to the crane for re-storing. Consequently, shuttle 3 does not return early enough to machine 2 to avoid delays in unloading the machine. These delays grow considerably when a truck arrives and the rolls it delivers have to be handled by the crane as well. To solve this performance problem the already-available second crane had to be used not just as a backup system but for simultaneously operating the store in parallel to crane 1. With this the estimated performance of the entire system improved tremendously, but not as much as needed for fulfilling the requirements.

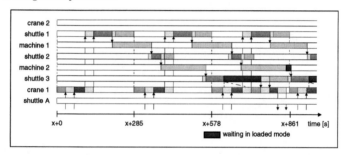

Figure 15.10: Deterministic analysis of system performance using a Gantt chart

Further steps in the deterministic analysis using the same methods as before helped to identify the shuttle-based transportation system in the work area as the remaining bottleneck. Due to its sequence-type design there was no possibility to improve the performance simply by adding another shuttle, for example. Because of this, alternative designs for the transportation system had to be found and analysed with regard to their performance. At this stage of the project, simulation methodology was finally applied because system and process complexity did not allow further analytical examination. For validation and comparison purposes a simulation model of the existing shuttle-based system including a simplified representation of the crane-functionality and store was built (see Figure 15.11-a). Afterwards two alternative modifications of the transportation system were modelled and tested, both of which physically separated

---
[1] A Gantt chart is a popular type of bar chart showing the interrelationships in the progression of time-related systems over time.

Chapter 15 Simulation and Logistics

the movement of rolls in the work area from the flows in the incoming area. Whereas the first modification stayed with the shuttles for moving the rolls and defined two separate crane areas, the second variant replaced the shuttle system in the work area by a system of circulating cars and allowed flexible, overlapping crane areas (see Figure 15.11-b). Both variations resulted in the desired improvement of the performance, but the proposed circulation system offered even more flexibility with respect to future increases in the system load. Here, it is only necessary to increase or decrease the number of cars circulating in the loop to adjust the system to performance requirements. The work area is now operated in such way that a car is loaded at one of the two entry points, moves the roll to the first machine, and waits there for the roll to be unpacked. The same car then moves the unpacked roll to the second machine, waits for the roll to be prepared for printing, and moves it to one of the two exit points of the work area. Further rolls can be handled in the same way by further cars following one another.

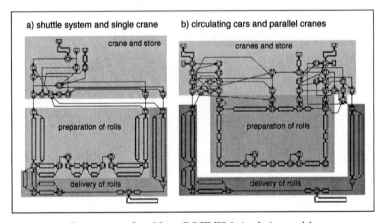

Figure 15.11: Simplifying DOSIMIS-3 simulation models

After comparing alternative possibilities for designing the roll transportation system in the work area and deciding on a system of circulating cars, a series of experiments was run with the respective model (see Figure 15.11-b) to find out how many cars should be attached to the work area to meet current load requirements. The number of rolls running through the work area (i.e. the throughput) was used as a performance indicator; the number of cars in the system should be as small as possible.

A comparison of the average simulation results for scenarios from 4 up to 8 cars circulating in the work area (see Figure 15.12) clearly shows significant differences in performance. If 4 cars are used the average daily workload is managed within 7 working hours (from 07:00 to 14:00) with a similar hourly throughput over this period.

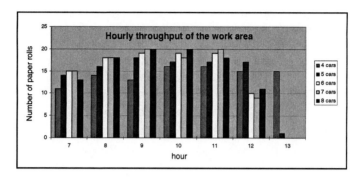

Figure 15.12: Simulation results for varying numbers of circulating cars

With an increasing number of cars the total working time required for coping with the daily workload decreases. If 6 or more cars are put into the system, even fewer than 6 hours are needed. On the other hand, the hourly throughput is not equally distributed anymore because of the extended warm-up and shut-down periods. Furthermore, it clearly transpires that there is no significant increase in the average hourly throughput according to whether 7 or 8 cars are used instead of 6. This might be the result of the required performance on the one hand and of the increasing traffic in the loop on the other. Against this background it is proposed to equip the transportation system of the work area with 6 cars in order to efficiently and effectively handle the current workload. In the case of an increased workload in future or at (e.g. seasonal) peak times one or two cars could easily be added; the implemented simulation model might also be used for further experiments.

Results and recommendations: In the course of the simulation project different components of the logistics system and varying aspects of the given problem were the focus of investigation. Accordingly, several methods were used to contribute to problem solving and at the same time to prepare simulation-based experiments. In the end a solution for modifying the logistics system was developed which leads to enormously increased system performance. The main findings of the project can be summarized as follows:

- ❑ Due to its design and technical parameters the implemented logistics system could never provide the expected performance.
- ❑ It turned out that the crane was not the only bottleneck, but that the work area for preparing the rolls of paper for printing was another major problem.
- ❑ The logistics system could meet performance requirements if both cranes already available are used simultaneously and the roll transportation system in the work

Chapter 15 Simulation and Logistics

area is designed as a system of circulating cars (see Figure 15.13) instead of the existing shuttle-based solution.

❏ The proposed solution requires the implementation of changes in the logistics system. To avoid crashes of cranes operating simultaneously a new control algorithm and software must be developed. The incoming area and work area need additional links to the paper store and crane areas; in the work area the track of the cars needs to be extended into a loop and 3 further cars must be added to the existing ones.

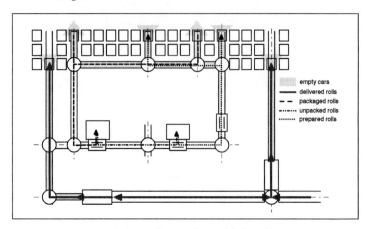

Figure 15.13: Paper flows in the modified working area

Implementation of the proposed changes and necessary modifications causes some additional technical and organizational effort. Although the benefit expected from this investment is quite high, additional costs and time could have been saved if simulation had been directly included in the planning process. Serious planning errors such as wrong calculations or inefficient procedures, which were exposed during problem analysis and simulation modelling, would have been eliminated before implementing the physical solution.

15.5.2 Simulation to Support Modification: The Case of a Pallet Flow System

System analysis problem and simulation tasks: A highly complex material flow system for pallets forms the interface and link between 2 warehouses (high-bay stores), 3 production areas, 2 order-picking areas, and the incoming-outgoing area of a company. As shown in Figure 15.14 there exist numerous relations with the crossing flows of raw

15.5 Cases in Logistics Simulation

materials, products, packaging material etc. Due to the increasing demand for storage capacity, production space and order-picking performance, the original module had been extended by a second, more modern one. As a result strict rules applied for which kind of material might be stored in which warehouse and certain functional restrictions for the different production and order-picking areas were in effect. This led to heavy traffic on the pallet flow system; the load did increase over time and is expected to continue to do so in coming years. Against this background the simulation project aimed at analysing the flows and system performance in the area and at estimating the maximum load the system could cope with.

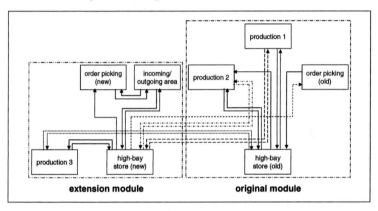

Figure 15.14: Pallet flows in the original and extension module of a company

Simulation model: A few years before this simulation project was launched the original module had already been subject to detailed simulation-based analysis. For the new study the existing simulation model for this part of the system had to be extended by the additional part. In this way the simulation modelling directly followed the historical development of the real-world system and faced similar challenges such as working within a given layout, enlarging or changing components, adding or modifying links. Despite this, the model-building phase of the project was much less time-consuming than in other projects in which it was necessary to start from scratch. After validating the resulting simulation model (see Figure 15.15) through the use of real data, a large number of experiments were run with increasing work loads under varying arrival strategies (e.g. equally distributed over time or in piles of jobs), with different arrival periods and even consideration of the influence of component breakdowns.

459

Chapter 15 Simulation and Logistics

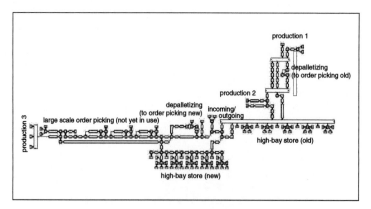

Figure 15.15: Simulation model of the pallet flow system

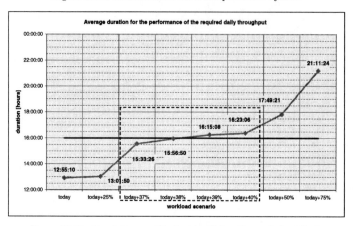

Figure 15.16: Simulation results for identifying the work load limit

Results and recommendations: The analysed pallet flow system was expected to handle the daily workload within a maximum of 16 hours. Consequently the average duration of the total handling time had to be used as a performance indicator. As shown in Figure 15.16 a step-by-step increase in the daily workload (in relation to the current work load) brought this value closer and closer to the permissible maximum. From this it can be concluded that the current daily workload could be increased by

15.5 Cases in Logistics Simulation

approximately 40 percent without requiring extra handling time. This conclusion is based on the assumption that the intensity of all flows grows equally and without shifting load from one relation to another. Whereas component breakdowns had no significant influence on performance, the arrival strategy and duration of the workload were identified as critical performance factors. The recommendation is, therefore, to spread as equal a workload as possible over as much time as possible (whilst still enabling the system to handle the entire load within the time limit). If the daily workload needs to be increased by more than 40 percent of the current level, a reorganization of the system and breaking-up of the crossing flows will become absolutely necessary. This challenging measure would provide the most lasting effects even in the case of increase rates below 40 percent.

15.5.3 Simulation to Support Logistics Operation: The Case of an Order Picking System

Logistics operation problem and simulation tasks: Order-picking systems are central components of any distribution centre. Performance requirements to be met by them depend directly on the sector, distribution strategy, and the required customer service level. In the case of a pharmaceutical company incoming customer orders are usually to be fulfilled and delivered the same day. For this, a complex order-picking system had been implemented. This system consists of 28 order-picking points (P1...P28) serving corresponding picking areas in a run-through rack (see Figure 15.17). They are linked by roller conveyors that form two loops for moving boxes. Each box is related to a specific order listing articles and quantities to be picked as well as the articles' location. A list of relevant destinations (order-picking points) to be visited by the box directly results from this.

After having entered the system at the box entry (B), the box is automatically moved by the conveyor system passing by the order-picking points of the loop. Every time the box arrives at a destination on the list and the respective order-picking point still has some empty space, it is pushed sideways out of the loop and waits for the picking units to be collected by a worker and put into the box. Then the box (with the current content) is pushed back onto the loop and conveyed to the next order-picking points. If a destination cannot be visited because of missing empty space, the box continues to move on the loop, either visiting the next destination on the list or circulating until the destination at which it had previously been rejected can be visited. At transfer points (T1...T4) boxes can change onto the other loop if its order-picking points also belong on the list of destinations. When a box has visited all destinations on the list it leaves the order-picking system on the shortest possible route via a checkpoint (C1 or C2). Here, the content of the box is checked for completeness and correctness before the box is forwarded to the packaging area.

As already explained, the order-picking system is a semi-automatic solution. Whereas the boxes move automatically, the picking is done manually. Here, each picking worker

Chapter 15 Simulation and Logistics

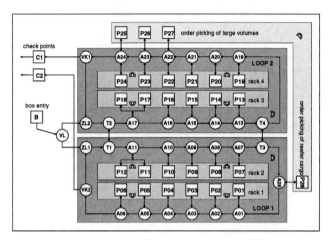

Figure 15.17: Material flow in an order picking system

usually operates more than one pick point. In order to improve the efficiency and effectiveness of the order-picking system with regard to the number of workers and working hours needed to perform the daily workload, a simulation project was launched. The project aimed specifically at proposing the best allocation to the pick points of a minimum number of workers.

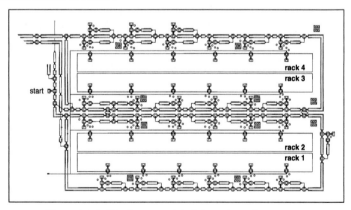

Figure 15.18: Simulation model of the order picking system

15.5 Cases in Logistics Simulation

Simulation model: Model design for representing the order-picking system and all physical processes run by it can be characterized as a standard problem, although the large number of elements produces some effort when using a component-based simulation package like DOSIMIS-3 (see Figure 15.18). Roller conveyors and further material flow elements are directly represented by respective simulation building blocks. The worker model as another standard component of the simulation package represents a certain number of order-picking workers including their work areas (i.e. allocation to pick points), individual activities (e.g. picking, box-handling, moving between different work places), and time model (i.e. shifts, breaks). So, the major challenge in model-building consists in creating a respective workload from the huge number of different articles (approx. 3,000) that closely matches the real-world scenario with its many and diverse customer orders. To be able to change the workload within the simulation experiments, it was not possible to use real customer orders as direct simulation input. Instead, a random generation of the workload was required. To derive an appropriate algorithm, real customer orders were analysed and destination lists resulting from them were put into tables with each row describing the order-picking points belonging to the destination list of one particular box.

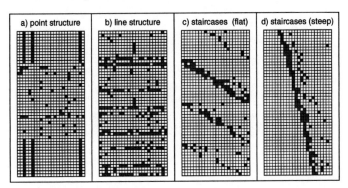

Figure 15.19: Typical structures of a box destination list

When looking at the tables from a distance, typical destination patterns can be recognized (see Figure 15.19):

- *Point structures* result from destination lists containing only a few order-picking points (fewer than 6 out of the 24 in the loops). They belong to small customer orders not consisting of more than 7 boxes.
- *Line structures* occur if a customer order contains only a few boxes but they visit a large number of order-picking points (each up to 22 out of the 24 in the loops).

Chapter 15 Simulation and Logistics

❑ *Staircases* can be found with large customer orders consisting of many boxes, because here each box has to visit just two or three order-picking points which may commonly be situated next to each other. The more boxes that belong to one customer order, the larger the resulting staircase.

The workload is now generated in two steps. At first the type and volume (in boxes) of the customer order is randomly defined and then for each box in the order an individual destination list is randomly created. Since the daily workload is given by the number of boxes to be handled by the order-picking system (throughput), the generation process stops as soon as the required number of destination lists has been defined.

Results and recommendations: To determine the best allocation of the minimum number of workers to the order-picking points a load-limit analysis for scenarios with varying numbers of workers was set up. The maximum number of boxes which could be handled by the picking staff within the working-time limit of 9 hours (including breaks) was chosen as performance indicator.

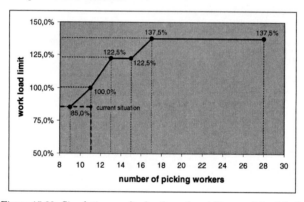

Figure 15.20: Simulation results for the order picking work load limit

On comparing the simulation results (see Figure 15.20) it can clearly be stated that the performance limit depends to a great extent on the number of workers allocated to the order-picking system: for the current situation of 11 picking workers (2 workers per rack operating 3 order-picking points each; 1 flexible worker per loop supporting the others as required; 1 worker operating the specialized order-picking points outside the loops), the workload could be increased by about 15 % in comparison with the current load to be managed. Without the flexible workers (i.e. 9 picking workers in total) the current load would form the load limit and no increase at all would be possible. Increasing the number of picking workers by allocating either more workers to the racks (and with this reducing the number of order-picking points to be operated by each of them) and/or more flexible workers to the loops will enable the order-picking system to cope with an even higher workload (an increase of up to 40% compared to the current worker allocation if 17 workers are appointed). With this also the absolute workload limit for the system has been reached and any further increase of the number of staff will not show any performance improvement. Even if each worker had to operate just one order-picking point, resulting in a total of 28 picking workers allocated to the system, the number of boxes to be handled by them (and the conveying system) could not be increased.

Based on these findings the following recommendations can be made:

- ❑ The workload limit depends to a great extent on the number of workers allocated to the order-picking system. But an increase in staff allocation does not adequately increase system performance.
- ❑ Allocation of 9 picking workers in total allows the order-picking system to cope with the current workload. In this case there is no need for flexible workers. The current workload also represents the workload limit for this scenario.
- ❑ Based upon the current allocation of 11 workers to the order picking system the workload could be increased by about 15%.
- ❑ The absolute workload limit of the order-picking system allows the handling of approximately 50% more boxes compared to the current situation. For this a minimum of 17 picking workers need to be allocated to the system. More workers do not lead to any further increase in performance, but might provide the system with some additional flexibility with regard to peak loads, for example.

15.6 Conclusions

Logistics simulation is one of the earliest and widest application areas of simulation methodology. Simulations are used not only to support the planning, modification, and operation of logistics systems and processes as illustrated by the case-studies (see Section 15.5); on the contrary, modelling, simulation, and visualization also enable illustrative and interactive logistics education: for example, by integrating simulation models and animation sequences in order to illustrate complex cause-effect-chains (or even networks); or by offering possibilities for simulation-based experiments directly to see and understand influences and how to make use of them. (For further discussion on the use of simulation to support learning see Chapter 14.)

Although discrete event simulation has been widely accepted in the logistics community, it is a fact that many logistics planning projects still run without any simulation. So, simulation projects do not accompany the planning and design of logistics processes and systems. Instead, they are not launched until doubt and uncertainty appear during functional tests of a technical and organizational solution or not even until the solution has physically been built and implemented. If unexpected problems then arise, reasons for failure need to be found and variants for reliable and speedy repairs need to be in-

Chapter 15 Simulation and Logistics

vestigated. Of course, simulation application at this stage supports problem solving as well, but with this late introduction some of the most crucial advantages of simulation methodology are thrown away. Instead, modelling, simulation, and visualization need to become an integral part of logistics design, implementation, modification, operation, and even training processes on much wider scale than is the case today. Preconditions for this are as good as they could possibly be:

- There is a wide variety of tools supporting modelling, simulation, and visualization in logistics (see Chapter 9). Simulation packages using building blocks for the implementation and use of a simulation model bring model building and simulation even closer to the logistics expert (see Section 15.3.2).
- There is a generally accepted standard procedure for running a simulation project in material flow and logistics (see VDI 1993). As in any other simulation project (see Chapter 16) logistics simulation projects also require the availability of sufficient simulation competence in the expected period of the project and the availability of license and permission to use an appropriate simulation package.
- Latest developments in the field of simulation to enable and support distributed and web-based simulation (see Section 12.3.3) or to offer web-based simulation services will also be of benefit to the logistics simulation user. Furthermore, major efforts are made to provide a domain expert with improved interfaces for data exchange and integration of software tools from different fields such as CAD, discrete event simulation, virtual and augmented reality, optimization etc. Within this context the term "digital factory" describes one of the most ambitious areas of research and development. It refers to planning approaches aimed at creating as real a computer model as possible of production processes in a not-yet-extant factory or manufacturing system. For this, not only software tools for the geometric representation of the structure of a plant or machine are used, but also simulation systems allowing the dynamic representation of the production process even in a 3D world by using virtual-reality models.

In the course of a simulation project really new knowledge is generated with the partners involved. Domain experts learn about the methodology, steps, and tools of simulation. Simulation experts gain increased knowledge and experience of the application area. As a side effect the understanding of system behaviour and processes is often improved, underlying (and not so well documented) control strategies can be figured out, or customer behaviour and order structures are understood. To benefit from these knowledge-transfer, knowledge-acquisition, and knowledge-generation processes in the long term, knowledge management approaches should be applied to logistics simulation and especially linked to logistics simulation projects (see Section 15.4).

15.6 Conclusions

Further Reading

Handbuch Logistik (Arnold et al. 2002, ch. A 2.4, pp. 41–61, *"Logistics Handbook"*, in German) is an interdisciplinary handbook that provides excellent access to the field of logistics. In four thematic parts a wide variety of relevant aspects and topics are presented and discussed in detail. Part A introduces basic concepts and logistics terminology and presents different techniques for modelling or optimizing logistics systems. Part B discusses key logistics processes in industry and commerce, whereas Part C provides basic knowledge on logistics systems and their material flow and information components for running the processes. Part D is dedicated to logistics management aspects and explains the economic and business constraints on logistics. The large number of authors, representing all related engineering and management domains guarantees high-quality, closely interrelated, up-to-date knowledge. Chapter 2.4, Part A, specifically deals with the topic of logistics simulation. An extended introduction into the subject is followed by simulation basics and general knowledge on simulation tools, before the procedure and steps of simulation projects are discussed. The chapter concludes by presenting application areas of simulation in logistics and discussing the potential related to this.

Modelling and Analysis of Manufacturing Systems (Askin and Standridge 1993) provides an introduction to the analysis of manufacturing systems using analytical and experimental models. This textbook brings together useful models and modelling approaches that address a wide variety of manufacturing system design and operation issues. By gathering all this information into one place, the text presents a concise, cohesive, and broadly-based view of the application of modelling and analysis in the manufacturing realm. The book is divided into four parts covering manufacturing systems and models (Part I), material flow systems (Part II), supporting components such as material handling systems and warehousing (Part III), and finally generic modelling approaches (Part IV). Thus the textbook is suited to the needs of both students and practitioners in the manufacturing sector. It provides a great deal of additional background to questions raised and discussed in this chapter.

Simulation von Logistik-, Materialfluss- und Produktionssystemen (VDI guideline 3633, in German) deals with simulation of systems in materials handling, logistics, and production on a large scale. It belongs to the set of more than 1,700 technical regulations developed and updated by the German Association of Engineers (VDI) to support students and practitioners by providing guidelines and working documents for daily use. VDI guideline 3633 is intended to consist of 11 parts; some of them are still under development. Main topics already covered by the guideline include:

- ❑ fundamentals and terms (Part 1)
- ❑ performance specification of the simulation study (Part 2)
- ❑ planning and evaluation of experiments (Part 3)
- ❑ selection of simulation tools (Part 4)

Bibliography

- integration of simulation into operational processes (Part 5)
- representation of human resources in simulation models (Part 6)
- simulation of costs (Part 7)
- machine-oriented simulation (Part 8)
- simulation and visualization (Part 11)

Hence it provides very useful knowledge for the practical application of simulation, taking into consideration the specifics of material flow and logistics as introduced in Section 15.3.

Bibliography

D. Arnold et al. *Handbuch Logistik* ("Logistics Handbook", in German). Springer, Berlin, 2002. pp. A2-41–61.

R. G. Askin and C. R. Standridge. *Modeling and Analysis of Manufacturing Systems*. Wiley, New York, 1993.

T. J. Beckman. The Current State of Knowledge Management. In J. Liebowitz, editor, *Knowledge Management Handbook*. CRC, Boca Raton, 1999.

European Logistics Association (ELA). *Revised ELA Terminology in Logistics*. ELA, Brussels, 2004. Unpublished, draft version.

C. Helms and T. Strothotte. Oracles and Viewpoint Descriptions for Object Flow Investigation. In *Proceedings of the 1992 EUROSIM Conference*, pages 47–53, Elsevier, Amsterdam, 1992.

G. Neumann and D. Ziems. Transparente Modelldokumentation und Resultatpräsentation schafft Vertrauen ("Transparent Model Documentation and Presentation of Results Increases Reliability", in German). In *Proceedings of Simulation and Animation '97*, pages 237–250, SCS, San Diego, 1997.

G. Neumann and D. Ziems. Logistics Simulation: Methodology for Problem Solving and Knowledge Acquisition. In N. Callaos, M. Bica, and M. Sanchez, editors, *Proceedings of The 6th Multiconference on Systemics, Cybernetics and Informatics*, volume XII, pages 357–362, International Institute of Informatics and Systemics, Orlando, 2002.

J. Tolujew. Werkzeuge des Simulationsexperten von morgen ("Tools of the Simulation Expert of Tomorrow", in German). In *Proceedings of Simulation and Animation '97*, pages 201–210, SCS, San Diego, 1997.

Verein Deutscher Ingenieure (VDI). *Simulation von Logistik-, Materialfluss- und Produktionssystemen – VDI-Richtlinie 3633* ("Simulation of Systems in Materials Handling, Logistics, and Production – VDI-Guideline 3633", in German). Beuth, Berlin, 1993.

Chapter 16

Simulation in Practice

Bernd Page

Contents

16.1 Motivation and Overview	469
16.2 Introduction	470
16.3 General Requirements for a Successful Simulation Study	472
16.4 Simulation Project Organization	477
16.4.1 Roles and Responsibilities in a Simulation Project Team	477
16.4.2 Simulation as a Consulting Service	478
16.4.3 Costs and Time Requirements for a Simulation Study	480
16.5 Methods of Data Collection	481
16.6 Typical Errors and Pitfalls in a Simulation Study	483
16.7 Conclusion	484
Further Reading	485
Bibliography	486

16.1 Motivation and Overview

In this chapter we will discuss how a simulation study can be launched in a practical context. We provide guidelines for the successful application of simulation beyond the academic field and address some questions which may arise before an enterprise commits to a simulation study; i.e.:

- ❏ Which kind of planning problems are suitable for simulation?
- ❏ What are the approximate time requirements for a typical simulation study?
- ❏ What are the costs of a simulation project?
- ❏ Is it worth investing in special simulation software?
- ❏ Which are the critical issues for the successful application of simulation technology?

Chapter 16 Simulation in Practice

These guidelines offer arguments, answers, and assistance for simulation users in enterprises and support management decisions to start simulation projects. Decision makers and specialists in industry should be able to make an informed decision in favour of or against the adoption of simulation technology – be it just for a given project or as part of an enterprise-wide strategy.

To achieve a project's objectives efficiently, we should assign special roles and responsibilities within a project team. External simulation consultants can be hired to compensate for missing in-house simulation experience, but smooth communication and cooperation between all parties is strictly essential.

Simulation projects are time consuming and costly. Depending on a project's scope we can conduct rather short studies over a couple of months, at a cost of a few thousand Euros, or we can commit to a long term project (e.g. lasting over than a year) with a price tag of more than 100,000 Euros. If such costs seem excessive, there are a number of options, such as limiting modelling detail, which can reduce both time and cost requirements.

Data collection is a crucial phase during a simulation study, and we can employ both *primary* (i.e. just for the study in question) or *secondary* (i.e. relying on existing data and files) methods to support this important activity. Because simulation is a data driven methodology, quality is a primary concern in either both cases. Simulation novices as well as experienced simulation specialists must be fully aware of typical error sources and pitfalls in simulation studies. These pitfalls can range from missing data to lack of management involvement.

In conclusion, simulation is a sophisticated technology for improved planning and decision making in complex situations. But there are cases where it should not be used, and a range of alternative approaches should be explored, many of which may both be less costly and less time consuming. However, if simulation is appropriate and the hints for a successful study summarized in the guidelines at the end of this chapter are followed, there is a good chance for successful deployment of simulation techniques in an industrial setting.

16.2 Introduction

In many industrial management problems simulation is often used as a synonym for solutions where a deep technical insight is missing. It is expected to support decisions on machine investments, staffing, operation schedules, sequencing strategies, or acceptance of work orders. Many times its potential is either underestimated, sometimes overestimated, or even completely misinterpreted. On the one hand, simulation is seen as a tool for precise forecasts of all consequences of corporate decisions, while, on the other hand, many believe that a simulation is nothing more than an improved production planning and control system (PPS). Both assessments misinterpret the potentials as well as the limitations of computer simulation. Simulation as a technology provides

16.2 Introduction

well-founded decision support and offers security of planning results. It helps to prevent wrong decisions and reduces risks. Although simulations can never pronounce a judgement as right or wrong, they can reveal consequences of possible causes of action. As already mentioned in Chapter 1, the main applications of simulation technology are:

- support for complex systems' analysis
- demonstration and illustration of complex processes
- decision support for system design and operation
- education and training

The description of system behaviour through simulation models has displaced many less flexible analysis methods (e.g. real life experiments) which played more important roles in the past. This is due to simulation's many advantages, such as:

- The costs of building a model and performing simulation experiments are usually only a fraction of similar experiments with a real system or analogous physical models.
- Observations of system behaviour over a specific time period can be condensed (i.e. slow processes can be accelerated) or extended (i.e. fast systems can be slowed down) at will. Thus observations which would otherwise defeat human perception in real world systems now become possible.
- The real system is not put at risk. Measurements or manipulations of real systems are unnecessary.

Decision support is a primary application for simulation technology in a corporate setting, in particular in production and logistics. Typical examples are:

- judgement of corporate strategies, such as the launch of new products, deployment of new technologies, or strategies for expansion
- assessments of likely success, prior reconstruction, or rearrangement of production lines
- exploring potential rationalizations of production and personnel costs
- risk analysis for investments

Simulation is also successfully applied to support the planning process of assembly, material flow, production, transportation, inventory, or information systems. Typical use cases are:

- checking functionality and expedience of alternative organization designs
- fine tuning of planning results
- education and training of decision makers with simulation games using enterprise models

Simulation technology offers planners and managers tools which are comparable to e.g. wind tunnels for aircraft designers. Model-based tests are often needed before production commences, either since accurate computations are impossible or because model structures are so complex or plagued with uncertainties that only systematic experimentation can yield a solution. Simulation technology enhances decision quality and security. It can contribute to making correct decisions more rapidly. Lengthy real life processes can be accelerated and realistically simulated in fast motion; e.g. within a few minutes. Relevant propositions can be deduced with required precision and certainty, with a relatively limited investment of resources. By increasing both quality and efficiency of understanding a complex system's behaviour the high degree of flexibility inherent in simulation technology also contributes to its popularity in industry. Improved understanding leads to identification of rationalization and cost reduction potentials and helps to avoid planning errors.

16.3 General Requirements for a Successful Simulation Study

There are a number of aspects which enterprises, project members, and simulation consultants must take into account, if they want to lead simulation projects to successful conclusion in a practical context. For example, they must ensure:

The right point in time for the employment of simulation technology in a project: A simulation project has to be put into place early enough at the beginning of planning the real system under construction. This is the only way in which we can ensure that sufficient time will be spent on the proper design and organization of all the required steps in a simulation; at an adequate level of quality and carefulness. Only an early presentation of simulation results allows for its integration into the planning process. Otherwise a simulation study only serves as an alibi and will make no significant impact during the planning process.

Realistic assessment of work load for the simulation study: A realistic estimate of the duration of the simulation study is a critical factor for its success. This information is needed to feed simulation results into the planning process as it advances and for adequately assessing required resources. These resources include internal as well as external personnel with specialized technical backgrounds (e.g. simulation consultants), suitable simulation software, and adequate computing resources. To gain approval for the study, fairly accurate cost estimates also have to be presented to top-level decision makers. These must not only include all the costs for external consultants and software investments, but should also estimate costs for the time company employees spend on the project. To exemplify rough cost estimates for simulation studies in the production industry, we can refer to the literature (see Košturiak and Gregor 1995, p. 6), where simulation costs of less than 1 % of total investment are quoted. Since simulation is only a small part of the planning process, a simulation study should not cost more than 10 % of the total planning expenditure.

16.3 General Requirements for a Successful Simulation Study

Good technical know-how of computer simulation and alternative methods: Project members who plan to conduct a simulation study must have the required specialized technical knowledge and substantial experience in the relevant subject areas in order to ensure the study's quality and success. A wide range of knowledge and experience in areas such as simulation technology's potential and limitations, model building and implementation, simulation tools and languages, statistical methods, experimental design and interpretation of simulation results – as introduced in this book – is essential. Information about which of the required resources are available within the company and where any additional ones can be obtained is also needed. These resources include simulation software tools, computing capacities and technical specialists. However, since there are always alternatives to the demand for simulation technology, a good understanding of alternative methods, such as mathematical optimization techniques, would be an asset.

Finally, good insight into the structure and operation of the modelled real system and the relevant technologies (e.g. manufacturing processes, transportation systems, production control) is essential. Typically, application specialists from within the participating enterprise will offer this background, while additional methodological know-how can always be added by hiring simulation consultants.

Examination of simulation's suitability for the project: Only if the problem under investigation is stated clearly and distinctly, we can decide whether computer simulation is the right option for the problem's solution. For example, a brainstorming session by the project team can offer a first stab at an ad-hoc solution to a problem or at least limiting the directions any associated simulation study may take. In some cases the considerable time and cost of a simulation study may prove difficult to justify and less costly alternatives will be explored before a final decision on method is made. Less complex and time-consuming alternatives to a simulation study include spreadsheet models, optimization methods, queueing theory, or statistical analysis. Often detailed data analyses with a statistical software package are sufficient to reach decent problem solutions in industry. If feasible, we can also employ a less complex and more compact analytical model, such as a standard linear optimization.

Adequate level of detail: Human nature favours completeness; i.e. modellers often succumb to the temptation to engineer perfect mapping studies. A good example is a physical model of an automobile to be tested in a wind tunnel. For the experiment's purpose (i.e. estimation of the aerodynamic resistance) we only need to include those aspects of the real automobile which are relevant for its aerodynamic resistance; basically body and wheels. We definitely do not need to represent aspects like the engine, steering wheel, seats, etc. The motto in practical simulation studies should always be: "A model must be as comprehensive and accurate as necessary, but as simple as feasible". Including needless details is always elaborate, error-prone, and costly.

Chapter 16 Simulation in Practice

Appropriate amount, quality, and format of data: Because all models are mappings of real systems characterized by large amounts of data at high resolution, simulation methods are very sensitive to the quality of their input data. The higher the degree of detail in a model, the more accurate and higher the resolution of the required data must be. Data collection and analysis are therefore very important steps in the computer simulation process. Before an enterprise launches a simulation study, the data situation must be checked carefully. While the simulation consultants may perform data analysis and evaluation, it is the responsibility of the participating enterprise to provide the required raw data. In this context the following questions should be asked:

- Does the data make sense?
- Is the data representative for this process?
- Is the data detailed enough for the project's goals?
- Are the time scale and resolution correct?
- How can we fill in missing data?

In some cases we can deal with inaccurate data of minor relevance by making assumptions and estimations with the assistance of the enterprise's employees. These typically will have a deep knowledge of the modelled system's operation or are often capable of making good guesses. Since simulation is an empirical approach, however, its quality very much relies on the quality of its input data, and there are limits for compensating for missing data. In general no simulation study should be started without a sound database, or at least an agreed upon procedure to collect relevant data "as needed".

Effective communication and user participation: Although simulation has been a well established technology for decades, not many employees are familiar with it. It may not be easy to explain the aims, scopes, and mechanisms of simulation to all participants in a simulation project; particularly those employees of an enterprise who have only a peripheral involvement. However, in order to avoid unrealistic expectations it is very important that all participants are informed about the potential as well as the limitations of the technology. There is often a typical communication barrier between simulation analysts (in-house or external) and members of a specialist department (e.g. logistics or production). This barrier has to be bridged and any misapprehensions must be rectified. The role of a simulation specialist is typically the one of the model developer, whereas a member of the specialist department plays the role of the model user. The gap between these two groups has to be bridged by effective communication and up-to-date documentation of project status. Only if users can understand what is happening in a simulation study and how this relates to the real world system, they can be gainfully integrated in the modelling process and will accept its results. Close cooperation and communication is also fruitful for the simulation analysts, since this enables them to absorb as much application domain knowledge as possible during model development. Such synergy will only occur if application specialists in the enterprise are closely involved in the model design. Since management is responsible for all final

16.3 General Requirements for a Successful Simulation Study

decisions, their early participation is crucial. Management must be informed on the goals of the project, should be invited to all important project meetings, and should be willing to lend their support to the project. Without effective communication and participation of users and management the success of a simulation study will very much be in doubt.

Adequate simulation tools: As outlined in Chapter 9, specialised software products for discrete event simulation are available in large variety. There are many different tools which might be suitable for a given simulation study: The market for simulation software has become huge and is not very transparent. Appropriate selection criteria for simulation software have been already discussed in more detail in Chapter 9. In this context we should only refer to the more important ones and again stress the relevance of choosing an adequate software tool as a critical factor for a simulation study's success. First of all, we have to make sure that the required modelling functionality is offered by the tool under consideration. For instance, if our system has not only discrete elements, but also elements of a continuous nature, the software tool should include discrete event as well as continuous simulation functions and should both techniques to be used in conjunction. Otherwise we run the risk of biasing the model just to fit the software's structure. Another important factor for modelling success is a tool's flexibility, since this allows more efficient model implementation for a variety of simulation problems. Program capacity (e.g. number of objects in the model, number of relationships, number of random processes, data storage) should not be overly restricting, so that larger scale models can still be implemented. In order to reduce the modellers' workload, model construction, implementation, and simulation experiments should be supported by powerful functions. User friendliness is also another significant requirement, which holds for software in general as well as for specialized simulation tools. However, in the field of simulation modelling the simulation specialists often become programming experts, who can handle complex software systems more easily than a casual user. Such power users sometimes trade user friendliness against speed of development or execution efficiencies. Intuitive model construction is a more dominant concern for casual users, who often will only deploy predefined, ready to run, parametrized simulation models (e.g. recurring simulations of an assembly line by production engineers). Such models will often have been developed by professional simulation analysts in a special department of an enterprise, who are themselves power users in the above sense.

It is clearly an asset if the effort required for training and adjusting to a new simulation tool is not too high. Good documentation including hands-on examples and a familiarity with the tool's implementation language (e.g. Java, in the cases of Java-based simulation tools, such as DESMO-J) are certainly helpful to restrict this investment and to help novices to become productive as quickly as possible.

Thorough model validation: Careful model validation is an indispensable requirement for any serious use of simulation models in practice. It should be obvious that

Chapter 16 Simulation in Practice

experiments with inadequate simulation models are a waste of effort and will at best produce irrelevant simulation results. Only meticulous, stepwise model validation can eliminate erroneous assumptions and will eventually lead to a credible model design. While model correctness can never be proven in general terms, the key requirement is for trust in and acceptance of a model's relevance and representativeness by the users in an enterprise whose problems it is designed to solve.

Correct statistical planning and analysis of simulation experiments: Discrete event simulations typically deal with stochastic models; i.e. they describe statistical experiments with random outcomes. Random numbers are therefore a central element of discrete event simulations. Random effects on model inputs (e.g. customer arrivals in a queueing system following a certain statistical distribution that is derived from the modelled system's empirical data) result in behaviours which may settle into statistical patterns over the duration of a simulation experiment. Similar to estimating input parameters, interpreting streams of "random" results requires a solid application of specialized statistical analyses.

For example, the length of a simulation run in terms of number of observations (e.g. number of customers served) or simulation time are experimental parameters which must be determined on sound statistical grounds. The effect of run lengths on simulation results depends on the model parameters' variances. Run lengths can strongly determine the precision of simulation results; see Chapter 7. A technically proficient design for a simulation experiment supports the extraction of model parameters which will yield predictions as close as possible to a real system's performance.

Proper interpretation of simulation results: Any stochastic simulation's results are statistical samples with some degree of *uncertainty* and any adequate interpretation must take the randomness of simulation experiments into account. Furthermore, these results must be related to the limitations, assumptions, and simplifications defined in an early phase of the modelling process. Only with this background in mind we can declare any experimental results to be *valid* and can relate them to a real system's behaviour.

Once validity is established, useful conclusions can be drawn and credible predictions can be made. Any problem solutions based on this information must then be sought in close cooperation of simulation analysts, departmental specialists, and management.

Detailed documentation of the simulation study: The value and long term impacts of a simulation study are strongly dependent on detailed documentation of all steps in a modelling cycle (see Chapter 1). In the long run such documentation preserves both a study's transparency and significance. Aspects such as initial conditions, starting situation, aims, and scopes at the beginning of the project must all be recorded. Modelling assumptions must be made explicit, and the model construction and implementation process must be described in detail. All simulation experiments and their results should be included in the documentation. Interpretations of these results and final conclusions and recommendations should be summarized in a management report.

16.4 Simulation Project Organization

16.4.1 Roles and Responsibilities in a Simulation Project Team

A solid simulation study requires an appropriate division of labour and responsibilities between the simulation specialists, frequently in the role of external consultants, and project members of a client enterprise. It is essential that they support each other and that each understands the duties of the others. One of the first and most important aspects of good project management is to identify key contact persons in the enterprise and among the simulation consultants.

This is a prerequisite for a smooth flow of communication, helps to avoid misunderstandings, and serves to ensure regular updates of all parties on project status. In simulation projects it is quite common to constitute project teams as shown in Figure 16.1.

Note that some people may wear several hats:

- The *manager* as decision maker holds the responsibility for the total budget and grants final approval of the project. S/he is not interested in technical details of the simulation study, but asks for brief summaries as decision aids, delivered on time.

- The *project leader* is responsible for the study's quality, for keeping to deadlines and for meeting the budget. S/he serves as both coordinator and central contact. In a cooperative project with an external consultant, there should be a project leader for both parties, who would then coordinate the project in close consultation. While they may delegate tasks as required, project leaders also have overall responsibility for project documentation.

- The *project members* of client departments are domain experts and own special know-how about the simulated system and are tasked to provide relevant information and data for the study. Often they will eventually be operational users of simulation results.

- The *simulation expert* (internal or external) defines the data requirements, constructs the simulation model, operates the simulation tool and runs simulation experiments. Although this is largely driven by the domain experts, s/he may also be consulted for technical support during the interpretation of simulation results.

Chapter 16 Simulation in Practice

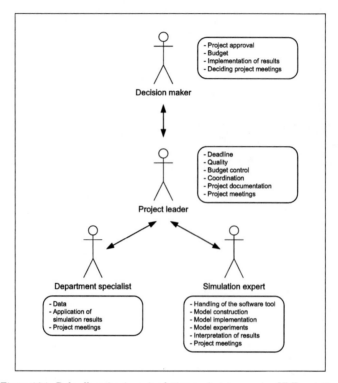

Figure 16.1: Role allocation in a simulation project team using UML notation (derived and extended from Rabe and Hellingrath 2001, p. 121)

16.4.2 Simulation as a Consulting Service

The first question an enterprise considering simulation based decision support must answer is whether to rely on internal staff or hire external simulation consulting services. If management favours the use of in-house expertise, it must ensure that the following preconditions are met:

- satisfactory source of qualified personnel with simulation background is available
- required data sources are available or easy to establish
- suitable simulation software for the application domain (e.g. production or inventory) is available

16.4 Simulation Project Organization

- sufficient computing power can be obtained
- qualified specialists can be hired to conduct in-house training
- realistic costs have been estimated for all personnel (internal and external) and resources
- the capability for proper checks and interpretation of simulation results is ensured

There are a number of advantages in cooperating with an external simulation consultant:

- a more objective and neutral perspective on the problem
- avoidance of conflicting views and interests in the enterprise
- bringing in know-how and experience from comparable simulation projects in different enterprises
- more efficient project management and implementation
- more realistic assessment of functionality and suitability of simulation software under consideration

Project success, however, strongly depends on close cooperation and communication between all parties.

If a decision is made in favour of using external consultants, the following services can be expected at different levels:

- basic services in simulation consulting:
    - analysis of modelling data provided by the customer
    - design and implementation of simulation models
    - running of simulation experiments
    - analysis of experimental results, deduction of insights, and recommendations for action
    - presentation of the simulation study's progress and results in regular project meetings (at least at a kick-off meeting, an intermediate project presentation and the final presentation)
    - project documentation
- additional services:
    - data collection and input
    - recommendations for action based on the simulation results
    - graphical animation of dynamic simulation output
    - preparation of simulation model for recurrent internal use
    - development of a specialized simulation tool

16.4.3 Costs and Time Requirements for a Simulation Study

Because it clearly depends on the size of the project, it is not easy to indicate an order of magnitude for the costs of a typical simulation study. However, a sum of 5,000 to 100,000 Euros for simulation consulting seems to be a realistic estimation for the cost span of a typical simulation project (see Rabe and Hellingrath 2001, p. 129). It should be noted that internal costs should not be neglected in such calculations; e.g.:

- time spent by internal personnel on the simulation project
- opportunity costs of internal project leader
- costs of meetings and interviews
- costs of data collection

If the project proceeds without consultant support, we must also take the following cost factors into account as basic investment when getting started with simulation (see Rabe and Hellingrath 2001, p. 130):

- simulation software license: 3,000-80,000 Euros
- technology/hardware: 2,000-25,000 Euros
- employee training (inclusive labour cost): 1,000-25,000 Euros
- informed selection of a simulation tool: > 5,000 Euros

The average duration of a simulation study also depends on its size. We can distinguish between:

- short simulation studies: 2 months
- average simulation studies: 2-6 months
- long simulation studies: 6-12 months
- very long simulation studies: > 12 months

There are a number of options to reduce costs and time:

- We can limit the level of detail to the absolutely necessary. In this way less effort must be spent on modelling, programming, and experimentation, and we need fewer and less detailed data. We can restrict ourselves to the data at hand without any additional work related to data collection. In many cases it may be feasible to substitute domain experts' estimates for missing data.
- We can reuse and modify already existing models. This becomes more attractive if past model development had already taken future reuse into account. In this case we may be able to draw on a library of reference models for complete model classes (i.e. parametrized models for specific problem domains) which only need to be enhanced and adapted for the new study.
- Selection of suitable software for the relevant class of problem can increase productivity and therefore reduce costs.
- Close communication and coordination between simulation consultant and internal project members can also help to keep costs down.

16.5 Methods of Data Collection

Data collection is an important phase during systems analysis. All quantitative and qualitative states of a system which are relevant for a simulation study's objectives are identified and recorded.

As part of this process we distinguish between *primary* and *secondary* data collection – as shown in Figure 16.2. The presentation again follows Rabe and Hellingrath (2001, Ch. 12.4.2, pp. 154–170 and Ch. 12.5, pp. 171-173). In primary data collection information is gained solely for purposes of the specific simulation study, while we must rely on existing documents and information sources for secondary data collection.

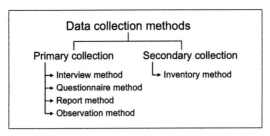

Figure 16.2: Data collection methods
(adopted from Rabe and Hellingrath 2001, p. 171)

Interview method: The interview method is based on questioning domain experts; i.e. department employees who own deep know-how of the system under investigation. These interviews can either be standardized or non-standardized and could be open or "under cover". In a standardized interview all questions are prepared in written form beforehand and then asked in predefined form and sequence. Additional questions are not permitted. In contrast to this, questions can be asked in any order in a non-standard interview. Additional questions are permissible and the interview may feel more like an informal chat. Interviews can take the form of individual questioning of experienced employees as well as questioning a whole group or conference. Group interviews usually address members of the domain department, whereas conference interviews bring employees from many different departments together. Beyond formal interview questions any discussions within the group can be of great interest.

Questionnaire method: Here employees with relevant background knowledge of the problem domain receive written questionnaires with predefined questions in parallel. They are then invited to answer these clearly and thoroughly. Questionnaires can cover standard questions as well as more differentiated ones.

Chapter 16 Simulation in Practice

Report method: The report method is similar to both the questionnaire and the interview method – as described above. Information is gathered from qualified employees and then structured and summarized in a report. This report can follow a predefined structure and minimal content requirements, or it can be in a free format with individual content.

Observation method: The observation method monitors an interview by close observation and interpretation of answers right at the moment of occurrence. These observations are then analysed to yield additional insights. Different forms of the observation method can be distinguished, depending on the relationship between observers and observed objects:

- open and "under cover" observation
- direct and indirect observation
- structured and unstructured observation

In an *open* observation an observer is clearly visible for an observed subject, and people are aware that they are observed. In an *under cover* observation observers do not reveal themselves. If an observer is monitoring and recording system states and behaviours right at the time when they happen we talk about *direct* observation. A very common approach in direct observation are measurements of time consuming activities or system arrivals at random times. The goal is to derive statistical distributions and parameters for a simulation model, e.g. for client arrivals in a service system.

Inventory method: The inventory method is an activity carried out by a special inventory team, with the intention to not rely solely on knowledge of people in a domain department. The method mainly consists of studying written documents containing information on work flows, enterprise operation, and the overall structure of the system under investigation. Similar to the yearly inventory of stock, suitable information and data sources are gathered and analysed. Documents used for this purpose could be organization charts, work schedules, job descriptions, task plans, internal statistics and reports, operating figures, or training materials.

Structure of input data relevant to simulation: A system investigated with simulation technology (e.g. a production system) can be described by a set of data classified into three categories; i.e. system load data, organizational data, and technical data (see Rabe and Hellingrath 2001, p. 154). This classification is shown in Figure 16.3.

The amount of data and the time interval to be covered mainly depend on model complexity and the required level of detail. To avoid unnecessary effort and redundancy, data collection should focus only on the main purpose of the simulation. Most of the enterprise data mentioned in Figure 16.3 is readily available in business information systems. However, such data is often not very consistent and its harvesting from decentralized computer systems may require a high degree of additional effort. In some

16.6 Typical Errors and Pitfalls in a Simulation Study

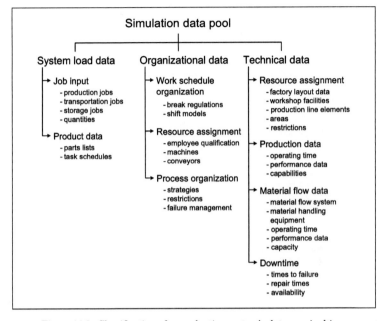

Figure 16.3: Classification of a production system's data required in a simulation study (adopted from Rabe and Hellingrath 2001, p. 154)

cases a special data collection campaign is even required in order to have all necessary modelling data at hand.

Checking all gathered data for correctness, completeness, and timeliness can ensure consistent simulation results. The more precise and reliable the input data, the higher the quality and informational value of a simulation study's results can be. This observation reiterates the significance for and influence of the modelling cycle's data collection phase for the whole simulation study.

16.6 Typical Errors and Pitfalls in a Simulation Study

One major obstacle for a successful simulation project is an ambiguous definition of the aims and scopes of a simulation study. An excellent model may well offer a perfect solution for the wrong problem.

Chapter 16 Simulation in Practice

Reasons for such mismatches of models and problems can be that
- needs and requirements of users are largely ignored;
- communication between simulations analysts and domain departments is poor;
- aims and scopes of the study are neglected during model construction;
- gradual shifts of simulation goals during a project remain undetected instead of being fixed in written form and agreed upon by all parties; or
- users hold tacit and erroneous beliefs about limitations and scope of the model's application.

Another source of error is poor data quality, particularly if data has not been thoroughly checked. Where data requirements were underestimated at the beginning of the study, additional unforeseen effort must sometimes be invested in data collection. To reduce the data collection effort, some input data can occasionally be replaced by estimates from domain experts with deep insight knowledge.

Sometimes a model may include too many details and become overly complex and unwieldy. Such a high degree of model complexity leads to both data collection (e.g. high data requirements) and implementation problems (e.g. complex program structure). Inadequate plausibility checks of simulation results lead to poor model quality and credibility. Model utilization can also be seriously impaired if documentation is incomplete.

Finally, inadequate cooperation within the project team and missing support and involvement of relevant decision makers will jeopardize a project success.

16.7 Conclusion

We have discussed in some detail under which circumstances simulation technology can successfully be applied in industrial practice and where sources of errors may lie. We also claimed that simulation technology should not be applied unless certain conditions are met. Some indicators which signal where simulation projects may be inadvisable are:

- demands for a short project duration and high pressure for timely completion
- very late project stage without any realistic chance of influencing relevant design decisions
- insufficient simulation know-how
- very limited resources
- very large and complex systems which change continuously; i.e.:
    - many system parameters fluctuating at all times
    - instable system structures
    - many overlaying, highly randomized influences and boundary conditions
- poor data provision

16.7 Conclusion

However, if the circumstances for a simulation study are more favourable, considerable benefits can be gained from simulation technology. For example, we can use a simulation model as a test bed for technical or organizational systems prior to its real world implementation, thereby reducing costs, development time, and risks. We can use simulation to improve the quality of and feel more confident about complex decisions. Quite often we also can make good decision substantially faster. A simulation study can offer a better informed view of a system's operation, and it can improve our awareness of crucial performance data. Eventually it may even lead to a better data pool for future decision making (with or without simulation).

In essence, simulation is an effective technology for improving our understanding of systems, and deeper understanding can help us identify opportunities for a system's performance's improvement. Many costly mistakes can be avoided by competently applying simulation technology during a planning process.

To conclude our discussion on simulation in practice, we reiterate some basic principles for applying simulation technology as a decision aid:

- Simulation always assumes prior goal and scopes definitions and cost assessment.
- Before simulation is applied, all alternative, less time-consuming, analytical methods should be considered.
- Simulation studies must be concluded before the final decision on an investment is made.
- Simulation technology must not replace for reasoned planning.
- Mapping accuracy in the modelling process should not to be as high as possible, but only sufficiently precise for achieving a study's goals.
- Simulation results are worthless and misleading if the database is fragmentary, the model validation poor, or the simulation results are interpreted incorrectly.
- Simulation results are only as good as the cooperation and communication in the simulation project team.

Further Reading

Handlungsanleitung Simulation in Produktion und Logistik – Ein Leitfaden mit Beispielen für kleinere und mittlere Unternehmen (Rabe and Hellingrath 2001, Ch. 12, pp. 117–190, "*Instruction Simulation in Production and Logistics – A Guideline with Examples for Small and Medium-Sized Enterprises*", in German) is a helpful report on simulation case studies in a number of smaller and medium-sized companies. It focusses on the domains of production and logistics. Case studies are situated in Germany and the book is written in German. It demonstrates the potentials of computer simulation in industry by presenting the results of a research and development project sponsored by the German Federal Ministry of Education and Research, where a number of industrial partners were brought together under the supervision of the Fraunhofer Institute for Manufacturing Plants and Construction Technology in Berlin. Most of the book documents ten selected case studies (Chapters 2 to 11), which report very interesting hands-on experiences in applying simulation technology to industrial practice; e.g. new material flow concepts for production line reorganization, restructuring a limited-lot production, flexible factory planning, or planning and evaluation of manufacturing cells. Chapter 12, where principles for guiding a simulation study are explored, is the most interesting and relevant for our purposes. It shows how a simulation study can be performed in a practical setting and highlights the issues that must be considered. The discussion gives answers and arguments as well as recommendations for conducting and managing simulation projects. Suggestions on when and how to apply simulation are made. A number of useful check lists for simulation practitioners (e.g. for data collection) are also included. This chapter adopts many ideas from the book.

The *Handbook of Simulation – Principles, Methodology, Advances, Applications, and Practice* (Banks 1998, Chapter 22 and 23, pp. 721–764) collects contributions of leading simulation experts and covers the principles, techniques, and applications of discrete-event simulation. More than most other books in this field it offers a single definitive source for key information on all relevant facets of discrete-event simulation methodology and its application in major industries. As an acknowledged standard it is frequently quoted in many Chapters of our book. In the context of simulation practice, we should particularly look into Part V of the handbook. This section is titled "Practice of Simulation", and the two Chapters "Guidelines for Success" and "Managing the Simulation Project" present a lot of useful hints and guidelines for conducting successful simulation studies, satisfying customer needs. Together with the Chapters on selected applications in Part IV (e.g. manufacturing, transport, logistics, health care) these sections provide a fairly complete picture on simulation practice.

Bibliography

J. Banks, editor. *Handbook of Simulation – Principles, Methodology, Advances, Applications, and Practice.* Wiley, New York, 1998. Chapters 22 and 23.

J. Košturiak and M. Gregor. *Simulation von Produktionssystemen* ("Simulation of Production Systems", in German). Springer, Vienna, 1995. Chapter 4.

A. M. Law and W. D. Kelton. *Simulation Modeling and Analysis.* McGraw-Hill, New York, 3rd edition, 2000. Chapter 13.

K. J. Musselmann. Guidelines for Simulation Project Success. In J. D. Tew, S. Manivannan, D. A. Sadowski, and A. F. Seila, editors, *Proceedings of the 1994 Winter Simulation Conference,* pages 88–95, 1994.

M. Rabe and B. Hellingrath. *Handlungsanleitung Simulation in Produktion und Logistik – Ein Leitfaden mit Beispielen für kleinere und mittlere Unternehmen* ("Instruction Simulation in Production and Logistics – A Guideline with Examples for Small and Medium-Sized Enterprises", in German). SCS-Europe, Erlangen, 2001. Chapter 12.

Authors

Main Authors

Bernd Page received a PhD in applied computer science from the Technical University of Berlin (Germany) and a Masters degree from Stanford University (USA). After graduation he worked as a scientific assistant at the Technical University of Berlin. Prior to his appointment to a professorship for Applied Informatics at the University of Hamburg (Germany) in the mid-eighties he also served as a scientific associate in the Environmental Information Systems Group of the German Federal Environmental Agency in Berlin. Since his university appointment he has been involved in research, teaching, and applications mainly in computer simulation and environmental informatics. Professor Page has published widely, resulting in a large number of papers for national and international conferences and several books.

Professor Page was a cofounder and has for many years been the chairman of the working group "Informatics for Environmental Protection" in the German Informatics Society (Gesellschaft für Informatik). Among other activities he has promoted a working group on environmental modelling and simulation tools.

More recently Professor Page has intensified his interests in modelling logistic systems, an area where discrete event simulation tools such as the DESMO-J framework, which has been under development by his research group for many years, can be applied very effectively. His current research is guided by the idea of combining economic and environmental aspects of logistics models (i.e. "ecologistics") and centers on the design of suitable tools for such models' construction and use.

Professor Page has held a large number of research and development grants for public and industrial projects. He currently leads a funded project investigating applications of E-learning to computer simulation. He has been a visiting professor at a number of international institutions including the Alberta Research Council (Canada), the University of Canterbury (New Zealand), Smith College (USA), and the University of Stellenbosch (South Africa).

Professor Page can be reached at `page@informatik.uni-hamburg.de`. His personal web page can be found at `http://asi-www.informatik.uni-hamburg.de/personen/page`.

Wolfgang Kreutzer received his PhD in applied computer science from the University of Frankfurt (Germany). After working as a scientific assistant at the University of Frankfurt he has been a lecturer in computer science at the University of Otago (New

Authors

Zealand) and an assistant professor of computer science at the University of Hawaii (USA). Since 1981 he has been employed as a senior lecturer and (since 1991) as an associate professor at the University of Canterbury (New Zealand), where he has also served as head of the Computer Science Department.

Associate Professor Kreutzer has published a large number of papers and books, many of which focus on simulation program design and construction. He has held visiting professorships at various universities and has been a keynote speaker at international simulation conferences.

Associate Professor Kreutzer has taught simulation and conducted research in related areas for many years. His current interests focus on the use of visual representations and animations in simulations, programming languages and multi-media systems.

His E-Mail address is wolfgang@cosc.canterbury.ac.nz. His web page can be found at http://www.cosc.canterbury.ac.nz/~wolfgang/.

Coauthors

Björn Gehlsen is a research associate at Dresden University of Technology's Department of Traffic and Transport Sciences. With the group for Traffic Modelling and Econometrics, he is mainly concerned with self organization concepts for traffic control and the exploration of traffic network properties and structures.

He received his diploma (MSc) and a PhD in computer science from the University of Hamburg. He first focused on operations research and heuristic optimization methods for NP-hard problems. Later he worked on different research projects on traffic simulation and on concepts for accessing distributed databases. In his doctoral thesis, he investigated techniques for the integration of simulation tools with optimization methods, using distributed system technology.

Dr. Gehlsen is a member of the Association for Computing Machinery (ACM), the German Informatics Society (Gesellschaft für Informatik), and the German speaking simulation society ASIM. His E-Mail address is gehlsen@hamburg.de.

Johannes Göbel studies business information technology at the University of Hamburg. Focal points include harbour logistics, environmental informatics, and discrete event simulation. The latter is also the intended base for his diploma (MSc) thesis within the research group of Professor Page (planned for 2006).

His E-Mail address is johannesgoebel@web.de.

Gunnar Kiesel studied computer science and geography at the University of Hamburg (1997-2004) and completed his studies with the diploma (MSc) degree in computer science. From 2003 to early 2005 he contributed to the "E-learning components for simulation teaching" project at the Department of computer science. He wrote his Diploma Thesis within the research group of Professor Page, concentrating on the possibilities of integrating simulation E-learning components in web-based learning management systems, benefiting from his long year experience as a freelance web developer.

Gunnar Kiesel works as application developer at IT' Services & Solutions since March 2005.

You may contact Gunnar Kiesel at gkiesel@de.ibm.com.

Nicolas Knaak obtained his diploma degree (MSc) in computer science from the University of Hamburg, Germany in 2002. In his diploma thesis he developed parts of the agent-based simulation framework FAMOS based on the DESMO-J simulator.

Since then he has been working as a scientific assistant and PhD candidate in the simulation group led by Prof. Page at the University of Hamburg. He has taught courses on Java programming, algorithms and data structures, and computer simulation. From 2001 to 2003 he worked on a funded research project dealing with the agent-based simulation of city-courier services.

His current research interests are UML modelling as well as the verification and validation of Multi-agent systems. At the moment he is preparing his PhD thesis on the validation of Multi-agent systems by means of simulation and data-mining techniques.

His E-Mail address is knaak@informatik.uni-hamburg.de and his personal web page can be found at http://asi-www.informatik.uni-hamburg.de/knaak.

Julia Kuck started her studies of computer science at the University RWTH Aachen (Germany). After receiving a pre-degree in 2002, Julia Kuck attended the University of Hamburg to achieve her diploma (MSc) in computer science in 2004. During her studies in Hamburg, she mainly focused on discrete event simulation. Within the research group of Professor Page, Julia Kuck made her diploma thesis, which concerned the potentials of automatic, statistical analyses of simulation experiments. Since 2005, Julia Kuck works as a Research Staff Member of the Institute of Computer Science III at the University of Bonn (Germany). Julia Kuck researches and teaches mainly in the area of information retrieval.

You may contact Julia Kuck at kuck@iai.uni-bonn.de and her personal web page is reachable at http://ir.iai.uni-bonn.de/people/persons/julia_kuck.

Tim Lechler studied computer sciences at the University of Hamburg, focusing on simulation. He participated in a research project combining traffic control and simulation before he developed the DESMO-J discrete event simulation framework as part of his Diploma in 1999. After achieving his degree in computer science (MSc) in 2000, he hired as software developer at the very traditional Berenberg Bank (founded 1592) to develop modern Java based cient/server applications. The biggest impact that simulation had on his life was meeting his wife Martina in a simulation seminar in 1993. He still monitors the evolution of the DESMO-J framework and its applications, but

Authors

most of his resources are consumed by his daughter Pia Marie (2.5 yrs) and his son Leif Timon (10 wks).

Ruth Meyer studied computer science and biology at the University of Hamburg (1989-1997) and holds a diploma (MSc) degree in computer science. From 1997 to early 2005 she has worked as a research assistant with the Department of Computer Science, University of Hamburg, in several research projects on discrete-event and agent-based simulation and the application of E-learning to computer simulation. She is currently in the final stages of completing her PhD which has focussed on agent-based simulation and explicit representations of space.

Since May 2005 she is a research associate with the Centre for Policy Modelling at Manchester Metropolitan University in Manchester (UK). Her research interests lie in the areas of agent-based simulation, spatial modelling, simulation methodology, and environmental informatics.

Ruth Meyer can be contacted at r.meyer@mmu.ac.uk. Her web page can be found at http://cfpm.org/~ruth/

Gaby Neumann received a diploma in materials handling technology from the Otto-von-Guericke-University of Technology in Magdeburg and a PhD in Logistics from the University of Magdeburg. Between 1994 and 2002 she was Assistant Lecturer at the Institute of Materials Handling and Construction Machinery Technology, Steel Construction, Logistics of the University of Magdeburg. Since 2003 she has been Junior Professor in logistics knowledge management. Since 1991 she has been also working as part-time consultant in logistics simulation. Gaby Neumann publishes frequently; she is author/co-author of numerous papers and presentations at national and international conferences and a series of E-learning modules in logistics. Her current activities and research interests are mainly linked to fields like problem solving and knowledge management in logistics, logistics simulation and planning, and especially technology-based logistics learning, didactics of teaching logistics, as well as logistics competence profiling and assessment. She organizes or co-organizes workshops and conferences in these fields, is involved in international programme committees of conferences in the field of simulation, coordinates the European logistics educators network for providing new technologies for logistics education inside the European Logistics Association (ELA-LogNet), and has been or is being involved in a couple of respective projects.

Her E-Mail address is gaby.neumann@mb.uni-magdeburg.de. At http://www.uni-magdeburg.de/ifsl/fachgebiet/wissensmanagement.php her personal web page can be reached.

Volker Wohlgemuth studied computer science at the Universities of Hamburg, Germany and Christchurch, New Zealand (1991-1997). In 1997, he earned his diploma (MSc) degree in computer science from the University of Hamburg. Since 1997 he has worked as research assistant with the Department of Computer Science, University of Hamburg as well as senior software developer and key account manager at the ifu Hamburg GmbH. In 2005 he received his PhD in applied computer science from the University of Hamburg (Germany). His research interest lies in the field of modelling and simulating business systems with regard to their effects on the environment.

His E-Mail address is wohlgemuth@informatik.uni-hamburg.de. His web page can be found at http://asi-www.informatik.uni-hamburg.de/personen/wohlgemuth/.

Index

A

Abstraction 4, 6, 8, 12, 20, 43, 264
Activity 28, 131
Activity diagram 77, 105
    Action 77
    Activity partition 80, 86
    Data token 83
    Decision node 78
    Documentation applet 426
    Fork and join node 80
    Interruptible activity region 86
    Merge node 78
    Object node 83
    Queue stereotype 84
    Receive signal action 82
    Resource stereotype 85
    Selection stereotype 84
    Send signal action 82
    Start and end node 78
    Time signal reception 83
    Token-semantics 78
Activity-oriented modelling 131
    Check 131
    Condition queue 132
    Example .... *see* Logistics system
    in DESMO-J .... *see* DESMO-J
    Model design 131
Agent
    Definition 340
    Properties 340
Agent architecture 343
Agent platform 360
Agent simulation 347
Agent-Group-Role model 355
Agent-supported simulation 347
AgentUML 359
Animation 8, 257, 382, 425
    Features 257
    of conceptual model 213
    Offline 242, 257
    Online 257
    Reasons 257

Applet .... *see* Java
Application-specific simulation tools 245
    ARENA 245
    DOSIMIS-3 .... 245, 442
    NETWORK 245
    SEE WHY 245
    SIMFACTORY 245
    WITNESS 245
Artificial society 350
Assertion checking 219
ATMOS 251
Autocorrelation 173, 184, 186
Automata theory 251

B

Batch mean data collection .... *see* Data
    collection
Batch mean test 178
BDI architecture 346
Behaviour graph 225
Behaviourism 407, 409
    Simulation 414
Blended learning 406, 421, 429
Bonferroni, method of 184
Box plot 226
Building blocks 249

C

C, C++, C# 54, 243
CAD systems 241, 257
Calibration 222
CBT 405
Central limit Theorem 182
Chi-square test .... *see* Statistical tests
Class diagram 65
    Aggregation 67
    Association 67
    Class 66
    Composition 67
    Generalization 67
    Interface 67
Classification of simulation tools 247
    Degree of specialization 251

Index

Level of application 247
Modelling concept 249
Type of system 248
Client/server pattern 380
CLOS 54
Cognitivism 408, 409
  Simulation 413
Common Object Request Broker Architecture *see* CORBA
CommSy 427
  Design 428
  Project room 427
Communication 354
Community system .... *see* CommSy
Competitive tasks 345
Component-based simulation *see* Distributed simulation
Composition .... *see* Object-orientation
Computer-based Training .... *see* CBT
Computer-supported cooperative learning *see* CSCL
Conceptual distance 45
Conceptual model 12, 212
Conceptual model validation 15, 199
Confidence interval 180, 186, 187
Confidence level 180, 186
Congruential generator *see* Random number generation
Constructivism 408, 409
  Simulation 413
Container shipment model ...... *see* Logistics system
Conway's rule 176
CORBA 246, 378, 380
Coroutine 101, 148, 244, 274
Course management system .... *see* CMS
Cross-correlation 184
Crossing the mean 176
CSCL 428
Cumulative distribution function .... *see* Distribution function

D

Data collection 15, 19, 170, 265, 278, 470, 474, 481, 484
  Batch means 148, 186
  in DESMO-J .... *see* DESMO-J
  Independent replications .. 185, 373, 390
  Input data . 159, 164, 170, 185, 382, 474, 482
  Interview method 481
  Inventory method 482
  Observation method 482

Primary/secondary 470, 481
Questionnaire method 481
Report method 482
System load data 482
Data mining 228
Deadlock 376
Debugging 220
Declarative modelling 357
Delphi 243
Dependency graph 213
Descriptive analysis 170
DESMO-J 101, 250, 263, 334, 420
  Activity-oriented modelling 266, 317
  Black box components 265, 276
  Class hierarchy 266, 279, 281, 285
  Combining events and processes 274
  Conditional waiting 284, 287, 317
  Data collectors 265, 278
  Debug 283
  Distributions 277
  Entity 264
  Error 283
  Event 268, 294
  Event list 265, 268
  Event-oriented modelling .. 266, 268, 294
  Experimentation 280
  Hierarchical modelling constructs ... 291
  High-level modelling constructs 284
  Hot spots ... *see* White box components
  Internet laboratory 422
  Interruption of a process 290, 324
  Lifecycle 98, 273
  Master-slave cooperation .. 284, 288, 320
  Model 280
  Modelling example 293
  Packages 265, 276
  Process 273, 307
  Process-oriented modelling 266, 273, 307
  Queues 276
  Random numbers 277
  Report 283
  Reportable objects 265
  Resources 284, 285, 314
  Schedulable objects 265
  Simulation applet 425
  Simulation time 269
  Synchronization 284
  Trace 283
  Transaction-oriented modelling . 266, 314
  Web tutorial 421
  White box components 265
Developer's bias 207

494

Index

Didactic concepts 410
Digital factory 466
Discovery-based learning .... see Discovery-driven learning
Discovery-driven learning 411, 421
Discrete event .... see Event
Discrete event model design 97
Discrete event modelling styles .. 98, 129, 249
    Activity-oriented . see Activity-oriented modelling
    Combination of processes and events 134, 274
    Comparison of processes and events . 117
    Event-oriented ..... see Event-oriented modelling
    Process-oriented .. see Process-oriented modelling
    Termination .... see Stopping rules
    Transaction-oriented .... see Transaction-oriented modelling
Discrete event simulation . 11, 23, 25, 27, 149, 266
    Internal processing strategy 29
    Language requirements . see Simulation language
    Main process 29
    Monitor 29
    Paper and pencil exercise 32
    State changes 27
    Stopping rules 23, 29
Discrete event simulation package .... see Simulation package; DESMO-J
Discrete event simulation software .... see Simulation software
Distributed simulation 373, 375, 376, 466
    Batch orientation 380
    Component-based simulation ... 376, 378
    Distributed synchronization .... see Synchronization
    Environment 382
    Fault tolerance 374
    Interactive tools 380
    Modes 376
    Parallel simulation 376, 377
    Partition of state space 377
    Partition of time axis 377
    Web-based simulation 377, 380
Distribution function 31, 161, 164, 165
Distribution, empirical 164, 170
    Continuous 164
    Discrete 167

Distribution, statistical 31, 147, 161, 165, 170, 265
    Bernoulli 165
    Binomial 165
    Chi-square 171
    Continuous uniform 31, 161, 166
    Discrete uniform 161, 165, 168
    Erlang 166
    Exponential 161, 163, 166
    Fixed value 165
    Geometric 165
    Negative binomial 165
    Normal 164, 166
    Poisson 165
    Rectangular .... see Continuous uniform
    Standard normal 170, 182
    t-distribution 183
    Triangular 166
Distribution, theoretical ... see Distribution, statistical
DOSIMIS-3 .... see Application-specific simulation tools

E

E-learning 402, 403
    Simulation 412
Educational theory ...... see Learning theory
Eiffel 54
eM-Plant .. see Integrated simulation systems
Emergence 342
Empirical data 164
Empiricism 204
Encapsulation .... see Object-orientation
Entity 24, 98, 108, 152, 264
    Lifecycle 25, 98
    Method 24
    State 24, 27
    Time property 24
Event 25, 27, 108, 146, 152
    DESMO-J 268, 294
    Distributed simulation 375
    External event 27
    Internal event 27
    Parallel event 26
Event list 26, 29, 109, 117, 146, 147, 150
    DESMO-J 265, 268
    Distributed simulation 375
    Documentation applet 426
Event-oriented modelling 108, 294
    Embedded in a process-oriented model 134, 274
    Event routine 109

495

Index

Example .... *see* Inventory
    system; Logistics system; Production
    system (combined styles)
    Implementation 268
    in DESMO-J .... *see* DESMO-J
    Model clock 108
    Model components 108
    Model design 108
    Scheduler 109, 147, 265, 426
    State changes 108, 117
Excel 243
Experimental learning 408
Expert review 213
Extend .... *see* Integrated simulation systems
eXtensible Markup Language ...... *see* XML
eXtreme Programming 202

F

Falsification 203
FAMOS framework 363
FIPA standard 360
Fortran 243
Framework .... 55, *see* Simulation framework

G

GA 394
    Candidate solution 394, 395
    Fitness 395, 396
    Generation 395
    Genetic operations 395, 396
    Genotype 395
    Globally parallel GA 397
    Individual 395
    Initialisation 396
    Mutation 395
    Parallelization 394, 397
    Parameter encoding 394, 396
    Phenotype 395
    Population 394, 395
    Probabilistic strategies 394
    Recombination 395
    Reproduction 395
    Selection 395
    Solution space 394
    Template 396
    Termination 396
General purpose programming language . 243,
    see C, C++, C#; Delphi; Fortan; Java;
    Modula
General requirements for simulation tools 240
    Flexibility 240
    Interactivity 240
    Readability 241

Reusability 240
Structure 241
User friendliness 240
Genetic algorithm .... *see* GA
Goodness of fit .... *see* Statistical tests
Gravel pit model 32, 66, 70, 78, 88, 92

H

Harbour logistics .... *see* Logistics system
High level Architecture .... *see* HLA
Histogram 226
HLA 378, 380
Human-computer communication 40

I

Independent replications . *see* Data collection
Information hiding .... *see* Object-orientation
Inheritance .... *see* Object-orientation
Initialisation ...... *see* Simulation experiment
Integrated simulation systems 245
    CREATE! 245
    eM-Plant 245, 250, 254
    Extend 245, 248, 252
    Simplex III 245, 248
Intelligent Tutoring System .... *see* ITS
Interaction diagram 87
Interoperability 374
Inventory system 24, 109
    Components 110
    Event-oriented implementation 113
    Example 111
    Goals 109
    Inventory costs 112
    Ordering policy 111
    Shortfall costs 112
Inverse transformation . *see* Random number
    generation
ITS 408

J

JADE agent platform 361
Java 54, 144, 243, 263
    Applet 148, 149, 380, 424
    AWT 144
    Beans 246
    Discrete event simulation modelling *see*
        DESMO-J
    Garbage collection 146
    Java as simulation language ... 144, 149,
        264
    Javadoc 145, 152, 209
    JDK 144
    Numerical accuracy 162

Index

Platform Independence 148
Servlet 380
Swing 144
Thread 101, 144, 148, 274
java.lang.Math 151, 170
java.util.Collections 147, 151
java.util.LinkedList 156
java.util.Observable 148, 280
java.util.Observer 148, 278, 280
java.util.Random ... 147, 151, 154, 163, 164, 168, 277
Jobshop system ...... see Production system

K

Knowledge 446
   Acquisition 404, 408, 412, 429
   Creation 451
   Repository 450
   Sharing 448
   Source 449
Knowledge base 357
Knowledge management 406, 446
Knowledge-based simulation systems 251
   DYNAMIS 251
   PLATO-SIM 251

L

Learning Content Management System ... see LCMS
Learning software 405, 409
Learning theory 407, 409
Linear congruential method .... see Random number generation
Linear transformation
   of a normal distribution 182
LMCS 406
LMS 405
LogEduGate 415
Logistics 436
   Education 465
   Key performance indicators 438
   Operation 438
   Planning 438
   Problem solving 439
   Process 437
Logistics simulation 436, 440
   Experiment 443
   Knowledge 446
   Tools 442
Logistics system 117, 293, 437
   Activity-oriented implementation .. 131, 317
   Event-oriented implementation . 124, 294

Example 119, 453, 458, 461
Goal 119
Process-oriented implementation ... 121, 307
Transaction-oriented implementation 129, 314

M

M-learning 406
Machine-oriented description 101, 249
MANTA model 349
Marginal standard error rule ...... see MSER
Material-oriented description 101, 249
Mean .... see Statistical estimators
Mental complexity 39
   Abstraction 43
   Reductionism 43
Meta-model 63, 224
Microsoft .NET 54, 246
Model 5
   Analytical model 4, 10
   Behaviour 6, 19, 24, 389
   Components 19, 98, 108, 378, 381
   Continuous simulation model 11
   Design model 7
   Discrete event simulation model . 11, 23, 97
   Event-driven 11
   Explanatory model 7
   External model 6
   Formal model 6
   Harbour model ..... see Logistics system
   Inventory model ... see Inventory system
   Logistics model .... see Logistics system
   Mental model 6
   Models as model components 19
   Optimization model 7, 10, 391
   Predator-prey 12
   Predictive model 7
   Production model see Production system
   Queueing model ... see Queueing system
   Simulation model 4, 9
   Stochastic model 16, 21, 31, 161, 393
   Time trajectory 11
   Time-driven 11
Model checking 214
   Program abstraction 221
   Trace-based 221
Model clock .... see Model time
Model design . 13, see Conceptual model, 473
Development cycle .. see Modelling cycle
Discrete event model see Discrete event model design

Index

Model documentation 209
Model implementation 15, 143, 264
Model parameters
    2^k-factorial design 190
    Choice 189
Model time . 24, 26, 28, 98, 100, 108, 146, 265
    Distributed simulation 375
Model validity 206
    Benefit/Cost ratio 207
Model-to-model analysis 222
Modelling concept of simulation tools 249
Modelling cycle 12, 45
    Construction effort 21
    Errors 21
Modelling styles   *see* Discrete event modelling styles
    Hybrid modelling 242
ModL 254
Modula 243
Morphological box ... *see* Simulation software
Movement 357
    Gradient following 357
    Random walk 357
MSER 177
Mulan agent platform 361
Multi-agent system 341
Multi-agent-based simulation 347
    Applications 349
    Properties 348
    vs. event-scheduling 351
    vs. object-oriented simulation 352
    vs. process-interaction 352
Multiple simulation runs ..... *see* Repeating simulation runs

N

Neural network 343

O

Object diagram 68
Object-orientation 39–56
    Class 44, 47
    Class library 45, 55
    Composition 47, 48, 55
    Delegation 47
    Encapsulation 46
    Information hiding 46
    Inheritance 47, 48, 55
    Model construction   *see* Object-oriented analysis and design
    Polymorphism 46, 55
    Property 55
    Representation of models 250

Scientific method 42, 43
Object-oriented analysis and design .. 49, 133
    Bottom-up design 50
    CRC Cards 52
    Data dictionary 52
    Protocol analysis 52
    Rapid prototyping 50
    Top-down design 50
    Use case .... 52, *see* UML
Object-oriented programming language ... 53, *see* C, C++, C#; CLOS; Eiffel; Java; Simula; Smalltalk
Objective function .... 10, *see* Simulation optimization
Occams razor 8
Operational model validation 16, 200
Operations research 4, 190
Optimization   10, *see* Simulation optimization
Organizational structure 355

P

Package diagram 68
Paradigm shift 55
Parallel simulation *see* Distributed simulation
Petri nets 249, 250
    Design/CPN 250
    PACE 250
    Renew 250
Philosophy of science 203
Polymorphism .... *see* Object-orientation
Pragmatism 205
Process 28, 98, 148
    DESMO-J 273, 307
    Distributed simulation 375
    Stationary state 174
Process list 29, 100, 117
Process synchronization 426
Process-oriented modelling 98, 148, 307
    Embedding events 134, 274
    Example .... *see* Logistics system; Queueing system; Production system (combined styles)
    Implementation 101, 273
    in DESMO-J .... *see* DESMO-J
    Lifecycle 98
    Model clock 99
    Model components 98
    Model design 101
    Model time management .. *see* Scheduler
    Scheduler 98, 99, 265
    State changes 98, 117
Production system 134

498

Index

Combined process/event-oriented implementation 136
  Components 134
  Example 135
Programming language .... *see* General purpose programming language; Object-oriented programming language
  High level 40
  Low level 40
  Very high level 40
Programming style
  Functional 41
  Imperative 41
  Logic-based 41
  Object-oriented 41–56
Pseudo-random number generation ...... *see* Random number generation
Pseudo-random numbers 24, 31, 162

Q

Quantile 183
Queueing system 24, 102, 250
  Closed queueing system 102
  Components 102
  Example 103
  Open queueing system 102
  Process-oriented implementation ... 104
  Resources 102
  Transactions 102

R

Random number generation 31, 147, 161
  Distributions in DESMO-J .... *see* DESMO-J
  Inverse transformation method . 31, 163, 164, 168
  Linear congruential method 163, 168, 277
  Middle-square method 162
  Normalized random numbers 31, 162
  Reproducibility 31, 162
  Seed 31, 163
  Stream 31, 161
Rationalism 204
  Critical 203, 204
Reductionism 43
Repeating simulation runs . 173, 184, 242, 254
Rule interpreter 357
  Backward chaining 358
  Forward chaining 358

S

Scheduler .... *see* DESMO-J; Event-oriented modelling; Process-oriented modelling

Sensitivity analysis 223
Sensitivity coefficient 223
Sequence diagram 88
  Communication role 88
  High level constructs 90
  Interaction fragment 91
  Lifeline 88
  Message 88
  State invariant 90
  Time constraint 90
SeSAm 364
Simula .... *see* Simulation language
Simulation 3, 9, 387, 470, 484
  Application 16, 471, 484
  Continuous 11
  Discrete event .... *see* Discrete event simulation
  Distribution . *see* Distributed simulation
  Hybrid 242
  Limitations 20, 483
  Parallel ...... *see* Distributed simulation
  Potential 470
  Quasi-continuous 11, 242
Simulation consultants 470, 477, 478
Simulation experiment 16, 173, 185, 242, 387, 443
  Analysis 16, 173, 242, 382, 476
  Application of results 17
  Documentation 16, 476
  Initialisation 29, 280
  Length .... *see* Sample size
  Observation 185, 476
  Presentation 16
  Results .... *see* Analysis
  Sample size 179, 188, 476
  Validity 476
  with DESMO-J 280
Simulation framework 246, 264
  Black box 264
  Language-level 264
  White box 264
Simulation language 144, 244
  Activity-oriented 245
  Dynamo 244
  Efficiency 145
  Future event management 147
  General requirements 144
  GPSS 244
  Interactivity 144
  Modularity 144
  Process interruption 148
  Process-oriented 245

499

Index

Queues 147
Random Numbers 147
Readability 145
Reporting results 148
Simscript 41, 244
Simula 41, 244, 264
Simulation clock 146
Simulation-specific requirements 146
State variables 146
Statistical evaluations 147
Structure 145
Temporary objects 146
Simulation optimization ... 10, 190, 373, 387, 388, 391
    Assumptions 388
    Candidate solution 388, 392, 394
    Exhaustive search 388
    Genetic algorithm .... see GA
    Initial state 391
    Integration simulation/optimization . 388
    Model 391
    Multi-criteria optimization 393, 394
    Objective function 387, 389, 392
    Optimal solution 391
    Optimization within simulation 390
    Output parameters 391
    Pareto-optimal solutions 393, 394
    Problem 389, 391
    Realizability 389
    Scenario 387, 391
    Search space .... see Solution space
    Solution space 388, 391, 393, 394
Simulation package ...... 244, see DESMO-J
    Event-oriented 244
    GASP, GASP/1 244
    ModSim 244
    Process-oriented 244
    SimPas 244
    SLAM 244
Simulation project ... 389, 448, 469, 472, 477
    Analysis of experiments 476
    Benefits 471, 485
    Choice of simulation tool 252, 475
    Communication 474, 479, 484
    Costs 470, 471, 480
    Data .... see Data collection
    Decision support 471
    Documentation 476
    Errors and pitfalls 483
    General requirements 472
    Interpretation of results 476
    Level of detail 473

Statistical planning 476
Suitability of simulation 473
Technical know-how 473, 479
Time requirement 470, 471, 480
User participation 474
Validation .... see Model validation
Work load 472
Simulation project organization 477, 478
    Consultants . see Simulation consultants
    Manager 477
    Project leader 477
    Project members 477
    Simulation Expert 477
Simulation results   see Simulation experiment
Simulation software .. 240, 247, 264, 442, 475
    Application-specific tools .... see Application-specific simulation tools
    Classification ...... see Classification of simulation tools
    Criteria for selection 259
    Development speed 475
    Flexibility 475
    General requirements ...... see General requirements for simulation tools
    History 243
    Integrated system .... see Integrated simulation systems
    Knowledge-based systems .... see Knowledge-based simulation systems
    Modelling functionality 475
    Morphological box 251
    Petri nets-based modelling see Petri nets
    Simulation-Specific requirements ... see Simulation-specific requirements for simulation tools
    Survey on simulation tools 260
    Universal simulation systems 246
    User friendliness 475
Simulation study ..... see Simulation project
Simulation time 24, 98, 108, 146
    Distributed simulation 375
Simulation tool ...... see Simulation software
Simulation world view 249
    Machine-based . see Machine-orientated description
    Material-based . see Material-orientated description
    Modelling styles .... see Discrete event modelling styles
Simulation-based learning 402, 412
Simulation-based optimization .... see Simulation optimization

Index

Simulation-focussed learning 402, 419
Simulation-specific requirements for simulation
    tools 241
    Data collection 241
    Model construction 242
Simulation-specific requirements for simulation
    tools
    Analysing simulation results 242
    Simulation experiments 242
Simultaneous confidence interval 184
Smalltalk 54
Software metrics 221
Spatial modelling 356
    Graph-based 357
    Grid-based 356
SPIN model checker 215
State variables 5, 7, 10, 12, 24, 375
Statechart 70
    Choice 72
    Junction 72
    Orthogonal region 75
    State 71
    Transition 71
Stationary state of a process 174
Statistical estimators
    Sample mean 180, 185, 187
    Sample variance 180, 186, 187
Statistical tests
    Chi-square 170
    Degree of freedom 172
    Goodness of fit 170
    Hypotheses 171, 229
    Kolmogorov-Smirnov 173
    Null hypothesis 171
    Poisson process 173
    Significant result 172
    Test statistic 171
    Type I/II error 172
Statistically independent 161
Steady states 174
Steepest ascent, method of 191
Stereotype .... 64, *see* UML
Stochastic model .... *see* Model
Stochastic process 173
Stochastic variable 31, 161
Structural validation 213
Subsumption architecture 344
SugarScape model 350
Swarm library 362
Synchronization .... 374, 377, *see* Process
    synchronization
    Causality constraints 374

Conservative strategy 375
Deadlock 376
Lookahead time 376
Optimistic strategy 375, 376
Rollback 376
Strategies 374
System 3, 4, 389
    Analysis 4
    Attributes 5
    Behaviour 4–6, 19, 24, 170, 387
    Boundary 4
    Closed system 5, 438
    Complexity 5, 18, 21
    Components 4, 24
    Constraint 388
    Cybernetic system 5
    Dynamic system 5
    Elements 5
    Object .... *see* Element
    Open system 5, 437
    Properties .... *see* Attributes
    Scenario 387, 389, 391
    State 5, 28
    Structure 24
    Theory 5
Systems
    Non-stationary 188
    Terminating systems 188

T

Temporal logic 214
    PLTL 214
Test first approach 219
Test statistic .... *see* Statistical tests
Testing 199
    Acceptance test 218
    Black box 218
    Integration test 217
    Regression test 218
    Simulation specific requirements 219
    System test 218
    Test case generation 218
    Unit test 217
    White box 218
Time series 225
Time slicing 27
Timing diagram 92
    General value lifeline 92
Tracing 220
Transaction-oriented modelling 129
    Blocks 129
    Deadlock 129
    Example .... *see* Logistics system

501

Index

in DESMO-J .... *see* DESMO-J
Model design 129
Request 129
Transaction 129
Transient phase 174, 188

U

UML 52, 60
   Definition 60
   Diagram .... *see* Activity diagram; Class diagram; Object diagram; Package diagram; Statechart; Timing diagram
   Diagram types 62
Use cases .. *see* Object-oriented analysis and design
Utilitarian validation scheme 205

V

Validation   15, *see* Model validation, 198, 475
Validation process 199, 200
Validation techniques
   Classification 210
Variance .... *see* Statistical estimators
Variance reduction techniques 191
Verification 15, 198, 200
   Qualitative 216
Visualization .... *see* Animation
   of model results 225
   of traces 226

W

Warm-up phase 174, 242
WBT 405
web services 380
Web-based simulation .... *see* Distributed simulation
Web-based Training .... *see* WBT

X

XML 380